THE COMPLETE LIBRARY
OF
CHRISTIAN WORSHIP

THE COMPLETE LIBRARY
OF
CHRISTIAN WORSHIP

Volume 4, Music and the Arts in Christian Worship

ROBERT E. WEBBER, EDITOR

Book 2

StarSong
PUBLISHING GROUP
Nashville, Tennessee

Produced for Star Song Publishing Group by the Livingstone Corporation. Dr. James C. Galvin and J. Michael Kendrick, project editors.

Star Song Publishing Group, a division of Jubilee Communications, Inc.
2325 Crestmoor, Nashville, Tennessee 37215.

Library of Congress Cataloging-in-Publication Data

Music and the arts in Christian worship / Robert E. Webber, editor.—1st ed.
    p. cm.—(The Complete library of Christian worship : v. 4)
   Includes bibliographical references and index.
   ISBN 1-56233-014-4 (v. A)—ISBN 1-56233-140-X (v. B)
   1. Public worship—Encyclopedias. 2. Church music—Encyclopedias. 3. Christianity and the arts—Encyclopedias. 4. Drama in public worship—Encyclopedias.
5. Religious dance, modern—Encyclopedias. 6. Liturgical language—Encyclopedias.
I. Webber, Robert. II. Series
BV290.M87   1994
246.7—dc20   93–1515
                                          CIP

Printed in the United States of America
2 3 4 5 6 7 8 9 — 99 98 97 96 95 94

CONTENTS

Part 2: MUSIC IN WORSHIP

Part 3: THE VISUAL ARTS IN WORSHIP

List of Illustrations and Tables

Preface to Volume 4

The authors and editors of this series recognize that modern society is in the midst of a communications revolution involving a shift from print to multisensual media. Not surprisingly, contemporary worship renewal is caught in this tension between the older written and more verbal forms of communication and the proliferation of newer multimedia communication. This shift needs to be seen in the context of the history of communication, particularly communication in worship. The Old Testament descriptions of tabernacle and temple worship portray a worship that was highly visible, sensual, and tactile. The presence of God's beauty and majesty was expressed in vibrant colors, motions, gestures, and sounds. The space in which worship took place was like the vault of heaven.

This setting of worship was changed by the destruction of the temple and the introduction of a simpler synagogue worship. Christian worship began in synagogues and in the home, so it naturally followed the simpler pattern of the synagogue. But after the conversion of Constantine, the Roman world of the West and the Byzantine world of the East restored art, architecture, icons, frescos, and various styles of music and motion to congregational worship.

Nearly a millennium later, Reformation Protestants, influenced by the innovation of print, shifted worship away from the visual. They emphasized plain buildings and a less ornate worship setting but continued to develop music, particularly hymns and songs for worship. Still, the importance of the visual was largely lost to Protestant worship, in contrast to Eastern Orthodox and Roman Catholic churches, both of which retained highly visual elements. Many of these differences continue to this day.

The communications revolution of the twentieth century has challenged all Christians to reevaluate their position toward music and the arts in worship. Today's worship leaders are investigating the history and tradition of music and the arts in worshipping communities and are contributing new creations and compositions. Fittingly, *Music and the Arts in Christian Worship* addresses the issues of worship in a multisensual society and explores the communication between God and the worshiping community through imaginative and effective means. In keeping with the other volumes of *The Complete Library of Christian Worship,* this volume addresses music and the arts from a biblical, historical, and theological view with an eye toward their effective use in contemporary worship.

I hope you will find *Music and the Arts in Christian Worship* to be informative, challenging, inspirational, and above all useful in your efforts to renew worship.

The Lord be with you.

Robert E. Webber, Editor

PART THREE

The Visual Arts
in Worship

Historical, Philosophical, and Theological Perspectives on the Visual Arts in Worship

Christian worship is an inherently visual event. Both the setting and the actions of worship need to be seen as well as heard. The visual dimensions of worship are important on several levels. Some visual components are functional, such as fonts, tables, and pulpits. They each serve the most essential actions of worship, proclamation, and sacramental celebration. Others are simply part of the environment of worship. Stained glass windows, flowers, and banners all affect the spirit of Christians gathered to listen and to celebrate. Some visual components present concrete images and symbols, such as the cross or a loaf of bread. Others feature abstract designs, such as a banner filled with vibrant texture and color.

Throughout the centuries, the church has tended to emphasize the aural and textual aspects of worship. In recent years, however, churches have explored the potential for the visual arts in worship with great energy. What churches need now are both careful theological reflection on the role of the visual arts in worship and creative artistic applications that are feasible for congregations with a variety of resources.

Throughout the history of the church, the role of the visual arts in worship has often been controversial, with debates being waged on both theological and cultural grounds. The first articles in this chapter briefly describe this history and explain some of the primary theological arguments involved in these discussions. Then, the remaining articles present philosophical and liturgical rationale for both why and how the arts should be used in worship. They are written by people from a variety of worship traditions, and they are both instructive regarding these traditions and prescriptive for how the various traditions can learn from each other.

270 • A BRIEF HISTORY OF THE VISUAL ARTS IN WORSHIP

The history of the visual arts in worship can be traced from biblical times to the present. The twentieth century has witnessed a virtual explosion of the visual arts in worship. Understanding the use of visual arts in the past helps us understand their proper use today.

Worship is a way of experiencing the truth about life and gives insight into the meaning of life. It is concerned with a religious interpretation of the world—with creation, fall, redemption, and the fulfillment of the universe. In worship these truths are not only said, they are sung, danced, dramatized, and seen through art. Therefore, visual art in worship functions as means of proclamation of the gospel.

Visual Art and Worship During Biblical Times

Although the second commandment prohibited the people of Israel from making a graven image of God, there was no lack of artistic symbolism in the worship of Israel. For Israel, God was a spirit who could not be imaged. Nevertheless, the prohibition against imaging God in no way detracted from the creation of artistic symbols that communicated the presence of God in worship. These symbols, particularly those commanded by God to adorn the tabernacle, are described in Exodus, Leviticus, Numbers, and Deuteronomy. The instruction regarding the ark of the covenant is representative of the symbols of Hebrew worship:

> They shall make an ark of acacia wood; two cubits and a half shall be its length, a cubit and a half its breadth, and a cubit and a half its height. And you shall overlay it with pure gold, within and without shall you overlay it, and you shall make upon it a molding of gold round about. And you shall cast four rings of gold for it and put them on its four feet, two rings on the one side of it, and two rings on the other side of it. You shall make poles of acacia wood, and overlay them with gold. And you shall put the poles into the rings on the sides of the ark, to carry the ark by them.
>
> The poles shall remain in the rings of the ark; they shall not be taken from it. And you shall put into the ark the testimony which I shall give you. Then you shall make a mercy seat of pure gold; two cubits and a half shall be its length, and a cubit and a half its breadth. And you shall make two cherubim of gold; of hammered work shall you make them, on the two ends of the mercy seat.
>
> Make one cherub on the one end, and one cherub on the other end; of one piece with the mercy seat shall you make the cherubim on its two ends. The cherubim shall spread out their wings above, overshadowing the mercy seat with their wings, their faces one to another; toward the mercy seat shall the faces of the cherubim be. And you shall put the mercy seat on the top of the ark; and in the ark you shall put the testimony that I shall give you. There I will meet with you, and from above the mercy seat, from between the two cherubim that are upon the ark of testimony, I will speak with you of all that I will give you in commandment for the people of Israel. (Exod. 25:10-22)

These symbols belonged to the worship of Israel and were the context for a meeting between God and God's people—"there I will meet with you" (v. 22). These symbols were not to exist outside of worship as art objects, but inside worship as the symbols of God's presence. Consequently, they became the essential link that expressed the meeting of Israel with God.

In subsequent years, the people of Israel developed a variety of symbols to communicate God's presence in worship—the table for the offering of bread, the seven-branch lamp stand, the tabernacle made of cloth, the veil across the Holy of Holies, and various priestly vestments.

A substantial change occurred in the Christian era. First, the church recognized Jesus as the image of God (Col. 1:15). The God who could not be imaged—who was literally unimaginable—became human, a real, living icon of God who visited the earth and lived among the people. The glory of God had become incarnate, born of a woman, had lived, died, risen from the grave, and ascended into heaven, and was now seated at the right hand of God (Eph. 1:19-23).

Second, the primitive church, recognizing God's presence in Jesus, retained the symbols he had ordained as their links with God through him. The symbols of his teaching, such as the parables and sayings, were collected and incorporated into the writings of the early church, which were read and taught in worship. Jesus had also used common elements of life as objects of his actions and signs of the gospel; these too—bread, wine, oil and the water of baptism—were retained as signs of his continued presence. Unlike the Jews, then, Christians believed God had been imaged in the face of a human person. And, like the Jews, Christians continued the practice of expressing the presence of God through symbolism in worship. A powerful example is found in Hebrews, where Christ is portrayed as the fulfillment of all the Old Testament symbols—the covenant, the sanctuary, the sacrifice, the curtain of the temple, and the sacrificial victim on the altar.

Visual Art and Worship in the History of the Church

Although much of the art from the first three centuries of the church has been destroyed, there is sufficient evidence to suggest that early Christians were active in symbol making. The fish, the loaves of bread, and the *Chi-rho* monogram appeared frequently in worship places throughout the empire. The most important evidence of symbol making is found in the Christian house church at Dura Europa, which is believed to be typical of the kind of worship structures existing throughout the Roman empire in the first three centuries of the church. Here is a description of the wall paintings found in that house:

> Next to Adam and Eve hiding their nakedness we see Christ carrying the lost sheep on his shoulders. Further on, the holy women are making their way

to the tomb carrying torches. . . . Then some miracles are depicted: the paralytic, healed by Christ, carrying away his bed; and Jesus walking on the water in the storm, stretching out his hand to St. Peter. We also find the woman of Samaria at the well, and David, who has just slain Goliath.

After the conversion of Constantine, a new flurry of artistic activity arose within the church. Eusebius was so impressed with the architectural changes that he wrote, "the cathedral is a marvel of beauty, utterly breathtaking." He went on to say, "the evidence of our eyes makes instruction through the ears unnecessary." This was the beginning of the idea that arts in the church could be a form of communicating the gospel and the history of salvation to the people, even those who were illiterate.

This "insight of the eyesight" of which Eusebius speaks stands in continuity with past developments of art in worship, but the content of the art changed dramatically. Whereas the art of the catacombs and early churches saw Christ as the good shepherd, the emphasis in depictions of Christ shifted to express the new relationship of the church to the state, a relationship of power not service, of strength not weakness. Christ was now the *Pantokrator,* the ruler who reigns over heaven and earth. Enthroned in the apse of the newly consecrated basilicas, the ascended and exalted Lord brings order to heaven and earth. Both types of imagery had biblical bases and warrants, but the older imagery was overshadowed by the new because of the new political reality.

The embracing of artistic imagery by the church was challenged significantly during the iconoclastic controversy of the eighth century. Led by emperors of the eastern empire, a party in the church opposed—sometimes violently—the veneration of icons of Christ, the Trinity, the Virgin Mary, and the saints as idolatry. The opinions of bishops, popes, theologians (especially John of Damascus), monastics, and the people, however, weighed heavily against the iconoclasts, and at the last of the ecumenical councils (Nicaea, 787) veneration of icons was restored and defended. The theological argument behind the decision was that iconoclasm amounted to a denial of the Incarnation, and that veneration of icons was not worship of them as God.

Thus the centrality of Christ to both the heavens and the earth is aptly depicted in the art, architecture, and worship of the post-Constantinian church, the development of which extended through the medieval era. In the worship of post-Constantinian Christianity, Christ is seated on the throne in the heavens and, as in the depiction of Revelation 4 and 5, the heavenly throng is gathered around him in worship and praise. When we earthlings gather to worship, we join the heavenly throng.

This theme was and remains the keynote of Eastern Orthodox liturgies, which has always seen worship as a participation in and anticipation of the heavenly banquet, the supper of the Lamb. In the West this imagery was somewhat countered by preoccupation with penitential themes. But eucharistic liturgies in both east and west began with the command to "lift up your hearts"—to the eternal sacrifice of the Lamb in heaven, which is also his wedding feast. Consequently, the art and architecture of worship from Constantine through the medieval period, took on the symbolism of heavenly worship. This included:

1. Architectural symbolism (the church is often laid out in the form of a cross; high domes and arches raise the perception upwards and evoke a sense of awe)
2. Mosaics (depictions of biblical scenes or of the saints assembled around the triumphant Lord)
3. Icons (images of the heavenly reality, especially in the East; Jesus, Mary, saints, prophets, apostles; scenes of the annunciation, death, Resurrection, Ascension, exaltation, judgment)
4. Minor arts, such as:
   - glass, gold, silver, and ivory carvings
   - stained glass windows
   - wood and stone carvings
   - elaborate altars and pulpits
   - flaming candles
   - ornate tapestry
   - artistic objects such as chalice, patens
   - artistically decorated books, often the texts of the gospel
   - elaborate vestments based on imperial models

Whatever the particular theological theme of the art work—art of the church in this period was never arbitrary, but always had a recognizable theological point—these objects were seen as expressions of the gospel and the history of salvation in concrete form. Many of the people in the Middle Ages were illiterate, and the services were in ancient languages that the people no longer spoke or understood. Consequently the works of art in the church became a major means of instruction in biblical history and theology for the people. Medieval apologists called the stained glass windows, sculptures, and paintings of a church the *biblia pauperum,* the "bible of the poor."

The development of art and architecture in worship was suddenly changed with the emergence of Protestantism in the sixteenth century. While Anglicanism and Lutheranism retained a sense of the importance of symbolism in worship, Calvinists, Zwinglians, and Anabaptists, and their modern successors, pietists, revivalists, evangelicals, fundamentalists, and charismatics largely neglected art in worship and continued to do so until recently. In the sixteenth century some Reformers went so far as to smash altars and sculptures, to remove carvings, candles, and artistically designed books, to throw away vestments, and to whitewash mosaics, frescoes, and other wall paintings.

As worship lost the "insight of eyesight," it gradually became either more intellectual (as in worship where the sermon predominated) or more emotional (as in worship where feeling predominated).

———— **Visual Art in Worship Today** ————

Today there is an equal concern among Catholics and Protestants to recover the arts in worship, although they are coming from different cultural contexts. Since the medieval era, Catholics have tended toward use of ornate secondary arts, a use which has nearly obscured the primary symbols of pulpit, Table, font, and the assembled body. On the other hand, most Protestants, by their neglect of both primary and secondary symbols, have created a style of worship that is bare of visual imagery, resulting in intellectualized worship. Today both Catholic and Protestant Christians seek a worship environment that emphasizes the centrality of primary visual symbols and allows secondary symbols to act as servants of the primary symbols.

This mutual concern to recover the rightful place of the primary and secondary symbols in worship grows out of the recovery of the meaning of symbol in worship. All Christians—Orthodox, Catholic, and Protestant—are gradually recognizing the revelatory nature of symbols. They see that the purpose of art in the church is to serve as signs that relate faith to the history of salvation and evoke true insight, just feeling, and genuine worship. As such, they disclose the hidden meaning of reality and create the possibility for encounter with that meaning. They act as signs, symbols, and images that develop a sense of community, a sense which has always belonged to the whole church around the world throughout history.

There are also common rules for the use of art and symbolism in worship. The first is that major attention must be given to the primary symbols of the worshiping environment—the arrangement of the worshiping assembly and the placement of biblical symbols such as the Table, the pulpit, and baptismal font or pool. The second rule is that secondary symbols should flow from the congregation rather than be imposed upon it. Symbols such as banners, vestments, furnishings, windows, and the like should reflect the common experience of a particular local congregation. Finally, visual symbols must be within sight of everyone in the congregation in order to be effective. If "eyesight is insight," all art which either directly refers to God's acts of salvation or which assists in the communication of these truths must be seen.

Robert Webber

271 • HOW CHRISTIANS HAVE APPROPRIATED THE ARTS

Christians have responded to various art forms in many ways over the centuries. Four typical responses are described in this article. These approaches to art in general necessarily influence how the Christian community approaches the visual arts in worship.

From the very beginning God's people practiced the arts. Adam composed the first poem in the world, about Eve:

> Bone of my bone,
> Flesh of my flesh,
> She shall be called wo-man,
> For she was won-from man. (Gen. 2:23)

Aaron's sister Miriam choreographed a dance to celebrate Israel's deliverance from the pursuing Egyptians (Exod. 15:20). God gave Moses blueprints for the tabernacle's architecture and the ark with its sculptured angels made of gold and decorated candlesticks (Exod. 25:9-40). The Lord poured out specially the Holy Spirit upon silversmiths Bezalel and Oholiab so they could practice their arts with special skill (Exod. 31:1-11).

David wrote many songs and hymns for use in worship (Psalms). Solomon's artisans carved, with God's specific handwritten approval (1 Chron. 28:11-19), bas-reliefs of flower blossoms, palm trees, and angels in the Holy of Holies (1 Kings 6:23-25); and the artists carved hundreds of pomegranates on the free standing columns arranged like sentinels in front of the temple (1 Kings 7:13-22). Musicians and a Levite band of instruments frequently accompanied worship (2 Chron. 5:11-14 and Psalm 88 subtitle).

The Bible also tells us that from earliest history people who did not fear the true God practiced art as well. Lamech's son Jubal played the harp and flute (Gen. 4:21), and Lamech's own oratory was boastful bombast (Gen. 4:23-24). The ziggurat tower at Babel was an architectural monument to human pride (Gen. 11:1-9).

The Bible uses without prejudice all kinds of literary art, from Jotham's fable (Judges 9:7-20) and Samson's riddles (Judges 14:8-18) to the majestic poetry of many psalms and passages like Isaiah 40. God has even revealed his will in Scripture through a dramatic chorus of voices like the book of Job and the artful parables of Jesus (e.g., Luke 10:30-37; 16:19-31).

The point is not whether followers of Jesus Christ should be busy in art or not. Since the very creation of the world the problem has been whether these arts have been fashioned and used by men and women as vehicles of praise to the Lord or whether they have been conceived and executed as expressions of human vanity.

For centuries, Christian craftsmen practiced their art as a service to the church. Nobody thought of art as "fine art," as if art were something utterly special for and by itself. Guilds of painters, sculptors, and architects were on a par with guilds of weavers, silversmiths, and carpenters. Music and literature were the skills of tradesmen called musicians and minstrels. The medieval church put all such artistry into its service.

Art was conceived by Christians as (1) *a liturgical means for worshiping God.* Plainsong became Gregorian chant used in the Mass. Rhetoric was converted into pulpit homilies. Sculpture ranged from

baldachin to gargoyle; artists in lead, colored glass, and precious stones taught catechism lessons in brilliant, stained glass windows; architects preached Gothic cathedral sermons in stone. Artistry was understood to be a worthy natural means by which talented men could lift their neighbor into a church experience of God's grace.

As the church lost its monopoly control over cultural life during the Renaissance, and as art came into existence as "fine art," patronized by rich nobles at their courts even more than by archbishops and popes, a new position firmed up on the relationship of Christians to the arts. Art was given its independence from being an audio-visual aid for ecclesiastical worship, but Christians still wanted art not to contradict biblical truth. Art was to be (2) *autonomous but bound to the general norms or beauty, truth, and goodness* of humanity and God's natural world.

The idea that art had its own inviolate realm separate from explicit Christian indoctrination meant art became somewhat secularized. Fifteenth-century frescoes of Bible stories on inner church walls gave way to sixteenth-century portraits of wealthy people for their homes. The change from devotional poetry, which one could use like prayer beads, to medieval romance like *Roman de la Rose* and Dante's *Divine Comedy,* continued. The tale remained devout, like Spenser's *The Faerie Queene,* especially in its allegorical dimension, but the story was one of human love and ordinary experience that had no Bible story prototype. Morality plays in the churchyard gradually turned into the enormously rich dramas of Shakespeare in the playhouse. Many Christians felt comfortable with the theater, painting, and poetry as they were developing as long as these arts did not undercut their Christian beliefs.

Another position taken by Christians on the arts is that art is normally (3) *a sensuous temptation that is dangerous to faith.* This view has inhibited followers of Christ from participation in the arts. If one believes that composing, performing, or viewing art is playing with fire, then one withdraws from that kind of activity. Sometimes only certain arts have been prohibited—like theater, painting, and dance—while others—like song, music, and poetry—are permitted. The first are considered earthbound and physical while the others are more spiritual in nature.

Christian iconoclasts of the eighth century A.D.

destroyed thousands and thousands of sculptures, paintings, frescoes, mosaics, and illustrated manuscripts because the pictured images had occasioned a cult of icon worshipers and misled the populace into trusting such images as if they were akin to miracle-working relics. English Puritans destroyed art in churches during the seventeenth century in the fervor of ecclesiastical politics, but also because they did not believe sensible art could lead one to spiritual realities. Eighteenth-century European pietism tended to be restrictive of artistic expression for similar reasons. Pietistic Christians are hesitant about imagination and are fundamentally distrustful of artistic illusion because it seems to be deceptive rather than straightforwardly true.

One final important way Christians have viewed art in history is the way of accepting it as (4) *a God-given mouthpiece for human witness* of the Lord's great works or for cursing our existence. This position, which the historic Protestant Reformation set in motion, believes that for art to be Christian, art does not need to be narrowly liturgical. Art is also not intrinsically normative nor is it intrinsically more seductive than any other human activity. Art is simply a certain kind of cultural calling that has its own legitimacy as a sensible, crafted, allusively symbolic artifact. Art can be a vehicle of insight thanking God for his mercies in our world or a vehicle of hate and blasphemy, no matter how expertly done, depending upon the spirit it embodies.

John Donne's amorous sonnets or his poem on "The Will" (1633) treat human passion with large, redemptive horizons. Rembrandt's *Flayed Ox* (1655) depicts the stunning glory of ordinary meat hanging in a butcher shop. *The Well-tempered Clavier* by J. S. Bach (1723) presents keyboard music that resounds with toccata-like joy and intricate contrapuntal rhythms that celebrate a creaturely rich world. Such poetry, painting, and music exemplify the way Christians can witness of our redeeming Creator's handiwork within the artistic idiom, irrespective of the "topic."

These four basic historical positions on how Christians should best conceive, practice, and relate to the arts represent roughly the major groupings within the worldwide Christian communion today. Each position shows certain strengths and weaknesses. How do Christians most responsibly come to terms with the utter secularization of the arts without trying to set back history? If Christians stay away from the arts (position 3), godless people have undisputed control of the arts media and can expand the influence of their worldview. If Christians adopt the best artistic forms current (position 2) or try to utilize professional, secular artistry without adapting it to the church's missionary outreach (position 1), Christians' cultural expression may be co-opted. If the Christian community tries to develop its own particular style of art (position 4), it runs the risk of being permanently off, amateurish, and obscurantic.

But the deep secularization of modern art is a fact. Surrealistic painting, by and large, calls into question the sanity of ordinary life and most traditional values. Salvador Dali (1904–1989) posited a Freudian universe and painted everything he treated into an erotic, hallucinatory vortex—even when he took biblical themes. The canvases of Rene Magritte (1898–1967) are fascinating artistic achievements which juxtapose objects in a way as disturbing as the unanswerable *koans* of Zen Buddhism. Martha Graham's choreography is also rigorously erotic, reaching for a new dance idiom of mythic power that repudiates the aristocratic niceties and elegant pirouettes of classical ballet. Many great innovators in modern art have been intensely self-conscious of their rejection of a bourgeois, Victorian worldview and their commitment to a non-Christian primitivism.

Much contemporary architecture, painting, and instrumental music rightly give Christians pause today, too, because of their hard-bitten secularity. It became possible around 1900 to use concrete and reinforced cement to construct buildings. Under the influence of the Bauhaus and architect Le Corbusier (1887–1965), large buildings of all sorts became standardized into functional shells with unobstructed interior spaces (e.g., movable partitions for walls); practical metals like aluminum, nickel, and chrome intensified the feel of cold brightness inside such structures already occasioned by the profusion of physical and electric light. In effect, office buildings, classrooms, and homes took on the aspect of being factories, which quite naturally provided little personal and private space. Painters like Malevich (1878–1935), Mondrian in his later works (*c.* 1917–1944), and Josef Albers (1888–1976) used a very restricted range of forms to construct what look like geometric blueprints in paint, and they did it with repetitive ingenuity and tenacity. Such rigorous, purist art, however, has a tendency to sterilize life.

An additional complication to the problem of how Christians are to confront both sexually aggressive art and the dehumanizing technocratic style around us is the fact that so much art today is mass produced and mass consumed. A futuristic novel like Kurt Vonnegut, Jr.'s *Cat's Cradle* (1963) sells hundreds of thousands of copies. A brilliant portrayal of aimless violence as a way of life and death, like Stanley Kubrick's film *A Clockwork Orange* (1972), is seen by millions of people. Self-righteous pornography like *Oh! Calcutta* runs for years on stage in London and New York. Mindless entertainment, pop star culture, and films interrupted by paid advertisements immerse children from infancy to adolescence. Superb means of mass communication rain secular art upon the earth with an almost brainwashing effect.

Christian families are called upon to face the secularized arts today in the strength of the Holy Spirit (John 16:13) and to show themselves approved of God (2 Tim. 2:15-16). But how can we do that with respect to the arts? The answer is that Christians must first of all become deeply rooted biblically, so that their faith life flowers as a rich plant unafraid in God's world, rather than as a poor, undernourished stick in the mud. Second, they must study both the nature and the history of art so they will not be fooled into approving or judging the wrong things.

Let me mention a few examples. The subject matter or topic of a novel or film provides little clue as to its worth or insight. Seduction can be graphically portrayed in a text like Proverbs 7:6-23, to our edification, or twisted into a scene that dirties and bores our sensibility, as in *Last Tango in Paris*. It is also a mistake to demand "beauty" and "harmony" from painting and music as if distortion and dissonance violated artistic norms. Grunewald's famous Isenheim altarpiece of Christ's crucifixion (*c.* 1510–1515) is grotesque and unpleasant, but an impressive presentation of our Lord's agony. Schoenberg's atonal *Variations for Orchestra* (1928) is important music that wakes a listener up musically to the important tensions we really know in our day. "Creativity," too, is more often a slogan than a sound idea for helping us to judge whether a given painting is truly art or bogus. A "creative" person can be one who uses his gifts to glorify God or one who idolizes frenzied experimentation (witness certain paint-dripping canvases by disciples of abstract expressionism). If one thinks of art as "creative," and if "creativity" is colored by the romantic adoration

of "artistic genius" so that the necessary element of craftsmanship in art is neglected, one goes wrong in approaching art.

The most important thing for Christians to understand is that the arts are skillful and thoughtful manmade objects characterized by allusiveness. All the arts—music and sculpture as well as drama and poetry—present an artist's religious perspective in ambiguity. Art is not by nature a confused matter, but art is by nature a *fused presentation of knowledge necessarily rich in suggestion.* It is both normal and normative for the arts to be oblique and symbolical in the way they bring things to our attention as spectators, readers, or audience.

If poetry tries to be as straightforward as a roadway sign, it will be poor poetry. If poetry or painting is overly complicated, like a crossword puzzle, it will also be defective. But poetic, painterly, and musical knowledge are not at core "verbal" or "propositional." Poetry, painting, music, and all the arts present knowledge that can certainly be talked about and analyzed, but the final character of artistic knowledge it that it is knowledge full of nuance.

Calvin G. Seerveld[42]

272 ◆ HISTORICAL PERSPECTIVES ON THE REFORMED VIEW OF THE ARTS IN WORSHIP

Of all the theologians and church leaders who are cited as being opposed to the use of visual arts in worship, Protestant Reformer John Calvin is perhaps the most famous. The following article describes the cultural context in which Calvin worked and the specific nature of his views on the visual arts in worship, suggesting that Calvin was more concerned with confronting idolatry than with opposing the visual arts in worship.

Liturgy is a muscular word, an image derived in part from its intrinsic visual quality. The worshiping community gathers around the Table, pulpit, and baptismal font. Water is sprinkled; bread is broken and wine poured; hands are folded and knees are bent; collection plates are passed. Because of the visual nature of liturgy, the church from its very beginning perceived the opportunity to teach and edify itself by producing works of art that would enrich these various aspects of its liturgy. More importantly, there was little distinction, if any at all, between art for life and art for worship, as the church understood that the spiritual was discerned through the material.

But during the sixteenth century, distrust of symbols began to take root in the European church. The Protesters rejected many forms of liturgical art. Leaders of the Reformed tradition, in rethinking the role and use of symbols and iconography, forged so strong an understanding of the arts that it is reflected in almost every Reformed church building to this day. In one of the most astonishing transitions in the history of the church, the church reversed its role from artistic proponent to artistic opponent, all in a time-span of less than a generation. John Calvin was one leader responsible for this fundamental shift.

──────── **Calvin in Context** ────────

In the sixteenth century, Christians belief emphasized God's immanence. God was believed to be always close to earth working miracles and protecting Christians through venerated relics. The great domes of the basilicas were held in place by large, over-proportioned columns, not because the domes required such heavy pillars to support them, but because the dome, representing the orb of the universe, was being tied down close to earth and the church. Europe pulsated with expectations of the miraculous. Medieval Catholicism held that the actual body and blood of Christ could be found in the consecrated host. The practice of obtaining and housing icons and relics became big business, for the power of God was thought to be in and around the pieces of bone, wood, canvas, or fabric.

This is the world into which John Calvin was born and a world he would, in turn, shape and change. In particular, Calvin redefined the understanding of God's presence in the world. For Calvin and the other Reformers, the medieval church limited access to God's grace to ways that were too one-sidedly "visual" in their orientation. The Reformers, instead, asserted a transcendent understanding of the presence of God. In this awareness, God ruled from Heaven, though his power permeated the world. The centerpiece of Calvin's theology is not so much humankind grasping for concepts of God, but a gracious God revealing himself to humankind. As such, basing his reasoning in part on John 4:24 and the second commandment, Calvin asserted that true worship of God does not happen through the aid of worldly trappings, but only through the Spirit of God.

The second matter that characterized the world

of the sixteenth century was the rise of humanism. The rise of biblical scholarship urged a re-emphasis on the Bible as the standard for worship instead of tradition. The printing press aided literacy and learning. Rhetoric led to the exaltation of the spoken word, encouraging a revival in preaching. For the learned Reformed leaders, these verbal, scholastic expressions came to be invested with greater authority and value in worship than its visual aspects (Philip W. Butin, "Constructive Iconoclasm: Trinitarian Concern in Reformed Worship," *Studia Liturgica* 9:2 [1989]: 133–139).

At the root of this theological paradigm shift was a revived interest in Neoplatonism. This phenomenon was an expression of the Renaissance at the time of the Reformation. In the manner of Neoplatonism, Lefèvre, Calvin, and other Reformers seem to have favored the spiritual over the material as a more vital contribution to Reformed worship.

Yet, the Reformed are not primarily antimaterial or antiaesthetic. Rather, as Carlos Eire points out in his recent and thorough treatise on the subject, Reformed iconoclasm was primarily an attempt to avoid all idolatry (Carlos M. N. Eire, *War Against the Idols* [Cambridge: Cambridge University Press, 1986]). Reformed aesthetics, therefore, stems from a broad, theologically motivated concern to avoid all forms of idolatry in worship. Admittedly, it was formed largely as a reactionary defense, in response to various criticisms of perceived liturgical abuses. Calvin argues for simple, direct (i.e., nonvisual) communication with the Deity.

──── **Calvin's Biblical Understanding** ────
of Aesthetics

As Calvin forged his aesthetic theology, he was prone to reference two key Scripture texts. First, Calvin's theology emphasized the role of the law, as summarized in the Decalogue. In particular, the first and second commandments were persuasive in warranting the expulsion of anything considered idolatrous. A second text, John 4:24, was also prominent. In John 4:24, Jesus, as exegeted by the Reformers, was calling for true worship as worship "in spirit and in truth." A Reformed liturgic—shaped by the writings of Zwingli, Bucer, and Calvin—is influenced by these two texts. These texts are the basis of the ongoing Reformed concern to avoid idolatry, while also contributing to an essentially positive thrust that promoted the idea of "true worship." This may be illustrated through a discussion of John

Calvin's development of what constitutes "true worship" and a right understanding of Reformed aesthetics.

Although Calvin never explicitly writes about aesthetic theory *per se,* his approach can be discerned from his writing on liturgical art and icons, particularly from his various warnings about worshiping relics (John Calvin, *An Admonition, Showing the Advantages Which Christendom Might Derive From an Inventory of Relics,* in *Selected Works of John Calvin: Tracts and Letters,* vol. 1, ed. Henry Beveridge and Jules Bonnet [Grand Rapids: Baker, 1983]). In addition, some of his commentaries and sermons provide us with his thought about beauty and the arts.

To understand Calvin's view of aesthetics, it is necessary to pull together his reflections upon the nature of art and the nature of worship; it is these two areas that Calvin does explicitly address, often in tandem. Understanding Calvin's view of aesthetics grows out of studying Calvin's theological reflection upon nature, human nature, and the function of art.

Art is dependent upon beauty, says Calvin, and beauty comes only from God. In fact, Calvin often interchanges the words *art* and *beauty.* Beauty, as expressed through the arts, is related to God and his existence as Creator. Calvin believes that God's beauty is transcendent but that it can be perceived in the created physical world and in moral order. In describing God as the author of physical and moral creation, Calvin clarifies how God is able to be known as the Trinity. God, the Father, created the heavens and earth; he is the consummate artist, since he formed the world and everything in it. These creative acts of God, the paradigm artist, are exhaustive and complete (John Calvin, *Institutes of the Christian Religion* 1:5 [Grand Rapids: Eerdmans, 1959], 59). Jesus Christ, the second person of the Trinity, came to earth and exhibited a perfect spiritual beauty. His spiritual presence, self-sacrifice, and love exemplify the lovely. The Holy Spirit, the third person of the Trinity, exhibits moral beauty, placing in the hearts of people such virtues as love, justice, goodness, wisdom, and compassion.

In addition to seeing God's beauty as revealed by the Father, Son, and Holy Spirit, Calvin also believes that humankind, in both the physical and spiritual sense, is beautiful. We are the chief creatures of God's creation. We are made in God's image: awesome, mysterious, complex, and beautiful. These attributes are vestiges of the *imago dei* (the image of God) and testify to heavenly grace, even though they are sullied by sin.

True Worship and Aesthetics

Calvin's understanding of art had implications for the use of art in worship. His view of liturgical art involves an understanding of the worshipers and the effect of beauty upon them. Visual imagery was thought to be too powerful a force, especially in the relic-packed Catholic churches of Calvin's time, to be used successfully in worship. As beholders of art are sinful and have a natural inclination toward idolatry, the majesty of God was to be guarded from any idolatrous confusion with images used to worship or represent him, the very issue addressed so directly in the second commandment. Thus, in order to resist the temptation to idolize and worship the works of creatures rather than the creator, Calvin railed against the use of many art forms in worship (Calvin, *Inventory,* 290).

Calvin was more interested in worshiping in "spirit and in truth" (John 4:24); that is, worshiping the Creator directly without relying on works of his creatures. To this end, Calvin's worship environments were purged. Altars were removed and plain tables were brought in. The pulpit—representing the preaching of the Word—took central place; the centrality of the Word was represented architecturally by placing the pulpit in the middle of the chancel. Baptismal fonts were brought to the front of the sanctuary, forming a triangle with pulpit and table. Organ cases were closed (at least during the worship service proper) and relics and icons were removed. All these actions brought the central acts of worship before the congregation in a clear, simplified way (James White, *Protestant Worship: Traditions in Transition* [Louisville: Westminster/John Knox Press, 1989], 65–66). The result was a re-formed Reformed worship service that simplified the visual and accentuated the verbal.

Later Calvinist Manifestations

Later expressions of Calvinism continued to glean the implications of its original concern to avoid idolatry in worship. The Puritans, for one example, were heavily influenced by the Calvinistic aesthetic. More recently, Dutch Calvinist thinkers such as Abraham Kuyper and Herman Dooyeweerd sought to refocus the problem of idolatry by warning against the idolatrous potential of misdirected worldviews. Another Dutchman, Gerardus van der Leeuw, though he takes Calvinism down a different path, nevertheless expresses again the role of Christ as the unique expression of God, who alone is worthy of ultimate loyalty. Karl Barth focused the problem of idolatry on idols of culture, race, and state. Reformed churches, in short, following the model cast by John Calvin, have always intentionally attempted to counteract anything that would replace Christ as the central focus of the church or worship. This can especially be seen in recent attempts to counteract nationalism, militarism, racism, and sexism.

Yet it cannot be denied that the Reformed concern to avoid all forms of idolatry has come with a cost: a cost many perceive to be the loss of imaginative and artistic expressions in worship. In a grand irony, many see the perceived lack of creativity to be unrepresentative of the Creator God—the God so many Calvinists are attempting to worship in a nonidolatrous way. And, though confessionally Trinitarian, many see Reformed worship as predominantly the worship of God the Father, with little emphasis on God as revealed in Jesus Christ or as revealed in the mysterious nature of the Spirit.

Fortunately, this understanding of Calvinism and the practice of it are changing. The ecumencally oriented liturgical movement has facilitated an openness to new expressions from the broader streams of Christian worship, albeit sometimes slavishly uncritical and eclectic in its borrowing.

Calvin's concerns remain valid for today. Reformed worshipers agree that they must not, in the rampant liturgical renewal, confuse an image with its reality, or a symbol with the reality symbolized. A distinction must be maintained, the Reformed insist, between symbol and adornment. Symbol is necessary; adornment should be used judiciously, if at all. We must not develop an autonomous taste for the sensuous or romantic. Nor can we delight only in the forms we have produced, unable or unwilling to discern the enabling grace of God in and through the forms. Likewise, the iconoclastic urge must continually be tempered so that the connection between the mystery of God and the beauty in creation and in our creativity is maintained.

Thus, the chief contribution of the Reformed tradition is to insist that all imagination and art is a servant to the word of God. The Reformed liturgist is one who asks, "How can every action, color, banner, anthem, sermon point away from itself to God?" And the Reformed Christian is one who sings with the English hymn writer William Cowper, ". . . the dearest idol I have known, whatever that idol be, help me to tear it from thy throne and worship only thee."

Randall D. Engle

273 • THE AFRICAN RECOVERY OF THE ARTS

In the midst of poverty and starvation, Christian faith and native talent in Africa are inspiring a wealth of art for worship. This art is one means by which African Christians express their faith while borrowing from their indigenous cultures.

Africa is a continent crucified by famine and war, pestilence and poverty. For Christianity, however, it is a continent of resurrection. Even as older churches in Europe and the United States are emptying, faith is thriving in the sprawling lands south of the Sahara. As is so often the case, spiritual strength is inspiring—and being inspired by—an outpouring of artistic creation. "We are on the verge of a golden age in African Christian art," proclaims Jesuit Father Engelbert Mveng of Cameroon. "The movement cannot be stopped and it is bursting out in flower all over Africa."

Not since Europe's Renaissance has such a large and varied body of living Christian art been produced. In inaccessible rural workshops, thatched-roof villages, and teeming urban slums, a firmament of fine artists inspired by Christian themes is emerging from within a much larger community of folk artisans. The movement is thriving in spite of serious obstacles. Most artists lack patrons, lucrative markets, and substantial schooling. With tools, paint, and canvas in chronically short supply, Africans work with whatever materials are handy. Wood is thus the most popular medium. If stained glass is too costly, colored resin is applied to window panes. If sculptors lack marble, they mix cheap pebbles and concrete. If budgets keep church buildings modest, they are brightened with imaginative decorations and vibrant vestments.

Styles range from garishly colored representational paintings to serene abstracts. The themes are the same ones that inspired a thousand Renaissance masterpieces: the Nativity, Madonna and Child, and gripping Bible stories. The most common subject is Christ's agony on the cross, a visual testament to the Africans' own suffering. But Zairian Catholic sculptor Ndombasi Wuma, like many Protestants, refuses to depict the Crucifixion. Says he: "I believe in the risen Christ. Why should Christ be anguished?"

African art is created not for museums or living rooms but for the community. Its function is fourfold, says Elimo Njau, a Tanzanian Lutheran painter. Art "makes Christianity African," provides a new context for worship, stimulates devotion, and teaches the meaning of the Bible through imagery. Many works are signed collectively; others are anonymous. At Sims Chapel, Zaire's oldest Baptist church, even Sunday school children played their part: their crude drawings provided the basis for the chapel's stained-glass windows.

Before the missionary era, the only Christianized black nation was Ethiopia. Its austere art style remained largely unchanged since the Middle Ages. When the first missionaries arrived in other parts of Africa in the fifteenth century, they sought to stamp out tribal religions and with them idols, ceremonial masks, and ancestral images. The artistic tug-of-war intensified during the nineteenth century as the number of Christian missions mushroomed.

The latter-day art boom was fostered by Roman Catholic missionaries. Among them were Brother Marc (Stanislas Wallenda) from Belgium, who founded Kinshasa's Academy of Fine Arts in 1943, and Father Kevin Carroll of Ireland, who in the same era came to work among Nigerian craftsmen. Most white missionary bishops back then, Carroll recalls, "thought we were wasting time." Political independence and the increase of black clergy accelerated the process that European Christians call adaptation or inculturation, meaning the incorporation of local culture into Christianity. Today Nigeria has Africa's largest corps of artists and artisans, and Zaire probably boasts the most important assemblage of sheer talent.

Inculturation often means nothing more controversial than transplanting the classic Bible stories into black African settings. A white policeman accompanies Jesus to Calvary. The crucified Christ wears a crown of cactus thorns. The three Wise Men bear gifts of kola nuts and chickens. More saucily, South African linocut artist John Muafangejo shows Satan urinating in fear before an angel. Sometimes even modest experiments produce scandal. Cheap reproductions hang beneath the Stations of the Cross carved by Kanutu Chenge for a Catholic

church near Lubumbashi, Zaire. They are there to appease a congregation shocked to see Pilate dressed as an African chieftain and women with tribal headbands witnessing the Crucifixion.

Serious theological problems can arise when Africanization uses symbols and myths from the pre-Christian faiths. Fearing syncretism in a continent where communion with the spirits and ancestors remains a powerful belief, most Protestants are exceedingly cautious about all the visual arts. Zaire's indigenous Kimbanguist Church strictly forbids decoration except on preachers' and singers' robes. But many Anglicans, once hesitant, are enthusiasts for the new church art. Methodist theologian Dkalimbo Kajoba encourages art so long as it is for "decoration" not "adoration."

Since the Second Vatican Council, Roman Catholicism has shown the most readiness to embrace Africanization. One of the boldest steps came in 1967, when the newly built St. Paul's Church in Lagos opened its doors to reveal frankly pagan symbols and statues. A black Nigerian priest protested at the time, "You are taking us back from whence we came—paganism." But prominent Nigerian artist Bruce Onobrakpeya notes that the Yorubas "worship God through the spirit Orisha, who will pray to God for them and obtain the blessings they desire—not so very different from parishioners kneeling before a statue of the Virgin." The decorations remained.

Abayomi Barber, a Nigerian who makes the sign of the cross over each painting he creates, sees profound value in tribal cultures. "The birth of a child, coming of age, marriage, death and the spirits of our ancestors—all these needed to be illustrated and represented as supernatural manifestations. This is the basis of our art. We are still interlinked with nature."

The most sensitive question is how to portray Jesus Christ. Some tribes show him with a huge head to symbolize great wisdom or a massive chest to convey strength. But should he be depicted as an African? Urban Christians are more open to this than believers in the bush. Commissioned by the Catholic Cathedral in Kananga, Zaire, Enkobo Mpane created his first Bantu Christ from ebony in 1969. Parishioners rejected the work, so it hangs in a nearby convent. "Our parishioners still think of Christ as a Jew and not an African," reports Arley Brown, a U.S. Baptist teaching in Kinshasa. But Nigerian Anglican architect Fola Alade insists, "If Jesus is the Son of God, how can he be just a Jew?"

For many African artists, the act of creation itself is a religious experience. Zaire's Mwabila Pemba, a specialist in beaten copper, rises daily at 5 A.M. to pray and believes that as he works he is "in the hands of a divine force." He is among multitudes who speak of creating through prayers, dreams, and inspiration from the Bible. Africans know that this makes them oddities among the world's modern-day artists. Ben Nhlanhla Nsusha, who recently returned to Johannesburg after five years of study in London, says the young artists in England "can't understand the way I think. They never do religious subjects."

Africans are anything but embarrassed about this cultural distinctiveness. Cecil Skotnes, one of the handful of creative white religious artists in South Africa, insists, "Urgency is the basis of all great art. This urgency is no longer apparent in European or U.S. art." That judgment may be too sweeping. Yet there is no question that African Christian art, serene and savage, florid and austere, stands virtually alone in the vigor and authenticity with which its practitioners seek to express the inexpressible.

Richard M. Ostling[43]

274 • Liturgical Aesthetics

The aesthetic dimensions of Christian worship encompass not only written liturgies and rubrics, but also the ways in which the liturgy is brought to life. This article addresses the rich and varied ways that these aesthetic dimensions are realized, including the liturgical expressions of time and space, the visual and the aural, the cognitive and emotional, the eternal and the culture-bound.

The term *aesthetics* derives from a Greek root meaning "of or pertaining to things perceptible by the senses, things material (as opposed to things thinkable or immaterial)" (*O.E.D.*). Since the 18th century the term has come to designate the theory and interpretation of the beautiful in art and in nature. Liturgical aesthetics comprehends both the modern and classical meanings of the term. Thus the scope of this article includes the concept of beauty in relation to prayer and ritual as well as reflection on the sensible signs and various "languages" of worship such as time, space, sound and

The Crucifixion (Angola). The crucified Christ, flanked by the two thieves, in a nineteenth-century sculpture by an unknown artist.

silence, movement and gesture, sacramental sign-acts, and the artistic environment.

Relations between beauty, the human senses, and the worship of God are both obvious and difficult to trace in their complexity. Liturgical worship requires corporately shared forms into which a community of faith enters to give expression to adoration, praise, thanksgiving, and petition. Because liturgy is more than texts and rubrics governing the correct performance of ritual acts, the "poetics of liturgical celebration" is of primary importance. The study of literary qualities of texts is only one strand in such a poetics. Since the mystery of God's self-communication in Word and sacrament is always in and through specific forms, the poetics of liturgical celebration constitute a simultaneously theological and anthropological inquiry. Poetics as the study of how living discourse utilizes the powers of language is here applied to the broad range of liturgical utterance and to the arts of ritual enactment.

Liturgy possesses great formative and expressive power over human imagination, thought, emotion and will. Speaking theologically, we may say that, over time, Christian liturgy forms persons in the paschal mystery that it signifies and at the same time brings to communal expression the lived experience of the gospel. From a phenomenological or anthropological point of view, liturgy may be said to form human persons (and communities) in specific symbol systems and fundamental ways of being in the world. At the same time, liturgical rites become the means of expressing primary identity and passional self-understanding. Both the formative and expressive dimensions of liturgy require structure and particular elements—words, actions, symbols, music and related art forms. But what gives such elements and the structure of the rites life is style—a particular way of celebrating the rites. As Aidan Kavanagh has observed, ". . . the artful symbolism which is the liturgy is never secured in the abstract or in the general. It is accomplished in specific acts done by people in certain places at given times" ("The Politics of Symbol and Art in Liturgical Expression," in *Symbol and Art in Worship* [Concilium: Religion in the Eighties, no. 132], Luis Maldonado and David Power, eds. [New York: Seabury Press, 1980], 39). Liturgical aesthetics investigates what is signified and experienced and how it is so signified and experienced in actual worshiping assemblies.

If Christian liturgy is understood as a complex of communal sign-actions and texts brought together in symbolic patterns about the Scriptures, the font, and the Table, then liturgical aesthetics studies the perceptual elements and the art of ritual enactment which render these human activities alive with significant form. If Christian liturgy is understood as an epiphany of the mystery of the divine self-communication, then liturgical aesthetics must address the question of how the style of celebration opens access to understanding and participation in that which theology cannot explain but can only comprehend in wonder and adoration. Both conceptions of liturgy and both methodologies are necessary.

Liturgy and Aesthetics: Historical Ambiguities

The matrix of artistic creativity for pre-Reformation cultural life in the West was the Christian liturgy. Liturgical art was, to a great extent, the fountainhead of popular art, and the cultural imagination was permeated with biblical stories and liturgical images. Such an historical period furnishes ample evidence of the power of liturgy to shape and receive cultural modes of perception. By contrast, the prophetic side of Christianity has from the beginning been suspicious of human imagination, voicing objection to the dissociation of the aesthetic from the ethical or the holy. The words of Amos echo in other historical periods: "Take away from me the noise of your song; to the melody of your harps I will not listen. But let justice roll down like waters, and righteousness like an everflowing stream" (Amos 5:23-24). Furthermore, the iconoclastic impulse to resist the uses of art emerges in the name of holiness to guard against idolatrous confusion of images with the divine reality they are to represent or express.

At the outset Christianity had considerable reservations about the arts and a relatively unadorned liturgy. The immoralities of songs in the context of pagan rites provided good reason for such suspicion. The pattern of life that was associated with music and the other arts of the theater was cause of great concern to the church. There was an asceticism in the earliest monastic movements that regarded the ease and even the sensuality of the post-persecution church as apostate. While the prophetic biblical traditions feared idolatry, the use of music, for example, seemed at home in the chanting of psalms. But the traditions springing from the philosophy of Plato also influenced the early church. Aware of the enormous emotional power of music, poetry, and dance upon the human psyche, such traditions regarded artistic endeavor as traffic with the ambiguities of sensuality. The strictures against flute-playing in Plato's *Republic* emerged in the Christian assembly's initial resistance to the use of instruments in worship. The mistrust of matter and images itself led to a chaste role of iconography in the early buildings. Gradually, especially in the East, the idea of the icon as an image which mediates but does not contain the sacred, emerged.

The theological and philosophical suspicions of art and of the aesthetic power of liturgy surfaced virulently again with some of the Reformers of the sixteenth century. The systematic destruction of images and religious art in places such as Zurich in 1524 at the hands of the Zwinglian town council testify to the fear of external rites, material form, and visible symbols. The suppression of all music in the liturgy seems even more extreme, especially at the hands of such an accomplished musician as Ulrich Zwingli. Yet such a reduction of the aesthetic dimensions of Christian worship among the Reformers resulted from an enormous drive to purify and to spiritualize worship forms in a period when the aesthetic and symbolic profusion of the Roman rites seemingly overwhelmed the central mystery of God's gracious acts and the primary symbols of faith. The sixteenth-century simplifications were partly a result of a new stress on Scripture as a primary source for liturgical norms arising in that period; but they also depended upon an opposition between reason and emotion, alongside a dualism of spirit and the physically sensate. Luther was not such a liturgical purist. In fact, as the liturgical iconoclasm of the Reformation grew more extreme, he spoke, even while defending simplification of the rites, of his eagerness to "see all the arts, especially music, in the service of him who gave and created them." The liturgical aesthetics of the three magisterial Reformers—Luther, Calvin and Zwingli—show a remarkable range of differences among themselves respecting the material forms that worship employs. None of them refers substantially to the earlier traditions which struggled with these same tensions, namely those of the early patristic figures, most especially St. Augustine.

It was St. Augustine who asserted that, despite human sin and limitation, divine providence could yet work through the human experience of beautiful things to illuminate the ground of all human perception and understanding in God. For Augustine, the recognition of truth and beauty in and through the created order (the physical and the sensual) revealed a divine lure turning human beings away from desires linked with sensuality and mortality to love of God. Before him, Basil, in his treatise *On the Holy Spirit,* had argued that honor given an image would move on to its origination in God. In contrast to the early theological suspicion of the arts and to the more extreme views of the Reformation, there has been an alternative tradition from Augustine to Aquinas, rediscovered in later historical and cultural periods—as with the nineteenth century Oxford Movement and neo-Thomist revivals associated with Jacques Maritain and Etienne Gilson —which regarded aesthetic activity and its liturgical bearing as defined in light of the relation of God to all human perception and to the goodness of the created order itself.

The history of styles of celebration and the "ceremonial" employed in liturgical rites has shown wide extremes in the history of the church, especially in the West. This fact shows that the aesthetic dimensions of Christian worship are ingredient in any change, whether of complex elaboration over time, or of dramatic reform and simplification. The last third of the twentieth century is witnessing one of the most extraordinarily complex periods of reform and renewal in the history of the Western churches. The emergence of liturgical aesthetics as a discipline is partly a necessary outcome of these developments.

Liturgy as Art: Symbolic Form and Mystery

Any consideration of liturgical aesthetics must begin with the acknowledgment of this ambiguity in the long history of Christian faith and artistic expression. Still there remains the fact that liturgy itself employs cultural forms in imaginatively powerful ways. Liturgical action does not simply use art, it *is* art—dialogue with God in symbolic form. To speak of liturgical aesthetics, then, is to refer to that which is ingredient in the enactment of the rites, both sacramental and nonsacramental. There is an intrinsically aesthetic character to all liturgical celebration and environment. This fact is at the heart of what liturgy is, according to the *Constitution on the Sacred Liturgy* of the Second Vatican Council. The liturgical assembly is the articulation and expression of the saving mystery of God in Christ, and of the nature of the church. The symbolic action of the liturgy is also an experience and manifestation of the church and a participation in the mystery of the triune life of God which animates the world. Such manifestation and participation is always in and through specific cultural forms: language, symbol, ritual sign-acts, music, gesture, visual and tactile environments.

Explorations in the domain of liturgical aesthetics, therefore, seek to interpret and to understand the various relations between beauty and holiness in particular liturgical contents. Bearing in mind the ambiguities of the human imagination per se and the possibilities of mistaking the symbol for the reality symbolized, liturgical aesthetics proceeds on the assumption that there is an ultimate connection between beauty and the reality of God. Liturgical aesthetics is based on the fact that liturgy is a complex art form and that right praise and thanksgiving to God require the engagement of the full range of human emotion, intellect, and will. Liturgical worship employs corporate shared forms that invite and engender a fully human participation, neither exclusively cognitive (mental) nor exclusively emotive or volitional.

The symbolic value and the beauty of the various elements of the liturgy derive from the material and form of each, while the sacredness or holiness derives from the mystery of the events celebrated "in, with, and through" Jesus Christ. These principles are based on the claim that God has created all things and called them good and has become incarnate in Jesus Christ, gathering an historical human community—always culturally embedded and embodied—for worship and service in the world. Liturgical aesthetics is thus rooted and grounded in the doctrines of creation and incarnation. All things are rendered holy by virtue of creation and the redemptive action of God, and are to be so regarded and brought to expression in communal worship of God. Liturgical worship respects the difference between creature and Creator, employing the things of earth to signify the glory and mercy and justice of God. This calls for a fundamental religious sensibility oriented to splendor and to appropriate sobriety and awe in the use of language, symbol, gesture, and the various languages of the rites.

Yet there is also a permanent tension involved in the use of material objects, the domain of the senses, and the imaginative powers of human art. This is because human beings are not in full harmony with the created order, nor is any human community or culture congruent with a fully transformed world. Our liturgies remain "east of Eden" and captive to the limits of human cultural perception as well. In short, Christian communities remain sinful and culturally bound. This means that whatever significant form is realized in liturgical celebration conveying the self-giving of God, we still "see through a glass darkly." Hence liturgical aesthetics must always point to an eschatological self-critique of the use of forms. This permanent tension in liturgy as art is but a reflection of the situation of faith—we live in a good but fallen creation, between the initiation of redemptive history and its consummation. Any given liturgical aesthetic belonging to a particular time and culture requires a counterpoint in a religious sensibility oriented to that which transcended culture, that "which eye has not seen, nor ear heard," which God has prepared for the children of earth.

The eschatological reservation concerning the cultural embeddedness of all aesthetic dimension of Christian liturgy will be made more explicit at the end of this essay. To a discussion of various languages and the aesthetic dimension of all liturgical rites enacted we now turn.

Time and Space

From the beginning, Christian liturgical celebrations involved the use of cultural modes of communication, language itself being a primary instance. The words and texts employed in the liturgy operate within a complex of nonverbal phenomena. The sense and force of the words employed in worship depend radically for their range and depth upon the nonverbal features of the rites and how they are enacted. The meaning of a sung text, for example, has a greater aesthetic range than the same text recited. The same text or gesture—or their combination—has a different connotative range in different seasons or feasts during the church year.

Among the primary nonverbal languages that constitute the poetics of liturgical celebration is time. Because liturgical rites are temporal, unfolding the juxtaposition of text, symbols, and ritual acts over time, participation is itself a temporal art. Within the duration of a single liturgical rite, for example, a eucharistic celebration, the meaning of the texts and the symbols are cumulative and dramatic rather than self-contained. Each text or gesture or liturgical subunit may possess its own determinate sense, but the significance and the broader radiations of meaning can only be discerned in light of the whole pattern. Worship may be impoverished, of course, by lack of coherence or structural dislocation, illustrated by the proliferation of sequences in the Renaissance period. Thus the poetry of an Entrance hymn or a festival Gloria may be fully grasped only after its connection with the praise and thanksgiving of the eucharistic prayer is sounded. The remarkable complexity and aesthetic power of images in the Exsultet at the Easter vigil does not fully unfold until the temporal process of reading and hearing the whole sequence of readings is completed and the baptismal covenant is sounded. Liturgy is a temporal art and is, in this sense, properly analogous to music, to drama, and to dance. This is why liturgical participation requires a sense of the "dance" and the "drama" of the rites, even when these art forms do not appear explicitly. The temporal art of liturgical celebration is in this respect intrinsically musical and dramatic.

The language of time also works in the accumulative associative power of specific elements within a rite. Thus, the aesthetic range and significance of eating and drinking together takes time. In everyday life we come to understand the multiple levels of meaning of such acts only after we have had meals together on birthdays, after funerals, on anniversaries and through the changing seasons of human lives in a wide range of ordinary circumstances. Symbols deepen as human beings mature with them. The source of the inexhaustibility of primary symbols is located here. At the level of texts the same is true. The same antiphon or full responsorial psalm, when used in different seasons of the year, yields a different range of potential value and force in texts (hymns, psalms, prayers, and lections).

The language of time also involves discipline in cycles of the week, the day, and the year. The aesthetic depth of liturgical participation is related to the experience of feasts and seasons. The liturgical year is a treasury of the church's memories of who God is and what God has done. The temporal cycles of day, week, and year intersect with the sanctoral cycle of holy men and women to form a powerful hermeneutical pattern.

A second nonverbal language is that of space. Because the liturgical assembly occupies a place and arranges the furnishings in that space, a pattern of acoustic, visual, and kinetic perception is set up. The places form environments that house the action of the liturgy. Each space and its interior arrangement may be said to possess specific aesthetic properties, encouraging specific kinds of actions and discouraging others. Some spaces invite a static and sedentary approach to God—in fixed auditoria, for example. Others invite freedom of encounter and movement, or uncluttered contemplation. The visual focus of the room has a profound effect upon the poetics of textual images and the function of vestments, vessels, gestures, and the uses of light within the liturgy.

There is also the history of the use of the building and the interior spaces which influences the tone and style of the liturgical celebration. So in a space where families have gathered for generations, where weddings, funerals and rites of passage have taken place, where the very sound of sung prayer has given association to the action itself, the aesthetic values of the space may dominate or even conflict with the actual style of celebration. At the same time, how we arrange furnishings—altar, ambo, font, musical instruments, presider's chair, the paschal candle—bears strongly upon what can potentially be brought to expression within the assembly.

Sound and Sight

Within the temporal-spatial setting, the acoustic and visual domains come into play. The art forms of music, whether congregational, choral, or instrumental, depend in larger measure on the properties of the building and the arrangement of the space. The relationship of sound and silence is crucial to music; but it is also part of the intrinsic music of the rites themselves. So all liturgical utterance has pitch, rhythm, intensity, and pacing. The silences between words spoken and sung are as important as the sounds themselves, for together they create the primary acoustical images of praise and prayer. Analogously, the pace, intensity, rhythm, and tone of ritual actions are part of the hidden music of the rites enacted.

The aesthetics of sound and sight are not ornamental to liturgy, but are intrinsic to the very nature of liturgical celebration. Thus music is not to be conceived primarily as something "inserted" into the rites. Rather, explicit music should seek to bring to expression the implicit music of the rites. The implicit music is at one and the same time related to the juxtaposition of texts, ritual acts, and symbols, and to the specific rites in their context. The actual acoustical experience of prayer or of preaching may carry more force than the semantic context of the actual words. Thus fully articulate musical liturgy is more festive and generates a greater range in levels of participation. At the same time, the style and quality of music must be judged appropriate to the nature of the rites and the nature of the assembly.

Following Vatican II, the United States Bishop's Committee on the Liturgy published documents pertaining to the aesthetic dimensions of Christian liturgy. *Music in Catholic Worship* (1972, 1983) and *Liturgical Music Today* (1982) present complementary sets of guidelines concerning music in the liturgy and provide a theological groundwork for integrity in liturgical music. The earlier document deals with the role of music, both instrumental and choral/vocal in various rites, while the latter proposes criteria for planning and conducting liturgical celebrations.

The whole liturgical environment is to be served

by the arts—this is the primary concern of a third document, *Environment and Art in Catholic Worship* (1978, English/Spanish edition, 1986). Particular emphasis is placed upon the liturgical assembly as a servant to God's created world and its calling to be "sign, witness, and instrument of the reign of God" (par. 38). Precisely because the assembly seeks to remember and to cultivate the redemptive power of God, it must nurture a climate of wonder, awe, reverence, thanksgiving, and praise. Therefore liturgy must seek what is beautiful in its total ethos as well as in the specific objects, gestures, sign-actions, music, and related art forms employed.

In these documents the acoustic, visual, and kinetic dimensions of liturgical celebration are integral to one another. The confluence of these arts in liturgy enables the assembly to discern the presence of God in the whole of the symbolic actions. The materials and the form are to reflect the beauty and dignity of the rites they intend to serve. Special focus is devoted to the climate of hospitality, the experience of mystery, the reality and efficacy of the range of symbols through word, gesture, and movement. A paragraph in *Environment and Art* concerning the concept of the beautiful in Christian liturgy is especially noteworthy:

> Because the assembly gathers in the presence of God to celebrate his saving deeds, liturgy's climate is one of awe, mystery, wonder, reverence, thanksgiving, and praise. So it cannot be satisfied with anything less than the beautiful in its environment and all its artifacts, movements and appeals to the senses. . . . The beautiful is related to the sense of the numinous, the holy. Where there is evidently no care for this, there is an environment basically unfriendly to mystery and awe, an environment too casual, if not careless, for the liturgical action. In a world dominated by science and technology, liturgy's quest for the beautiful is a particularly necessary contribution to full and balanced human life (par. 34).

Liturgical Aesthetics and Human Emotion

The relation between liturgy and human emotion is complex, but it is evident that Christian worship forms and expresses particular patterns of emotional dispositions in human beings. Music, poetry, dance, symbolic actions—all these have to do with the affective capacities in human life. Liturgy may be regarded as a time and place where the language,

sign-action, and symbols concerning the divine shape and express deep human emotions as gratitude to God, hope, repentance, grief, compassion, aversion to injustice, and delight in the created order. The Christian life itself is characterized by the having of such emotions and their having become wellsprings of attitude and action in life. The language of Scripture, prayer, and the sacraments has to do with elemental features of human existence: emotions linked to birth and death, suffering, sin, and oppression as well as with desire, joy, hope, and happiness. These deep emotions are not simply named or described in the language of liturgy; they are evoked, portrayed, sustained, and refined in the rites.

Holy fear, repentance, and amendment of life depend upon sharing deeply in the mystery of prayer and ritual action as in the shared meal of the Eucharist. The language of the liturgy in descriptive, ascriptive, and performative force shapes us in particular affectional ways of being by addressing God and being open to God. So eucharistic participation points toward a life of gratitude and self-giving. The very fourfold action of taking the bread and cup, blessing God over them, breaking the bread, and giving the gifts presents the pattern which the eucharistic community is to live out in daily life.

To learn gratitude to God or awe or love of God and neighbor one must learn to pray with the church. The graciousness, the holiness, and the love of God create the possibility of authentic worship. But the experiential power and range of liturgy is required in turn for the deepening of such dispositions. The integrity of the art of common prayer and ritual action requires that such gratitude, awe, and love is not confined to the liturgical event itself. That is, these religious affections are not simply aesthetically held states of feeling. Yet without the aesthetic dimensions of participation in and through the forms, no sacramental self-understanding in life can emerge. As *Environment and Art* rightly observes:

> In view of our culture's emphasis on reason, it is critically important for the Church to reemphasize a more total approach to the human person by opening up and developing the non-rational elements of liturgical celebration: the concerns for feelings of

conversion, support, joy, repentance, trust, love, memory, movement, gesture, wonder. (par. 35)

Christian liturgy that seeks emotional and symbolic authenticity and depth must always pay attention to the materials and the forms employed. Language that is only clear or cognitively precise with no overplus of poetic meaning will diminish the power of the symbols to hold together multiple levels of meaning. If the ritual actions are perfunctory or merely efficient, the texts and symbols will be diminished. If the music is always immediately accessible and without surprise or tension or durability, the texts wedded to such music suffer reduction in imaginative power and metaphoric range. The quality of texts, gestures, movements, and the form of the symbols is critical to levels of participation. Attention to each element and to their interrelation in the whole pattern of the liturgy is necessary to the power of liturgy to draw us, as church, into the gospel proclaimed and the saving mystery enacted. This is what leads Joseph Gelineau to say, "only if we come to the liturgy without hopes or fears, without longings or hunger, will the rite symbolize nothing and remain an indifferent or curious 'object.' Moreover, people who are not accustomed to poetic, artistic, or musical language or symbolic acts among their means of expression and communication find the liturgy like foreign country whose customs and language are strange to them."

——— Liturgical Style and Culture ———

The question of style is not a matter of mere technique. If it were so, we could produce awe-inspiring liturgical rites by manipulating lighting and symbols. But the aesthetic dynamism of authentic liturgical celebration is the opposite of manipulation and magic; it is the opening of the mystery of the realities signified, proclaimed, and ritually participated in. This "opening" is a matter of faithfulness and attentiveness to the whole environment of worship. Each unit or element of the liturgical assembly, and each "sub-rite," invites a particular quality of disposition which is appropriate to the nature of the rite and its context. This goes together with honesty and integrity of materials and the aesthetic adequacy of the forms. Both the leaders and the assembly as a whole share mutual responsibilities for the art of the liturgy. The presider and other specific ministers become focal points and representations of the prayerful participation of the

assembly. Activities of gathering, singing, praying, reading, listening, bowing, touching, eating, and drinking all require a heightened sense of receptivity and active participation as a community of mutuality. The cultural variables here are many, since different cultures exhibit differences in behavior in the course of such activities.

The church's teaching and catechetical approach to preparing the worshipers—both long term and immediately in the room of celebration—cannot neglect the aesthetic dimensions of specific cultures. The study of liturgical forms and teaching the primary symbols of faith must create a hospitable environment. Assisting the worshipers to participate fully in the musical forms, for example, requires sensitivity to the range of musical styles available to the people. Giving the assembly a model of good "performance practice" in responsorial psalmody, the hymns or sung responses can open up new dimensions of the cultural heritage. The problems of musical participation raise all the issues of liturgical participation. Creating appropriate spaces of silence for reflection on the readings and in relation to the sign-acts and symbols is part of the nonmanipulative art of the liturgy.

The poetics of celebration requires examination of the specific cultural context of the assembly. In our post-conciliar period, new emphasis is being placed on the modes of expression indigenous to the social and cultural history of the people. If the liturgy is to signify the divine/human interaction, then modes of appropriating and sharing the basic symbols must be mediated in and through the language, music, visual, and bodily style of the people. The aesthetics of liturgy thus demands that we know the differences between, for example, patterns proper to a North-American cultural tradition formed principally in Northern Europe and patterns that are Afro-American or Hispanic.

At the same time, the symbolic action points to realities which are in tension with all inherited cultural assumptions and patterns of behavior. The permanent tension in the poetics of liturgy is between the necessity of local cultural modes of perception (expression and interpretation) and the common culture of Christian faith and life. Only by maintaining this tension can we also assert specifically Christian faith and life over against the assumptions of much postmodern and technological culture. Though each subculture has its own integrity, there is a manner of celebration which is Christian, stemming from the particular claims of the paschal mystery. There is a way of enacting the rites which is ultimately the human reception of what God has done in creation and in Jesus Christ. This has been referred to by Gelineau and others as the "paschal human in Christ"—a manner enacted in particular cultural languages that evidences "both reserve and openness, respect and simplicity, confident joy . . . and true spontaneity. . . ."

Afterward

Liturgy belongs to the created world and thus is an art, for the created order belongs to God. The aesthetics of authentic liturgy concerns the intrinsic means, not simply the eternal decoration, or the rites themselves. Without such aesthetic considerations as honesty of materials, quality of craft and performance, appropriateness, proportionality, and integrity within the liturgy of the art forms and the people, the whole of the liturgy is diminished in its symbolic power.

Yet, lest we take delight only in the beautiful forms we have managed, and not discern the enabling grace of God in and through the forms, the final word must be eschatological. All artistic effort is itself proleptic as well as participatory in God's creativity. The mystery celebrated is never exhausted or fully contained in the liturgy. Liturgical rites authentically celebrated point beyond themselves to the eschatological vision and the "heavenly liturgy" of Christ of which all earthly celebrations are but hints and guesses. This way all attention to the aesthetics of Christian liturgy is but a servant of the vision of a created order transformed and reconciled to the life of God. There all that is creaturely will be permeated with light, dance, and song. Insofar as we experience the prefigurement of that reality in particular times and places, the aesthetics of liturgical celebration become congruent with the holiness and the beauty of the triune life of God, at once incarnate in the world and yet transcendent in glory beyond all created things.

Donald Saliers[44]

275 • SYMBOLS AS THE LANGUAGE OF ART AND LITURGY

Symbols are a primary means by which the truth of the gospel is communicated. They communicate to us through all our senses and on many levels, to our thinking and our feeling, our memory and our imagination. Further, symbolic language serves to unite Christians, giving them a common reference point and experience that transcends divisions within the Christian community.

Artists Are Primary Communicators

We can't do anything right in the work of reform and renewal of the church if we do not first realize its importance. We are not decorators to a reality that is essentially abstract and cerebral. We are, in fact, primary communicators, ministers, and evangelists, since our work is in and with and for the Sunday assembly where the faith community celebrates its identity as church and shares its nourishment—where humans are formed, not merely brains informed. We are communicating the gospel at a level that precedes, and is fundamental to, all theologizing and all administration.

What is the symbol-language of our "primary and indispensable source," the liturgy, and how are environment and arts part of it? By the terms *symbol* and *symbol-language* I mean primarily the stories of the Bible proclaimed in the Sunday assembly and the actions we call sacraments done by the Sunday assembly. Environment is the skin, the space, the enabling scene of that assembly, that proclamation, that action. Its arts are the skills of music, rhetoric, movement and gesture, design and craft in the making and using of all things necessary for sacramental worship (from architecture and images to vessels, vesture, utensils, and books, and so on).

Communication among human beings, including what Jews and Christians believe is God's revelation, puts environment (its shapes, colors, textures, smells, flavors, tones) and all the imagining and skills we call the arts right at the center of the enterprise. So when poor, deluded creatures dismiss environment and art considerations in any of the ways with which we are so depressingly familiar, what they are really doing is dismissing the way God touches us, loves us, the way God reveals the divine design and will, the way in which we are invited to share the vision of God's reign, justice, and peace for all, liberation and reconciliation for all, and therefore the way we are to know ourselves as church and our mission in the world. There is nothing luxurious or precious about these concerns.

Symbol-Language Appeals to All Our Human Levels and Faculties

Unlike our prose discourse and our verbal formulas, so terribly limited by their vocabulary as well as by the time and place in which they are conceived, the symbol-language of liturgy is comprehensive, classic, and seminal.

Since we believe the biblical covenant and the paschal mystery are God's invitation to a new way of life, a new orientation of our lives, and not merely to an oath of allegiance or a set of ideas or a party line, symbol-language is its favorite as well as its most adequate communication. Symbol-language appeals comprehensively to all of our human levels and faculties and to the whole species in all of its variety. Its types are deeply imbedded in our common human roots, escaping the Babel of our different languages, customs, ways. It engages not merely the listening and idea mechanism but the entire person, through song and speech and silence, through gestures and other forms of movement, through touch and taste and smell and sight and hearing, through its evoking of memory, recollection, fantasy, imagination—acting out in liturgy (rather, enabling the Sunday assembly to act out) the liberating and reconciling deeds of God in living rite, as the commitment of the baptized.

From the liberating bath of immersion into baptism's newness to the reconciling meal, where we share equally one holy bread, drinking from one holy cup, in the Eucharist's solidarity—in every rite of public worship, this multidimensional symbol-language admits the inadequacy of our feeble words, respects the terrible mystery of God, excludes no means that might, however obliquely, penetrate our defenses with vision and with hope.

But this can't be unless we take it seriously, unless we play hard at it, unless we give our ears and our hearts to those biblical stories, our minds and our bodies and our imaginations to those sacramental actions and gestures. When the liturgy thus becomes ours, our very own, we can begin to catch the vision of God's reign, of what we and our world must become—liberation and reconciliation.

And the stories and the actions and the gestures will not grab us in this way until we learn to absorb them fully, with no abbreviations and no shortcuts: space—not constructed on the model of the auditorium but made for liturgical action; the baptismal bath—immersion, done to the full; the Lord's Supper—bready bread, broken, shared; real wine—poured out and drunk from common cups. *Significado causant.* The sacraments have their effects through what they signify—our experience of them. We have been positively ingenious in depriving and robbing the sacraments of their signification: by our "practicality"; by our desire for convenience; by our aversion to work. Our liturgical world has been verbal—anything else being incidental. Opening up the nonverbal to signification and experience is a revolution that has hardly begun.

Symbol-Language Unifies Us on a Biblical and Sacramental Level

Symbol-language is catholic, universal, not only in its comprehensiveness but also in its classic character. It is a great gift to have covenant sources that reveal God's design and make us partners in its realization—and do it in a classic way, a way that applies to all times and all places. No blueprints. No party line. No concrete instructions for exactly what must be done right now in our lives, in our political and economic organization, in our other cultural and social affairs. Those things God trusts us to work out with the talents we have been given and in concert with the rest of the human family. Only the direction, the orientation, the goal is clear in the Word of God who is liberator and reconciler—justice and peace. Everything is to be measured by that direction. And it is that direction in our sources, as well as their ambiguity about our concrete steps today, that invites a multitude of different insights and interpretations . . . and with all of these joined in the church we make a bit of progress toward consensus. That's why at our best (and we are rarely at our best) we are so loath to stifle controversy. Because we are all so limited individually (none of us being the whole Christ), it is through our sharing of different interpretations about what to do that we may eventually arrive at some common interpretations as the body of Christ.

That classic, catholic character makes a lot of people nervous. What it wants to do is challenge us to respect each other and be open to learning from each other, recognizing our need of each other, to be, as church, the body of Christ. If we have a deep unity on this symbolic biblical and sacramental level, then we can trust each other to grow up and bring our own consciences and human gifts to a common solution of problems. But if we have lost that deep and classic oneness, then there is nothing left but a sect, a party line, a forced and literal conformity on a relatively superficial level.

Reform and Renewal Are the Very Nature of the Church's Existence

Another characteristic of the symbol-language I am discussing is its seminal, unfinished, evolving, developing nature. God's revelation itself is progressive, as the Bible, Judaism, and Christianity prove, and indicates a living tradition, a continuous creative process, by which God draws human history inch by inch toward a fuller realization of the freedom and oneness God has already given us in faith. That is why reform and renewal are the very nature of the church's existence and not merely an era or a diversion in its story.

What a relief! Who could abide the church if we thought it were a finished, completed, perfected reality? Any more than we could abide ourselves as individuals, if we thought we had no possibilities of change, of growth, of development! Our understanding and living of the Good News is always in process, conditioned by our time, our place, our culture. All that is in God is dynamic, moving (not standing still and not retreating) toward God's reign of justice and peace. We imagine and experience in rite and bring to our work and world possibilities of greater justice, firmer peace, more freedom from oppressors or addictions, more oneness in diversity for all God's children.

Art always sees nature, the world, and humanity not as inert, static, fully developed accomplishments of the past, but as en route, on a journey, full of promise and of as yet unrealized possibilities. True art will have nothing to do with a static, rearguard, the-old-times-were-the-good-times conception of life or of the church. In art we bring our human intent, our express desire, our will and commitment to a work of creation. Not resting in what has been but increasing the good, the true, and the beautiful, drawing what is to be out of what is with our imaginations and our work.

In this seminal character, this openness to growth and development, the arts are like the gospel itself. No wonder they are so bound up with its symbol-language and that their ministry is so indispensable to its proclamation and celebration.

How Do We Go about Our Project?

Now to a few remarks about the means we use for our project. How do we prepare an environment that enables and enlists the arts that serve this critical symbol-language of our rites? Power corrupts, as we all know. To approach our function in these matters without reflection on that fact of human experience would be foolish indeed. Clericalism and what was for a time considered clerical power are fading—not rapidly enough, but fading nonetheless.

One of the great gifts of the reform efforts thus far since the Second Vatican Council has been a stemming of our perennial drift toward idolatry, a purification of our notion of God, the holy otherness of God, that has, as its complement, the rediscovery that we are all creatures, no matter what hats we wear or what offices we occupy. All of us are gifted in different ways, yet all of us are limited. Relating again the clergy and any other specialized ministries to their basis in the common ministry of the community of the baptized has shattered the long-tolerated illusions about exclusive clerical connections with the divine. Slowly we regain a healthy notion of church, including a recognition of our need of specialized ministries—a need that does not require pretension.

We must not be apologetic about this development, as if this health were somehow a weakening of ministry or offices of leadership. It is their strength, and this conciliar era is a gift of God. This moment of reaction is merely another instance of our well-proven resistance to repentance.

Now that we are beginning to move from what had become an autocratic to a more communitarian and consensual sort of decision making, we have to remember that the new committee, although it is more representative of the community than the old autocrat, is no more than the autocrat a source or guarantee of competence. The committee has to do the same searching for artists, architects, designers, craftspeople as the autocrat had to do. When the autocrat did not do this searching and finding and freeing of appropriately competent artists, and instead assumed that because he had the job he had the gifts, we witnessed the environmental and artistic mess of our recent past. If the new committee is going to act in the same way, the results will be just as disastrous.

Committees and collegial structures of all sorts are necessary and important developments in the church. But we must not confuse their function with any of the particular competencies that environment and art require. A liturgy committee, for example, should have a basic understanding of the faith community and of the full, conscious, active participation of all its members required by its liturgy and of what the rites require in terms of personnel and equipment. But when it comes to the ministry of reader, the committee has to search for that particular trained talent of public proclamation. The old autocrat who understood human limits (many did not) searched out, employed, and paid individuals with appropriate training and talent for the job to be done. The new committee must do the same and should be able to do it more effectively, given its representative character and its presumed knowledge of the community and its resources. It is a tragedy when the new committee simply inherits the old autocrat's power, without any feeling of responsibility for seeking and hiring those highly individual and particular competencies and charisms. One of the marks of the church, as a community whose common ministry is liberation and reconciliation, should be a deep respect and reverence and gratitude for the gifts of others and a feeling of need for them. We recognize this when we are dealing with tasks of plumbing or bricklaying. We tend to forget it when we are dealing with building or renovation, with design and the arts in worship.

Conclusion

We pray and think and talk about how our faith communities and local churches can create environments and solicit arts that will not only embody but also encourage and enable the kind of human experience through symbolic communication we call liturgy. We are given the thankless task of being goads, prodders, gadflies, stingers of consciences (including our own). We get tired. We'd like to have somebody pat us on the head and say "Thanks . . . thanks!" But if we are serious about where we are or are coming from, our job is to struggle against human nature's preference for the misery it knows, its fear of the new and different. But when the job is done and the space begins to form the faith community that worships in it and with it, encouraging and enabling with its awe-inspiring beauty and its

warm human scale and hospitality, the full, conscious, active participation of the entire Sunday assembly—then, if we are still alive, we can bask in glory. For now, however, it is all uphill.

Robert Hovda[45]

276 ◆ How Symbols Speak

Symbols, including liturgical symbols, communicate to us on many levels. This article explores the profound nature of symbolic communication, based on the approach of scholar Paul Ricoeur, and offers suggestions for how liturgical symbols can be made to speak more clearly and profoundly.

The whole program of the liturgical revival may be summed up with the apt phrase used by Robert Hovda in a variety of places: "Let the symbols speak." We long for our communities to be clear about the great central signs and actions that bear Christianity and speak it authentically to our time. We want to "unshrivel" these symbols and let them stand forth, ample, gracious and full, occupying the whole time and space of the liturgical assembly's gathering. We want to see anew that these symbols are the actions of a whole community, not objectified things under the control of a clerical few. And we want to learn anew how to take seriously the rich implications of these symbols as they propose to us new ways to see ourselves, our world and our cultures held under the great mercy of God.

A growing ecumenical consensus tells us what these authentic symbols of Christianity are: they are a people washed and anointed into common life; they are that people gathered for the reading and interpretation of the ancient Scriptures; they are that people eating and drinking at a table of thanksgiving; and they are the lesser—but still important—signs that link individual or family life to the assembly's symbolic purpose or reconcile alienated persons into the assembly.

We do not necessarily have such wide agreement on what exactly it would mean to present these symbols in their unshriveled fullness, or to build and to live following their implications. How large shall the pool of washing be? How does the speech of the assembly come to be marked with the same kind of symbolic authenticity we are seeking for the enacted signs? What does the communal character of the action mean for the nature of leadership and authority in the assembly? What are the links between the symbolic vision of the liturgy and social criticism? Just what is it that the symbols are saying?

We are working on these questions, and working hard, but the underlying question is always the same and always the most important: how can we foster this renewal of our symbols and our life? Or to say it again, what exactly shall we do to let the symbols speak?

Ricoeur's Criteriology

A variety of scholarly analyses exist to assist us in this work by helping us determine how symbols do their "speaking" at all, how they *mean*. One of the most useful of these is the phenomenology or "criteriology" of symbols found in the introduction to Part 1 of Paul Ricoeur's classic study, *The Symbolism of Evil.* The discussion occupies only a few pages, but reflection on the structures of meaning proposed there may be very helpful for our task of letting the symbols speak.

According to Ricoeur, in every authentic symbol three dimensions are present: the cosmic, the oneiric (of or relating to dreams), and the poetic. A symbol is (a) a thing in the world in which the sacred is manifested to our community; (b) a thing which then figures in our dreams or, more generally, in our own psychic histories; and (c) a thing around which words and songs and names gather powerful meanings. Only on the basis of these dimensions or functions of a symbol ought one proceed to distinguish yet a fourth function or dimension, the reflective. A symbol is also (d) a complex of meanings that may "give rise to thought," that may feed concept and doctrine.

Thus, to take one example, from earliest times the sun and the moon have presented themselves to some human groups as the basic—indeed, the most primary—manifestations of the sacred. Night and day and the cycles of seasons and tides experienced in relationship to the cycles and positions of the sun and the moon made those heavenly bodies available as symbols of the very cosmic order itself. To encounter the sun (or, in a transposition, the moon) was to encounter that beyond our world which held our world together. Moreover, the burning, blinding fire of the sun was an analogue to the human experience that real order always has to do with danger restrained or transformed. The sun rises. The world has a center. And if all is well, in balance with moon and water, the sun does not burn us up.

Sun and moon rise also in our dreams. the terrify us or they save us. They give us light for hunting or for working or for living. Their duality becomes the focus for our experience of father and mother and so of our own sexual identity. We fly with them. We become the center of meaning and order. But not quite. We hunt with the moon, or are hunted. We reign with the sun and are burned up.

So the poets have a great resonance in us when they begin to sing. And their words and epithets and metaphors make even deeper the meaning we see in objects in the sky or the material that is interpreted in our dreams. Their words seem to carry the tribal order and our own psychic history. The word is itself the thing—the symbol—it names. "Great Light," the poets sing. Or "Father" or "Mother." They sing the tales of Phaethon or Icarus or Diana. Or they make a day the first day or the second and name it after one of the great lights. Then when the sun or moon rises on the tribe's horizon or in our dreams, there is the name and the story and the order of the week.

What comes first—cosmos or dream or word? We do not really know; and Ricoeur is not proposing a history. His structure simply proposes that it is useful to see that all three aspects are present in any symbol, and in primary symbols all three—the cosmic order, the dream power and the poetic word—are the same. Of course, what is meant by the dream power, the "oneiric," is not just the functioning of the symbol in our dreams; it is all that the symbol does in our individual psychic lives. For us now the symbol does not even exist as "thing" apart from the word, but the word interprets and makes available a powerful cosmic and psychic experience.

A New Poetics

But in the Judeo-Christian tradition, at least, the poets speak on: the great lights, they say, and the days and weeks they rule are creatures, made by God. God—a word for that giver of order who is beyond all names and all natural necessities—may fly and burn and reign like the sun, may rise as the sun of righteousness. But God is not the sun. And, for Christians, Sunday is the order-giving first day now, chiefly because it is the day of assembly around the risen *Christ,* not the risen sun. Still, in this new poetics the old cosmic and oneiric powers still resonate, bringing the order and the fears suggested by the sun to names we use for God or for the assembly's day. And classically the positions of the sun and the moon were used to determine the dates of the great feasts on which the story was told of the salvation of God who is beyond the sun. So classic iconography has sun and moon on either side of the image of the crucified.

Surely, among Christians, further discourse on the doctrines of monotheism and of creation will be assisted by including some reflection on the cosmic, oneiric, and poetic functions of the symbolism of sun and moon, as well as on the transformation of this symbolism in the new poetics of the Bible. The symbol, says Ricoeur, gives rise to thought, and the thought is illuminated by rerooting it in its symbolic matrix. What Christians mean by "monotheism" is not so much a philosophical position derived from the experience of one sun in the sky and the suppression of the symbol of the moon, as it is the event that happens, in the conception of God and the world, when the new poetics says: "*God* made sun and moon!" The "event" that happens in the poetry, this revolutionary and surprising turn, must always be borne in mind in reflection on doctrine, or the doctrine is distorted into philosophy or ideology.

It is interesting, of course, to anyone who cares about symbols, to note that while we are all taught that the universe does not circle around either the earth or the sun, we still so mark our days and seasons with the passages of sun and moon as to bring to them, to quote Ricoeur again, a postcritical "second naiveté." It is no wonder, then, that homiletic calls to hope for the sun of righteousness are still so moving to us, or that the Christmas and Hanukkah feasts that occur in the dark time of the sun's return still have such a hold on our culture, quite apart from their Christian or Jewish content, their "new poetics." Teachers and preachers and liturgists should note that even in this scientific age there is still room for the surprise, the discovery, the joy of the biblical poetics. "This light you long for at Christmas, lighting fires and candles and tree-lights against the darkness, midwinter protest—this light of order and peace already shines in the darkness itself. Christ born, God come among our darkness and injustice and death—this is the sun. It shines in the bread in your hands, the cup at your lips."

Basic Christian Symbols

But neither sun nor moon, though they have determined festal dates and given a name to the assembly day and lent imagery to our preaching and our hymns, is the primary symbol of the liturgy. A bath, an assembly-for-the-Word, and a shared meal—these are primary. Can Ricoeur's schema of "cosmos, dream, word" illuminate *these* symbols and help us to see what we are doing in letting them "speak?" Or, rather, can we apply to these primary symbols of the assembly the adaptation of Ricoeur's schema that I have used here: cosmic meaning, psychic power, poetic names and songs; then the new poetics of the Bible and so the symbols as the grounds for concept and doctrine?

Yes.

Take the symbol *meal*. Many communities of human beings have encountered a cosmic revelation of the sacred in a laden table: the food represents the cooperation of the fruitful land or the giving forest with human culture and work; the food means the survival of the tribe or family, the circle of shared eating, against famine and death. Because of these meanings, the food of a meal comes to signify more than its momentary utilitarian value. It stands for peaceful order and life; indeed, it carries intimations of a larger order than that enjoyed by this circle eating now. The symbol *meal* is used to integrate others into the community or to give an occasion for the enactment of secondary symbols that also manifest something of what we think to be this universal order: who eats first? who is admitted? what foods are there? what is the order of eating? The power of the symbol is heightened, of course, because it tames and transforms its opposite. We eat to live. But just so death is suggested: without eating we would die, and even now our life depends on the death of plants and animals which the forest or our agriculture have given us. In eating we are at the edge, the limit, of our possibilities. We know ourselves to be contingent, dependent, on that which is outside us—so we are before the sacred.

I also eat and drink in my dreams. I eat the tree or am eaten by the beast. I drink the magic cup or the stream that is the beloved. I come to a room that has been prepared for me or I am embarrassed or terrified at a common meal. Such might be images in anyone's dreams. Eating or being eaten, slaking thirst or being poisoned, being terrified or richly delighted at a common meal—it is no wonder that there should be such oneiric themes since, generally in my psychic life, I face in hunger my limit, my death. And my earliest knowledge of another, and so of my emergent self, was at eating, was looking up across the breast at one who responded to my hunger. Eating, then, has always been communal.

At the same time, it has always been powerfully, personally intimate. My contingency says: perhaps in that food there is order and peace for me.

And the poet sings. There are songs at the meal, telling what the tribe or community knows to be most true and using the order suggested by the meal as the occasion to tell it. There are histories and tales and stories of other meals—stories of fears and hopes and necessary labor—which thereby become part of what is eaten. Words are said to interpret the course of the meal, and names are created for the food and for the meal itself, as the singers broaden and complicate the reference of the cosmic symbol and deepen the material of my dreams. The words, the eating and the dreaming are one "thing," one powerful symbol.

God's Surprise

That "thing" is material for the biblical poetics; indeed, says the faith, it is material for the very grace of God to speak to us an unexpected mercy. So, for Jews and Christians, God is the source of food, and the principal words of the meal are words of thanksgiving. Such thanksgiving witnesses to an order of the world—"dominion of God" is one major metaphor in the meal prayers that transcends the security of the tribe or family or nation. Eating and the words are one "thing": they are thanksgiving. And there are stories and songs at the meals, stories of God's great mercy for a poor people, and mercy making this people free. The meals themselves become witnesses to the covenant with this God. The people do not die; they eat and drink with God. These are covenant meals and sacrificial meals and festal meals and the Passover meal and the promise of the final, great, nation-feeding meal on the holy mountain.

The old cosmic, oneiric, and poetic resonances are all still around—the hope for land and culture to be united in order, the longing for life-giving food, the inclusion of references to death. But now they are surprised: God is the giver of land and culture and hope and life; the gift is to all peoples, and the real order is not given by our too early, foreclosing, frequently murderous "order."

Still, the biblical surprise goes on. Jesus eats meals of the dominion of God and eats them with outsiders and excluded ones. Jesus' own death is interpreted by a meal. Finally, the community's meal, whereby it means to gather its gathering of many lost and poor ones into an assembly to witness to

God's order, receives Jesus' witness, his death and risen life, as its principal food. And already in the letters of Paul and James, Christians begin the long critical process continuing until today, which asks whether the meal sufficiently represents the new order and justice of God. Eating and drinking, words of thanksgiving, Jesus' witness, his body and blood, a community of outsiders made the people of God—these, by God's grace, are all one thing.

The old cosmic, oneiric, and poetic references have been received and broken and reshaped. There is no salvation, finally, in our dreams or in our ancient symbols, no hope beyond our own necessities and projections. But in surprising grace God saves all that we are—our hopes and our fears and even our dreams and symbols and stories.

Much of the same sketch could be made of *water* or of the symbolic complex *word-in-assembly*. So, for example, water is met as the cosmic order, as chaos tamed, as the source of fruitfulness. It is dreamt about as drowning or birth, as washing or sex. And stories are told of the community that lives by the water, defeats the water, survives the water, finds and drinks the water. Such water is received in the biblical poetics and then in Jewish and Christian ritual. But now, for Christians, its full force is broken open at a new thing—order and birth and the slaking of thirst where we thought there was only death, in the midst of human life in this world. God comes among us to share our lot and our death, and that sharing is washed over us to make us a new people, witnesses to God's order, alive with God's life.

And so word-in-assembly has been, as with the ancient reading of *Enuma elish* at the new year, the creation of the world each year afresh: people gathered around ritual word was a symbol of the cosmos. It has been oracle and the hope for a word for me. And it has been stories and songs of a people gathered to hear proclaimed the great charter or the fearful royal decree. In the biblical poetics, it is the assembly of Israel to hear God's word, God's law; it is the people being in the covenant; it is the final assembly of all the nations. And then it has become, in the great surprise, the assembly of this collection of folk today to hear the word, to hear Jesus Christ risen, "beginning at Moses and all the prophets."

Implications

Such reflections as these might follow from Ricoeur's criteriology. And, indeed, much more could be said for each of the levels of meaning and each of the primary symbols of Christian assembly. But this much is enough to suggest some answers to the questions we posed in the beginning. The pool should be very large, so large as to evoke the cosmic and oneiric references. The speech of the assembly, taught by the biblical poetics, should function symbolically more than didactically, so that it keeps alive cosmic, oneiric, and poetic resonances while bringing them into new crisis. The critique of order at the meal must continue with a new emphasis on the breaking of false authority and the welcoming of outsiders to the center. These must become part of what the symbols are saying.

Finally, this schema of symbolic meaning itself proposes three theses that can guide our thinking about renewal:

1. The primary symbols in the assembly need to be recovered as full signs that readily evoke the cosmic, oneiric, and poetic. In such a fuller presence these symbols will be better able to evoke ourselves and our hopes for the world, our sense of humanity located in a cosmos, our fears, and failures.

2. But we are not about a new paganism; there is no great hope in our symbols and dreams, but rather in these greatly evoked and greatly broken in the poetics and grace of God. The recovery of the symbols needs to be accompanied with a profound recovery of biblical catechesis and preaching, of mystagogy into the surprise of Jesus Christ. He is the bread and the water and the Word.

3. This twofold recovery will protect us from a continuation of the use of symbols as mere illustrations of doctrine or as proposals of ideology. Such renewal will instead urge that doctrine is reflection on the crisis of full symbols when they are used of Christ. And when the symbols are allowed to speak they propose a new world order greater than our justice, already present in God's gift and forming us to lives of witness.

Gordon Lathrop[46]

277 • THE RELATIONSHIP OF VISUAL AND VERBAL ELEMENTS IN WORSHIP

The following article describes how visual and verbal elements have been used throughout the history of the church, noting how the modern church has not allowed visual elements to have a significant role in worship. It goes on to describe how the visual arts can be revived and how we can learn to communicate and receive theological truths through the visual arts.

In the life of the church, the visual arts have ranged from being conspicuously pervasive to being totally absent. In no period was art as central or so important as in the Middle Ages, nor, in contrast, so programmatically and theologically absent as in the Reformed tradition beginning from the sixteenth century as well as in many churches that grew on English soil. Although such extremes do not define our time, their impact has left us with considerable ambiguity about the place and role of the visual arts in the church.

History sheds only partial light on the sources of this ambivalence. For the Middle Ages we can point to the proliferation of saints and the ascendancy of Mary to a special place in redemptive history, both widely depicted in the arts along with biblical figures, Christ and the Godhead. At that level, one would assume that the Reformation would stand for the removal of the saints and of Mary, with concentration instead on Christ and biblical subjects in works of art. But the total abolition of the arts in the Reformed churches, sometimes with frightening evidences of violence, indicates that more than the subject matter was involved.

Idolatry, of course, was the pivotal word, and the second commandment was interpreted to mean that images, not just false images, were to be destroyed. But for images to be considered idols meant that something had happened, for up to the Middle Ages an image remained an image and was not confused with the reality it represented or mirrored. But already in the Carolingian period images were viewed with suspicion, not because they would be confused with what they imaged, but because they were *only* images. Relics were considered more important, for they provided tangible realities in which God was literally as well as symbolically present. Seeing and touching such realities was more important than experiencing images in which the divine was not physically present. But in the subsequent medieval history, images, as well as the consecrated elements, were interpreted as if they were relics. Then images became idols, or so the Reformed tradition understood them.

That this could happen discloses something about the visual. It too, like other sensibilities, can be a power for good or evil. In much of the Middle Ages, seeing was more important for the public than hearing. The consecrated elements were lifted up to be seen, and it was believed that seeing the elements made it unnecessary for all to partake or to hear what was said.

What a reversal, then, when the Reformed tradition based everything on hearing, and its derivative, reading, along with the abolition of the visual. But what had happened to the visual in the Middle Ages now occurred with respect to the verbal. The initial symbolic power of language took on a literal meaning, as the verbal increasingly and variously was understood as propositional statements of truth, or a fundamentalist reading of Scripture, or a spiritual or moral reduction of content to management proportions. Emphasis on the words in the Word had brought a new form of idolatry.

What we need, of course, is a rightful view of both the visual and the verbal. They represent one reality through two modalities, each appropriately important and necessary for the full expression of our humanity. Theologically, considerable progress has been made in recovering the imaginative power of language, a development that bodes well for an alliance between the visual and the verbal. But among those responsible for services or worship, a preoccupation with the dynamics of the worship service has led to a conviction that only that which directly serves the liturgy has an appropriate place. Some liturgists have declared that the better the work of art, the more it interferes with liturgical practice or the worshiping community. That outlook encourages the use of poor art, including the inordinate profusion of banners, with the result that only art which has no power of its own, that is, only art that can be used for purposes other than what art conveys, is acceptable. Such a reintroduction of art is neither dangerous nor helpful; such art is simply banal.

The reappropriation of the visual for the church, for which theological seminaries can be a vehicle— and for which some have taken responsibility—requires taking the arts seriously on their own terms.

Scripture is not directly helpful on that point, for some passages are positive; some are negative. In addition to the problem of how the second commandment is to be understood, there is reference in 1 Kings (7:14) to Solomon's bringing Hiram from Tyre to do works of bronze, and in Exodus 31 (vv. 1-11) an artist named Bezalel is mentioned as doing works in various media for the temple. Concepts of beauty play their part in the Psalms and in sections of the New Testament, as in the lilies of the field, though these passages point to the works of God, not the works of the artists.

The other arts—music, drama, and dance—also have had an ambiguous relation to the church, but, unlike the visual arts, they have been more widely accepted. It is surely ironic that many churches will not shrink at spending large sums of money for a new organ, but not a penny for paintings or sculpture. The plea for the organ rests, of course, on the fact that music has made its way into the worshiping life of the congregation, even though, in principle, music is not necessarily dependent on the organ. Surprisingly, literature as an art form does enter into biblical consciousness. Perhaps that is because Scripture itself is a literary form, thereby making it a natural medium for those who expound Scripture, sometimes with quotations which at their best shed new light on biblical passages.

Music and literature, while banished from the church at certain periods, are art forms that have nevertheless made their way within it. They confirm rather than challenge the worship life of the community, though to be sure avant-garde music and literature can create a stir within the church.

What is it about dance and the visual arts that makes the church uncomfortable? Undoubtedly, it is because both are sensual. In dance for the church, that art form is frequently stylized to the point that it merely illustrates biblical passages and has been deprived of much of its sensual nature as dance. But sensuousness defines the very essence of dance and the visual arts.

We have come full circle. The Reformed tradition, in its fight against idolatry, defined the spiritual over against the material or sensual. Hence Reformed churches, Presbyterians, Congregationalists, Baptists, or those who eschewed such connections, such as Quakers, abolished the arts, for in their way of perceiving the spiritual, the material or sensual was not a medium through which the spiritual could be manifest. Theologically, that was the great divide between the medieval world and the Reformed tradition, with Lutherans and Roman Catholics accepting that the spiritual was also manifest in materiality and through the senses, even though the latter had been abused in the past. On this issue, the Anglicans, reflecting England's self-conscious Protestant stance, were also originally suspicious of the arts; but in the nineteenth century they returned to more Catholic sensibilities.

In recent decades, spirituality has invaded the consciousness of most of the churches. Derived from the Catholic tradition, but understood partly in Protestant terms, spirituality has become a bridge on which the spiritual, the material, and the sensual have come together again. Without judging either the defects or contributions of spirituality as a movement, one can say that it has become a vehicle for overcoming the split between the spiritual and the material or sensual. Hence, it places us in a more favorable ethos with respect to the visual.

Just as the disappearance of the visual in Protestantism and its transformation in Catholicism was a theological issue, so its reemergence today is theological. This reemergence involves how we understand our various sensibilities, that is, how all our senses may be related to moral, religious, aesthetic facets of existence, involving both emotional and intellectual ingredients. One way of understanding the human scene is to admit that hearing, seeing, feeling, tasting, smelling—all of which belong to our humanity—do not form a unity. It is as if, theologically speaking, there were a split among our senses, and some of them were considered safer than others. No one would challenge the role of hearing, giving preeminence to speaking and to the printed word. More recently, we have witnessed the dominant characteristic of television and its technique of telling us what to hear through seeing. Hence it is more a verbal than a visual source of understanding. But while we accept the role of hearing, and its consequences for good, seldom do we face what may be called word pollution. For some reason, word pollution is not considered as dangerous or bad as the abuse of the other senses. In contemporary life, the verbal is surely as abused as was the visual in periods of the Middle Ages.

All of our senses belong to our humanity. Therefore, to bracket one or more out because it or they present problems, also deprives us of the good that belongs to each sensibility, that is, it leaves out something that belongs to our created humanity. That is too high a price to pay, for we are called to be fully human. Leaving out part of our humanity makes us less than that which was intended in creation, for each sense gives us something, which, while related to what the other senses convey, is

also unique. The intermixture of the senses is surely evident in biblical and religious language, such as "having the eyes of our hearts enlightened," or "taste and see how good the Lord is." Surely, the word in proclamation and the word in sacrament are the same word; yet, in each the mode of reception also provides us with perceptions that come to us only in that way.

Stressing the visual as well as the verbal demands visual as well as verbal literacy. The expression "I know nothing about art but I know what I like" has to go. Would one really accept ignorance as an ideal anywhere else in life? No sensibility is to be trusted unless it has been honed. An informed sensibility is the fruit of work and discipline. Just as we are schooled in the verbal, we must be schooled in the visual. Yet, schooling in the visual requires disciplines appropriate to that sensibility. While there are analogies between the verbal and the visual, schooling in the visual is not the same as schooling in the verbal.

The visual requires a discerning eye. While our distinguished artists have a special talent, as do our distinguished writers, talent is not enough. Without the disciplined exercise of the medium, which comes only with practice and learning, and usually with the help of teachers, talent burns itself out and provides nothing of enduring or transcending value.

For those of us with lesser talent, the development of a discerning eye is especially important. That can happen in two forms, sometimes separate, sometimes combined: (1) by engaging in the practice of an art form, such as painting or sculpture, or (2) by repeated seeing and careful study of works of art. Traditional learning, whether through lectures or books, about the works of art is appropriate, but as an adjunct to seeing.

Learning to paint or sculpt introduces one to the special dynamics of seeing as evident in the creative process. It has the special character of interiority, in which there is an immediacy that can hardly be secondhand. When guided by those with exceptional talent, we enter into the special world of seeing, where the eye is the pulse directing the arms and hands in the use of brush or chisel. Such an experience creates forms of perception that will make us see the world differently.

By entering directly into the making of art, those with little talent may still learn the special way in which the eyes inform and form works of art. If the process becomes recreation rather than creation, human purposes may still be served, but one has not entered into the world of art. Those with little talent for the education of their own eyes need to accept and understand the difference that talent makes in the creation of art. In the visual, as in the other arts, we need to accept the range from the average to the excellent, an outlook we have learned to accept in music. While the excellent in the arts may statistically be small in volume, it provides all of us with the unimpeachable power and structure of the visual. The excellent, too, is not without its dangers, for such creations express an audacity dangerously close to creation itself. But in such creations we may also come to know the power of the human eye in imaging God and seeing ourselves as created in the image of God.

For many, probably most of us, the discerning eye will be developed by the repeated seeing of works of art, an habituation that creates its own discipline and satisfactions to the point that not to see is to feel deprived of a part of one's very being. Here it is important to be specific, for merely wandering around in museums can be debilitating. It is important to start somewhere, such as choosing four or five artists that seem to interest one. Then repeated seeing of the same works, as well as other works by the same artists, creates seeing patterns of new discoveries that become the basis for widening one's horizons. In the context of such seeing, information about the works and the artists will be enriching, but is not a substitute for seeing. In fact, information is detrimental to seeing when the printed word or the verbal defines what one is to see. Information rightly provides a helping hand, but when an end in itself, it substitutes the verbal for the visual. Sad to say, there are art historians whose studies of the iconography or social setting can be carried out without actually seeing the works of art, an exercise that has been dubbed "art history without art."

Hence, the recovery of seeing as a human discipline is essential as a prelude to the recovery of art within the church. The loss of the visual was more pronounced in Protestantism than in Catholicism. But even Catholicism began to substitute plaster saints for authentic works of art, thus providing reminders of the verbal rather than creating the fresh perceptions required of art and its appropriate seeing, which is the function of great art.

Given that seeing is so much a part of our lives, it plays a role even when we ignore it. Both space and

the forms and shapes around us affect us, whether or not we are conscious of them. Hence, poor art also affects us negatively, even unknowingly. But the obverse is also true, that significant art and architecture stimulate genuine seeing that enriches everything with which we come in contact, that stretches us, that makes us comfortable on the other side of being as comfortable as an old shoe.

Surely it is ironic that the poor or the oppressed have a greater interest in what feeds the human spirit—the visual arts, theater, and indigenous cultural ingredients—than do the conservatives or the liberals who translate justice primarily into economic terms. The drive against spending funds for architecture and art when money should be given to the poor is a liberal guilt trip that contrasts markedly with the attitudes of the poor, who have no such hang-ups. Of course, extravagance is a problem; but we also know that the funds used for art and architecture would not make a significant dent in the problems of oppression.

One cannot live without the necessities of life. But there is more to life than survival. How we determine what is "more important" becomes an essential ingredient in how we perceive the needs of our society. For some, beauty and aesthetic dimensions are as necessary to the human spirit as anything else. Perhaps it is the aesthetic dimension that makes ethics full-orbed in its concern for the human spirit. It is the aesthetic dimension that makes humanity human.

Part of the problem is that liberals and conservatives alike often fail to see aesthetics and the arts as integral to being human. For liberals and conservatives, art is entertainment, or an interest that is fashionable or *au courant*. Hence, they show a schizophrenia about the arts, either deriding them or courting them, but they do not see them as part of one's very humanity. A greater danger results when society attacks the fundamental nature of humanity. Theodore Gill makes the point that a part of Bonhoeffer's resistance to the Nazis came from an aesthetic revulsion to its limited, inverted, cynical view of what it means to be human. It is not by accident that revolutionaries, whether from the right or the left, first attack the vanguard artists. Such artists are always pointing to aspects of humanity denied or being suppressed in the culture. Many people say that the arts are not important, but why do the same people attack them so vehemently when the message of the arts does not coincide with what they believe? The arts look to the future; though, to be sure, the arts can also be reactionary when they are simply a part of the establishment or are being coopted by it.

The New Testament demonstates clearly that Jesus was concerned about the poor. But, as Theodore Gill reminds us, his first miracle was turning the water into wine, when Jesus was the life of the party. And of course we all know of the story of Mary and Martha, surely an approbation of considerable waste when one thinks of the cost of the ointment. In short, there are aesthetic dimensions to the New Testament as well.

Everything can be abused, and aesthetics can become an avoidance of social responsibility. But aesthetics can also be true to ethics, to that wedding in which humanity is enriched in all its facets, its physical, spiritual, and beauteous aspects. The Expressionist painter Barnett Newman wrote that the first human was an artist, that is, a human being whose imagination created worlds that made this world worthwhile.

In a world of competing visions, the aesthetic relation to the ethical can provide conceptions of the human that make us unafraid, that make our diversity a source of enrichment, that stretch our humanity, and that create common cause in our quest for an enriched humanity. The visual and the verbal express our rich humanity through diverse modalities, and the question of God will become real again when our humanity is wide and deep enough to be encompassed by its source, that is, the God who as Creator is also redemptive.

John Dillenberger[47]

278 • A CALL FOR RECOVERY OF THE VISUAL ARTS IN ANABAPTIST WORSHIP

Traditionally, Anabaptists have been wary of the visual arts in worship. This article, however, observes that modern culture presents unique challenges that were not present during the early Anabaptist opposition to the arts and that can be met by artists. Thus, the article calls for a union of art and ethics and a dual concern for both the transcendent and immanent, resulting in an intentional and imaginative use of the visual arts in worship.

Our problem with the arts is rooted in our rather uncritical adherence to Anabaptism. Any resolution must begin with a recognition that the Anabaptists joined other reformers in throwing out the baby with the bath water. All the senses were employed in Roman Catholic faith and worship. But in the interest of reforming the church of the day, or even recreating the New Testament church, a significant narrowing occurred; the Word—the written Word and the heard Word—became the front and center focus for the mainline reformers. The Anabaptists added a significant qualifier: the acted Word, or better, the incarnate Word.

In the reformation process, what happened to all the other senses—sight, sound, smell, touch, taste? Particularly for the Reformed and the Anabaptists, these senses were at best adiaphora, at worst dangerous distractions from true Christian faith. The arts were thus casualties of the Reformation, and to this day they struggle to regain legitimation within the reformational traditions—not least the Mennonite tradition.

Proposal with Reference to Mennonites and the Arts. A series of theses—not ninety-five, only an immodest eight—outline a modest proposal regarding Mennonites and the arts.

Thesis I: All theologizing, and all thinking about the Christian faith, is relative to a context, to a historical situation. Language, culture, economic conditions, and political dynamics shape the questions and provide contour to the answers.

The discussion of Mennonites and the arts in our day is not without context, not without history. Certain internal and external dynamics to the Mennonite tradition bring us to this moment when artists consider their corporate place in the larger Mennonite community. Space need not be taken here to analyze why this discussion arises now rather than some years ago. A comparative note may, however, be interesting. Whereas in earlier centuries the arts flourished among the Mennonites in Holland, they are less prominent today. The current renaissance of the arts among Mennonites is primarily a phenomenon of the immigrant Mennonite cultures like those of North America. Why this is so is a question for another essay.

Thesis II: Anabaptist theology in the sixteenth century was defined, at least in part, over against a Roman Catholicism that was rich in its sense of the transcendent world and its aesthetic correlates, but weak in its response to the immanent world and its ethical correlates.

The restitutional impulse tends to overreact, to

confuse manifestation with essence. The Anabaptists largely assumed traditional theological commitments; they assumed the reality of the transcendent order, so they paid little attention to such matters. In order to recapture ethics they abandoned aesthetics. The two were considered alien to each other. Anabaptists joined Zwingli in his iconoclasm, smashing organs and even, for a time, negated the legitimacy of singing. Aesthetic perversions required the exorcising of the aesthetic, they seemed to say. (This is detailed in Rodney J. Sawatsky "Symbol as Reality: Christianity as Art" an unpublished lecture presented to the symposium on "The Arts and the Prophetic Imagination: Expressions of Anguish and Hope" at Bethel College, North Newton, Kansas, January 13, 1991.) The degree to which the aesthetic served as a necessary pillar of the transcendent was apparently unrecognized. Transcendence, however, was not their problem.

Thesis III: Mennonites, in their quest to be faithful to their Anabaptist origins, have wrongly assumed that they must continue to emphasize precisely what the Anabaptists emphasized, because they have failed to contextualize theological emphases. Accordingly, four centuries later Mennonites still do not have a place for aesthetics.

The Editorial Committee of the recently published *Mennonite Encyclopedia V* did not include an article on aesthetics. I must, as a member of that Committee, take part of the blame for this omission. My sense is that even Mennonite artists tend to reduce aesthetics to ethics, and so they too may not have noted this oversight. If Mennonites think in terms of the classical trinity of the good, the true, and the beautiful, they have a limited place for beauty and are concerned primarily with the good. This parallels another tendency among Mennonites, namely reducing theology to ethics or collapsing the question of truth into the quest for goodness. Such narrowing of the agenda fails to consider the late twentieth-century context and functions as if the sixteenth-century worldview remains alive and well.

Thesis IV: Since the world in which or over against which we shape our theology is so profoundly different today than in 1525, we are not faithful to our forefathers and foremothers by repeating their response to their culture. Indeed in our day we may well need to say precisely the opposite of what was said on some matters in the sixteenth century. (For a parallel discussion see: Walter Klaassen, "The Quest for Anabaptist Identity," in *Anabaptist-Mennonite Identities in Ferment,* Leo Driedger and Leland Harder, eds. [Elkhart, Indiana: Institute of Mennonite Studies, 1990].)

We live in a world where a transcendent and a personal God is not assumed. The opposite is true. We are the measure of all things; we will make and remake the world; we are the creative and the creators; we will mold, make, and realize ourselves. If there is a god at all it is a god of self, of nature, or of community, or of justice. All is immanence! Human action and human being are all.

The Anabaptist concern to recapture a place and role for the immanent, for human decision and human action is victorious in our day, but with the victory has also come defeat. For the Anabaptists, ethics were always related to God; they were a response of obedient faithfulness to God. The transcendent referent of our action is, for the most part, lost in modernity.

Sadly, the sense of a transcendent God is being eroded not only outside but also inside the church. We struggle against great odds to maintain a sense of the superhuman dimension in our understanding of reality. Theology is so readily reduced to psychology and politics. Perhaps this is why some are drawn to Anglicanism, Pentecostalism, or even the occult, where transcendence still seems a reality.

Hence to be countercultural, to challenge the world, to be nonconformist, to be biblical, to be faithful to Jesus today will necessarily mean being different from the reformers of the 1500s. Today we need less human action and much more of God's reality, or better said, we need to place all human action in relation to God's reality.

Thesis V: Words, literal words, are very limited vehicles to communicate transcendent reality. Metaphors, symbols, icons, and harmonies nurture the imagination with rumors of angels. If ethics were a necessary corrective in the sixteenth century, aesthetics is the necessary corrective for the late twentieth century.

Our artists carry a heavy burden in our day. We need them today more than ever before to create new metaphors, symbols, and icons that connect us spiritually, emotionally, and imaginatively with the God who is beyond our grasp.

Thesis VI: While in the sixteenth century we emphasized ethics and basically negated aesthetics, today we should not follow suit by emphasizing aesthetics to the exclusion of ethics. The two need not be and ought not be over against each other, but rather close partners in the Christian cause.

Yet, Mennonite aesthetics has too often been subsumed under ethics. Out of their own sense of alienation and marginality in relation to both the church and the larger society, as well as out of their own sensitivities to the injustices around about them, Mennonite artists have repeatedly painted the picture of human brokenness and played the sounds of human discord. Their message has been that of the ethical prophets crying "woe, woe." Surely little can sensitize as profoundly to human evil as the arts can.

But does our world not know all about brokenness? Is such imitation of brokenness really prophetic, or is it simply falling into lockstep with cultural inertia? What we lack is a vision of peace and of wholeness rising out of the ashes. We have all kinds of pretty and nice and superficial, but above all we lack *beauty!* We desperately need a recovery of aesthetics.

Thesis VII: The modern assumption that aesthetics is all in the eye of the beholder must be challenged. Aesthetics in this century has been completely relativized. Beauty no longer is premised on any objective criteria. Subjectivism and individualism reign. In turn, self-indulgence is the constant temptation of the artist.

If the arts can be a major means to regain a sense of the transcendent in our materialistic, scientific, technological world, then art and the artist will necessarily move beyond subjectivism and individualism to consider both the larger community and a more objective understanding of beauty.

Art, by definition, is a lonely task. It is not a function of a committee. It is an expression of individuality, of individual imagination and creativity, but not necessarily an expression of individualism. Art at its best is not created simply for the artist, or for fellow artists, but for the edification of the larger human community.

Regaining some objective criteria for beauty is difficult. Yet we desperately need to try. Ethics have faced the same morass. Yet ethicists, especially Christian ethicists, have refused to opt for a complete relativistic subjectivism. Surely Christian artists must do the same with aesthetics.

The cultural norm says aesthetics is dead. A countercultural response insists that normativity in the arts as in ethics is alive and well and living in the Christian community.

*Thesis VIII: A primary arena, although defi-*nitely not the only arena, for the artist's call in the postmodern world is in public worship.* It is in and through worship that the God who is not limited by time and space, by human action and imagination, is best known (See John Rempel, "Christian Worship: Surely the Lord is in this Place," *The Conrad Grebel Review: A Journal of Christian Inquiry* 6 [Spring 1988]: 101-118).

Words are of great importance in worship. Our preaching and our prayers desperately need to relearn the power of well-crafted and well-delivered words. Indeed words, both written and spoken, need to be reclaimed for their symbolic and poetic possibilities and power. Yet words are limited. The nonverbal arts offer us vehicles to realize the reality of the transcendent more powerfully than can any preached word.

If the arts are to fulfill their calling in worship, they will point not to the artist, but through the art to God. This kind of art in recent decades is relatively rare. But it is the kind we all long for, and which is vital to a renewal of a multidimensional cosmos in which God is alive, moving, and being.

Rodney J. Sawatsky[48]

279 • A CALL FOR THE RECOVERY OF VISUAL ARTS IN REFORMED WORSHIP

The Presbyterian Directory of Worship provides authority and guidance for artists and liturgists who desire to proclaim the gospel through various art forms. This article describes this document and imagines new possibilities for the role of the arts in Reformed worship.

There has never been a time when the arts have not been present in the development and language of human expressions of faith in the Presbyterian church. The *Directory for Worship suggests* possibilities for worship, *invites* development in worship, and *encourages* continuing reform of worship. Incorporating all the arts in worship as a form of proclamation and prayer is clearly lifted up throughout the *Directory for Worship.*

Possibilities

In the Christian tradition, the arts have always been essential. Today there is no corporate act of worship by any group of Christians that does not appropriate some aspect of the arts to enact and proclaim its praise and prayer. In the processional or recessionals, the choir director's movement, the physical gestures of the clergy during the sacraments, dance and drama are present. The shape of space, the placement of the pews, the pulpit, the lectern, Communion table, and baptismal font all create and sculpt environmental art in worship. *The Directory for Worship* liberates us to move toward integrating all the arts:

> Christian worship joyfully ascribes all praise and honor, glory, and power to the triune God (W1.0000). Heart, soul, strength, and mind, with one accord, . . . join in the language, drama, and pageantry of worship (W1.2000).

These opening lines, taken from chapter 1 of *The Directory for Worship,* no longer allow us to shy away from understanding praise and proclamation as expressions of doxology. We enter worship simultaneously at three levels: *socially,* connecting human beings with God and with each other; *publicly,* involving practices and beliefs; and *systematically,* a collective ensemble of practices, sentiments, and beliefs which are carried out in "liturgical" acts.

We participate in a public "ritual," "festivity" or celebration. In the Reformed tradition, religious celebration is carried out in community. Community or *communitas* is a direct and spontaneous modeling of relationships. To celebrate is to perform rituals publicly and formally. Our liturgical heritage is corporate, public, and inclusive. Worship embraces not only the individual but the community, providing space, environment, language, sights, sounds, smells, and pageantry that allows one to feel confronted by God and oneself. Religious practices, rituals, or rites can be identified in three simultaneous and harmonious ways: (1) by what is shown, (2) what is done, and (3) what is said.

Invitations

Historically, the art forms in liturgical settings of the Protestant faith have not been rich and elaborate architecture, painting and sculpture, or spectacular and thought-provoking drama or dance, but limited to the art forms of oratory, testimony, and sermon. We have fallen short of the enormous gifts and richness of the expressive art forms, gesture, dance, and mime. We have done somewhat better with the visual arts: painting, sculpture, vestments, paraments, and banners. In his recent article entitled "Worship as Art, Evangelization, and Mission" (*Reformed Liturgy and Music* 23:107–113), Horace Allen, Professor of Worship at Boston University's School of Theology, writes: "Praise means art, and art in Christian praise means light, song, and cult, as essential expressions of the freedom of God for us and of ourselves for God."

Continuing Reform

If we are to understand anything about ourselves, the world, and God's continual creating and recreating activity, we cannot ignore the forms of expression that come to us through the arts. Not only is worship art, but the arts are worship, doxology, and proclamation. The *Directory for Worship* makes every effort to grant us this freedom within its guidelines and suggestions. A quick glance at the index to the *Directory* gives several citations for dance, drama, music, and a category entitled "general."

All works of art are instruments and objects of action: actions on the part of artists and actions on the part of the public. It is true that works of art carry the convictions and concerns of the artist, and this has been described in works of dance, drama, sculpture, painting, architecture, vestments or music. The arts are expressions of the world behind them. Art historians, anthropologists, and sociologists can find vivid representation of this in the remarkable and prophetic masterpieces of the Renaissance. For example, one cannot stand before the fifteenth-century tapestries of *The Hunt of the Unicorn* at the Cloisters without experiencing the world behind, within, and revealed. They speak words while moving beyond linguistics. They dance and sing without musical notation or physical movement. These tapestries proclaim!

The rejection and dismissal of art forms in the Christian community has left a huge void in our worship life. The *Directory for Worship* offers an opportunity, under the guidance of the session of a particular church (W1.4004), for new possibilities to be explored and new ministries to be utilized.

It is important that the artist touch the lives of people around him or her. An artist's gifts and talents are a public expression of ministry. The difficult struggle is, and continues to be, the issue of motives and of "good taste." It is sad that we have to single out the arts, for this issue is present in the life and work and mission of the entire church. We are free to allow the spoken and written works of art to be presented, and criticized later, but the visual and performing arts creates human vulnerability and a prejudgment is often required . . . or demanded.

The aesthetic value and quality of liturgical arts will lie in their unity and integrity. It is important not to deposit a dance here, a banner there, and a drama in between during worship. The *Directory for Worship* clearly offers a process, a guidance for the freedom to use the arts in worship. It does not attempt to place a value or merit system on any one of the arts, but correctly invites all the arts to be considered in the development of liturgical art forms. The cultural and ethnic diversity in this country does not allow the *Directory for Worship* to isolate any particular art form nor dictate what is appropriate and when it should or should not be used. It does not qualify or quantify artistic designs, actions, or objects. An art form that is aesthetically excellent when considered in isolation may be inappropriate, out of place, even jarring when included in a liturgical setting. The opposite is also valid. A vestment, banner, painting, or sculpture displayed on the street, on the beach, or in a supermarket may not have a meaningful place in a service of worship. Many factors in a liturgical whole must be considered if the arts are to be aesthetically assessed. St. Thomas Aquinas in *Summa Theologia* 1.184 Q.39. art. 8, says:

> . . . beauty includes three conditions, integrity or perfection, since those things which are impaired are by the very fact ugly; due proportion or harmony: and lastly brightness, or clarity, whence things are called beautiful which have bright color.

A beautiful work of art is the consequence of a harmonious cooperation of the inner and the outer. The artist, dancer, actor, composer, feels an emotion and moves towards what is to be sensed, then on to the work of art. The work being exhibited in a public space, or in a community, is what is sensed by the observers until it rests in their emotions.

Aesthetic tastes differ. Some aesthetic aspects may give one person satisfaction while giving another person no satisfaction whatsoever, and causing him or her acute distress. And within the structure of church governance the *Directory for Worship* in harmony with the *Form of Government,* assigns the responsibility for worship to the session including: ". . . those who lead worship through music, drama, dance, and other arts" (W1.4005). Art in worship is and will constantly be struggling to achieve whole-

ness and integrity. Sessions and worship committees will find the *Directory for Worship* a document that is descriptive, prescriptive, and theological, making this part of our constitution a creative and instructive piece of educational material.

Conducting Worship

The arts are tools, tools of expressing a ministry, expressing a life message. The word read, sung, enacted, or proclaimed includes these tools of ministry. The question raised by *The Directory for Worship* is this: Do we allow a ministry through these tools? Do we consider art, dance, drama, music, or other media in the same way we have considered the tools of a typewriter, print, pen, brush, and ink? Often on the front of a worship bulletin one can read the titles *Ministers* or *Minister of Music.* Is it possible someday to read *Minister of Liturgical Arts?* A few churches have tried naming and identifying a ministry of arts. Individual congregations have established this only after careful and conscious education, preparing, and providing leadership training and congregational understanding.

Liturgical art, or using the arts in worship, is participatory in character; it is the art of a community. The word proclaimed, whether it is through music, art, drama, or dance is proclamation because it is exhibited in community.

> Drama and dance, poetry and pageant: indeed most other human art forms are also expressions through which the people of God have proclaimed and responded to the word. Those entrusted with the proclamation of the word through art forms should exercise care that the gospel is faithfully presented in ways through which the people of God may receive and respond (W2.2009).

Praise God from whom all blessings flow!

Barbara Miller[49]

280 • A CALL FOR THE RECOVERY OF THE VISUAL ARTS IN CHARISMATIC WORSHIP

Art is a gift from God. The Bible itself records many examples of the arts. Written by a leading mime artist in the charismatic community, this article defends the importance of the arts for the Christian life and in Christian worship.

Throughout Scripture, God has used dramatic expression to communicate his will and his Word. This might be in mime, acting, storytelling, parable, allegory, song, dance, gestural communication, or sign. God's Word is full of examples of ministry through arts. However, we have failed to see what is obviously there. Why? Simply because we _read_ the Bible instead of _seeing_ it. We read what they enacted. There are numerous examples of the arts in prophecy. Mime is recorded over forty times in Scripture. Over one-third of the ministry of Ezekiel was done in mime. Parables, as a form of storytelling, are used over forty-nine times; the majority of them were spoken by Jesus. Parable, in a general sense, is seen over 250 times throughout the Old and New Testaments. The Song of Solomon is a narrative allegory. The life of Hosea was a living prophetic drama. Hosea 12:10 brings out many important points about the arts:

1. God chooses to speak through the use of the arts
2. The artist is a minister of God, separated unto God, and under the direction of God
3. The ministry of the arts is a prophetic call

If we can understand the drama and art found within Scripture in a living, dramatic way, we will gain a richer comprehension of God's word, and therefore, of God.

Jewish Mime

Jewish mime, seen when a prophet uses gestures and movements to communicate his message, is delivered in three ways:

1. Actions with no narrative
2. Actions with narrative before or after
3. Actions with narrative given at the same time

Eighty percent of communication is nonverbal. This makes the message delivered with mime powerfully clear and very well communicated. Those who would no longer hear the word of the Lord . . . could see it.

The eight messengers who used mime were Agabus, Ahijah, the angel in the book of Revelation, Elisha, Ezekiel, Hosea, Isaiah, and Jeremiah. Mime is used to show God's judgment (1 Kings 11:30-40), to show God's provisional will (2 Kings 13:15-19), to illustrate judgments of shame (Is. 20:1-6), to foretell and warn (as seen in the prophesies of Ezekiel and Jeremiah), and to make clear the results of one's

actions (Acts 21:1-11)—the list can go on. Mime is used to clarify, illustrate, and demonstrate.

The Ministry of the Arts

In these days when God is restoring all things to their proper place, there will arise again a ministry of the arts. All expressions of creativity are from God, who alone is the creator (Gen. 1; John 1). It is by his breath and gift that we create and express ourselves artistically. We might misuse this gift, as many have, but the gift is still from God. How shall we use these gifts?

"Each one should use whatever gift he has received to serve others, faithfully administering God's grace in various forms. If anyone speaks, he should do it as one speaking the very words of God. If anyone serves, he should do it with the strength God provides, so that in all things God may be praised through Jesus Christ. To him be the glory and the power forever and ever" (1 Peter 4:10).

The Uses of Art

Art can bring a person recognition with dignity and honor (Exod. 28:2, 3, 39). It can speak of the glory of the heavens, as the tabernacle is a faint copy of heaven's glory (Exod. 24:9-18, 25:40; Heb. 8:5). All things are done to glorify God. His creation shows us his truths. If we paint a waterfall, we do not need to justify the painting by putting a Scripture on it, as many do. The waterfall itself is a testimony of the power and glory of God (Rom. 1:20). Art can communicate glory, beauty, and joy, which are godly of themselves. However, the arts can be and have been used to bring people to repentance, salvation, and a greater revelation of God. This time from the start, the very start. Loving God, that is where it all begins. Using our God-given bodies to express ourselves: to each other in a hug, to God in uplifted hands, and in the movements of drama. All art is the extension of our longing to love and communicate with God . . . and everyone loves . . .

Todd Farley[50]

281 • THE ROLE OF THE ARTS IN WORSHIP

The arts in worship are never to dominate, intrude, or distract. They serve the action of worship and act as vehicles through which a communication between human beings and God takes place.

Worship renewalists recognize that the primary purpose of the worshiping assembly is to celebrate the saving acts of God through Christ. They also recognize that because God's work in Jesus Christ is directed toward the whole of creation, the worship of God is best experienced when the creation is symbolically set free to worship God in the context of the church's celebration. Consequently the arts, which use the materials of creation and are expressions in the image of God of God's creativity, may become avenues of communication through which God encounters worshipers. They in turn are enabled to respond to God. When music, drama, space, movement, color, furnishings, objects, and the environment of worship become vehicles through which an encounter with the message of God's salvation takes place, creation not only enables worship, but also sets worshipers free to worship.

The Theological Basis

The place of the arts in worship is grounded in the incarnation of God in Jesus. Essentially, the Incarnation means that God became part of creation, which had been disturbed by sin, in the womb of the virgin Mary. Bearing the fallen creation, God in Jesus died to destroy the power of death over creation and was raised to restore creation to newness of life (Rom. 8:18-22). Thus, the incarnation, death, and resurrection of Jesus restore the created order to its original state. Consequently, when the restorative work of God in Jesus is celebrated in worship, creation acts as a worthy vehicle for God's encounter with us. Even as God chose to encounter us in the flesh of the man Jesus, so God continues to use the physical, tangible, and concrete stuff of creation to encounter us. Thus the arts are vehicles of communication.

The Arts as Vehicles of Communication

The celebration of God's act of salvation in Christ is not and should never become a purely intellectual act. Worship is an experience that engages the whole person—body, mind, senses, imagination, emotions, and memory. Since the arts in particular communicate to these various aspects of the human person, they act as important vehicles of encounter. Redemption restores the whole creation and the whole person; both creation and persons are to be represented in worship.

But the arts constitute an indirect rather than a direct form of communication. As a nonverbal language, they are forms of symbolic communication through which thoughts, feelings, and intuitions are conveyed. The arts touch us deep within the recesses of our being and elicit a response from the subconscious, irrational, and suprarational part of us. As such they deal with intuition, imagination, and emotion as well as with the thinking or will of the human person.

Unlike words, which have ready-made meanings, the arts are more of a mine in need of exploration. The worshiper may not even be aware of the reality they communicate. Instead, an artistic expression may take root and grow as a seed, imperceptibly and quietly; yet it affirms the mystery of the gospel, strengthening the worshiping community as well as an individual's faith.

Rules for Using the Arts in Worship

All regulations for using the arts in worship need to reflect the communal nature of that activity. Worship is more than a congregation of individuals gathered for personal and private devotion. It is the public act of the church: the communal recollection of the mighty act of salvation done by God for the whole church and the world. Therefore, the arts serve the public act of worship.

First, arts need to be characterized by simplicity. They should not to be attended by a multiplicity of words, which smother the symbolic action, nor should the actions of the arts be so complex that the message of the gospel they portray be hidden in symbolic clutter.

Second, quality should characterize all arts used in worship. Musical works, dances, dramas, or banners, done in a shoddy or haphazard manner, reflect on the message they convey. Care should be taken in all forms of communication so that they express the beauty, the majesty, and the mystery of God.

Third, art in worship needs to be appropriate for its task. It must be able to express its message in such a way that it does not interrupt the movement of worship (i.e., the rhythm of coming before God, hearing God speak, entering into intimate relationship with God at the Table, and being dismissed from worship).

In sum, art serves the action of worship and is not independent of the structure of worship. The service of worship is a drama which recalls the saving act of God in Christ; it is a drama of praise and thanksgiving, an offering of prayer, and an envisioning of the coming kingdom of peace and justice. Consequently, art is never a performance within this drama, but an intricate part of the whole. Art provides a poetic imaginative means of conveying the drama of redemption for the community gathered to celebrate God's work in Christ.

Robert E. Webber

282 • THE INTEGRITY OF FORM AND FAITH IN LITURGICAL ART

Art for worship must evidence not only aesthetic integrity but also fidelity to Christian truths. Specifically, liturgical art should reflect the theology and character of the worship that is enacted in the local congregation. The following article explains these claims and describes two examples of how they have been put into practice.

Cameras were flashing in the cathedral. I was standing next to a stone effigy of some monarch who lay on the lid of his tomb and stared confidently upward beyond a vaulted ceiling to a vaulted heaven that had been there when he died. All around the royal sepulchre tourists were poking their fingers in guidebooks. Several leaned their heads back to survey a deep blue stained glass window whose intricacies of lead patterned cherubim about a haloed Christ. Gazing frozen from the walls were medieval burghers posing as saints. One of them was pointing his finger in his own guidebook and looking as if he had discovered something much more worthy of attention than the birthdate of the duke who gave the altar.

Amidst the click of cameras and the shuffle of feet on stone a voice broke the air over a perfectly modulated sound system, loud enough to catch everyone's attention but soft enough to sound conversational in that cavernous space. We were welcomed to the cathedral and reminded that "this is above all a house of prayer," that living congregations continued to worship here, and that we were invited in Christ's name to join them. Then the voice announced we would have a brief prayer. We were asked to be still while an intercession was offered to God. We were given a few seconds to bow or kneel or sit, whatever our customary posture for prayer. Several people looked shocked: Prayer?! There followed a simple, powerful plea for the ill, the home-

less, the hungry, the mentally disturbed. After the Amen, the click of the cameras began immediately, although when I looked up I noticed several people were still praying. Perhaps they were seeing what the saint had been pointing to in his book for centuries: the force of Spirit in the heart of faith, the depths of reality, the visionary power of belief to take stone and wood and sand and lead and reshape them to the glory of the primal source from which they came, the rhapsodic conviction of unseen mysteries that guided the stonecutter's hammer, the mason's chisel, the carpenter's plane, and the glass maker's iron.

The First Concern: _____ Seeking an Integrity of _____ Form and Faith

The saint saw what we need to see before beginning any discussion of how to use art in the worship of the church. For the issue is not simply: What is aesthetically pleasing? Those photographers in the cathedral impatient for the intercession to end had clear ideas about that question. Yet no matter how perfectly focused their pictures, their perspective was distorted. They failed to capture the depth of faith from which all that splendid art had emerged. They may have caught the play of light and shadow, but they missed this greater truth: those windows, statues, carvings, and vaulted arches were more than objects of art. They were prayers, the yearning and praise of the heart externalized into materiality.

Sometimes our use of art in worship has the same "photographic" quality as the slides of those shutterbugs. I have watched liturgical dances, listened to anthems, looked at slides, and seen chancel dramas that pleased the ear and eye but left the soul empty. They were beautiful but failed to engage the congregation in the praise of God because they were unexpressive of the community's life and faith. That is why I never think of simply "bringing art into worship in order to enliven it some." A cathedral, a New England meeting house, a Bach chorale, and a black spiritual all possess the power to inspire because each embodies a blazing conviction about the precise, personal center of reality. Notice that the power is a function of something more than a particular artistic style. The cathedral and chorale share a mysterious complexity, while the meeting house and the spiritual are leaner witnesses to the Holy Breath of life. But all of them are characterized by *an integrity of form and faith,* a theological-aesthetic coherence that makes them effective bearers of the divine. Although earlier ages spilled ink and blood over the different theologies manifest in these outward signs of belief, we can now see that each was an authentic expression of faith for its own time and place. Each developed out of the central convictions of the community and connected to the life and experience of the worshipers.

Moving Beyond the Verbal Word

Therefore, our first task as worship leaders who want to use art in our services is to clarify our central convictions: What is our church trying to express and celebrate as a community of faith? We cannot answer this question simply by reclaiming what John Calvin wrote or by turning to any period or theology of the past as the final arbiter of what art belongs in our worship. If our ancestors who now live in the great cloud of witnesses had done that, we would have no cathedrals, meeting houses, chorales, spirituals or any of the other treasures that they left us! To use the past as a rigid authority would be to make the same mistake as the photographers in the cathedral who saw it as a museum rather than a house of prayer. Worship is not the atavistic act of an antiquarian society, but the vibrant engagement of living humanity with what is eternally true.

The appropriate use of art in liturgy requires that we first name those fundamental theological principles which shape our identity as Reformed congregations, and then explore how the Spirit of God is expanding those principles to embrace more of that truth which is beyond the grasp of any human formulation. In working with congregations, I often begin by exploring their concept of the Word of God, for it is central to Reformed worship. I find most churches restrict their understanding of the Word to what is verbal, though in fact the biblical concept bursts beyond the boundaries of speech. The *logos* (Word) of God created what we see and touch as well as what we hear. Furthermore, God saw that what was created was good. But our Reformed propensity to stress the ear as the gate to heaven has detached us from the materiality of the creation. Our worship in effect dis-incarnates the Word by being too exclusively aural. I am aware of the historic reasons for this in the Reformers' thrilling reclamation of the Bible as the church's book. However, to perpetuate their iconoclastic extremism is not to be faithful to the Scriptures they recovered. Until our Reformed congregations come to

terms with this weakness in our historic theology, we will feel uncomfortable with the introduction of visual art into our worship or we will do a poor job of it: banners so filled with words the symbols cannot be seen, bulletin covers of pallid piety, naves that are a pastiche of styles unrelated to our animating convictions. Reclaiming the visual and material expression of our faith will make us more faithful to the wholeness of the Word than we currently are. We will not be denying our tradition, but deepening and expanding the truth that gave it birth:

> The Word of God was from the start.
> The Word drove seas and land apart.
> The Word made rocks and living things.
> The Word raised up and brought down kings.
>
> The Word became a child of earth.
> The Word arrived through human birth.
> The Word like us was blood and bone.
> The Word knew life as we have known.
>
> The Word of God was human sized,
> The Word by most unrecognized.
> The Word by some though was received.
> The Word gave life when they believed.
>
> The Word had first made flesh from sod.
> The Word-made-flesh turned flesh toward God.
> The Word is working on flesh still.
> The Word is spelling out God's will.
>
> The Word shall be our life and light.
> The Word shall be our power and might.
> The Word above all wealth is priced,
> The Word by name is Jesus Christ.

Moving Beyond Biblical Citations

Along with an expanded concept of the Word goes a more accurate understanding of the canon of Holy Scripture. The term *canon* means "measure," not "boundary." When we say that the Bible is our canon we are indicating it is the *standard* by which we judge other experiences and expressions of the Spirit. To be biblical does not require confining ourselves to the Bible, but rather witnessing to the *reality* that the Bible proclaims. Artistic expression that is in touch with the Spirit may be more biblical than a worship service that profusely quotes the Scripture but never embodies the contemporary surgings and rumblings of the renewing, creating, ever-living God. The use of art in worship can be a way of enacting the Pentecostal promptings that echo in the hearts of worshipers satiated by verbosity and hungering for other dimensions of the truth:

> Wind who makes all winds that blow—
> Gusts which bend the saplings low,
> Gales which heave the sea in waves,
> Stirrings in the mind's deep caves—
> Aim your breath with steady power
> On your church, this day, this hour.
> Raise, renew the life we've lost,
> Spirit God of Pentecost.

These expanded understandings of the Word, of the meaning of "biblical," and how the Spirit comes to us are crucial prerequisites to the introduction of art into Reformed worship. Space limitations have allowed me only to identify the issues, but a worship committee seeking to enliven its services with art might well precede its efforts with study sessions tracing the meanings of "Word" throughout the Bible, and then share their findings through newsletter and sermon with the entire congregation. All of this may seem a tedious and complex process, but without such background work most efforts at revitalizing worship will either meet extreme resistance or be little more than passing fads. There may be one or two services where some beautiful work of art provides a temporary flash of excitement, but there will not be the sustained revitalization that brings the deep satisfaction of worshiping God in Spirit and in truth week after week.

Two Examples

Two visiting artists, made possible by a grant from the Luce fund, have brought this truth home to me on our seminary campus. The first was a professional choreographer and dancer, Garth Fagan. Before Garth did anything with our worship he sat down and talked with the community's worship leaders and participants. He asked them what they believed, what they were doing in worship, what they hoped would happen in their services. He acknowledged that it would be easy for him simply to come in with some pre-planned program, do it, dazzle us, and leave. But all that would remain would be a memory of when the "dance troupe visited us." Our own dance of faith, our own movement with the Spirit, would not have been touched or encouraged or deepened. Rather than teach us how to leap through the air or stand on our toes, Garth began at a much more basic level. He asked

us to walk to the front of the room with a Bible and then pointed out how many of us walked with slouching shoulders or timid steps—all of which contradicted the things we said we believed about the grace of God, the power of the Spirit, the good news of Jesus Christ. Then he helped us simply to walk and to stand with grace and assurance, to claim with our bodies what we affirmed in thought and word. The effect was astonishing. We began to incarnate our theology in posture and bearing.

From these simple initial exercises Garth moved to develop a service in which there would be a central liturgical dance related to Psalm 150. But again he did not simply create the dance on his own. He worked with volunteers from the congregation and developed from their gestures a simple pattern of movement that they could perfect and that the entire community would feel comfortable with. Throughout this time he joined with me and my colleague in music, Carol Doran, to blend appropriate prayers and hymns with the simple choreography. The result was a service that engaged both the most traditional and most innovative members of the congregation in a service of stirring praise.

Notice the pattern in all of this: the art form is not imposed from without but is carefully cultivated as an authentic expression of the community's faith. The success of the process depended on both the artist and the community. The artist supplied his extraordinary gifts of bodily discipline and grace, while the community supplied the theological conviction and eagerness to praise God with all that they were and could become. If either the artist or the community were closed to the other's world, then the process would fail. The mutual receptivity of each to the other gave the final service *that same integrity of form and faith* which I observed in the cathedral's carvings, arches and windows.

This year we are currently engaged in a similar process with a graphic artist, Willy Malacher, whose specialty is liturgical design. Once again, Willy did nothing until he had visited our community, worshiped with us, and talked about our beliefs and hopes. Then having listened carefully to us, he put together a stunning slide show tracing the development of different worship settings in the history of the church. He helped to train our primitive eyes to the effect of line, space, proportion, and color. He did not make us into great graphic artists—that was not his task—but rather, like Garth, he raised our consciousness of the disparity between our verbalized faith and our visual symbolization of that faith. Nowhere was this more apparent than in the contrast between a series of pictures of splashing, bubbling public fountains and the meager drops of water used in baptism. Willy pointed out that "If there is one thing Christ is not, it is stingy." Yet the paucity of our sacramental symbol proclaimed the exact opposite! Our verbal formulations are orthodox, but we practice visual heresy.

Having alerted our sleeping eyes, Willy began to work with us on a wall hanging that would give focus to a flexible worship space we have so far not focused with much success. He could easily have done the design entirely on his own, but he did not. He was eager to get the community involved. Therefore, he had each of us draw two sets of designs: the first to represent our hope of what we might be as a community; the second to represent our experience of the community as it currently is. Then these were placed in parallel horizontal rows on a wall, and each was interpreted by the creator. Now Willy went into action as an artist. He identified certain motifs that keep recurring—curves and circles in our first set of drawings, broken lines, and isolated geometric shapes in our second set. Then he took all of the drawings and used them to fuel his own artistic imagination and produced a design for a beautiful hanging that was amazingly expressive of who we are as a community and what we want to become. We are currently involved in purchasing the materials and producing the hanging and designing a special service for its dedication.

None of us has the artistic genius to come up with a design as aesthetically pleasing as what Willy did. But on the other hand, Willy needed our contribution to understand the yearning and praise in our hearts. Once again it was the accessibility of the artist and community to one another that made possible the creation of a work that has the right intuitive fit for our worship.

Achieving an Integrity of Form and Faith

Here then, summarized is *a process for achieving that integrity of form and faith* which makes the use of art in worship more than a gimmick or an awkward intrusion:

1. Clarify and amplify the community's theology to provide a framework for understanding why we are using art in the praise of God.

2. Talk with an artist to interpret the community's life and beliefs and to gain from the artist a perspective on the depths of reality to which our gabby religion may have blinded us.
3. Create liturgical art that grows out of the above dialogue, drawing on the community's faith and the artist's visionary powers.

There is a special excitement in working with a living artist, but the process doesn't have to be limited to that. My colleague and I have used the same steps by engaging worship committees in the study of composers, poets, and visual artists through books, records, and slides. Our guiding principle is not to turn each study into an art history course, but rather to ask with the committee: What is God's living Word to us through this artist's creation? Again and again congregations have been surprised and moved by the depths of the Spirit that have been revealed to them through the process. And each time the final result was a service that fit the community, that connected with its life and faith while expanding its vision.

The age of building cathedrals is long past. But the age of the Living Word who comes to us through the creativity of those in touch with depths of Reality is always with us. To work with such artists is to do more than upgrade the aesthetic level of our services. It is to respond to the Spirit who blows in unexpected ways and unpredictable places. Seen from this perspective, art in worship is more than taking pictures in the cathedral, more than dabbling with beauty to give Sunday's service a lift, more than an intriguing idea for the worship committee to consider. It is, instead, an essential part of the congregation's journey of faith, carrying them into the presence of the One from whom every good and perfect gift flows, including the riches of the creative artist:

> To climb the sacred footworn peak
> Where pilgrims long have trod
> Alert both eye and heart to seek
> The present living God.
>
> In spirit and in truth you'll find
> What words alone can't frame:

The source of pulse and breath and mind,
The primal wind and flame.

Thomas Troeger[51]

283 · THE NONVERBAL LANGUAGES OF PRAYER

When we think of prayer, we probably think of words that we speak, sing, or read. Yet human communication happens as much through nonverbal means as through verbal ones. This article probes the nature and influence of nonverbal communication and argues that it should be intentionally employed in worship.

Not long ago, a well-known magazine carried an article on what happens to Christians who participate in the Eucharist on a regular basis. Its fruits, according to the article, are joy, peace, love, and a sense of union. The editors were surprised to receive letters from many Christians in response to the article reporting that such feelings and participation are often not evoked by the liturgy. The liturgical movement since Vatican II has done much to remedy this situation, yet the problem continues. Today's Christians are determinedly loyal; many attend worship even though the experience often leads them to frustration, anger, and apathy.

The cause of our frustration lies partially in the way that we are educated. We are the products of a rational, logical, analytic, and scientific culture. Parochial schools, most public schools, and many colleges teach their students to think in only one of two styles of thought. Many people are not even aware of their ability to think and feel in nonverbal ways.

As an art educator, religion teacher, and painter, I have been excited by recent brain research indicating that there are two very different, equally conscious and cooperative styles of thought in the brain. This research reveals the brain to be two totally conscious, experiencing, expressing halves. The left half, we educate; the right, we don't. In most people the left consciousness gets all or most of the educational attention because the brain's left hemisphere controls our mastery of verbal language, which has often been mistaken as a gauge for intelligence.

Left and Right Hemispheres

Language is a linear, sequential form of expression: one word after another, one sentence after another. It cuts apart whole pictures—for instance, a historical incident—and describes each part one at a time. Isolated sequences are used to describe the people involved, the place, the reasons, the history that led up to the incident, and its results. Chance affairs, perhaps the weather, may have changed things; a book or a certain school may have influenced the participants in earlier years. Family life may have had its effect. In this manner, epic tales of history, philosophy, and theology come to be. To present anything like a whole picture of events and ideas we must build word on word, tome on tome.

The left brain also imagines itself a detached observer, unclouded by emotion. The left brain is clear and concise, cool and business-like; "business is business" is a typical left-consciousness phrase. The left brain also tends to focus on rules and procedures in its attempt to find cubby-holes for everything and everyone.

The other hemisphere of the brain (usually the right side) is programmed to take in the entire field or "gestalt" of events as they occur. The right brain can absorb the total picture, at once taking in the many influences of a story without dividing the facts or missing important connections. The languages for its fast, detailed, and interconnected grasping have their own styles of expression which are suitable to it and complementary to the other consciousness.

Each half of the brain has direct physical control of the opposite side of the body, coordinating movement and thought through the intimate connections of the bundle of nerves running between them. Until recent times the right side was considered a minor hemisphere because of our cultural bias for verbal language. As it turns out, however, the right hemisphere is programmed for a different operation. In contrast to the sequentially patterned logic of the left brain, the right brain senses shapes, forms, colors, and motions. Its experience in these modes gives rise to the languages we call art.

The right brain's experiences are sounds, silences, and rhythms. It speaks directly in music. The right brain experiences relationships of the body to other bodies and to tables, chairs, and trees; it speaks in body language and dance. It also experiences emotional relationships. It is imaginative and intuitive, and it can be more spiritually sensitive than its partner, the left hemisphere.

Except in certain areas of the United States, most schools have given short shrift to education in the arts and have played down symbolic, poetic, intuitive styles of thought and action. Yet when it comes to worship, people must cling to natural, holistic styles of expression and to dramatic, symbolic, intuitive, and musical modes. New styles of worship will become more problematic than helpful if art and speech are not equally represented. The acceptance of the vernacular has this danger, that meaning expressed verbally can be represented as more important than being. New understandings of the brain's native programming and abilities may be able to help Christians appreciate and respond to a more artistic and intuitive worship experience.

Overloading the Verbal

Drawing is a direct expression of the right hemisphere of the brain—one of its many nonverbal languages. Among many adults, it is also an underdeveloped talent. Its repression, a trauma many people experience, has a deep, direct effect on one's sense of self. For example, if children's drawings are not accepted as true expressions of their feelings and spirit, they will be disowned. In disowning their own creations, children also lose a sense of their own goodness. It becomes much harder for them really to believe in God's love and acceptance. Their reactions can't be put into words; their command of the verbal language is too small.

Adults do not completely express their feelings in words either. There are other languages in our repertory besides the verbal. We have, in fact, overloaded the verbal, powerful as it is. The result is a population with much the same aspect as a stage tree, all leaves and trunk on one side and next to nothing on the other, often needing to be held up by outside structures just to exist.

Often we do not fathom the depth of injury that a one-sided education does to our culture. But many adults now truly believe that they are not artistic. Often in conversation they will point to some overbearing teacher or older child, even a parent, who strongly criticized or painfully ridiculed their artistic creations. This rejection usually happens at about the third or fourth grade, an age at which children are especially vulnerable.

One person told of painting the mountains she had seen from the sea as she sailed in from her mother's home island where she had lived all her life. The teacher ridiculed her drawings because her mountains, the only ones she had ever seen, were brown, rounded, and mostly all the same height. Apparently, the teacher imagined that all mountains

were snow-covered peaks resembling the Alps or the Rockies. This woman never dared to paint again, although she needed this medium desperately to express some of the later experiences of her life.

A man in early middle age showed me a scar across his right knuckle; the art teacher had used the metal edge of a ruler to register profound disapproval of his drawing of a tree. Both tales are violent, although most of us only recognize the violence in the second one. We often seem not to recognize spiritual and emotional violence.

A wide range of acceptable behavior characterizes our use of art, music, dance, and symbolic imagery, and confidence in these abilities has become an imperative for human and spiritual growth. We must gently, but definitely, move away from the overly verbal, logical, and analytical modes of thought—no matter how much we in Western cultures have been steeped in these.

Liturgy is a spiritual experience that comes to us largely through these languages of the right hemisphere: solemn ritual, music, color, poetry, and story. The liturgy calls us to experience a deeply intuitive and personal response to the revelation of God whose word is Jesus Christ. Vestments, banners, and stained glass, the affective and physical poetry of the Psalms and dance, the parables and stories of salvation history require a response from whole persons. A one-sided emphasis on logical-analytical thought styles can make it difficult for us to feel this involvement. Didactic or doctrinaire styles of preaching and teaching will not help us. Neither will complaints from highly educated and dissatisfied musicians. Unworthy music is a symptom rather than a cause of the problem.

Unless Christians can grow in artistic, intuitive, imaginative, and symbolic styles of thought, participation in the liturgy will fall off and we will once more find ourselves sitting in the back pews watching experts perform the liturgy.

Remedial Measures

Here are a few basic ideas, guidelines, and suggestions that may help us to remedy this need. First, we may want to consider sponsoring a parish program for art education. The arts are the natural basis for spiritual experience. Visual art, poetry, dramatic movement, and music can be more expressive of God's presence in one's life than the mere effort to capture this presence in prose. In fact, faith will be more naturally and joyfully articulated as we learn to respond to Christ's presence in more visual ways. With self-acceptance in a world of colors, shapes, and forms comes an outpouring of joy that is already close to prayer. Thus a parish program for art education will be a program for liturgical renewal as well.

Second, just as we have many names for the Holy One, so there are a variety of artistic styles that express our experience in worship. For many people being good at art means producing a photographic image, but such images are rather the product of machines called cameras. Other kinds of images are possible for the magnificently complicated sensing, responding organism that is the human being. Childlike, impressionistic, and symbolic images may also be good art. We must recognize, therefore, our need for education specialists in the arts. If the parish has a school, or other educational facility or program, it should have no difficulty finding an art teacher for a reasonable salary. Good art teachers do more than conduct classes; they also help us discover the art that is part of daily parish life.

Third, music and harmonious movement are also valuable expressions of spiritual truth. Certainly, music as well as art needs to be taught, recognized, and affirmed as a part of daily life. Too often we concentrate so hard on concert performers that children who are not musically gifted are neglected. Then, just as the visual and musical art media are natural tools for comfortable expression in everyday life, so is the body a natural medium for direct expression. Some excellent dance or movement therapists and teachers live in large parishes. If teachers are not available locally, perhaps some of the music, dance, drama, or art teachers in the public schools can be invited in for some experimental sessions.

All teachers, whether they are parishioners or visitors, will need some materials on the liturgy. If they are good at their work and sensitive, they will be able to put liturgy and art together with their own knowledge and skills to help fulfill the needs of the worship assembly. Art educators and music educators are aware of the naturalness of these expressions.

Whether the programs focus on visual art, music or motion, teachers and students will need to recognize the self-critical, self-conscious fears of most people. Whatever our expertise in other areas—we may be engineers, counselors, mechanics, nurses, priests or parents—rejection of the right hemi-

sphere's natural use is endemic to our modern American culture. Perhaps the rush of the young to loud, overwhelming music, drugs, and alcohol reflects the extent of our problem. The back-to-basics movement and our current romance with science, computers, and budget resolutions must not be allowed to make matters worse. We must be careful not to present the arts as second-rate.

The sacramental life is a long series of actions and symbols, a combination of the verbal and nonverbal expressions of a community's spiritual experience. The arts can help us to be more easily and joyfully attuned to the rituals that open us to this presence of God in the life of the church.

Grace M. Donaldson[52]

284 • ENVIRONMENT AND ART IN WORSHIP: A ROMAN CATHOLIC DOCUMENT ON ART IN WORSHIP

This statement is the result of the cooperative effort on the part of the Federation of Diocesan Liturgical Commissions and the Bishops' Committee of the Roman Catholic Church. It addresses both theological and practical considerations regarding almost every aspect of the visual arts in worship.

1. Faith involves a good tension between human modes of expressive communications and God himself, whom our human tools can never adequately grasp. God transcends. God is mystery. God cannot be contained in or confined by any of our words or images or categories.

2. While our words and art forms cannot contain or confine God, they can, like the world itself, be icons, avenues of approach, numinous presences, ways of touching without totally grasping or seizing. Flood, fire, the rock, the sea, the mountain, the cloud, the political situations and institutions of succeeding periods—in all of them Israel touched the face of God, found help for discerning a way, moved toward the reign of justice and peace. Biblical faith assures us that God covenants a people through human events.

3. And then in Jesus, the Word of God is flesh: "This is what we proclaim to you: what was from the beginning, what we have heard, what we have seen with our eyes, what we have looked upon and our hands have touched, we speak of the word of life" (1 John 1).

4. Christians have not hesitated to use every

human art in their celebration of the saving work of God in Jesus Christ, although in every historical period they have been influenced, at times inhibited, by cultural circumstances. In the resurrection of the Lord, all things are made new. Wholeness and healthiness are restored, because the reign of sin and death is conquered. Human limits are still real, and we must be conscious of them. But we must also praise God and give God thanks with the human means we have available. God does not need liturgy; people do, and people have only their own arts and styles of expression with which to celebrate.

5. Like the covenant itself, the liturgical celebrations of the faith community (church) involve the whole person. They are not purely religious or merely rational and intellectual exercises, but also human experiences calling on all human faculties: body, mind, senses, imagination, emotions, memory. Attention to these is one of the urgent needs of contemporary liturgical renewal.

6. Historically, music has enjoyed a preeminence among the arts of public worship, and there is no clear evidence to justify denying it the same place today. The Bishops' Committee on the Liturgy, therefore, published guidelines (*Music in Catholic Worship,* 1972) encouraging attention to music, both instrumental and choral/vocal. This companion booklet, *Environment and Art in Catholic Worship,* offers guidelines to encourage the other arts necessary for a full experience in public worship. The two booklets, therefore, should be used together, complementing one another, by those responsible for planning and conducting liturgical celebrations. For that reason, music is excluded from the specific concerns of the following pages.

7. If we maintain that no human words or art forms can contain or exhaust the mystery of God's love, but that all words and art forms can be used to praise God in the liturgical assembly, then we look for criteria to judge music, architecture, and the other arts in relation to public worship. (Among the official conciliar and post conciliar documents which specifically address these questions are: *The Constitution on the Sacred Liturgy* [hereafter, *CSL*], chapters 6 and 7; *Instruction of the Congregation of Rites for the Proper Implementation of the Constitution on the Sacred Liturgy,* chapter 6; and the *General Instruction of the Roman Missal* [hereafter, *GI*], chapters 5 and 6.)

8. The reason for offering principles to guide rather than blueprints to follow was stated clearly by the Council fathers: "The Church has not adopted any particular style of art as her very own; it has admitted styles from every period according to the natural talents and circumstances of peoples, and the needs of the various rites. Thus, in the course of the centuries, she has brought into being a treasury of art which must be carefully preserved. The art of our own days, coming from every race and region, shall also be given free scope in the church, provided that it adorns the sacred buildings and holy rites with due reverence and honor, thereby it is enabled to contribute its own voice to that wonderful chorus of praise . . ." (*CSL,* no. 123).

I. The Worship of God and Its Requirements

Liturgy and Tradition

9. Liturgy has a special and unique place in the life of Christians in the local churches, their communities of faith. Each church gathers regularly to praise and thank God, to remember and make present God's great deeds, to offer common prayer, to realize and celebrate the kingdom of peace and justice. That action of the Christian assembly is liturgy.

10. Common traditions carried on, developed and realized in each community make liturgy an experience of the church which is both local and universal. The roots as well as the structure of its liturgical celebrations are biblical and ecclesial, asserting a communion with believers of all times and places. This tradition furnishes the symbol language of that action, along with structures and patterns refined through the centuries of experience, and gives the old meanings new life in our time, our place, with our new knowledge, talents, competencies, arts. Therefore, this celebration is that of a community at a given place and time, celebrated with the best of its resources, talents, and arts in the light of our own tradition (*GI,* Introduction, nos. 6–15).

A Climate of Hospitality

11. As common prayer and ecclesial experience, liturgy flourishes in a climate of hospitality: a situation in which people are comfortable with one another, either knowing or being introduced to one another; a space in which people are seated together, with mobility, in view of one another as well

as the focal points of the rite, involved as participants and not as spectators (*GI,* nos. 4, 5).

The Experience of Mystery

12. The experience of mystery that liturgy offers is found in its God-consciousness and God-centeredness. This involves a certain beneficial tension with the demands of hospitality, requiring a manner and an environment which invite contemplation (seeing beyond the face of the person or the thing, a sense of the holy, the numinous, mystery). A simple and attractive beauty in everything that is used or done in liturgy is the most effective invitation to this kind of experience. One should be able to sense something special (and nothing trivial) in everything that is seen and heard, touched and smelled, and tasted in liturgy.

13. Incarnation, the paschal mystery, and the Holy Spirit in us are faith's access to the transcendence, holiness, otherness of God. An action like liturgy, therefore, has special significance as a means of relating to God, or responding to God's relating to us. This does not mean that we have "captured" God in our symbols. It means only that God has graciously loved us on our own terms, in ways corresponding to our condition. Our response must be one of depth and totality, of authenticity, genuineness, and care with respect to everything we use and do in liturgical celebration.

The Opening Up of Symbols

14. Every word, gesture, movement, object, appointment must be real in the sense that it is our own. It must come from the deepest understanding of ourselves (not careless, phony, counterfeit, pretentious, exaggerated, etc.). Liturgy has suffered historically from a kind of minimalism and an overriding concern for efficiency, partly because sacramental causality and efficacy have been emphasized at the expense of sacramental signification. As our symbols tended in practice to shrivel up and petrify, they became much more manageable and efficient. They still "caused," were still "efficacious" even though they had often ceased to signify in the richest, fullest sense.

15. Renewal requires the opening up of our symbols, especially the fundamental ones of bread and wine, water, oil, the laying on of hands, until

we can experience all of them as authentic and appreciate their symbolic value.

The Personal-Communal Experience

16. A culture which is oriented to efficiency and production has made us insensitive to the symbolic function of persons and things. Also, the same cultural emphasis on individuality and competition has made it more difficult for us to appreciate the liturgy as a *personal-communal* experience. As a consequence, we tend to identify anything private and individual as "personal." But, by inference, anything communal and social is considered impersonal. For the sake of good liturgy, this misconception must be changed.

17. To identify liturgy as an important personal communal religious experience is to see the virtue of simplicity and commonness in liturgical texts, gestures, music, etc. This is easier said than done. But it does require a persevering effort to respect the church's mind in terms of its common feelings and simplicity, for example, by not drowning the action in a flood of words or by not making the action more complex than necessary in order to signify the gospel essentials.

The Sacred

18. An important part of contemporary church renewal is the awareness of the community's recognition of the sacred. Environment and art are to foster this awareness. Because different cultural and subcultural groups in our society may have quite different styles of artistic expression, one cannot demand any universal sacred forms (*CSL,* no. 123).

Quality and Appropriateness

19. This is not to say that liturgy makes no demand upon architecture, music and the other arts. To be true to itself and to protect its own integrity, liturgy must make demands. Basically, its demands are two: *quality* and *appropriateness.* Whatever the style or type, no art has a right to a place in liturgical celebration if it is not of high quality and if it is not appropriate (*GI,* no. 254).

20. *Quality* is perceived only by contemplation, by standing back from things and really trying to *see* them, trying to let them speak to the beholder. Cultural habit has conditioned the contemporary person to look at things in a more pragmatic way: "What is it worth?" "What will it do?" Contemplation sees the hand stamp of the artist, the honesty and care that went into an object's making, the

pleasing form and color and texture. Quality means love and care in the making of something, honesty and genuineness with any materials used, and the artist's special gift in producing a harmonious whole, a well-crafted work. This applies to music, architecture, sculpture, painting, pottery making, furniture making, as well as to dance, mime or drama—in others words, to any art form that might be employed in the liturgical environment or action.

21. *Appropriateness* is another demand that liturgy rightfully makes upon any art that would serve its action. The work of art must be appropriate in two ways: (1) it must be capable of bearing the weight of mystery, awe, reverence, and wonder which the liturgical action expresses; (2) it must clearly *serve* (and not interrupt) ritual action, which has its own structure, rhythm and movement.

22. The first point rules out anything trivial and self-centered, anything fake, cheap or shoddy, anything pretentious or superficial. That kind of appropriateness, obviously, is related to quality. But it demands more than quality. It demands a kind of transparency, so that we see and experience both the work of art and something beyond it.

23. The second point (to serve) refers both to the physical environment of public worship and to any art forms which might be employed as part of the liturgical action (e.g., ritual movement, gestures, audio-visuals, etc.).

The Serving Environment

24. By environment we mean the larger space in which the action of the assembly takes place. At its broadest, it is the setting of the building in its neighborhood, including outdoor spaces. More specifically it means the character of a particular space and how it affects the action of the assembly. There are elements in the environment, therefore, which contribute to the overall experience, e.g., the seating arrangement, the placement of liturgical centers of action, temporary decoration, light, acoustics, spaciousness, etc. The environment is appropriate when it is beautiful, when it is hospitable, when it clearly invites and needs an assembly of people to complete it. Furthermore, it is appropriate when it brings people close together so that they can see and hear the entire liturgical action, when it helps people feel involved and become involved. Such an environment works with the liturgy, not against it.

The Service of the Arts

25. If an art form is used in liturgy it must aid and serve the action of liturgy since liturgy has its own structure, rhythm and pace: a gathering, a building up, a climax, and a descent to dismissal. It alternates between persons and groups of persons, between sound and silence, speech and song, movement and stillness, proclamation and reflection, word and action. The art form must never seem to interrupt, replace, or bring the course of liturgy to a halt. If one uses film, for example, in such a way that one seems to be saying, "We will stop the liturgy for a few moments now in order to experience this art form," then that use is inappropriate. If, however, an art form is used to enhance, support and illumine a part or parts of the liturgical action or the whole action, it can be both appropriate and rewarding.

26. A major and continuing educational effort is required among believers in order to restore respect for competence and expertise in all the arts and a desire for their best use in public worship. This means winning back to the service of the church professional people whose places have long since been taken by "commercial" producers, or volunteers who do not have the appropriate qualifications. Both sensitivity to the arts and willingness to budget resources for these are the conditions of progress so that quality and appropriateness can be real.

II. The Subject of Liturgical Action: The Church

27. To speak of environmental and artistic requirements in Catholic worship, we have to begin with ourselves—we who are the church, the baptized, the initiated.

The Assembly of Believers

28. Among the symbols with which liturgy deals, none is more important than this assembly of believers. It is common to use the same name to speak of the building in which those persons worship, but that use is misleading. In the words of ancient Christians, the building used for worship is called *domus ecclesiae,* the house of the church.

The Action of the Assembly

29. The most powerful experience of the sacred is found in the celebration and the persons celebrating, that is, it is found in the action of the assembly: the living words, the living gestures, the living sacrifice, the living meal. This was at the heart of the earliest liturgies. Evidence of this is found in their architectural floor plans which were designed as

general gathering spaces, spaces which allowed the whole assembly to be part of the action.

30. Because liturgical celebration is the worship action of the entire church, it is desirable that persons representing the diversity of ages, sexes, ethnic and cultural groups in the congregation should be involved in planning and ministering in the liturgies of the community. Special competencies in music, public reading, and any other skills and arts related to public worship should be sought, respected and used in celebration. Not only the planners and ministers, however, are active in the liturgy. The entire congregation is an active component. There is no audience, no passive element in the liturgical celebration. This fact alone distinguishes it from most other public assemblies.

31. The assembly's celebration, that is, celebration in the midst of the faith community, by the whole community, is the normal and normative way of celebrating any sacrament or other liturgy. Even when the communal dimension is not apparent, as sometimes in communion for the sick or for prisoners, the clergy or minister function within the context of the entire community.

32. The action of the assembly is also unique since it is not merely a "celebration of life," reflecting all of the distinctions stemming from color, sex, class, etc. Quite the contrary, liturgy requires the faith community to set aside all those distinctions and divisions and classifications. By doing this the liturgy celebrates the reign of God, and as such maintains the tensions between what is (the status quo of our daily lives) and what must be (God's will for human salvation—liberation and solidarity). This uniqueness gives liturgy its key and central place in Christian life as seen from the perspective of an actual community. Just as liturgy makes its own demands on the environment and the arts, so too, does the assembly. When the assembly gathers with its own varied background, there is a commonness demanded which stems from our human condition. The commonality here seeks the best which people can bring together rather than what is compromised or less noble. For the assembly seeks its own expression in an atmosphere which is beautiful, amidst actions which probe the entire human experience. This is what is most basic and most

noble. It is what the assembly seeks in order to express the heart of the church's liturgy.

Contemporary

33. Contemporary art forms belong to the liturgical expressions of the assembly as surely as the art forms of the past. The latter are part of our common memory, our communion (which extends over time as well as over geographical boundaries). Contemporary art is our own, the work of artists of our time and place, and belongs in our celebrations as surely as we do. If liturgy were to incorporate only the acceptable art of the past, conversion, commitment, and tradition would have ceased to live. The assembly should, therefore, be equally unhesitating in searching out, patronizing and using the arts and media of past and present. Because it is symbolic communication, liturgy is more dependent on past tradition than many human activities are. Because it is the action of a contemporary assembly, it has to clothe its basically traditional structures with the living flesh and blood of our times and our arts.

Beautiful

34. Because the assembly gathers in the presence of God to celebrate his saving deeds, liturgy's climate is one of awe, mystery, wonder, reverence, thanksgiving, and praise. So it cannot be satisfied with anything less than the _beautiful_ in its environment and in all its artifacts, movements, and appeals to the senses (_GI,_ no. 253). Admittedly difficult to define, the beautiful is related to the sense of the numinous, the holy. Where there is evidently no care for this, there is an environment basically unfriendly to mystery and awe, an environment too casual, if not careless, for the liturgical action. In a world dominated by science and technology, liturgy's quest for the beautiful is a particularly necessary contribution to full and balanced human life.

The Human Experience

35. To gather intentionally in God's presence is to gather our total selves, our complete persons—a "living sacrifice." Other human activities tend to be more incomplete, specialized, and to claim one or the other facet of ourselves, lives, talents, roles. Liturgy is total, and therefore must be much more than a merely rational or intellectual exercise. Valid tradition reflects this attention to the whole person. In view of our culture's emphasis on reason, it is critically important for the church to reemphasize a more total approach to the human person by open-

ing up and developing the nonrational elements of liturgical celebration: the concerns for feelings of conversion, support, joy, repentance, trust, love, memory, movement, gesture, wonder.

Sinful

36. The church is a church of sinners, and the fact that God forgives, accepts and loves sinners places the liturgical assembly under a fundamental obligation to be honest and unpretentious, without deceit or affectation in all it does. If all distinctions have been stripped away, then basic honesty has to be carried through in all the words, gestures and movements, art forms, objects, furnishings of public worship. Nothing which pretends to be other than it is has a place in celebration, whether it is a person, cup, table, or sculpture.

Servant

37. Different ministries in such an assembly do not imply "superiority" or "inferiority." Different functions are necessary in the liturgy as they are in any human social activity. The recognition of different gifts and talents and the ordination, institution or delegation for the different services required (priest, reader, acolyte, musician, usher, etc.). is to facilitate worship. These are services to the assembly and those who perform them are servants of God who render services to the assembly. Those who perform such ministries are indeed servants of the assembly.

38. The liturgical assembly, as presented, is church, and as church is servant to the world. It has a commitment to be sign, witness, and instrument of the reign of God. That commitment must be reflected and implemented not only in the individual lives of its members, but also in the community's choices and in its use of its money, property, and other resources. Liturgical buildings and spaces should have the same witness value. Their planning should involve representatives of oppressed and disadvantaged parts of the communities in which they are located.

III. A House for the Church's Liturgical Celebrations

39. The congregation, its liturgical action, the furniture, and the other objects it needs for its liturgical action—these indicate the necessity of a space, a place, a hall, or a building for the liturgy. It will be a place for praying and singing, for listening and speaking—a place for human interaction and active participation—where the mysteries of God are recalled and celebrated in human history. The servant nature of the church in relation to the rest of the community in its area (and in the world) invites it to consider the broader needs of the community, especially in the community's deprived, handicapped, and suffering members, and therefore to consider a breadth of possible uses of its buildings.

Primary Demand: The Assembly

40. In no case, however, should this mean a lack of attention to the requirements of liturgical celebration or a yielding of the primary demands that liturgy must make upon the space: the gathering of the faith community in a participatory and hospitable atmosphere for word and Eucharist, for initiation and reconciliation, for prayer and praise and song.

41. Such a space acquires a sacredness from the sacred action of the faith community which uses it. As a place, then, it becomes quite naturally a reference and orientation point for believers. The historical problem of the church as a *place* attaining a dominance over the faith community need not be repeated as long as Christians respect the primacy of the living assembly.

42. The norm for designing liturgical space is the assembly and its liturgies. The building or cover enclosing the architectural space is a shelter or "skin" for a liturgical action. It does not have to "look like" anything else, past or present. Its integrity, simplicity and beauty, its physical location and landscaping should take into account the neighborhood, city and area in which it is built.

43. Many local churches must use spaces designed and built in a former period, spaces which may now be unsuitable for the liturgy. In the renovation of these spaces for contemporary liturgical use, there is no substitute for an ecclesiology that is both ancient and modern in the fullest sense. Nor is there any substitute for a thorough understanding of ritual needs in human life and the varied liturgical tradition of the church. With these competencies, a renovation can respect both the best qualities of the original structure and the requirements of contemporary worship.

Teamwork

44. Whether designing a new space for the liturgical action or renovating an old one, teamwork and preparation by the congregation (particularly its liturgy committee), clergy, architect and consultant

(liturgy and art) are essential (*CSL*, no. 126; *GI*, no. 258). A competent architect should have the assistance of a consultant in liturgy and art both in the discussion stages of the project (dialogue with congregation and clergy as well as among themselves) and throughout the stages of design and building. Recent competitions in the design of buildings for liturgy have indicated the advantages of such consultation.

45. The congregation, or local church, commonly acting through its delegates, is a basic and primary component in the team. The congregation's work is to acquaint the architect and consultant with its own self-image as church and its sense of the larger community in which it exists. It is important for the congregation and clergy to recognize the area of their own competence. This will also define the limits beyond which they should not go. Respect for the competence of others in their respective fields is essential for good teamwork.

46. If a community has selected competent and skilled persons, they will receive from the architect and the consultant, a design which will stimulate and inspire, as well as serve the assembly's needs as they have been described. When financial benefactors are involved, they have the same part in this process as the congregation and the clergy, subject to the same prior requirements of good liturgy.

47. A good architect will possess both the willingness to learn from the congregation and sufficient integrity not to allow the community's design taste or preference to limit the freedom necessary for a creative design. The architect will look to the congregation and clergy for an understanding of the character and purpose of the liturgical assembly. With that rapport, it is the architect's task to design the space, using contemporary materials and modes of construction, in dialogue with consultants who are expert in the areas of liturgical art, rites, acoustics and other specialized issues.

48. The liturgical-artistic consultant is an invaluable partner of the architect, for the purposes of space can be imagined and the place creatively designed only by a competent designer (architect) who is nourished with liturgy's tradition, its current shape, together with the appropriate furniture and other objects used. The feeling of liturgical action is as crucial as the craft of the designer in producing a worthy space and place.

Visibility and Audibility

49. One of the primary requirements of the space is visibility of all in the assembly: others in the congregation as well as the principal focal point of the ritual action.

50. Visibility speaks more to the quality of view than merely the mechanics of seeing. A space must create a sense that what is seen is proximate, important, and personal. The arrangement of the space should consider levels of priority in what is seen, allowing visual flow from one center of liturgical action to another. Furthermore, the sense and variety of light, artificial or natural, contribute greatly to what is seen.

51. Audibility of all (congregation and ministers) is another primary requirement. A space that does not require voice amplification is ideal. Where an amplifying system is necessary, provision for multiple microphone jacks should be made (e.g., at the altar, ambo, chair, font, space immediately in front of the congregation, and a few spots through the congregation). Since the liturgical space must accommodate both speech and song, there must be a serious acoustical consideration of the conflicting demands of the two. The services of an acoustical engineer can enable architect and builder to be aware of certain disadvantages in rooms that are exclusively "dry" or "live." A room designed to deaden all sounds is doomed to kill liturgical participation.

The Scale of a Space

52. The liturgical space should have a "good feeling" in terms of human scale, hospitality, and graciousness. It does not seek to impress, or even less, to dominate, but its clear aim is to facilitate the public worship and common prayer of the faith community.

Unity of Space

53. Special attention must be given to the unity of the entire liturgical space. Before considering the distinction of roles within the liturgy, the space should communicate an integrity (a sense of oneness, of wholeness) and a sense of being the gathering place of the initiated community. Within that one space there are different areas corresponding to different roles and functions, but the wholeness of the total space should be strikingly evident.

54. Planning for a convergence of pathways to the liturgical space in a concourse or foyer or other place adequate for gathering before or after liturgies is recommended. In some climates this might be outdoors. Such a gathering space can encourage introductions, conversations, the sharing of refreshments after a liturgy, the building of the kind of community sense and feeling recognized now to be a prerequisite of good celebration.

IV. The Arts and the Body Language of Liturgy

55. Liturgical celebration, because of its public and corporate nature, and because it is an expression of the total person within a community, involves not only the use of a common language and ritual tradition, but also the use of a common place, common furnishing, common art forms and symbols, common gestures, movements, and postures. But when one examines the quality of these common elements, one finds that an uncommon sensitivity is demanded. For these common elements create a tremendous impact on the assembly visually, environmentally and bodily. This section and those following will offer a basic orientation and some principles with regard to each of these elements. We will begin with the sense of the person in the space: the bodily movement.

Personal Gestures

56. The liturgy of the church has been rich in a tradition of ritual movements and gestures. These actions, subtly, yet really, contribute to an environment that can foster prayer or which can distract from prayer. When the gestures are done in common, they contribute to the unity of the worshiping assembly. Gestures which are broad and full in both a visual and tactile sense, support the entire symbolic ritual. When the gestures are done by the presiding minister, they can either engage the entire assembly and bring them into an even greater unity, or if done poorly, they can isolate (*The Directory for Masses With Children* [hereafter, *DMC*] bases the importance of the liturgy on the fact that liturgy, by its nature, is the activity of the entire person. See no. 33).

Posture

57. In an atmosphere of hospitality, posture will never be a marshaled, forced uniformity. It is important that the liturgical space can accommodate certain common postures: sitting for prepara-

tions, for listening, for silent reflection; standing for the gospel, solemn prayer, praise, and acclamation; kneeling for adoration, penitential rites. Those who suffer from handicaps of one sort or another, must be carefully planned for so that they can participate in the liturgy without unnecessary strain or burden.

58. Attentiveness, expressed in posture and eye contact, is a requirement for full participation and involvement in the liturgy. It is part of one's share in the life of the community and something one owes the rest of the assembly. Because of this, a space and its seating should be so designed that one can see the places of the ritual action, but further, that these spaces cannot be so distant that eye contact is impossible, for eye contact is important in any act of ministry in reading, in preaching, in leading the congregation in music and prayer. Not only are the ministers to be visible to all present, but among themselves the faithful should be able to have visual contact, being attentive to one another as they celebrate the liturgy.

Processions

59. Beyond seeing what is done, because good liturgy is a ritual action, it is important that worship spaces allow for movement. (See *Holy Communion and Worship of the Eucharist Outside Mass* [hereafter, *EOM*], nos. 101–108; *DMC* no. 34). Processions and interpretations through bodily movement (dance) can become meaningful parts of the liturgical celebration if done by truly competent persons in the manner than befits the total liturgical action. A procession should move from one place to another with some purpose (not simply around the same space) and should normally include the congregation, sometimes with stops or stations for particular prayers, readings, or actions. The design of the space and arrangement of the seating should allow for this sort of movement. There should be concern for the quality, the gracefulness, and the surety of this movement. Seating arrangements which prohibit the freedom of action to take place are inappropriate.

60. In the general movement of the liturgical rite, the role of the one who presides is critical and central. The area of presiding should allow that person to be attentive to and present to the entire congregation, the other ministers, and each part of the liturgical action, even if not personally leading the action at that moment. The place should allow

one to conduct the various ministers in their specific activity and roles of leadership, as well as the congregation in its common prayer.

61. In the above instances, audibility and visibility to all in the assembly are minimal requirements. The chair, the lectern and the altar should be constructed so that all can see and hear the person of the reader or the one who presides.

Ease of Movement

62. The proper use of furniture and other objects which have a symbolic function is important in ritual action. These objects are next in importance to the people themselves and their total environment. They are part of a total rite which everyone present should be able to experience as fully as possible. Thus, their placement and use should allow for ease of movement.

V. Furnishings for Liturgical Celebration

63. Because the Sunday eucharistic assembly is the most fundamental ecclesial symbol, the requirements of that celebration will have the strongest claim in the provision of furnishings for liturgy. Consequently, any liturgical space must take into consideration not only the general requirements of the assembly, but also the need for a feeling of contact with altar, ambo and celebrant's chair.

64. This primacy of the eucharistic assembly, however, should not discourage a liturgical life of greater richness and variety in the local church. In planning construction, renovation, or refurnishing of liturgical spaces, baptism and the other sacraments, morning and evening prayer, services of the word, prayer meetings and other community events should be kept in mind.

65. When multifunctional use of the space is indicated by the needs either of the faith community or of the surrounding city, town or rural area which the faith community services, a certain flexibility or movability should be considered even for the essential furnishings. Great care, however, should be taken in the design and care of movable furnishings that none of the dignity and noble and simple beauty proper to such objects is sacrificed. There is no reason why a movable altar or ambo need have a flimsy, cheap, or disposable appearance.

66. Normally the furnishings used in a liturgical celebration of any kind should be placed before the celebration begins and remain stationary during the celebration. Ritual action is not enhanced by the moving of furniture during a rite. A careful arrangement of furnishings is an integral part of liturgical planning.

Dignity and Beauty

67. Consultation with persons who are experts, at least one in liturgy and one in the arts, is not a luxury, but a necessity for those responsible for furnishing the liturgical space. Each piece of furniture has its own requirements, but at least two criteria are applicable to all of them, in fact, to any object used in any way in liturgy: (1) None should be made in such a way that it is far removed from the print of the human hand and human craft. When mass-produced items are chosen, care must be taken that they are truly suitable. Dignity and beauty in materials used, in design and form, in color and texture— these are concerns of artists for their work, for the furniture they build, and are not, unfortunately, the evident concerns of many mass manufacturers and merchandisers. (2) All furnishings taken together should possess a unity and harmony with each other and with the architecture of the place.

Benches or Chairs

68. Benches or chairs for seating the assembly should be so constructed and arranged that they maximize feelings of community and involvement (*GI,* no. 273). The arrangement should facilitate a clear view not only of the one who presides and the multiple focal points of reading, preaching, praying, music and movement during the rite, but also of other members of the congregation. This means striving for a seating pattern and furniture that do not constrict people, but encourage them to move about when it is appropriate.

69. Benches or chairs for the seating of those engaged in the ministry of music, instrumental or choral, should be so constructed and arranged that they have the advantages described above for congregational seating and also that they are clearly part of the assembly (*GI,* no. 274). Yet, the ministers of music should be able to sing and play facing the rest of the assembly in order to elicit the participation of the community without distracting from the central action of the liturgy. The same should be said of an individual cantor or song leader.

The Chair

70. Chairs or benches for the presiding minister

and other ministers should be so constructed and arranged that they too are clearly part of the one assembly, yet conveniently situated for the exercise of their respective offices. The importance of the personal symbol and function of the one who presides in liturgical celebration should not be underrated or underplayed, because it is essential for good celebration. The chair of that person should be clearly in a presiding position, although it should not suggest either domination or remoteness (*GI,* no. 271).

The Altar

71. The altar, the holy table, should be the most noble, the most beautifully designed and constructed table the community can provide (*GI,* nos. 259–270; Appendix to *GI,* no. 263). It is the common table of the assembly, a symbol of the Lord, at which the presiding minister stands and upon which are placed the bread and wine and their vessels and the book. It is holy and sacred to this assembly's action and sharing, so it is never used as a table of convenience or as a resting place for papers, notes, cruets, or anything else. It stands free, approachable from every side, capable of being encircled. It is desirable that candles, cross, any flowers or other decoration in the area should not be so close to the altar as to constitute impediments to anyone's approach or movement around the common table.

72. The altar is designed and constructed for the action of a community and the functioning of a single priest, not for concelebrants. The holy table, therefore, should not be elongated, but square or slightly rectangular, an attractive, impressive, dignified, noble table, constructed with solid and beautiful materials, in pure and simple proportions. Its symbolic function, of course, is rendered negligible when there are other altars in sight. The liturgical space has room for but one.

73. The location of the altar will be central in any eucharistic celebration, but this does not mean it must be spatially in the center or on a central axis. In fact, an off-center location may be a good solution in many cases. Focus and importance in any celebration move with the movement of the rite. Placement and elevation must take into account the necessity of visibility and audibility for all.

The Ambo

74. The ambo or lectern is a standing desk for reading and preaching (although preaching can be done from the chair or elsewhere) (*GI,* no. 272). One main ambo should be reserved for these functions and therefore not used by commentators, song leaders, etc. Like the altar, it should be beautifully designed, constructed of fine materials, and proportioned carefully and simply for its function. The ambo represents the dignity and uniqueness of the Word of God and of reflection upon that Word.

75. A very simple lectern, in no way competing or conflicting with the main ambo, and placed for the necessary visibility and audibility, can be used by a cantor, song leader, commentator, and reader of the announcements. It should be located for easy communication with both musicians and congregation.

Baptistry

76. To speak of symbols and of sacramental signification is to indicate that immersion is the fuller and more appropriate symbolic action in baptism (*Rite of Baptism for Children* [hereafter, *BC*], Introduction). New baptismal fonts, therefore, should be constructed to allow for the immersion of infants, at least, and to allow for the pouring of water over the entire body of a child or adult. Where fonts are not so constructed, the use of a portable one is recommended.

77. The place of the font, whether it is an area near the main entrance of the liturgical space or one in the midst of the congregation, should facilitate full congregational participation, regularly in the Easter vigil (Ibid., no. 25). If the baptismal space is in a gathering place or entry way, it can have living, moving water, and include provision for warming the water for immersion. When a portable font is used, it should be placed for maximum visibility and audibility, without crowding or obscuring the altar, ambo, and chair.

Eucharistic Chapel

78. The *celebration* of the Eucharist is the focus of the normal Sunday assembly. As such, the major space of a church is designed for this *action*. Beyond the celebration of the Eucharist, the church has had a most ancient tradition of reserving the eucharistic bread. The purpose of this reservation is to bring communion to the sick and to be the object of private devotion. Most appropriately, this reservation should be designated in a space designed for individual devotion. A room or chapel specifically designed and separate from the major space is important so that no confusion can take place between the celebration of the Eucharist and reservation (*GI,*

no. 276). Active and static aspects of the same reality cannot claim the same human attention at the same time. Having the Eucharist reserved in a place apart does not mean it has been relegated to a secondary place of no importance. Rather, a space carefully designed and appointed can give proper attention to the reserved sacrament.

79. This space should offer easy access from the porch areas, garden or street as well as the main space. The devotional character of the space should create an atmosphere of warmth while acknowledging the mystery of the Lord. It should support private meditation without distractions. If iconography or statuary are present, they should not obscure the primary focus of reservation.

The Tabernacle

80. The tabernacle, as a receptacle for the reservation of the Eucharist, should be solid and unbreakable, dignified and properly ornamented (*GI,* no. 277). It may be placed in a wall niche, on a pillar, or eucharistic tower. It should not be placed on an altar for the altar is a place for action, not for reservation. There should be only one tabernacle in a church building. A lamp should burn continuously near it.

Reconciliation Chapel

81. A room or rooms for the reconciliation of individual penitents may be located near the baptismal area (when that is at the entrance) or in another convenient place (*Rite of Penance,* nos. 12, 18b; *Bishops' Committee on the Liturgy Newsletter* 1965–1975, 450). Furnishings and decoration should be simple and austere, offering the penitent a choice between face-to-face encounter or the anonymity provided by a screen, with nothing superfluous in evidence beyond a simple cross, table, and Bible. The purpose of this room is primarily for the celebration of the reconciliation liturgy; it is not a lounge, counseling room, etc. The word *chapel* more appropriately describes this space.

Sacristy

82. A sacristy or vesting space should be located to favor the procession of cross, candles, book, and ministers through the midst of the congregation to the altar area.

Musical Instruments

83. Because choir, instrumentalists, and organ often function as an ensemble, they need to be located together in such a way that the organist can see the other musicians and the liturgical action directly or by means of a simple mirror (*GI,* nos. 274, 275; *Music in Catholic Worship,* no. 38). Organ consoles can be detached from the pipework and their connection supplied by flexible means. This allows for movable consoles, which may be an advantage, especially when the liturgical space serves other functions as well. However, self-contained organs, where console and pipework are united in a single element, are a possibility also, and can be designed so that the whole organ is movable. Organs designed for liturgical rather than concert purposes need not be very large; they should not be grandiose or visually dominating. But they should be superior musically, and as with all artifacts, the instrument and its casework should be authentic, beautiful and coherent with its environment. Proper space must also be planned for other musical instruments used in liturgical celebrations.

VI. Objects Used in Liturgical Celebration

84. Like the furniture, all other objects used in liturgical celebrations should be designed or selected in consultation with experts in both liturgy and art. Each should be not only suitable for its purpose, but also capable of making a visual or other sensory contribution to the beauty of the action. The two principles cited above are applicable to everything employed in liturgy.

Duplicated and Minimized

85. There is a cultural tendency to minimize symbols and symbolic gestures and to cover them with a heavy curtain of texts, words, and commentary. As a result there are two other problems in our use of objects in worship.

86. One problem is the tendency to duplicate signs and objects, a practice which seems to have multiplied in proportion to the symbols' diminution. (The converse is also true: the multiplication of symbols causes their very diminution.) A symbol claims human attention and consciousness with a power that seems to be adversely affected by overdose. For example, the multiplication of crosses in a liturgical space or as ornamentation on objects may lessen rather than increase attention to that symbol.

87. A second common problem in the use of symbolic objects is a tendency to "make up" for weak primary symbols by secondary ones. It is not uncommon for example, to make extensive and ex-

pensive efforts to enrich and enliven a Sunday eucharistic celebration without paying any attention to the bread that is used or to the sharing of the cup. Bread and wine are primary eucharistic symbols, yet peripheral elements frequently get more attention. It is important to focus on central symbols and to allow them to be expressed with the full depth of their vision. This may mean solutions which are less efficient and pragmatic.

The Cross

88. A cross is a basic symbol in any Christian liturgical celebration. The advantage of a processional cross with a floor standard, in contrast to one that is permanently hung or affixed to a wall, is that it can be placed differently according to the celebration and the other environmental factors (*GI,* nos. 84, 270; Appendix to *GI,* no. 270). While it is permissible for the cross to rest on the altar, it is preferable that it be elsewhere, not only for noneucharistic liturgies, but also so that in eucharistic celebrations the altar is used only for bread and wine and book.

Candlesticks and Candles

89. The same can be said of candlesticks and candles. When they are floor-standing, they can be arranged differently from time to time. The number can be varied according to the season and feast and the solemnity of the celebration. Like the cross, the candles should be visible without impeding the sight of the altar, ambo, chair and action (*GI,* no. 269, *EOM,* no. 85).

90. The Easter Candle and its standard call for very special dimensions and design. They occupy a central location in the assembly during the Easter season and a place at the baptismal font thereafter (*BC,* no. 25).

Books

91. Any book which is used by an officiating minister in a liturgical celebration should be of a large (public, noble) size, good paper, strong design, handsome typography and binding (*Bishops' Committee on the Liturgy Newsletter,* 1965–1975, 417). The Book of the Gospels or lectionary, of course, is central and should be handled and carried in a special way. The other liturgical books of the church, which contain the rites of our public worship tradition, are also worthy of venerable treatment and are a significant part of the liturgical environment. Each should be visually attractive and impressive. The use of pamphlets and leaflets detracts from the visual integrity of the total liturgical action. This applies not only to books used by ministers at the altar, chair and font, but also to those used in any other public or semipublic rite.

92. When a liturgical book is employed at a place other than altar or ambo, the book should be held by an assistant or acolyte so that the hands and body of the one who reads are free.

Vestments

93. The wearing of ritual vestment by those charged with leadership in a ritual action is an appropriate symbol of their service as well as a helpful aesthetic component of the rite (*GI,* nos. 297–310; Appendix *GI,* nos. 305–306). That service is a function which demands attention from the assembly and which operates in the focal area of the assembly's liturgical action. The color and form of the vestments and their difference from everyday clothing invite an appropriate attention and are part of the ritual experience essential to the festive character of a liturgical celebration (*GI,* nos. 308; Appendix *GI,* no. 308).

94. The more these vestments fulfill their function by their color, design, and enveloping form, the less they will need the signs, slogans, and symbols which an unkind history has fastened on them. The tendency to place symbols upon symbols seems to accompany the symbolic deterioration and diminution already discussed (*GI,* nos. 289–296).

95. Vesture may also be used appropriately on an altar or ambo or other objects at times, especially for festive occasions, not as "frontals" or "facades," but as decorative covering which respects the integrity and totality of the particular object (*GI,* no. 268). The fabrics used in these instances should be chosen because of the quality of design, texture and color.

Vessels

96. In a eucharistic celebration, the vessels for the bread and wine deserve special attention and care (*GI,* nos. 289–296). Just as in other types of celebration those objects which are central in the rite are a natural focus. When the eucharistic assembly is large, it is desirable not to have the additional plates and cups necessary for Communion on the altar. A solution is to use one large breadplate and either one large chalice or a large flagon until the breaking of the bread. At the fraction, any other chalices or plates needed are brought to the altar. While the bread is broken on sufficient plates for

sharing, the ministers of the cups pour from the flagon into the Communion chalices. The number and design of such vessels will depend on the size of the community they serve. To eat and drink is of the essence of the symbolic fullness of this sacrament. Communion under one kind is an example of the minimizing of primary symbols.

97. Like the plates and chalices or flagons, all other vessels and implements used in the liturgical celebration should be of such quality and design that they speak of the importance of the ritual action. Pitchers, vessels for holy oils, bowls, cruets, sprinklers, censers, baskets for collection, etc.—all are presented to the assembly in one way or another and speak well or ill of the deed in which the assembly is engaged.

Images

98. Images in painting or sculpture, as well as tapestries, cloth hangings, banners and other permanent or seasonal decorations should be introduced into the liturgical space upon consultation with an art consultant (*CSL,* no. 125; *GI,* no. 278). Like the furniture and other objects used in worship, they become part of the environment and are subject to its criteria of quality and appropriateness. In addition, their appropriateness must take into account the current renewed emphasis on the action of the assembly. If instead of serving and aiding that action, they threaten it or compete with it, then they are unsuitable.

99. In a period of church and liturgical renewal, the attempt to recover a solid grasp of church and faith and rites involves the rejection of certain embellishments, which have in the course of history become hindrances. In many areas of religious practice, this means a simplifying and a refocusing on primary symbols. In building, this effort has resulted in more austere interiors, with fewer objects on the walls and in the corners.

Decorations

100. Many new or renovated liturgical spaces, therefore, invite temporary decoration for particular celebrations, feasts and seasons. Banners and hangings of various sorts are both popular and appropriate, as long as the nature of these art forms is respected. They are creations of forms, colors, and textures, rather than signboards to which words must be attached. Their purpose is to appeal to the senses and thereby create an atmosphere and a mood, rather than to impress a slogan upon the minds of observers or deliver a verbal message.

101. Although the art and decoration of the liturgical space will be that of the local culture, identifying symbols of particular cultures, groups, or nations are not appropriate as permanent parts of the liturgical environment. While such symbols might be used for a particular occasion or holiday, they should not regularly constitute a part of the environment of common prayer.

102. Flowers, plants, and trees—genuine, of course—are particularly apt for the decoration of liturgical space, since they are of nature, always discreet in their message, never cheap or tawdry or ill-made. Decoration should never impede the approach to or the encircling of the altar or any of the ritual movement and action, but there are places in most liturgical spaces where it is appropriate and where it can be enhancing. The whole space is to be considered the arena of decoration, not merely the sanctuary.

103. Suitable decoration need not and should not be confined to the altar area, since the unity of the celebration space and the active participation of the entire assembly are fundamental principles. The negative aspect of this attention to the whole space invites a thorough housecleaning in which superfluities, things that have no use or are no longer used, are removed. Both beauty and simplicity demand careful attention to each piece of furniture, each object, each decorative element, as well as to the whole ensemble, so that there is no clutter, no crowding. These various objects and elements must be able to breathe and function without being smothered by excess.

Audiovisuals

104. It is too early to predict the effect of contemporary audiovisual media—films, video tape, records, tapes—on the public worship of Christians. It is safe to say that a new church building or renovation project should make provision for screens and/or walls that will make the projection of films, slides, and filmstrips visible to the entire assembly, as well as an audio system capable of fine electronic reproduction of sound (see *DMC,* nos. 35–36).

105. There seems to be a parallel between the new visual media and the traditional function of stained glass. Now that the easily printed word has lost its grip on popular communication, the neglect of audiovisual possibilities is a serious fault. Skill in

using these media in ways which will not reduce the congregation to an audience or passive state can only be gained by experience.

106. Such media, of course, should never be used to replace essential congregation action. At least two ways in which they may be used to enhance celebration and participation are already apparent: (1) visual media may be used to create an environment for the liturgical action, surrounding the rite with appropriate color and form; (2) visual and audio media may be used to assist in the communication of appropriate content, a use which requires great delicacy and a careful, balanced integration into the liturgy taken as a whole.

VII. Conclusion

107. When the Christian community gathers to celebrate its faith and vision, it gathers to celebrate what is most personally theirs and most nobly human and truly church. The actions of the assembly witness the great deeds God has done; they confirm an age-old covenant. With such vision and depth of the assembly, can the environment be anything less than a vehicle to meet the Lord and to encounter one another? The challenge of our environment is the final challenge of Christ: We must make ready until he returns in glory.

Bishops' Committee on the Liturgy,
National Conference of Catholic Bishops[53]

285 ✦ Bibliography on the History, Philosophy, and Theology of the Visual Arts in Worship

Adams, Doug. *Transcendence With the Human Body In Art.* New York: Crossroad, 1991. The volume explores the connection of the human body and subject matter in contemporary American art, especially the theological perceptions of such art where transcendence is expressed and experienced with the human body. Artists examined are George Segal, Stephen De Staebler, Jasper Johns, and Christo. Visual (47 illustrations) and verbal consideration.

Adams, Doug and Diane Apostolos-Cappadona, eds. *Art as Religious Studies.* New York: Crossroad, 1987. Scholarly and readable study of the visual arts in Judaism, Christianity, and religious praxis which sets the study in the larger context of edu-

cation as worship. Various authors consider visual art as instructive in religious symbolism, aesthetics as hermeneutics, religious meaning with respect to nudity and gender, religious transformation, pastoral care, social justice, and other subjects. Historical/philosophical. Illustrations and over 50 pages of bibliographies.

Apostolos-Cappadona, Diane. *Art, Creativity, and the Sacred.* New York: Crossroad, 1984. A collection of twenty-five essays on the history of religious art and philosophical perspectives on art and aesthetics.

Bishops' Committee on the Liturgy. *The Environment for Worship: A Reader.* Washington, D.C.: The United States Catholics' Conference, 1980. Fourteen essays that comment on the Roman Catholic document on the environment for worship reprinted in this essay.

Burch Brown, Frank. *Religious Aesthetics: A Theological Study of Making and Meaning.* Princeton, N.J.: Princeton University Press, 1989.

Cope, Gilbert. *Christianity and the Visual Arts.* London: The Faith Press, 1964. A collection of essays concerning the Christian themes in the history of art, including essays about the arts in the buildings for and actions of worship.

Digges, Mary Laurentia. *Transfigured World: Design, Theme, and Symbol in Worship.* New York: Farrar, Straus, and Cudahy, 1987.

Dillenberger, Jane. *Image and Spirit in Sacred and Secular Art.* New York: Crossroad, 1990. Dillenberger considers the images of women in Western art, interpretations of the human body in sacred and secular art, iconographic studies in traditional Christian art, and spiritual impulse in modern art. Art, symbol, and theme are integrated with Scripture study, church history, and theological analysis with cultural and art history. Illustrated.

Dillenberger, John. *The Visual Arts and Christianity in America.* New York: Crossroad, 1989. Focus on colonial period to the present. Consummate volume in four major parts, including: Protestant and Catholic Approaches to the Visual Arts; Nineteenth-Century View of Art and Architecture; Nineteenth-Century Art in Private and Public Life; and The Visual Arts in the Twentieth Century. Especially valuable for insights concerning religious views of artists, theological interpretations of style, clergy views of the arts, and emerging forms of art in the contemporary United States.

Eire, Carlos M. N. *War Against the Idols: The Reformation of Worship from Erasmus to Calvin.* Cambridge: Cambridge University Press, 1986. A history of worship in the Reformation, with particular attention to the Calvinist reforms regarding the use of art in worship.

Fischer, Balthasar. *Signs, Words, and Gestures.* New York: Pueblo, 1981. A theological treatise on the significance of the nonverbal dimensions of worship.

Garside, Charles. *Zwingli and the Arts.* New Haven: Yale University Press, 1966. A comprehensive historical treatment of the Zwinglian opposition to the arts in worship.

Hovda, Robert. *Strong, Loving, and Wise.* Collegeville, Minn: The Liturgical Press, 1983. An essay on the pastoral and theological dimensions of liturgical practice in Roman Catholic worship, with frequent reference to the role of the visual arts.

Kennel, LeRoy. *Visual Arts and Worship.* Scottdale, Pa.: Mennonite Publishing House, 1983. "Visual arts and worship are friends," asserts Kennel in a concise function-and-form argument for visual arts in worship. A biblical theology undergirds their necessity and value, and the author considers at least fourteen forms of visual arts in worship. Text includes strategy, responsible bodies, and both church and denominational statements concerning the inclusion of visual arts. Good bibliography.

Maldonado, Luis, and David Power. *Symbol and Art in Worship.* (Concilium: Religion in the Eighties, no. 132). New York: Seabury Press, 1980. A collection of essays that explore the cultural and philosophical dimensions of the arts in worship, including essays about the practice of the arts in Latin America and Africa.

Martin, James Alfred, Jr. *Beauty and Holiness: The Dialogue Between Aesthetics and Religion.* Princeton, N.J.: Princeton University Press, 1990.

Miles, Margaret. *Image as Insight: Visual Understanding in Western Christianity and Secular Culture.* Boston: Beacon Press, 1985.

Nichols, Aidan. *The Art of God Incarnate.* New York: Paulist Press, 1980. Discusses the nature of representing Christian themes, narratives, and images by the visual arts.

Power, David N. *Unsearchable Riches: The Symbolic Nature of Liturgy.* New York: Pueblo, 1984. A treatise on the multidimensional nature of Christian worship.

Rookmaaker, H. R. *Art Needs No Justification.* Downers Grove, Ill.: InterVarsity Press, 1978. Author issues a prophetic call in four short essays to Christian artists, craftspeople, and musicians to reenter and repossess the world of art that was forsaken as a profane vocation. The impassioned plea advocates a "reformation" of evangelistic, human "art with a difference" and a return to artists with "talent, intelligence, character and application."

Ryken, Leland. *Culture in Christian Perspective: A Door to Understanding the Arts.* Portland, Oreg.: Multnomah Press, 1986. A general view of the arts from a Christian perspective.

Schaefer, Francis A. *Art and the Bible.* Downers Grove, Ill.: InterVarsity Press, 1973. A very influential work by a renowned evangelical leader.

Seerveld, Calvin. *Rainbows for a Fallen World.* Pittsburgh: Shiloh, 1980. A theological treatise on aesthetics with important implications for the use of the arts in worship.

Van der Leeuw, Gerhardus. *Sacred and Profane Beauty: The Holy in Art.* New York: Holt, Rinehart, and Winston, 1963. One of the most significant contributions to religious philosophical aesthetics of the twentieth century. It includes a discussion of all the arts, from dance to poetry, visual arts to music, along with their theological implications.

Von Balthasar, Hans Urs. *The Glory of the Lord: A Theological Aesthetics.* 7 vols. New York: Crossroads, 1982. A comprehensive theological treatise by a renowned Roman Catholic theologian.

Veith, Gene Edward. *The Gift of Art.* Downers Grove, Ill.: InterVarsity Press, 1983. An inspirational book touching on aesthetics, history, theology, and criticism. Art includes all aesthetic forms, and the author's focus is that of enlightening the reader regarding the biblical understanding of art and religion. Interesting reading for the particular focus.

Walton, Janet R. *Art and Worship: A Vital Connection.* Wilmington, Del.: Michael Glazier, Inc., 1988. A case for the integral connections between worship and art, along with principles for the use of art in worship.

Wolterstorff, Nicholas. *Art in Action: Toward a Christian Aesthetic.* Grand Rapids, Michigan: Eerdmans, 1980. An introduction to philosophical aesthetics with frequent references to the aesthetics of art in worship.

❧ ⊞⌷⌷⌷⌷ ⌷ ❧

The Worship Environment

The space of worship ultimately shapes the beliefs, sensibilities, and understandings of those who worship in its confines. The congregation shaped in the open air of the forest will be different from congregations shaped by basilicas, homes, storefronts, and public halls. Only in recent decades have the effects of space on congregational life been considered seriously. Space dictates the ways in which people interact with each other and with other objects in their environment.

Over the centuries Christian traditions have developed styles of architectural design that have expressed their particular liturgical beliefs or assumptions. Presently, nearly all traditions are reevaluating their assumptions in light of historical studies and Vatican II reforms. Congregations are renovating old buildings or erecting new ones to encourage greater movement and interaction by the congregation in worship. The spatial relationship between the primary symbols of faith—the pulpit, Table, and font/baptistry—takes on significant importance as worshipers gather with and around them in the liturgical environment. Various structural, visual, and acoustical considerations are outlined in this section that must be attended to if God's people are to participate fully in the actions of worship.

286 • INTRODUCTION TO THE WORSHIP ENVIRONMENT

Since the arts in worship serve as vehicles of communication, the architectural space in which worship takes place is a matter of primary importance. Space speaks. It is a voice that says something about the action of worship. The symbolic objects of worship assist in communicating Christ's presence and ministry.

Christian Assumptions about Worship Space

Because space speaks, it is important to know what kind of biblical assumptions regarding the church and its worship should inform the Christian approach to worship space. Those involved in contemporary worship renewal agree on three biblical teachings about the church and worship that informs all thought about worship space.

1. The church is people. The church is not a building, a denomination, a judicatory, but the people who assemble to worship.
2. The building in which worship takes place is the house of the people. It is not the house of God, as though it were where God dwells.

God dwells in the people and is present in their assembly.
3. Worship is the action of the entire people of God. It is not something done to the people or for the people by a special class of ordained clergy. Worship is the work of the people.

These three assumptions point to a specific problem in the worship space of many existing churches that were not informed by these principles. Consequently, that space is not conducive to the type of worship advocated by those leading renewal. A brief overview of how space for worship was arranged through the centuries points out the problem.

Early Christianity. The use of space in the church's first three centuries was shaped by the three principles outlined above. For the most part Christians worshiped in homes that were renovated into worship spaces. Worship was people oriented in such spaces.

The Constantinian Era. After the conversion of Constantine and the Edict of Toleration (A.D. 313), the church was given huge Roman basilicas, which were turned into worship space for large gatherings. In these spaces the clergy was separated from the people, and worship was increasingly seen as the action of the clergy. Meanwhile, the participation of the entire body of worshipers went into decline.

The Medieval Era. By the thirteenth century the three biblical principles regarding the church and worship became obscured. The church was identified with the building, which was seen as the "house of God." The people became spectators to the action of worship conducted by the clergy. In Roman Catholicism, this view of space was retained until Vatican II (1963–1965).

Protestant Christianity. While Protestantism attempted to return worship to the people, it gradually turned the worship space into an educational space or an evangelistic space. Today many new Protestant churches, especially the megachurches, have created an entertainment space with a stage, stage lighting, and theater seats.

Contemporary Renewal. Twentieth-century advocates of renewal are returning to the biblical principles of church and worship. They want to end the spectator mentality of worshipers and return to the concept of the church as a people who assemble in a particular space to do the action of worship together.

Since the use of space in the past has both reflected a misunderstanding of worship and therefore an unbiblical design of space for worship, we must ask, "What are the characteristics of a space that indicate what we do when we worship?" These characteristics are three:

1. **Mystery.** Worship speaks the mystery of redemption through Jesus, the Christ who becomes present in worship to do for us what he did historically. A worship environment should speak this mystery, both the mystery of God's transcendence and the mystery of Christ's presence.

2. **Hospitality.** The environment of worship should express a feeling of warmth and congeniality, putting the people of the assembly at ease and making them feel welcome.

3. **Participation.** The environment should aid the participation of the people and should not hinder their actions in speech and movement.

The goal of an environment which speaks of mystery, hospitality, and participation is achieved through a careful consideration of both the primary and secondary aspects of the worship environment.

Primary Symbols of the Worship Environment

The primary symbols of the worship environment, which speak of the meaning of the action taking place, are the configuration of the assembly space and of the furniture of worship. A summary of the salient features of these two aspects of the worship environment follows.

1. **The Assembly Space of the People.** Since worship has to do with experiencing the saving presence of Christ, the people assembled should sit in a configuration that allows them to see each other and to participate with each other as they worship. Consequently, the abilities to *see,* to *hear,* and to *move* must be primary concerns of the seating arrangement.

2. **The Furniture of Worship.** The furniture of worship speaks to the presence of Christ in the assembled body. This furniture should be placed within the worshiping assembly in such a way that the action symbolized by each piece is allowed to speak the presence and work of Christ it represents. There are four pieces of furniture:

- *The baptismal font or pool.* Since this piece of furniture represents entry into the church, its most favored location is near the entrance door.
- *The pulpit.* A free-standing pulpit near the Table and in a place where everyone can see it reflects the revelation of God's Word.
- *The Table.* A free-standing table placed in a location near the pulpit and visible to all speaks of the death and resurrection of Christ.
- *The presider's chair.* A free-standing chair placed behind the pulpit and Table speaks to the position of Christ who presides over the assembly through the one who delivers the Word, celebrates the Table, and baptizes in his name.

Secondary Symbols of the Worship Environment

The secondary symbols of the presence of Christ in worship are the objects that speak of redemption. They are secondary, because they do not hold the same necessity for worship signified by the primary symbols. Nevertheless, these objects must be chosen with care and should reflect a concern for authentic workmanship. These objects include books, such as the gospel book or lectionary books, candles, crosses, Communion vessels, banners, linens, vestments, flowers.

The Worship Environment during Various Seasons of the Christian Year

In addition to the primary and secondary symbols of the presence of Christ, it has become customary to create an environment that speaks the particular biblical mood of each season of the Christian year. Here is a brief summary of the essential feature for each mood:

Advent. At one time Advent was seen as a penitential season. While penitence in preparation for the coming of Christ is still a part of Advent, Advent should be seen as a season of joyous anticipation. The Advent wreath with its five candles is the most obvious object to be placed in the environment for this season.

Christmas. The festivity of the birth of Christ is expressed by flowers—poinsettias and greenery. While the Christmas crib and manger scenes depict Jesus' birth, they should be placed in a place where they can be seen, but not before the Table or pulpit where they distract from the major symbols of worship.

Epiphany. The manifestation of Jesus to the world on January 6 ends the Christmas season. As such, January 6 employs the same environmental motif of Christmas. The season after Epiphany is ordinary or nonfestive time and should conform to the environment of that time.

Lent. Lent prepares worshipers for the events of Holy Week and is an austere season reflecting the sobriety of repentance.

Holy Week. The celebration of the triduum (the three days of Maundy Thursday, Good Friday and the Great Paschal, Vigil of Easter) should be seen as a single continuous event. This event is dominated by the special symbols of these liturgies—bread, wine, the washing of feet, stripping of the church, solemn processions, light, fire, water, and the cross.

Easter (Paschal). The joyful season of Easter is symbolized through floral art, celebrative vestments, and the use of the finest secondary symbols (see above) the church has in its possession.

Ordinary Time. The time after Epiphany and the time after Pentecost is characterized by an emphasis on Sunday as the original feast day of the Resurrection. This time is an especially appropriate time for artists within the church to express their creative talents for the ongoing celebration of the Resurrection.

Conclusion

Finally, it always needs to be kept in mind that worship is the ministry of Christ in his body. He is there to touch people, to heal them, and to make them whole. Everything in the environment of worship is the servant of Christ's action; the environment *serves* the ministry of Christ, as it serves the people. Anything that takes its place, interferes with, or hinders the ministry of Christ, is out of place.

Robert Webber

287 • HOW THE ARCHITECTURAL SETTING FOR WORSHIP FORMS OUR FAITH

Every liturgical space reflects the theological commitments of its designers. Every time a liturgical space is used, those ideals shape the experience of those who worship within it. Space for worship must be designed with concern for the theological and liturgical commitments of a given worshiping community.

In the valley of the Mohawk River in upstate New York stand two churches built just before the Revolutionary War. Both were built by German immigrants, both were built with the same local stone. But there the similarities end. Reformed Christians built the Fort Herkimer Church, while Lutherans erected the Palatine Bridge Church. The buildings show how far apart in faith their builders had grown in the two hundred years since the Reformation.

The Fort Herkimer Church is a preaching church par excellence. Every element in the building focuses on the pulpit, standing about twelve feet high with an elegant sounding board over it. No building is a better witness to the sovereign Word of God, which shapes both life and worship.

The Lutheran church, by contrast, is a sacrament church, gathered around the Communion rail that encircles both altar-Table and pulpit. God's presence in, with, and under physical objects is proclaimed by this building.

One comes away from each building with no doubt about the faith of its builders. The buildings are good examples of the ways in which faith can be expressed in stone and wood, plaster and glass. And each has been making its respective witness for well over two hundred years now. We think of Churchill's famous phrase when the rebuilding of the House of Parliament was undertaken: "We shape our buildings and ever after they shape us."

Certainly, these two churches were successful spatial efforts in expressing the faith of the pioneers. In their time, these buildings were not only adequate but were probably more satisfactory than the remodeled medieval buildings their builders had forsaken back home in the Rhine Valley. The new buildings were built with an intentionality to express a contemporary faith, not that of a previous age.

Space and Faith as Potential Antagonists

The problem for us is whether either of these buildings would be an adequate expression of our faith today. Of course, a building need not be old to be out of touch with our faith. In Burlington, Vermont, two cathedrals stand barely a block apart. Both were built after earlier Gothic-Revival cathedrals had burned down in the 1970s. In architectural style, both are contemporary but the Episcopal cathedral is strangely conservative in that the altar-Table and clergy seats are located in a distinct space, removed as a separate volume from the nave where the people and choir sit. The Roman Catholic cathedral thrusts the altar-Table into the midst of the congregation, and no one sits more than eight seats from it. One cathedral suggests that God is remote and transcendent, the other that God is near and immanent.

What if the building does not reflect our faith today? If not, it will fight us, and the chances are that the building will win. I would be reluctant to preach on the priesthood of all Christians at the Episcopal cathedral because the building would shout me down; in the Roman Catholic cathedral I would get a better hearing. Not only does space form faith but it can, and frequently does, deform and distort faith. Thus we are frequently caught in a conflict between the faith that we profess and the faith that the building proclaims. The most ironic sermon I ever heard was Pope Paul VI preaching against triumphalism in the church. But he preached

in St. Peter's Basilica, and Michelangelo clearly had the last word. The conflict is not usually that obvious but it happens in many of our churches every Sunday. The more subtle and undramatic it is, the more insidious and dangerous.

The conflict between space and faith is not to be taken lightly. Pastors have to develop a new sensitivity in learning to "read" space. We must learn to ask of any church space the same question we ask when making ethical decisions: "What is going on here?" Church architecture is not some innocuous muzak that we can afford to neglect. Rather it is an important constituent in forming the faith of the people who gather within it, perhaps the most important single factor in their formation.

Frequently, remodeling or renovating a church is one of the most significant occasions for reshaping the life of a community of faith. Too often, such opportunities become mere occasions for redecorating or accommodating a new organ. Renovations ought to be regarded as a vital change to rethink the mission of the church and to reinforce that mission by giving it physical form. Careful church renovation is not a luxury; it often is a necessity unless we are to continue in self-contradiction. Unless we are indifferent to the contents of the faith we teach, we have to take seriously the architectural setting of our worship.

At stake here is the sacramental principle that the outward and visible cannot be dissociated from what is inward and spiritual. Somehow Protestants still have trouble with this; the people who sell automobiles take it for granted. They give us power, glamour, affluence, all made of steel and glass. We are not called to be more spiritual than God. Buildings are faith in just the same sense that a kiss is love. Judas could dissemble, actors can pretend, but buildings are pretty honest statement of faith. In a very real way, space is faith.

Seeking Harmony between Space and Faith

As we become more sensitive to the relationship of space and faith, there is a certain grammar we learn as we discover what space is saying. We may note here two forms of speech. One, we recognize that *every space in churches exists in relationship to other spaces*. This forces us to raise questions about people and how they relate to each other, how they relate to the clergy, and how they relate to God. The arrangement of different spaces are primary concerns. What kind of space is provided for people to come together to discern the body of Christ? Are the clergy alone with God in the remote holy space of a chancel? Does the building suggest that God is somewhere out beyond the east window? The arrangement of spaces makes definite statements about such matters.

The second thing we have to think through is *what it is that people do when they come together.* Such activities usually focus on a particular liturgical center, a baptismal font or pool, a pulpit, an altar-Table. Here it is important to be clear about functions. What happens in baptism? Is it simply a sentimental occasion of Christian cuteness, or is it grafting a new branch onto the trunk so that the same energy that vivifies every part of the tree gives life to it, too? Does the whole community participate, or is it a private ceremony? And is it a genuine proclamation of God's will to forgive and cleanse or just a dry cleaning? All these questions and more must be asked about the design of the font and its location. One has to make up one's mind about some important theological issues first.

This is why worship reform and architectural renovation have to go hand in hand. You cannot reform the Lord's Supper with the altar-Table nailed to the wall. But a free-standing altar-Table will not be much of an improvement either unless one is deeply aware of what it means to gather a community about the Lord's Table to give thanks.

The baptismal fonts we have in many Protestant churches reveal what baptism has meant to us. They are an outward and visible witness that baptism has been a short and insignificant ceremony performed from a bowl tucked out of sight most of the time. In a perverse way, those bowls told just how unimportant baptism was in many of our churches. If we had really believed that baptism is union to Christ and incorporation into the church, we would not have been content with such diminutive fonts to proclaim so great a truth. In the South, Baptists tend to speak of being baptized and being saved as synonymous terms. Their baptismal pools are highly visible and important parts of the building, at least when they are being used.

We do better with pulpits, but there are questions to ask here, too. Do we preach "six feet above contradiction" (J. A. T. Robinson), or do we speak on our people's level? Is our preaching biblical, or is the Bible visually (and really) relegated to a separate lectern? How do we bring preacher, Bible, and people together in the most meaningful relationship? Our visible signs tell far more than we want to reveal. Liturgical reform must accompany any meaningful reform of space.

One word of caution is necessary. We do not want to tie knots in the future the way many congregations did in the 1950s when they built churches as if nothing in worship would ever change. Now we are more humble; we know that worship does change and so must our space. We shall not always express our faith in the same ways, and so the spaces of those who come after us will be different, just as our faith must be expressed in ways different from those who came before us. We can learn from the past, but we do not wish to impose it on our present or on the future.

James F. White[54]

288 • THE "PUBLIC LANGUAGE" OF CHURCH ARCHITECTURE

Church buildings should be designed with consideration of how the general public will relate to the space they define. Church architecture is one language by which the witness of the church may be made known. Church buildings may be valuable to a community both as a space for communal activity and as a symbol of what community stands for.

In a few pages of his classic book *The Shape of the Liturgy,* Gregory Dix described what it might have been like to come together for Christian worship in second-century Rome. It is very, very early on a Sunday morning, which was a working day in Rome. The setting is a somewhat generous home—typically a series of spaces surrounding the central *atrium* which might be open or covered. The *tablinium,* which is a couple of steps up, is the place of the bishop and elders. Others mostly assemble in the *atrium,* which has its pool, the *impluvium,* and the *cartibulum,* a small, blocky Table. There are many elements of the event that endure to this day, and others that we might well recover.

It is noteworthy that the architectural setting had a humane and domestic character instead of a monumental one. This was quite fitting for the Christian concept of worship; the assembly was a sort of family reunion. In sharp contrast to most other religions of the time, Christian worship was very much a communal occasion and not an exercise in personal piety.

Another interesting thing about the place is that though it had architectural dignity, it was what we would call a "secular" place; the architecture itself had no ecclesiastical features. For as Justin Martyr said in the year 155 when Rusticus, who was the prefect of Rome, asked him where the Christians worshiped, "The God of Christians is not circumscribed by place, but is invisible and fills all heaven and earth. He is worshiped and glorified by the faithful anywhere."

A third noteworthy characteristic is that the place was one of functional variability; it was not used exclusively for worship. Clement of Alexandria wrote, "We have no temples and no altars." Typically, the structure was sturdy and durable; but the artifacts of worship, the lamps for reading in the early dawn, the books, fabrics, and vessels were portable and kept in storage between times.

These are qualities that we can, and I think should, accept as continuities between the way early Christians conceived their places of worship and the way we conceive ours. Nevertheless, there was one very radical difference between worship in those early centuries and ours. Theirs was hidden from the public eye. Even when it was not secret, it was private. Neither the liturgy itself nor the structure that surrounded it was open to the public. There are circumstances like that in our world too, and those Christians who _must_ worship in secret must feel a particular kinship with the early Christians.

But our condition is quite different and much happier. We may have, if we wish, public worship; and we may build whatever we need and can. Their service and their public witness, _charisma_ and _kerygma,_ were apart from the liturgy and outside the place of assembly; ours need not be separate.

Buildings and Symbol Systems

What are the implications of all these similarities and differences for those who design and fund the buildings of the church?

What I have to say emerges from the fact that architecture is not only useful shelter, but language. It is a silent language, a symbol system through which Christians can communicate. They speak of themselves for one thing, reminding themselves Sunday by Sunday about the body of Christ—who they are and what they hope to be. And they speak to other people—the public—about the household

of faith and what it is that binds this household together as believers and as disciples.

We are not, by the grace of God, a secret society. We address the public. One thing we have to say is that we receive life as a gift from the Father, and through the Son, forgiveness. It is only reasonable then that Christians respond in the way they design their structures. People who receive gifts of grace and love respond, if they are grateful, with a kind of vivid joy. And so there ought to be a kind of liveliness and joy in the language of our architecture.

There are a million ways of accomplishing this, and I can't begin to tell you how. But I can say something about what a church building must not be. It must not be a dull, banal, prosaic, commonplace, architectural nothing. It must not be ugly. It must not seem to be something done only out of duty, or stinginess, a cowardly workaday drudgery. It should be a gift not in payment for but in response to a gift. A beautiful thing.

And of course it must not only be a gift of the congregation to itself, it must also be a gift from the family of God to others. For if we have received the gifts of life and forgiveness, and if we want to acknowledge the relentlessly loving God, we must be relentlessly loving in turn to the people about us—even in the way we build our buildings. Bonhoeffer described Jesus as being "the man for others" and said that it was only proper that his followers should also be for others.

So, if there is ever the impulse to say, "After all, it's only a building for ourselves so let's keep it down and not get too excited about it," think again. Architecture speaks, and the language is public.

On the other hand, if there ever is the impulse to say, "Let's build a great monument with a fine tower, so people all around can see it and say, 'That's where the Disciples go to church; they surely let themselves be known,'" think again. Is that tower just another self-serving billboard?

A Design for Others

The best way I can propose that Christians acknowledge God's gifts is to approach the work as a few of the congregations we have worked with have. They have said to themselves: "We want a building that isn't just for us; we want a building through which we can supply some of the unfilled needs of the community we belong to. It will be so planned and so available that it can be used for other purposes besides ours. And this will be our gift to the people around us."

What that meant, of course, is that they didn't build what we usually think of as traditional, single-use "sanctuaries." They grafted onto the oldest tradition instead and built places that could have varied uses. A Catholic parish agreed that if they were in earnest about being hospitable to non-Catholics, they ought to avoid the typical array of Catholic devotional accoutrements. So there are no holy-water stoups fastened to the walls (though there is a great vessel of running water at the door); there are no sculptured or painted stations of the cross (which exist instead only as signs in the floor along one wall); the only crucifix is one brought in on a staff when Mass begins; the stained glass is beautiful, but has no pictures of iconographic symbols; the tabernacle can be veiled with a screen; and the liturgical furnishings are movable, including the altar-Table. It is a place just about as secular as the house where the early Romans assembled. But that doesn't mean it isn't a fine place for the Mass. We call the place not a church, nor a sanctuary, nor a nave. And it surely isn't an auditorium. We call it a *centrum*—a fine hall for various kinds of assemblies of people, including liturgical assemblies.

A couple of other centrums we have designed have been used as banquet halls, even for such things as political dinners. Why not? They are noble rooms and anything that happens in them is made nobler by the environment. So a double gift is given: a place for the public event and an environment that bestows upon the event a dignity it wouldn't otherwise have.

What the church says in this public language is what it ought to be saying: "We are the people for others. And even our buildings are intended to be vehicles of service to others."

Symbols of Roots and Responsibility

Here is another sentence from the public language: Christians live in history, between memory and hope. Our present life is part of a thread that traces back to Jesus and beyond, and it will be spun on from us and through us into an unpredictable future. We have roots in the past, which we treasure.

Architecture supplies a visual and useful symbol of rootage and continuity. Human history is not in the end chaotic, aleatoric, a matter of chance and accident. We may not have a very complete or secure knowledge of the order of time, but we do believe in order, and in destiny. And we do believe that when God gives us the stewardship of a piece of land and the means to build a piece of the world, we must do it responsibly.

What does "responsibly" mean? It means that we build coherent structures that are meant to survive because we believe in history. Buildings that can be symbols of our sense of time, or our hope, and a good heritage for future generations.

We tend to look at old buildings in two ways. Sometimes we think of them as trouble; irritating, intractable, outworn candidates for the headache ball. And then there are those we cherish. They wear their datestones like medals of honor. What's the difference? Generally, the first kind of buildings weren't really good even when they were new, and they got worse. The second kind were done well and beautifully. So, we adopt them as symbols of our roots and history.

But, one may ask, why should we strain ourselves to build well when the future is so insecure, change is so certain, and it is such a burden to do things well? San Antonio is a great city to supply an answer. For here in San Antonio, we have five missions built by the Spaniards 250 years ago. They built simply, durably, and beautifully. Today those missions are the treasures of the whole populace. They supply a heritage even to people who haven't been in the city very long and aren't Roman Catholics. They are occasions for wonder and pleasure, and a sense of rootage in a transient and fractured society. And what if they are no longer place of worship? Those ancient Spaniards gave a gift to more people in that architecture than any of them might have thought possible.

Accommodating Change

As Christians we live in a context of change. We pray for change daily when we pray "thy kingdom come." We bivouac, we live in contingency, we look for reformation, for renewal, for growth, and for change. How then should the language of architecture deal with this and at the same time deal with permanence, durability, and roots?

If we start with the conception of the early Christians and of the centrum, rather than with the conventional single-use ecclesiastically oriented place of worship, incompatibility disappears.

A centrum is a piece of secular, earthy (not otherworldly) architecture. It is essentially a beautiful assembly hall, intended for people, but not shaped around any one particular configuration of people and furniture. There aren't any ecclesiastical motifs in the architecture. It's just a nice part of the world, and a durable, permanent one capable of accommodating change.

Consider what is likely to change. Even if the centrum's major use—perhaps for the time its only use—is worship, we know the patterns of worship will change. The numbers of people vary, the kinds of liturgical or paraliturgical events vary. And each condition of use has its own proper configuration of people and furniture, changing with the occasion and changing with the passage of time.

So in a centrum we may accommodate change—even invite change—because almost all the furnishings (as in the early Roman house-church) are movable.

It is these things, these artifacts, that make a place convenient to worship. And their portability and changeability is the symbol that our life as Christians is provisional, contingent, a life of _becoming_ as well as life of _being_. The people and the artifacts turn the place into a place of prayer.

Minnesota senator Hubert Humphrey once said, "The beginning of all practicality in politics is a vision of things as they ought to be." I think the statement is equally valid if you substitute the word _architecture_ for politics. For like politics, architecture is a reflection of people's self-understanding, and architecture, like politics, is the art of the possible. The beginning of all practicality in architecture is a vision of things as they ought to be. I'm going to suggest such a vision.

Somewhere in America

Imagine a fine big room that is vacant except for chairs arranged on three sides of a platform which is made up of sturdy, but movable modules. Someone brings in some plants and flowers in pots and vases. Some of these are put beside a pool of running water near the main entrance, some at other places around the room. The custodian hoists a great banner behind the platform. It is vermilion and white and has two words on it because it is Pentecost: "Fire! Fire!" He wheels out a cart full of hymnbooks and places this cart just outside the main doors. He opens the doors wide.

Some people come, take their books, and find seats. Ushers appear. More people come. The organist begins to play. A procession forms. Two people

bring in a rug and roll it out on the platform. Four men carry in, shoulder high, a fine Table. Two candle bearers bring lighted candles and set them down. A deacon brings a colored tablecloth with a Pentecost motif. Another one comes with a fine book on a pillow and puts it on the Table (the service book). Then the choir comes in, each with a candlestick (because it is Pentecost), and they part at the door and spread the candles all around the perimeter of the room. Then comes a crossbearer, with a staff and cross that is set in a position where it hovers above the heads of the people. And behind come the ministers who take their place.

The verbal part of the service then begins. But the service really began when the room began to be transformed (converted?) by the people and things that make it a place of Christian celebration. The movement and action aren't over yet. When the time comes to read the Scripture, another small procession begins—two candle bearers and the bearer of a fine and large Bible. Nothing trivial is to happen here, like reading the Scripture from the back of the service folder. And when the Communion service begins, an elder brings a white linen to spread on the Table over the colored cloth, and the Communion elements are then brought to the Table too. At the end of the service, while the people are still singing, the procession reverses, and the centrum again becomes just another very fine part of God's world, available for other worthy purposes.

So, architecture is a witness to being and becoming, certitude and contingency, the general presence of God in the world and the special presence of Christ in his body, the church.

A Noble Speech

There are a great many other things that this kind of approach to the language of architecture can reveal about the church. But now I ask you to think about the two words, _public language,_ in a different context. I take my clue from the language of speech.

We have seen in the last decades some remarkable changes in the texts of worship. For instance, the Roman Catholics switched from Latin to English or other local speech in the liturgy. That's the sharpest change perhaps and a very admirable one. But there have been others: an Episcopal priest wrote a book of prayers titled _Are You Running with Me, Jesus?_ One of my sons came back from camp a few years ago with a new Table prayer: "Rub-a-dub, thanks for the grub! Yeah, God!" and another came back singing, "Be present at our Table, Lord" to the tune of the Gillette razor jingle.

Perhaps you may have the same fears as I—that the public language of our worship is being depreciated. The intent has had a certain validity. The artificialities of the public language of worship had separated religion into a discreet category of life. The language had no currency. So it has been contended that worship had no relevancy.

Something similar has been happening in the architecture of worship. The artificiality of the Gothic and Georgian was held under siege by a generation of so-called modern architects. Georgian and Gothic are pretty well gone, and good riddance. But the old styles were followed by uncertain, sometimes brash, sometimes capricious new forms. "Get with it, get hep," many of them seem to be saying, and saying it too loudly. And more recently there has been a current that seems to use domesticity not as a paradigm but as a model. "The church is like a family," they seem to say, "obviously the church building must be an oversize rambler." Not long ago I was in a big new structure where the interior surfaces were wallpapered. And we've all probably seen new church buildings filled with the same modish chrome and plastic chairs that we see in restaurants and hotels. I'm all for using chairs, but not just any stackable commercial chair.

There is a difference between the everyday language and a public language. The everyday vernacular is surely acceptable for conversation and for private prayer. But liturgy is not conversation, and it is not private prayer. It is proclamation, or praise, or common prayer. Public language has its own style, cadence, and dignity. It is not esoteric, but it verges on poetry.

Some may object for fear that I am backsliding to the ecclesiastical jargon, the "language of Canaan," with its circumlocutions, its pious embroidery, and its indirections and pecksniffery—the kind of speech that substitutes "he died" with "he forsook the fragile tabernacle of this world." We've all heard this kind of quaint euphemism that weakens thought and camouflages reality. Architecturally, we do the same thing when we take the Latin cross—which is an image of the instrument of execution on which Jesus died—and camouflage it with sweet decorations or distort it into something elegant and pretty until it is no longer a symbol of the real tragedy and terror.

What we must have is a public language, both of speech and architecture, that is direct and real, noble and gracious. Listen to this:

> O God, for as muche as without thee, we are not able to please thee: Graunte that the workyng of thy mercie, may in all thynges direct and rule our heartes; through Jesus Christ our Lorde.

Terse, unsentimental, rhythmic, full of feeling. This is not the everyday vernacular. It is a public language, as good today as in 1549. The *thee's* and *thou's* have no inflated value, of course; *you* is just as good.

The virtue of Bishop Cranmer's prayers is not that they are ecclesiastical jargon, they aren't; they are a public language. For public language exists also in the secular world. For example: "Fourscore and seven years ago our fathers brought forth on this continent a new nation, conceived in liberty and dedicated to the proposition that all men are created equal." That's public language just as surely as Cranmer's. Public language in speech and architecture is quite distinct from the vernacular. It is secular, but it is not commonplace prose.

Bridges Are Needed

Can we make the architecture of our church buildings a public language? Neither ecclesiastical nor trivial, but direct, real, earthy, secular, vigorous, and at the same time noble, gracious, and beautiful? How shall it happen?

Clearly it won't happen by accident. It won't happen if we try to get by with half-skilled, half-educated, half-sensitized, and halfhearted designers. The distinction is much too subtle for mediocre sensibilities. We need the very best professional help we can get. There is one way toward the goal.

But there are aspects of this work that we can't expect many architects—even the best designers and most responsible professionals—to bring, ready-made, to the work. We won't find many of them very sophisticated in church finance. We won't find that they know much about church policy and the processes of decision making in church affairs. And we may find that they have not thought any more deeply about worship and theology and Christian piety than the typical minister has about the subtleties and complexities of architectural aesthetics and technology.

A bridge is usually needed. And that bridge is the consultant. A consultant can widen the people's horizons regarding architecture and deepen the understanding of the architect in the areas of churchmanship, worship, and theology—and in the relationship of these things to architecture.

The issue before us, of course, is not so much how we get where we want to be; there are various routes. But we must clarify our visions. And I think that if we are careful about that, we will find that we are rediscovering and recovering some of the most ancient patterns of church life and grafting onto the most elemental traditions of our faith.

Edward A. Sovik[55]

289 • THE CHURCH BUILDING AS A HOME FOR THE CHURCH

The church building is the home for God's people, providing identity and a place in the world. The article illustrates how the change in liturgical understanding since Vatican II has changed the understanding of what a church building wants and needs to be for God's people.

What does the building want to be? Architect Louis Kahn, whose work ranges from the Sears Tower in Chicago to the Unitarian Church in Rochester, New York, introduced this question into the discussion about architecture. Although the question has been posed in a variety of disguises throughout the history of architecture, Kahn's phrasing stands in stark contrast to the modernist preoccupation with function: _What should a building do?_ In light of Vatican II, its reformed liturgy, ecclesiology, and view of the world, Kahn's question may be asked more specifically: _What does the church building want to be?_

We may answer the question by showing how the church building has undergone a change in identity from the house of God to the home of the church. An appreciation of this change is now fundamental for designing church buildings and worship space. The new paradigm for the church building is, in light of the reforms, the home.

House of God—Home of the Church

Adapting an older church building to the liturgical reforms is often difficult and frequently unsuccessful. This indicates the radical shift in the identity of the parish building. The older buildings were not meant to house worshipers. They were meant to house God, and this was consistent with the theology inherent in the liturgy and popular piety of the times.

With the Counter-Reformation of the sixteenth century, the Roman church aggressively attempted to defend against the confusion introduced by the Reformation, especially regarding the Eucharist. For example, the Council of Trent reaffirmed the doctrine of transubstantiation, which holds that the substance of the bread and wine undergoes a radical transformation at the moment of consecration and becomes the body and blood of Christ, even though appearances remain the same. Reaffirmation of this doctrine renewed devotion to the consecrated host, a devotion that had its genesis in medieval church history and nourished later as reception of Communion waned. What people felt no longer worthy to receive, they could worship and adore from a distance. Thus, the consecration at the Mass became the _raison d'etre_ of the Mass.

Parallel with this devotion, preaching took on a life of its own outside the Mass. Architects then designed churches to feature the sermon and the consecration. The pulpit became prominent; acoustical projection became essential. However, except when the pulpit was in use, the focus was the high altar where the consecration could be seen. With the increasing focus on the consecrated host, the tabernacle found its place on the high altar. Thus, even after Mass, one could prolong that moment of consecration by gazing at the tabernacle, which typically was placed where the priest would have elevated the host. The tabernacle often included its own _balcacchino_ where a monstrance, which also served to keep the faithful focused on the consecrated host, could be enshrined.

The architecture of the church—from the reredos that embellished and augmented the tabernacle to the plan of the building—reinforced the importance of the tabernacle and the theology it symbolized. The lines of the church from the main entrance led the eye to the sanctuary, up a flight of stairs, to the high altar upon which the tabernacle rested, augmented by an elaborate backdrop. Here was the locus of God's presence, where one could witness the sacred moment and sustain it in worship and prayer.

In effect, the Tridentine church became a tabernacle to house the tabernacle that housed God. One came to church to pray to God who resided there. God's court could be found there, too, hence the various side altars and shrines for the Virgin and various saints. The church was a place to make a sacred social call in God's earthly dwelling.

We should not be too quick to denigrate such piety. It was practiced for centuries and was supported by a formidable theology. The greatest and most sophisticated architecture gave expression to it. Such architecture served the spiritual needs that today we run the risk of ignoring, forgetting, or denying.

The Essential Recovery

That piety, however, neglects the essential character of the eucharistic liturgy that the church needed to recover. To Christians, divine presence is not manifested primarily in objects and images, but in the community of believers, especially when they gather for the eucharistic liturgy.

Despite the long tradition of seeing the consecrated host as the primary manifestation of God's presence, the documents of Vatican II, along with subsequent documents, emphasized the primary importance of the assembly. The assembly not only has the right and duty to be present at the liturgy, it has the right and duty to take an active role in it. The liturgy, which formerly was a rite performed by one man for a passive congregation, became a ritual celebration demanding the activity of all present—from actively listening to the Word of God to moving around an altar in song and prayer. Sacred objects, instead of helping to focus attention on a consecrated host, now facilitate the liturgical action. In short, what was formerly the house of God has become the house of an active congregation.

The difference between the house of God and the house of the church reflects the difference between two significantly different kinds of prayer. Since Vatican II, both private passive prayer and active public prayer have been encouraged. However, they require different times and, perhaps, even different spaces. The house of God is suitable for private prayer, which calls for quiet and solitude. Even when devotions are done in common, they are essentially passive. Gestures, movement, and active responses are typically detrimental. Such prayers engage the imagination, experience, and emotions and may be deliberately inspired by sacred images and objects.

True community prayer is exactly the opposite. Because it requires the faithful to gather together as a community, it is predisposed to socializing. Enter-

ing the church quietly, saying a prayer, and waiting for Mass to begin is no longer appropriate. Community worship requires the active participation of people: to greet each other; to sing and pray with one voice; to wish each other peace; to break bread and share it; to drink from the same cup. The eucharistic liturgy still engages the feelings and imaginations of the congregation, but this occurs less through extraneous visual images beheld by the individual and more through the word, action, and symbols of the liturgy made available to the entire assembly.

Where Is the Sacred?

This shift in the nature of the church building also reflects a shift in the way the church perceives herself—from militant and triumphant to personal and serving. With *Gaudium et Spes* the person received renewed recognition and importance. With *Lumen Gentium* the people of God recovered their identity as a church of disciples and servants. With *Sacrosanctum Concilium* the Sunday assembly assumed a vital significance as the visible manifestation of the body of Christ gathered again to remember and reenact the saving work of the Lord.

The church needs a new architecture to house its people, its liturgy, and its other activities. This new architecture must have a "good feeling in terms of human scale, hospitality and graciousness. It does not seek to impress or even less to dominate." A monument or temple of exaggerated proportions is no longer deemed appropriate.

The document *Environment and Art in Catholic Worship* suggests another possibility. "The congregation, its liturgical action, the furniture and other objects it needs for its liturgical action—these indicate the necessity of a space, a place or hall, or a building for the liturgy."

Since the council, architects like E. A. Sovik and Frederic Debuyst have designed such halls and parish buildings fully equipped with portable altar, movable platforms, stackable chairs, office rooms, classrooms, and what Sovik calls the *centrum,* a space large enough for a congregation to meet for any number of reasons, only one of which is the eucharistic celebration. The new space is meant to facilitate and house the activities of a parish or faith community. The main centrum becomes a space that can be adapted to the needs of a large group, but primarily it provides space for the celebration of the Eucharist.

One might question the appropriateness of this multipurpose hall for the liturgy. As *Environment and Art in Catholic Worship* indicates, ''such a space acquires a sacredness from the sacred action of the faith community which uses it.'' At the same time, the community of the church and her liturgy find their home in the space because the space is sacred. This is not a simple matter of cause and effect, but a matter of mutual relationship between the space the community. What is sacred about the space must be sustained by its design and ''feel.'' To use the metaphor from modern architecture, the model of the multipurpose hall is in danger of becoming nothing more than a machine for worship. To paraphrase Frank Lloyd Wright, the church building is a machine for worship, but architecture begins where the machine ends.

Look Homeward

Environment and Art in Catholic Worship, with its emphasis on hospitality, graciousness, and human proportion, suggests that the church building should be a home, a dwelling. A home is more than shelter, more than a skin to house the inner activity. Like Heidegger's understanding of ''thing,'' a dwelling gathers ''world.'' It is the space where life occurs. It serves as a reference and orientation point. The home, the dwelling, becomes for the household part of the fabric of its life together. Home is the place where the person creates his or her world. It is the place where the person is at home in the world. This is not a matter of convenience, appliances, or decoration, but a matter of meaning, harmony, and integrity.

What are the characteristics of the home that might be pertinent to the church building?

First, the home is both a public, or at least a semipublic, and a private place. It shelters, facilitates, and becomes integral to the ritual activities of the household. At the same time, it allows and fosters spontaneity, individuality, and solitude. As the place that gathers world, establishes and maintains meaning, it must be instrumental in gathering family and friends and in gathering the self. It must help designate the subsets of the world that stand for the world and that are progressively more intimate: friends, family, lover, self. It thus articulates one's relationship with the world.

Second, the building becomes home when the household takes possession of it. This is not accomplished by the exchange of title deeds. The classical Romans had the custom of carrying and moving their household gods with them. The household ''moved in'' when the gods were established in the house. The household moves in when the spirit of the family meets the *genius loci,* the spirit of the place, and the two are wedded, shaping each other and accommodating each other. The family takes possession when those tokens, those things which stand for the family, are established and when the new place embraces the rituals and the uniqueness of the individuals who contribute to the household's spirit. This is not an immediate occurrence, but one that takes time and that resists manipulation.

Third, the home must stand over and against its surroundings as well as respond to them. As the subset of the world, it is of the world and opposite to the world. To maintain a sense of the mutual relationship between the home and the world, the home includes something of its surroundings: plants and animals, for example. The house, built of materials like stone and wood, assumes characteristics of its environs, while open windows for view and air allow for interpenetration of the world within and the world without.

The fourth follows from the third. Even as the home articulates the distinction between outside and inside, it must also celebrate the transition from one to the other. Entry into the home is carefully arranged so that it becomes something of an event. One removes outer garments, proceeds through a vestibule, and so on. The home is supported architecturally by a porch and a door that is an integral part of the structure, but more than a machine for gaining entry. All this conspires to promote a feeling of hospitality and welcome. The dwelling opens its arms and enfolds the one who enters and then sends them on their way.

Fifth, the house needs a center around which the household gathers. In some cultures and at certain times, this was the hearth or the fountain in the middle of the courtyard. Perhaps now it is the kitchen. But it must become the center for the group's most intimate and significant experiences. It must provide a means for preserving former experiences and for documenting the history of the household. The hearth is perhaps the best example of this. Favorite chairs were placed around the hearth. Pictures and family relics were displayed on the mantelpiece. The center is the place within the space that gathers the household, gathers meaning.

It is the center of the world; the place where the family is most at home; the place where the family leads its guests to be at home with them.

Thus, the house as home facilitates relationship and communication as well as the withdrawal from them. It is a place replete with meaning and memory, a place which encourages and ritualizes the activities which are sacred to family.

Moving In

The church building is a public facility, but people who use the church building are bound together by a faith which makes them more a family than a random collection of people on independent paths.

Although there is a communal aspect to the church building, the design of the building must allow for the need to withdraw, to be alone, to pray. The building which houses the people of God and becomes the facility for their prayer and worship must accommodate both public and private prayer.

To be at home in the church building, the community must take possession somehow and move in. The household gods must be established, so to speak. The spirit of the community and the *genius loci* must embrace. This is achieved in a number of ways and on a number of levels. First, the design of the church must communicate the presence of God, whether the community is assembled or not. Through its eloquent beauty, it must bespeak the presence of the holy. For Catholics, the "household God" moves in when the blessed sacrament is reserved and the red lamp burns. The blessed sacrament testifies to the lasting presence of God. The "household gods" move in when the patron is adopted and the beloved Virgin finds a home.

In terms of its surroundings, the church building, like the home, must stand over and against its environs and, yet, relate to them. By separating the space for the people of God, the building thus groups the people and gives basic architectural expression to the unity of those who assemble there, but which does not extend beyond the walls to those who do not believe. Yet the church serves as a witness to the world. To be entirely self-enclosed, with no relation to the world, would frustrate the community's essential duty to the world.

A sense of welcome and hospitality must be woven entirely into the fabric of the building. This does not take the place of a welcoming community, but architecture has the capacity to help make hospitality possible and more likely. Moreover, even when the community is not assembled, the solitary visitor ought to feel welcome to enter and pray. A church, especially in a busy urban area, has the responsibility to be a place where one can withdraw momentarily in order to recollect oneself. Such a welcome can be achieved through the combination of several elements: a vestibule; light; warmth; color; familiarity; and a place for coats, hats, bags, and so on.

Hospitality is not merely a matter of functionality. The design of the church must embrace the community and the individual. It must reveal the God who summons a people to gather. The break in the boundary, the entrance, must serve as the invitation and the point where the building begins to reveal itself.

Finally, the church building needs a center where the most significant actions of the community can be experienced. This center is where the Eucharist becomes "the summit toward which the activity of the church is directed" and "the fount from which all the church's power flows." Although this place is conducive to and may be used for other events such as concerts, other artistic performances, meetings, and prayer groups, its vital importance as the space for the Eucharist must not be compromised or violated. Any activity that divorces the sacred experience of the liturgy entirely from the space is a questionable practice. The space acquires its sacred nature from the activity of the community, but the sacred is not so transient a characteristic that it can be disregarded immediately after the sacred activity is completed. Like the house, the church building becomes part and parcel of the sacred activities of the community and cannot be violated without violating the sensitivities and the dynamic of the community.

The Second Vatican Council reestablished the church as a people called to holiness and to be witnesses of the good news to the world. It also reestablished the Eucharist as the activity of that people, a ritual that asserts their identity in relation to God. In light of this, what the church building wants to be is a dwelling for this people, the place that allows them to be, the center of their lives, which holds and communicates the meaning of their lives. Nothing is so expressive of this meaning as the eucharistic liturgy, and the church building that houses this sacred activity becomes an integral component of it. More than a platform or a facility for their activity, the church building becomes the place where this people gathers its world and its greater meaning, which is not finally thought, but felt. It is where religion is articulated and restored through the community's experience of God. The church building is that existential foothold where the community is at home.

Thomas R. Slon[56]

290 • THE CHURCH BUILDING AS A SETTING FOR LITURGICAL ACTION

The following comments discuss the relationship of the design of the worship space to the actions that take place there. The function and significance of these actions provide the needed guidelines for liturigical architecture.

The church building and setting for the liturgical assembly. Nothing more, but nothing less. Liturgical worship happens in space, and space is shaped into place by the meaning people discover within it. Jews and Christians have shaped space into place by discovering that the Creator abides throughout creation. Christians especially can never forget the spatial concreteness the Incarnation entails. God did not become a movement, a concept, an ideal, or even a committee, but a man of flesh and bone with a parentage, friends, a language, a country, a home. He inhabited not just a time but places, streets, rooms, countrysides, and by his presence in the flesh he changed them all. The memory of this has never died because his continuing presence by grace, faith, and sacrament still does the same in the world through his body, which is the church, enfleshed locally in the liturgical assembly.

It goes counter to Christian instinct, therefore, that the place in which the church assembles should be devoid of all evidence of his presence or that this presence should be regarded as temporary, capricious, or discrete so as not to restrict him or inconvenience the assembly. He restricted himself by becoming incarnate, and the assembly's only inconvenience is his real absence.

Raw space becomes liturgical place through the change his presence by grace, faith, and sacrament causes. Liturgical place is thus not a monument to the pastor's tastes or the locale in which the assembly feels most comfortable. Jesus Christ's incarnate presence caused notable discomfort even for those who loved him best, and he is reported to have resorted to violence on one occasion when faced with the obduracy of the temple clergy's tastes. Liturgical place belongs to the assembly only because the space it occupies is first his. He alone makes it a place by specifying its meaning as distinct from all others. To this specification the assembly can only be obedient; for it the assembly can only pray even as it cooperates with him by faith in its specification.

What the church building shelters and gives setting for is the faithful assembly, the church, in all its rich diversity of orders from catechumen to penitent, from youngest server to eldest bishop. As it meets for worship of the Source and Redeemer of all, the assembly is the fundamental sacrament of God's pleasure in Christ on earth. The eucharistic food and drink are the sacred symbol of this ecclesial reality, which Paul calls simply Christ's body. Christian instinct has been to house this assembly as elegantly as possible, avoiding tents, bedrooms, and school basements.

The assembly uses its place to do something in. This is the liturgy, by which the assembly celebrates the nuptials of all things with their Creator. Because the celebration outstrips being merely an instruction, a pageant, a meditation, a preachment, or an act of therapy, the assembly as a rule has kept its place open for movement on the part of all. Furniture is used for public purpose and for those who find it difficult to stand or move.

The strong and elemental openness of liturgical place makes for dynamism and interest. It is a vigorous arena for conducting public business in which petitions are heard, contracts entered into, relationships witnessed, orations declaimed, initiations consummated, vows taken, authority exercised, laws promulgated, images venerated, values affirmed, banquets attended, votes cast, the dead waked, the Word deliberated, and parades cheered. It is acoustically sonorous, rarely vacant of sound or motion. It possesses a certain disciplined self-confidence as the center of community life both sacred and secular. It is the Italian piazza, the Roman forum, the Yankee town green, Red Square moved under roof and used for the business of faith. It is not a carpeted bedroom where faith may recline privately with the Sunday papers.

Find the most serviceable places for altar, font, and chair and leave them there. Altars on wheels, fonts that collapse, and presidential chairs that fold away do not free but neuter liturgical place. Since crucial values are perennial rather than disposable, they flock with usage to sustained focal points and thus help to reduce raw space into human place. Crucial values so incarnated become roots for people's lives. Gymnasia rarely play a profound role in most people's maintenance of a secure identity.

Altar and font normally should be fixed, elemental, and powerful in their simplicity, free-standing to allow access from all sides, and worthy of the assembly that surrounds them. The amount of space surrounding each should be scaled to the size of the assembly. Neither altar nor font should be so close to the other as to compete for attention or to confuse each other's purpose, dignity, and quite different kinds of liturgy. The altar is a Table to dine upon. The font is a pool to bathe in, a womb to be born from, a tomb to be buried in. Bathing and dining areas are rarely found in the same room, except in churches.

The presidential chair should be modest but not trivial. It is best located not primarily in reference to the altar but to the assembly, perhaps in an opened area in the nave of the church facing both lectern and altar along with the rest of the assembly. This would shift the ceremonial focus of the liturgy, except for the eucharistic prayer, into the midst of the assembly itself, where it seems to belong given the nature of Christian worship. Outside baptism and the eucharistic banquet, the form this worship normally takes is that of a liturgy of the Word in which the Word is heard and responded to by the whole assembly, ministers included. Locating the ministerial area and president's chair in the midst of the assembly may thus be the most versatile arrangement.

As the name implies, the lectern is a reading stand rather than a shrine competing with font and altar. The shrine of the gospel book is the altar. The shrine of the gospel itself is the life of the faithful assembly which celebrates the Word liturgically. The gospel book, which is "sacramental" of all this, is constantly in motion, being carried, held, opened, read from, closed, and laid rather than left somewhere behind votive lights or under lock and key.

The altar and the baptismal font are the primary spatial foci of the liturgy. The altar Table is kept free of contraptions such as elaborate bookstands, pots, cruets, plastic things, electrical apparatus, aids to piety, and the efforts of floral decorators. The book of the Word and the sacrament of the Word are adornment enough.

The baptismal area is kept free of rumpled vestments, cotton wads, stacks of reading material, and folding chairs. The pool itself is kept clean. It contains what is called "living water" not because things grow in it but because it moves to give life to those who lie in death's bonds.

Liturgical things are designed for the assembly's purpose. The church building houses the assembly. It is neither a museum for ecclesiastical art nor a pious attic. All it contains should possess a sober splendor congruent with the assembly and its sacred intent.

Bread and wine should be just that, not plastic disks and grape juice, not corn chips and lemonade. The assembly uses bread and wine as food and drink in the Eucharist. These should be present in form, quality, and quantity to correspond with a banquet's usual liberality, keeping in mind, however, that this banquet's purpose is not to fill bellies but to give thanks to the Source and Redeemer of all things. The Eucharist, like the Supper that remains its prototype, fills one with more than food, rejoices hearts with more than wine.

Cups, plates, flagons, and bread boxes should be ample. Cluttering the altar with many small cups is logistically and symbolically inelegant. Use one cup of some significance together with a clear glass or crystal flagon large enough to fill smaller cups for Communion later. The same principle holds for the bread plate: Use a single large one from which breads can be transferred to smaller plates for Communion later. The Eucharist that becomes a fast-food operation might be compared to a baptism that proceeds from eye-droppers or aerosol cans.

Vestments are sacred garments rather than costumes or billboards. They are meant to designate certain ministers in their liturgical function by clothing creatures in beauty. Their symbolic strength comes not from their decoration but from their texture, form, and color. The basic vestment of major ministers is the stole, which bishops and presbyters wear around the neck and deacons wear over the left shoulder. No other ministers wear stoles in the Roman Rite. Ministers ordained to lesser orders may wear albs. When lay persons carry out liturgical duties it is more fitting that they wear their own clothes as members of the assembly, which is no mean dignity in itself. Dalmatic, chasuble, cope, and miter can be handsome garments and should be worn as complements to the assembly whose purpose at worship is never merely utilitarian but festive.

Books are means rather than ends. Even so, they should be worthy of the Word they record and of those among whom the Word has taken flesh.

Good images are neither accidents nor fantasies but knowledgeable accomplishments that go beyond what can be observed either now or in time past. As John Meagher says, they are meant to evoke the presence of mysteries the mind has glimpsed, to remind us of the ancestral heritage of worship, to tease us out of mere thought lest we forget that history does not fence in truth, that we may not substitute critical understanding for reverence, that our knowledge is not so complete or accomplished as we often assume, and above all that our memories mix with our longings and our joys to put us in touch with our deepest sense of home.

Churches are not carpeted. While rugs and runners may occasionally enhance liturgical place by adding festal color, carpeting in quantity wearies the eye and muffles sound. Even with a good electronic sound system, which is a rarity, a carpeted church often has all the acoustical vigor of an elevator. The ambiance of a carpeted church, moreover, is too soft for the liturgy, which needs hardness, sonority, and a certain bracing discomfort, much like the Gospel itself. Liturgical ambiance must challenge, for one comes to the liturgy to transact the public business of death and life rather than to be tucked in with fables and featherpuffs. The liturgy challenges what Quentin Crisp calls the general notion of Christianity as a consolatory religion, as something nice that Jesus of Nazareth could say to those who turn to him for comfort.

Furniture is significant and kept to a minimum. Pews, which entered liturgical place only recently, nail the assembly down, proclaiming that the liturgy is not a common action but a preachment perpetuated upon the seated, an ecclesiastical opera done by virtuosi for a paying audience. Pews distance the congregation, disenfranchise the faithful, and rend the assembly. Filling a church with immoveable pews is similar to placing bleachers directly on a basketball court: It not only interferes with movement but changes the event into something entirely different. Pews are never mentioned in Roman rubrics, nor is there any record that being without pews has ever killed Christians in significant numbers.

Banners are decorative images, not ideological broadsides or opportunities for tricky piety. Rather than a festal gesture for the assembly, banners often are a form of disposable ecclesiastical art bearing disposable thoughts which foster a disposable piety. Such banners should be disposed of.

Aidan Kavanaugh[57]

291 • FROM DEVOUT ATTENDANCE TO ACTIVE PARTICIPATION

This article argues for an environment of worship that encourages the full participation of the people and complements the symbolic meaning of the actions of worship, particularly the sacraments. It is written in the context of Roman Catholic worship, but reflects the concerns of nearly all highly liturgical traditions. Many of these have been emphasized throughout the Christian church, given the recent phenomenon of liturgical convergence.

We are all aware that today's liturgy requires a different kind of space than the liturgy of yesterday. But different in what ways? Just what adjustments are required? It may be helpful to reflect on some of the differences between past and present needs. Both new building and remodeling require attention to them.

Before Vatican II, the church building was, above all else, a place for *devoutly attending Mass.* Mass was celebrated as a drama in the sanctuary to be *watched* by those attending. The primary mode of communication was *visual,* signaled in architecture by the central, elevated, and normally very large high altar, and signaled in rite by the dramatic elevations of the host and chalice at the peak moments in the Mass. Any number of secondary elements served that visual concentration: precision movement by celebrant and ministers, symmetrical side altars and candles, deep sanctuaries drawing the eye forward and upward. Virtually everything else was subordinated to that central function of the church building as a place for devoutly attending Mass. Devotional services outside Mass took place before the altar and normally culminated in benediction. Other services either took place outside of church (e.g., anointing of the sick) or were carried out in relative privacy in corners with a bare minimum of ceremony (e.g., penance, baptism).

Today's liturgy is the result of a reform that sought

to replace devout attendance with active participation. Today's ideal worshiper is not a spectator, but one who is part of what is taking place. The people in the pew concelebrate the liturgy with the ministers in the sanctuary (see #54 of the *Instruction of the Roman Missal* for the strongest possible statement of this understanding of the people's role at the liturgy). This displaces the visual as the primary mode of communication. To be sure, watching is an indispensable element of participation in any public act. But watching is not the *only* element in active participation. People are expected to sing, respond vocally, listen, and, above all, to feel themselves as a real part of what is taking place.

The absolute centrality of the altar has also been displaced by the restoration of the importance of the proclamation of the Word and the communal celebration of sacraments other than the Eucharist. Respect for the presence of Christ on the altar has been balanced by respect for his presence in proclaimed word and worshiped assembly and for his action in all the sacraments.

The arrangement of the church building requires that these enrichments of Catholic perspective be taken fully into account. Many experts now prefer to speak of the environment for worship rather than speaking of church building and furnishings. The term is indeed appropriate. Liturgy is an activity that communicates on many levels and in diverse ways, and it is only when all of these various modes of communication (hearing, feeling, seeing, smelling, tasting, sensing movement) are integrated and work together that the liturgy can work well. There is a genuine ecology of worship that should unite Word and sacrament, people and ministers, Christ and church.

When that ecology is neglected, we have to cope with a liturgy that is confusing and distracting, because it does not clearly signal what we are doing. For example, any number of recently built or recently remodeled churches have a large altar in the center of the sanctuary, flanked on either side by lectern and music stand. This says, and says loudly, that the Word is only a mere appendage to the sacrament, on more or less equal par with commentary, announcements of parish schedule, and the songs of the liturgy. It is not enough to reduce the size of the music stand. The prominence of the Liturgy of the Word, not only for Mass, but also for the other sacraments and for common prayer, requires that we rethink the proportion between altar and lectern. If

our worship is to signal the importance of the Word, then the place of proclaiming the Word will have to *look* important. One of the ways to make it look important is to scale down the size of the altar. As long as the altar is located in the dead center of the sanctuary and is as large as it normally is at present, the altar will be perceived as the only important focus of attention. The conventional elongated altar is an inheritance from the medieval Mass-with-back-to-people and is totally unnecessary now that it can be seen in front of the celebrant.

In fact, our oversized altars confuse the kind of sign that the altar is supposed to be. The point of turning the altar around was not simply to make it visible, but to make it visible as the Lord's Table around which we gather. But our very large altars inevitably mean that the gifts are swamped in a sea of linen and unnecessary decorations. The average large altar makes the Eucharist look more like starvation rations with window dressing than the banquet of the kingdom. A smaller altar, say four feet wide, would force the removal of flowers and candles to other places where they belong and allow the gifts to look more like a generous banquet.

The height of the floor on which the altar stands is an equally critical matter. The point of turning the altar around and moving it forward is to create a sense of unity with the congregation. That sense is destroyed when the altar stands in an excessively elevated sanctuary or when it stands on steps that are too high. In contemporary liturgy, dramatic elevation of the altar is a distraction. An altar is easily visible without seeming remote if the floor beneath it is elevated six inches for every thirty feet of distance between altar and people. In other words, an altar which stands a hundred feet from the back pew should stand on a floor twenty inches higher than the floor of the nave. If it stands higher, the congregation senses distance and remoteness from the altar.

Scaling down the altar and placing it lower than it once was is a real departure from the practice of the past, and some may see this as demeaning the altar. Emotions aside, it must be observed that the altar does have a different function now than it did in the past. In the old liturgy, it was *the* liturgical center. Now, the importance accorded to work, to congregation, to the communal celebration of the other sacraments means that it is *a* liturgical center, functioning in relation to lectern and to the people gathered around it.

Also, the primary mode of according a sense of importance to the altar in the old liturgy was its dramatic visibility. Now, the importance of the altar can be dramatized ritually with the shift of ministers from lectern to altar after the liturgy of the Word, with the offertory procession, with the visibility of the gifts on the altar, with speaking aloud the eucharistic prayer. We no longer need to rely so exclusively on elevation and size to make the altar appear as a thing of importance. Some new churches are being built with the altar to one side of the sanctuary.

This solves several problems at once. The lectern can come into its own, suggesting the importance of Word as well as sacrament. The vexing problem of the celebrant's chair is also solved. When the chair is at the side, its use makes the celebrant seem to be in temporary retirement from the celebration. When it is placed directly behind the altar, the chair either has to look like a throne or the congregation must live with looking over the top of the altar at a bodiless head. In this plan, the chair requires no pedestal or only a very low one, and the celebrant can be readily seen by most of the congregation. The greatest advantage of this plan is that chair, lectern, and altar _together_ constitute a strong focus of visual attention. Credence tables, music stands, and devotional appointments can be readily seen as the secondary items that they are. Radical as this plan may look at first sight, it is also the one which most readily accommodates either a statue or a tabernacle at the side without distracting attention from the liturgical action itself.

Contemporary liturgy requires a larger and lower sanctuary than we normally had in the past, and not only because there are more ministers running around the sanctuary than there used to be. The ministers represent the church at the altar, and so the sanctuary should be experienced as an extension of the place where the people are. In some older churches, this is an architectural, financial, or emotional impossibility. In such cases, some kind of makeshift will be inevitable. But in other churches, the only barrier is imagination.

Another acid test of liturgical ecology is the placement of the font. There is a general awareness that baptism should be celebrated as much as possible as an action of the entire assembled church. It is often indicated by placing the font somewhere at the head of the nave or in the sanctuary. Placing the font at the front does mean that people can see more

readily, and there is much to be said for this concern. But there are requirements beyond mere frontal visibility. One of the most important is room for candidates (or parents), sponsors, and ministers around the font. Not all sanctuaries readily provide this sort of room. The font should also be visible to the eye as a thing of importance and dignity. This does not necessarily require that it be of immense size. But when the font draws no more attention to itself than a music stand or credence Table, or is rivaled by the tabernacle, it does not have the proper place of importance in the sanctuary.

There is still something to be said for having the font at the back of the church, near the entrance. There is nothing to be said for its being kept in the small and generally invisible baptisteries of the past. If the main aisle is wide enough, the font should stand there. Placing the font in the back suggests in a dramatic way that baptism is an entry into the church, especially if it can be used for holy water, instead of the conventional little bowl. There is an almost superstitious fear of having people touch the font or the water in it, a curious inversion of piety that makes the water more important than those who are baptized. This should be firmly resisted. The real difficulty with the font in the back is not that people cannot see, but that they generally cannot turn around comfortably during a baptism. If pews had a little more space between them, it would be possible to turn around without peril to nylons and kneebones. It should also be noticed that the word _font_ means "fountain" or "pool," not the sink suggested by the style of the average font. Indoor plumbing has been around for a while, and it is time that the church makes use of this convenience. Priests and catechists deplore the fact that most ordinary Catholics are so tied to the baptismal symbol of washing that everything else escapes them. A real fountain with moving water would suggest life, movement, celebration, as no font without running water can.

Active participation demands that processions play an important role in the liturgy. There is nothing like a parade to get people involved in a civic event, and the procession is the religious counterpart of a parade. A generous aisle that cuts through the midst of the assembly is a must, as is generous space between pews and sanctuary. Almost every rite of the church, to say nothing of the need for room for such necessities as wheelchairs and bassinets (this writer does not approve of the leprosarium called a "cry room"), demands that there be free room for movement.

Closely related to the processional space is the entrance and exit space. A truly appropriate entry to a church would say loudly and clearly that this is a place of significance and a place that gives welcome. Outside, even a small patio entrance would do this. Inside, there should be room for conversation, informal greetings, and real entrance rites. It is not surprising that priests are often reluctant to begin a wedding, a funeral, or a baptism at the entrance to the church. Many of them are not places where most of us would care to linger, much less pray in! Some newer or remodeled churches have the sacristy near the door. Then, not only the space, but also the ministers give welcome to the people, who have come to pray with them. Places used for genuine social occasions, like theaters and good restaurants, have just such generous entrance spaces. Places which have a more utilitarian purpose (like supermarkets and take-home eateries) allow you to move as quickly as possible from parking lot to counter. The question is, do we want the church to seem like a spiritual supermarket or a place that houses a serious social occasion?

Many people complain that new or remodeled churches are "cold," and the complaint is genuine. Some are cold because of insufficient attention to lighting and color or because of poor arrangement. Some are cold because of puritan housecleaning that removes all touches of the past. With careful planning, such things as statues and vigil lights can be placed where they are still accessible for devotion, but not a distraction from communal worship. Some innovations are utterly tasteless—like tabernacles resembling microwave ovens or the refusal to use old and perfectly serviceable pieces of furniture that do not match a new decor. Any room that has all new furniture has a certain sterility and flatness because it conveys no sense that this is a room whose users have a common past.

But it should also be realized that the newer church building is much more suitable for public, communal celebration than it is for private devotion. Nothing is colder than an amusement park in the winter or a good restaurant in the early morning, because those are places meant to be filled with people socializing. The more a space is functional for public gathering and communal celebration, the less it is apt to be a pleasant place for solitude. Our newer churches probably require devotional

chapels or corners that invite private prayer and reflection. This would be a far happier solution than the compromises that now afflict our churches— old high altars left in place for the reservation of the blessed sacrament, vigil lights burning before abstract Madonnas, and all the rest. Compromise is an excellent political principle, but it is liturgically disastrous. Good liturgy calls for wholehearted affirmation, and a church that is neither here nor there is anything but a strong affirmation of what we are about.

If a parish does not have a sense that certain things from the past are liturgical distractions, then perhaps its liturgical sensibilities need further education. Improvement of the celebration and understanding of the liturgy may be more necessary than remodeling of the building. Better, perhaps, to make a few absolutely necessary changes and to live with a makeshift for a while, than to do a full scale remodeling that will saddle the next four generations with the problems of their grandparents. Remodeling ought to be done with an eye to further and later improvements. If compromise is inevitable, and sometimes it is, then it should be carried out in such a way that those who are able to make further improvements will not have to undo everything that has been done in the present remodeling.

Ralph Keifer[58]

292 • PULPIT, FONT, AND TABLE

The following article examines every aspect of the worship space, reflecting the unique perspectives of the Reformed tradition. With regard to many concerns, the similarity of the Reformed view with other views expressed in this chapter is quite striking—a reflection of how much various worship traditions have learned from each other. One point of contrast among traditions concerns the understanding of the sacraments and how that understanding is reflected in the design of the worship environment.

Church buildings are really quite unnecessary! In fact, early in its history the church did not have buildings. If the church were again to be without buildings, it certainly would be hampered, but it would not lose anything essential to its life. All that is needed is some space, a Bible, some water, a loaf of bread, and a bottle of wine. This is true because it is the community that the building houses that is primary. The community of God's people gives the building its meaning, purpose, and dignity. The building has little meaning apart from the community that gathers in it.

However, buildings are important. They are important because of their function. They accommodate the gathering of people and provide a place where the Word can be preached and the sacraments celebrated. It is not easy to maintain the community apart from some place to meet. Furthermore, the building either helps or hinders the church in understanding its true God-given nature. Whenever a congregation builds or renovates its space for worship it ought to ask itself, "How can the space for worship best serve to build up the community in Christ?"

Form Follows Function

Modern architecture works from the premise that form follows function. This means that buildings are designed from the inside out. Worship space is, therefore, to be built to serve the liturgy in the best possible way. Care needs to be taken to ensure that our buildings do not get in the way of the liturgical actions. Worship should never *be shaped* by the architecture; worship should always *shape* the architecture. Peter Hammond wrote, "The task of the modern architect is not to design a building that *looks like a church*. It is to create a building that *works* as a place for liturgy" (Peter Hammond, *Liturgy and Architecture* [New York: Columbia University Press, 1961], 9).

When planning space for worship, we need to consider first the nature and needs of the worshiping community and seek to answer questions such as, "What is the church, . . . its purpose, . . . its mission?" "What is the meaning of worship, . . . of the sacraments, . . . of preaching?" "How can space for worship help us understand worship?" "What are the actions and movements of the liturgy, and how can the building best accommodate them?" Only by beginning with this kind of a functional analysis can the resulting space adequately serve its purpose. A congregation should never ask an architect to start plans until it has come to understand the nature and function of its life together as a community of faith. It is the responsibility of the congregation to articulate this self-understanding to the architect so that it may shape the design.

The importance of starting with a definition of function becomes clear when one realizes that the reverse of the principle "form follows function" is

in some sense also true. A building always tends to shape what takes place in it. John A. T. Robinson made this point:

> The church building is a primary aid, or a primary hindrance, to the building up of the Body of Christ. And what the building says so often shouts something entirely contrary to all that we are seeking to express through the liturgy. And the building will always win—unless and until we can make it say something else. (John A. T. Robinson, "Preface," in *Making the Building Serve the Liturgy*, ed. by Gilbert Cope [London: A. R. Mowbray & Co. Ltd., 1962], 5)

It is important to so shape the building for worship that, when it is used, it will shape us in accordance with the best insights of our faith.

Space for Corporate Worship

Space for worship should help a congregation understand that Christian worship is basically communal. Many church buildings encourage an individualistic view of worship and contribute little to a corporate sense. A building designed for corporate worship should somehow seem incomplete until the people gather together in it.

It is important to consider how the expression of worship's corporate nature should shape the form and location of each of the liturgical spaces:

A. the place occupied by the congregation;
B. the area for the choir;
C. the space for baptism;
D. the space for proclamation;
E. the space for the Lord's Supper; and
F. the space required for processions and the movement of the people.

For example, the location of the people will either suggest a group of individuals in a spectator role or a community participating in the action.

A single unified space, rather than the two-room chancel/nave, best underscores the unity of God's people by including both ministers and laity. The single space also helps eliminate the implication that God is more real in the area screened off from the people where the ministers conduct worship.

Edward A. Sovik suggests that we might see the entire worship space as chancel rather than a remote part of the space. The liturgical centers—pulpit, font, and Table—would be dispersed throughout the space rather than placed together in a single area. Perhaps people then would more readily recognize that they are part of the liturgical action and not mere spectators. Sovik describes the concept:

It can be helpful if we will allow the space to have many foci, so that the congregation can sometimes feel itself to be the center, and sometimes the pulpit, and sometimes the Table, and sometimes the choir, and sometimes the prayer desk, and sometimes the reading desk, and sometimes the baptismal font. And so we would allow the focus to move to wherever the action of the liturgy naturally takes it. This, it seems to me, could make liturgy and architecture companions in a much more effective way than they usually are. (Edward A. Sovik, "Fundamentals for Church Builders," *Your Church* 7 [July-Sept. 1961]: 33)

Certainly the long, narrow nave, with people lined up row upon row in military fashion facing a distant chancel, does not contribute to a sense of community or participation. On the other hand, the semicircular arrangement does contribute to a sense of community, for it is the natural way people group themselves, as may be seen when a crowd gathers about a speaker in a public park. The semicircular arrangement helps us be aware of others and assists a group in being a community rather than a faceless crowd.

Even so, while worship's corporate aspect is fundamental, we must not lose *the sense of the holy* in our zeal to recover a communal sense. To replace the former otherworldliness with mere sociability would be to move from one extreme to another. The church is a community, but it is *a community bound together with its Lord*. It is the body of Christ. There needs to be a balance between the sense of community and the sense of the holy.

Hospitality—Simplicity—Flexibility

A church building should express a true hospitality. It is a place for people. This is in keeping with the concept that the church is a household, the family of God. It should therefore convey warmth and not be cold or pompous. On the other hand, it must avoid an atmosphere of "clubiness" or living-room coziness in which God is thoroughly domesticated.

Contemporary liturgical architecture will also express a simplicity. Superfluous elements will be eliminated. The focus will be clearly upon the essentials. Churches are so often cluttered with nonessentials that the primary things are not readily recognized.

Contemporary liturgical architecture also demands a flexibility unknown in the past. The space for worship should accommodate different kinds of services in varying circumstances and occasions. Flexible seating and movable furnishings greatly aid this. Flexible space will also provide the extra benefit of accommodating other congregational activities, thereby enabling the congregation to more adequately fulfill its servant role. When the space for worship is also used in ways that support its mission to the community, the relationship of worship and service come into clearer focus.

In speaking of the need for simplicity and flexibility, one should not conclude that what is being described is the typical multipurpose hall, which is often erected as the first stage of a congregation's activities. On the contrary, many of these buildings, designed to serve every function, end up serving none well and most poorly. A variety of functions are possible and desirable, but those functions need clear definition, and the space designed accordingly. Furthermore, there are numerous alternatives to the steel folding chairs once characteristic of first units. Seating is now available that is attractive, comfortable, interlocking, and stackable. (The desirability of flexible space is convincingly presented in Edward A. Sovik, *Architecture for Worship* [Minneapolis: Augsburg, 1973].)

A common problem with the minimal worship space of the typical first unit is that it does not help persons be sensitive to the numinous, to the mystery and majesty of God. Being devoid of the artistic and aesthetic qualities, they fail to point us beyond ourselves. Art mediates a sense of the numinous, because there is a kind of mystery in it which is truly beautiful. It transcends our rational ways of thinking and often moves us to wonder and awe. Beauty as well as truth and goodness are ingredients of our faith and are important to our being fully human.

Therefore, space that is ordinary, banal, or ugly fails to serve the Christian community adequately. We cannot afford to build spaces that dwarf the human spirit. The space for worship with its liturgical centers, together with the objects used in that space (e.g., the vessels used in the sacraments, the Bible itself, vestments, paraments), needs to be planned with artistic sensitivity. Care needs to be taken to avoid what is cheap, tasteless, or sentimental, for such fails to point us to God. Neither is there a place for elaborate ostentation. Simplicity and good taste should prevail. When worship space is artistically designed, embodies a proper balance of space and light, and speaks with theological and liturgical clarity, it will help lift us beyond ourselves.

Particularly important in liturgical space is the character of the liturgical centers—pulpit, font, and Table. These furnishings provide for the material objects that are essential to Christian worship, as the following diagram shows.

Liturgical Centers

Essential Liturgical Actions	Primary Physical Requirements	Enabling Furnishings
reading of Scripture, preaching	Bible	pulpit
baptism	water	font
Lord's Supper	bread and wine	Table

Around these three centers the community of faith organizes its life of prayer and praise. These three centers not only fulfill their utilitarian purposes, but also symbolize the actions that are central to the life of the community. Even when they are not in use, they communicate something of the meaning of the actions they enable. Care should be taken therefore to ensure that each center clearly and unambiguously expresses the true nature of the action identified with it.

The Pulpit

Even though the proclamation of the Word is not dependent upon a pulpit, the pulpit is likely to remain as the principal place from which the Scriptures are read and the sermon is delivered. The presence of this liturgical center further symbolizes the centrality and authority of the Scripture in the life of the community of faith. As such, it should clearly express the authority of God.

Where should the pulpit be placed? In early Christian churches, the preacher delivered the sermon while seated in a throne behind the Table. During the late Middle Ages, a recovery of preaching by the mendicant friars resulted in pulpits being placed on the wall on the side of the nave. For much of post-Reformation history, in Protestant tradition, the pulpit has dominated the space in front of the people, virtually eclipsing the Table and font.

Acoustics are the main consideration for location of the pulpit. It is helpful when a wall is located immediately behind the pulpit to help amplify the voice. It is not such a great problem in a small building, but a wall at a considerable distance behind the preacher results in the sound of the voice being blurred. A pulpit placed too far forward may result in acoustical problems.

Perhaps the best location is against the wall, but off center. It has been pointed out that a pulpit located off center is about as effective acoustically as a central pulpit against the wall, provided the path of reflected sound is not over sixty feet longer than the path of direct sound (Ade Bethune and Thomas A. Drain, "Some Plans on Renovating the Sanctuary for the Renewed Liturgy," _Liturgical Arts_ 33 [Aug. 1965]: 108). Therefore, the acoustical advantages of a pulpit against the wall are not lost by moving it off center away from the Table, thus freeing each liturgical center to possess its own space. Care should always be taken to avoid remoteness from the people.

At the same time, it is important in fan-shaped seating that the people are in front of the preacher rather than at the extreme left or right, and certainly not behind the preacher. Unless the people are in front of the preacher, they will not feel they are being addressed. A fan-shaped seating rather than a full horseshoe shape is preferable therefore, since it avoids too sharp an angle at the sides of the preacher or celebrant at the Table. The preacher can comfortably address the entire congregation without undue awkwardness turning from side to side. Since the choir is also part of the congregation, it should not sit behind the preacher any more than any other portion of the congregation.

An attempt should be made to have the best acoustics possible, with the ideal being to eliminate the need for a public-address system. A public-address system detracts and makes rapport between preacher and congregation more difficult to achieve. If a public-address system is necessary, it should reinforce the voice without distorting it, with the microphones hidden from view of the congregation.

The problem of acoustics goes beyond considerations about the pulpit. It is equally important to be able to hear those officiating at the Table and font. By giving proper attention to the acoustics of the entire space, a public-address system may not be needed except in the largest buildings. In an acoustically live building, voice, song, and musical instruments are stimulating.

The visibility is another consideration for the location of the pulpit. It should therefore be elevated sufficiently, so that the minister may be seen by everyone. However, it should not be so high that the minister is isolated from the people. Vertical separation is even more difficult to overcome than horizontal separation, since it results in an awkward head angle for those seated near the pulpit.

The design of the pulpit should express a balance of intimacy between the preacher and people, on one hand, and the authority of the Word, on the other. If too large and dominant, the pulpit will convey a sense of hierarchical structure and undue austerity. Preaching then tends to become oratory, formal, and impersonal. On the other hand, an insignificant pulpit magnifies the preacher rather than the preacher's role as minister of the Word. James A. Whyte points out that an insignificant pulpit tends to "destroy the sense of the rule of the word in the midst of the people" (James A. Whyte, "The Theological Basis of Church Architecture," in *Towards a Church Architecture,* ed. by Peter Hammond [London: The Architectural Press, 1962], 108).

Practicality would require spaciousness in the area surrounding the pulpit to enable ample freedom of movement on the part of those participating in the liturgy. A movable pulpit is a distinct advantage to meet the needs of varying situations. Preaching is not the same for every worship occasion.

Care should be taken in the lighting of the pulpit. It is better to have some well-placed lights in the ceiling, illuminating the pulpit area as naturally as possible, than to have a small desk light to light up the manuscript (and the preacher's stomach), a practice that often leaves the face in gloom. Often, pulpit lamps create glare and are never appealing visually. The light should not be so strong that the preacher cannot see the congregation. The preacher should not be in the spotlight like an actor on a stage. To establish rapport requires that both congregation and minister see each other. Overhead lighting creates distorting shadows and should be avoided.

A clock built into the pulpit, visible only to the preacher, is a good feature. A small shelf out of view of the congregation to hold hymnal, service book, and papers is a convenience.

The pulpit should be designed so that the Bible is visible at all times during worship. The pulpit Bible, when not being read, can be placed in a niche or front panel on the face of the pulpit. Thus it, has its own place of honor. A pulpit designed so that the Bible is its dominant feature will express the relationship between sermon and Scripture. This eliminates the preacher's manuscript being shuffled on top of the opened Bible or closing the Bible and tucking it away on a shelf in the pulpit. In recommending that the Bible have a place of honor, Theodor Filthaut, a Roman Catholic, writes that the place provided

> ought always to manifest that love and veneration which are paid to the book as the instrument of God's word. Then too, the cabinet or shelf ought to be constructed in such a way that the book (which like the receptacle ought to possess artistic value) can be seen by the faithful. This book does not serve for the perusal of casual visitors. It should be looked upon as the sign of the presence of God's word in the church. This would give clear expression to the fact that the church is not only a church of the sacrament, but also of the word. (Theodor Filthaut, *Church Architecture and Liturgical Reform* [Baltimore: Helicon Press, 1968], 65.)

The Bible itself, the quality of its binding, its size and visual appeal, should say that this book is of great significance for Christians. It is through the sacred Scriptures that we hear the Word of God. The Bible shapes our faith and the way we live. No small hand Bible or paperback edition can visually communicate the centrality that the Scriptures have in Christian worship. We tend to respond causally to whatever is treated casually. We could learn a great deal from the respect Jews give to the scrolls and the way they are used in synagogue worship.

As is common in Scotland, the Bible might be brought into the assembly during an entrance or processional hymn, and then enthroned in its place of honor. It is important that the Bible carried in procession or enthroned in a place of honor be the same Bible whose pages are opened and from which the lessons of the day read.

A pulpit of significance is located in First Presbyterian Church, Lawrence, Kansas. It is approximately seven feet wide with a book rest of approximately six feet in length. Behind the pulpit is a sounding board in the form of a plain wall that extends upward toward the ceiling for about twenty feet. It is about nine feet wide and is painted white. In the upper right corner of the sounding board is a single column speaker for amplification. It has a pleasing appearance against the dark brick color of the interior of the room. The sounding board is used as a projection screen. Space is provided in the pulpit for an overhead projector, which is sealed from view when not in use. This space for proclamation thus provides for a variety of forms of proclamation.

Whereas a pulpit has a clear and important function, a lectern is not essential to worship. When a lectern is used for reading the Scripture and the preaching is from a pulpit, a division between the reading and preaching is suggested. In ordering worship, preaching and the reading of the lessons should not be separated. Preaching is to immediately follow the readings, thereby underscoring the interdependent relationship of one with the other. Just as this is true in ordering worship, it is equally true for the spatial arrangements. The reading of Scripture and preaching should be from a single center, the pulpit.

Although a lectern is unnecessary, there are occasions when a speaker's stand other than the pulpit is desirable. A portable lectern, attractive in design and made to harmonize with the other furnishings, could be provided for such occasions and can be placed when and where needed.

In building or renovating worship space, it is important to anticipate the space needed for a variety of appropriate proclamation forms such as the dialogue sermon, drama, dance, and audiovisual presentations. Although nothing can fully replace a pastor who lovingly interprets the Word to the people, proclamation need not always be in the form of monologue.

Unencumbered space is required for movement and drama. Movable furniture is also desirable, so that it may be relocated as the need emerges. If movable seating is utilized, the entire space can be adapted, as the need requires, to accommodate the varied forms of proclamation. Nevertheless, it is desirable that the space around the Table and the pulpit in its usual arrangement be open and spacious, unencumbered and uncrowded. Thus, other forms may be easily provided for without the need to move pulpit and Table.

Lighting is again an important consideration in planning for other forms of proclamation. A theatrical appearance should be avoided. An audiovisual room might be located nearby to enable simultaneous projections and to provide for ease in using tapes and recordings. Where a room is not possible, convenient and adequate electrical outlets need to be provided for both power and sound. The projectors may be hidden from view of the congregation by well-placed banners. A white wall surface is desirable, which would eliminate the need for setting up portable screens, which are always intrusive. Speakers need to be built in at appropriate places for the best acoustical effects. The use of audiovisuals may require that some windows be neatly and easily darkened. The space needs to be radiant with light, symbolizing resurrection joy, but should also have the ability to control the light easily and to direct it where it is wanted.

Those responsible for planning the space need to anticipate the various forms that are to be accommodated and build flexibility into the structure that will free the space for use in a variety of ways.

The Font

The space for baptism is too often the neglected liturgical center. Many churches have no visible evidence that baptism is practiced. It is central to Christian worship, because it is through a washing with water in the name of the Trinity that one is initiated into the Christian community. This sacrament is a clear sign of God's grace, of our cleansing from sin, of our dying and rising with Christ, of our incorporation into the body of Christ, and of the gift of the Holy Spirit. All that the gospel means is focused in this sacrament. The font with its surrounding space, the baptistry, should therefore serve more than the utilitarian function of accommodating the ritual washing. It should be the ever-present symbol of Christian initiation.

Given the centrality of this sacrament, where should the place of baptism be located? What should the font be like in order to give baptism the prominence it merits?

In early centuries, Christians built separate buildings to accommodate baptism. Later, fonts were placed in alcoves at the entrance to the nave. Since the Reformation, Protestants have usually baptized persons before the congregation with fonts located near the pulpit and Table.

The communal dimensions of baptism would rule out a separate building for us. It would also rule out an enclosed space in the narthex. In neither location could baptism be celebrated in the presence of the congregation, nor could the people participate.

Nevertheless, *when baptism is celebrated at or near the entrance of the nave, it becomes a strong symbol of entry into the body of Christ.* There are ways of locating the place of baptism at the entrance without sacrificing the presence and participation of the congregation. The limitations can be overcome if there is no wall separating the baptismal space from the worship room. The removal of the wall would be an economic advantage in making the space serve double duty as an entry and as an open space to accommodate people gathered around the font for the baptism.

Another possibility would be to provide a space for baptism between the narthex and the worship room. Worshipers would pass through the baptismal space as they enter to worship. Any drawbacks hindering a communal celebration of baptism would be reduced if the walls between the baptistry and the worship room were quite open in design.

Perhaps a better alternative would be to locate the place of baptism within the worship room itself. We are quite familiar with the provision of space near the Table and pulpit. The advantage of this location is that people can see, hear, and participate in the sacrament. However, even though the Reformers chose this location to emphasize incorporation into the community, it does not clearly convey this. Nor is the relationship of baptism to the Eucharist and the Word read and preached conveyed simply by placing the font in close proximity to the pulpit and Table. Furthermore, clustering the liturgical centers together results in little movement in worship and contributes to confusing focal points.

There is great symbolic strength in restoring the baptistry to a position at the major entrance into the nave, but preferably inside the worship room. It can be located at the side of the entrance, although a clearer symbolism is conveyed when the font is placed in a space between the door and the seating space, where worshipers must pass around it as they enter. The Christians of the community may be reminded repeatedly of their own baptism through which they entered the Christian community.

The importance of the sacrament is emphasized if sufficient space is provided around the font, enabling part of the congregation to move in procession to it for the baptism. The rest of the congregation could still see, hear, and participate by standing and turning to face the baptistry. Movable seating would be a distinct advantage so that space could be opened up as needed. A baptistry located in this position does not compete with the pulpit and Table. It has its own appropriate space and is able to maintain its own distinct integrity. The relationship of baptism to the Eucharist and the reading and interpreting of Scripture is clearly seen. Baptism is recognized as the way we enter into that community where the Scripture and Eucharist mark the continuing style of the Christian life.

Some efforts have been made to locate the font in the center of the main aisle in the midst of the seating space. This may also symbolize entry into the community, but such an arrangement tends to be crowded and may unduly separate the seating areas. It also can accommodate only a few people at the font, unless movable seating can provide flexibility for baptismal occasions.

There have also been attempts to symbolize the entrance motif of the sacrament in front of the congregation. In these buildings the font is the first liturgical center seen upon entering, even though the font is actually located in front of the people.

In one such building the font is located near the pulpit and Table, but is on an outside aisle leading from the entrance. It is directly visible as one enters the door from the narthex, since the doors open at the corner of the room. A small room above the aisle lowers the ceiling between the entrance and the baptistry, thereby leading one's eye directly through an area of reduced light to the font which is bathed in light from a glass wall on the side of the nave. Neither the Lord's Table nor the pulpit are visible from the entrance. They come into view as one enters the seating space. (This church, St. George, Rugby, England, is described, together with the plan, in J. G. Davies, *The Architectural Setting of Baptism* [London: Barrie Rockliff, 1962], 155. This book is a particularly valuable in tracing the history of baptismal space and the ways the contemporary church is providing for baptism. It is well illustrated.)

Another example combines both the symbolism of entrance with baptism before the people by having an indirect path into the nave. "Along the route one passes a pair of glass doors which open on the baptismal font and allow a glimpse of the chancel area and worship space beyond the font." ("An Inner City Mission Church," *Faith and Form* 1, Special Issue, p. 19. It is a description of Emmanuel Presbyterian Church, Chicago, Illinois.) The font is associated thereby with the entrance, while still being located before the assembled congregation.

Together with the baptistry being located in an open space between the major door and the pews or at the entrance to the space occupied by the worshipers, these examples successfully combine the symbolism of entrance, while still providing opportunity for the congregation to hear, see, and participate. If the font is to be located in relation to the pulpit and Table in a manner similar to these examples, it should not compete with the Lord's Table and the pulpit. Each will have its own distinct space. The greater advantage may still be to locate the font away from the pulpit and Table releasing each liturgical center for its own unique action.

There is something to be said in favor of a baptistry in which one must step down into the font area. Stepping down symbolizes identification with Christ's death and burial. Stepping upward after baptism symbolizes rising with Christ to newness of life. Where this is done, some sort of railing is needed for safety reasons. A paschal candle located in relationship to the baptistry is a reminder of baptismal resurrection. It is appropriate that the baptismal space have artistic beauty. Light streaming through colored glass could further symbolize new birth and new life. Provision for kneeling should be made for the baptism of older children and adults.

The font, set within its own unique space, should be of significant prominence, of ample size and visibility, denoting the importance of baptism. It should not resemble a Victorian birdbath in which the font is insignificant, and especially the kind in which a small glass dish is used in the rite.

The font should be made of stone, marble, ceramic, cement, or some other durable material that is not damaged by water drippings. Because wood is damaged by water, wooden fonts should be avoided. Carvings, relief design, mosaic, or other artistic expression may depict various aspects of the sacrament's meaning.

The font should be convenient to use for adults, children, or infants. The basin portion should be a minimum of two feet in diameter, which will facilitate easily the pouring of water into it, the scooping of a generous amount of water out of it, and the dipping of an infant into it. (A noteworthy example is the font in St. Richard Church, Jackson, Mississippi, pictured in Frank Kacmarcik, "The Berakah Award for 1981," _Worship_ 55 [1981]: 377.)

An effective provision for baptism in one church is a large ceramic basin about two feet in diameter. The basin and a matching pitcher are placed on a table at the entrance to the worship space. There they remind the faithful of their own baptism as they enter. This arrangement provides a flexibility in use, enabling a variety of locations for the baptismal action. The basin can be moved to the midst of the people for a baptism, and then placed once more at the main door. The baptismal vessels should be prominent, in the direct path into the worship space, and thereby obvious to all who enter.

Since immersion is the most dramatic use of water in baptism, forcefully portraying our dying and rising with Christ, some congregations may want a font that is large enough for the immersion of an adult. It is important to keep in mind that a large font can accommodate a variety of modes of baptism, whereas a small font will allow only limited use of water and will be unduly confining.

The font should speak clearly that it is a receptacle for water. Water is clearly the important feature of large fonts and in fonts that are designed so that water recirculates. In this last font, water is seen and heard when entering to worship, since it always contains live, running water symbolizing new life. To see and hear the baptismal water when one enters to worship is a reminder of our own baptism and all the meanings associated with it. (A fine example of such a font is in the United Methodist Church, St. Charles, Iowa, pictured in E. A. Sovik, _Architecture for Worship,_ 94.) In small fonts, the font itself as a furnishing tends to become the focus rather than the water in it.

Aids for administering the sacrament would include a ewer, or pitcher, for pouring water into the font (if water is not in the font at all times) and a baptismal shell for use when pouring water over the head of the candidate. The ewer can also be used to pour water over the head of the candidate leaning over the font. The water, as it is poured, falls over the head and into the basin of the font. A generous amount of water should be used, so that it may be seen and heard. This sacrament calls for more than just a dampening of the forehead. The generous use of water will more clearly indicate that baptism is a washing. As a part of the baptistry, a ledge is desirable to accommodate the service book, ewer, shell, and towels.

Drama is heightened when parents, family, and friends form a procession to the font for the baptism and stand with the ones being baptized. If water is not in the font at all times, it may be poured into the font during the rite, immediately prior to the prayer preceding the actual baptism. (Suggestions for baptismal practice are developed in Harold M. Daniels, "Celebrating Baptism," in *Worship in the Community of Faith,* ed. by Harold M. Daniels [Louisville: The Joint Office of Worship, 1982].)

The importance of baptism will be more readily recognized when it has its own space with a font of significant proportion and design is celebrated in a liturgy that is sensory in character and unfolds baptism's manifold meanings.

The Lord's Table

The Lord's Table, set in the midst of the assembled congregation, visually symbolizes week by week the presence of Christ in the midst of the faith community. This symbol of Christ's presence also speaks of the community that Christ inaugurated, which gathers around the Table on each Lord's day. E. A. Sovik points out that the Communion table is the symbol of the family of Christians, just as the dining table is our strongest symbol of being one when we are gathered at mealtime at home. The meal we have together around the Communion table provides us with our strongest sense of unity as the family of the Lord. (E. A. Sovik, "A Portfolio of Reflections on the Design of Northfield Methodist Church," *Your Church* 13 [Sept.-Oct., 1967]: 53–54.)

The Table should be *free-standing,* enabling the celebrant to officiate from behind it. Reformed Christians have insisted upon the fact that the Communion table is a table and not an altar. It should, therefore, look like a table, preferably with a central support and with a top that extends well over the edges of the support to assure the graceful draping of the linen. The top needs to provide adequate space for all of the Communion vessels and the service book. The length and width ought to be in proportion to the area in which it is located. Six to eight feet long is probably ample; the standard height is from 36 to 42 inches. It should be constructed as perfectly as possible from the finest materials.

It is desirable for the Table to be *movable*. This would make possible varying placements of the Table in celebrating the Lord's Supper and would be adaptable to different circumstances and occasions.

Art used in the Table and in its environs should enhance the sacramental action, ensuring that the artistry does not detract from the action. Artistic Communion vessels can convey the importance to the occasion and enhance a sense of the holy. The Table and its setting should foster a joyous, festive spirit, for the Eucharist is "the joyous feast of the people of God."

The Table needs to *stand in equal prominence to the pulpit*. When constructed of the same material and design as the pulpit, it will imply the unity of Word in Scripture with the Word in sacrament. If placed in the center of light concentration, it will help focus the attention of the people. However, the lighting should not isolate the Table from the congregation.

The Table should be *fully visible to the congregation at all times*. In many churches built about the turn of the twentieth century, the Communion table lacks prominence. When the Table is placed on the floor in front of the pulpit, one is aware of it only when walking down the center aisle. Too often it is the place to put flowers and offering plates, obscuring its purpose.

When raised on a low platform, the Communion table can be seen over the heads of the congregation. One step ordinarily suffices, especially if the congregation is seated in a semicircular configuration around the Table, rather than in a long narrow nave. Certainly no more than three steps are needed, not raising it to a point that it is isolated from the people, thereby making it a "holy island." If more than one step is used, they should be broad, inviting easy access. If the design features the pulpit, Table, and font across the front of the room, the steps ought to extend from wall to wall. If the Table is extended into the midst of the people, the steps should surround the platform on three sides.

It should be self-evident that the Table is the Table of the congregation. It must be *accessible* with no rail separating it from the people. The Table should not appear to be set on a stage, but impress the congregation by standing in its midst. Obviously, identification with the Table is much more readily achieved if it is central, with the congregation sitting around it. This conveys a sense of involvement in the action of the Supper. The pastor celebrating from behind the Table is a reminder that the Lord is in the midst of the congregation. Generous space around the Table will facilitate freedom of movement on all sides. The people must be so related to the Table that there is a rapport with the celebrant, but not so close that the space about it becomes crowded.

It is preferable that the people receive the sacrament at the Table rather than merely being in its presence. To receive the sacrament at the Table involves one's choosing to take the bread and wine, rather than being passively served. In standing around the Table people more readily sense their place within the family of God.

The manner in which the Lord's Table is used should clearly speak of the character of the sacrament. Therefore, _only those articles used in the eucharistic liturgy_—the Communion vessels with the bread and wine, and the service book—_should be placed on the Table._ Whenever such things as flowers, a cross, and a large, open Bible are placed on the Table, making it a shrine to focus the attention of the congregation, the primacy of the Supper is dissipated. Candles may be set on stands around the Table. Flowers may be placed elsewhere in stands. A cross may be located on the wall behind the Table or suspended above the Table. The Bible should be associated with the pulpit where it is read and interpreted.

Offering plates should have their own place apart from the Table. To place them on the Table confuses the nature of the sacrament. The sacrament should speak clearly that God's grace is prior to our response, that it is God who takes the initiative. It is therefore preferable that another place other than the Table be provided for the offering, such as a credence Table or a shelf near the Table.

It is appropriate that the Lord's Table be used for all portions of the service, except the reading and interpretation of Scripture. This was Calvin's practice. The Table is a more appropriate place for prayer than the pulpit, the place of proclamation. An alternate possibility is to lead the confession of sin and the prayers of the people in the midst of the congregation. Such practice clearly conveys that these are the people's prayers.

The Lord's Table should be treated with the respect entitled it. Although we do not make it a fetish or place it under a taboo, we do expect that the Table be respected. It ought not be a place for coats or piles of music during choir rehearsal, a convenience to Sunday School teachers for their lesson materials, a countertop for ushers to count the offering, or a station for tellers to count ballots. It is true that it is only a table, but it is the appointed place to set forth the clear sign of God's grace-filled acts.

Respect for the place of sacramental activity naturally flows from a deep appreciation of the significance of the sacrament itself, for which it is the sign. The Lord's Table will stand in our midst as a clear sign of God's presence only when it is allowed to express simply, clearly, and without ambiguity the Supper, which is central to the life of worship.

Summary

The reading and interpretation of Scripture, baptism, and the Lord's Supper are the indispensable actions of Christian liturgy. Around these three actions the church orders its prayer and praise. Since each action is central to the church's life, the pulpit, font, and Table are to be given prominence. In order for the essential character of Christian worship to be clearly seen, without distortion or ambiguity, each center is to be designed with great care. Each needs its own separate and uncrowded space. No single center should dominate, deny, or distort the significance of the others. The locations ought to express both the distinctiveness of each as well as their unity and interdependence. The space for worship should clearly say that it is through baptism that one enters the community, which is continuously nourished by Scripture and Eucharist.

More than anything else about a building, these three liturgical centers aid in our growth in Christ and help root us in the essentials of the faith. As parts of the actions they enable, these centers can assist us to understand the meaning of the gospel, to shape us into a Christian community, and to keep before us the essential character of Christian worship. They can do this only when they are carefully designed, shaped by the liturgical action, informed by solid theology, and in continuity with historical tradition.

Harold Daniels[59]

293 • SPACE FOR WORSHIP: A BAPTIST VIEW

In addition to concerns raised in earlier articles, Baptist churches are designed in order to facilitate communication among worshipers and to serve as settings for evangelistic services.

It can be generally said that most Baptist churches are characterized by certain building features that are determined by Baptist theological emphases:

- An emphasis on the centrality of the Bible means that the pulpit is usually centrally located.
- The emphasis on believer's baptism and a regenerate church calls for the baptistry to occupy a prominent place in the building.
- The importance of the public invitation, or the altar call, means that the congregation should be close to the minister and the pulpit; the evangelistic emphasis also means it should be easy for people to move forward to make decisions. The emphasis on intimacy and immediacy is also causing some younger ministers to use pulpits that are slender stands.
- Allowance for the choir to help in the evangelistic invitation means it is usually behind the pulpit. A recent movement toward a semicircular style of auditorium has seen some churches moving the choir to the side.
- The Lord's Table is usually in front of the pulpit.

For economic reasons and in order to encourage fellowship, many churches have smaller auditoriums and are holding multiple services. High steps are avoided in order to make it easier for people to come into the building.

Since they major on outreach, Baptists are especially interested in better ways to communicate. Provision is being made for visuals with rear projection screens. Consoles for special lighting effects are being installed. Development of sound systems that can encompass the entire congregation is characteristic of some of the new churches. Architectural provision is also being made for large youth choirs and for musicals and drama in the worship center. Larger foyers are provided in certain urban centers to encourage fellowship both before and after services. In many pioneer fields, multipurpose buildings are used.

One problem Baptists confront is how to gain a sense of transcendence without building high ceilings. Problems related to building costs and heating and cooling have raised serious questions about the wisdom of constructing buildings with high ceilings. A theological teaching brought to bear on this problem says the biblical emphasis is more on a journey-and-return motif after the redemptive pattern of the Prodigal Son, rather than that of an upward-and-downward motif. The context is one of man revolting against God, God's redemptive love

plan, and man's response and return. While some architectural means of emphasizing transcendence should be utilized, the dominant biblical emphasis is on journey and return. That means evangelism and missions. The architectural emphases mentioned above are thus of primary importance.

John P. Newport[60]

294 • SPACE FOR WORSHIP: A BRETHREN VIEW

Noting that the New Testament does not advocate retaining the elaborate rites and liturgical spaces of Old Testament Judaism, the Brethren tradition emphasizes simplicity in its design of the worship space. The Table, with its bread and cup, are the only symbols present.

Christian Brethren assemblies heartily agree that worship is congregational, that architecture must not draw a distinction between "us" and "them," and that all too often Protestant worship has been more of a talent show than a remembrance of Christ. Emphasis on symbolism in church architecture and in the form of worship will promote rather than attenuate both clericalism and sacramentalism.

The emphasis on symbolism is appropriate enough for Old Testament worship, as evidenced by the detailed instruction given to Moses regarding the tabernacle and the priesthood (Exod. 25–31). If the goal of church architecture is to incarnate the meaning of worship in space, as some have claimed, would not the Old Testament analogy lead us to expect some evidence or instruction along this line in the New Testament? The absence of New Testament examples is understandable, for the early church had neither the freedom nor resources to build cathedrals. The absence of New Testament instruction is another story.

In contrast to the detailed pattern given Moses, simplicity characterizes New Testament worship. "The hour comes and now is," said Jesus, indicating a change from what had gone before, "when the true worshipers shall worship the Father in spirit and in truth" (John 4:23 NKJV). Were he referring only to the Samaritan sanctuary, his words might be interpreted as an endorsement of Jewish religion. His introduction, "Neither in this mountain, nor yet at Jerusalem" (v. 21), implies not only the abandoning of a central religious shrine but also the significance of any building anywhere. "God is a Spirit," and henceforth true worship must be in keeping with that truth (v. 24).

Shadows, examples, patterns, and _figures_ are the terms used for Old Testament worship in the book of Hebrews (8:5; 9:1-9, 23-24; 10:1), implying that the symbolic—like the rest of the Levitical system—was to be done away, replaced by a reality unrelated to man-made edifices (Heb. 10:19-25; 13:10-16).

So it is that the simple Table with its bread and cup appear to be the totality of New Testament symbolism in worship. The church buildings of Christian Brethren assemblies have been in keeping with this understanding of Scripture. Even the use of crosses as decorations has been avoided. Scripture texts will often be found on the walls, being truth itself, rather than symbols of the truth.

The pulpit will be on a raised platform for purposes of visibility and acoustics, but not as marking the exclusive territory of a clergy class. The Communion table will always be on the main floor, never separated from the people, even by an altar rail. The Brethren reject the distinction between clergy and laity, and the bread can be broken by (and so must be accessible to) any person in the congregation.

In earlier days it was common to rent rooms or halls for church services. Chairs were arranged in a square with the Table in the center for Communion services and Bible studies. They were arranged auditorium fashion for public preaching.

In recent years it has been more common to build attractive chapels, install pews, and place the Communion table at the front. But worship still centers on an hour-long Communion service. Meditative hymns are interspersed with prayers, Scripture readings, devotional messages, and even periods of silence. The goal is that the heart and mind should be fixed on the reality of Christ in keeping with his command, "This do in remembrance of Me."

James A. Stahr[61]

295 ✦ SPACE FOR WORSHIP: A PRAISE-AND-WORSHIP VIEW

The praise-and-worship tradition involves a variety of worship leaders who usually lead services from a center platform or stage. This article suggests ways of seating and arrangement on the platform that may maximize communication between the worship leader, the worship team, and the worshiping people.

Many churches have asked about practical ideas in platform arrangements of musicians and singers. Naturally, it is impossible to cover every situation in every church, because of the many variables in congregational size, physical space limitations, and so on. But by carefully considering the following suggestions you will find some that are applicable to your situation. These will be especially helpful for those considering future platform positioning and for those involved in new building plans.

Worship Leader's Proximity to the Congregation

Some churches have a platform that is quite far removed from the congregational seating either by height or by horizontal distance. Because a good worship leader will often take his cues from the response of the people, too much distance can hinder this vital interaction. Sometimes, worship leaders prefer to have a large distance between them and the people, usually because they feel that distance somehow gives them more credibility or authority (i.e., "I am the leader"). However, if a person is committed to leading people in worship (as opposed to just putting on a show or being "up in front"), he should seek the proper balance concerning proximity. For extremely large congregations this may be impractical, but for most churches the worship leader can be easily positioned close to the congregation. The closer the placement of the primary worship leader or team to the congregation, the better the interaction. Even those in the back do not have to be that far removed from the leader.

The Rhythm Band

The rhythm band is usually considered the musical core of a church's worship team. Sometimes it makes up the entire worship team. A rhythm band consists of drums, bass, guitar(s), and keyboard(s); they are the basic instruments that carry the rhythm and play the harmony on which the melody is built. Other instruments (flute, violin, oboe, harp, etc.) are considered solo instruments and are less foundational. Therefore, they are not considered a part of the rhythm band.

It is important that the members of the rhythm band be placed close together. There is a tight rhythmical interaction that takes place during praise and worship and during services and rehearsals. When these musicians are not in close proximity to one another, there can be real problems with tempos, rhythms, chordal progressions, and basic communication.

Most of us have observed that many churches have an organ on one side of their platform and a piano on the other side. Some churches even put drums on the opposite side of other percussion instruments (congas, timpani, etc.). Although such an arrangement looks nice aesthetically, musically it is ineffective. These key foundational instrumentalists should be positioned near each other to allow them the musical interplay that they need. For instance, the bass player can match some of the drummer's kick-drum patterns.

Worship Leader's Sight Line to Key Musicians

Just as the rhythm-band members must have interaction with one another, the worship leader must be able to interact at least with certain key musicians. This is, of course, assuming that the worship leader is not one of the rhythm-band members. If he is, then the necessary interaction is simple. If, however, the worship leader is not a rhythm band instrumentalist, then certain arrangements are vital. The most significant of these is the sight line to both the drummer and the lead accompaniment instrumentalist (usually piano). The worship leader must be able to indicate desired tempo changes to the drummer at any time. In the same way he must be able to communicate key changes or song changes with the main accompaniment instrumentalist. Without this communication his leadership is greatly hindered. If the worship leader has an unobstructed view to these two primary musicians, then communication is much easier. Simple hand signals to indicate tempo changes, modulations, song endings, etc., are very effective, if the primary players are within easy view.

Vocalists

The primary vocalists are usually as follows: worship leader singing melody (with occasional improvisation), two or three "natural ear" harmony singers, an additional melody singer, especially if the worship leader does a lot of embellishment work or improvisation. These primary vocalists should be positioned close to each other in the same way as the rhythm band. This will help them in hearing one another and avoiding clashing harmonies. If monitors are used, this can help immensely, especially if the vocalists can be given a vocal-oriented monitor mix. Obviously, each of these primary vocalists should have their own microphone to help obtain the proper levels in the overall sound, house-P.A. "mix," if at all possible.

Other vocalists (e.g., choirs, etc.) should not be close-miked in the same way as the primary vocalists. One or two microphones at a proper distance for choir singing is adequate. The end result gives more of a group sound, which adds musical weight. It also gives an example for others to see in worship. These choir singers can be positioned off to the side as long as they can hear, preferably through monitors, the instruments and other vocals. Many churches making the praise-and-worship transition simply leave their choirs where they have always been positioned.

Other Instrumentalists

Additional instrumentalists outside of the rhythm band need to be handled carefully. They can be placed away from the rhythm band with proper monitors, although it is helpful to have them as close as possible. Individual miking of these instruments is usually not necessary, although occasionally a solo by a certain instrument may be miked. For this, there are two options. One is to have a designated person with a handheld microphone go to the instrumentalist and hold the mike for the duration of the solo. The other option is to utilize one or more stationary microphones, depending on the number and location of instrumentalists, for the instrumentalists to go to. Some instruments, such as a cello, do not work well with this set-up. One additional note: Separate your instruments according to other proven arrangements, such as those of symphonic orchestras or like some other larger churches that have already made this transition.

Visual Projection Equipment

Many churches are now using overhead transparencies or slides to project lyrics onto a screen or wall for the congregation to sing. Although under the best circumstances these are very effective, sometimes there are problems. Placement of the projector can be crucial.

Proper use of overhead projectors includes two major considerations. (1) The words should be easily viewed by the entire congregation. Sometimes two projectors are needed, one on each side of the room. Very often, without two projectors, many of the people in attendance will be unable to fully participate. (2) The projector(s) should not interfere with the musicians. Some churches have the projector positioned so that it actually shines in the eyes of the musicians! This can be a real problem if they are trying to read music! There is also a potential for blocking the sight lines between musicians. Make sure the projectionists communicate with the musicians to avoid any problems.

Finally, keep in touch with other churches in your region. Call them up and occasionally drop in to see any changes they have made in their arrangements during the year. As in any area, use the "common sense" approach to your specific problems, changes and challenges that face your people or building. Where there's a will, there's a way. And do not forget, where there is no way, God will make a way.

Keep in mind that Scripture does not give us any guidelines about platform arrangements. The practical advice we offer here are suggestions only. They've come from our own worship-leading experience, and, hopefully, will be beneficial to you and your church.

Psalmist Magazine[62]

296 • THE PROBLEM OF WORSHIP RENEWAL IN PRESENT WORSHIP SPACE

Many existing church structures present problems for current efforts at worship renewal. In particular, these structures may fail to emphasize the primary symbols of Word, font, and Table or altar. They may also significantly restrict movement around these primary symbols and leave little room for the congregation to gather for worship. This article outlines some of these problems and is therefore instructive for congregations who may be designing new spaces for worship or renovating old ones.

A generation ago the debate about architectural style revolved around theological perspectives. On the one side of the debate were those who argued that the only appropriate architectural style was the "centre-pulpit church." On the other side of the debate were advocates of a "split-chancel church." The former would have looked like many church buildings that were built in the late 1800s, whose prominent feature was supposed to be a dominant, central pulpit that emphasized the essential role of the reading of Scripture by the clergy and the preaching of the sermon. The latter building would have appeared much like any Anglican church of the day, with a long choir and a visible Table at the end of the sanctuary, and with a smaller pulpit to one side of the chancel with a lectern or reading desk for the Scriptures at the opposite side. The advocates of this style believed that it gave a balanced emphasis to Word and sacraments. By placing such a "balance" within an almost medieval structure, the advocates of such a style were often derided by the other party as being more "high-churchy."

Today that debate is totally out of date. With the acceptance of new service books that give expression to the fruits of almost a century of biblical and liturgical research, none of the old buildings and their architectural styles give adequate expression to the new realities. The dominant role of the clergy in worship is no longer acceptable. Choirs are no longer seen as "religious performers" in some Victorian concert hall, providing entertainment to the congregation as a means of alleviating the weariness associated with long pastoral prayers and even longer sermons contained within worship that gave practically no active role to the people. Consequently, there is a growing awareness that our church buildings give inadequate expression to the new forms of worship. While some of them are capable of interior modification to address these realities, many congregations will look to new buildings as their congregations grow. Others will look to new buildings as older congregations that are growing smaller are amalgamated and relocated on new sites. Properly addressed, this can be an exciting and stimulating time in the life of a congregation.

What's Wrong with the Old Architectural Style?

Most church buildings are characterized by flaws that prevent free worship. Generally, there is practically no movement space at the front of the sanctuary. Many churches have relatively small Communion tables that have been crowded under the pulpit and must be moved out for celebrations of the sacrament in order to allow the minister to sit behind it facing the people. This leaves barely enough room for the servers to move from their seats to receive the elements at the Table for distribution to the people. On those occasions when the people come forward to receive the Communion at the Table, movement past the Table by the people is awkward. This same lack of movement space at the front of the church is very noticeable at weddings. Here, in many churches the Table must literally be moved from its central position and placed to one side, blocking a side aisle, in order to enable the prie-dieu to be located in front of the bride and groom, and to allow space for the minister to stand there as well. As it is, the entire first pew on either side of the main aisle must be left empty.

The same lack of space is also very evident in celebrations of baptism. The baptismal font, in churches that do not have a pool, should be one of the most prominent items of liturgical furnishing. Yet, because it occupies too much of that small space that may be needed for other purposes, it is placed to one side, along a sidewall, while at other times it is removed entirely from the front of the church. At baptisms, it is placed within this small space to one side of the Table, and those being baptized are crowded around it with the feet of people in the front pew again being a hazard.

This lack of movement space becomes very apparent whenever a funeral is held. The church is the proper place for funerals, especially for people whose lives have been closely associated with the worship of God, and even more especially where that association has taken place in this building. However, the lack of space to place the coffin and the lack of space to move about it, together with the numbers of steps that must be climbed to get into the church building in the first place, often discourage people from having the funerals of loved ones take place here. Because of the limitations of space, the Table must be moved in order to accommodate the coffin, and the candles that visualize the light of the world, who is the Christ who gives us hope at such times of sadness, are also crowded onto the rails surrounding the Pulpit rather than being able to stand significantly at the head of the coffin.

Such lack of movement space is not just a logistics problem for people. Much more importantly, it is a hindrance to the setting forth of those pieces of liturgical furnishings that symbolize the very core of our faith. Like so many church structures that are based to some extent on the Victorian concert hall model, the pulpit and the pipe organ are the domi-nant visual elements. For many churches this has had the effect of singling out the sermon in the Liturgy as the central element of worship. The somewhat hidden Communion table indicates a poor understanding of the centrality of the sacra-ment alongside the preaching of the Word. In many church buildings the pulpit area is also extremely confined. While there are the customary three chairs behind it, the space is often so small that it becomes almost a gymnastic feat to move more than one person around from chair to chair. Conse-quently, the very structure discourages the use of lay readers, thus once again centering out the Min-ister as the official "worshiper" on behalf of every-one else. The large pulpit Bible solemnly set on this pulpit thus becomes disengaged from the peo-ple and appears to be the domain of the minister. All of that is simply bad theology and communicates a message that is contrary to the message that is being given verbally from that same pulpit by the minister!

Like most older buildings, the seating in the sanc-tuary is represented by fixed pews set in rows one behind the other on both sides of a central aisle. It is almost impossible to establish a sense of "commu-nity" in a building where, for the most part, you are looking at the back of someone's head. This form of seating arrangement carries with it all the theology of the Middle Ages, where the laity in the nave of the church were physically separated from the sig-nificant actions of the clergy in the choir area at the front of the building. We need to remember that earlier tradition did not place seating in the church at all, much like the Eastern Orthodox practice, and people were able to turn around, move, and mingle; to rub shoulders with each other in such a way as to make no mistake that this was a community of the faithful gathered together to offer their worship and devotion to God.

Consequently, one of the "musts" for a new building will be the need to provide seating in some-thing like the half-round so that people can see each other. With a large central area devoted to pulpit, Table, and font, and with the seating located around that focus, people will be able to recognize them-selves as a community of people gathered together around those visual symbols of God's presence among us rather than a group of individuals focus-ing on a religious lecture and entertained every now and then by a choir. In this proposed arrangement the choir would be seated in one section of the curved pews, able to be seen by the congregation so that the choristers could cue the people for their participation, but also very be evidently identified as part of the worshiping congregation rather than a body of entertainers. Such a seating arrangement requires careful thought relative to the placement of the pipe organ. Whatever the mechanics and sound demands of that placement require, the organ should not be seen as the most visible artifact in the building.

Such a plan would solve the problem of movement space at the front of the church, making many things possible, including much more lay participation than is possible now. Weddings would be vastly improved, and funerals caskets would be able to be placed and moved with much greater effect and dignity than is now possible. Such a seating layout also enables more people to be gathered together but kept within much closer proximity to each other than is ever possible with a long, narrow nave. With such seating, it would also be possible to leave gaps at aisles where wheelchairs could easily be placed, enabling handicapped people to be physically and visually a part of the congregation. With a church building built at ground level, without any steps anywhere approaching it or in it, the handicapped will be encouraged to attend the worship of God. That none do so now is not caused by the congregation's unwillingness to accept them. It is simply the fault of the building that does not accommodate them.

Another problem posed by many present buildings is the lack of gathering space. Many buildings have a narrow narthex at its main entrance. Imagine a Sunday congregation of between 100 and 120 on average moving from the sanctuary following the benediction into a narthex that measures ten feet by twenty feet, already filled with several tables, coatracks, and containers for food-bank donations, and you can readily appreciate that it is not a mingling space! It is, however, important to provide a sufficient space outside the sanctuary where people can congregate prior to worship and greet each other following worship without being jostled and pushed or made to feel that they have to move on for fear of blocking someone else's approach or departure. Many new churches have an expansive

narthex and a kitchenette where tea and coffee are prepared for fellowship times after worship. This large, bright, and cheery gathering place is an excellent companion space to that of the sanctuary.

The Structure and the Church Year

All of this concern for adequate architecture to enable adequate worship to take place impinges heavily on the subject of the church year and its expression. Beginning in Advent, a building without adequate visual space surrounding pulpit, Table, and font leaves little room for the use of such symbols as the Advent wreath with its candles. Where such visual symbols can be easily seen in a central location relative to the people, its use assists in focusing attention on the theme of each Sunday in Advent. The appearance of chrismon trees or Jesse trees should not be relegated merely to church-school classrooms. With sufficient room to accommodate their presence in the sanctuary, they can again add visual focus to children's participation in the Advent season's devotional acts each Sunday. As Christmas approaches, the need for suitable space in which to place the crèche is also important. Within many of our traditions, the use of a Christmas tree carries on customs that many Lutherans claim credit for beginning. In my present church structure, all of these make their appearance, leaving the front of the church totally crowded and less effective than they might otherwise be.

Each season of the church year carries with it potential for changes in color through banners, antependia, and drapes. In older buildings, these can only be used as the building permits. A new structure provides an architect and the people with the opportunity of reflecting on the good use of color to highlight the change of ecclesial seasons. Walls thus have more significance than just structures to keep the roof and the floor apart! This usefulness of the visual in the form of changing color needs to be given thought in the design of the structure.

Holy Week and the triduum cry out for adequate space for the special services that mark this highlight of the church year. Gathering space outside the sanctuary proper is essential for the formation of processions that often precede some of these rites. Open space around the pulpit, Table, and font becomes necessary for the adequate use of candles in the Tenebrae. In my congregation, the movement of elders in relation to the Great Entry of the elements in the form traditional to the Church of Scotland is a feature of our Maundy Thursday celebration of the sacrament. Clear space to enable the gathered congregation to see what is happening is essential to the effectiveness of the movement, something that is now lessened by the design of the present building. The special and particular needs of the high holy seasons have traditionally been overlooked completely in much of Protestant church architecture. With the renewal of concern and interest in matters liturgical among many Protestants, the time is now ripe for the appearance of buildings that give adequate expression to the full range of Christian worship.

James A. Thomson

297 • SIX ARCHITECTURAL SETTINGS AND WORSHIP RENEWAL

The assembled body of Christ is a primary visual symbol. The way people are seated affects the ways they relate to each other in worship and has much to do with their experience of community. There are six different architectural settings for worship currently in use. Each setting is briefly described and illustrated below with comments on its relationship to worship renewal.

Configuration is the heart of the seating issue. Here again we are guided in particular by *Environment and Art in Catholic Worship, #68.* The arrangement must support all liturgies (Sunday Eucharist as well as funerals and weddings but other liturgies as well). It must also support singing, provide for emergency egress, and may need to be as functional with dozens as with hundreds. Configurations are here put into six categories. Each has its own characteristics and personality. All of the diagrams below have an identical scale and seating capacity (approximately 780 people for 18-inch seat spacing and 670 people for 21-inch spacing).

1. **Gothic Plans** are normally long and narrow with transepts and often with columns. Formality and hierarchical order dominate, with the climax occurring far from most of the seating. This configuration, especially when the capacity is large, is simply not able to function in support of the vision of liturgy articulated by Vatican II and the following reforms. It may support strong participation

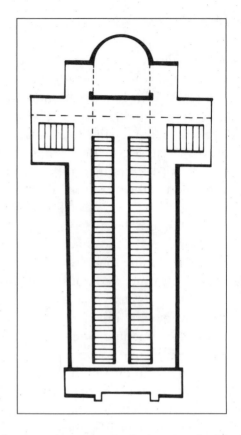

through song, but can do little to uphold a strong and ongoing sense of assembly action.

2. **Processional** is an efficient pattern in rectangular spaces. Its regimented order is common in our present spaces. Processionally oriented actions fare well here, but not communal actions. From the similarity to theaters and other settings, we tend to think of ourselves as an audience in this setting.

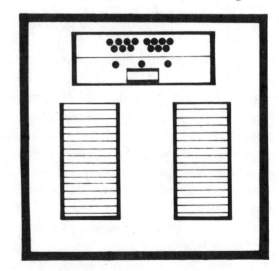

3. **Antiphonal,** reminiscent of monastic seating, uses the processional aisle as the center of liturgical

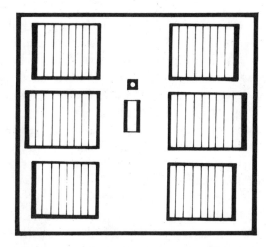

action as well, allowing for a large, flexible area. With the action in the midst of the assembly, proximity and interaction are good, but the line of view may suffer with larger capacities; bending the pattern lessens this problem. This plan fits readily into many spaces and can handle large capacities.

4. **Juxtaposed** lacks a shared focus, which increases the challenge of executing effective liturgical movement and ministerial actions. The multiple orientations tend to fragment the gathered community.

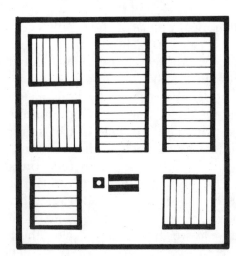

5. **Central** evokes theater-in-the-round. Its geometry suggests a highly interactive, close-up, participatory worship process, while creating distinct seating "neighborhoods." This plan, perhaps more than others, needs a great awareness of choreography and acoustics.

6. **Radial** is amphitheater shaped, usually with a flat floor. Chairs are more easily accommodated in radial layouts and provide greater flexibility for the size of the assembly and for seasonal variations. Radial seating supports processions and community

interaction. Capacities above eight hundred introduce awkward "rear-guard" areas, which are better used only for occasional overflow seating.

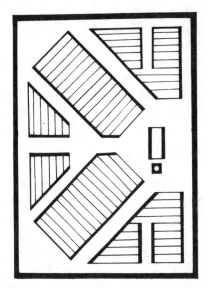

Conclusions. Liturgical practices and goals should have the greatest weight in determining the approach to seating. If seasonally responsive arrangements are intended, the extent and purpose of such flexibility ought to be carefully defined and the various configurations well investigated. Flexibility requires more versatile sound and lighting systems, which increase design complexity and associated costs.

In renovation, an existing structure's size and shape act as constraining "form givers" to the seating pattern; this will often result in a hybrid configuration. In fact, older Gothic and processional forms are often adapted very well to the antiphonal, radial, and other patterns. In new construction, the need to attach to an existing building and/or site limitations sometimes inhibit the seating solution. More often, the seating pattern should be a priority so that it can give form to the architecture of the building, not only shaping its floor plan but also influencing the three-dimensional form.

Bill Beard[63]

298 • HISTORICAL AND THEOLOGICAL PERSPECTIVES ON ACOUSTICS FOR THE WORSHIP SPACE

One of the most important aspects of the worship space is its acoustical properties. This is so because of the importance of sounds in worship, the sound of verbal proclamation and musical prayer and praise.

"What no eye has seen, nor ear heard, nor human heart conceived, what God has prepared for those who love Him, God has revealed to us through the Spirit" (1 Cor. 2:9-10).

On a visit to the city of Meissen, Saxony, in early May of 1985, I was given an opportunity to tour the magnificent Gothic cathedral, the construction of which was begun in the year 1260 and largely completed late in the 15th century when the lower portions of the west towers were built by Arnold of Westfaha (Cf. Paul Liebe and Hermann Klemm, *Meissen: Der Dom und seine Geschichte* [Berlin: Evangelische Verlagsanstalt, n.d.], pp. 11–36). The woman who guided us through the cathedral began the tour by saying, "We would not build a building for the church like this today because we have a different understanding of the church." What a church understands itself to be determines what kind of building it builds and, simultaneously, what kind of acoustical requirements it expects of its building.

Our guide in Meissen was giving simple expression to an observation by French sociologist Emile Durkhelm (1858–1917), who said, "A society is not simply the mass of individuals that comprise it, nor the territory it occupies, nor the things it uses, nor the movements it carries out, but *above all it is the idea that it has of itself* (Quoted by Leonardo Boff, *Church: Charism and Power* [New York: Crossroad, 1986], 41). The idea that the medieval church had of itself was that of "salvation institution," a society whose leaders could confer salvation upon its individual members, provided that those members fulfilled the minimum conditions required for salvation (Cf. Avery Dulles, *Models of the Church*

[Garden City, New York: Doubleday and Company, Inc., 1974], 31–39). Since the minimum conditions required for salvation consisted of participation in certain sacraments, the buildings constructed in the high Middle Ages were intended for the administration of baptism and the medieval Mass. Baptism was administered outside of the gathered congregation, usually with no more than family members and friends in attendance. No attention to acoustics was required for its administration.

Buildings were constructed chiefly for the administration of the medieval Mass, the main sacrament for the congregation assembled on Sundays and Holy Days. Although the mass was "said" or—on festive occasions—"sung," it was meant to be primarily a visual event rather than an audible event. It was mean to be seen, not heard. Bard Thompson has described the "three conceptions" that attained prominence in the Middle Ages: (1) the Mass as an "epiphany" or God amongst men, which focused attention upon the reality of the eucharistic presence, upon the consecration at which it occurred, and upon the priest by whose action it was effected; (2) the Mass as a sacrifice offered unto God for the benefit of the living and the dead; and (3) the Mass as an allegorical drama of the whole economy of redemption (see Bard Thompson, *Liturgies of the Western Church* [Cleveland: The World Publishing Company, 1961], 48).

Even though the events were available to the eye, the Mass was directed toward God, not toward the congregation. The "drama" of Christ's sacrifice upon the cross was once again offered to God by means of the "consecration," which transformed the elements of bread and wine into Christ's sacrificed body and shed blood. Because the consecrated bread, now Christ's body, could be preserved in more or less elaborate tabernacles, the building became literally "the House of God." The ever-burning lamp indicated the location of God, who was there, available for the prayers and devotions of the individual worshiper.

The Lutheran Reformation of the sixteenth century articulated a different understanding of the church with very significant implications for the spaces that such an understanding required. The Augsburg Confession defined the church as "the assembly of all believers among whom the Gospel is preached in its purity and the holy sacraments are administered according to the Gospel" (Theodore G. Tappert, ed., *The Book of Concord* [Philadelphia:

Muhlenberg, 1959], 32). The focus here was not on the leadership of the community but on the baptized people. They were regarded as visible, available to the eye, when they gathered. Their gathering was identified as "church" by what took place when they gathered, namely, the proclamation of the Christian good news and the administration of the "holy sacraments" identified and defined by that Christian good news. The primary sacrament that took place in the gathering of the baptized people was the Holy Eucharist. But in the Christian gospel, as the Lutheran Reformation understood it, the Holy Eucharist was not directed toward God as a representation of Christ's sacrifice. It was directed toward the people as God's good news to them that the great benefit of Christ's sacrifice is *for them*. It was available to them here and now in the promise of Christ to be present as the One who was crucified for them, namely the promise to give them his body and blood under the forms of bread and wine for their forgiveness, life, and salvation.

Both proclamation and Eucharist were meant for the ear as well as for the eye. The buildings of the Christian community were no longer to be understood as houses for God. They were to be houses for the People of God, spaces in which they would be addressed by the Word of God and participate in a sacrament in which the presence of God was promised to them through bread and wine, which they were to eat and drink. Hence Luther could say that "the church is a *Mundhaus,* the place of the mouth and salutary speech, not a *Federhaus,* the domain of the scribe" (Cited by David Lotz, "The Proclamation of the World in Luther's Thought," *Word and World* 3:4 [Fall 1983]: 347). In Luther's own words:

The gospel should really not be something written, but a spoken word which brought forth the Scriptures, as Christ and the apostles have done. This is why Christ himself did not write anything but only spoke. He called his teaching not Scripture but gospel, meaning good news or a proclamation that is spread not by pen but by word of mouth. (Martin Luther, "A Brief Instruction on What to Look for and Expect in the Gospels," *Luther's Works,* American ed., vol. 35 [Philadelphia: Muhlenberg, 1960], 123)

In 1523 Luther directed that the words of Christ used in the Eucharist were "to be recited in the same tone of voice in which the Lord's Prayer is sung at another place in the Canon; so that it will be possible for those standing by to hear" ("Formula Missae et Communionis of 1523," in Thompson, *Liturgies of the Western Church,* 112). "The Peace of the Lord" is "to be announced with face turned to the people, as the bishops were accustomed to do" (Ibid.). Three years later Luther wrote that "in the true Mass . . . of real Christians, the altar could not remain where it is and the priest would always face the people as doubtless Christ did in the Last Supper" (Ibid., 130–131).

Thus both proclamation and sacrament would now require church builders to take acoustics into account. The first space constructed under the influence of the Lutheran Reformation was the chapel for the castle of the Elector of Saxony at Torgau. It has a free-standing Table on a platform raised two steps above the floor, accessible to communicants on all four sides, and a prominent pulpit. (A photograph of the interior of the chapel is reproduced in Peter Manns, *Martin Luther: An Illustrated Biography* [New York: Crossroad, 1982], p. 200, plate no. 82.) Luther preached the sermon at the dedication of the chapel. In his sermon he added prayer to the acoustical activity of the gathered people of God.

Therefore God very wisely arranged and appointed things, and instituted the holy sacrament to be administered in the congregation at a place where we can come together, pray, and give thanks to God. . . . And here the advantage is that when Christians thus come together their prayers are twice as strong as otherwise. . . . Prayer is nowhere so mighty and strong as when the whole multitude prays together. (*Luther's Works,* American ed., vol. 51 [Philadelphia: Muhlenberg, 1959], 337–338)

It is impossible to claim that Protestants followed their own Reformation insights in understanding both church and liturgy so that this understanding determined the construction of buildings for worship. In fact, Protestants and Catholics alike were affected by a variety of influences upon buildings and worship, most of which were not especially attentive to the acoustical dimension of the Christian gospel.

However, attention to the eschatological horizon of the New Testament in recent decades has given Protestants and Catholics a new and increasingly convergent perspective on the Christian gospel, on ecclesiology, on worship and Eucharist that has profoundly affected the approach to Christian architecture. I want to summarize briefly what I think that eschatological horizon is, what its effects have been, and what its implications are for Christian architecture and its acoustical dimension.

1. The witness of the New Testament is that the Christian gospel is profoundly eschatological. The proclamation of Jesus can be summarized by the Gospel of Mark: "The time is fulfilled, and the kingdom of God is at hand; repent, and believe in the gospel" (Mark 1:15). The witness of the earliest disciples proclaims that Jesus has been raised from the dead. Jesus is therefore the Messiah, and the messianic age has begun. Jesus' resurrection is a radical revelation of the *eschaton,* the outcome of history. Because Jesus has been raised, he and no one else determines that outcome. The kingdom of God has begun and will finally triumph. Death no longer has the last word. The resurrection of Jesus affirms Jesus' mission, proclaims his death as redemptive, and confers the eschatological Holy Spirit on the community of Jesus' disciples.

2. The community of Jesus' disciples is called to be a witness to the resurrection of Jesus, a witness to the breaking in of the kingdom of God. The event of Jesus' resurrection, which calls the disciple community, also shapes what the community does when it gathers for worship.

    a. The disciple community appropriates anew the Scriptures of Israel and the remembrance of Jesus as it listens to the reading and exposition of lessons from the canon of the Scriptures. The disciple community has its matrix in Israel and in the mission of Israel's messiah, Jesus of Nazareth. It is marked by its attention to "apostolic teaching" (Acts 2:42).

    b. The disciple community engages in prayer in the name of Jesus. The prayer formula given to the circle of Jesus' disciples (Luke 11:1-4) means participation in Jesus' mission. It is the foundation for all prayer in the community. Prayer in the name of Jesus means attention to the needs of the community for its mission of witness to the kingdom of God.

    c. The disciple community celebrates in anticipation the banquet of the messianic age (Isa. 25:6-8). The meal of the community includes the following: first, the offering of bread and wine as symbolic of the offering of all the baptized to the purposes of the kingdom of God (Rom. 12:1-2); second, the thanksgiving of the community under the leadership of the presiding minister as the way in which the community receives the promise of Jesus to be present with his body and blood in, with, and under the bread and wine; third, the eating and drinking through which the death of Jesus is proclaimed as shaping the community for its mission in and on behalf of the world as the body of Christ.

    d. The disciple community sings the "new song" by which it celebrates the victory of God and anticipates the final eternal praise of God in the eschaton.

3. All of these elements, essential to the worship of the gathered community, require the ear to receive as well as the eye. The gathering of the community for attention to the Scriptures of Israel and the apostles, for prayer in the name of Jesus, for the eucharistic banquet of the messianic age, and for the new song of God's victory is, and is meant to be, *visible,* that is, available to the eye. It is meant to be seen in such a way that this gathering can be distinguished from other gatherings, that is, as church rather than as a meeting of stockholders, a musical concert, an instructional class, and so on. But these visible activities have an audible dimension. Scriptures are meant to be read and expounded so that those present are addressed, so that those who have ears to hear can hear. Prayers are said so that those present can assent with "amen" or can raise their own voices for the amen of others. The bread and cup are not just distributed for eating and drinking. That would not yet be the messianic banquet under the conditions of anticipation. Rather the bread and cup need to be taken up into the words of blessing and remembrance, thanksgiving and proclamation, by which bread and cup are audibly linked with the promises of Christ (Eric W. Gritsch and Robert W. Jenson, *Lutheranism* [Philadelphia: Fortress, 1976], 83–84). The new songs are sung in such a way that the whole community is drawn into the praise and anticipation of eternity.

What had not, prior to Jesus' resurrection, been disclosed to eye and ear and human heart has now been revealed through the eschatological Spirit. It is now available to eye and ear and heart. What is made visible and audible can now be received in faith. It must be visible and audible for faith to occur, for "faith must have something to believe—something to which it may cling and upon which it may stand"

(Martin Luther, "Large Catechism," *The Book of Concord,* p. 440).

Hence architecture for Christian worship needs to create space in which speaking and hearing, addressing and responding, sharing a meal in the context of promissory eschatological words, and singing the new song can take place. We need attention to acoustics in such a way that no artificial amplification of the human voice is needed. Architects can be attentive to such requirements for Christian worship. Eliel Saarinen designed a building for Christ Lutheran Church in Minneapolis, Minnesota, in 1951 in which the human voice could be heard by more than six hundred persons without amplification. Musical leadership was still required to come from a balcony in the rear, so only speaking leadership could be seen as well as heard. But Saarinen gave attention to hearing. The chapel of Trinity Lutheran Seminary in Columbus, Ohio, designed by McDonald, Cassell, and Bassett, Inc., and completed in 1983, allows the musical as well as the speaking leadership to be seen. Attention to acoustics is such that a congregation of six hundred can hear speaking without amplification. Singing the new song takes place in a space that the music critic of the Columbus *Dispatch* described as "like sitting inside a gigantic cello" because it has both resonance and clarity.

The church is called by its gospel, its liturgy, and its mission to give attention to acoustics *in advance* of constructing its buildings, not after the fact. For "what no eye has seen, nor ear heard, nor human heart conceived, what God *has* prepared for those who love him," God has revealed to us through the Spirit.

Walter R. Bouman[64]

299 • ACOUSTICAL DESIGN FOR CONGREGATIONAL SINGING

Congregational singing can be effectively stymied or greatly encouraged by the acoustical properties of the worship space. Recent trends in church architecture have unfortunately led to the use of more acoustically absorbent materials, which is harmful to this important aspect of worship. The following article provides helpful advice to remedy this problem.

Perhaps the greatest challenge in architectural acoustics is the worship environment. The acoustical characteristics within a worship space must cover the gamut from pristine clarity for the spoken word to enveloping reverberance for the pipe organ. The demands for room responsiveness exceed those of traditional concert halls and multipurpose performance facilities.

A closer examination reveals an even greater richness in this range of acoustical qualities. The speech end of the spectrum must accommodate all types of voices, from lay readers to seasoned preachers who will utilize every available nuance of the dynamic range—from tumultuous shout to intimate whisper to poignant silence. Through all this, the Word must be understood throughout the entire congregation.

At the opposite extreme is the pipe organ, capable of a dynamic range and frequency spectrum that can exceed that of a full symphony orchestra. And somewhere between the auditory alpha and omega are the choir and solo voice. They too must convey the Word with warmth and clarity, while encouraging and supporting the participation of the congregation.

Many of the difficulties of combining, within one structure, the requirements for speech intelligibility and musical resonance have been solved. Yet, if there is one facet of church acoustics that might be thought of as the neglected stepchild, it is the provision of appropriate acoustics for congregational singing.

Acousticians serving as consultants in church building projects, whether a renovation or new design and construction, are typically presented with a list of priorities during the initial stages. These invariably include a statement calling for "excellent acoustics for congregational singing." However, as the project develops, this program element is frequently overshadowed or forfeited in compromise to other perceived needs.

Church renovation or construction projects involve an extraordinary variety of needs and priorities among the clergy and congregation. A church building project is, after all, a multifaceted undertaking and will typically involve

1. **An organ.** The selection and cost of an organ can be a major issue. Usually a committee is appointed to study alternatives and make recommendations. They may spend a year or more touring neighboring churches, interviewing organists, and debating the pipe-versus-electronic and tracker-versus-electropneumatic issues. The installation of a significant instrument can easily

exceed $500,000 and have major architectural and aesthetic ramifications.

2. **A choir or music program**. Here too a committee may be selected to address questions of placement of the choir, provisions for rehearsal space, new robes and robe storage, and so on.

3. **A sound-reinforcement system**. Another committee or perhaps one of the other sound-related committees should be responsible for the sound system. The system must amplify speech intelligibly and perhaps include provisions for music reinforcement, recording, playback, and so on. It must also be visually unobtrusive and preferably invisible.

4. **Furnishings and finishes**. The visual elements of the project call for many decisions regarding materials and colors, religious and art objects, seating, lighting, etc. This particular facet of the project is a major preoccupation for the architect who is deeply concerned about the impression the space will make, an overwhelmingly visual impression.

Too often the priority of congregational singing is overwhelmed by the high cost and visibility of other elements. When this happens, it is often assumed (or hoped) that if the worship space is designed to provide good acoustics for speech, organ, and choir, then it will naturally provide a welcome environment for congregational song. This is a reasonable-sounding assumption, but it is not necessarily true. To appreciate this, we might ask what is really known about the acoustical requirements for congregational singing and how these relate to those for speech intelligibility, organ, and choir. Before addressing these issues directly, let's briefly consider a more fundamental question.

What Is Meant by Good Acoustics for Congregational Singing? This is indeed an intriguing question. When it comes to the qualities of the singing voice, research in acoustics has been primarily concerned with trained voices in the performance environment. This is not an appropriate paradigm for the common parishioner who may or may not be able to carry a tune, who may or may not even enjoy singing. Published studies dealing with the ordinary voice are generally geared toward open-plan offices, speech interference, telecommunications, and the like.

Let's take a less pedantic approach, then, since there is little scholarship regarding the "optimal acoustics for the untrained voice as applied to congregational singing." Let us consider some reasonable assumptions to motivate the formulation of acoustical requisites for congregational singing.

1. The environment should provide support and encouragement for the untrained voice. It should sufficiently enrich and enhance the quality of the ordinary voice so that the singer feels encouraged to sing out, to participate in the communal act of lifting the voice in praise.

2. The acoustic response of the space should impart to each individual in the congregation a sense of being a part of the assembly, an assurance that one is not alone or unduly exposed.

3. The environment should convey to each parishioner the awareness that, as small as one's contribution may seem, it is a meaningful part of the whole.

To summarize, the ideal environment ought to enhance the quality and fullness of the voice, provide a sense of envelopment, yet provide a sense that one's simple gifts are an essential part of the whole and that this whole is profoundly greater than the sum of its parts. We seek, in essence, a sonic analog of unity, echoing the concept of the oneness of the assembly, while acknowledging the sanctity of the individual.

This is, perhaps, a rather grandiose concept; it surely exceeds the aspirations of even the most accomplished acoustician. But the concepts embodied in these lofty ideals suggest some well-understood acoustical principles. An insightful interpretation of these requirements can provide the proper acoustical conditions for congregational singing. Let's take a brief look at some of the fundamentals involved.

Reverberation. Most people have some familiarity with reverberation time, the quality of sustain that occurs in large, hard-surfaced spaces. One need not be an acoustician to have some sense of the sound enhancement provided by a cathedral with a six-second reverberation time, a space where it takes six seconds for a sound to fade to inaudibility. Some of the more erudite may be aware that concert halls typically provide a reverb time of two seconds or more for symphonic music and that a pipe organ requires more than three seconds. There are many well-established benchmarks for "optimum" reverberation times for all types of environments and all forms of music. There are, however, no comparable reverberation criteria for congregational singing.

Nonetheless, reverberation is unquestionably a major and necessary factor for enhancing the quality of the ordinary voice in worship spaces. It also increases the loudness of a sound. Reverberation is, after all, made up of the myriad returns of acoustic energy from sound-reflective building surfaces. This energy combines with the original sound and increases the apparent loudness of the source. You might think of the analogy of a light source in a room. If the wall surfaces are covered with a dark, nonreflective finish, the overall illumination throughout the space will be less than if the finishes are light and reflective.

Sound-Absorbing Materials within the Worship Space. In most churches designed for good acoustics, there is a minimum of sound-absorbing material. In fact, in most churches, the single greatest sound absorber is the congregation itself. The fully clothed person provides about as much sound absorption as four to six square feet of conventional acoustical ceiling tile. A congregation of one thousand can provide as much sound absorption as an entire suspended acoustical ceiling over the nave!

It is fairly well-known that a certain amount of sound absorption is required to prevent echoes and to control reverberance. But it is not generally known that the performance of a sound-absorbing material is strongly dependent on the location of this material relative to the sound source.

If a sound source is located quite far from a sound absorber and if this source is also projecting its sound away from the absorber, then the sound will have an opportunity to develop. It will blossom and begin to fill the room volume before the absorption begins to produce its sound-suppressing effect. In a church, these are generally the conditions that exist for sounds produced by the choir and organ. The major sound absorber (the congregation) is relatively far from the choir and organ, and both are oriented so that their sounds project directly into the full room volume. These conditions allow these sound sources effectively to utilize the available reverberation of the worship space.

If, on the other hand, the sound source is located near a major absorbing surface, the sound is di-rected (more or less) into the absorber, then the sound will be absorbed before it has a chance to be enhanced by the reverberance of the space. As we shall see later, these conditions fairly well describe those that exist for the voices in the congregation. In fact, it is a common perception, from within a congregation, that the choir and organ sound reverberant, while the congregation sounds rather dry in comparison. This is primarily a result of the proximity of the congregation's voices to the sound absorption provided by the clothed bodies throughout the congregation's seating area.

Sound-Reflecting Surfaces. Acoustically reflective surfaces are especially important for the support and distribution of unamplified sounds. A choir, if located near sound-reflective surfaces, can project its sound more fully and uniformly. A properly oriented overhead reflector can have enormous beneficial effects by projecting sound to the assembly and distributing sound among the choir members. A choral shell would be a real asset for a church choir, but such performance-oriented furnishings are considered by many to be inappropriate in the house of the Lord. Acousticians often attempt to introduce architectural elements that will perform the same functions as a choral shell while respecting the aesthetics and sanctity of the worship environment.

In much the same fashion, the voices of the congregation could make beneficial use of nearby reflecting surfaces to help distribute their sound throughout the assembly and provide support. However, only those singers near the perimeter will derive any advantage from sidewalls. There are rarely any usable overhead surfaces for the congregation since the needs for long reverberation require large room volumes and comparably great ceiling heights. The only available reflective surfaces are the pews and surrounding floor area.

Acoustical Requisites for Congregational Singing

We can summarize this review of acoustical factors with a statement of the obvious: Long reverberance and supportive reflections provide the foundation for delightful and awe-inspiring sound qualities of the archetypal church. These same factors greatly enhance the sound of the organ and choir, and add a larger-than-life grandeur to speech.

It seems reasonable to assume that these qualities should also lend themselves to the needs for congregational singing. They do. But they do not assure it. Nonetheless, large room volumes and long reverberation times are basic and minimum requirements for an environment that will encourage participation in congregational singing. We need to look just a bit further to see why these necessary conditions may not be sufficient.

Location and Disposition of the Sound Source. There is one feature of congregational singing that distinguishes it from nearly every other musical acoustic setting: The sound sources and receivers are in virtually the same location. Even more important, the sources and receivers are at the same physical height. There are few, if any, equivalent situations in musical acoustics. (There are some parallels in the acoustics of rehearsal rooms and stages, but the context and objectives are quite different.)

It should be evident that the height of a sound source, relative to the listener, is an important acoustical consideration. From an elevated position, sound is projected more efficiently and uniformly. The architectural acknowledgment of this principle is evident in the traditional form of music performance spaces. The principle is equally applicable in worship spaces. For example, the elevation of the chancel and celebrant takes advantage of the sound projection made possible by this simple height differential. The organ pipes and choir are typically elevated for the same purpose and are often located in a loft. Even within the choir, we typically find risers to take advantage of the enhanced projection of sound made possible by being elevated. Loudspeakers for the spoken liturgy are also placed as high as possible. Comparing these examples with the conditions in the congregation, we see that the assembly is at a decided disadvantage.

Another closely related factor is the directivity of the voice. The greatest concentration of sound energy from the untrained voice projects forward and down at a slight angle. Within the congregation, this tends to direct sound into the back of the person immediately in front. Most of the sound will be absorbed by clothing. What little remains to be reflected and scattered will be further absorbed by neighboring worshipers.

Pew Cushions and Carpeting. For the needs of congregational song, the use of any form of sound-absorbing material in and around the congregation is detrimental. It is not that these materials are the only cause of a poor environment for congregational singing. But, if we examine the most commonly occurring conditions in worship spaces, even in highly reverberant spaces, we see that the congregation already has several strikes against it:

- The congregation is typically on one level (except where there is a balcony) and cannot take advantage of the benefits to sound distribution provided by elevation, raked seating, or tiers.
- There are few, if any, proximal surfaces to produce supportive sound reflections and to distribute sound throughout the seating area.
- The congregation is engulfed in a sea of highly effective sound absorption. The ordinary clothing worn to services is absorptive enough, and in cold climates heavy outer clothing can increase the amount of effective absorption by 50 percent or more.
- To make matters worse, the normal directivity of the voice projects the sound energy from each member directly into this body of absorption.

The introduction of further absorption in the congregation in the form of pew cushions and carpeting is truly the final blow. It should be clear from the presentation above that this is a matter of physical fact, not simply the knee-jerk reaction of most acousticians who, as everyone knows, are always lobbying against the introduction of sound-absorbing material of any sort.

In fact, pew cushions and carpet produce, simultaneously, two effects that are directly contrary to the acoustical requirements for congregational song:

- They absorb sound and do so in a highly efficient fashion because of their proximity to the sound source.
- They occlude the floor and pew surfaces. These sound-reflective surfaces would otherwise be available to provide supportive reflections and to scatter sound among the assembly.

Pew cushions are generally considered to be a comfort issue as well as cosmetic concern. In truth, sitting on a contoured wooden pew for an hour is not a great discomfort. People of all ages are quite willing to sit in far less comfortable seating for even longer periods. Ballpark bleachers and park benches are two examples that immediately come to mind. This is really a matter of perception and priorities.

If pew cushions simply cannot be avoided, there are some alternatives that can minimize sound absorption. Cushions made with vinyl covering or fabrics with latex or vinyl backing will provide less sound absorption that the more common fabric upholstery. There are also closed-cell foams and alternative padding materials that offer adequate comfort without absorbing as much sound.

Carpeting is generally an aesthetic matter. There are many attractive hard-surfaced alternatives (for example, quarry tile, wood parquet, etc.) which would not introduce further absorption in and around the congregational seating area. If carpet is required for safety or to minimize the sound of foot falls, use the thinnest material possible and cover only the minimum area necessary.

Other Factors. Mechanical-system noise is of great concern in worship spaces. A noisy ventilation system can ruin speech intelligibility and cause distractions at the most inopportune moments. This same noise can have detrimental effects on congregational singing.

Consider the fact that background-noise generators are used in some open-plan offices to provide speech privacy and to reduce distraction from conversations and activities in neighboring areas. In such environments, an electronically produced "white noise" is used to drown out sounds from adjacent areas. The artificial noise effectively isolates areas by blocking or masking normally audible sounds. It is much like the effect of running water drowning out conversation in your home.

However, for congregational singing, we need to maximize communication within and throughout the entire sanctuary. A noisy background can greatly reduce the sense of support you would perceive from those singing around you.

Priorities and Compromises. Much of the foregoing has been a restatement of the oft-heard indictment against carpeting and pew cushions in the worship space. Hopefully it has shown that if acoustics for congregational singing are a priority, then there are few options available, few concessions that can be made. There are no conventional methods that can offset the negative effects of sound-absorbing materials in and around the congregation.

It has also acknowledged the fact that church building projects evoke conflicting priorities that call for compromise. There will surely be incompatibilities among the major areas of the project, for example, liturgy, architecture, and acoustics. There will even be disparities within these areas such as the conflicting acoustical requirements for speech and music. However, the acoustical characteristics required for choir, organ, and congregational singing are wholly compatible. These same characteristics (with a properly designed speech-reinforcement system) will provide the responsiveness necessary for the full range of liturgical oratory and actually enhance the richness and uniformity of speech distribution among the assembly.

It can be as compelling and uplifting as that which exists in any collective experience. While we might all wish for better singing voices, we must acknowledge that in some endeavors our God-given gifts are limited, but that we can be more than we are individually by being part of the whole. This is, perhaps, an idealized concept of the power of congregational singing, but proper acoustics within the sanctuary can help bring this concept to fruition.

Dennis Fleisher[65]

300 • QUESTIONS TO ASK ABOUT YOUR WORSHIP SPACE

This article asks the kinds of questions that force congregations to think about the power of their worship space to form worship that is faithful to the gospel and meaningful to all participants. The questions are asked in light of the Reformed tradition, but can be modified to reflect the specific theological commitments of any given worshiping community.

The sanctuary is the setting for most corporate worship experiences. Either by design or by interest, the worship committee often finds itself involved in the custodial concerns and mechanics of presenting meaningful worship in that space. While mechanical concerns are not to be ignored, theological messages presented by the setting need to receive attention as well. The worship committee can be the bridge between the congregation's level of understanding of worship and the clergy's role in utilizing the symbolic in response and instruction.

Take time to look objectively at your worship setting. Do the furnishings and architecture and symbols represent your congregation's theology of worship? Do they tell a faith story or reflect socioeconomic values? Does the building focus on God, or has the building become the thing that we worship?

The Room. What message is communicated by the room itself? Does it generate a sense of awe or a sense of community? Do you want it to be a place for responding in worship—or a place for observing worship? What can be done to make a tiny church feel awe filled? What can a large worship space do to provide a setting for "community"? Does the church with movable seating communicate an active, alive faith, or careless disregard for tradition? Most of all, is what you see in your sanctuary consistent with the theology of worship?

The Pulpit. Where is the pulpit located? Is the clergy "removed from" or "among" the people? Does its placement say what you believe about the relationship of clergy and laity?

The Table. Is it clear that the Lord's Table is a table and not an altar? Is the Table intentionally placed either "removed from" or "among" the people? Would there be a powerful message in changing its location on some occasion? Does the congregation understand the symbolism of whatever arrangement or placement you are utilizing or tolerating?

The Baptismal Font. Where is your baptismal font or bowl located? Calvin would have placed it near the pulpit (the Word) and the Lord's Table to indicate the unity of the three. Some of us, on the other hand, have begun to appreciate the placement of the font by the entrance to the sanctuary as symbolic of baptism as an entrance rite into the life of the church. What can be communicated if the baptismal font or bowl is very small or usually stored in a cupboard in the kitchen?

Other Visual Symbols. Are your symbols, including the cross, selected and placed with an eye to message? Are the symbols, especially banners, ever changed, changed seasonally, weekly, or only when convenient? Have memorial gifts distorted the faith story? What is the value of floral arrangements? Can they enhance the liturgical year in addition to reflecting the seasons of the calendar? Does the lighting of a candle or candles, especially a paschal candle, have symbolic value in your congregation, or is the lighting a housekeeping matter understood only by clergy?

Recently I heard of a church building program in which every design decision was made with an eye to its potential value for teaching and experiencing the faith. I also visited a sanctuary in which the baptismal font was padlocked and the chancel cross so small as to be nearly imperceptible. I am curious what a caring worship committee might do with each of these "problems." In the first case, the power of the theology of the building and furnishings cannot be sustained if the symbols are neither taught nor the space utilized consistently with their understanding. In the case of the second church, it is necessary to recognize the power of symbols for everyone in order to correct the messages now being communicated unintentionally. In careful planning of new worship space, the potential for empowering or at least stimulating the congregation by design and furnishing is immense. But the constraints of the already-designed or misdesigned facility requires even more of the committee if the building is to say what we believe.

It is God that empowers our faith journey, but the use of the space has the power to detract or enhance the journey. The issues will not produce ultimately right answers, but will assist the faithful in understanding. We must take worship seriously enough to not miss opportunities to teach the faith and to carefully call it out in all that we do.

Karmen Van Dyke[66]

301 • THE PROCESS OF BUILDING AND RENOVATING A CHURCH

The article illustrates the importance of identifying a process for making decisions in building and renovation projects. The final product will satisfy the community's needs only in proportion to the time spent in soliciting opinions, educating the members, and consulting experts.

Stakes are high when modifying worship patterns. The way people worship does not just reflect their beliefs—it cultivates and shapes those beliefs as well. The early church identified this mutual interaction between the liturgy and faith through reflecting on its own experience. The contemporary church is recovering the significance of this insight as it applies it to the design or redesign of a place of worship. To move ceremonial objects in a church, let alone to shift the walls or the orientation in a worship space, moves sensibilities in ways which help or hinder. How do we judge what assists or obstructs? Who makes these judgments?

For eight years I have been helping communities throughout the United States build or renovate their places of worship. As a consultant, I came to each group wanting to listen to the members' expectations about their place for prayer. As a liturgist, I responded with the best of my training, in hopes that the final product would embody informed judgments and serve generations of Christians well.

After working with diverse communities, I have noticed a pattern that deflates spirits and depletes energies. I have confirmed this pattern with my liturgical colleagues. I wondered whether it would help if someone who regularly encounters these problems could alert those who are approaching the renovation or building of a church. The situation seems parallel to offering assistance to a couple approaching marriage. How can a young couple know the potential problems if they have never been married before or have never been part of the preparations for a family member's or friend's wedding? The same is true for renovating or building a church. How can a parish community know the pitfalls if it has never ventured into such a project before?

There is no need to reinvent the wheel. Too often, each worshiping community takes up the task of renovating or building a church as if it has never been done before. Communities need not work in a vacuum; information is available upon which to base informed decision making.

"Never Again"

Renovating or building of worship space can be like having a baby. Sometimes it is hard to know what is going on. Sometimes it just hurts. Sometimes the stirring of new life is felt along with the sense that this might work and come out all right after all. When the renovation or building comes to term, the feeling is—one hopes—that it was all worth it. Unfortunately, this is not always the case.

The quality of the product depends upon the quality of the process. If the method of approaching the renovation or building is slipshod, the end product will likely be the same. As James White put it in *Introduction to Christian Worship,* "The process is as important as the product—especially when it comes to the people of God collaborating around the design of their space for *worship."* What good is it if Christians go for the jugular in order to build a lovely church where they can celebrate their care for God and for one another? It happens all the time. Christian, atheist, and other-than-Christian architects and engineers have told me they approach the building of a church as if they are daring to go where angels fear to tread.

Who has the ultimate decision-making power? This should be clear to all from the outset. Too often, confusion reigns in this area, and various individuals or groups misconstrue their roles as deliberative rather than consultative. Will final decisions be made by the pastor or by some committee? Are there constraints (e.g., the budget) over which the local community has little or no control? Is it out of the question, for reasons beyond local control, to consider a building on property other than the existing one? Will eventual decisions made at the local-church level need additional approval from some hierarchical body within the Christian tradition? *Someone needs to offer a clear lead.* Presenting the method or approach for decision making clearly can help both to allay fears and to provide data for a choice to get involved. Those convening the process need to think and plan carefully before beginning. Muddling through these questions with a large group of people leaves a wake of dead bodies or, more accurately, broken spirits. To proceed intelligently, a community may need outside assistance if local leaders have little expertise in renovating or building churches. This is all the more reason to proceed with caution and not in haste.

Let Every Worshiper Speak

Before renovating or building a church, everyone who desires to pray in the new worship space ought to be invited to speak his or her mind. Whoever chooses to be part of the smaller group overseeing the project needs to develop the skills of listening to worshipers who wish to speak. No matter how kooky or strange a reflection may seem, it still needs to be received with care, even if not with agreement. It is not helpful to offer impulsive responses while listening. There is no need for immediate judgment and quick closure. If people perceive, even incorrectly, that the pastor or some select group is attempting to railroad something through, they can react as if someone is running away with a precious part of their lives. If you do not give people the time and space to voice their concerns and to sense that their perspectives are considered, you seed the project with disaster.

CAUTION: Some people interpret careful listening as implicit agreement with what has been spoken. In one way or another, after all have had their chance to speak and to be heard, the pastor or project leader needs to speak and to be heard. Without becoming defensive, the leader needs to provide some direction (at least concerning method) by way of response. Leaders need to make it clear that the project will not be the result of each person having an equal voice. The process for building or renovating a church is not democratic. Many Christians in the United States find the nondemocratic process difficult to accept, because it is so different from other parts of their life. Following the culture in this instance, at least uncritically, does not serve a community well.

Solicit the view of each person, listen to it, and promise to take it into consideration. But do not in any way pacify people in the short term with an ambiguous response that could be misconstrued to mean "Your way will win in the end" or "If you just convince enough people (and maybe circulate a petition), then you can get your way." The all too common dynamic of "the squeaky wheel gets the grease" breeds an unhealthy spirit of competition and, more importantly, divides a community. A building project should not be a contest of wills. However, inviting opinions about what to do with the community's worship space is potentially explosive. The person in charge needs to be politically savvy and must be able to make clear which norms must be used when making decisions.

Knowledge of Criteria

In the end, the spectrum of opinions needs to be sifted in light of a hierarchy of criteria, the most decisive of which are liturgical. Surely there are competing values: aesthetics (what individuals consider pleasing); devotional taste (how individuals prefer to relate to God and others in church); cultural sensibilities (what people expect because of culture and custom); ecclesial understanding (what people believe about the relationships within the church—lay with clergy, the assembly with God, worshipers with each other); and financial realities (what people consider essential given limited funds, what people would want if additional sources of revenue could be found).

Once the consultation is completed, the liturgical criteria must be given priority. Values other than liturgical ones do matter and must temper decisions by, at the very least, improving the quality of understanding between the worshipers and the leader-

ship. Values other than the liturgical ones, though, should not be determinant.

One of the most effective and liberating tools the church has at its disposal is knowledge. From a broad-based knowledge of liturgy, people can make informed choices for their renovation or building project. If knowledgeable people are not available locally, the parish should invite competent outsiders to help the members, or at least the leader, understand more about the liturgical principles operative in this situation. For example, in the Roman Catholic tradition, those who will deliberate and decide upon the eventual shape of worship space need to understand, at the very least, the *Constitution on the Sacred Liturgy* and *Environment and Art in Catholic Worship*. Structural engineers, artistic consultants, or architects should not be given the power to make decisions without demonstrating knowledge of the liturgical criteria.

Often I have seen well-intentioned but undereducated leaders of a renovation or building project relinquish decision-making power to individuals who claim liturgical competence. In reality, these artisans have made choices in brick and mortar, wood, and glass that betray priorities other than the liturgical ones. The end product, while lovely in its own way, does not serve the gathered community at prayer. Having a beautiful building does not necessarily mean having a good place for worship (see Bill Brown, AIA, "Space as Servant of the Assembly," in *Building and Renovation Kit for Places of Catholic Worship*).

Timing

Timing is no small issue when modifying or building a church. It takes time to raise the funds necessary to complete the project. It takes time to raise the consciousness of those worshipers who are ready and willing to learn. If the leaders show a desire to learn, this will go a long way in fostering the receptivity of the worshipers to learning and possible change. The leaders must show that they do not know it all. Learning needs to happen on many fronts. Some individuals will not be ready and willing to learn more about liturgy, but will want only to voice their preconceptions. Others will grow through the intelligent presentation of liturgical information, provided you offer it with care. This will take time. Those who tend to prefer quick decisions and action may be hard-pressed by the extended efforts needed to educate others. But the time and the effort put forth to help others understand are worth the trouble.

A few years ago, I explained to a beloved aunt the thinking behind the renovation of a church on which I had worked. With exasperation, she stated passionately her desire for the *traditional* church. I realized that my heart and my head were responding in different ways. With my heart, I felt compassion for my aunt who did not like this unfamiliar approach to how a church "should" look. With my head, I knew that *traditional* goes beyond the twentieth century, and that the thinking behind the renovation I had explained was rooted in early church understanding and practice.

How *traditional* should Christians be? What should educated Christians use as the ultimate criteria for the design of liturgical space? The best of contemporary liturgical thinking has patristic roots. All the same, we need to be patient with people, like my aunt, who feel less and less at home in places of worship that are outside their experience. Feelings cannot be rationalized away, but people can be invited to reexamine them in light of new data. On many occasions new learning has served to initiate remarkable movement. Will everyone learn? No, of course not. Will some people reconsider their perspectives in light of education? Yes. Will the numbers be sufficient to justify the time it took to offer education? As the American educator Derek Bok said: "If you think education is expensive, try ignorance."

The community needs to avail itself of the best thinking. This is especially true at the beginning. Doing this will benefit the community for years to come. Relegating decisions to popular opinion or to power broking will lead to a finished product with which nearly everyone will have problems. It will be like the horse that was put together by a committee and ended up looking more like a camel.

Worship is too important to be left to less than the best we can bring.

T. Jerome Overbeck[67]

302 • BIBLIOGRAPHY ON THE WORSHIP ENVIRONMENT

Books on the worship environment most often discuss both church architecture and the design and placement of the primary symbols in worship. This bibliography covers materials relevant to both chapters 11 and 12.

Arndt, Elmer J. F. *The Font and the Table*. Richmond: John Knox, 1967. A brief overview of the place of the primary symbols in traditional Protestant worship.

Atkinson, C. Harry. *How to Get Your Church Built*. New York: Doubleday, 1964. A comprehensive guide to the process of designing a worship space that could serve as a helpful complement to more recent (but often less complete) books on the subject.

Beiler, Andre. *Architecture and Worship*. Philadelphia: Westminster, 1965. Beiler's work is a sketch of the relationships between architectural conception and a theology of worship from the primitive church to the present. Pagan and Jewish temples are introduced as important to the development of church buildings. The volume includes an essay by Karl Barth, "The Architectural Problem of Protestant Places of Worship."

Bond, Francis. *The Symbolism of the Baptismal Font in Early Christian Thought*. Washington, D.C.: University of America Press, 1951. A historical discussion concerning the rich symbolism associated with baptismal fonts.

Brown, Bill, ed. *Building and Renovation Kit for Places of Catholic Worship*. Chicago: Liturgy Training Publications, 1982. An overview of the nature of worship space, following advice for every step of the building process, from hiring an architect to making decisions about landscaping and acoustics.

Bruggink, Donald, and Carl Droppers. *Christ and Architecture*. Grand Rapids: Eerdmans, 1965. "Church architecture is a matter of theology, not style," asserts Bruggink, and one can only meet the needs of churches after pursuing questions of history and theology. This volume is a wealth of information on the subject, complete with pictures, illustrations, floor plans, landscape drawings, and many planning imperatives. Bruggink shapes the argument in part one, while Droppers gives substance to the edifice in part two. This is a primary sourcebook and should be consulted along with *Faith Takes Form* (1971), by the same authors/publishers.

Clowney, Paul, and Tessa Clowney. *Exploring Churches*. Grand Rapids: Eerdmans, 1982. This book is a unique and practical guide to the rich cultural heritage in Christian church buildings worldwide. A field guide shows the development and use of buildings, with the main body of the volume alerting the reader to architectural changes that reflect shifting emphases on belief, praxis, and place in society. All traditions are represented. Diagrams, models, illustrations, and plans. Especially suited for introduction to a building committee or those who enjoy touring churches. Glossary of terms.

Cope, Gilbert. *Making the Building Serve the Liturgy*. London: Mowbrays, 1962. Theologians, pastors, bishops, and architects combine to consider liturgical theology that conforms to Anglican congregational requirements and its selection in architectural principles and precepts, space and substance. The "application" section reports on a number of older parish buildings that have been transformed (renovated) and new construction that conforms to these requirements. Pictures and illustrations.

Dahinden, Justus. *New Trends in Church Architecture*. New York: Universe Books, 1967.

Davies, J. G. *The Architectural Setting of Baptism*. London: Barrie and Rockliff, 1962. A very comprehensive historical sketch of the fonts that Christians have used for the sacrament of baptism.

Debuyst, Frédéric. *Modern Architecture and Christian Celebration*. Richmond: John Knox, 1968. Debuyst is critical of modern structures "with no specific sacral character." His work is an attempt to remedy analytic buildings with synthetic or organic tendencies by reintroducing the imperative of celebration as a way to reshape buildings. The book is a survey of churches with respect to their ability to facilitate liturgy and celebration.

Filthaut, Theodor. *Church Architecture and Liturgical Reform*. Baltimore: Helicon Press, 1965. A brief overview of each aspect of liturgical space in Catholic worship.

Fitzpatrick, James M., and Thomas G. Simons. *The Ministry of Liturgical Environment*. Collegeville, Minn.: The Liturgical Press, 1984. Brief consideration of the liturgical environment advocating a "quality" approach to buildings and furnishings, and the reintroduction of craftsmanship and quality art to the worship space. Listing with commentary regarding essential furnishings in worship space. Source: Catholic. Booklet: "The Ministry Series."

Geerdes, Harold P. *Worship Space Acoustics*. Washington, D.C.: Pastoral Press, 1989. Booklet guide to overlooked area of church planning. Concise and complete primer on the subject with helpful suggestions, photos, and diagrams. Subjects: music and speech; sound reinforcement; organs and instruments; rehearsal and storage spaces; and renovation and modernization. Source: Reformed. Glossary and bibliography.

Gieselmann, Reinhard. *New Churches*. Stamford, Conn.: Architectural Book Publishing Co., 1972. The volume is a stunning pictographic record of modern churches with floor plans and landscape drawings. Minimal text illuminates both theology and philosophy of shaped spaces and their architectural significance. All traditions will be served by this consulting "must."

Hammond, Peter. *Liturgy and Architecture*. New York: Columbia University Press, 1961. Also *Toward a Church Architecture*. London: Architectural Press, 1961. Two works that anticipate the vast reforms that would follow Vatican II.

Hayes, Bartlett. *Tradition Becomes Innovation: Modern Religious Architecture in America*. New York: Pilgrim Press, 1983.

Henze, Anton. *Contemporary Church Art*. New York: Sheed and Ward, 1956. Henze contributes an introductory survey of the potentialities of modern art in the church, which includes theological and philosophical rationales for inclusion of statuary, icons, furnishings, celebratory articles, vestments, glass, mosaics, and enamels. Pictorial.

Huffman, W., and A. Stauffer. *Where We Worship* (Study Book and Leader's Guide). Minneapolis: Augsburg-Fortress, 1987. A Lutheran perspective on church architecture, complete with a study guide for use in the local parish.

Kennedy, Roger G. *American Churches*. New York: Stewart, Tabori, and Chang, 1982. The volume is a color survey of more than one hundred U.S. church buildings. Interior and exterior pictures are combined with text linking each edifice to the operative philosophical/theological imperatives that shaped it.

Kuehn, Regina. *A Place for Baptism*. Chicago: Liturgy Training Publications, 1992. A complete discussion of the images, style, location, and function of the baptismal font, along with many photographs.

Lockett, William, ed. *The Modern Architectural Setting of the Liturgy.* London: S.P.C.K., 1964. A collection of essays representing a variety of worshiping traditions.

Lynn, Edwin C. *Tired Dragons: Adapting Church Architecture to Changing Needs.* Boston: Beacon Press, 1972. Specifically addressing the challenge of adapting or redefining an older building in light of new or changing patterns of worship.

Mauck, Marchita. *Shaping a House for the Church.* Chicago: Liturgical Training Publications, 1990. A helpful, popular guide to current thinking about church architecture that includes many examples. A good introduction for building committees to some of the issues involved in designing a space for worship.

Middleton, Arthur P. *New Wine in Old Skins: Liturgical Change and the Setting of Worship.* Wilton, Conn.: Morehouse, 1978.

Mirsky, Jeanette. *Houses of God.* Chicago: University of Chicago Press, 1976. Mirsky's work surveys "artifices of eternity" from all of the great religions—approximately one-third are Christian. She contends that church buildings should be "serious, vital, lofty and dangerous qualities, because the worship of God should not be off-handed." Pictorial. Illustrations.

Riedel, Scott. *Acoustics in the Worship Space.* St. Louis: Concordia, 1986. A brief overview of the acoustical problems inherent in the design of a space for worship, including a helpful discussion of the complex terminology of acoustical sciences.

Smith, Peter E. *Building Materials and Aesthetics.* Chicago: Liturgy Training Publications, n.d. A discussion of the various types of building materials available for church construction and an argument for the use of classic and organic materials.

Sovik, E. A. *Architecture for Worship.* Minneapolis: Augsburg, 1973. Combining theology, ecclesiastical tradition, architectural theory, and aesthetic appreciation, this architect advocates constructing beautiful, simple "non-church" worship spaces that are both hospitable habitations and contemporaneous, appropriate witnesses in culture rather than "cultic structures" of the past. Sovik's solution, the *centrum,* becomes the focal point of his discussion. A number of church renovations are also discussed. Illustrations, models, and photos. Source: Lutheran.

Sovik, E. A., ed., *Acoustics for Liturgy.* Chicago: Liturgy Training Publications, 1992. Essays by an architect, acoustician, church musician, theologian, pastor, and organ builder on the problems of acoustics in a worship spaces.

Turner, Harold W. *From Temple to Meeting House.* Hawthorn, N.Y.: Mouton de Gruyter, 1979. Turner proceeds from the thesis that Christian places of worship repeatedly fail to express the distinctiveness of their own religious tradition. Beginning with the Old Testament temple, he moves through primitive structures, the medieval period, and into the modern era, asking whether church buildings are numinous houses for God or community houses for God's people. The unique volume moves from phenomenological analysis to theological synthesis, is very thought-provoking, and should be considered necessary for a thoroughgoing study of the subject.

Vosko, Richard. *Through the Eye of a Rose Window: A Perspective on the Environment for Worship.* Saratoga, Calif.: Resource Publications, 1981. A brief overview of each liturgical space, including the font, altar, gathering space, and related aspects to the environment for worship, including seating arrangements, acoustics, and various art works.

White, James F. *Protestant Worship and Church Architecture: Theological and Historical Considerations.* New York: Oxford University Press, 1964. A history of Protestant architecture.

White, James F., and Susan J. White. *Church Architecture: Building and Renovating for Christian Worship.* Nashville: Abingdon, 1988. The single best overview of architecture for Protestant worship spaces. Covers each aspect of the worship space in light of the various liturgical services that it needs to accommodate, including baptism, the Lord's Supper, funerals, and weddings.

⚘ TWELVE ⚘

The Primary Visual Arts for Worship

Cultural and historical developments have directly influenced the ways that color, form, and design have been used in the worship environment. In semiliterate societies, the illustrated word carries more meaning and, therefore, more power than the read or printed word. Visual art creates a context that can demonstrate relationships between people, objects, and concepts more efficiently than other media. Contemporary North American culture is becoming image dominated. Television, film, photography, advertising, and computerized graphics are shifting the balance of communicative power between word and image. The visual arts in worship can not be avoided or ignored in the present age. They are an important means of communication with God for artist and participant, drawing worshipers into the story of faith in affective and spiritual ways. The different visual forms discussed in this section point toward a greater awareness of the visual aspects of worship and congregational life.

303 • AN INTRODUCTION TO THE PRIMARY VISUAL ARTS IN WORSHIP

There are three primary liturgical furnishings for the setting of worship: the pulpit, the Table (or altar), and the baptismal font (or pool). The size, shape, and placement of these furnishings vary according to the setting in which worship takes place. The following comments relate to the current understanding of the place and function of the primary symbols in a renewal worship.

The Pulpit

In the early church there was no such thing as a pulpit. Pulpits were invented during the medieval era and did not become popular until the fifteenth century. In England, pulpits did not become standard until 1604 when James I ordered that pulpits be established in every church. In liturgical churches, a divided chancel promoted the use of two pulpits, one for the readings of the Old Testament lessons and epistles, another for the reading of the gospel and the sermon. Protestants insisted on one central pulpit, usually placed on a raised platform with the Table under the pulpit on the level where the people sat.

It is now generally agreed upon by liturgists and scholars that only one pulpit is necessary. It should be simple and close to the people to express symbolically that God is near. The design of the pulpit should emphasize the Bible that it holds and should not draw attention to itself. It may be adorned with a cloth hanging in the color of the season, as long as the cloth does not take attention away from the Scripture. In brief, a pulpit should not be an end in itself but should serve the Scripture. It expresses the importance of the Word of God in the midst of God's people.

Because of the reintroduction of balance between Word and sacrament in worship, the pulpit should be neither large and dominating nor small and inconspicuous in relation to the Table. It should be set on the same level as the Table and to its left (as viewed from the congregation). It is best to make it out of the same material and design as the Table to show the unity of Word and sacrament.

The Table

The use of the Table is derived from the Last Supper when Jesus sat at a table in the Upper Room with his disciples and instituted his supper. It is not clear, however, when the Table became associated with sacrifice and thus received the name *altar*. The earliest name for the place of the eucharistic action was *table*. As the central object in the early church, the Table was free-standing and simple. In small worship settings the people gathered around it to celebrate the death and resurrection of Christ.

Gradually the Table came to be called the altar, the place of sacrifice, and it became the object of increased attention artistically. In some cases, very large altars were built (e.g., Lady Chapel of Ely had a sixteen-foot altar); in other places, altars with columns and a canopy (*ciborium*) were built. In many churches, the altar became the major artistic focus, having numerous carvings of the apostles, saints, and biblical scenes. Most altars were dressed with elaborate altar hangings, crosses, and candles. The altars came to be placed against the back wall of the church at a great distance from the people. This was consistent with the growing hierarchy of the church, the dominance of the clergy over the people, and the clericalization of worship.

In the Reformation, Protestants cleared their churches of these altars, smashing and demolishing many of them. Clearly this action was a sign of their rejection of the belief that Christ was resacrificed on the altar in favor of a simpler interpretation of the sacrament. Large and conspicuous altars were replaced with small inconspicuous tables set below the pulpit, the new dominant architectural symbol of the Protestant church.

Today the balance between Word and Table, which represents a return to the practice of the early church, is emphasized by using a simple table with plain liturgical utensils. Furthermore, the Table has been moved away from the back wall to the front of the nave inviting all the people to participate in the worship that takes place around the Table. In renewed Protestant churches, the Table is now larger and placed in the center or off center where both Table and pulpit visually express the unity and centrality of Word and Table.

Baptismal Font or Pool

In the early period of the church, new Christians were baptized in local pools or rivers. However, as congregations began to build their own places of worship, especially after the conversion of Constantine, places for baptism in the church building became increasingly important.

At first baptismal places were either separate buildings or adjoining rooms off the narthex. Pools were usually square or rectangular, reflecting the shape of the Roman baths or of tombs. Since baptism is associated with death to sin, the shape of a tomb was a strong factor in the architectural development of baptismal pools. Thus, like many tombs, baptismal pools were built in a circular fashion with six and eight-sided designs.

In the late medieval era, detached baptisteries were no longer built, and a font was placed inside the church. The specific symbolic expression of death to sin through baptism into Christ weakened. Gradually, a space in the church, usually near the entrance, came to be the place of baptism and entrance into the church. It became the norm to erect a font for pouring or sprinkling as infant baptism, not adult baptism, became the prevailing practice.

In Protestantism, the baptistery nearly ceased to exist. Calvinists simply used a portable basin. Anglicans and Lutherans placed a small font near the door. Baptists, while having a pool, usually hid it under the pulpit area so that it had no visibility, except when in use.

In the twentieth century architects have been returning to the idea that a particular space for baptism is the way of visually expressing the new importance placed on baptism. The earlier conviction that baptism is a participation in the death of Christ and, therefore, a baptism of death to sin has been restored in renewed worship. There is a need to express this biblical truth in a spatial way.

In modern Roman Catholic churches, a space designated only for baptism is created in the new church buildings by relegating baptismal spaces to one side of the church in the entrance hall or the narthex. In many new Protestant churches, the font or pool is in the back of the church near the entrance, but in a space of its own where the people within the congregation may move to and gather for the celebration. While new attention is being given to the baptismal space, no one standard configuration has emerged. What occupies the attention of congregations and architects is the concern to provide a space for congregational participation, a space that visually represents what is happening, and a shape for the pool or font that expresses the meaning of being buried with Christ in a death to sin. By arranging the pulpit, the Table, and the baptismal font (or pool) visually in a manner appropriate to their function, the church proclaims the central message of the Christian faith.

Robert Webber

304 • Evaluating the Place of the Lectern, Pulpit, and Bible

This article clarifies the purpose of the lectern (here discussed using the synonymous term ambo), pulpit, and Bible. Embellishments that characterized these items in earlier times are less appropriate when the action of proclamation is emphasized over the adoration of beauty.

The proclamation of sacred Scripture is of central importance in liturgical celebration. The lector proclaims the Word of God from the book at the ambo. The ambo and book are active elements in the liturgical action and should not be perceived simply as inert objects. They derive their special quality from the holy action itself in which the body of Christ celebrates liturgy. Ambo and book are symbols in the action of the living Word of proclamation.

There is a trend in our celebrations toward excessive, or the wrong kind of, reverence for the book itself. One of these trends is lifting up the book after the proclamation while announcing, "This is the Word of the Lord." This focuses on the book, as if it were the reference point of the announcement. This is misleading. The proclamation by believers to believers is the Word of the Lord, not the book.

Enthroning the book is another way to suggest that the physical book—its pages, its writing, rather than faith proclamation—has the primary call upon the assembly.

We must ask ourselves whether we are in danger of doing with the action of proclamation what we did with the action of eucharistic meal sharing. Are we shifting the focus from the action itself to the elements of the action? With the Eucharist, our attention went from meal sharing by the assembly to the tabernacle. With the liturgy of the Word, we are

in danger of shifting from proclamation to the book and its ambo-throne.

The elements of bread and wine in the eucharistic action are critical in the faith action of meal sharing. The book is crucial in the faith action of proclamation, but the focus needs to stay clear.

The liturgy of the Word is an active and participatory communal experience. Nourishment from the Word of God in Christ is the experience. Participation in the proclamation by lector and hearers is the event of faith that unfolds in the liturgy of the Word, and this is the experience that counts.

In the Middle Ages, the book was much larger than today's book and often covered with precious metals encrusted with jewels of breathtaking beauty. In an era of superstition and illiteracy, when only the clergy and a few other elite could read, the front and back covers of the book were decorated with biblical images. As a kind of icon, the splendidly decorated book was a glimpse into the world beyond, summoning one's imagination to search the precincts of mystery. When the book was not being used in the liturgical action, it was sometimes suspended over the assembly, manifesting in this way Christ's presence to the community. Like the tabernacle, the book was where Christ's presence was preserved, a piece of dazzling beauty that, when opened, revealed the presence. The more jewels, the more real the presence must have been! All the while, however, the possibility existed that one might worship the book rather than venerate the presence manifested in the book.

Vatican II and the mandate of the *Constitution on the Sacred Liturgy* emphasizes that "the treasures of the Bible be opened up more lavishly so that a richer fare may be provided for the faithful at the table of God's Word." This summons does not suggest that we should open up the biblical treasures by prominently displaying the open book on the ambo or by creating wonderful covers for the book or building beautiful ambos for its enthronement. The "richer fare" refers to a broader scope of the biblical content being made available regularly to the praying assembly. The reference is to active participation in the faith-event of proclamation.

A visual symbol used in liturgy is a visual form of an experience or an action. The symbol is an action, not a thing. It is an event. The word *symbol* should really be heard as a verb, because it is an action that reveals an experience. Opening up symbols, furthermore, does not require that the symbol be reinvented. It is the reshaping of the symbol, in the culture of the people, that makes the experience richer and, thus, makes it possible for people to own the experience. Making the ordinary extraordinary is what makes the old new again and creates emotional involvement in the event.

To participate fully and to experience the liturgy of the Word does not mean merely being able to see the book when the lector announces, "This is the Word of the Lord!" Participation means active listening and grasping the Word that is shared. Our former understanding of liturgical space as the house of God (*Domus Dei*), with its interest in sacred objects, needs to be enlarged by the ancient church's sense of the liturgical space as the house of the church (*Domus ecclesiae*). When the community gathered, its priorities had to do with the community action. Experience is the primary symbol, not the book or the ambo where the book is placed or from which it is read.

Book and ambo are critical elements in the experience of proclamation. The sacred text, printed and bound with beauty and handled with reverence, is proclaimed at the ambo, the place that is the table of the Word of God. This table provides nourishment for the hungers of the assembly. Its form, scale, and materials establish its identity and dignity, while providing balance and support in relation to the altar table.

Historically, the ambo was not a piece of furniture that evolved into a pulpit. Early Christian worship in the homes of community members placed the Scripture proclamation and homily in the midst of the assembly. Basilicas, which replaced home liturgy, had the presider (bishop) speak from the *cathedra* (chair) that was placed in the apse behind the altar. Other clergy used the sanctuary steps or a raised platform; it was this area that was the ambo. The ambo was a place, not a piece of furniture.

In the Middle Ages preaching often occurred outside of Sunday liturgy. This led to the development of the pulpit. As the book of Scripture used for preaching became smaller, the pulpit became larger. Eventually, the pulpit developed an overhead canopy that functioned as an acoustical soundboard, a necessary feature because the pulpit was so far removed from the congregation.

Until recently, the pulpit was overdecorated with multiple symbols and was large, often overshadowing the altar. It overwhelmed the preacher and functioned as a theatrical device meant to entertain the passive congregation.

Like the medieval book cover, the pulpit encouraged imagination through its decoration. Indeed, it became a liturgical "thing" separated from everything around it, an elaborate stage built up before the audience but separate from it. Very much like pews with closed ends that removed their occupants from everyone else, the pulpit was the stage for one person, separated from everyone else. The idea of active participation in a shared proclamation of Word was not central.

Although ambos are to be substantial in character, their design should be open so that the book and the proclaimer will be perceived as part of the gathered assembly. *Environment and Art in Catholic Worship* suggests reshaping the ambo as a symbol whose primary function is table of the Word: "Like the altar, it should be beautifully designed, constructed of fine materials and proportioned care, fully and simply for its function." The liturgical documents do not suggest making the ambo look exactly like the altar. They encourage a clarity appropriate to its special function. Though both Word and Eucharist nourish, they have individual requirements in the way they do so.

The long tradition of the church as patron of the arts needs to be opened up again. When symbols are reshaped into vernacular forms, the community can make the symbols their own. The ambo, properly located and designed, can provide a sense of place for a new and lasting experience. Ambo should be part of the architectural space that provides an environment of clarity and excitement demanded by the symbols we use. The old is new and the ordinary extraordinary.

Mario Locsin[68]

305 • EVALUATING THE PLACE OF THE ALTAR OR TABLE

This article argues that the altar should serve as a focal point in the worship space. It discusses both the theological rationale for this idea and how it can be achieved through spatial arrangements and seating patterns. It is presented from a Roman Catholic perspective but introduces ideas that can inform discussions in many worshiping traditions.

Liturgy documents, rituals, and commentaries published since the Second Vatican Council clearly indicate that the altar table is to be a focal point in worship spaces and that it is to be central to the gathered assembly. These sources paint a striking picture of the whole assembly gathered about the altar table. Why then is the altar table in most Catholic places of worship still located at one end of the room?

One answer has to do with how a community understands the different roles required for the eucharistic liturgy. Another answer is found in the research that deals with the psychology of space, e.g., territoriality and seating factors. Both answers affect the location of the community table. The case studies depicted in this article show that it is possible to return the Table to the community.

Assembly as Celebrant

Does the worship space say that the assembly is the celebrant of the eucharistic liturgy? Or does it say that the priest presents the liturgy to the assembly? In a technical sense, liturgy is shaped by different roles and actions. A community that understands this principle can identify appropriate architectural settings for various liturgical ministries and movements. These spaces are then specifically designed according to the needs of each ministry.

For example, choirs and musicians are ideally arranged together in a flexible, elevated area in view of the rest of the assembly. Hard surfaces and finishes, adequate light and acoustical equipment are essential to this ministry. The same consideration should be given to all other ministries including the assembly. (Here some readers will have different opinions regarding the ministerial nature of the assembly during the liturgical act. To be involved in a ministry requires a commitment and willingness to learn how to carry out the ministry in exemplary fashion. One wonders if assemblies are ready for this kind of involvement.) Nevertheless, we must remember:

> Liturgical services are not private functions, but are celebrations of the Church, which is the "sacrament of unity," namely, the holy people united and ordered under their bishops.
>
> Therefore liturgical services pertain to the whole body of the Church; they manifest it and have effects upon it; but they concern the individual members of the Church in different ways, according to

their differing rank, office and actual participation. (*Constitution on the Sacred Liturgy*, 26)

Although many communities have worked hard to improve liturgical ministries, the arrangement of the worship setting, in many cases, works against the efforts of liturgy planners to involve the assembly. Long straight rows of seats, bolted to the floor, facing the priest who presides from an elevated platform at one end of the room, creates a divided environment for worship that renders the assembly passive. This type of setting does not foster the bonding of the assembly.

The place of worship can help the assembly in its liturgical role by gathering participants around focal points (e.g., the Table) and not dispersing them. The environmental needs of the assembly include:

- ample, barrier-free spaces for gatherings and processions
- unobstructed and well-spaced seats
- good sightlines
- good acoustics
- comfortable temperature
- appropriate color schemes
- accessible focal points

This last factor means the assembly is arranged in such a manner that it has visual, acoustical, physical, and psychological accessibility to the major furnishings used for worship (font, ambo, Table).

If the Table is located in a space that says, "KEEP OUT!" the worshiper will sense *"the Table does not belong to me"* and *"the Eucharist celebrated on that Table does not belong to me—it belongs to the priest who gives it to me."* This is perhaps why some people have resisted extraordinary eucharistic ministers. In their minds only the priest has the power to do the eucharistic act which traditionally took place in a special part (sanctuary) of the room where only the priest was once allowed. Here power and space are connected. Poor, powerless people do not own vast amounts of territory. People with power have lots of space.

Spatial Arrangements

In most worship places the architectural settings for the presider's chair, the ambo and the Table are still remote and distant from the assembly. These furnishings are usually found in the territory traditionally set aside for the ordained. Although the

Roman Catholic church requires an ordained priest to preside at the eucharistic liturgy, the placement of the Table should not suggest that the Mass is an action delivered by the priest to the assembly.

However, the usually remote location of the Table should not surprise us. Robert Sommer, who has researched the behavioral basis of design, wrote, "Because social and spatial orders serve similar functions, it is not surprising to find spatial correlates of status levels and, conversely, social correlates of spatial positions." (*Personal Space* [Englewood Cliffs, N.J.: Prentice Hall, 1969]). In this sense one can see how certain Catholic ritual conventions have created spatial hierarchies that are difficult to change. Furthermore, Sommer says "the ancients placed great value on chairs and thrones in which their political and religious leaders sat. . . . Seating position is an important part of diplomatic protocol with people often seated according to a complicated formula of rank and status."

The traditional hieratic arrangement of Catholic worship spaces (the sanctuary for the priests and the nave for the laity) can be analogous to the barnyard pecking order alluded to in Sommer's work. In the barnyard, the top fowl (i.e., roosters) can roam where they please while the lower birds are restricted to small areas. Rails may have been taken down, but the distance factors in many houses of worship sustain the division and outline territories for different castes. There does not seem to be any significant or theological reason for maintaining a spatial pecking order in places of worship. In fact, the only reason for elevated platforms is to provide adequate sightlines.

Moving the community Table, the ambo, and the presider's chair into the midst of the assembly can help erase any semblance of division, territoriality, and ranking during the eucharistic liturgy. The centralized setting will affirm that all worshipers (priest and people) are the celebrants and that every person present has a particular role to carry out. It says that the Table belongs to all. Further, reducing the distance between the assembly and the Table (often by as much as 50 percent) will provide better sightlines, eliminating the need for very high and inaccessible platforms.

Seating Patterns

The arrangement of seats in a place of worship can affect the "performance" of the participants in the liturgy. Humphrey Osmond, in his classic 1950s study on airports, prisons, and hospitals (in C. Goshen, *Psychiatric Architecture,* 1959) made the distinction between sociofugal and sociopetal settings (see figure below). Quite simply, the sociofugal arrangement—straight rows of seats—discourages interaction among people and drives them to the edge of the room. We find such arrangements in airports, theaters, and churches. Ever notice how people will occupy the end of a pew while the middle of the row remains empty? These people are choosing the optimum seating location, suggesting they are probably not comfortable in that space. (The need for privacy, another important environmental factor, is not discussed in this article.)

Irwin Altman wrote that "strangers who expect to deal with one another are likely to seek an optimum interaction distance; deviations from this distance

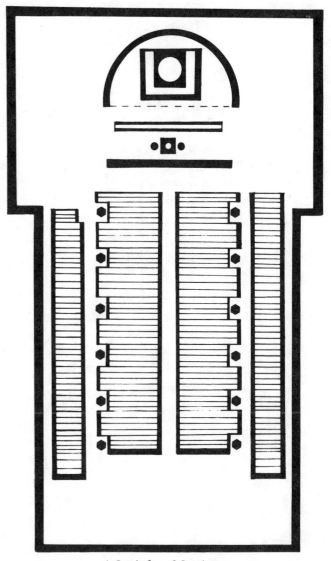

A Sociofugal Setting

(much closer or much farther) are unsatisfactory. This is in relationships between strangers in which there is an explicit expectation of interaction" (*The Environment and Social Behavior* [Pacific Grove, Calif.: Brooks/Cole, 1975]). Could it be that most Catholic worshipers are not comfortable with the expectations placed on them during the eucharistic liturgy? Perhaps, over a period of time, a more inviting spatial arrangement could foster a gentle understanding of the liturgical act?

A sociopetal pattern, seats arranged in a circular type setting, encourages interaction, focuses people on the center of the room, and brings them together. We find this arrangement at the dining room table where family and guests eat and drink as friends. A worshiping community striving for energetic involvement in the liturgical event will discover that

a more sociopetal arrangement of seats will begin to shape the participatory behavior of the assembly. However, communities with worshipers who do not like to look at each other while praying have to solve the societal problem before addressing the liturgical problem. Such shy people will naturally move to the optimum rows.

Placing the Table in the midst of the worship setting will help the assembly bond over time and focus its undivided attention on the actions taking place at the Table. Restoring the Table to the worshipers is an important part of the renewal of the liturgy and can no longer be overlooked.

Richard S. Vosko[69]

306 • SCRIPTURAL PERSPECTIVES ON THE ALTAR

The altar was a significant part of Old Testament worship, serving as a place for ritual sacrifices and symbolizing the presence of God. In the New Testament, Jesus Christ fulfilled and superseded Old Testament sacrifices by his sacrifice on the cross.

The English word *altar,* which is derived from the Latin *altare* and probably related to *altus* ("high"), is defined in Webster's dictionary as "a raised structure or place on which sacrifices are offered or incense is burned in worship." It is possibly rooted in the Latin verb *adolere* ("to worship," "to burn or cause to go up in smoke"), so that the word came to signify "a place of sacrifice."

In the classical world and the ancient Near East, the altar was a place where gifts were offered to the gods; it was a symbol of the hidden presence of the divine. The gods were invited to consume the gifts which were often transformed or transferred, through burning, from the material to the spiritual realm. The most primitive altars consisted simply of a large stone or pile of rocks; in some areas they were mere mounds of earth strewn with special grass.

Israelite Religion

The function of the altar for the Israelites was basically the same as it was for the ancient Near Eastern peoples, but there were some significant differences. The Hebrew word for altar is *mizbeah* (a place of sacrificial slaying), which is rooted in the word *zabah,* meaning "to slaughter as a sacrifice." In addition to animals and birds, other objects of-

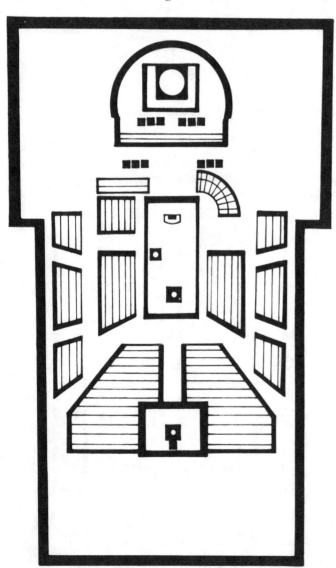

A Sociopetal Setting

fered on the altar were wine, grain and incense. At times altars served non-sacrificial roles, such as witness (Josh. 22:26-29) and as a place of refuge after one had committed a crime (1 Kings 1:50-53). For the Israelites the altar was above all a symbol of divine presence. People built altars to remember that God had intervened in human history in a special way at a particular time and place; hence they served as memorials of divine favor (Gen. 33:20, 35:1-7; Judg. 6:24). Altars were also the place of libations and sacrifices. If at one time or another simple stones were used as altars (Judg. 6:20; 13:19), most of the time the people built actual altars with care so they were satisfactorily adapted to their proper purpose (Exod. 20:24-26).

Abraham and Jacob built altars to commemorate a special revelation of God's presence and activity (Gen. 13:18; 35:7). At the altar, renewed communion with God was achieved. Gifts were removed from the human sphere and transferred to the divine by being placed on the altar. The gifts symbolized the people who offered the gifts; the altar itself symbolized God. Hence gifts placed on the altar symbolized the union of the people with their God. This union was explicitly expressed by blood rituals. Blood itself was the primary symbol of life which had its source in God. The blood was sprinkled on both the altar and the people. Because God and the people shared in the same blood, they shared in the same life and so were in union with each other.

Some of the altars, including the altar of holocausts and the altar of Incense in the Temple of Jerusalem, had horns at each corner. Their original purpose is unclear, but they came to be looked upon as a sign of God's protective presence, thus affording sanctuary to those who took hold of them (1 Kings 2:28). For the Israelites, however, the altar, at least in its early stages of development, was less a utilitarian object than it was a sacred symbol of the encounter between humankind and God. But for the descendants of the patriarchs the altar as a place of worship tended to take on more value than the memories of the theophanies which were at the origin of the altars. This primacy of place over memorial is reflected in the fact that ancient places of pagan worship such as Bethel (Gen. 35:7) and Shechem (Gen. 33:19) were taken over by the Israelites without any reference to a special encounter with God. Although the law required that pagan altars be demolished (Exod. 34:13, Deut. 7:5, Num.

33:52), the Israelites often simply consecrated them to the true God by means of their own sacrificial offerings (1 Kings 3:4).

By concentrating so much attention on their altars the Israelites often forgot that the altar was not holy in and of itself, but only because it was a symbol of the living God. They likewise often failed to distinguish carefully between their use of altars and that employed by their pagan contemporaries. Solomon, Ahab, Ahaz, and Manasseh even went to far as to tolerate pagan altars (1 Kings 11:7-8; 16:10-16; 16:32; 21:5). The prophets for their part scolded the people for multiplying altars (Amos 2:6-8, Hos. 8:11; Jer. 3:6).

The primacy of God was strongly reasserted when the worship of the chosen people was centralized at Jerusalem (2 Kings 23) where the altar of holocausts in the temple focused the religious life of Israel. The Psalms bear witness to the fond place the altar held in the hearts of the people (Psa. 26:6, 43:4; 84:1-4; 118:27).

Among the Israelites, many of the priestly functions were closely associated with altars. The priests were above all men of the sanctuary, for their primary role was to offer sacrifices. As special mediators between God and the people, they presented to God the offerings of the people and they transmitted to the people the blessings of God. Their distinctive role was exemplified by Moses, who offered the sacrifice of the covenant (Exod. 24:4-8), and by Levi, who became the head of the whole line of priests (Deut. 29:38-42). On the Day of Atonement, the high priest carried out his role as supreme mediator by offering sacrifice to obtain the pardon for all the people's sins (Lev. 16). The priests became exclusively ministers of the altar while the Levites took care of the purely material chores (Num. 3:6-10).

New Testament

That Jesus acknowledged the special holiness of the altar is indicated by his calling down woe on the Pharisees for their attempt to discourage oaths sworn by the temple or the altar and shifting the oaths to less important things such as the gold of the temple or the gifts on the altar (Matt. 23:18-21). It is by altar and ultimately by God symbolized by the altar that the gifts are sanctified. To approach the altar for sacrifice is to draw near to God; if one's worship is to be worthy, this cannot be done with anger in one's heart (Matt. 5:23-24).

Jesus not only purified the worship of the Israelites, he put an end to it. His own body was and still is the new temple (John 2:19-21); he himself is our altar. He is also the prefect victim offered to God; likewise he is the perfect priest who offers the victim. In Jesus, temple, altar, victim, and priest are all one.

In writing to the Corinthians, Paul affirmed that when Christians partake of the body and blood of the Lord they partake at the altar which is the Lord; they share his table (1 Cor. 10:16-21). There is no reference to the traditional altars in his letter. Likewise the author of the letter to the Hebrews makes no reference to an altar for the eucharistic sacrifice. When he says, "We have an altar from which those who serve the tent have no right to eat" (Heb. 13:10), he is either referring to the cross or to the very person of Jesus.

There are a number of references to altars in the Book of Revelation (Rev. 6:9; 8:3, 5; 9:13; 14:18; 16:7). Above all the author speaks of the heavenly altar under which rest the martyrs slain for the Word of God (Rev. 6:9) and on which flames cause abundant fragrant smoke to rise to God (Rev. 8:3, 5). These flames symbolize Christ who is the one altar of sacrifice whose fragrance is perfectly pleasing to God. As the author of the letter to the Hebrews asserts, Christ is the one who "offered for all time a single sacrifice for sins . . . For by a single offering he has perfected for all time those who are sanctified" (Heb. 10:12, 14).

In the New Testament the significance of the traditional altar of the Israelites is eclipsed by Christ, for in the new Jerusalem there is neither temple nor altar. The Lord God Almighty and the Lamb are the temple in the heavenly city (Rev. 21:22).

Kevin Seasoltz, O.S.B.[70]

307 • ADVICE ON THE USE OF THE TABLE

The visual appearance of the Table or altar is important in communicating its meaning. This article offers advice for how to present the Table so that it will serve as a symbol of Christ's presence with the people at worship.

The holy Table is the physical focal point of every eucharistic place. It must never be overpowered by decorative architecture or suspended crosses; never compromised by the proximity of other major objects such as chair, tabernacle, or baptismal font; never trivialized by minor objects such as

bookstands, microphones, cruets, flower vases, devotional aids, and the like being left on it. Roman tradition, despite lapses here and there, has always regarded the holy Table as the main architectural symbol of Christ's abiding presence among his people, recalling to them constantly their fundamental nature as a Table fellowship in him. The Table in this sense is a "blessed sacrament" in its own way and should be treated with the same degree of reverence accorded the sacrament of Christ's body and blood. That the integrity of both these sacred symbols of his abiding presence in the Church be maintained is the reason why the reformed liturgy reasserted the Roman tradition of reserving the eucharistic species in a place other than on the eucharistic place's holy Table. Altar ornaments such as candlesticks, reliquaries, flower vases, crosses, and the like must be scaled to the Table and are best removed when the Table is not in use. The Table itself should be free-standing, accessible from all sides, more square than long in shape, and itself scaled to the space it occupies. It should have a strong and elemental simplicity to it and possess a certain mass which remains visually constant from whatever angle it is viewed. The space around it should be flat and adequate to accommodate numbers of people and without complicated risers which endanger access and render the space fussy. The holy Table is not an idol but a sacramental symbol of the presence of the Unseen. It is consecrated by water and oil similar to the way a Christian is consecrated in baptism.

Aidan Kavanaugh[71]

308 • ACTIONS OF REVERENCE AT THE EUCHARIST AND THE DESIGN OF THE TABLE

Christians in many worshiping traditions use a variety of ritual actions to indicate their reverence for the worship of God and participation in the sacrament of the Eucharist. This article explains what these actions of reverence look like and how the architectural design of the sacramental symbols can enhance their meaning.

We were well trained from earliest childhood and had been so for countless generations. When we entered God's House, after having made the sign of the cross with holy water, we genuflected toward the tabernacle (on or above the main altar) and then entered a pew where we knelt in prayer. In many cases the ritual had become perfunctory, but we knew the etiquette of entrance into God's presence. Whether coming into church for private prayer or Mass, we knew how to get started. We knew that the genuflection was a special mark of honor and greeting to Christ sacramentally present in the tabernacle.

Things have changed. Now Roman Catholics entering new and/or renovated worship spaces seem at a loss as they perceive that the tabernacle, the central focus of liturgical etiquette in the experience of Catholics more than 30 years old, has been relocated within or outside the main worship space. The *altar,* with the ambo and presider's chair, has replaced the tabernacle as the visual center of the worship space. Rarely do we see, however, a new etiquette of entrance consonant with this re-arrangement. It would seem that the sacramental presence of Christ in the tabernacle was so central to Catholic piety that its absence causes ritual confusion.

The confusion is a testimony to the loss of an ancient element of popular Catholic spirituality—devotion to the altar.

The restoration of the altar to its former architectural prominence is not an exercise in archaeology. It is an attempt to give physical expression to the centrality of eucharistic celebration in our common life. The altar is not itself the center but is one of the elements which makes the eucharistic act possible.

The reformed Roman Sacramentary bears witness to that more ancient reverence for the altar which was once so integral to the piety of all the baptized. The Sacramentary directs the presider at the Eucharist to reverence the altar as part of the introductory rite. This the priest does by first bowing before the altar, then approaching it and kissing it. He also has the option of incensing the holy Table. This is an etiquette of greeting. The Table of the Lord is perceived to be a symbol of Christ who is himself altar, victim and priest, table of fellowship, food and drink, host and fellow guest.

Just as the etiquette of the dinner party continues through the event and does not come to end with the rituals of entry and greeting, so the ritual directives of the Roman rite reveal "good manners" which bear witness to a deep altar spirituality. Whatever is placed on the Lord's Table is set aside exclusively for God's service. The Scriptures may be placed there until borne in honor to the ambo for the liturgy of the Word. During the preparation of the gifts, the deacon assists the priest in setting upon the altar in clarity and simplicity the bread and wine over which the eucharistic prayer shall be proclaimed. The text of that prayer is the only object to be placed on the altar with the bread and wine.

What about an altar etiquette for all the baptized? In fact, the presider models manners for all the congregation. Just as we reverence Christ present in the tabernacle, so the tradition calls us to reverence Christ's Table, the locus of the eucharistic place of identification between Christ's act of self-offering and our daily Christian service.

Look at the altar. Bow deeply and deliberately to it before taking your place in the congregation. This is an act of attending to the presence of the One who has called us together to hear his Word and share his flesh and blood. It is good liturgical manners. It is a way for the whole person (body and spirit) to enter into contemplative prayer.

The ritual etiquette elaborates a spirituality.

- This Table is honored by being allowed to *stand free* and unencumbered. Allowing space is an act of hospitality. The altar is to be allowed its space so that it may be an instrument of liturgical hospitality for the community.
- This Table is honored by being *in harmony* with the other appointments which enable our worship. If sacraments are "visible words," then the altar must allow the table of God's Word, the ambo, its space and not be out of balance or in conflict with it or the presider's chair. Much less should the size, shape, or visual impact of the Lord's Table ever dwarf the presider and/or other ministers. The altar, like good ritual music, serves the church's ritual prayer; it does not draw undue attention to itself.
- This Table is honored by the *vesting* which celebrates its crucial role in our worship. Nothing cheap or poorly crafted should adorn it. Altar cloths are not foundation fabrics for words or theme statements. Altar cloths are vesture as much as the chasuble and alb.
- This Table is honored by *keeping it free* of anything and everything which is not the focus of eucharistic prayer. It is no longer a shelf for the cross and candles, much less for flowers, statues, reliquaries, missalettes, songbooks, homily notes, parish announcements, mass intentions, or the list of deceased to be prayed for during the month of November. It is certainly not the repository for pumpkins (Halloween or

Thanksgiving), toys (Christmas), rings (high school celebrations), or diplomas (graduation ceremonies at any and all levels). A good rule of thumb is: if it is placed on the altar, it is consumed in the celebration and reserved for the sick (the sacrament of Christ's body and blood), constituent of and reserved for liturgical celebration (vessels and books) or is placed in archives of religious communities (profession charters). Anything else belongs somewhere else.

The Table of the Lord, like our dining room and kitchen tables, is a bearer of memories. To this Table Christians bring their tears and their joys, their dying and rising with Christ. As such a vessel of individual and collective memory, it is an object worthy of contemplation as much as any icon or statue. Indeed, the more we see our lives joined to the ongoing paschal offering of Christ, the more we will see the altar as a symbol of that great communion. In time the altar becomes a partner in our dialogue of prayer. The Byzantine tradition admirably sums up this rigorous sort of devotion to the altar when it directs the priest to bid farewell to the altar as he is about to leave the sanctuary at the conclusion of the Divine Liturgy:

Remain in peace, holy altar of the Lord, for I do not know whether I shall return to you or not. May the Lord make me worthy of the vision of you in the assembly of the first born in heaven. In this covenant I trust.

Remain in peace, holy and propitiatory altar. May the holy body and the propitiatory blood which I have received from you be for me for the pardon of offences and the forgiveness of sins and for a confident face before the dread judgment seat of our Lord and God for ever.

Remain in peace, holy altar, table of life, and beg for me from our Lord Jesus Christ that I may not cease to remember you henceforth and for ever.

Andrew Ciferni[72]

309 • HISTORICAL AND THEOLOGICAL PERSPECTIVES ON THE BAPTISMAL FONT

The placement and appearance of the baptismal font has been the subject of many debates throughout the history of the church. This article traces many of these discussions and offers suggestions for current practice.

Questions about the scale and location, the symbolism and importance, of the baptismal font, indeed about the relationship of baptismal washing to initiation, are crucial to our generation. The issues are so complicated, however, that some parishes are refusing to decide about the location of fonts and are building churches without them. Many other churches have abandoned permanent fonts in favor of stainless steel basins, plastic bassinets, or glass punch bowls.

Contemporary practice seems to be repeating that of the middle decades of the sixteenth century, when reformers abandoned the abuses and popery of Rome in order to create places and rites that would focus on fundamentals: the assembly gathered around the candidate. The reformers set aside all else—no salt, no blowing in the ears, no oil, no candle, no clothing and sometimes, as with the Anabaptists, no water at all—hoping to find the fundamental meaning of this sacrament, which all agreed was given by mandate of the Lord Jesus Christ.

The search is an emotional one. We argue about the font, because we know that as baptism captures our identity, so it becomes a symbol of our struggle for the church's survival in this age. Not only is this notion appropriate but also it is in keeping with the history of baptism. No place has been so layered with meaning, so laden with iconography, as the place of baptism. No archaeological remains have been more consistently in evidence than the font. Even when the church's worship took place in private Roman houses, the baptisteries were clearly set apart. No table, no reading stand, no presidential chair, no plate, no cup, no cross survives that period. But the font was already rich in iconography.

Patristic Sources

We will better understand the place of the font in contemporary church architecture if we begin with a review of the primary sources, the patristic literature concerning the baptismal washing, especially the baptismal literature dating from the second century. This information exists in three forms: Christian apologetic, ritual descriptions and texts, and homilies or catecheses.

We often operate with two assumptions about the

first centuries of the church: first, that the various churches throughout the empire held the same beliefs and celebrated the sacraments in the same way; and second, that the era was primitive and therefore theologically undeveloped. Both assumptions are false. Churches in the first four centuries witnessed active research in biblical and philosophical sources. There were theological debates between Christians and political and religious discussions among Christians and Gnostics and others. There were theological and practical differences between the East and West—even in the way they kept their calendars. All of these factors yielded a rich matrix for baptism.

The word _baptism_ comes from the Greek _baptizein,_ meaning "to dip repeatedly." The sacrament that we refer to as baptism was at first called "enlightenment," as we read in the writings of Justin (_c._ 160). Baptism was called enlightenment because it bestows the fire of the indwelling Word, the pillar of light, Christ, who scattered the darkness and spread the light of truth. It was also understood as initiation, a term for the process of becoming a member of the community. If one considers the _process_ as initiation, then the _act_ of baptizing, though meaningful in itself, is part of a broader constellation of rites.

Although the word _baptistery_ does not occur until 350 in the writings of Cyril of Jerusalem (_Mystagogical Catechesis I_), archaeology has shown us that baptisteries existed as early as 235, for example, at the Roman house church in Dura-Europos. To consider these sources as evidence of a universal practice, however, would be a mistake. That a wide variety of practices continued long after fonts were in use suggests, perhaps, that neither the place of a font nor its specific qualities is as important as the water and the action of washing.

The _Didache,_ written in the early second century, represents Syrian practice. It is concerned with the qualities necessary for the water; namely, that it be cold (or at least not hot) running water. Practically speaking, these requirements eliminate the cistern in favor of either a fountain or a bath with living water. Justin, writing from Rome in 160, says that there must be enough water at baptism so that one can be washed. Hippolytus, also writing from Rome in 215, requires that the water be pure and flowing.

Tertullian, writing from North Africa after 195, approaches the matter more boldly, by saying that all water is made sacred by invoking God. For him the waters of baptism become the waters of creation, pure and aboriginal. The Acts of Judas Thomas, written in Edessa, now Turkey, describes the baptism of Gundaphorus at a Roman bathhouse in the third century. (The bathhouse was closed for preparation seven days before the baptism.) The same source describes the baptism of Mygdonia at a fountain. Finally, the History of John, Son of Zebedee, written in 350 in Caesarea, has the most elaborate architectural setting for the act of washing. The baptism of Tyrannus takes place in the theater at Ephesus in a specially constructed cistern 22 inches deep.

The earliest literature does not conclude absolutely that a font is needed. Water is water, and almost any water is appropriate. But how does the water get its meaning? If fountains, amphitheaters, and Roman baths are all acceptable, is there anything in patristic literature that makes water a symbol all to itself? Is it a sacred object?

Blessing the Water

If specific legislation required the use of fonts, then perhaps we could say that water is, in and of itself, a sacred object. There is no such text, however, and yet the water is meaningful. Its identity comes from two sources that are deeply interdependent: texts of blessing and theological descriptions of washing. And we know that once a blessing is proclaimed, no earthly matter may pollute it. It is simply pure.

As the patristic age developed, references to a blessing of the water became more numerous. Neither the _Didache_ nor Justin mentioned a blessing over the water. Hippolytus referred to such a prayer, but he did not describe it. Finally, Tertullian (in North Africa, _c._ 195) called it an invocation of God that brings the spirit upon the waters. Thus, the act of washing is the spirit washing, and the waters become the waters of creation.

Texts of blessing begin to appear about 350, in Serapion and Ambrose, for example, but also in the Syrian text of the History of John, Son of Zebedee. In the Syrian text, the scene is set in the large amphitheater in Ephesus, with the priests of Diana deserting the white marble temple for a newfound Christian faith. As the sun sets, they step forward, cutting a line across the open edge of the theater. John, the presbyter, calls down the Spirit of God on the improvised font, saying:

Glory to you, Father, Son and Spirit of holiness, forever. Amen. Lord God Almighty, let your Spirit of holiness come and rest upon the oil and upon the water. Let these people be bathed and purified from uncleanliness; let them receive the Spirit of holiness through baptism. Yes, Lord, sanctify this water with your voice, which resounded over the Jordan and pointed out our Lord Jesus, saying, "This is my beloved Son." Yea, I beseech you, Lord, manifest yourself here before the assembly who have believed in you.

After these words, fire blazed over the oil, and John took the priests of Artemis and washed them clean, baptizing them in the name of the Father, Son, and Spirit. Then bread and wine were brought forward.

This text opens many horizons for us. Its focus is not on the water and the oil *per se,* but on the effects of the acts of washing and anointing. Nevertheless, it is the water and the oil that are made, that is, identified. Moreover, the whole washing is public, which is not the case in our other sources; and finally, the washing relates to the ritual actions before and after it, especially to the Eucharist that follows the washing.

The basic meaning of the baptismal water in the History of John is that of a bath of purification and a gift of holiness. This view of redemption is as appropriate for the city of Ephesus as it was for the apostle Paul. The primary biblical type is the baptism of repentance and faith given by John at the Jordan.

This is not, however, the only identity given to the water in the patristic sources. Theodore of Mopsuestia, speaking for the Church of Antioch in the fifth century, describes the blessing as an invitation to the spirit to give the water power of conceiving and becoming the womb of sacramental birth. This is a typical Johannine creation image and the second major interpretation of the act of washing: to be baptized is to be made new in the waters of rebirth.

We think of Adam, like Christ, asleep in the garden that God has made. In his sleep, Eve is begotten as bride and newborn, a child fed by Adam's flesh and blood. Together, Adam and Eve are companions just as Christ and the church begotten in Christ's flesh and blood are companions. This image describes a new beginning, gentle and fresh. It is the opening of one's eyes to new creation and seeing the hand of God still smeared with the earth from which we came.

Creation, destruction, and new creation, sin and death, forgiveness and resurrection, converge on the cross and death, burial and resurrection of the new Adam, Jesus Christ. These two approaches to the water are a convergence of Pauline soteriology and Johannine eschatology. Together, they describe the soul of the water.

The Act of Washing

After the blessing texts come descriptions of the act of washing. They are remarkably similar in the writings of Cyril, Ambrose, Chrysostom, and Theodore. After the catechumenate, the season of Lent and election, scrutinies and exorcisms, the rite at the font takes place. First, those to be baptized stand in an outer darkened chamber, symbolizing renunciation of the past. They face the west, the night, sin and death and Satan; and they disavow them. They undress, and their whole bodies are anointed with rich oil.

Second, they are led gleaming to the pool and in the shimmering light of lamps, confess the faith and are led into the font step by step. There, guided by the hand of the deaconess or deacon, they are plunged into the dark cold waters and emerge three times. This is accompanied by a formula of baptism. They are then led out of the pool, anointed, touched, kissed, and fed.

What happens in this baptismal act is precisely what the prayer over the water invoked: a candidate is changed into Christ the crucified one and the new Adam. He or she is born again or transubstantiated.

Although the washing and anointing were pivotal points in the initiation process, they were not absolute. If death should come before the water, the catechumen or elect was still buried as a Christian. Further, to die as a witness to Christ replaced the baptismal washing absolutely, for martyrs are washed clean in the blood of the Lamb.

These texts for the blessing of water and the description of the rite were soon translated into architectural forms and images that we must now explore.

The Iconography of Fonts

Fonts in the East and the West had three similarities: they were essentially shallow baths, built for adults, and located in special rooms. In fact the Constantinian church plan was an assembly of rooms set aside for a variety of purposes.

The size of the fonts varied greatly. The smallest

was 96 centimeters wide by 1 meter and 61 centimeters long; the largest, located at St. John Lateran, was 8 meters wide (approximately 25 feet across). The general depths were between 50 and 65 centimeters, about 24 inches. One font in Greece, however, was a full meter deep. No font seems to have been deep enough for total submersion, which means that the act of washing was an immersion.

The basic character of the fonts as baptismal baths is the primary and anthropological iconography of the font. The bath signifies a ritual place of washing, not because one is soiled but because one descends into the font having one identity and ascends from it with another. This datum is transcultural and archetypal; it is just as true of Qumran, the Ganges River, and the Taurobolion of Methra.

There is also a basic religious iconography associated with the decoration of fonts, which is what makes them Christian places of washing. The iconography of the fonts corresponds to the known prayers of blessing and popular homilies. Those prayers and homilies explored the passages concerned with water in the Hebrew Bible and applied them as parallels to the Jesus event. The recurring images are primarily concerned with creation, redemption, and purification.

Images of Creation

In general, the creation typology is prevalent in the Eastern church, which celebrated initiation at Epiphany. Redemption typology was preferred in Roman circles. The West celebrated initiation at the Paschal vigil or Pentecost. Purification typology is found in the East and the West, in Orthodox and Arian churches.

The creation typology makes baptism an act of returning to the origins of the earth. Because the font is the place of new creation, images of Christ's incarnation are the demarcation point. Creation is glorified in the event and evil overcome. The new creation imagery is drawn from nature. Some of the specific images are taken from the Psalms, but other biblical sources are also apparent. Among these images are peacocks (as symbols of eternity); deer (slaying snakes and slaking their thirst); fruit trees, as in the Garden of Eden; the four rivers of Eden; Adam and Eve; stars (as a symbol of creation and of the covenant with Abraham); birds; and a baldachin or apse to symbolize the vault of heaven.

The creation typology prefers the circular font as a sign of new creation and birth, thus also affirming the long tradition of the circle as the symbol of fullness.

These creation images are found on many tombs, such as the Galla Placidia in Ravenna. Many churches also have a similar iconography.

Images of Redemption

The redemption typology takes its imagery from the cross of Christ and his entombment. The shapes of the fonts are often quadrilateral or even cruciform. Three steps lead into the font and three out of it, so that the neophyte's descent into the water parallels the three days Jesus spent in the tomb. Cardinal Danielou describes the descent into the font as a seven-step process. Three steps are taken in the name of the Trinity, and three represent the time in the tomb. The seventh step, the step out of the font, is the Sabbath rest God took at the completion of creation.

The deluge, Noah and the Ark, the dove, and the eight survivors of the flood also contribute to the redemption imagery. The number eight plays an important part: not only were there eight survivors for the new world, but also it was the eighth day, the day after the Sabbath, that Jesus chose to inaugurate the new era. This eschatology is clearly found in the eight-sided fonts in Hagia Sophia and St. John Lateran. The symbolism of eight sides also relates to the creation typology.

The six-sided font is also an image of redemption, for it represents the sixth day, the day of Jesus' death and the day God created man and woman. Further redemption images are the harrowing of hell, the crossing of the Red Sea, the slaying of the leviathan, the apocalyptic image of the throne, and the glorified cross.

Each image suggests a new era begotten in the waters of death and ushering in the last days. All that is evil has been overcome in the triumph of the cross. Satan flees, and all the heavenly hosts fill the sky with hosannas, for the Lord is risen and the people are set free as in the great Exodus.

Images of Purification

The third source of icons associated with baptism celebrates a purification typology. This imagery, crossing all architectural settings, is focused primarily on John's baptism of Christ in the Jordan, a baptism of repentance and faith. To this scene are added the purification of Joshua coming through the Jordan as he enters the chosen land and Elijah who passes through the waters of Jordan before he is taken up in the fiery chariot. We also see this symbolism in the purification of Naaman, the leper, who is washed clean in the Jordan. At Ravenna there are two primary fonts with the Jordan scene, the Arian baptistery and the Orthodox baptistery.

Guidelines for Our Practice

The architectural decoration of ancient fonts is an explicit iconography; it places the fonts within an intelligible framework. We must do more, however, than simply repeat the three sets of images. We must also try to retrieve the primary symbols. Thus, the baptismal bath is much more significant to us than the slaying of the leviathan. As authentic as the multiple images of creation, redemption, and purification are, they should be subordinate to the anthropological images of the bath and descent into the font. This is what the ancient church really cared about, the essential meaning of the font.

With one eye on the authenticity of the ancient experience and another on today's needs, we can draw out a few basic guidelines for our efforts to revitalize our baptismal practice.

First, it is the act of washing, not just water, that carries meaning. We have tended to theologize symbols rather than experience them, in part because we accepted the patristic era's typology, but not its anthropology. The patristic period was marked by the process of doing rather than the static realism that makes objects sacred apart from the rites that give them birth and sustain them. The act of washing, not water as pure symbol, is the bearer of meaning.

Second, we should look upon the washing as a public action focused on the individual. When the Roman church started celebrating baptism privately, the font became a symbolic "door to the sacraments" rather than a place of ritual action. The sixteenth century reformers abandoned the locked basin at the entry in favor of simple bowls placed on or near the altar, thus permitting the presence of the assembly as a witness to God's grace. So if we begin to look at the place of baptismal washing as a place of dynamic ritual and assembly, we will be appropriating the valid insights of the reformers.

Third, the act of washing should be seen in a wider constellation of rites, especially anointing and Eucharist. With the initiation rites of 1969 and 1972 dealing with the baptism of infants and adults, the Roman liturgy has once again placed baptism in its broadest ritual context. This emphasis on process and a wider constellation of rites comprising the sacrament of initiation stems from a patristic theology that sees the bath as a generous gift of God. This could mean a balance between works and grace, or between process and gift.

Fourth, the shape, depth and iconography of the font should support a basic theological understanding, namely that the act of washing is based in the full adult experience. When infants became the primary candidates for baptism, architecture responded to the practice and began to raise the fonts from the basins that sat in the floor to containers on pedestals because they were more convenient. In the patristic literature, fonts are places of water that can be entered, places in which the adult's coming to faith is the paradigm. Respecting this insight will call for dramatic changes in the architectural setting for baptism. Fonts will become baptismal pools rather than pieces of furniture.

Fifth, and finally, we must consider the location of the font. As I mentioned earlier, the patristic period developed fonts in specially designed rooms. Today the location of the font is necessarily in a place of assembly, to accommodate our new awareness of the community's role. We must look, therefore, for a public place. The two locations most frequently used are the sanctuary and the entry. I feel, however, that neither of these is the best solution to the problem.

If ritual is something to engage in and not simply to watch, we have a principle for locating the font apart from the sanctuary as it is presently conceived. Further, if the end point of worship is the Table, we have a principle for maintaining the stational character of the patristic period. While this may not imply a separate room, it does require a separation. As for the second image of the baptismal font as "the door to the sacraments," a font in the entry tends to eliminate totally the public character of the washing. Unless the entry allows for total community assembly, we have a symbol without a function. It is clear that we need deeper experiences of community ritual to reveal to us the best location for baptism "in the midst" of the assembly.

The patristic evidence has silhouetted the wrong turns we have made in the past; it challenges us to probe the issue of the font as symbol of our identity. Most of all it calls us to move our focus from status symbols to process within community. The whole process of initiation is an interaction between individuals coming to the assembly and the assembly's dialogue with these persons. The font and all the other symbols—words, gestures, objects, places—serve that holy process through which God comes to life in our love for one another.

James Notebaart[73]

310 • THE FONT AS A PLACE FOR BURIAL, BIRTH, AND BATH

The sacrament of Christian baptism presents a variety of symbolic meanings. In one ritual act, the new Christian is buried with Christ in his death, is birthed to a new life with Christ, and is washed of sin and impurity. This article explains the relationship of these meanings and their implications for the design of baptismal fonts and the practice of baptism today.

Water creates and destroys, brings to life and drowns. Without water people and animals and plants wither and die. Water extinguishes fires; it cleanses and refreshes. God created water for life and death and bathing. It is God's instrument for salvation and destruction. As the waters of the flood brought death, so the waters of the Exodus—"swept by a strong east wind"—brought life.

Christian baptism is also water for life and death and bathing. Wherever abundant water flows, there is a setting for baptism: Jesus was baptized in the Jordan River (Mark 3:9-11), and Paul baptized Lydia in a river near Philippi (Acts 16:13-15). Rivers, lakes, and the sea continued to be the usual sites for baptism for two or three centuries. In the second century, however, because Christians were still under persecution, baptism may sometimes have occurred in the bathing rooms and courtyard fountains of private homes and in small public baths.

Early Baptisteries

In the third and fourth centuries, particularly after the emperor Constantine ended the persecutions in 313, special places for baptism were constructed or adapted. Baptisteries were buildings, or sometimes separate areas within buildings, which contained baptismal pools known as fonts. At that period in church history, adult baptism was the norm, and baptism generally occurred during the Easter vigil. To accommodate all the candidates for baptism and to provide privacy, the baptisteries in the West were usually detached or only loosely attached to churches.

Examples of such early baptisteries still exist in Italy in such places as Ravenna, Grado, Lomello, and Rome (San Giovanni in Laterano) and in Fréjus, France. In addition, excavations have revealed other important paleo-Christian baptisteries in Italy: San Tecla in Milan (the Ambrosian baptistery), Castel Seprio, Torcello, Concordia Sagitarria, Aquileia, and San Marcello in Rome. The form of these early baptisteries and their fonts varied by geographic area and related to the architectural origin, the sacramental mode and the theological meaning of baptism.

The baptisteries seem to have at least two architectural antecedents. First, they have been influenced architecturally by martyria and mausolea, which were often quadrilateral, circular or octagonal. The fourth century baptistery of San Giovanni alle Fonti at San Tecla in Milan, for example, was modeled after Maximian's mausoleum at San Vittore. Moreover, its plan bears a striking resemblance to the extant chapel of San Aquilino, attached to San Lorenzo in Milan, which was originally built as a mausoleum and was also modeled after the San Vittore mausoleum. Also remarkable is the eleventh-century trefoil baptistery at Concordia Sagittaria, Italy, which exactly reproduced the nearby fourth-century trefoil martyrium; the martyrium itself, in fact, may have been transformed into a baptistery for a period of time.

A second architectural antecedent of baptisteries seems to have been the *frigidarium,* the cold section of Roman baths which was usually octagonal, circular, or quadrilateral. The baptistery of San Giovanni in Laterano in Rome is one example of a baptistery built over a preexistent bath. In the Constantinian era, its plan was very similar to two *frigidaria* in Pompeii.

Interpreting the Font

Fonts, more than the baptisteries in which they were located, deserve our particular attention, since it now appears that separate or detached baptisteries would contradict an emerging ecumenical consensus regarding baptismal theology and practice. According to this consensus, baptism is a part of corporate worship, to be celebrated in the congregation's presence and with their involvement.

The oldest font known to us dates from the early third century. Found in a house church in Dura-Europos (in what is now Syria), this font had the rectangular shape of a coffin. In Italy from the fourth century on, hexagonal and octagonal fonts became common. Round fonts were also found in many areas in the early church including the earliest font at the Lateral baptistery in Rome. Cruciform fonts (square, like the Greek cross) existed in Greece, Asia Minor, Syria, and Egypt.

The shapes of fonts have been interpreted according to differing theological emphases, especially burial, birth, and bathing. Paul stressed the paschal nature of baptism in his letter to the Romans:

> Do you not know that all of us who have been baptized into Christ Jesus were baptized into his death? We were buried therefore with him by baptism into death, so that as Christ was raised from the dead by the glory of the Father, we too might walk in newness of life. (Rom. 6:3-4, RSV)

This paschal motif was central in the baptismal theology of Ambrose, Cyril of Jerusalem, John Chrysostom, and Theodore of Mopsuestia (Hugh M. Riley, *Christian Initiation: A Comparative Study of the Interpretation of the Baptismal Liturgy in the Mystagogical Writings of Cyril of Jerusalem, John Chrysostom, Theodore of Mopsuestia, and Ambrose of Milan* [Washington, D.C.: The Catholic University of America Press, 1974]), and it is a common theme in patristic writings about baptismal fonts. In the late third century, Origen referred to the font as a sepulchre (*In Romanos 5:8*). A century later Chrysostom wrote that "it is as in a tomb that we immerse our heads in the water" (*In Joannem 25:2*) Ambrose of Milan, also in the late fourth century, described the font as being like a grave and a tomb (*De sacramentis 2:20* and *3:1*).

It is not surprising that baptism was usually celebrated at the Easter vigil, or that many early fonts were interpreted as symbolizing this understanding of baptism as death and resurrection with Christ. Octagonal fonts, which probably originated in the Ambrosian baptistery in Milan and can still be seen in excavations there, symbolized the eighth day, the day of resurrection, the eschatological dawning of the new age. The fifth-century Lateran font, which can no longer be seen, was also octagonal.

Hexagonal fonts suggested the sixth day as the day of Christ's death. Such paschal symbolism was particularly powerful when a hexagonal font was in an octagonal baptistery—an arrangement which can still be seen in Italy in Aquileia, Grado, and Lomello—because when the candidate for baptism

"entered the hexagonal font, he knew he was to die with Christ, but as he left the font and stood once more in the eight-sided room he also knew that he was to walk in newness of life" (J. G. Davies, *The Architectural Setting of Baptism* [London: Barrier and Rockliff, 1962], 21). Another shape, the cruciform font, symbolized the victory of Christ's resurrection.

A second major theological emphasis connects baptism with birth as in this text from the fourth gospel:

> "Truly, truly, I say to you, unless one is born anew, he cannot see the kingdom of God." Nicodemus said to him, "How can a man be born when he is old? Can he enter a second time into his mother's womb and be born?" Jesus answered, "Truly, truly, I say to you, unless one is born of water and the Spirit, he cannot enter the kingdom of God." (John 3:3-5; RSV)

Theologically, the font was seen as a womb or a mother. Clement of Alexandria wrote in the early third century that God "begot us from the womb of the water" (*Stromata 4:25*). Almost two centuries later, Augustine described the font as "the womb of the church" (*Sermones 56, De oratione dominica ad competentes*). The fifth-century Latin inscription which can still be seen on the architraves in the Lateral baptistery includes many phrases interpreting baptism as birth. Leo the Great, who may have composed the Lateral inscription, also preached about the parallelism between baptismal water and the womb. Round fonts have also been interpreted as suggesting this birth imagery.

A third theological understanding is of baptism as a bath for cleansing us from sin. Paul wrote to the Corinthians: "You were washed, you were sanctified, you were justified in the name of the Lord Jesus Christ and in the Spirit of our God" (1 Cor. 6:11; RSV). In the second century, Justin Martyr described baptism as a washing. In the next century, Cyprian of Carthage wrote frequently of baptism as washing and cleansing. It is interesting that some early baptisteries were located near or constructed over Roman baths; whether this was done for symbolic reasons or simply to connect Christians to a source of water is a matter of debate.

Despite their varying shapes, early fonts—literally pools—were always large and held abundant water. The Lateran baptismal pool was twenty-eight feet in diameter—easily accommodating the two most common modes of baptism. Immersion involved dipping the candidate's head in the water; affusion involved pouring the water over the candidate's head. In both cases, however, the candidates were standing in the water when they were baptized. Affusion as well as immersion suggested burial; water was poured over the candidate just as earth was cast on a corpse. Submersion (completely plunging the candidate under water) does not seem to have been practiced in most places in the early church because the fonts were relatively shallow.

From the sixth to the eight centuries, adult baptisms declined in number—probably due to the high infant mortality rate and parental fears resulting from Augustine's doctrine of original sin. When fonts no longer needed to be large enough for the immersion of adults or to be located in detached baptisteries to insure privacy, they were placed inside churches, usually near the main entrance. They were still relatively large—to accommodate the immersion of infants—and traditional in shape, either octagonal (suggesting resurrection), hexagonal (death with Christ), rectangular (tomb), or round (birth).

The Loss of Primary Symbols

From the Middle Ages until the present time, baptismal space has deteriorated both functionally and symbolically. As affusion (pouring) and aspersion (sprinkling) became widespread, the fonts became smaller and smaller. What was originally a river and then a pool eventually became a shallow "birdbath" and finally a small bowl. In addition, in the thirteenth century, when people began stealing the consecrated water in the font to use for witchcraft, locked covers were placed over the fonts. The covers soon became elaborate and decorative, and eventually the covers—not the water itself—became the primary visual symbol, until it was no longer possible to interpret the font with its water as either womb or tomb or even as bathtub.

As a result, today's popular understanding of baptism is often trivial. Baptism is seen as a nice little ceremony, rather than as a consequential event of death and life. Few of us perceive baptism as the profound event that Cyril of Jerusalem described in a sermon to newly-baptized Christians in the fourth century: "You died and were born at the same time. The water of salvation became for you both a tomb and a mother" (*Mystagogical Catecheses 2:4*). In-

deed, so little water is commonly used for baptism today that even the washing or cleansing motif is impossible to perceive.

Baptismal Space Today

The trivialization of fonts through the centuries resulted largely from deteriorating baptismal practices. Now, these practices are changing for the better. New and revised baptismal rites across the ecumenical spectrum have attempted to let the rite itself—its texts and actions and setting—demonstrate its profound meanings. Because we learn the meaning of the sacraments from what we do and what we see, the poor baptismal practices of centuries have taught us a poor baptismal theology.

One of the most important changes in baptismal practice today is the growing ecumenical awareness of the sign value of water, and thus the use of more abundant water in the rite. The Roman Catholic Bishops' Committee on the Liturgy has written: "To speak of symbols and of sacramental signification is to indicate that immersion is the fuller and more appropriate symbolic action in baptism" (*Environment and Art in Catholic Worship* [Washington, D.C.: United States Catholic Conference, 1978], 39). The remarkable ecumenical document, *Baptism, Eucharist, and Ministry,* agrees:

> In the celebration of baptism the symbolic dimension of water should be taken seriously and not minimalized. The act of immersion can vividly express the reality that in baptism the Christian participates in the death, burial and resurrection of Christ. (Faith and Order Paper 111:Baptism V 18 [Geneva: World Council of Churches])

Four centuries ago, in 1519, Martin Luther also affirmed the practice of immersion. He wrote that it is

> demanded by the significance of baptism itself. For baptism . . . signifies that the old man and the sinful birth of flesh and blood are to be wholly drowned by the grace of God. We should therefore do justice to its meaning and make baptism a true and complete sign of the thing it signifies. ("The Holy and Blessed Sacrament of Baptism," *Luther's Works,* ed. E. Theodore Bachman, vol. 35 [Philadelphia: Fortress Press, 1960], 29)

Immersion and even affusion—if the pouring is done with an abundant amount of water—more fully convey the meaning of baptism than mere sprinkling. The point is not how much water is necessary for baptism to be efficacious, but rather how much water it takes for us to realize the radical nature of baptism. A few drops cannot communicate the rich biblical meanings of baptism.

Renewing Our Baptismal Spaces

Baptismal space in a church building will encourage or inhibit a congregation's development of mature baptismal practices and understandings. An insignificant font kept in a corner for occasional use does not signify the permanent baptismal foundation for the Christian life. A font in any location, if it holds only a minimal amount of water, does not teach us to understand baptism as burial or birth or bath. A small bowl of water placed on the altar for baptism does not reflect the centrality of baptism in the life of the church.

Form follows function and meaning. If baptismal practices are to be renewed to make clear the meaning of baptism, then our baptismal spaces must also be renewed to enable those practices and that meaning. Water is the central symbol of baptism:

> All the things suggested by water—washing, life sustenance, refreshment, drowning, birth, creation, flood, Exodus, Jordan—support and enrich the proclamation of incorporation. The first five of these meanings connect with people's experience of water outside of liturgy, and they communicate in a supraconceptual way. For example, one cannot really explain the refreshment a shower brings after a strenuous game. The latter four meanings are conditioned or learned, and they depend upon one's knowledge of biblical history. It is water signalling on all these levels which gives depth and breadth to what is proclaimed about incorporation into Christ. Baptism is not solely a verbal event; it is a total experience. (Eugene L. Brand and S. Anita Stauffer, *By Water and the Spirit: Pastor's Guide* [Philadelphia: Parish Life Press, 1979], 25)

The most important factor about the font is the amount of water it can hold. The *Lutheran Book of Worship* (1978) suggested in its rubrics that "a font of ample proportions for the Sacrament of Holy Baptism should be part of the furnishings of the church" (*Minister's Edition,* p. 30). In the same year, *Environment and Art in Catholic Worship* advocated the same principle. A font should be large enough to accommodate at least the immersion of an infant, or ideally, the immersion of an adult. (A good example of the former is the font at St. John the Evangelist Roman Catholic Church in Hopkins, Minnesota; and of the latter, at St. Peter's Lutheran Church in Manhattan.) Even if immersion is not now practiced in a parish, the profusion of water will help people recognize the biblical water images used in the baptismal liturgy.

To communicate central baptismal imagery, a font should contain enough water that one could bathe or even drown in it. If possible, the water should be running and heated. Also, in our era when good stewardship of the earth certainly involves water conservation, the water in a font should probably be recirculated.

What, then, should be the shape of a font? The ancient octagonal and hexagonal shapes still have much to commend them. With good pastoral teaching, the shape of the font can help convey the meaning of baptism as burial and resurrection with Christ. Such emphasis seems especially important in our culture in which the denial of death is pervasive and the scandal of the cross less appealing than cheap grace.

Round, cruciform, quadrilateral, and other shapes of fonts are also possible; a remarkable new cruciform font for the immersion of adults has been constructed at St. Charles Church in London. Care should be taken, however, to avoid "cute" shapes such as shells.

Before determining the shape for a new font, a careful study of symbolism should be undertaken by the planning committee—to be followed by a program of thorough and ongoing catechesis with the entire congregation and prospective members when the new font is completed. The shape of the font is less important than its size, however, and this, too, is a matter for good catechesis.

It is not necessary for the font to be adorned with symbols. The water it holds is the central symbol, and the font itself—its size, shape and location—is also a symbol. Other symbols on the font may detract. This is not to disparage art, but only to suggest that symbols on symbols are not necessary. Likewise, it is no longer meaningful to put covers on fonts. In our culture baptismal water is not considered supernatural (though it is used for a holy purpose) or magical, and there is no need to prevent people from stealing it as they did in medieval times. It is far better to let the water be visible and tangible.

The location of the font is a matter of symbolism

and of good liturgy. First, the Word of God, the Eucharist, and baptism are three separate ecclesial acts. As there are three worship acts, so there should be three worship spaces, the pulpit, the altar and the font. Placing the font in the chancel obscures this distinction. In addition, as it minimizes the amount of movement in the liturgy, it reduces everyone's participation to passive roles.

Second, what is symbolized and enabled by the location of the font? The most appropriate location seems to be inside the main entrance to the worship space, with adequate space around it. Such a location symbolizes baptism as entrance into the family of God, the church. It is good for the font to be located so that the people must walk around it as they enter the nave, and thus be reminded each Sunday of their baptism. When baptism is celebrated, the baptismal party (and perhaps others in the congregation, especially children) gather around the font; the rest of the congregation turns to face it (even as it turns to face a bride when she enters for a wedding).

The area around the font is known as the baptistery. The paschal candle may be placed near the font (except during the weeks of Easter, when it is located near the altar) as a reminder of the primary connection between baptism and Easter. A small shelf or table is also useful in the baptistery, to hold items needed for baptism, such as oil for anointing, a towel, the baptismal garment, and the small baptismal candle.

Proclaiming the Profound

Baptism is a profound and radical act—profound because it draws us deeply into Christ and the paschal mystery, and radical because it grafts us onto the very roots of the Christian faith and into the body of Christ. Baptism is a cosmic and individual act because it makes each of us a part of salvation history. It is also a profoundly personal act with radical corporate consequences because it makes each of us a child of God and simultaneously incorporates us into the communion of saints.

Baptism is an act of termination and new beginning, a time of _transitus_—the most important passage of our lives. The words of Ash Wednesday remind us abruptly of the reality of life on earth: "Remember that you are dust, and to dust you shall return." All too soon we, too, will be but skeletons disintegrating into dust, like the remains that stare out at us from the burial niches of the catacombs.

Born from the wombs of our mothers, we move inexorably toward tombs in the earth.

But there is another reality of life in Christ: reborn in the font, the direction we move in is reversed, for the font is both a watery womb and a life-giving tomb. In baptism we move from death to new birth, from burial to resurrection, from darkness to light, from the stain of sin to the cleansing power of grace, from ourselves into the family of God. We are never the same again because the chaos and self-centeredness of our lives are washed away, and we are joined to Jesus Christ. The waters that drown us are also the waters that give us life.

Baptism is a profound and radical act of burial, of birth and bath. The sacrament is not a trivial event, but it is trivialized by insignificant fonts and small amounts of water. Baptism is not time for minimalism; it is, rather, a time for signs and actions consistent with its radical and profound meaning. Only large fonts holding abundant water can proclaim and enable baptism's wonderful consequences: death and life and salvific cleansing.

S. Anita Stauffer[74]

311 • FONTS FOR FUNCTION AND MEANING: SOME WORTHY EXAMPLES

Once the theological rationale for the design of the font has been established, artists, architects, and craftspersons face the challenge of shaping a font that reflects those convictions. This article describes three thoughtful examples of recently constructed fonts.

How can baptismal fonts be designed so that they enable ritual fullness and signify sacramental richness? That is, how can fonts be designed for both function (the immersion of adults and infants) and meaning (baptism as passage with Christ through death into life, as new birth, and as salvific washing)?

The church in the first three centuries did not need fonts; it used natural bodies of water for baptism. In the fourth through the sixth centuries, large baptismal pools were constructed, and the remains of many of them can still be visited in Europe and the Middle East. Today, however, we have inherited the minimalist fonts of the Middle Ages, and these often tiny fonts are neither adequate for the ritual actions of the baptismal liturgy nor appropriate for our renewed appreciation of baptism's profound meaning.

Fortunately, in the past two decades in the United States we have witnessed the design and construction of more adequate and ample fonts, and this article will highlight three of the best. These fonts share several very important characteristics. First, each is part *of* the space, not a furnishing *in* the space. Second, each is provided with running water in a quantity that enables the immersion of both infants and adults. Third, though the locations vary somewhat, in each case the location is related to entrance, an important baptismal image. Fourth, each is freestanding, thus providing space for the baptismal party and congregation to gather around the font.

Indianapolis, Indiana

In his 1986 renovation of the Roman Catholic Cathedral of Saints Peter and Paul in downtown Indianapolis, architect Edward A. Sovik provided an octagonal above-ground immersion pool, 5 feet 6 inches in diameter, with water approximately 20 inches deep. In overall appearance the pool resembles the ancient octagonal pools which can still be seen in northern Italy. The Sovik pool is located just inside the main entrance to the cathedral nave; a beautiful and imposing paschal candle stands beside it. The interior of the pool is polished granite, and some sections of marble arcade from the pre-renovation cathedral were used in the exterior sides. City water is used. The water does not recirculate, for reasons which, according to Sovik, are both practical (costs and pump noise) and symbolic (divine grace flows constantly). The water temperature and rate of flow can be controlled, and the pool can be drained for occasional cleaning. A removable stile facilitates entrance into and exit from the pool by adult and youth candidates for baptisms. The surrounding floor is terrazzo, so there is no damage from dripping water when neophytes go to the restrooms in the rear corner of the nave to change (a distance of about 40 feet).

Requested to provide a way to prevent children from climbing into the water, Sovik designed a brass wire "fishnet" which can be hooked into the interior of the pool about an inch below the water surface. It is easily removed when baptism is celebrated. Given the height of the pool, it seems unlikely, if not impossible, that a child could accidentally drown in it, but Sovik's solution is certainly worthy.

At one side of the pool is an upper granite basin, circular on the inside (to symbolize the infinite, according to Sovik) and square (the finite) on the exterior. This upper basin is for infant baptism and is a source for water for making the sign of the cross when entering the worship space. The interior is 24 inches in diameter and about 5 inches deep. Water flows into the upper basin and then through a brass spout into the lower pool (although the lower pool itself can also be filled directly).

The font has several strengths. Its location is optimal, both liturgically and symbolically. Its appearance is beautiful in itself and in its setting within the renovated cathedral. Its octagonal shape "speaks" the eighth day, the new day of resurrection which we enter through our baptism. It holds a large amount of water—enough water to drown in or bathe in—and thus it is a fitting vessel for holy baptism. Its size accommodates the baptism of people of any age.

The only criticism of this font regards the provision of the separate upper basin; it seems unnecessary. The lower pool itself, the top rim of which is 28¼ inches high, could easily accommodate baptizing infants by either immersion or affusion (pouring), and the water is easily accessible to hands for blessing oneself upon entrance to the nave. Double-level fonts are becoming common (and, as they go, this one is well designed and visually well connected to the main pool), but in this case, it is not necessary. In a society where theological debate continues about the merits of infant baptism, it would seem better for liturgical churches not to have multilevel fonts which may suggest that infant baptism is different from adult baptism.

Concord, California

The font at the new St. Francis of Assisi Roman Catholic Church in Concord (east of San Francisco) is a below-ground cruciform pool set within an octagon. Designed by architect Frank Mighetto, the building was completed in late 1986. The pool is approximately 6½ feet across, with water about 2½ feet deep. On two opposite sides of the cross are three steps into and out of the water—thus enabling descent into the waters as well as passage through the waters, both principal baptismal images. The interior of the pool is faced in attractive blue porcelain ceramic tile. The slightly raised slate tile octagon on which the pool is placed is symbolic of the eighth day. The paschal candle stand is placed on one side of the raised octagon.

At one side of the pool is a 30-inch raised stone font for infant baptism; it is a 9-inch deep octagonal basin within a square base. Water is pumped into the raised basin and then flows over one edge into the lower pool. The water is heated, recirculated for conservation, and filtered to inhibit algae.

The font is located within a narthex which, because of an ingeniously designed colonnade, creates the appearance of an octagonal baptistery at the main entrance to the nave. Just as the church itself resembles an early Christian basilica, the baptistery/narthex gives the visual hint of an ancient baptistery. Adjacent to the narthex are restrooms which may be used as changing rooms for adult baptism. The narthex floor is slate tile, so splashed or dripped water is no problem.

This is an impressive font, functional and powerful in its visual and symbolic impact. Mighetto has done well combining two principal motifs of baptism—death (cruciform pool) and resurrection (octagonal shape used for base, infant baptism, and baptistery area). Materials and colors are good.

Still, one wonders whether the location of the baptistery separate from the nave is the best idea. True, the entrance motif is clear. And true, the doors between this baptistery and nave are large. But perhaps it would have been better for liturgical reasons to locate the font within the nave itself or in such a way that it is clearly visible from every seat in the nave. A second possible criticism is the provision of the separate basin for infants, although here entrance blessing in the below-ground pool would be difficult (in contrast to Sovik's raised pool in Indianapolis). Infant baptism in the lower pool would require the priest to enter the water. A third criticism relates to the placement of many plants around the entire perimeter of the pool. Presumably it is to keep children from climbing into the water, but surely there are better solutions if in fact this is a problem (remember Sovik's solution in Indianapolis). The near-jungle of plants greatly distracts from the font.

New York, New York

Saint Peter's Lutheran Church in Manhattan, dedicated in 1977, has a large above-ground immersion pool at the entrance to the worship space. The font gives the impression of a square with $9\frac{1}{3}$-foot sides, although one corner is cut off for the steps down into it. The rim of the pool is 34 inches above the ground, and the water level at the bottom of the steps is 22 inches. The pool is constructed of granite, the same as the floor of the entranceway and nave. The architect was High A. Stubbins, Jr., with interior design by Vignelli Associates.

The water can be heated and recirculated. There is no purification system, and the pool is emptied weekly for cleaning and then refilled with fresh water.

The location of the font at the rear corner of the worship space is excellent both liturgically and symbolically. All persons entering the worship space must pass by the font, and they can easily dip their fingers in the water to trace on themselves the sign of the cross in remembrance of their baptism. Adults being baptized must descend into the water, a good baptismal image. Infants can be baptized by either immersion or affusion without the pastor entering the water.

The shape of the font, however, lacks the symbolic impact of those at Indianapolis and Concord. While it holds abundant water, the shape itself does not teach anything about the meaning of baptism. The other weakness of the space is the failure to provide nearby changing rooms.

Conclusion

While none of these fonts are perfect, they are all worthy examples of attempts to provide fonts which make an adequate statement about baptismal theology and which enable and encourage significant ritual action.

S. Anita Stauffer[75]

Secondary Visual Arts for Worship

Complementing the Table or altar, font, and pulpit in a space for Christian worship are a variety of secondary visual arts that heighten the impact of the primary visual arts, serve the function of the primary visual arts, and contribute to the celebrative ethos of the worship space. These secondary visual arts include contributions by sculptors, weavers, potters, painters, and a variety of other artists and provide many opportunities for ongoing contributions by visual artists to the worship life of the local congregation.

312 • An Introduction to the Secondary Visual Arts in Worship

Because worship celebrates the gospel, the most visual images of worship are those which express the body of Christ assembled around Word, Table and font. Consequently, secondary symbols must serve the primary symbols by pointing to them and never dominating or overpowering them. The following secondary symbols have an important place in worship and will function well as servants of the primary symbols.

Table (Altar) Hangings

In the early church, cloths were probably not placed on the Table. However, by the third century there is evidence that a silk cloth covered the Table. By the fourth century, Christians began to decorate the cloth with embroidery and jewels, so much so that a warning against paying too much attention to the cloth was issued by John Chrysostom, the Bishop of Constantinople. Over the decorated cloth another linen cloth was placed for the celebration of the Eucharist. In the medieval era this top cloth was replaced by a frontal cloth which hung down the front of the altar (now placed against the back wall of the church). In renewed practice today the Table is either left bare or an inconspicuous cloth is spread. Elaborate cloths are shunned since they tend to call attention to themselves and detract from the sight of bread and wine, the dominant visuals of the action taking place at the Table.

In traditions where the Table is set with bread and Communion dishes holding the individual cups, a cloth covers the elements until the service at the Table begins. Many churches are eliminating the cloth, because it gives the appearance of a covered body. By allowing the elements to be seen, the image of the resurrection is communicated. This symbol is in keeping with the emphasis of renewed worship on the presence of the risen Lord at the Table.

Banners

The use of banners to communicate ideas and create feelings goes back before Old Testament times. The armies of the Egyptians, the Persians, and the Assyrians used banners. The various tribes of Israel adopted them as well (Num. 2:2). In medieval times, tapestries of wool, linen, and silk made of bright colors and embellished with gold threads were made by simple folk for use in worship. In modern times, banners have been rediscovered and revived for use in the worship.

There are three basic rules to keep in mind about the use of banners in worship. The first is that they are not decoration. A banner is never a piece of art-work placed somewhere in the church to add color or serve some aesthetic purpose. The second rule is that a banner communicates. It says something about what is happening in the specific worship service in which it appears. Therefore, thirdly, banners have a limited use and are not to be thought of as permanent fixtures in a worship setting. A banner may be associated with a season such as Advent or Lent. It could be hung on the wall during the entire season. It could be used for the entrance procession, placed in a stand during worship, and used again in the recessional.

If these three rules are followed, banners will retain their function as servants of the Word. On the other hand, churches that choose to decorate their worship space with many banners hanging from the ceiling or on the walls will find that their presence will overpower the primary symbols; they will clutter the space and detract from the main focus of worship with too many messages.

Candles

The significance of candles in worship is not related to the candle itself, but to the light it projects. Christ is the light of the world, and the light of the candle speaks this truth.

The use of the candle in worship probably goes back to the paschal vigil service held on the night before Easter dawn. The service began with the lighting of fire, emphasizing Christ, the light. From this fire a single candle, known as the paschal (Passover) candle, was lit. It was used as the main candle in worship that year, lighting other candles used in various worship settings.

Throughout history the candle has been used in various ways. In the Roman Catholic church it has been customary to burn six candles on the altar, seven if a bishop is celebrating the Eucharist. In Eastern Orthodox worship, a seven-branched candlestick stands on the altar. Most Protestant churches have used candles for special services, such as Christmas Eve, but have rejected the use of candles in the sanctuary during worship.

In modern worship renewal, it is customary to set two candles on the Table of the Lord as symbols of Christ, the light of the world. Two lit candles may also be used at the reading of the gospel as acolytes stand on both sides of the reader.

Numerous candles may be used in processions and with the entire body of worshipers, particularly in services that celebrate the birth or resurrection of Christ.

Since there are no universal rules about the use of candles in worship, each congregation determines its own use, keeping in mind that candles are never mere decorations, but reminders of Word, Table, and font.

Chalice and Paten

The chalice is the cup which holds wine, symbolizing the blood of Christ shed for the forgiveness of sin; the paten is the dish which holds bread, symbolizing the body of Christ broken for our salvation. These liturgical utensils of the Table have been the object of considerable artistic attention throughout history because of their functional importance.

Today artists both privately and commercially are expressing the importance of the body and blood of Christ through chalices and patens that fit aesthetically into the larger artistic environment of the church. It is important in making or purchasing a chalice and a paten to keep in mind their functional roles. They are not decorations and should not call attention to themselves. Their roles as servants of the primary symbols of wine and bread should be kept in mind.

After the Reformation, many Protestant churches introduced individual cups in place of the chalice. Today many churches are returning to the chalice or using both chalice and individual cups. Where individual cups are used the dish that holds them is usually made of pewter or silver and serves the primary symbol well. However, the introduction of plastic cups as a replacement of the original glass cups poses a problem. Plastic does not serve well the importance of Christ's shed blood. It tends to cheapen the primary symbol and detract from its importance. If the individual cups are retained, it is advisable to return to the glass cups even though considerable time is spent in cleaning them.

Color in Worship

Over a period of time, certain colors have developed meanings that serve the seasons of the Christian year. The use of color in worship is not rooted in any biblical precedent, but in developments in the medieval era. For the first thousand years of the church, vestments were always white, and color was used indiscriminately in the church. During the twelfth century colors were organized according to different seasons and various festivals. By the early thirteenth century Innocent III ruled that white is for feast days, red for martyrs' days, and black for penitential seasons. Today various colors are used to correspond with the seasons:

Advent:	Royal blue or purple. Royal blue is a kingly color representing the second coming of Christ the King, and purple is the color of repentance.
Christmas:	White or gold. These are colors for festive occasions.
After Epiphany:	Green. This is the color for ordinary time signifying continuity.
Lent:	Purple for penitence.
Holy Week:	Black for sobriety.
Easter:	White and gold for festivity.
Pentecost:	Red for the martyrs of the church.
After Pentecost:	Green for continuity.

Colors are also used for specific occasions:

Baptism:	White or red.
Confirmation:	White or red.
Ordination:	White.
Marriage:	White.
Funeral:	Violet, blue, or black.
Dedication of a Church:	White.

Colors may be used on the following items: vestments, pulpit hanging, Table cloth, and banners.

Cross

A variety of crosses appear in many churches—Orthodox, Catholic and Protestant. The use of the cross as a visual symbol has a complicated history. An empty cross was used very early, symbolizing the Resurrection. Processional crosses, for example, can be found as early as the fourth century. In the twelfth century realistic crucifixes with the suffering Christ were introduced, mainly by the Franciscans.

Today, both the crucifix and the empty cross are used in worship: one symbolizing the death, the other the resurrection of Christ. In many churches a large cross may appear on the wall as a symbol of both death and resurrection. Care should be taken that such a cross does not become the dominant symbol in the church, overpowering the primary symbols. It is best when the cross is made in a design and material complimenting the primary symbols of pulpit, Table, and font or pool. When used in a processional, a cross is placed in a stand next to the Table and used again to lead the recessional.

Glass

Stained glass windows originated in the medieval period. Their original purpose was to tell a story, the deeds of a biblical character, or the proclamation of a message, such as the judgment.

Today stained glass is still used in many churches, although the cost prohibits its lavish use. There are a number of different kinds of glass: (1) architectural glass is a stained glass that is actually built into a building's architectural design and functions not only as a visual art, but as an integral part of the building's structure; (2) translucent glass is designed to cast a light into the sanctuary. Thus "opaque" glass allows for a considerable amount of light, even colored light, while "beveled" glass casts a pure prism of color, and "clear brown" glass, because of its lines, will sparkle with light in the glass itself; (3) overlaid glass is glass upon which a colored plastic film has been applied; (4) painted glass is glass on which a scene has been actually painted then baked on; (5) opalescent glass is a heavy thick glass that has a scene glued onto it. Instead of reflecting light, it absorbs light and displays its colors; (6) leaded glass has been assembled by strips of lead oxide and affixed to the glass with metal joints soldered together with putty.

In contemporary worship renewal, glass has a place as long as it does not call attention to itself. Its should create a mood and not be an image to ponder. As such it should speak to the unconscious mind, not the conscious mind. It should assist the gospel and its primary symbols by evoking feelings of joy and wonder, trust and love. The true function of glass is to create an atmosphere in which the worshiper senses the power of God's love and transcendence.

Liturgical Books

In the medieval era it became customary to adorn the books from which the services were read, especially the gospel book, with symbols of beauty, such as pictures set in the midst of jewels.

In contemporary worship renewal, artistic attention is being paid again to books used in worship. The emphasis is on simplicity of design so that the books do not become objects of attention, but objects that serve the gospel by creating an atmosphere of respect.

Projection and Lighting Techniques

Due to the advances of technology in recent decades, it is possible to create "projected environments" for a particular occasion of worship. Slide projectors, overhead projectors, and various lighting techniques can be employed in a variety of ways to create such an environment. Various images can be projected onto walls, ceilings, or screens to trigger the imagination. Because this kind of visual imagery easily can be an end in itself, quickly overpowering the more subtle communication of the primary symbols of Table, pulpit, and font, it is important to use these technologies sparingly.

Pyx

A pyx is a box or receptacle that houses the consecrated elements of bread and wine reserved for the sick or shut-in members of the church.

The practice of reserving the elements for those absent from worship is mentioned by Justin Martyr in the middle of the second century. In the early centuries of the church, the elements were probably taken to the sick and shut-in immediately. However, by the fourth century the reserved elements were kept in the church, probably in the sacristy. Consequently, the necessity arose of making a receptacle where they were kept. By the ninth century regulations concerning those boxes were issued, resulting in containers that were not only artistically beautiful, but kept in places where they could be seen and adored. In some cases they were kept in private rooms, and in others hung from a chain in a beautiful box over the altar.

In contemporary worship renewal the pyx should be kept in an open, but inconspicuous place. It may be artistically beautiful to reflect the importance of the elements it houses, but it is not to call attention to itself and detract from the primary symbol of the Table.

Vestments

Vestments, or the clothing worn by the worship celebrants, originated in the fourth and fifth centuries. During the first three centuries of Christianity the celebrant wore the civilian dress of the Roman empire: the alb, stole, and chasuble. During the fourth and fifth centuries, Roman dress changed under the influence of the barbarians, who introduced trousers and shirts. However, Roman dress for the celebrants of worship did not change. The consequent differentiation resulted in a distinct clerical dress for worship.

Throughout history the vesture worn by the clergy has undergone considerable change, expansion, and development. The details of these changes need not be outlined here. Nevertheless, it is important to note that where a vestment became a "thing in itself" and lost its relationship to worship, the art of vestments became cluttered and overdone.

Most Protestants rejected the wearing of vestments. While Anglicans and Lutherans continued to use vestments, many of the Reformed bodies wore the Geneva gown, a black robe similar to an academic gown with white tabs attached to the collar. In America, many pastors, particularly those of the Presbyterian tradition, wore a Prince Albert suit, a black coat with tails and striped trousers, a dress outfit popular in the nineteenth century.

As a result of the twentieth century renewal, many churches are returning to the ancient use of the simple alb, stole, and chasuble.

An alb is a long white robe secured at the waist with a belt; the stole is a wide strip of cloth that hangs around the neck and down the front of the body. It is a sign of pastoral and priestly office and thus worn only by the ordained. The color of the stole is normally the color of the church season. It may be adorned with a cross or a symbol of the church season. The chasuble is originally an outer cloak worn over other clothing. Liturgically, it is worn during the celebration of the Table by the celebrant as the eucharistic garment. The color of the garment depends on the season of the church year. It may also be adorned with symbols depicting the particular event celebrated, or it may bear symbols of regional or ethnic importance.

In choosing or making vestments, several matters should be kept in mind: (1) a vestment is a liturgical apparel and not a mere costume. Therefore, it speaks of the role, office, or function of the celebrant in the sacred action in the assembled community; (2) a vestment should be chosen with regard to the space in which it is to be used. It should serve the space and not overpower it or be a dominant factor within it.

Who should wear what vestment in a service is as follows:

Clergy Presiding Over the Table:	Alb, stole, and chasuble.
Clergy at a Noneucharistic Service:	Alb and stole.
Deacon:	Alb and stole.
Child Server or Acolyte:	Alb or white shirt/blouse with dark pants/skirt.
Lay Eucharistic Minister:	Alb or street clothes.
Lector:	Street clothes.
Choir:	Robes.
Cantor:	A robe with the opposite color of the choir robes.

Summary

A visual art never exists in worship as an end in itself. What is of first importance is the celebration of the gospel which takes place at the pulpit, the Table, and sometimes at the font. These primary symbols are served by many secondary symbols, whose function is always to signify the primary action or to assist this action. Consequently, their appropriate place must always be carefully planned lest they overpower the primary symbols and thus function in a negative rather than a positive way.

Robert Webber

313 • THE SIGNIFICANCE OF ICONS IN ORTHODOX WORSHIP

The Eastern church has long valued the significance of icons as sources of revelation in worship. With insights from the Eastern Orthodox churches, the theological rationale and traditional practice of iconography is described here in terms of its role in worship.

Windows on the Holy

There is an old story about a child in a Sunday School class who is asked by her teacher, "And who are the saints?" Thinking of the elaborate stained-glass windows lining the nave of the church, the child responds, "They're the people that the light shines through."

In a certain sense, that is the task of the liturgy: to be, like the saints (or the stained-glass windows), a means through which God's light might shine, might reach us. And that has always been the pri-

The Genevan Gown. This black robe, tailored like the traditional academic gown, with bell sleeves and white collar tabs, is favored by many Protestant denominations. Its use can be traced back to John Calvin's Geneva.

mary role of iconography as well: to be a window, a doorway, a glimpse of the light of God's kingdom.

Yet to Western eyes, icons can often seem dark, sad, primitive. Icons without interpretation are meaningless: flat paintings, mysterious, and filled with the unknown. They can touch us only when we learn to use their language; for while Western Christianity tends to be rational, icons speak directly to one's intuition, to one's heart.

Icons are not only illustrations of biblical stories but also they are the embodiment of an ancient practice of meditation on these stories. The Western Christian's experience of icons is similar to entering into a church where an unfamiliar liturgy is being celebrated: until the language has been learned, until the meaning behind the words and the gestures has been absorbed, then indeed the observer is in foreign territory. One has to be educated, through usage and experience and love, until finally the intrinsic values become meaningful; then one can fully participate.

But for both liturgy and iconography, once their meanings have been assimilated and internalized, they are transformed into gateways, new ways of expression, new ways of reaching out to God—and, for many, new ways in which God might touch us.

The Encounter

The icon is an encounter, a moment in time and space where everyday life connects with the holy. Entering an Orthodox church gives one, immediately, the impression of having entered into a different world. Strange and intricate metal lamps hang from the ceiling. The nave of the church is separated from the altar area by a high screen, called the _iconostasis,_ covered with icons. Incense drifts about on the air. The dome overhead is painted with yet another icon, an image of Christ looking down from on high, raising a hand in blessing. Pillars that support the church are painted with images of the apostles, pillars of the church in a less literal sense. Nothing is gratuitous; nothing is superficial. The sense of being in a different world is intentional, for an Orthodox church is decorated to represent the kingdom of heaven. There is no disorder, but instead a sense of heavenly peace, order, and grace.

The Orthodox church is an important environment for the icons, for they too are meant to emphasize something much more profound than that which immediately meets the eyes. There is no sense of "looking at" icons in the same way that one might normally approach art. If anything, we do not look at the icons, but they instead look out at us. Icons are considered to be as much a medium of revelation as the spoken or printed Word. The grace and truth of God is not limited to the intellect; it can enter the soul through the eyes and the heart as well.

The liturgy, too, is a medium of revelation, a moment of encounter between the soul and God. There is a sense, almost, of being involved in a dance with the holy, a movement, a meeting, an experience.

The iconostasis separating the nave from the altar existed in Christian churches from very early times, as can be seen from some of the writings of St. Gregory the Theologian and St. John Chrysostom; it is thought by many that they were originally an adaptation of the curtain covering the ark of the covenant in Jewish temples. Although it is easy to construe the separation as representing elitism on the part of the clergy, who alone may be on the altar side of the screen, it is more in keeping with the Orthodox mind to see the screen as emphasizing the mystery of God. It divides the human world from the divine, but also unites those worlds into one image in which all separation is overcome and reconcilation is found.

In the center of the iconostasis is a door, called the holy door, with a figured top; this is the entrance into the altar area. Only the clergy may enter, but, significantly, they may go through only at specific moments, as required by the liturgy. So we see the clergy not as a privileged class, but as the servants of the liturgy, the servants of God, the servants of mystery.

Immediately above the door is an icon of the Last Supper (often called the mystical supper), separating out the sacerdotal office of Christ expressed in his action as priest. It brings the faithful into the mystery of the Eucharist, the primordial liturgical action, by providing an image for the action and a space in which that action takes place.

It is also significant that the screen can be seen as being punctured by the door: the smooth progression of icons is interrupted by this entrance into the altar area. It is not an incidental feature of the iconostasis, for it is important to see the many ways in which our lives and our world are punctured by the presence of God reaching through and getting involved with us. That too is the role of the liturgy: a particular, sanctified space in our lives where God can reach through and touch us.

An Expression of the Faith Community

The liturgy is composed of people playing different roles. The assembly, including the celebrant or officiant, the choir, the deacon, the director of music, the lectors, the preacher, the chalicists, all have specific, assigned roles within the liturgy which make it a complete, whole act. Each role is different, yet each role is vital to the whole. Without any single one, it becomes unbalanced, askew, diffused.

In the same way, many people take part in the creation and use of an icon. The icon begins with the idea, the need, the commission; centered and grounded in prayer, the concept for an icon is given birth. The parish priest, a parishioner, or the community of faith may decide that the need for an icon is present. The icon-painter, or iconographer (for icons are said to be written, not painted), is then engaged to take on a work of spiritual expression. This is a strictly liturgical art, combining all parts of the liturgy into a theology at a different level than that which is written and appeals primarily to the mind of the worshiper.

Just as the icon is seen as a means to an end, so too is the iconographer, fulfilling the work of externalizing a spiritual reality. The iconographer is the servant of God, the Orthodox liturgical tradition, and the sacred legacy of prayer that lies at the heart of the Orthodox church. Therefore the iconographer enters into a period of prayer and fasting, a time of preparation, before beginning work on an icon; for divine inspiration is necessary in order to produce something that will be inspirational.

The iconographer is not free to express his or her own thoughts or ideas; icons are part of a given tradition and must follow the rhythms of that tradition. The methods for painting the icons have been elaborated over centuries of practice; the gestures, the symbols, the faces themselves follow a prescribed pattern that does not allow for deviation. What is being depicted is not the power and mastery of the artist, but the traditional teachings of the church.

Similarly, the liturgy contains certain moments that allow for individual expression, but the liturgist in general is held to prescribed patterns, rhythms, cadences. The liturgy expresses the teachings of the church, not the dynamism of the celebrant. Christians are formed by the ways in which they pray: if prayer (and the liturgies and icons that flow from prayer) is sloppy, haphazard or capricious, then so too will be people's lives and their theology. Just as the community of faith has a right to know what to expect when entering into the worship of God in the church, so too does the community have a right to know what to expect when using icons in prayer and worship.

These patterns are a clue to the icons' meaning and give us the key to touching and entering into their mystery. Holiness is depicted as it cannot be in earthly life, where saints pass by us daily without our knowing—by halos and bright colors. There is no source of light in an icon, for there are no shadows in the kingdom of God. Icons have no reflections, no point of view, no dramatic shafts of illumination. Iconographers call "light" the background of the icon and make it gold. Eyes are large and luminous, for they have seen God's glory. The nose is narrow, the mouth small because there is less need for physical satisfactions. Figures are elongated, purposely, to prevent idolatry; they are clearly representations and not graven images. The Christ child is always shown as being larger than life, for he is not a helpless baby, but a crowned king.

The teachings of the church occur, again and again, in simple additions to the icons. After the Council of Nicaea, the Greek letters alpha and omega were added to icons of Christ in order to stress the teachings on his divinity. In the same way, Athanasius is always portrayed as holding the Scriptures which he fought so long and hard to preserve.

The liturgy, rhythmically and in simplicity, also upholds these teachings. The Nicene Creed is part of many liturgies. Versicles and responses contain Scripture passages, repeated week after week, until they become intrinsic to the life of the worshiper. The Eucharist celebrates a belief held in common by the community of faith, and burial rites reflect the church's teachings concerning eternal life.

So it is that liturgy and iconography weave together the story of the church, the story of the community of faith, held in common and repeated over the centuries in time honored rituals. And all people—iconographers, liturgists, worshipers—have equal and important parts in them.

Glimpses of Truth

Icon comes from a Greek word that means "image." This is the same word used in Genesis to describe God's creation of humankind in God's own image. It is the same word used by the Pauline author of the letter to the Colossians when speaking of Christ: "He is the image of the invisible God" (Col. 1:15). An image is an imprint, a shadow, a reflection of something that cannot be duplicated. An icon is an image, the image of something greater than can be understood in human terms.

If the icon can be seen as liturgy, then the liturgy too can be seen as an icon. Both tell us who we are in relation to God and the community of faith; both give us a point of reference. And when they "work," when they are beautiful, haunting, and filled with a longing for God, then there is a crowning on the whole effort, the seal of conformity of image to prototype, of symbol to what it represents: closeness with God.

Neither liturgy nor iconography pretends to be anything other than an image; neither seeks to duplicate the splendor and majesty of the kingdom of God. Both give us glimpses of it; both give a space in which to reenact it; both hold out the tantalizing promise and assurance of God's love here and now. Neither the icon nor the liturgy promises to be perfect, but both promise to be truthful. In a sense, the liturgy itself is an icon of God's presence in the world, reflected back through our humanity, imperfectly, but always truthfully.

The Icon in Liturgy

Just as the liturgy can be seen as an icon, so too can the icon be seen as a participant in the liturgy, drawing the faithful, through its images, into closer union with God.

The people portrayed in icons do not gesticulate; there is nothing disorderly or chaotic about their movements. Rather, they officiate; there is always a liturgical character to movement in an icon.

They can be seen, therefore, in a real sense, as officiants at a liturgy, leading the community of faith into a closer, deeper relationship with the triune God. The icons fill the ache for beauty, for holiness, for grace, that is in all of us; and they do so by imparting the grace of the Holy Spirit, the holiness of God, the beauty of Christ. The icon is the way and the means; it is the prayer itself. Not surprisingly, therefore, icons are used in conjunction with meditative or contemplative prayer, complementing the prayer of the liturgy with the prayer of the heart.

There is the key. There is no reason why God cannot touch us in many different ways: through our minds, hearts, and senses. Just as the meaning of the gospels is hidden in symbolism, so too is the meaning of the icons understood only through the heart that takes them into itself. As Westerners, we have been taught that science and logic will explain everything. It is difficult for us to conceive that the language of intuition can lead to eternal truths. Yet this is the language touched on by the icons and the liturgy: the language that speaks directly to the soul.

As the various liturgies take place in the Orthodox church, the community of faith finds its eyes drawn to the iconostasis, to the images that glow with the light of God. It is all one whole: words, incense, music, icons. It is the soul speaking to God in a language that the intellect cannot hear.

If liturgy begins in worship, then it must continue in the world. For liturgy is not only an encounter in which God is revealed to God's people, but also a response to that encounter: the people of God carrying out God's work in the world.

Nor do the icons stay in church. A visitor to the home of any Orthodox family is struck immediately by the role of the icons in everyday family life: they adorn the walls, they are significant people who have special meaning in this particular household. A china cupboard, its doors flung open, holds icons and candles, a point of reference for the family's prayer life. Small children run to it and bring out their favorite icons for the visitor's inspection: this is my name-saint, one will say, and launch into a description of that saint's life and attributes. I like St. Nicholas because I am engaged, and he was kind to young brides, shyly adds an older sibling. They are a familiar and almost cozy part of the household, and they serve to teach the children about the church.

Indeed, no one can visit an Orthodox church and look at all of the icons without coming away with a strong sense of that church's beliefs. Gospel scenes are depicted. Parables are portrayed. Judas and the devil alone have their faces averted; all others are shown directly, glowing with the light that they have touched. Gentleness and strength shine through. It is an educational experience, and a humbling one.

The places in which we worship are important. As Christians, we can never divorce ourselves from our setting, since our theology is essentially an incarnational theology. This concreteness—we worship a God who became human—has always been a part of established Christianity. Just as we are challenged by the Incarnation, so too should we be challenged by the spaces that we choose for our liturgies, by our surroundings.

The icons are part of those surroundings, and they are part of that incarnational theology. God's love is shown for us in our stories, our beliefs, and the lives of people around us: icons, images of who God wants us to be. They are not always comforting or comfortable, just as liturgy is not always comforting nor comfortable.

Icons and the liturgy are all doorways into stillness, into closeness with God. If we involve ourselves with them, we too can enter into that stillness. If we participate wholly, with our hearts and intuition, we just may discern the voice of God.

Jeannette Angell-Torosian[76]

314 • A GLOSSARY OF TERMS FOR SACRAMENTAL VESSELS

Along with the Table or altar, the vessels used for sacrament are also important in communicating its meaning. This article defines many of the terms used in describing sacramental vessels.

Chalices are commonly made of precious metals, or at least plated with such metals. Other materials, such as glass or ceramic, are also suitable, provided they are not porous. As the most conspicuous of the sacred vessels, it is desirable that chalices be well designed and finely crafted. It is also important that they not be top-heavy.

Patens intended for wafer bread ("well" patens) are usually designed to fit on top of the chalice, which is a convenience when bringing the vessels to the altar at the offertory. Patens intended for leavened bread are, of necessity, considerably larger, as well as being deeper. They also may be made of any suitable material. It is desirable that the paten used be large enough to hold all the bread to be consecrated at the service. When necessary, additional patens can be brought to the altar at the time of the breaking of the bread and used in the distribution of Communion.

Flagons are pitcher-like vessels, frequently with hinged covers, used to hold additional wine to be consecrated at the celebration. Like chalices, it is important that they be made of non-porous materials. In some places, the people's offering of wine is brought to the altar in a flagon, which is then used to fill the chalice. An attractive carafe or decanter may be used instead. When the amount of wine to be consecrated is small, a glass cruet of suitable size is commonly used.

Ciboria are chalice-like vessels, with covers, used to hold the consecrated bread. They are convenient vessels for holding the reserved sacrament but, because of their chalice-like appearance, are not recommended for use during the liturgy.

Pyxes are small vessels, frequently shaped like pocket watches, used to take the consecrated bread to the absent. Ciboria are sometimes referred to as standing pyxes.

Bread boxes are small vessels, either round or square, with covers, used to hold wagers to be placed on the paten at the offertory. Such boxes may also be used, in place of a ciborium, for the reservation of the consecrated bread.

Cruets are used not only for wine, but for the water to be added to the chalice and for the washing of the priest's hands. It is helpful if the necks of the cruets are wide enough to make cleaning them easy. Stoppers are frequently easier to deal with than flanged metal covers.

Lavabo bowls are now generally the size of finger bowls. The original custom, however, was the washing of the priest's hands, not merely of the fingers. The earlier practice and the use of bowls large enough for this purpose is recommended here.

Patens and chalices used to communicate the sick and shut-ins are commonly smaller than those used in church. It may be questioned, however, whether they should be so small as to look like toys. The bottles for wine provided in many "private Communion" sets, moreover, are difficult to fill and even more difficult to clean. In many cases, a small attractive bottle with a wide neck and a plastic-coated stopper will be found to be more practicable.

Ampullas are vessels designed to be poured from, used for the blessing and consecration of holy oils. They may also be used in administering such oils at public services. Between services, the oils are kept in tightly sealed bottles, labeled "Sacred Chrism," or "Oil of the Sick," as the case may be. Such oils may also be administered from "oil stocks," small cylindrical metal objects, packed with cotton, into which some of the oil has been poured.

Ewers are large pitchers with a wide spout used to fill the font at Holy Baptism or to add to the water already present in the font.

Baptismal shells are commonly small and made in the shape of sea shells. With the recovery of the tradition of using a significant amount of water, however, shells that are both larger and deeper are desirable. At the baptism of adults by total affusion, a large wide-mouthed vessel with a handle will be found most convenient.

Howard E. Galley[77]

315 • THE SIGNIFICANCE OF LITURGICAL VESTMENTS

This article discusses both theological and historical perspectives on the use of vestments in worship, referring both to vestments for worship leaders and for important objects used in worship.

In the movie *Back to the Future,* a young man is transported in a time machine back to the teenage years of his parents (the 1950s). When he is first discovered, his parents' peers call him Calvin because so much of his clothing bears Calvin Klein labels. Sporting the names of famous designers on seat pockets, sleeves, and shirt pockets is a mark of status in our time. This has rarely, if ever, been so before. Within recorded history, however, clothing has always been more than a mere extension of the skin for purposes of warmth and protection.

Clothing communicated relationships and meanings within a community. Although all the Maori of New Zealand may wear cloaks made of bird feathers, the pattern of the feathers distinguishes one group from another. The contrasting patterns of Chinese and Japanese clothing reveal that the Chinese were predominantly a hunting society, while the Japanese were largely agricultural.

English kings, earls, dukes and counts can be identified by the shape of their crowns and the number of ermine tails on their ceremonial robes. Denim jeans and flannel shirts are unacceptable attire at board meetings of Merrill Lynch, and the wearing of three-piece pinstripe suits at a gathering of Hell's Angels could be dangerous.

The Alb. This is usually a long, straight, white robe, secured at the waist with a belt. It is collarless and, in most traditions, has narrow sleeves.

Vesting the Ministers

So it is with the presence or absence of ritual vesture in communities of Christians. To proscribe all ritual vesture is to communicate a clear theological position and to raise the problem of what suit or dress is appropriate for the leader of this Sunday's assembly. To prescribe only academic vesture for the preacher and leader of worship is to say something loud and clear about the community's understanding of the liturgical act. Churches with "high" sacramental traditions are also taking a theological and ritual stance by continuing to use special liturgical vesture for some or all of their liturgical ministers.

Before we begin to focus on the artistic quality of liturgical vesture, we need to look at the liturgical and pastoral judgments to be made about these elements of our sacramental prayer. *Music in Catholic Worship* (USCC, 1972) reminds us that no artistic criterion is without its pastoral and liturgical implication. The application of words or shopworn religious signs to a chasuble, for instance, reduces this noble garment to a sandwich board and tends to reduce the liturgy itself to a medium of information rather than formation. Not only is a lightweight polyester confirmation "stole" poor art; it also gives rise to ministerial confusion, since the stole is a vestment specific to the ordained minister.

Vesting the Assembly

The use of fabrics in worship goes far beyond the obvious vesting of the presider, since to vest or not to vest an object, person, group, or action indicates the reverence we have for them. Since the *Constitution on the Sacred Liturgy,* official liturgical documents have stressed the assembly as the primary symbol in Christian worship. How is this reflected in the use of the textile arts?

How do we vest the entire space where the assembly gathers? Do we still pile hangings around the altar and the presider's chair and on the front of the pulpit? Does an assembly have any sense that hangings give an added seasonal dimension to the entire space? Is the particular importance of ritual objects underlined by the coverings they bear? The draped cross on Good Friday, the veiled tabernacle, the lectionary covered in precious fabrics—these objects still speak to us of the glory that shines through them. In the same way the roles of the various ministers can be more clearly symbolized if the ministers are clothed in gracious vesture.

Devotion to the Chasuble

The textile arts, like the other arts that serve the liturgy, have changed over the centuries. The ample vesture of early presiders gradually became shrunken and stiff panels, worn fore and aft. This shift from the classic conical *planeta* to the less significant "fiddleback" or "Roman" chasuble charts the development of ministerial roles, especially the presider's, vis-à-vis the entire assembly's ownership of its liturgy. The conical chasuble is admittedly a garment that does not allow for a wide range of free arm movement. The celebration of the Eucharist, however, in which each ministerial rank (including deacons, acolytes, and lectors) performed only those actions proper to its own ministry, revolved around a vision of the presider as one who did nothing but preside.

The bishop or priest prayed the orations, preached (from a seated position), and raised his arms only at the end of the entrance, offertory, and Communion processions and during the eucharistic prayer. Taking the gifts, setting the Table, and handling the vessels were all done by less encumbered ministers. When some of those ministers, the deacons, did wear chasubles, they did so in a way that changed the shape of that garment (the *planeta plicata* or folded chasuble). The *dalmatic,* a full-sleeved tunic, came to be identified with the diaconal role because the deacon could "work" better in that beautiful garment than in the fuller but more confining *planeta.*

Historians of liturgical vesture are accustomed to presenting charts that show a gradual process of cutting away the long sides of the chasuble in order to free the arms of the presider. As the presider assumed more of the various ministerial roles during the Eucharist, the presider's distinctive garment, the chasuble, became smaller and smaller. The more the Eucharist was dominated by the priestly office, the smaller, stiffer, and less beautiful the chasubles became. In a sense, one could teach the history of eucharistic development—and therefore, the history of the church—by tracing the evolution of the chasuble.

Fabric Coverings

We can follow a similar route for the vesting of objects. Icons, engravings, and book illuminations abound with illustrations of pious Christians covering their hands with plain linen cloths as they handle the altar vessels. The same simple yet ample cloths often cover these same vessels. Gospel books, pastoral staffs, and vessels for holy oils are covered and carried in the same way. As these objects became minimalized, their coverings became stiff little flaps on which insignificant images were painted or embroidered. Because the objects were reduced as effective signs, and because the actions in which they were employed were no longer open and full, their coverings no longer spoke to the community. Chalices, grapes, and wheat came to be applied to the coverings of bread plates and wine cups to signal that something significant was being covered.

Enter the Banner

The vesting of the great assembly space has evolved more in our own day than in previous centuries. Though we know that magnificent tapestries have occasionally covered the walls of some churches, we have little historical information on significant vesting of worship spaces prior to the modern era.

A banner is of its nature temporary—it identifies particular groups in the entire assembly or procession, or it gives a special but temporary highlight to some person, group, object, or action during a liturgical celebration. A wall hanging, though not permanent, usually has a special place throughout a liturgical season. Banners move into a liturgy and move out; wall hangings are in place before the assembly gathers and remain in place for weeks, months, or even years.

Banners and wall hangings are used more frequently today than at any previous time. Because so many of our first efforts in liturgical renewal treated worship as a communicator of information, banners and wall hangings made their entrance in the great

American tradition of the billboard. More and more, however, our assembly spaces are being graced by simple but bold statements of color and abstract design that give greater allowance for the eye's ability to be caught more powerfully by the imagination than by theological aphorisms or slogans.

Promise for the Future

These remarks may sound like a psalm of lament. They were intended, however, to point out how truly significant vesture is as one of the elements in the ensemble of arts that makes up liturgical prayer. Now, more than ever, visual, graphics, and handicraft artists are being called on to design and execute altar coverings, banners, wall hangings, vesture and lectionary covers worthy of our growing awareness of the power of the liturgy in which these objects are used. We have moved from the felt-and-burlap stage to hand-woven textiles, finely crafted tapestries, and freeform fiber works. Now we know that the kind of chasuble that sells in gross lots (often to bereaved families who then donate them to the parish) is not fit for any liturgical assembly (and especially not for foreign missions). For the first time, pastors and parish liturgical committees are willing to commission vesture and hangings designed for a particular space with its own unique play of light, wall finishes, and floor textures. The freeing of the Christian imagination in public prayer has opened the door to a significant revival of the textile arts in worship.

No element of life and no art is insignificant to a particular liturgical celebration. In the past two decades, we have learned to recognize music as a central element of worship and not simply as decoration. At first we spoke of liturgy and music, then of liturgical music and finally of musical liturgy. In the past decade, we have also taken a particularly critical look at the shape of our assembly spaces, the quality of light and acoustics, and the worthiness of liturgical furnishings. From the beginning of our liturgical reform we have criticized the quality of translations and new texts. As we become more aware of the crucial role of language, we are beginning to enjoy freshly composed texts that voice our common prayer in a language both evocative and challenging.

We are just beginning to look at vesture and the textile arts. Perhaps we Americans are reluctant to give too much attention to something so clearly decorative as fabric, its shape, color, cut and flow.

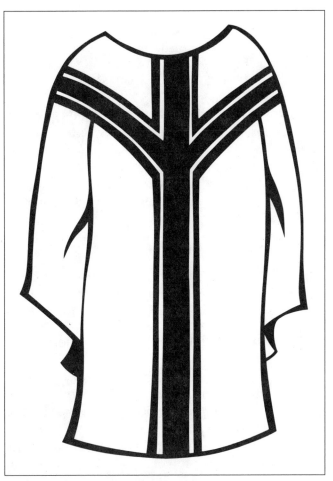

The Chasuble. _This cape-like garment, worn over other liturgical garments, originated as an outer cloak worn over other clothing. Its appearance has varied at times throughout church history._

But in fact the nonverbal world—the colors we behold, the textures we feel and touch—beckons us across the threshold of the spirit.

Andrew D. Ciferni[78]

316 • THE USE OF LITURGICAL VESTMENTS

Vestments, which have a long and venerable history in liturgical practice, provide many opportunities for artistry and creativity. The following article outlines guidelines for the use of vestments, taking into account both the history of their use and the differences of a variety of worship traditions.

"And you shall make holy garments for Aaron your brother, for glory and for beauty. And you shall speak to all who have ability, whom I have endowed with an able mind, that they may make Aaron's garments to consecrate him for my priesthood." . . .

And of the blue and purple and scarlet stuff they made finely wrought garments, for ministering in the holy place; they made the holy garments for Aaron; as the Lord had commanded Moses. (Exod. 28:2-3; 39:1, RSV)

In Exodus is seen the beginning of a long tradition that is still with the church, that is, the tradition of wearing special garments for worship. The tradition affects the laity as they dress in their "Sunday best" to attend public worship services and the clergy as they wear various types of robes and other garments to lead public worship.

—————— **History Within Christianity** ——————

As the Christian church grew, special garments were adopted by its leadership in the style common to the upper lay classes of imperial Rome (Gregory Dix, *The Shape of the Liturgy* [London: Dacre Press, 1945], 399). This style was the *linea* (a long linen robe with long, close sleeves) above which was worn a *tunica* (a garment that ended at about the knees and had short sleeves) and above that was the *chasuble* (a round piece of cloth with a hole for the head in the center) worn on formal occasions or when one was outside (Dix, p. 400). This was the common costume of the clergy, civil servants, and senators and remained so even after lay styles had changed to the more military style invading barbarians had brought to Roman territory in the fourth century.

The first recorded appearance of special liturgical vestments was in A.D. 330, when the emperor Constantine presented such a garment as a gift to the new cathedral in Jerusalem. The vestment was a robe, probably in the style of the common linea, tunica and chasuble, made of gold tissue to be worn by the bishop when presiding over baptism during the Easter vigil (Dix, p. 399). We see in this development that the style remained that which was common to the upper lay classes, but the material of liturgical garments was becoming quite elegant.

The first move to a special liturgical garment was the adoption of the *pallium* near the end of the fifth century. The French clergy had sought to adopt the pallium, a scarf of secular office, as a special badge of ministry, but they were rebuked by Pope Celestine I in A.D. 425. Celestine said that he wanted ". . . bishops distinguished by life not robes, by purity of heart not by elegance. . . ." (Dix, p. 401). Celestine's opinion did not prevail; by the late fifth century the pallium was adopted by clergy of all orders as the liturgical vestment of the church.

Soon other developments in liturgical vestments became popular. The *maniple,* which began in Egypt and reached Rome in the sixth century, was a sort of large handkerchief or napkin worn on the left arm or carried in the left hand. The tradition of it stayed with the church until the twelfth century, when the maniple became embroidered bands on the left sleeve of many vestments (Robert Lesage, *Vestments and Church Furniture* [New York: Hawthorne Books, 1960], 10). The traditional tunica also developed a slightly longer form with larger sleeves and was renamed dalmatic. The dalmatic was worn without chasuble. The dalmatic was accepted in the late sixth century as the distinctive vestment of deacons in the Western church (Dix, p. 402).

By the seventh century a special costume had been adopted as the official clerical vestment of the church. In A.D. 633, the Council of Toledo ordered the restoration of alb (another form of the ancient linea), stole, and chasuble to a priest who had been unfrocked and was being restored to orders (Dix, p. 403). This account witnesses to the official acceptance of these garments as vestments strictly for the clergy.

During the fourth and fifth centuries the unwritten policy of the church was to celebrate the liturgy in the garments of everyday life. These garments were perhaps made of finer material and were more colorful than much of the common lay clothing, but in style and manner of wearing they were essentially the same. The use of symbolical liturgical vestments, like those of the Old Testament, was strictly avoided.

By the end of the eighth century special vestments were developed largely due to the conservatism of the clergy. While much of lay society had turned to barbarian and military fashions during the sixth and seventh centuries, the clergy retained the old "civilized" fashions of imperial Rome. These fashions were later adopted and developed into official garments of the clergy. Three points may be made concerning the early history of Christian liturgical vestments:

1. Prior to the fourth century, the "domestic" character of worship was asserted to prevent the church from adopting special ceremonial robes as was the practice of vestment common in pagan mystery religions.

2. There was no real intention of creating a distinction of dress between clergy and the laity at liturgy.

3. By the Middle Ages such a distinction had appeared accidentally because the clergy kept the old costume long after the laity had discarded it and eventually the idea of special clergy dress was accepted as right and desirable in itself (Dix, pp. 404, 409–410).

When the church reached this third point of acceptance, many more elaborate liturgical costumes developed that were used to display clerical rank and distinguish clergy from laity.

With the coming of the Reformation, Calvinist and Lutheran groups reacted against the elaborate vestments of the Roman church and adopted the black Geneva gown. The Geneva gown was the proper garb of the educated men of the Reformation period and became the proper garb of the new Protestant clergy. It was a sign that these were scholarly and educated men. The black gown became a symbol of importance of a rationalistic approach to Christianity. The only ecclesiastical garment borrowed from Catholicism was the stole, as a sign that the person wearing the stole was a minister conducting worship (Joseph A. Culpepper, "Clothed for God's Glory," *The Disciple* 8:3 (Feb.1, 1981): 13–14; Albert W. Palmer, *The Art of Conducting Public Worship* [New York: Macmillan, 1939], 97).

Current Fashion

In many traditions and congregations the pastor chooses to wear, or as a congregation's norms may dictate, a plain dark business suit in which to lead worship. The tradition behind this practice stretches back into the early church tradition of wearing the daily garb of the upper classes. Certainly in the United States a strong case can be made that the business suit meets the requirement of common, everyday clothing, which does not separate clergy from laity. It points to the fact that the gospel relates to the everyday world and that the clergyperson is one of the priesthood of all believers.

The disadvantage of this style is that there is little celebrative mood conveyed by the business suit and less of a feeling that the pastor is putting on special garments for worship as a visible act of the service of God in the office of ministry. As more women enter the ministry, some feel we must deal with the question of what they should wear in worship, what is proper and whether radical differences in dress styles between male and female pastors emphasize sexist tendencies. Clearly, there are better choices for liturgical vestments.

The Geneva gown is still the prevalent style in much of the Reformed tradition. It is serious in appearance and is a symbol of the importance of the acts that occur during worship.

Major objections to the continued use of the Geneva gown are that its dark colors are somber and, thus, do not lend themselves to festivity in worship. For the majority of its history it has been used more in academia than the church and, thus, it is more properly an academic garment than a liturgical one. The use of hoods and addition of doctoral bars place even stronger emphasis on the academic side of the garment. Furthermore, the Geneva gown developed as a masculine garment. By using this gown as the liturgical vestment of the Reformed tradition, women in ministry are forced to adopt a traditionally male vestment. The Geneva gown is appropriate for worship in some instances, but other styles should also be considered.

The last of the current liturgical fashions to consider is the alb. It has an ancient tradition, which dates back to the linea of the early church in imperial Rome. It is usually a simply cut white robe with a great deal of versatility. In its original form in secular Roman society, it was the garment worn by both men and women. Current styles remain appropriate for either sex. The alb has widespread use today in Roman Catholic, Episcopal, and Lutheran traditions, and there is growing use of the alb in other traditions (Culpepper, p. 14).

The basic problem with the alb is the fact that it may not be readily accepted by some congregations—but this should not deter its adoption by the church.

The Future

Dressing in special ways can truly be another manner in which we glorify God. Furthermore, the tradition of dressing in some form of liturgical vestment is an ancient one, reaching back to the Exodus stories, and one which was rediscovered and reinterpreted by Christianity.

The alb is perhaps the most appropriate liturgical garment. In style it is less sexist than other current fashions. The white color lends itself to joy and celebration. The simplicity of the garment allows it to be quite versatile, i.e., stoles and chasubles of various design and color may be added designate to the seasons of the church year and various liturgical celebrations.

The alb is used in many traditions and, thus, is a symbol of the oneness of the body of Christ. The Geneva gown, on the other hand, emphasizes the division of the body of Christ by reminding us of the violent reaction during the Reformation against the practices of the Roman Catholic Church. Simplicity and modesty should be guiding principles, along with the desire to aid the congregation in celebrative worship.

The Geneva gown is still a useful garment, especially in most Reformed churches, and should be considered as an important liturgical vestment. A pastor may possess a variety of special liturgical garb to be used at various times and places.

A final word must be said about the importance and use of color in liturgical garments. When used with a keen sense of what is right and pleasing to the eye in a given situation color can be one of the greatest liturgical aids. These same basic rules apply to choice of textured and patterned material for vestments and linings. (See E. A. Roulin, *Vestments and Vesture: A Manual of Liturgical Art* [Westminster, Md.: Newman Press, 1930], 41–53.)

We are moving into an age with the most exciting possibilities for liturgical vestments. The changes ahead will lead to more practical, more celebrative, and more versatile garments. The changes, especially in Protestant traditions, will also help ground liturgical garments in the larger history of the entire Judeo-Christian tradition.

Kevin R. Boyd[79]

Prince Albert Suit. *This popular late-nineteenth-century suit was favored for some time by many Protestant preachers.*

317 • A GLOSSARY OF TERMS FOR LITURGICAL VESTMENTS

Many technical terms are used to describe the variety of vestments and textile arts used in worship. These terms are defined here.

The vestments worn at the Eucharist are derived from the dress-up clothing of the late Roman Empire, the dominant culture of the world in which Christianity first took root. The only exception is the stole, which is a sign of office.

The basic garment is the *alb,* which is properly worn by all ministering at the service. Some albs are intended to be worn under other vestments, are put on over an *amice* (which is simply a neck cloth), and girded about the waist with a rope cincture. Other albs are designed to be seen, are more tailored in appearance, and frequently require neither an amice nor a cincture.

The *surplice* is a medieval variant of the alb. It is appropriately used as a substitute for it by all except the priest-celebrant, the concelebrating presbyters, and the ministering deacons.

The *cotta* is a shortened surplice. It is also far less attractive. Its use is not recommended, even for choristers and young servers.

Priests' stoles are worn over both shoulders, and hand straight down in front.

Deacons' stoles may be worn in three different ways:

a. Over the alb (and under the dalmatic), over the left shoulder, drawn across the chest and back, and fastened on the right side.
b. Over the alb (and dalmatic), with the center under the right arm, and the ends drawn across the chest and back and over the left shoulder to fall front and back.
c. Over the alb (and dalmatic), with the center on the left shoulder, and the ends hanging straight down front and back.

The _chasuble_ is the distinctive vestment of bishops and priests at the Eucharist. (It is also worn at the Good Friday and Holy Saturday liturgies.) Some modern chasubles are designed to have the stole worn over them. Most chasubles are not, however, and look best when worn over the stole. Chasubles worn at celebrations facing the people should be as attractive when seen from the front as from the back.

The _dalmatic_ is the distinctive vestment of deacons, and its use is not confined to the Eucharist. It may be worn at all celebrations or only at the more festive times and occasions.

Chasubles and dalmatics, as pointed out above, began as articles of clothing, and it is desirable that they appear to be such. Their essential beauty should derive from their cut and choice of fabric, rather than from embroidery or other ornamentation. It is not necessary that the fabrics chosen should be "ecclesiastical"; decoration that suggests "slogans" should be avoided.

A _cope_ may be worn by bishops and presbyters at services that do not include the Eucharist.

The use of _frontals_ to decorate the altar is very ancient. In their classic form they fall to the floor, sometimes on all four sides, sometimes only on the front and back. In the latter case the "fair linen" that covers the top of the altar falls to the floor at the ends.

Howard E. Galley[80]

318 • BANNERS IN WORSHIP

Banners are found in sanctuaries of large cathedrals and small rural churches. This article offers some means for evaluating the purpose and qualities of banner art.

Improving Liturgical Banners

The Song of Solomon sings, "His banner over me is love," and other scriptural allusions remind us that flags, standards, and banners were an ancient art. (See for example Exod. 17:15, 16; Ps. 20:5; 60:4; Song of Sol. 2:4; 6:4, 6:10; Jer. 50:2.) Indeed, Constantine's substitution of the cross for the Roman eagle on his army's banners is legendary. But what of the contemporary use of banners in the church?

A recent survey of church art in our county revealed that the visual art most often being produced by both Protestant and Catholic churches is the banner. Many small rural parishes, county seat churches, and the congregations adjacent to college and university campuses are enthusiastically reviving interest in liturgical textile art.

It is also apparent, however, that there is a wide range of quality in the banners displayed. In fact most banners, while showing our contemporary desire for variety in the worship environment, also demonstrate the churches' need for thinking more carefully about the theological, liturgical, and artistic principles involved in banner art.

Many churches first approach banners as a project in Christian education undertaken by youth or by children in the church school. Undoubtedly a banner can be a useful tool for teaching the symbolism of important themes in biblical theology. Typical is the attempt to express a joyous response to God's love since banners are often seen as celebratory implements like flags in a parade, a not unlikely comparison.

But a red felt banner with the slogan "Smile, God loves you" in variegated colors is not necessarily the most effective means of expressing the wonders of divine grace, however sincere the fledgling banner makers may be. The search for fresh ways of giving form to faith will surely avoid trite phrases and clichés.

Theological Criteria

How then can we encourage better banners? First, because there has been a long controversy over the proper use of images in church, some theological criteria need to be established. Shall there be an attempt to portray the Christ, or shall only symbols be used? Shall new visual metaphors be encouraged, or shall only familiar signs like the cross and dove appear? Shall banners be used only on special days of the church year, or should they become fixtures like the national flag?

Rather than being simply an aid to devotion, or a gimmick to "get the kids involved," a good banner can be a significant offering of praise to God for the creation and redemption of life. The banner may express our gratitude for spiritual gifts or may put us in touch again with the anguish of suffering and sacrifice. A banner may affirm an important conviction, as when an Epiphany banner reminds us of the worldwide thrust of the gospel.

Designers of church banners, then, will have the same theological principles to guide them as church musicians, architects, or dramatists. They will know that the best banners grow out of the life of a community, just as flags emerge from the life of nations. If God speaks in history, then the artist needs to have studied the history and contemporary witness of the church which commissions the banner. All banner makers, whether amateur or professional, need to think carefully about the theology of the church and of the particular occasion(s) on which the banner will be displayed. Somehow the artist must discover links between the reality of God in the midst of a worshiping people and visual forms available in the textile art of banners.

Closely liked with a church's theology is its liturgical practice, so some knowledge of liturgy is important for banner markers. Too often, banners made by children and youth have been hung for a Sunday service when the young persons had special responsibilities for the worship, but then the banners were left hanging for many months afterwards, whether or not they were appropriate. This illustrates our need to recall that banners, unlike permanent windows, can have a temporary utility by highlighting a theme for a particular Sunday or season in the church year.

Enlisting Artists

Artistic excellence is also difficult to achieve with untrained eyes and hands. Composition, color design, and manipulation of different materials such as rough burlaps or satins—these are considerations not unlike musicians' concern with rhythm, tonality, timbre, phrasing, and the like. While many churches, even rather small ones, give at least minimal recognition and pay for the skills of organists or choir directors, few churches carefully select a person with visual artistic skills to oversee and direct the production of banner work. Perhaps be-

cause of iconoclastic views of art, particularly in Protestant churches, we have not enlisted the help of people with art training.

Yet such artistic persons live in even the most isolated communities. Art teachers in the public schools, photographers, and persons in newspaper advertising have skills which could dramatically improve the banners produced even in church schools. Many artists probably would be quite flattered to be asked to design a challenging, interesting project such as four banners based on Old Testament readings for the Advent services.

What are some new possibilities for creating interesting banners? One answer is to have the banner take shape before the eyes of the congregation throughout a season. During the seven weeks of Lent our congregation saw a single banner progress from a plain purple hanging to a fully imaged work on Easter Sunday. On each Sunday a different symbol of Christ was added, yet integrated so that a visual unity was achieved along the way as well as at the end. Thus a stump produced a shoot which became a vine which grew to cruciform shape and included white flowers for Easter. The ever-changing banner was a real interest-grabber, although we probably erred by trying to include too many images in one banner.

Where can banners be displayed? I have seen good banners in the entrance halls, over doors, and from balcony railings as well as from rods suspended from ceilings and walls of sanctuaries. Pulpit antependium hangings and Communion table paraments are essentially banners. Small banners representing the twelve apostles were hung from the aisle candle holders during one service. In a special service with clowns and mimes, a central banner was suddenly unfurled from its rolled up position by a tug on a securing string which released the velcro binding

A procession of banners is, of course, a compelling visual experience, particularly when combined with stirring music by instruments and voice, for as Marion Ireland's book *Textile Art in the Church* has shown us, "Religious flags and heraldic flags are by nature processional, and therefore mobile" (Marion Ireland, *Textile Art in the Church* [Nashville: Abingdon Press, 1966], 69). And how many churches have hung banners outside to line entrance walks or to flutter in the breeze from doorways or even steeple towers? That is often done by galleries, theaters, and such stodgy institutions as museums; why not by churches?

Design Principles

What, then, makes good banner design for churches? Marion Ireland's classic book discusses six basic principles: organic unity, theme, balance, rhythm, hierarchy, and evolution (Ireland, pp. 181–192). We can summarize her discussion by certain questions that a designer of banners needs to address:

1. Does each part contribute to the whole, or do unnecessary elements distract from the unity?
2. Does the banner have a dominant theme identified by some preeminent shape, color, line, or meaning?
3. Does the banner have a balance of color, line, and form within itself, and does it balance with other visual elements such as the windows of the sanctuary?
4. Does the rhythmic repetition of color, line, or form strengthen the design?
5. Is there a hierarchy of elements so that each part is appropriately related to the dominant theme?
6. Does the design progressively lead the eye toward the central visual meaning of the banner?

People respond to textures and shapes as well as to colors and movement. A crucifixion banner was constructed by a Hiram College student who used rough materials to match the mood of her subject: burlaps, wools, and leathers were joined in a semi-abstract design which is more powerful because of the textures used. In a Thanksgiving banner by another artist, a shimmering blue satin was used for sky effects, this material contrasting vividly with the warm tones and textures of the earth shapes. Rich embroidery of bright colors, metallic threads, and rickrack set against a black background created a majestic design in another banner to emphasize the crown of life from Revelation with its background of suffering.

Shapes can be varied also from the usual vertical rectangle. Long triangles or inverted arches may echo stained windows, while narrow horizontal strips over doorways may provide significant entrances and exits for worshipers. The Newman Center at Kent University produced a huge circular

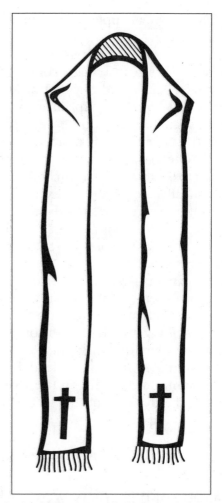

The Stole. *This strip of cloth worn about the neck and over the robe is usually a sign of pastoral office. Today it is commonly the color of the current church season (purple for Lent, etc.) and often embroidered with liturgical symbols.*

banner on a frame, perhaps one of the most unusual forms to utilize, although one often seen in museums and galleries which display contemporary examples of textile art.

Certainly designers should be encouraged, if they have the skills, to experiment with abstract shapes. The chaplain at Hiram College commissioned a creation banner, but no particular direction was given to the artist such as "reproduce Michelangelo's fingers of God and Adam." From the artist's imagination emerged a swirl of blue and green forms, clearly evoking the organic forms of the earth and the wave forms of the ocean, while not literally reproducing either. Such a banner is harder to dismiss than a simple banner saying, "LET THERE BE LIGHT." The eye and mind trace again and again the blues and greens as they interact in curvilinear loops. Meanings are multiple and metaphoric rather than literal.

This banner, then, reminds us that symbols can take different forms in the visual medium. Protestant churches have been word-oriented in liturgy and musical art, which perhaps explains why most banners being created today contain language. But words can be spoken or sung more effectively than portrayed in the visual arts, unless particular attention is taken to make the very form of the letters and words artistically pleasing with excellent calligraphy. The banner normally should be more a window or a stage than a book: a focus for meditation, or an occasion for reflection on the drama of God's presence in the world.

Makers of banners have the opportunity to renew a congregation's sense of the beauty of God. They can provide a changing environment which matches the shifting moods of music or the moving themes of the church year. By their movement in procession, and their display inside and outside of churches, banners can enliven the worshiper's awareness of the dynamic quality of faith which is rooted in the living God.

Thomas Niccols[81]

319 ᐧ CANDLES AND LIGHTS IN WORSHIP

Lights serve both a utilitarian and symbolic function in worship. This article traces the history of candles, lamps, and other lights in worship and suggests ways that the symbolic function of these lights can be maintained.

The first recorded use of lights in Christian worship occurs in the New Testament (Acts 20:8). There the use was obviously utilitarian, since the service was being held at night. By the third century at the latest, however, the bringing in or kindling of the evening lamp(s), whether at home or at a meeting of the church, was understood as a symbol of Christ, "the light (that) shines in the darkness" (John 1:5), and was frequently accompanied by a prayer of thanksgiving and/or a hymn. The Order of Worship for the Evening in the prayer book is a conscious revival of this practice, while the service of light at the Great Vigil of Easter is a special form of it.

Given this symbolic understanding, it is perhaps not surprising that the city churches built in the fourth century, after Christianity had been legalized, were supplied with sources of light for evening ser-

vices that were far in excess of what was needed for adequate illumination. Lamps filled with olive oil (usually with floating wicks) were suspended before and above the altar, sometimes in clusters. Tall candlesticks, standing on the floor, were placed in the chancel and nave, and chandeliers bearing lamps or tapers illuminated the ceilings.

Lights were also used at the tombs of martyrs, many of which had churches built over them. Some of these were lamps that burned continuously; others were votive offerings of the faithful. This same honor was later extended to include pictures and images of saints.

No lights at all, however, were placed on the altar itself, which was considered too sacred to bear anything more than what was actually needed for the celebration of the Eucharist.

The fourth century also witnessed the beginning of the practice of burning at least some of the lamps at the altar by day as well as by night—and not just at service time—a practice which is the basis of the tradition, which lasted for centuries, that at least one lamp should burn continuously in every church. (This tradition is still faithfully observed in many Lutheran churches, and should not be confused with the custom of burning a lamp before the reserved sacrament—a practice which was unknown before the thirteenth century.)

Such lavish displays of light were not, of course, possible everywhere, and especially not in the hundreds of small country churches built in the following centuries. For many, probably most of them, the single, ever-burning lamp provided the norm. Additional lights, as needed and available, were used in service time, and on festivals extra lights were added.

None of the lights mentioned thus far, it should be noted, are specifically connected with the celebration of the Eucharist. The only special use of light at that service was the practice of carrying candles at the reading of the gospel.

It was not until the eleventh century that candles were placed on the altar itself, a practice that was originally confined to the greatest festivals. These candles were lighted for the morning and evening services as well as the Eucharist, and were removed at the end of the feast. This same period also saw a change in the shape of altars, from that of a cube to a shallow object as much as twelve feet long. Far more space was available than was needed for the vessels and altar book; and in many (though not all) churches, candlesticks, in varying numbers, gradually appeared to fill up the space. In larger churches, elaborate rules were devised, specifying the number of candles to be lighted on or about the altar on particular occasions.

Much of the polemic of the Protestant Reformers was directed against lights, especially those which burned before images and relics—practices which had, indeed, given rise to much superstition. The English Injunctions of 1547 demanded the removal of all lights except for "two upon the high altar, before the sacrament." Attempts to abolish these as well were thwarted by the death of King Edward and the accession of the Roman Catholic Queen Mary.

The reign of Elizabeth I saw the disappearance of candles from the altars of virtually all Anglican parish churches. The use of two, however, was carefully preserved in chapels royal, in most cathedrals and college chapels, and in the private chapels of bishops and lay nobles. In some places, at least, they were lighted at all services, not only at Holy Communion; and in other places (or during certain periods) were treated merely as decorations, and not lighted at all except when actually necessary.

The general recovery of the use of lights in Anglican churches occurred in the nineteenth century, which also introduced a distinction, unknown to history, between "eucharistic candles" (two candles placed on the altar itself and lighted only at celebrations of the Eucharist) and "office lights" (the number of which sometimes suggested that Morning Prayer was more deserving of a great display of lights than the Holy Eucharist). The continuance of that distinction is not recommended.

As the preceding summary indicates, there has been no consistent tradition with regard to the use of candles.

The use recommended here, as a norm, is the burning of two candles at all services. These lights may be placed on the altar itself or on the floor at either end of it.

Alternatively, two torches may be used. These are carried in the entrance procession, placed in stands on the floor at either end of the altar, used at the gospel procession, and carried during the procession out. At services at which there are no servers to carry them, they are put in place before the rite begins.

If a larger number of candles is desired, torches may be used in addition to the two candles which burn on or near the altar.

In some places, processional candlesticks are used in place of torches. These are tall lightweight candlesticks, carried with one hand under the base and the other around the candlestick itself. When not being carried they are placed on the credence, or on the floor, or on a convenient shelf or shelves.

Where space permits, the use of additional lights on the principal feasts and in festal seasons is suitable. Such candles may be placed, for example, in standard candlesticks on the floor of the chancel, or in sconces on the walls. In some buildings, extra lights may also be placed in the nave. Such candle holders should not, however, be considered as fixed ornaments, and should be removed from the church in seasons when they will not be used.

Traditionally, candles used in church, and especially those on or about the altar, are made of beeswax. The Episcopal Church does not, however, have any rules on the subject, and other substances may be used as well.

In some churches, because of drafts, the use of "followers" on candles is a necessity. Metal ones, however, diminish the beauty of candles by obscuring the glow that the flame casts into the top of the candles themselves. When needed, therefore, clear glass or plastic followers should be preferred.

Whenever possible, it is desirable that candles that are burning at the conclusion of a service remain lighted until the congregation has departed.

During the fifty days of Easter, the paschal candle is lighted for all services. The most suitable place for it is near the ambo. At other times it is appropriately placed near the font and lighted whenever baptism is administered. The prayer book also provides for its use at funerals (p. 467).

In planning new churches, and in remodeling old ones, it is suggested that consideration be given to recovering the practice of hanging lamps over or in front of the altar, either singly or in a cluster. Such lamps may be lighted for all regular services, or the use of some or all may be reserved for the more festal occasions.

The burning of a lamp before a picture or icon of the patron or some other saint or of the Virgin and Child (at least on occasion) is an attractive practice, and is not today likely to be the cause of superstition.

Howard E. Galley[82]

320 • THE SYMBOL OF THE CROSS IN WORSHIP

The one symbol used in perhaps every tradition of worship is the cross. This article presents advice on appropriate ways that a cross may be displayed in the worship space.

It is desirable that there be only one cross visible in the chancel during the celebration of the liturgy. Depending on the architecture of the building and its furnishings, such a cross may be simple and unadorned, or elaborately decorated.

In a church with a free-standing altar, a fixed cross may appropriately be placed on the wall behind it, or it may be suspended over it. While it should be large enough to be seen, it should not be so large that it appears to lessen the importance of the altar itself.

When there is a cross above or behind the altar, the processional cross should be placed out of sight, or at least in a place where it is not facing the congregation, during the course of the liturgy.

An attractive alternative is to use the processional cross itself as the cross to be visible during the service, a practice which is very ancient. After being carried in the Entrance procession, it is placed in a stand in a convenient place in the chancel, such as behind or beside the presidential chair; at the end of the service, the cross is carried in the procession out. Such a usage also makes possible some seasonal variety where that may be desired, an elaborate cross for days of special festivity and a simpler one at other times.

At services at which the cross is not carried, it is put in place before the rite begins. It may also be left in its stand outside of service time as a focus for private devotion.

The bearer of a processional cross holds the staff perfectly upright (not tilted forward), with one hand just below the cross and the other further down the staff, with the palms of both hands facing the bearer.

The custom of veiling the altar cross on Good Friday serves a practical purpose. By being concealed from view, it does not "compete" with the wooden cross brought in and placed in the sight of the people after the solemn collects (*Book of Common Prayer*, 281). The practice of extending the veiling to the whole of Holy Week can be defended on devotional grounds; the congregation looks forward to seeing the cross unveiled. But the value of extending it back another week, which became the Roman practice (now merely allowed and not enjoined), or to the whole of Lent (which became the custom in northern Europe) is not apparent, and especially when it involves veiling crucifixes during the season in which they are most appropriate. The practice of extending the veiling is not recommended here.

Howard E. Galley[83]

321 • FLOWERS IN WORSHIP

Flowers are commonly used in the worship space but are not always subject to the same level of reflection as other aspects of the environment. This article presents some basic suggestions regarding the use of flowers in worship based on both liturgical and practical considerations.

A liturgist and a florist make a good parish partnership, especially if the two encourage each other to imagine the best possible marriage of available plant materials to how these are used in worship. Here is a primer on flowers, written to jog the imaginations of anyone with responsibility for the parish worship environment.

Cut Flowers and Force Blossoming Branches. These flowers can add life and color to those things in liturgy that are most important: perhaps a wreath of alstroemeria around the processional cross, a great blossoming plum branch set near the paschal candle, a bed of seasonal flowers under an icon in the gathering place, a few white gardenias floating on the baptismal waters, rings of roses to crown the confirmed.

When selecting flowers, respect the season and learn the traditions associated with certain flowers: anemones for Good Friday, asters for Michaelmas, snowdrops for Candlemas, black locust for Pentecost. All of this will become less arcane for the parish if year by year you draw into worship the flowers not so much of greenhouses but of fields, orchards, and gardens.

Many cut-flower arrangements add tedium to our worship. Sprays of gladioli, mums, and ferns look like what they often are: leftovers from weddings or funerals. While it may be wonderful to share such flowers, they often appear in the Sunday assembly on an erratic schedule, with little regard for the season. It is better, although ambitious, to come to depend on certain parishioners who take responsibility to use "leftovers" to best advantage, livening them up with garden flowers, rearranging them, even giving them away if they are inappropriate. Such people have the important task of maintaining a consistency in the use of flowers on Sunday.

Spring-Flowering Bulbs: Daffodils, Tulips, Amaryllises, Hyacinths, Freesias, Irises, Lilies, Crocuses. This wide range of flowers, available December through April, are generally inexpensive, fragrant, and splashy. The flowers ride atop homely foliage. Flowering bulbs are short-lived, good for just one Sunday. (Lilies and amaryllises last for two, maybe three weeks.) You can get another Sunday's worth out of them if you have some way of keeping them at 40 degrees (not freezing) during the week.

Flowering bulbs can spark up grouping of longer-lasting flowers. They're often used on Easter Sunday but rarely at Christmas. Why not add a few pots of white tulips among the poinsettias, or a broad range of spring flowers rising from the straw of the creche? Blood-red amaryllises or a crock of violet crocuses fit on Palm Sunday, perhaps near the cross.

Flowering bulbs are best up close. A single pot placed in the vestibule or gathering space is more hospitable than a mass of these flowers behind the altar. Great banks of them in a warm church can create a horrible odor. Leave that for conservatories where the temperature can be kept low.

Cool-Weather Flowering Plants: Azaleas, Cineraria, Cyclamens, Calculations, Primulas, Hydrangeas, Martha Washington Geraniums, Chaffinches. Like oysters, these plants are mostly available in months with an "R" in them. If they get conditions they favor, they have very long-lasting flowers. (A cyclamen can bloom for six months straight.) All need 60-degree temperatures and lots of sun. Most fall apart—especially azaleas and hydrangeas—if the soil dries out or remains waterlogged for just a few hours. Yet even under the worst conditions, many will remain beautiful a month.

The ubiquitous chrysanthemum falls in this category. True mums are cheap and long-lasting, but with the exception of the pastel, daisy-type ones, they belong to autumn. It's worth your while to learn what cyclamens, calceolarias, and cinerarias are. These tongue-twisters are spectacular, with the same usefulness as mums, but they look much more fitting in spring. "Cineraria" means "rising from the ashes," a nice bit of Eastertime lore, and you won't find a brighter blue flower to grace a baptismal font.

Potted plants look better if you order them with-out foil and ribbons, knock the root balls out of their original containers, then arrange them in giant pots—such as the several-foot-wide Italian terra cotta pots found on occasion at garden centers. (Partially fill them with sand or perlite.) Tilt the flowers to their best advantage and stuff into the pot as many plants as possible. One super pot of the same type of plant looks better than a scattering of smaller pots.

Tropical Plants. They make beautiful occasional visitors to church, but otherwise they need to be kept in a greenhouse or other good growing conditions. Perhaps tropical plants will remain healthy in those very few churches flooded with natural light. For example, a spectacular flowering hibiscus in a plant store won't last a month in a dimly lit church, and even under more favorable conditions all the flower buds will likely drop unopened.

The poinsettia is an example of a flowering tropical plant. In good conditions they can stay colorful all winter, but in most churches they drop their leaves by Epiphany.

Foliage plants tend to become permanent fixtures that can create a problem no different from any clutter in the worship place. They get neglected. Most tropical plants look out of place during autumn and during Lent or Eastertime (what does a schefflera contribute to a worship environment in spring?), and they look especially bad alongside Christmas greens.

Only rarely have I seen foliage plants make a contribution to the iconography of worship. As an example of their good use, behind a baptismal font a creeping fig *(Ficus pumila)* had been allowed to form a delicate tracery as it grew over a stone wall. It seemed the same sort of artistry as might go into the creation of bonsai. Another example was the placement during Lent of (rented!) succulent plants in the gathering area near the niche where the parish's processional cross remained through the week.

A Few Guidelines. A very large quantity of flowers and greenery put in the worship place often winds up looking like a transplanted rock garden, and it easily reminds people of the places we often see such banks of plants: shopping malls. Surrounding fonts with plants may speak of "life" to some, but it can obscure many more subtle understandings of the significance of the font. For similar reasons, it isn't good to use the altar or ambo as a backdrop for plants or to use plants in such numbers as to cause an assembly to notice their cost more than the delight of their profusion.

As a general principle, flowers or plants should be used as iconography—sacred images that draw us into the divine. During certain seasons and days of feasting, we relish being surrounded with such living "icons," images of the Creator, God incarnate, God our Savior. During certain seasons and days of fasting, we put aside such iconography to remind us of our exile and the distance we have yet to travel on our journey. And during all the other times of the year, we get small glimpses into heaven, Sunday by Sunday, through such reminders as a handful of cattails or a noseful of lilacs.

Peter Mazar[84]

322 ✦ STAINED GLASS IN THE WORSHIP SPACE

One medium of art that has been almost exclusively associated with Christian churches is that of stained glass. Some basic considerations regarding stained glass are mentioned here.

Light. In the beginning God created light. Since that time, it has been a source of fascination. Such fascination has been important in the art forms of Christian places, so much so that a prime criterion for judging the success of a religious building has been the way in which light enters the spaces. The craft of the glass maker thus has its important place.

Glass. We marvel at the wonderful ways stained glass plays with light. Glass is thought to have been invented by accident; Phoenician sailors found glasslike remains in the embers of their beach fires over five thousand years ago. Glass was long considered a precious material, used in molded vases, mosaic tile, beads, and imitations of gems. Glass was not used for glazing windows until 1500 years ago, and the earliest evidence of such window glass is in buildings for worship.

Colored glass originated from our ancestors' inability to make clear glass. Such glass is not really "stained"; the colors come from metal oxides fused to or suspended in the glass while it is liquid. "Art glass" is a more appropriate term today, one which can refer also to clear glass which has been acid-etched, beveled, engraved, sandblasted, or textured. These are all ways to modulate the quality of light refracted through the glass surface. Color is only one of the qualities available to the artist working in glass.

Between the Glass Pieces. The materials which hold the glass pieces together must also be carefully chosen. Since medieval times, lead channels have been in common use. In the last 100 years, glass fabrication methods have changed; copper, foil, epoxy, and zinc are now used as structural members.

Cost. The cost of art glass is generally determined by its size (square feet being the unit of measure). Price varies according to the types of glass used, the way it is held together, and the installation conditions. More significantly, the intricacy of the design and the number of glass pieces per square foot are primary cost determinants. Art glass suitable for a worship space typically ranges from $75 to $150 per square foot, not including the window frames and installation. For glass with painted figures of scenes, the median price is between $200 and $350 per square foot.

Collaboration. In church building and renovation, it is important that the architect, artist, and fabricator work together to explore all the design possibilities. Working with the parish representative, this team enhances the likelihood of a compatible marriage of the art glass to the architecture.

Steven J. Melahn[85]

323 ✦ SCULPTURE IN WORSHIP

At times a piece of visual art opens possibilities for creating sermons or reflections on Scripture readings in worship. Sculpture is an art form that can lend itself to such proclamation or contemplation.

That art can enrich worship is freely acknowledged. To understand why art can enrich worship calls for a variety of approaches. Mine will be that of a sculptor who has dealt primarily with the story of Christ and his disciples. For over forty years my vocation has been the work of an ordained Presbyterian minister. Wood sculpture, on the other hand, I regard as an accomplishment. It is quite natural that I should have had a lifelong interest in how the church might use both sculpture and painting in worship. I find it encouraging that in so many churches the visual arts are now being explored with appreciation, so that the title of this article could be reproduced with many helpful variations by a growing number of people who are knowledgeable in art.

Why Talk About It at All?

There are several common warnings for those contemplating the use of visual arts in worship. Do not show art as a mere illustration of something else. It should not be a handy prop to embellish an otherwise bald and probably unconvincing tale. It is commonplace in art criticism that the sculpture or painting should stand on its own merit without attempts to enhance its impression by talking about it. If it has a life and vitality of its own, any explaining would seem to be worse than irrelevant. This is the reason that artists, as a rule, do not give critical accounts of their own work. They are silent about their method of composition. We seldom get a peep into their technical workshop where, of necessity, they must withdraw into an inner environment. How beauty is conjured out of technique is their own secret. Epstein in his autobiography tells of a reception given in London for Rodin. Not being used to making speeches, Rodin responded very simply with few words. Another sculptor, named Tweed, got up and began a long discourse, commencing, "If Rodin could express himself . . ." (Sir Jacob Epstein, _An Autobiography_. [New York: Vista Books, 1955], 220). That must have approached the record for the most impertinent speech ever made.

Granted verbosity is an enemy of art. It is my considered judgment that some talk is not only helpful but absolutely necessary if the fullest use is to be made of art in worship. The best thing, of course, is to persuade the artist to share some of his or her basic feelings about the meaning of the creation—not easy to arrange, but wonderfully rewarding when it can be worked out.

Failing to have both original art and a willing artist, congregations should consider the wide range of excellent color slides of good art. Often some patient searching can turn up just the comment by the artist that will help them understand his or her spirit's absorption in what was made. An example of what can be found is Andrew Revai's book _The Coventry Tapestry_ (London: The Pallas Gallery, 1964), based on conversations which Revai had with Graham Sutherland, the creator of that great tapestry. They were talking about Sutherland's sensitivity to the events in the gospels, which deal with suffering and cruelty. The artist answered that having

lived through the epoch of Buchenwald and the twentieth century's violence and cruelty, it would be unnatural not to be touched by these events. And then he added surprisingly, "It is true to say, however, that I believe it to be much more difficult to invent a valid equivalent for tenderness" (Revai, _The Coventry Tapestry_, p. 82). What a moment for a worship leader, using the background of the artist's words, to focus a slide of the head of Christ in glory in Sutherland's tapestry. Perhaps there will be people present who have had the privilege of worshiping in Basil Spence's rebuilt cathedral who cannot forget the spell evoked by the great central image.

Helpful interpreters of art will often surface. Sometimes they may even be found in the pulpit. Let me give another effective example in this area of worship. One of the most gifted preachers of our time was the late Austin Farrer. In a book of his sermons entitled _The End of Man_ (London: SPCK, 1973) there is one with the title "Epstein's Lazarus." It was preached in New College Chapel, Oxford, where Epstein's sculpture stands so that it will be passed as people come and go from the chapel. Farrer was moved to preach on this theme after reading an eloquent poem on the Epstein sculpture by A. L. Rowse. The resulting sermon is a model of how a meditation on a work of art can bring home the claims of God.

A Leopard-Skin Coat and Emmaus: An Example of Sculpture in Worship

It is time that I discuss the use I have made of my own sculpture in worship. In a way it all began when I had my first piece of sculpture displayed in a really good museum. The occasion was the 1960 North Carolina Annual Exhibit at the State Art Museum in Raleigh. My accepted piece was a carving of _The Walk to Emmaus_ with the two disciples and the Stranger who joined them, done in the likeness of Appalachian mountain people with whom I feel at home. Passing through the museum one day I found a stylishly dressed lady in a leopard-skin coat standing by my sculpture. She was obviously puzzled by the title, for she said to her companion, "Emmaus? Emmaus? It must be a place in Austria." As usual, when I should have used the opportunity to say something meaningful, the oracle was dumb and space not. So they drifted away, and my little Emmaus figures were left alone in a large gallery filled with abstract and studio art. I suppose I did not deliberately start to wonder how the truth of Emmaus could be made central to people who drop into our museums. That conviction has its source in a gospel deeper and far more lasting than any approach through aesthetics. But something was stirring in me about one way to make meditation on the life of Christ a more meaningful thing for some people in the church's worship.

When I began the sketches for my *Walk* on Good Friday, 1960, I was moved with the thought that Rembrandt had dealt with the Emmaus theme eighteen times and that Evelyn Underhill had written to a friend who was visiting Palestine, ". . . wonder if you went to Emmaus; that is one of the bits I should most like to do" (Margaret Cropper, *Life of Evelyn Underhill* [New York: Harper and Brothers, 1958], 189). Obviously this Easter story in Luke's Gospel had stirred great souls down through the church's ages. Shortly after this exhibit, when our church sanctuary burned, I began work on a relief sculpture after Rembrandt's 1648 Louvre painting of *The Supper at Emmaus* to be placed in the rebuilt church over the baptismal font so that the carving and the font might be a visible reminder of the two sacraments.

In 1968, I found just the piece of crotch walnut I wanted to do my own interpretation of the supper at Emmaus. It was a massive block 14″ x 18″ x 26″, really too heavy for one person to lift. I modeled a bare table with only the broken bread and a traveler's canteen. One of the chairs was an old fashioned three-corner design seen in old mountain cabins. In the months of working on the sculpture, I thought often of the words of a Nobel Prize-winning French novelist, François Mauriac:

"It seems to me there is one page of the Gospel for each one of us. . . . For my part I have walked all my life with the two tired travelers who entered Emmaus in the evening—Christ was dead, they had lost everything. . . . Who among us is not familiar with the inn at Emmaus? Who has not walked on this road in the evening when all seemed lost? . . . We followed a road and Someone walked at our side. We were alone and yet we were not alone." (Francois Mauriac, *The Son of Man* [New York: Collier Books, 1961], 48–49)

That winter and spring of carving gave me the opportunity to do what I hoped the finished sculpture would help others to do. It was to meditate on

a gospel scene by what Evelyn Underhill called, in a wonderfully apt phrase, "chewing the evangelical cud."

> When day is spent He turns
>   Stone into bread.
> One table gesture burns,
>   And hearts are fed.

Show and Tell Within Limits

Over the years I have been able to carve nearly thirty pieces depicting the life of Christ and his disciples. Their use in worship has been varied. Sometimes, placed in a sanctuary, two or three of them were used as the basis for the sermon. For instance, two from the opening chapters of John's gospel, *John Pointing to Christ* and *Jesus at the Well,* were central in a sermon on "Beginnings in John's Gospel." Both sculptures stood out as quite ordinary scenes—a man pointing two friends to a greater friend, and a thirsty man asking for a drink. Yet in each narrative there are mysterious words, "The Lamb of God" and "living water." Together they make good examples of the two stances from which C. H. Dodd believed the narratives in the gospels should be approached—matter-of-factness and mystery. For me, at least, this must be a controlling impression in any worthy art that deals with Christian themes.

Most often my work has been displayed with various gatherings in churches that wanted to explore the use of visual art in worship. The range of settings has been pretty wide. The one common denominator has been the inevitable row of banquet tables that, even with long experience, brings on a suppressed shudder. (Do no churches have adequate stands for displaying sculpture?) But that is all part of the job, and again and again there has been the joy of helping to create an atmosphere in which people could worship the Lord who moves among us with the secret of His power.

Involved in presenting art to congregations, one is tempted to overvalue the very thing one loves. I have to remember the sardonic things Isaiah had to say about those who carve images out of wood. A needed corrective comes from the wise words of Dr. Johnson, who expressed his distrust of religious poetry in his *Life of Waller:*

Contemplative piety, or the intercourse between God and the human soul, cannot be poetical. Man admitted to implore the mercy of his Creator, and plead the merits of his Redeemer is already in a higher state than poetry can confer. (Samuel Johnson, *Lives of the English Poets,* vol. 1 [London: J. M. Dent and Sons, 1925])

It is queer that anyone could think that pigments on a brush or a chisel chipping on wood might speak to us about God and our destiny. Byron dismissed sculpture and painting as "those two most artificial of the arts." In his penetrating, "wicked" way, he described Michelangelo's marvelous sculptures in the Medici Chapel as "fine frippery of great slabs of expensive stones to commemorate fifty rotten and forgotten carcasses" (Leslie A. Marchand, *Byron: A Portrait* [Chicago: The University of Chicago Press, 1970], 265). There are more pressing uncertainties when one faces up to the priorities of discipleship in such a day as we face in the 1980s. Auden wrote in 1948,

> The present state of the world is so miserable and degraded that if anyone were to say to the poet: "For God's sake, stop humming and put the kettle on or fetch bandages. The patient is dying," I do not know how he could justifiably refuse. (Charles D. Abbot, ed., *Poets at Work* [New York: Harcourt, Brace, and Co., 1948])

Ditto for 1984.

These are troubling doubts, but they have not kept me from spending time on carving. Maybe I have been turning over plates of those wonderful wood carvings of Tilman Riemenschneider done nearly five hundred years ago dealing with the same gospel stories, and suddenly I want to do another sculpture. After all, life without worship is hard put to sustain meaning. So I turn again to Evelyn Underhill. She is writing to the poet Margaret Cropper:

> How wonderful that you are doing a Passion Play and let me think of it. Seems to me making such things as this does count for people like you. . . . It is given to stimulate other people's sense of God, and so adds to the total prayer energy, which is the ultimate job. I always console myself like that when I find myself spending time having happy notions for addresses instead of attending to Him in a more obvious way. P'raps it is part of the price we have to pay for our particular vocation. (Cropper, *Life of Evelyn Underhill,* 170)

John Walker[86]

324 • TEMPORARY ART IN WORSHIP

Many artistic works are created for a specific time or purpose; the artist does not intend for such temporary art to exist beyond the limits of the temporal space. The primary images and symbols of Christian faith are important sources for these works whose purpose is to unlock their hidden meanings or to reveal new ones.

The Rationale for Temporary Installations of Art in Worship

Historically the visual arts have been an important part of the life of the church. Most of the production of art has been permanent and of intrinsic value. It has been used as a visual voice instructing worshipers in scriptural truths by means of illustration and symbol. Other work—mainly architecture—has been designed to provide environments which are appropriate for meditation and worship, to assist both the performance of the liturgy as well as to provide an appropriate ambiance for devotional exercises. In addition, the visual arts may be used as embellishment for sacred objects and places in much the same way as we wrap a present in beautiful paper and ribbon to set it apart from an ordinary box.

Temporary art, in contrast to the more intrinsically valuable permanent forms of religious art, is designed to have a short life span. In recent years there has been a desire by some Christian artists to create works which serve to complement a thematic focus within a particular worship service or series of services. This art aids the congregation in understanding the truth that is being taught from the Scriptures. It has a supporting role within the service, and as such, needs to be made with that intention in mind. Most of these artists share a philosophical conviction that the art object itself does not have intrinsic worth. Accordingly, they limit how much money is spent for materials and how much time is spent on the execution of the work. By nature, temporary works function best within these limitations. A primary goal in making temporary art is to avoid undue attention on the work itself and to have the work point beyond itself. If it fails on this point, the work is viewed as profane. For artists working in this genre, it is a constant struggle to create works with artistic integrity, fine craftsmanship, and an appropriately supportive role in corporate worship.

There is ample evidence that we are helped in our understanding of both material and spiritual reality through visual symbols. Using symbols as a vocabulary, the Christian artist can effectively use his/her artistic gifts for the good of the church. If the Christian artist assumes that the artistic gift has been given by God, and if there is a sense of obligation to the local body of believers to be a good steward for the benefit of the body, then doing art as an aid to worship will be a natural result.

The Power of Symbol in Temporary Art

A symbol is a sign which stands for something else. Through the imagination and the ability to make conceptual connections people invent symbols. We transform our knowledge and experience of the world and our inner subjective existence into codes, patterns, and visual configurations that represent reality by abstract means. A symbol is an image that expresses meaning indirectly; it is a surrogate image, a stand-in for other factual information.

The meaning of an image may not be understood to everyone seeing it. Its meaning is recognizable only to those who are initiated or who are able to use the imagination to make symbols. This fact divides symbols into two types: universal and particular. An example of a universal symbol is bread. We need no code or explanation to understand its meaning. One form of bread, a pretzel, is a particular symbol. We need an explanation apart from its literal message if it is to become a meaningful referent. In this case, the explanation is that a medieval monk awarded pretzels to children as an incentive for memorizing prayers. The shape was inspired from the folded arms of children in prayer. Once this connection is given, the pretzel becomes a symbolic pointer to some idea outside of itself. This mental function is what the German psychiatrist Herbert Siberer called auto-symbolization, a process by which our minds transform disparities into unified picture symbols.

An important value of a symbol is its ability to bridge the gap between the temporal and spiritual, the seen and the unseen. When used in this way, it is important to keep the distinction clear between symbol and reality; the symbol is merely a pointer, or sign of the reality. A wedding ring is not the reality of marriage, it is a sign that one is married.

There is ample scriptural support for the use of the symbol in art as an aid to worship. Our Lord himself taught spiritual truths through symbols, including the mystery of his own passion through the symbol of the Eucharist. Once seen and understood, the symbol becomes a messenger of truth. John's gospel is filled with examples: bread, vine, branches, light, shepherd, door, salt, water, wine. These are a small part of the extensive ready-made glossary for use by the artist in the service of the church. The use of these symbols informs beyond propositional statements. Symbols help us to understand some of the paradoxes of the very nature of Christ. For example, he is presented as both lamb and lion. Other symbols of Christ are just as diverse: grapevine, cornerstone, pioneers, door, bread, water, bridegroom, wine, rock, foundation, and so on. Because these are symbols or metaphors, one is able to hold many of these images in the mind simultaneously.

When using these symbols, and other newly invented ones, it is necessary for the artist to make sure the uninitiated are led into an understanding of their particular significance. Written explanations incorporated into bulletins is an efficient way to teach the meaning of the symbols. Verbal explanations during the homily or sermon are appropriate and helpful, enabling both the words and the visual forms to have a consonant impact on the congregation.

How Temporary Art Works

The start for artists making art as an aid to worship is to invent works that revolve around the major themes of the church calendar. This is the easiest due to the wealth of images that have come from art history and have established traditions in the church. The cross, crown, candles, cup, bread, lamb, lion, basin of water, towel, significant colors, circle, triangle, square, and numbers are a few of the important symbols that have been in use from the earliest days of the church and, for the most part, have their roots in Scripture.

In addition to creating works based on the major themes of the church calendar, the artist may invent works that support the theme of a sermon or series of sermons. Often this necessitates a combined effort of artist and minister together with the ideas of a worship committee. To begin, there needs to be advance planning that gives attention to the scriptural source of the theme or themes. It is helpful to have ongoing conversation about the salient points of a given Scripture lesson and the visual images that the passage suggests. Next, the images need to be translated to simple symbols that will not complicate the fabrication of the idea. This proves to be the greatest challenge to the artist's problem-solving ability. At this point it is useful to consider materials that will make it possible to make an object out of the idea. Contemporary Christian artists working on temporary installations have found that materials such as felt, nylon, gauze, and paper allow for both inexpensive production and great potential for creativity. Three dimensional works are often rendered in lightweight wood and foam board. Some artists have approached the work as set-design and have gained experience from this art form. The work is similar in concept and process to theater and installation art.

In one church during Advent season the theme of Christ emptying himself of his glorification to become as a servant and a sacrifice was made into a work, which supported ideas from a variety of texts including Philippians 2, 2 Corinthians 9:9, and Matthew 14:15-21. The top zone of the work consisted of blue and purple velvet representing the heavenly realm and royalty of Christ in that realm. Purple is the color of sorrow and penitence. The work was constructed to give the effect of descent. Under this top part was a series of six golden baskets, five filled with loaves of bread and one filled with two fishes (real bread and real smoked fish). This was a visual reminder of Matthew's account of Christ's feeding the multitude. Under this lineup of filled golden baskets were six empty baskets representing the needs of humanity and the potential of being filled. These were gray in color and were six in number to correspond to the six golden baskets and to represent the six works of mercy tending the hungry, the thirsty, the stranger, the naked, the sick, and the prisoner (Matt. 25:35-37). Under the gray baskets were torn, dirty, gray-dyed cheesecloth, representing the contrast to the royal, heavenly cloth in the top area. Humanity is in a needy condition but always with the potential of God's grace cleansing and enrichment through the redemptive work of Christ the Savior.

Alva Steffler

325 • BIBLIOGRAPHY ON THE SECONDARY SYMBOLS IN WORSHIP

Bangert, Mark P. *Symbols and Terms of the Church.* Minneapolis: Augsburg-Fortress, 1990. A pamphlet appropriate for use in church education programs.

Dean, Beryl. *Ecclesiastical Embroidery.* London: B. T. Batsford, 1958. A complete discussion of the contribution of embroidery to vestments, altarcloths, veils, and other cloths used in the context of worship in highly liturgical churches.

Benson, George Willard. *The Cross: Its History and Symbolism.* New York: Hacker Art Books, 1983. A comprehensive history of what has become (but was not always) the most prominent Christian symbol.

Ferguson, George. *Signs and Symbols in Christian Art.* New York: Oxford, 1954, 1989. A catalogue of a vast number of symbols used in the history of Christian art, along with 350 illustrations.

Hope, William St. John, and E. G. Cuthbert Atchley. *English Liturgical Colours.* New York: Macmillan Company, 1918. A classic work on the significance attributed to colors in the worship environment.

Ireland, Marion P. *Textile Art in the Church: Vestments, Paraments, and Hangings in Contemporary Worship.* Nashville: Abingdon Press, 1971. A comprehensive overview of the use of the textile arts in the worship environment in both history and recent practice. Especially helpful are the numerous photographs throughout.

Kapikian, Catherine A. *Through the Christian Year: An Illustrated Guide.* Nashville: Abingdon Press, 1983. A book of sketches that correspond to the seasons of the Christian year.

Lesage, Robert. *Vestments and Church Furniture.* New York: Hawthorne Books, 1960. Complete description of Roman Catholic practice prior to Vatican II.

Moe, Daniel. *Christian Symbols Handbook: Commentary and Patterns for Traditional and Contemporary Symbols.* Minneapolis: Augsburg, 1985. Includes helpful patterns to aid in reproducing these symbols on larger scales.

Pocknee, Cyril Edward. *Cross and Crucifix in Christian Worship and Devotion.* London: Mowbray, 1962.

Limouris, Gennadios, ed. *Icons: Windows on Eternity: Theology and Spirituality in Colour.* Geneva: WCC Publications, 1990. Essays on theological, historical, aesthetic, and spiritual dimensions of iconography.

Miller, Madeleine. *A Treasury of the Cross.* New York: Harper and Brothers, 1956.

Mayar-Thurman, Christa C. *Raiment for the Lord's Service: A Thousand Years of Western Vestments.* Chicago: The Art Institute of Chicago, 1975. Includes hundreds of photographs along with essays by Aidan Kavanaugh, Donald Garfield, and Horace T. Allen.

Mayo, Janet. *A History of Ecclesiastical Dress.* London: B. T. Batsford, 1984.

Norris, Herbert. *Church Vestments: Their Origin and Development.* London: J. M. Dent and Sons, 1949.

Post, W. Ellwood. *Saints, Signs, and Symbols.* Wilton, Conn.: Morehouse-Barlow Co., 1962, 1974. An illustrated listing of the most common symbols used in the Western church.

Rest, Friedrich. *Our Christian Symbols.* Cleveland: Pilgrim Press, 1959.

Ritter, Richard H. *The Arts of the Church.* Boston: Pilgrim Press, 1947. Discusses the full range of use of the arts in the church, including a discussion of painting, sculpture, and the furnishings of the worship space.

Webber, F. R. *Church Symbolism.* Cleveland: J. H. Jansen, 1938.

West, Edward N. *Outward Signs: The Language of Christian Symbolism.* New York: Walker and Company, 1989. A complete, illustrated guide to the various symbols of the Christian tradition and related terminology.

Whone, Herbert. *Church Monastery Cathedral: A Guide to the Symbolism of the Christian Tradition.* Short Hills, N.J.: Ridley Enslow, 1977.

❧ FOURTEEN ❧

Planning and Creating Visual Art for Worship

=====

As the preceding chapters point out, the use of visual arts in worship involve a complex set of theological, liturgical, and aesthetic issues. Undoubtedly, these issues need to be addressed by skilled worship leaders, planners, and artists. This chapter addresses some of the concerns involved in planning and creating visual arts for worship.

=====

326 • PLANNING VISUAL ARTS FOR WORSHIP

This article gives practical advice for planning art for worship, focusing particularly on temporary art. It argues for the importance of planning art that coordinates with other aspects of the worship service and that is characterized by simplicity.

The Artist in Cooperation with Worship Planners

The cooperation of the pastor and the worship committee is essential for an artist to make any meaningful visual contribution to the worship service. The *total* service needs to be taken into account when we alter the worship environment: the kinds of songs we sing, the readings, and the sermon all may suggest a particular mood—affirmative, confessional, devotional, or celebrative. That mood should be reflected in the worship environment where God's people gather.

The Christian church uses colors to mark the moods of the various seasons of the church year. The Advent color has traditionally been purple, but recently blue-purple or even dark blue has been used to separate this season from Lent. Christmas, because it is one of the holy days of the church, is colored white, as is Epiphany. During these days and seasons the designated colors should dominate the worship environment.

Images that are introduced into the worship environment should connect with either a song, a reading, or the sermon. By definition, symbols are visual reminders, so if an image stands alone, it will lose its purpose—its connection with the service. That is why it is so important to plan ahead, to attempt to integrate the total service by talking with everyone who will be contributing to worship. The ideas and concepts that emerge from such a dialogue will best serve your particular congregation. Everyone will know why a particular image is used; it will be a meaningful element in the total worship experience rather than just a decoration.

Visual Planning

But how does one begin this process? Start with the biblical texts the pastor has chosen for the sermons; begin, by reading and listening.

To illustrate how this process might work, take a close look at some of the first Sunday of Advent readings from the *Common Lectionary Year B*. You gain a number of insights simply by listing the concepts expressed in the various lessons. Some are abstract; some are visual. For the purpose of this general study, here are a few from the RSV, underlining those that have specific visual possibilities.

• **Isaiah 63:16–64:8 (First Sunday in Advent).**
rend heavens, come down, mountains quake,

fire kindles, *fire* causes *boiling,* make name known, heard nor seen, a God like you, *unclean, filthy garments,* wither like a leaf, iniquity like *wind,* Father, like *clay, potter,* all are work of thy hands

- Psalm 80:1-7 (First Sunday in Advent). *face, shine upon,* tears, save
- Mark 13:32-37 (1st Sunday in Advent). take heed, keep alert
- Isaiah 40:1-11 (Second Sunday in Advent). every *valley,* every *mountain, grass* withers, *flower* fades

If all of these texts will be part of the worship service, and especially if the sermon deals with the Isaiah text, the pot from the first Sunday and the flower from the second Sunday could be combined into one image. If you have a potter in your congregation, it may be effective to ask her to create a pot during the service. That pot will serve in weeks to come as a reminder of the message for this day.

Keep It Simple

When creating images, it is important to remember two things: simplicity and proportion. By keeping an image *simple,* the trap of becoming overconcerned with detail is avoided. For example, the profile of a pot allows people to recognize it as a pot; fancy decorations or a three dimensional effect are unnecessary. All that is important is the symbol—it reminds us that God is the potter and we are the clay. People may not understand the symbol when they first enter the sanctuary and have not yet been told the story. But when they leave, the meaning of the visual image should be clear.

In addition to simplicity *proportion,* or relationships within the overall image, should be remembered. How big in the space of the banner should the pot be? What emphasis, what kind of focus are we trying to create? How does the church sanctuary influence the decisions made about the size of the image?

Most of those who contribute to filling the worship space with symbol and color quickly discover that each church sanctuary presents demands as well as solutions. They also find that their congregation's unique style of worship has a lot to do with the types of visuals designs that will be effective in worship.

Chris Stoffel Overvoorde[87]

327 • EVALUATING VISUAL ART FOR WORSHIP

Visual art is made for communication and expression, and thus must be evaluated for how it accomplishes these tasks in a liturgical context. The evaluation process must be sensitive to be theological and aesthetic considerations. In particular, arts for liturgical use are best presented and evaluated in the context of the Christian year or the particular Sunday for which it is created.

The visual arts present opportunities to look at long-standing prejudices and ideas about art in worship and to search for fresh ideas in a field shunned by many faiths for a long time. It is presumed, in this article, that what we are evaluating is temporary art, rather than architecture or more permanent additions, such as sculpture, stained glass, or furnishings.

The Broader Questions

Many of us are untrained in the visual arts. We are vaguely aware that art can decorate our walls, and that some people collect art, and that some institutions enshrine it for the rest of us to venerate. We can appreciate art that pleases us. We can even find a place for visual art in worship, especially during Christmas, when our secular life holds such a strong promotion of nostalgia. Creches and greens are then a part of the times and do not offend our sense of appropriateness for our worship spaces.

Is this how we evaluate the function of art in worship? Is it to entertain? Does it provide the traditional image to particular festivals? Do people have to like art for it to be acceptable in worship?

Many of us have tolerated another form of art—that which *instructs* or *gives a message.* We permit slogans or cliches to appear on our walls, brightly colored, in the form of banners. Occasionally we even abandon words, substituting instead a cultic vocabulary of esoteric symbols or crests from creeds of the past. Our favorite medium for this is felt and Elmer's Glue, and we often "design" by vaguely copying examples from religious catalogues or poster books. We even totally ignore the space it will show in, disregarding color or size as relevant considerations. Such religious "propaganda," such it is because its function is to persuade or educate us, attracts our attention for a moment or two, but seldom goes beyond this. It is quickly dismissed or overlooked beyond a first glance.

Should art used in worship be the Word made

visual? Should it explain, justify or connect an illustration as illustrative of a theme or idea from Scripture or sermon? Is it less important than other parts of worship?

Another tradition of the visual arts has been that of the icon or religious image that serves as a _meditative focus for prayer._ Usually these images are stylistically and iconographically predictable. Their function is to become transparent to our experience, almost magic in their ability to transform our humble words to prayers fit for the Holy to hear.

Is there religious art and secular art? Is subject matter the most important quality to consider in evaluating such art? Can religious subject matter ever become kitsch? Or sentimental?

There are dangers in attitudes like these that are used to evaluate visual art in worship. Many of us are uncomfortable with sentimental religious experiences, sensing with embarrassment their inability to address the complex and conflicting questions and priorities before us today. We see cloying sweetness and innocence leading toward indifference or hostility toward the world as it is. We also are jaded by fads and by slogans, and are impatient with cliches. Our artists often sell out to our aesthetic limitations, choosing instead to approach us as yet another client for a commission, yet another advertising design challenge. They do not give us art, but a product they think will please us.

We hunger for truth, honesty, and freshness. We wither without our imaginations. We cry out for visions of glory. We want our sons and daughters to dream dreams, our old ones to see visions, and our men and women to prophesy. I believe it is here that we must begin to evaluate art that is used in our sanctuaries for use in worship.

Specific Ideas

What, then, is appropriate for worship? Obviously such an evaluation begins with a clear understanding of what theme or season is highlighted on a particular Sunday. It is probably more appropriate to look backwards at credal images on Reformation Sunday than on Pentecost. Thorns belong more to the austerity of Lent than the abundance of Epiphany. Many churches find art for worship flowing naturally when particular Scriptures guide not only the sermon and music, but all other aspects in the liturgy. Use of a lectionary or similar long-range plan makes such creativity practical.

There are certain aesthetic considerations in vi-

sual art that have parallel sensitivities in the other arts. Visual art is evaluated by these criteria: composition, color, scale, harmony, counterpoint, and the environment in which the piece is hung. Usually scale is the most difficult concept to grasp. Many of us simply make things too small! A grand scale, like one would use in stage-set design, conveys of itself a graciousness and majesty that automatically adds a sense of glory and importance to worship.

One of the reasons artists make art is for self-searching and self-expression. When working for a congregation, this cannot be the focus. Here we are making art for _communal use_ and _common expression._ Here the work is not for self, but rather for _communal identity._ When our own experiences can be made broad enough or transparent enough in their meanings that the community can use them or claim them, they can be appropriated. But even here, it is not personal testament as much as _corporate vision_ that works.

The strongest criteria of the quality of art appropriate for worship is its ability to evoke, to involve, to refresh, to provoke, or engage the worshiper on an emotive rather than a rational level. Such art allures us, calling forth response before calling for explanation. It is often very difficult to talk about it at all. Often images based on an emotional response to the Scripture or theme of worship for that day are the place to begin. Usually these are semiabstract in form, engaging our imagination rather than instructing us.

There are not categories of spiritual feelings and nonspiritual feelings. We must be ready to accept the intensity of all the feelings evoked and integrate them with faith experiences.

Finally, for the work to have integrity, it best arises out of the people themselves. It is created for their own community in a particular time, for particular occasion, in a specific site. This is perhaps the most difficult dimension of evaluation. Not every church is able to claim artists among their own, nor find artists willing to work within the assumptions and needs of the church. Making visual art is a talent and skill, like making sermons, or making music. Unfortunately the church has done much to discourage the artist from participating in worship as an artist.

In summary, how is work evaluated? Does it work aesthetically? Especially the scale? Is it integrative, as the other parts of the worship service are? Is it communal in its nature rather than personal or esoteric? Does it evoke rather than instruct? Does it merely decorate? Does it have courage and integrity? Is it imaginative? Does it arise from the work of the people themselves?

When art arises from these parameters, it belongs naturally in worship. It adds a dimension which is unapproachable by any other means. But diminishing of any of these parameters by compromise or carelessness seriously weakens this gift.

Yet it is our visual artist who can most clearly show us a vision that hints of the Kingdom of Shalom. It is God's glory which is reflected whenever one works from courage, integrity, and imagination. It is God's love made visible in yet another way when the abundance of such art is showered upon us with the lavishness and sensuality: a gift that is bestowed with love made visible.

Nancy Chinn[88]

328 • An Artist's Perspective on Creating Visual Art for Worship

The following article examines the process of commissioning and creating visual art for worship from the point of view of an artist, exploring in particular the unique concerns of the liturgical artist.

After fourteen years as a professional craftsperson, working in pottery and fiber, I have become increasingly interested in making things for use in worship. The occupation of "dressing the church" uses many of my past experiences and skills, but it brings with it a new set of problems—personal and professional. The following reflections developed as I wove vestments, hangings, and altar cloths. I hope they will strike a chord with others who can develop them more fully and more deeply.

A Question of Design

As I do liturgical design work, one question repeatedly comes to mind: What is the difference between designs for the liturgy and other designs? I don't feel any different doing liturgical work, and there is no apparent difference in the design processes. I gather information from a client and find out as much as possible about the space in which the object will be used. I show samples, swatches, and sketches to elicit responses; then within the limits of available materials and technical skills, I produce the best design possible. That's pretty

straightforward, though not easy. Any artisan who does commission work or custom orders has a healthy respect for the difficulties involved in communicating with clients and in satisfying them with the resulting product.

Many conflicts and tensions are built into the design process, and picking one's way through them is a balancing act. The artisan has to balance conflicting responsibilities. Details of planning or producing, for instance, require constant attention, while one's vision or image of a beautiful creation shimmers in the future. Such a "stereoscopic vision" must be held in focus for the goal to be attained with any success, or the result will lack clarity.

Another conflict or tension exists between the desire to spare no expense to produce the most beautiful object possible and the real limitations placed on the artisan's time and the client's pocketbook. Sometimes the design process is unexpectedly prolonged by something as simple as the unavailability of a required material. But such stumbling blocks, conflicts and tensions can become the steppingstones to where one wants to go. This is a matter of making good use of the time at hand to think about and experiment with design possibilities.

The process is almost the same whether the commission is for an altar cloth or a bed quilt, but the completed works will be used in distinctly different ways. Liturgical design work is done for a community rather than individual, and that community uses the work for a sacred purpose: to enhance worship.

Designing for a Community

Even though the artisan may deal with one individual who represents the worshiping community, that person must convey the needs and desires of the whole group. The artisan needs to ask the right questions and gather as much information as possible before proceeding, but the design is not produced by committee; it is the responsibility of the artisan alone. If the proposed design is not acceptable, it may be modified; another design can be worked out or another artisan hired.

The resulting design should express or reflect the nature of the particular community, but it should also point that community to what it might become. This prophetic quality, or prescience, is an elusive but important element of art that challenges the body of worshipers, encouraging response and growth. If "we become what we behold," as Psalm 34 suggests, then all the visual elements in a church are vitally important. The community's response to the completed work can be a powerful dynamic when it gathers to worship and when it goes forth into the larger community.

In addition to considering the community for which a work is executed, one must also carefully consider the sacred purpose of the completed work. This purpose is realized when the object is taken out of the artisan's control and put to use. At that moment this "work of human hands" is made holy. If the artisan is in the congregation, it is a humbling and poignant experience to see the vestment of chalice or altar cloth used in the context of worship.

A designer must understand that the object is made holy, not by human efforts alone, but by being offered and used for a sacred purpose. This fact frees the designer from the worrisome feeling that only saintly or religious people can make sacred objects. No human being is adequate to this task, and if this fact is not fully accepted, some problems are bound to arise. For one thing, if the artisan feels "unworthy," there will be an almost compulsive temptation to multiply the use of sacred symbols on the work. This multiplication has a "desanctifying" effect, for the harder we try to "make" something holy, the more we are assured of failure. The multiplication of symbols weakens the power of the object. By accepting the fact that the object will be transformed more by use than by symbols, the artisan is free to do what he or she does best. Creative energies can then be focused on making a beautiful form through which the liturgy can come alive and flower in the community.

This topic of the object's holiness has personal parallels for the artisan. On our own, we might achieve virtuous lives with great effort. But we cannot make ourselves holy; God alone does this. We can offer ourselves to God and cooperate with God's actions in our lives, or we can choose not to. We can receive the Lord's blessings joyfully and gratefully, or we can take them for granted. We can share God's gifts with others or keep them to ourselves. But if we offer ourselves to God, as the work of the artisan is offered, then God can use us for God's own purposes.

Respecting One's Craft

God's work in completing the process of liturgical design does not diminish the importance of the artisan's effort. We must bring to any work we do for churches a sense of reverence and respect, but not to the point of timidity or immobility. Being self-conscious is as much a difficulty as being insensitive to the work's importance and potential. Fear of doing something that is unintentionally funny, absurd, or even scandalous—something that will be shown as a "bad example" in someone's slide show at next year's liturgy conference—must be overcome again and again. Otherwise one will do only what is "safe," repeating something that succeeded in the past. That course of action results in work that has a deadly, sanitized look. Removing the risk means removing all the things that invigorate a work; it is the death of creativity. "Playing it safe" won't displease or offend anyone, but neither will it move people to smile with joy, shed a tear, or pray spontaneously.

I have resolved this tension between safety and risk by making the best work I can. Then I show it to someone whose judgment and taste I respect, for comments and criticism. This dialogue helps me to grow and try out new ideas. Looking at other works, traditional and contemporary, also helps.

People who are interested and knowledgeable in liturgical design are difficult to find. When I do find them, I consider them gifts. Various people appear in my path when I need them, and for that I am grateful. Both their encouragement and their critical comments have helped me to continue working in the liturgical field when confidence wavered or when logic could provide no answers. One such resource person I met through a magazine article, and we developed a correspondence. I met another when friends brought someone into our shop. Others came from a design workshop and a visit to a seminary to look at a vestment collection.

I value my dialogue with these people who are vitally interested in a rather specialized field of design work for which good books and periodicals are hard to come by. These people are clergy and lay, women and men, of various ages and backgrounds. What is important is that we share a common vision: we want to create beautiful things to be used for a sacred purpose by the worshiping community, and we each have different abilities to contribute to that end.

Catalogue versus Craft

Why order custom-made work when articles can simply be ordered from a catalogue? While there is nothing inherently wrong with ready-made vestments or altar cloths, they can never replace objects crafted with the personal skill, inspiration and creativity of an artisan. Never having the chance to commission original art would be a great loss to the community as well as to local artists and artisans. The presence of something unique and beautiful is a great gift; it calls forth peace and healing—even conversion—at deep, unspoken levels in both the artist and the viewer. Thomas Merton said, "Sacred art is theology in line and color, and it speaks to the whole man. . . . The material elements of the image become as it were the vehicle of the Holy Spirit, and furnish Him with an occasion to reach souls with His hidden, spiritual power" (Thomas Merton, *Disputed Questions* [New York: Farrar, Straus, and Giroux, 1976], 156).

When parishioners make a vestment or an altar cloth, they often think that materials must be ordered from a church goods catalogue; yet actually, they could purchase the same fabric locally. In a local store, they can examine the material, or ask for a courtesy discount, or have the owner order just what they need. But some church goods catalogues suggest that their fabric is special, beyond the ordinary; the fact that it costs more than local goods only seems to enhance its desirability. Catalogue prices for mass-produced items are often so high that an experienced artisan can produce work at competitive prices. Catalogue prices, after all, reflect the cost of employees, accountants, equipment, and 200-page annual color catalogues. Responding to the desire for crafts, some suppliers list handmade or handcrafted items, like carved crosses from Italy, that cost thousands of dollars. Imported crafts are not necessarily better than domestic crafts; artisans working in this country can produce equally authentic and beautiful objects, and at less cost.

Adapting the Ordinary

Why can't an artisan's ordinary production items be purchased for use in church? If you buy a handmade iced tea pitcher and goblets to hold and serve the consecrated wine, you are not making use of the artisan's ability to design something special for liturgical use. The maker of a custom Communion set considers such important aspects of the design as the capacity of the vessels, their size in scale to the altar, the extra stability required and ease in passing them from hand to hand. Such a design takes time and should be done sensitively. Artisans should pray for the grace to do simple and subtle liturgical design work. Obvious solutions, such as putting a cross on an existing iced tea pitcher or sewing the word *Alleluia* on a spring hanging to make an Easter banner, do not make good liturgical design.

The obvious does not invite us to go deeper, to reflect, to look, to wonder. Sensitive use of color and symbol in church design work is a natural means to lead us into supernatural realities with all their mystery. The obvious solution ("Alleluia!") has a bullying quality that brings out our defenses or numbs us; subtle solutions lead us gently, gracefully, into worship. "Where there is revelation, explanation becomes superfluous" (Frederick Frank, *The Zen of Seeing* [New York: Random House, 1973], 28).

For an artisan, the completed work becomes a prayer to which the community can say "Amen." Freedom, however brief or fleeting, can be found by losing oneself in such a work. Though questions linger, their importance fades. What matters to me at the creative moment is that both the artisan and work serve a sacred purpose and become incarnations in which God's spirit can live.

Mary Lou Weaver[89]

329 • COMMISSIONING A STAINED GLASS INSTALLATION

This article gives helpful advice for planning or commissioning a stained glass work, describing the process that might be used and important decisions that need to be made by both the artist and the commissioning congregation.

Stained glass, from its origins, has been an integral element of church architecture because of its inherently dynamic qualities. While it stimulates our visual senses, it stirs us emotionally toward a more reverential sensitivity, encouraging introspection and contemplation. Stained glass complements the liturgical action by infusing the place and people with a heightened sense of purpose.

However, like all aspects of building or renovation, the successful use of stained glass depends on careful and thoughtful planning. These notes will focus on the steps involved in commissioning stained glass work rather than aesthetic or stylistic considerations.

The Parish Team

A committee or task force for procuring stained glass should be formed early in the design of the project to work with the building team and the parish as a whole. This group is best comprised of a member of the building or renovation committee, the architect, the pastor or a representative, and several interested parishioners who reflect the diversity of the congregation but who are also knowledgeable in the arts. Five to seven members is a good size. This team is then charged with selection of the artist or team of artists, with design review, parish communication, and cost control. (Editor's note: We would encourage parishes to include an art consultant on the overall building/renovation committee. This person would also be included on the task force dealing with stained glass.)

The committee should begin by learning at least a bit of the history of stained glass and by visiting stained glass installations in the area to familiarize themselves with the scope of the medium. Then they are ready to determine the role of stained glass in their building. Important factors are:

- **Purpose**: e.g., to express ideas, beliefs, feelings
- **Light**: e.g., aesthetic effect, control, level of brightness, emphasis, color
- **Effect**: e.g., quiet, calm, meditative, exciting, dynamic, joyful
- **Expression**: e.g., realistic, symbolic, abstract
- **Style**: attitude toward traditional or contemporary

Artist/Studio Selection

The committee can go to an independent artist/designer, or to a studio with a staff artist/designer. There are arguments to be made for either. The committee should consider both possibilities. Sources for learning about possible candidates include the architect, other churches, local arts organizations, and national organizations such as SGAA and IFRAA.

Initially, the committee should request from each candidate a brochure describing the person's work, slides, and photos, a resume with references and a list of previous commissions. By reviewing these materials, the committee can reduce the number of candidates to a manageable few. Each of these should then be invited for an interview. At the interview, the committee and the artist view and discuss the artist's work; the committee shares with the artist their thoughts about the parish's project, about the process, and possibly about the concept. The committee should inquire about costs, insurance, length of time for design and production, background and experience of any other persons who would be involved through the artist.

This selection of an artist should be made as soon as possible after the schematic (preliminary) design of the building or renovation so that the artist/designer can collaborate with the architect during the further development of the design. This allows for a high degree of integration between stained glass and the building itself.

Contracting the Artist

After the selection of the artist or studio, the relationship between the artist/studio and the parish (owner/client) should be set down in a contract. A complete contract usually involves the following:

- Well-defined scope of services to be performed by the artist/studio
- Description of the work and responsibilities involved in performing the scope of services
- The work schedule and temporal conditions of the work's performance
- The cost/fee for the contracted work and an explicit payment schedule
- Any terms or conditions that are peculiar to the project

The Design Process

The stained glass design process begins with a contract that commissions the artist. (Note that sometimes people suggest that the artist be selected by means of competitive [and unpaid] design submissions. This begins design process before the artist is a member of the team and thus removes the possibility of productive interaction between the artist and other team members. The result of such competitions is often inferior art, and the whole process is unfair to the artists who are not selected.)

The first phase of the design process begins with meetings between the committee and the artist to share perceptions of the role stained glass will play in the project. The artist then initiates preliminary designs for the committee's consideration. This process does not imply that the committee tells the artist how to design. Rather, the shared impressions and the interaction help the artist to become more sensitive to the character and personality of the community being served.

From these discussions, the artist prepares the final designs, preferably in a transparent form so that the effects of transmitted light are better understood. It is also beneficial if the artist provides a sample panel, or prototype, that demonstrates the materials and techniques that are proposed for use in the windows.

Upon approval of the final design, the committee's work is essentially complete, although visits to the studio during production may be warranted and helpful. The success of the installed windows is, to a great extent, the result of the work of parishioners and building team members through their involvement in the early phases of the process.

Kenneth F. von Roenn, Jr.[90]

330 • THE ARTIST-IN-RESIDENCE IN THE LOCAL CONGREGATION

One creative approach in integrating the visual arts into the life of the local congregation involves employing an artist-in-residence. In return for studio space and appropriate monetary remuneration, the artist-in-residence is available to create visual arts for worship, to instruct worshipers about the nature of the visual arts in worship, and to involve members of the congregation in the design and fabrication of the arts in worship.

Art and theology are both about the discipline of the imagination. Thus, they have a natural affinity, one with the other, making an advocacy role by the church for artistic expression in process and product a wise investment. In fact, the local parish provides an optimal setting for a resident artist and gives the congregation and artist alike the mutual benefit of each other's imaginings.

The sense of awe and wonder triggered by watching a resident artist work kindles the religious imagination. The reality of radical faith is brought to light when watching an artist trust a creative process to reveal resolution. The presence of grace is experienced when watching an artist transform material and transcend the medium by creating a whole greater than the sum of its parts.

The intermingling of creative processes with religious ideas is productive for the church and empowering for the artist. This mutually beneficial arrangement lifts up the notion that applied creativity is an essential resource for building our world, while the faith of the church lifts up the notion that the capacity to create is a reflection of our being in the divine image. By building on the intrinsic relationship between the artistic and spiritual dimensions of human existence, an artist-in-residence program promotes the idea that the artistic vision and the vision of faith see possibility in all things.

Although the following discussion sets forth parameters for a visual artist's residency, its concepts are adaptable to residencies of artists working in nonvisual mediums (dance, music, drama, or other arts). Furthermore, the issues and suggestions outlined in this discussion are pertinent to churches of contrasting membership size. Only slight modifications are required in establishing an artist-in-residence in a small church of approximately 200 members as opposed to a corporate-sized church of 2,000 members. (See Arlen Rauthge's *Sizing Up Your Church* for a definition and discussion of categories of congregational size.)

In a large church, it is politically astute to align the arts committee with another (worship, liturgy, education, or music) for support or status. As a catalyst for arts activity, the arts committee negotiates between professional staff and members of the congregation, recommending to both on behalf of the other.

Since the arts committee functions to enhance the life of the congregation through art, and since art is easily dismissed or misunderstood, this committee must supplement all of its programming with a persistent educational agenda. First, however, the committee must educate itself. An organized study of several books that bridge art and theology will enable the members to field such questions as: "What is religious art?", "What is Christian art?", "What is sacred art?", "What is liturgical art?" Members will be prepared to point out invalid distinctions as well as amplify meaningful ones. If asked, "Is the best church art the best secular art, or what purpose in Christianity should art serve, or can a non-Christian artist produce a work of art for liturgy?" committee members will answer by asking more questions. Compelled to such discourse with the congregation, committee members animate interest and understanding of the arts and lay the groundwork for the appointment and arrival of an artist-in-residence.

It is wise to select an artist who not only is professionally competent, but also is articulate and engaging. Give the artist ample room. Convert a Sunday school classroom to a studio. Such a room often exists in a heated building otherwise empty during the week. Forty hours per month of working time on behalf of the church is an equitable exchange for a modest salary and in-kind contribution of space and utilities. Give the artist a key and expect him or her to come and go at will, creating in the studio a place where the creative process is given high visibility for the church. The congregation and the artist need at least a year together to realize the benefit of each other. A renewal contract or a contract with another artist is a viable option at the end of the first year.

Traditionalism versus innovation is the critical issue the church faces in committing to an artist-in-residence, and the arts committee helps the congregation understand this issue. The artist works at the boundary between tradition and innovation. A work of art by nature has the capacity to take a person to a new place of being because the newness of the experience excites, distresses, delights, disturbs, challenges. The role of the artist, like that of the priest, is a prophetic one.

The arts committee helps to integrate the artist with the professional staff and advocates for his/her presence in planning sessions. Inclusion achieves two major things: first, the artist has time to incubate, a critical step in the creative process when the artist wrestles with ideas and searches for solutions; second, the artist is not ghettoized, thereby enabling his/her works to be understood as essential to the life of the church rather than "extra," like frosting on a cake or stripes on a pair of stockings. If the artist is well integrated into the staff and understood and accepted as one of them, his or her visual proclamations will be taken in stride much the same way the pastor's work is.

When West Coast artist Nancy Chinn was artist-in-residence with a congregation in San Francisco, she appointed two committees to work with her—one, a Dream Committee, and the other, a Recruitment Committee.

The Dream Committee, comprised of approximately half a dozen members from the congrega-

tion, interacted with Nancy regarding the use of sanctuary space around themes of worship. Referring to the appointed Scripture for that week or season, Nancy would ask, "What does this Scripture mean to you? What are the feelings this Scripture evokes from you? What is the mood we are trying to get across with this theme?" These questions provoked a "feeling" response, enabling Nancy to incubate ideas and visualize creations.

The Recruitment Committee, also comprised of members of the congregation, helped paint, fabricate, cut, install, and otherwise construct the work designed by the resident artist. Thus the work in the sanctuary became the work of the people. This work, inspired by Scripture, might accompany the procession, amplify the reading of the lessons, embellish a prayer, accompany the bringing of the gifts, elaborate upon the sermon, or surface during dismissal. With the help of this committee, the artist designed the work (a painted paper carpet down the center isle with images of Holy Week on which congregants walk); organized the project; worked out mechanics of installation (e.g., a concealed drop-line system supportive of an evocative swoop of red, orange, and yellow ribbons during Pentecost, or 1,400 cut and folded paper dove images during Epiphany); and instructed people how to work with the chosen artistic medium.

The artist embodies and enfleshes the Word with the aid of the community in other ways. He/she might offer intergenerational "how-to" workshops during off-school times that thrive on the spontaneity of children and adults of all ages. Retreats which lift up the creative process as a meditative process, sessions with Sunday School teachers helping them incorporate the artist's expertise in their teaching situations, an artist's chat on Sunday morning about work in the church studio or a dialogue sermon about applied creativity as rootedness in the divine image, all represent possibilities for engagement.

It is empowering to the artist to interact with a nurturing community. Furthermore, artists need space and the church needs the fresh insights of its artists. Why not risk such a relationship? Without risk, art and theology will not take us to an enlarged vision of reality where the religious imagination can take flight.

Catherine Kapikian[91]

331 • BIBLIOGRAPHY ON THE VISUAL ARTS IN WORSHIP

Allison, Laura. *Celebration: Banners, Dance and Holiness in Worship.* Wilmington, Pa.: SonRise, 1987. Everything you've wanted to know about banners, from theology to tote bags. Excellent ideas and planning resource with stunning color pictorials and graphics. Includes ideas for making stands, hangars, and carrying cases. Short section on dance focuses on garments appropriate for suggested dances. Third part emphasizes holiness as integrator of worship.

Beall, Patricia. *The Folk Arts in God's Family.* Sylva, N.C.: Celebration: 1984. Narrative history of the creative artisan/performer Fisherfolk, intermingled with a theology of arts ministry with missionary focus that includes worship, education, and festivity. Practically oriented writing discusses "unlocking" arts gifts and leadership necessary to maximize impact. Hundreds of readings, prayers, poetry, dances, mime and dramas, and some graphic arts. How-to section regarding workshops for every discipline. Ecumenical/renewal.

Bryans, Nena. *Full Circle.* San Carlos, Calif.: Schuyler, 1988. Excellent, concise volume proposing an end to the "estrangement" of religion and the arts by providing a rationale for initiating an arts ministry. Primer on spirituality and the arts; changing attitudes in the church with list of educational programs offered at various colleges/ universities; and an introduction to the four "languages" of worship and implications for worship, education, priestly, and prophetic roles of an arts ministry. Great quotes/footnotes and bibliography. Source: Methodist. Audience: Varied.

Gurak, Eileen. *Using Art in Sunday Worship.* San Jose, Calif.: Resources Publications, 1990. A very brief overview of the contribution of the visual arts to vestments, use of color in the worship space, and liturgical banners.

Knutson, Tekla, and Lynn Bloom. *Expressions of Faith: A Handbook for Visual Arts in the Church.* Minneapolis: Augsburg/Fortress, 1989.

Krier, Catherine H. *Symbols for All Seasons: Environment Planning for Cycles A, B, and C.* San Jose, Calif.: Resource Publications, 1988.

Moe, Dean. *Christian Symbols Handbook.* Minneapolis: Augsburg, 1985.

Ritter, Richard H. *The Arts of the Church.* Boston: Pilgrim Press, 1947. Classic and complete volume which considers both the worship environment and those who move through it. Church buildings, fittings, and furnishings; church literature, drama, and dance, painting and sculpture, and the "art of common worship" are all considered.

Post, E. Ellwood. *Saints, Signs, and Symbols.* Wilton, Conn.: Morehouse-Barlow, 1974.

Snyder, Bernadette, and Hazelmai Terry. *Decorating for Sundays and Holy Days.* Mystic, Conn.: Twenty-Third, 1983. Referenced to Cycle A church calendar. Small volume combines excellent creative and contemporary decorative ideas with Scripture references, prayers, and a reflective element. Seasonal, temporary designs with good visual components. Volume for Cycle C also available. Source: Catholic. Audience: Varied from family to parish.

Snyder, Bernadette, and Hazelmai Terry. *Decorations for 44 Parish Celebrations.* Mystic, Conn.: Twenty-Third, 1983. "Enhancing worship experiences tastefully and simply" is the theme of the book. Each suggestion is divided into three parts: *Reflection*—statements concerning liturgical theme and decorations; *Preparation and Decoration*—descriptive how-to section; and *Remember*—planning tips to involve and invite participants. Especially suited to more liturgical traditions. Source: Catholic/Episcopalian.

Also, for ideas for creating liturgical banners, see several of the resources published by Resource Publications, San Jose, California, including: George Callopy, *Extraordinary Banners for Ordinary Times;* Diane Guelzow, *Banners with Pizzaz: A Step by Step Guide;* George Callopy, *It's a Banner Year;* Jill Knuth, *Banners Without Words;* Adelaide Ortegel, *Banners and Such.*

PART FOUR

Drama and Dance
in Worship

FIFTEEN

Introduction to Drama
in Worship

Important in worship are not only the arts that we hear (music) and see (the visual arts), but also the arts that involve both seeing and hearing (drama and dance). These arts are complex and challenging, both to the artist and to the worshiper. They communicate messages at many levels, either by presenting an idea or image or by representing a significant event or narrative. Careful reflection and instruction is necessary to insure that artist and worshiper alike understand the appropriate role of drama and dance in worship and the unique language of each art that allows it to fill that role. The following chapters present arguments for the inclusion of these arts in worship, along with guidelines for their appropriate use and examples of each that can be used and adapted in local congregations.

Moments of heightened awareness, slowed or accelerated in pace and characterized by tension or pathos, are the small dramas of everyday life. Drama is part of living; it is also an inevitable part of worship. The liturgy itself has a dramatic quality, featuring dialogue between God and his people and heightening the worshipers' awareness of God's presence. In addition, drama in worship may recreate an important scriptural narrative or portray a scene from modern life that elicits or requires a scriptural response. Articles in this section give some historical background regarding the relationship of drama and worship, describe various types of drama appropriate for worship, and offer guidance for developing drama ministries in the congregation.

332 • A BRIEF HISTORY OF DRAMA IN WORSHIP

Worship as the celebration of God's saving acts in Christ is itself dramatic, enacting the relationship between God and his people and reenacting the living, dying, and rising of Christ. The article below traces this theme throughout the history of Christian worship.

Drama and Worship During Biblical Times

Hebrew worship, beginning with the early sacrifices made by Abel and his successors Abraham, the patriarchs, and the priesthood of Israel, is a dramatic portrayal of the relationship that men and women have with God. In the sacrifices of the Old Testament, a common pattern emerges, which, at its very heart, is a powerful four-part drama. First, the worshipers went through an extensive preparation and personal cleansing, followed by a ritual of preparing an animal for slaughter. Next, the animal in a cere-

monial rite was "offered" as a gift to God, who is the giver of all gifts. Then, in another ceremony the animal was butchered, and certain parts were burned on the altar. Finally, both priest and people shared a great feast together with God as they ate the animal that had been offered. In this dramatic action the "stuff" of every day life, which came from God, was offered to God, and returned by God to the people for the feast in which God shared. In this drama the true meaning of life was portrayed in a powerful four-act play.

This sense of dramatizing a relationship to God is central to all Jewish worship and finds a significant place in the feasts of Israel. The Shabbat is a dramatic remembrance of God's creative act; Passover a reenactment of the Exodus; Shavuoth, or Feast of Weeks, a celebration of harvest; Rosh Hashanah, or the Feast of Trumpets, a drama of the new year; and Yom Kippur, the Day of Atonement, a drama of returning to God; Sukkot, the Feast of Tabernacles or Feast of Booth, a dramatic remembrance that Israel lived in booths or huts when God called them up out of Egypt. In all these celebrations Israel told and acted out the story in worship which was directed to God. Drama was the underlying structure of worship.

The same approach to worship is found in New Testament times. The service of the Word is a dramatic retelling of God's great acts of creation, the Fall, the patriarchs, the Exodus and formation of Israel, the prophets, the coming of Jesus and his birth, life, death, resurrection, ascension, and coming again. This is story and drama at its best, a play about the meaning of the world and of our lives within world history.

Furthermore, the Eucharist or Lord's Supper is the great drama of God's saving act in Jesus Christ. (The connection the dramatic feast of the Old Testament has with the eucharistic drama and feast of Christian worship is more than coincidental.) Here, as in Israel, the drama of redemption is acted out and symbolized in the taking, blessing, breaking, and giving of bread and wine. This drama has an affinity with eating and drinking at home, with the drama of life continually nourished. It is not a casual drama to be taken lightly or not played well. Rather, it is a dramatic reenactment of the most important event in history, the event through which a new creation was birthed, an event that marks the beginning of the steady march of creation toward becoming the new heavens and the new earth.

Drama and Worship in Subsequent History

The dramatic nature of worship shown above is found in the practice of worship from the very beginning of the Christian era and has remained a fundamental aspect of worship through history. Variations can be seen in the intensity with which the drama of worship has been celebrated. In the early church the Eucharist was always celebrated with an awareness of its drama and mystery. As worship became public and was celebrated in large basilicas, later churches, and cathedrals since the fourth century, the dramatic nature of the service was stressed through an increased number of processions and ceremonial actions centering around primary actions of the liturgy, such as the reading of the gospel and the celebration of bread and wine. The only major departure from the dramatic sense of worship in history is the emergence of modern Protestant worship. This form of worship is largely directed toward the intellect. But even here dramatic elements are often unknowingly expressed in the style of preaching and in the manner of handling Communion.

In addition to the Sunday drama, the festivals of the church year were developed as dramatic memorials of God's acts of salvation. Primarily these services of worship are clustered around Christmas and Easter. While the services of Advent, Christmas, and Epiphany were dramas of the coming of Christ and his manifestation to the world, the most intense dramatic celebrations are during Holy Week—Palm Sunday, Maundy Thursday, Good Friday, the Paschal Vigil, Easter Sunday, and Pentecost.

Drama Within the Liturgy

While the dramatic nature of worship has always been expressed through the service of worship itself, the idea of drama or small dramas within worship has not fared as well. Christian worship began in the Roman era when theater was crude, degenerate, and characterized by a considerable immorality. Consequently drama, the theater, mime, puppets and such were viewed by Christians with distaste and even horror. When Constantine was converted and the empire was "Christianized" somewhat, Christians dealt a decisive blow to drama and theater.

During the medieval era, the Catholic church restored drama as a way of communicating the stories of faith and educating the people. The earliest forms of drama were developed around the events of Holy Week. On Palm Sunday, the church held a procession with a person riding on a donkey; on Good Friday a cross was wrapped in cloth and laid inside an empty tomb in the chancel; and on Easter Sunday the empty cross was dramatically displayed to celebrate the Resurrection. Another early form of drama known as the trope, meaning phrase or clause, became a dramatic insertion in the liturgy. The following trope, *Quem Queritas* ("whom seek ye"), is found in the introductory portion of the Mass as early as A.D. 925:

ANGEL: Whom seek ye in the tomb, O Christian?
THE THREE MARYS: Jesus of Nazareth, the crucified, O Heavenly Beings.

ANGEL: He is not here, He is risen as He foretold. God and announce that He is risen from the tomb.

Soon plays like the *Quem Queritas* were expanded into full dramatic productions and eventually spread all over Europe, expanding beyond into the medieval market place. Three kinds of plays were developed: (1) *mystery plays,* which dramatized Bible events such as Creation, the lives of various persons (e.g., Cain and Abel, Noah, Abraham, etc.), the birth, death and resurrection of Jesus; (2) *miracle plays,* which featured Christian saints such as St. Nicholas and Joan of Arc; (3) *morality plays,* which probed human conduct and dealt with the clash between vices and virtues; the most famous of these plays is *Everyman.* While drama had its start in the church and flourished in the liturgy and the courtyards of churches, it eventually became increasingly baudy and secular. In 1250, Pope Innocent III threw the players out of the church, but they continued to perform in the outdoors.

Drama within the church did not fare well during the Reformation, the Puritan era, or during the seventeenth through the nineteenth centuries. Only now in twentieth-century renewal worship is drama finding its place back within the church.

———— Drama in Worship Today ————

In the twentieth century, drama within the church has come full circle and is making a comeback in worship. The dramatic nature of every service of worship, the dramatic character of the great festivals of the church year, and the use of small dramas within worship are all matters of interest. Generally, three criteria are used to measure the dramatic character of these services: (1) the emotional and physical involvement of the congregation; (2) the presence of crisis and conflict in the drama; and (3) the reenactment of an important spiritual experience or the rehearsal of that which is to be performed in the world.

There are certain forms of drama which are inappropriate within worship, yet appropriate in educational situations like Sunday School, recreational situations like church parties, or family worship. Youth plays, drama games, skits, puppets, clowns, and parades are all forms of drama that are useful means of communicating truth, but are not generally acceptable within a morning worship of Word and Table. Because the great drama of the Christian faith is expressed primarily through Word and Table, the use of small dramas must always serve these two focal points and never replace them or even overshadow them. Consequently, the forms of drama recommended in a service of worship among renewalists is that of choral reading, storytelling, and chancel drama. These are especially useful in the service of the Word, where they heighten important aspects of the scriptural text.

Robert Webber

333 • THE VALUE OF DRAMATIC REPRESENTATION

Drama is an extremely powerful means of communication, able to depict a narrative from many points of view and to portray the cosmic themes in situations that touch everyday life. The planning and execution of drama is also beneficial in that it can use a the gifts of a variety of people from all ages in a congregation. While not addressing drama in worship directly, the following article raises important issues that should be considered regarding every dramatic moment in worship.

The interest in drama in Mennonite circles is slowly growing. There are not only more requests for plays to be presented for special holidays or to illustrate specific topics, but there is a growing interest in the essential nature of drama and an appreciation of its power.

The word *drama* means "a thing done." It suggests an action, a piece of work, a worthy task for the human being. John Jay, a former drama professor, presently a minister of the gospel, says drama is a means of "enfleshing the word." So it is not only "a thing done," it is the abstract made concrete, the metaphysical joined to the physical. Its dynamic is like that of the "word" becoming "flesh." By taking on human form, Christ showed the Father; it was in his life and death that he focused and made visible to the human eye the struggle between God and the devil—between good and evil. He showed us truth.

Since the fifth century B.C. the word *theater* has meant "seeing place," a place where the enfleshed word in action could be seen by a group. In spite of our fear and suspicion of the theater, the word still means the same thing today: it is the place where the group, the community, can sit back and watch an enactment of the conflicting forces of life which, taken to their ultimate source, are the forces of good and evil.

The conflict is usually in the form of a fictitious story (usually fictitious) that in some essential way represents reality. But the dramatic story is different from the short story or the novel: the tale is told not primarily from the point of view of the main character, but from various points of view. This objectivity allows the viewer to see the whole development of the conflict: its beginning, its development, and its conclusion. Moreover, the viewer is enabled to see the interplay of opposing forces in all its complexity: the many faces of evil, its insidious entry into our lives, and its propensity to masquerade as good. But this interplay also shows us how good can come out of evil and win the day. The sermon tells us about this; the drama allows it all to be played out before us, turning the bright truth upon "the whole." Because it is in story form, we are less likely to be defensive.

In this process we often see and hear things we do not like. Some characters may well offend us by their actions and their language, as people do in life. This is not to say that any evil act is either stageworthy or useful in presenting life with its many conflicts—a certain decorum and restraint must be observed. But to show only what we confirm and applaud, to force all characters to speak virtuously and sensitively, is to diminish the action and to deny the essential nature of the conflict. The morality of a play cannot be faulted for its parts. It must be judged as a whole, and on what it all comes to—the final resolution.

All this is to admit that drama has its disturbing elements: it stirs up rather than soothes. It is just as likely to reveal our vulnerability and weakness as it is to point us to our source of strength and our potential for good.

Balance and objectivity are not the whole of the argument in favor of drama. The objectivity does not preclude a certain identification with the characters on the stage. From their position in the auditorium, the observers are able to identify first with one and then another. As they enter into another person's struggles, fears, aversions, and despair, they are made vulnerable, but are also enabled to recognize and face the darkness within themselves. In the process they vicariously "learn by going how to go" (Roethke).

A drama is like a dream that simultaneously raises thought and emotion in order to bring us new insights. And as we enter into the world of the play, we invariably sense that the essential struggle does not lie in the world around us (our neighborhood, the society, or the system) but rather in our inner world. The dialectical power of a great drama clarifies the struggle and brings it home to its source—which is the human heart.

All of this speaks of the high seriousness of drama. To stage a drama is to take a certain risk and to work hard. But there is a reason why the written script, which is the basis of the dramatic production, is called a play. To fully enjoy a drama as an audience member, one must be willing to play. The playwright wants to give pleasure to the audience. People do not attend a drama with the attitude of going to work, but to be at leisure. And the audience says of the actors, "They are playing their parts." What is the nature and importance of this "play?" What should be the aim? Does drama build the body which is the church?

In drama, playing means entering into an imaginative world in which we temporarily free ourselves from the structures of "real life." Whether purely for pleasure or for both pleasure and some other purpose (e.g., sharing a vision), a world on stage in which actors imagine themselves to be the people of the play. As the restrictions of "real life" are temporarily lifted, people are given the freedom to explore something new or something hidden deep within themselves. There is a certain abandonment in play that allows us to leave our everyday serious or inhibited self at the door and to call upon the "child within"—that aspect of personality which allows us to be spontaneous, eager, carefree, and readily in touch with emotion. In doing this we may reawaken thoughts and feelings, ways of behavior, and ways of seeing the world that have lain dormant for a long time. In the reawakening we enrich and rediscover ourselves.

One of the special features of a dramatic production is its intergenerational character. Many plays call for people of various ages. As the octogenarian "plays" with a child of seven, or with a teenager, the gaps between the generations are inadvertently bridged. A peculiar bonding takes place as people of different statures and ages commit themselves to a task that calls for a certain element of risk, commitment, and play.

Another benefit accruing to the church family is the drama's ability to call forth a wide variety of gifts in the church. Even a short one-act play may call for a number of imaginative and courageous people to act the parts, technicians to produce sound and light, artists to design the set and programs, crafts-people to build sets, sew costumes, and make props. Finally, people with organizational skills are needed to direct and produce the play. A dramatic production is not only play; it is also work, as anyone who has ever participated knows.

The plays that embody a Christian theme and that also "play well" on the stage are scarce. Understandably, church audiences are more concerned with the content than the form. The person educated in drama is often more concerned with the play's artistry, because he or she knows from experience that unless the piece "plays" on the stage, it is difficult to communicate its truth, however important that may be. Plays that meet with the approval of both groups are hard to find. Many plays that would be spurned by the professional director, who can choose from hundreds of well-wrought scripts, will work to a greater or lesser extent in the church, particularly where there is excitement and eagerness for dramatization. It is not unusual for a production to assume more significance than the script itself.

Then too some worthy plays may incorporate ideas that may make a Christian director uneasy. It is possible, in cases where the playwright is still living, to negotiate permission to change or to delete something potentially offensive if it is not substantive to the play. I would caution against the easy tendency to make changes in the script, but I admit having changed some lines now and then, particularly when they present a theological problem.

Some plays are more suitable for the church college than for the church itself because of their length and difficulty. While I would encourage even the inexperienced group to begin working and playing at short plays (called sketches, not skits), I would discourage them from beginning with anything longer than a one-act play. To "enflesh the word" takes considerable time and energy. A church director will generally find people in the church blessed with various skills mentioned above. Team work is of the essence and pays valuable dividends.

Some plays are most useful to the church if they are performed as readers' theater. Although this style of presentation does not preclude memory work, it most often allows people to sit and hold script in hand while reading their parts. It should be noted that stools are not a necessity. Various boxes may be used for different levels, and in the case of a very short play, readers may stand. Anyone interested in using this style might be advised to buy a good manual on readers' theater.

In her book *Eighth Day of Creation,* Elizabeth O'Connor says, "When we describe church we like to say that it is a gift-evoking, gift-bearing community—a description based on the conviction that when God calls a person, he calls him into the fullness of his own potential."

Esther Wiens[92]

334 • Types of Drama for Use in Worship

This article joins others in this chapter in arguing for the intentional and imaginative use of drama in worship. Its unique contribution is a helpful explanation of the various types or varieties of theater that can be incorporated into worship.

Incorporating the art of theater into the worship setting is an important and exciting ministry. To accomplish this, we must deal not only with practical matters regarding how a drama ministry might be launched in our churches, but also with the complicated history of drama in worship. We must understand and accept the nature and limitations of the form and see the art of theater in its large intended creative context—as an art form with the capacity for revelation, praise, challenge, and comfort. Theater does not merely use language or the symbols of love; it can enact love. It can show us the love of parents, of friends or brethren. Theater can also challenge us by exposing sin while reminding us that we are not alone. It is a collaborative art form that places words and ideas in action through character. It isn't merely oral or sermonic; it's oral, physical, and visual.

One of the things that intrigues me is the complex history of the theater and the church. As far as we can ascertain, theater actually arose from the impulse of religious celebration and from the need to express the longings of a people for their creator. Through dramatic ritual, humanity gained a glimpse of the divine. In certain periods—notably the Greek and medieval—theater became primary avenue for religious expression. Yet, even within those periods, ecclesiastical suspicion fell on theatrical practitioners. As Jonas Barish points out in *The Antitheatrical Prejudice* (Berkeley: University of California Press, 1981), "Thespis, who gave his name to the art of acting, was called a liar by Solon because he was

A Modern Band*. Contemporary worship is frequently led by a band with electronic and rhythm instruments.*

pretending to be someone else" (p. 1). As a church, we are no different. We too are uncomfortable with those who would make their living by dissimulation. Actors of this lowly art were and are still segregated, set apart as somehow unworthy or unclean. As historians note, often theater was abandoned by institutionalized church, left to thieves, prostitutes, and vagabonds, further polarizing it from the church and, at times, mainstream society. And be-

cause no dialogue between believing and unbelieving people occurred, the theater began to live up to its reputation. For example, H. R. Rookmaaker, in his book, *Art Needs No Justification,* wonders where the Christians were in the eighteenth century when humanism was born. Humanism in this period managed to re-direct society away from the needs of the human spirit so that it might seek after pleasure and power. Rookmaaker posits that those believing societies had turned to a purely pietistic Christianity and rejected the arts. "Too easily, large areas of human reality, such as philosophy, science, the arts, economics and politics were handed over to the world, as Christians concentrated mainly on pious activities" (quoted in Harry Farra, "Theater Position: A Report to the Strategy Planning Task Force," Geneva College, 1991, p. 5).

This antitheatrical urge has persisted to the present. We readily accept the awesome power of this art to destroy but rarely acknowledge its capacity to heal as well. The church responded to theater too often by pulling away, allowing for an increasing secularization of the medium and eventually resulting in out-and-out hostility. In some denominations, the impulse for keeping theater away from the flock was a matter of theological priority. In his book *Contours of a World View* [Grand Rapids: Eerdmans, 1983], Arthur Holmes makes this perceptive comment:

> Traditions with a strong emphasis on the physical in creation, incarnation, and sacrament, like the Roman Catholic and the Anglican, have generally been productive in the arts. Traditions that stress a law-governed creation, such as the Reformed, have put creative energies into government and work. The Anabaptist tradition, emphasizing God's provision for human needs, has attended to work and works of compassion and healing. American Evangelicalism's theology focuses largely on sin and grace, and its most creative outlet has therefore been in evangelism and missions. Theology naturally gives direction as well as meaning to creativity. But a complete and balanced theology should direct it into every area of responsibility: art, science, society and church. (*Contours of a World View,* 205–206)

Interpreting this statement correctly implies that we have always asserted the validity of the arts but have placed our energies for the most part elsewhere. Incorporating drama in worship will constitute a huge risk for many constituencies. Theater can engender very strong reactions, especially when it disturbs the comfort of those used to more traditional methods of worship. The theater is viewed by many with suspicion and a bit of fear. "What does it have to do with us?" they ask. "It doesn't belong in the service. Worship isn't entertainment. We've got our focus all wrong. Drama is all right as long as it stays with the children, but keep it away from the traditional service." Those who view theater in this man-

ner see theater as an enemy, a Goliath, a force that threatens from without. It's foreign and secular. To many, it simply doesn't belong.

And, in their defense, it is true that worship is not an entertainment. Theater not incorporated properly into the service can seem like mere show. My most effective collaborations have occurred when my pastor and I mapped out specifically the goals and scriptural themes for the service. When I first started doing this; however, there were a few times when the coordination wasn't there and the congregation was left thinking *why was that included?* or *so what?* That shouldn't happen.

How do you get started? And how do you avoid some basic pitfalls? Let's talk about a beginning: the basic nuts and bolts of incorporating theater into your service, the types of occasions that theater may be suitable for within your individual churches, and the different styles of theater possible.

The Process of Starting a Drama Ministry

Purposes. There are several different functions or purposes of scripts in worship. A first function would be the use of drama for sermon illustrations. Lasting from five to ten minutes, they provide physical illustrations of a service's sermon or homily. These are perhaps the most common and popular methods of incorporating theater into your worship, but they are frequently limited by time restrictions and therefore can express only a simple point, not complex ideas. Generally, the tone of these pieces tend to be lighter and more comedic.

A second type might be called evangelical illustrations. Their time length can vary depending on the occasion. They can also take the form of a five- to ten-minute sketch. These openly proclaim the gospel as a means of grace and salvation in the church, to bring people to the altar, or to call us to our knees.

A third type are theatrical plays. These are longer dramatic pieces that on special occasions replace a sermon or homily. The best plays pose questions and don't offer pat solutions; theater is not meant to take the place of a sermon.

Setting. Any worship setting may be appropriate for theater in your church. Plays can be a part of either morning or evening services, a youth or children's worship proper, or they can highlight seasonal events, celebrations of church calendar, retreats, and so on. Your purpose, occasion, and performing space will dictate the length and degree of seriousness of such plays.

Theatrical Style. In addition to understanding the different types and intentions of scripts possible in any of your worship services, you also must have some knowledge about the variety of expression possible with theater. There are many different styles of theater to contend with as well. There are four basic theatrical styles that are appropriate for use in worship: reader's theater, choral staging, realistic representation, and presentational performance.

Readers' theater is a script-in-hand interpretation that reenacts (rather than represents) the actions in the text. It may be used with virtually any type of material or theme. Readers' theater performances may be formal and static or have limited staging. Churches often use them where physical facilities and sightlines are problematic.

Readers' theater may be performed with either *static staging* or *limited staging.* In static staging, the actor's focus is directed to the audience. Actors don't relate directly with their fellow actors; instead, they choose a point out in the audience where the character they address is located. The actors cross their focuses so that the illusion is maintained that the performers are speaking to each other. (If actor B stands onstage to actor A's right, actor A looks out in the audience to the right at a diagonal. Actor B does the reverse. Thus, focuses are said to be crossed.) Limited staging, in contrast, does involve some movement, generally to indicate characters entering or exiting, and to focus the audience's attention on specific actors. In reader's theater, the manipulation of gesture and body positions are still possible. This is especially essential when actors are playing multiple roles and the uniqueness of individual characters needs to be portrayed.

Choral staging is an ensemble performance that may be either script-in-hand or memorized. This style also works well for churches that have spaces with limited performance capabilities. Patterns of movement among the actors are the key to this style of representation. Most often they take the form of geometric patterns: v-shapes, x-shapes, diagonal lines, squares, circles, semicircles, and so on. Choral staging minimizes the role of individual characters. Actors may speak both in unison or in concert. The group is the character: individual characters are not represented in this style. (Individual voices, perhaps, but they are simply reflective of the whole unit.) This style works well with nonnarrative forms, including poetry, psalms, and more abstract prose.

Realistic representation involves a fully memorized performance. This style may have grand or modest production values in setting, costume, and lighting. In this style the action proceeds as if it is really happening, the virtual present. It represents reality, the reality we observe in day to day life. The actors behave as if the audience were not there to witness their activities. The actors are perceived as real people (three-dimensional). Gestures and physical movement should be as natural as the space permits.

Presentational performance is a fully memorized performance. Generally, production values center on the performer and not the setting (e.g., Madeleine L'Engle poetry). The action is directed out to the audience as a presentation of content rather than a representation of reality. Actors are performers representing themselves. Most often they don't assume the role of other characters. If they do portray a character, that character is most likely to be a stock character or stereotypical character, not a three-dimensional character. This style works well with musical venues, revue-style sketches, poetry, and some prose.

Scripts. There are several types of scripts that may be employed in a worship setting. First, you can employ a literal rendering of Scripture, taking a passage from the Bible and performing it as it is written. Second, you can choose a script that interprets a scriptural event, aligning it in time very closely to the actual biblical reference. Third, a script could be chosen for its application of a scriptural event in contemporary terms, transplanting the events into our culture. Fourth, you may determine the best way to communicate your message is to chose a script that represents contemporary cultural satire. These types of scripts look at the world we live in and expose our cultural values for what they truly are. Finally, you may choose to employ a script that combines cultural illustration and confession. These comment on the human condition and expose our fears, concerns, and failing.

Organization. How do you set up a ministry? Having a coordinator in each model is crucial, as is identifying and describing the parameters of the ministry. One possible model for such a ministry is ACTS (Actors Committed to the Teachings of the Savior), involving a lay minister but relying on no support from the church administration except with special events programming. (ACTS was primarily an internal support ministry that provided sermon illustrations once a month and helped in a special evening of evangelism). Another model is that of Parable Players, a para-professional outreach ministry involving direct administrative support from the church. The artistic leader, a Ph.D. in theater, was a volunteer, but the actors (some academically trained, others not) were paid a small honorarium per performance. This outreach ministry toured regionally with two different full length plays in its repertoire, performing on average eight times per month. The repertoire could change from year to year, and all roles in each play were double case, allowing for an interesting mixture of actors from performance to performance. Another model is used at Willow Creek, a large nondenominational church in the suburbs of Chicago, where a professional staff (led by an artistic director with a Ph.D.) provides drama once a week. The ministry involves staff writers and performers in addition to congregational members. Whatever you do, start off small, producing no more than one to three events per year. Build a core of people interested in committing to this ministry. Send lay ministers to workshops and lectures to aid in training. Let your ministry grow through interest, not by decree.

More than Evangelism

To conclude, it is my hope that the majority of Christian people can think of more than Bible drama when they consider church and theater. Theater used strictly as a tool to evangelize limits its power to communicate to us. Legitimizing theatrical endeavor by slapping an evangelical label on it reduces art to function. Stuffed with facts, dramatic form frequently labors to express tracts and dogma, quoting faithfully and duly Scripture texts that should resound and roar in our minds and hearts. Why not use a sermon to preach the message of salvation and allow theater to relate to drama of human experience?

You see, this is one of theater's greatest strengths: to hold a mirror up to nature and allow us to see ourselves. And in seeing to change and grow, to mature in the things that matter. Theater can share the Gospel in a powerful and exciting way; it can evangelize when done well. But it can also show us the reality of living in a fallen world and what sin does to our lives. It can show laughter and pain, joy and despair. It can also bind us together as a common people. Stuart Scadron-Wattles, artistic director of Theater & Company, a Canadian Equity theater that produces works from a biblical perspective, believes that "we should find ourselves moving from the use of drama to achieve certain religious ends into something broader and more demanding: the dramatic expression of the kingdom of God."

The most truthful statements about God's goodness, his creation, and the fallenness of his creatures should be derived from the church. However, as Nigel Forde of Riding Lights Theater Company in England points out, "The reason that the most trenchant, memorable, and truthful statements about ourselves and the universe come from outside the Christian church is that Christians are all too easily shocked by reality; they want the truth to be completely beautiful. Whereas the real truth about truth in a fallen world is that it is likely to be both beautiful and horrible, both pure and filthy" (_Theatercraft: Creativity and the Art of Drama_ [Wheaton, Ill.: Harold Shaw, 1990], 101). We need to be truthful in our churches and allow mature discussions to flourish to nurture and challenge us. Too often when we shove some material aside and say that it's secular, we create walls between acceptable discussion material and unacceptable, Christian and secular. Think of theater in a broader perspective in your church. "It is the imagination that shows us the truth of what is going on around us. It is imagination that makes art not a copy of life, not a snapshot, but an appraisal, a vision, sometimes a prophecy" (Forde, _Theatercraft,_ 110).

Theater can break down barriers and create new avenues of discussions among the members of your congregations. In _The Antitheatrical Prejudice_ (p. 266), Jonas Barish writes:

> The theatrical process works to complicate our judgments and disarm our vindictiveness. It makes us apprehend [theatrical characters] as feeling beings like ourselves, in whom virtue may be strong or nearly as strong as vice, but for whom circumstances may have been stronger, who have struggled painfully but at length unsuccessfully against their passions. And so, as it makes us less judgmental, it validates our claim to be teaching us something. It educates by widening our imaginative range.

Nigel Forde puts it this way: "Theater does not browbeat man into accepting a rule or message written in flaming letters on stone. Rather it opens his eyes and enlarges his sympathies. If it is written on anything, it is written in water; it soaks in and nourishes the parts that other wise would not be reached" (Forde, *Theatercraft,* 109). That's my prayer for our work in the church: that it would break the stone hearts we carry within us and make us eager to walk in love, as Christ's ambassadors on earth. I know that means making a small beginning first. But I don't want to leave you stuck at "GO." I pray that you catch a vision for the incredible revelatory promise that a reconciliation between theater and church holds.

By grace we can create. Arthur Holmes says, "A world amenable to human creativity, and human creativity itself, bear witness to their creator. These are living God's good gifts, evidence of his continued creativity in human affairs" (*Contours of a World View,* 204). Through theater in our churches we can bear witness to our Creator God. Finally, I'd like to leave you with a comment by Lee Krahenbuhl, professor of theater at Judson College:

It is the Lord's work to demolish walls that divide. When theater makes us less judgmental, when it teaches us something by widening our imaginative range, when it eliminates labels, it continues to work. I find it interesting that the same Hebrew name with we translate *Jesus* via the Greek of the New Testament, *Y'shua,* is in the Old Testament translated *Joshua*—through whom God brought the walls of Jericho tumbling down.

A theater ministry in your church could tear down a great many walls. And build the kingdom.

Debra L. Freeberg

335 • THE FESTIVAL MUSIC DRAMA

The festival music drama as described here is a type of drama in which the entire congregation plays a role. It involves many of the traditional elements in a worship service, reordered so that their dramatic quality is realized. The central theme is always that of the life of Jesus Christ, which is presented in dramatic fashion to give believers an opportunity to celebrate Christ's victory and to present the gospel narrative to unbelievers. An example of a festival music drama is included in the next chapter of this volume.

The festival drama is an innovative type of musical drama that enacts the significant events in the life of Christ for the purpose of celebration and evangelism. Its unique characteristics are (1) the full participation of the congregation in a group role, and (2) the incorporation of many worship elements such as singing, Scripture reading, prayer, confession, and sermon.

In each festival music drama, Christ is the central character. All the dialogue and actions lead up to climatic moments of praise and celebration of who Jesus is and what he has done and continues to do for us. Festival music dramas may celebrate Christ's birth, his death, and resurrection, and can also celebrate his adoration by the magi, his baptism and temptation, his transfiguration, his Holy Week descent into grief and suffering, his ascension, and his second coming.

The festival music drama is designed not only to celebrate Jesus, but to be an evangelistic outreach. While participating Christians are celebrating Jesus, the nonbelievers in attendance will see and hear the joyful sound of Christians' acclamations and singing. The nonbeliever will also witness the story of Christ's love and salvation. After each presentation, he or she will be given an opportunity to respond to what has been witnessed.

The first distinctive characteristic of the festival drama is that it is participation oriented, not performance oriented. The congregation becomes actively involved in the story since it is given the role of shepherds/shepherdesses, villagers, servants, or worshipers in the temple. From beginning to end, the congregation sings and dialogues, most often during a worship action. It also participates in processions, pilgrimages, or other journeys. Its members perform many other simple rituals such as carrying candles or offering gifts. It also participates by receiving or giving symbols or central images.

Also unique to the festival music drama is the use of stages or stations throughout the church, such as the aisles, the right and left sides of the sanctuary, or church hall. In this way, it resembles pageant.

The festival music drama is as musical as it is dramatic. Throughout the presentation, various types of congregational, responsorial, antiphonal, and choral music occurs. While choirs are used in the festival music drama, they are given a dramatic role; they never sing to the congregation, but with it or during a congregational action.

A second distinguishing facet of the festival music

drama is its inclusion of worship elements, such as the call to worship, sometimes a confession, prayers, reading or recitations of the Scriptures, and also a sermon. These worship elements are part of the story line and may not be clearly identified, since they are reframed into a dramatic framework. A lead character is also a worship leader. He or she "directs" the congregation in much the same way a pastor or music minister directs a congregation. While the festival music drama is not designed to be a worship service, it could be considered a celebration service.

The concept of the festival music drama is based upon the celebration of the three pilgrim festivals found in the Old Testament: the Feast of Passover, Feast of Pentecost, and the Feast of Tabernacles. Three times a year the Israelites went to Jerusalem for one or two weeks to observe these feast days. While the Bible does not clearly indicate all the types of services and celebrative activities that took place, other sources do indicate that there were elaborate ceremonies and several celebrative events.

One such event might have been some form of dramatic enactment. During each festival, a "festival scroll" was read. These included such biblical books as the Song of Solomon, Esther, and Ruth. These narratives were read by one priest, but other priests may have made certain movements acting out what was being read.

The festival music drama has also an historical antecedent in the medieval liturgical drama. Originally short dramatic scenes or tropes were sung before the Mass. However these tropes became too dramatic, so they were expelled from use. They developed into full length music dramas that had several liturgical elements.

Christmas and Easter are the two primary festivals; however, the celebration of Christ's second advent and final establishment of his kingdom on earth has the potential of becoming a third major festival. This festival is already found in the Lutheran and Catholic churches. There is a strong biblical exhortation for all believers to look forward to Christ's return. The festival music drama is one way the Christian church can celebrate this future glorious day. The model used to demonstrate the festival music drama is based upon the Feast of Christ the King, since it not only shows the what and how of this musical drama, but will give an idea of how this day can be celebrated.

This participatory festive music drama is offered as another way for the Christian community to joyfully celebrate the greatest events in history. At the same time, it will be a witness of the gospel to unbelievers.

James Speck

336 • READERS' THEATER IN THE CHURCH

Readers' theater is a form of drama well-suited to the church. It attempts to present a text rather than to represent or portray an event. It minimizes the staging that may be difficult in some worship spaces. This article describes both the history of readers' theater and gives suggestions for its use in the church.

Readers' theater is a dramatic hybrid which combines the oral interpretation of literature with the theatricality of performance art. Readers' theater has been a viable expressive art form for centuries. The Greeks used a chorus of chanters to link stories and episodes in their plays. The chorus served as a reminder of plotlines or as a transition from scene to scene. The performers in chorus might comment also on the philosophical nature of the play or give a moral pronouncement evident in the performance. The ancient Hebrews composed group chants, praises, and prayers to augment their public worship. Many of the Psalms have verses intended for antiphonal or call/response choral effects in worship. The Catholic Mass emerged with segments of group reading/recitation, so that the words and the Scriptures could be heard in the vaulted expanses of the large basilicas and cathedrals. In 1945 the term _readers' theater_ was first applied to a Broadway oral recitation of Sophocles' _Oedipus Rex._ Later in 1951, the first major readers' theater production was presented on Broadway: George Bernard Shaw's _Don Juan in Hell,_ a difficult act to produce from his play, _Man and Superman._ Four prominent actors, dressed in formal attire and carrying black notebooks, stood behind lecterns and brought the philosophical scenes to life by means of vocal and physical expressions. In more recent times, the evolving art form of readers' theater has been apparent in staging decisions of such prominent Broadway plays and musicals as _You're A Good Man, Charlie Brown; Evita; Godspell; Nicholas Nickleby;_ and _The Grapes of Wrath._

Though used in the secular performance arena, readers' theater has its roots in religious communication. As early as the tenth century A.D., the German nun Hroswitha wrote plays about biblical characters and saints, not intending that these plays would be acted, but that they would be read aloud in the confines of a monastery. Today, ten centuries later, we need to rediscover the legacy of Hroswitha and look to "RT" as a performance option for today's churches.

Although the word *readers* implies that performers read their scripts, today's RT performances may or may not have scripts present. "Readers" means that performers offer a text, the words of literature, and ask the audience to imagine what is happening. The readers need not wear actual costumes, sit on actual sets, or have makeup that actually reveals their character. Readers can present more than one character in a performance, (a narrator, a male or female, young or old, funny or sad) by means of vocal variety and nonverbal gestures so as to suggest an imaginative landscape without elaborate lighting or set design. "Theater" recognizes that mere reading without expression or drama cannot sustain interest or imagination. Readers can be expected to move in place, use mime actions, or move in and out of scenes. Multimedia (music/slides/video/film) can be presented simultaneously to augment the imagined scene. Wearing apparel with colors suggests mood changes or character traits. Eye contact may be with the audience, in off-stage pointing (suggesting imagined interaction between characters), in on-stage eye gaze, or in indirect soliloquy musing. Stools, blocks, ladders, and levels can be used to turn a stark stage area into an arena of creativity and imagination.

Thus, a definition of readers' theater is formulated: *readers' theater is the presentation of prose, poetry, or dramatic literature by two or more performers in such a manner that the words are theatrically offered and recreated in the minds of an audience so that all involved can consider the persuasive intent of the literature.* Readers' theater is not superior or inferior to conventional drama. It is another art form. Conventional drama requires that literature be scripted in a dramatic form, where, in most cases, exposition is discovered in dialogue. RT has no such restrictions. Readers can dramatize narrative portions of short stories, novels, essays, newspaper articles, or poems. Conventional drama normally requires a pictorial space, a specific limited playing arena, usually box-like with sets and curtains, lighting, and theatrically actualized reality.

Readers' theater uses *acoustic* or *found space:* the whole environment, including the audience's minds.

Readers' theater may be the most practical dramatic outlet the local church has in these modern times. While not every church has facilities that allow for fully staged dramatic productions, every church has space that can be creatively used for RT performance. Readers' theater scripts may consist of single works, written specifically for RT format. Readers' theater may emphasize its abilities to stress persuasive messages by thematically linking various literary selections with original transitions, creating a collage or combined script. A special form of RT called *chamber theater* combines staged drama with narrative prose literature. Narrators in a chamber theater are considered characters, but may have manuscript notebooks with the literary text present and visible. Other personae in the cast may be fully costumed and respond as if in a staged drama. Variations of the RT form can be viable and extremely creative for performance options.

Frequently, readers' theater makes use of the "split-line" technique, dividing a sentence between multiple readers for effect. Generally, the tempo and pacing of RT performances move at a faster pace than traditional drama. Most audiences can sustain interest in a 30- to 45-minute readers' theater production, but short sketches or vignettes also work well as lead-ins to sermons or other forms of public communication. Performers need to be aware that their voices and nonverbal communication share most of the intent and help assist the audience in recreating the described scenes on the platform of their own minds and imaginations.

Preparations are identical for the RT performers and the traditional dramatic actor. The difference in art form is one of degree in actuality and imaginative response. Good believable acting and dimensional credible readers' theater preparations are essential for any performance.

Blocking or staging an RT requires as much creativity as staging a proscenium drama. In the church sanctuary, you may choose to block your performance on one of three axis planes: the x-axis, the y-axis, and the z-axis. The x-axis consists of right to middle to left stage, the straight-line-across-the-stage effect. The y-axis places readers along the upstage/downstage continuum, up and back away from the audience. The z-axis is vertical and can be varied by means of short to medium tall boxes or ladders or levels. RT makes use of clusters of performers, angles of performers, motivated movements of performers. Effective blocking attempts to keep all readers visible when in a scene. Power areas of the stage are central to the action, and any major character or action should be blocked to the center of the audience's visual attention.

Readers' theater can be an important addition to the ministry of any church. It can be used as an important and creative evangelistic tool as well as a teaching mechanism. It can reach and teach people through strong messages, coupled with humor and dramatic pathos. RT can join with a strong biblically based pulpit ministry to share the good news of God's grace and the dependability of Christ's faithfulness to us. Christian readers' theater dramatizes principles that may have been preached or taught to congregations for years. We live in a media age. Radio, TV, and film have turned us into dramatic consumers. Christian readers' theater can take the performing art of drama and use it to share the deep truths of Christ as we strive to impact our world for him.

Todd Lewis

337 • DRAMA AND PREACHING

Drama and preaching are both means for communicating biblical truths. Yet they are fundamentally different in their most typical forms, with preaching presenting a message and drama representing a narrative. This article gives helpful historical perspectives to the use of drama in worship, as well as guidelines for the appropriate relationship of preaching and drama in worship today.

Two places in which we have a right to expect to hear the truth spoken are the pulpit and the stage. For that reason, if for no other, preaching and drama should each find an ally in the other. Sadly, this is not and has not been the case.

Drama in the church arose out of the liturgy in a period preceding the Protestant Reformation, that is, before the proclamation of the Word had assumed a central place in Christian worship. For that reason, many elements in the liturgy were receptive to the introduction of dramatic material: the responsive sections, the liberal and expanding use of music, the clergy's colorful vestments, symbolic actions and gestures, and the architecture of the church or cathedral.

Perhaps the single most important development leading to drama's emergence in the church was the widespread medieval practice of troping. The custom of beautifying the service of worship by inserting _tropes,_ or verses, could hardly have occurred in early Reformed churches. The idea that the worship of God needed any kind of beautifying introduced an aesthetic concern that the Reformers would probably have considered irrelevant if not irreverent. Any attempt to make liturgy aesthetically satisfying would have underlined the part played by human sensibilities in the worship of God. For those who held the human imagination to be vain and profitless, such beautifications were perceived as leading away from the pure worship of God and toward human self-aggrandizement. Not accidentally did the Puritans in England engage in a steady conflict with the secular theater. It was during Oliver Cromwell's twelve-year rule that all the theaters in London were closed. Naturally, then, nothing that smacked of theater would find acceptance in the churches.

In Reformed churches, it was chiefly the centrality of the Word that worked against dramatic development. To some degree all the Reformers, for different reasons, eventually emphasized the service of the Word over the celebration of the Eucharist. These services—Lutheran, Zwinglian, Calvinist—tended toward simplicity, the reduction of opportunities for congregational participation, and the abandonment or simplification of clerical vestments. Preaching became absolutely central. The Word of God was proclaimed and explained. The service shifted from mysterious rite toward and instructional and educational experience.

This centrality of the Word and the simplicity of the liturgies, especially those of Zwingli and Calvin, diminished the elements that made drama possible: dialogical progression, symbolic action, and symbolic vestments. Calvin, struggling with the question of how Christ is present in the Eucharist, said: "I will not be ashamed to confess that it is too high a mystery either for my mind to comprehend or my words to express; and to speak more plainly, I rather feel than understand it" (quoted in S. F. Brennen, et al., _A Handbook of Worship_ [Philadelphia: The Heidelberg Press, 1941], 50). The Reformer's apparent discomfort with the mysterious action in the Mass, represented by the doctrine of transubstantiation, helped to push reformed worship in a direction toward which it was already oriented biblically, that is, the predominance of the ear as organ of perception. In the Mass the eye was predominant, for it was the moment of the elevation that medieval crowds rushed from church to church to see. In the Reformed tradition, the prominence of the word shifted the emphasis from the eye to the ear as the chief organ of perception, as it was in the Hebrew Bible: "Hear, O Israel . . ."

This emphasis on the ear is of course not totally antithetical to drama, but the shift does not particularly encourage the art. Drama performed is essentially an art that appeals to the eye. The Greek word from which our word "theater" is derived is *theatron,* which is literally "the place of seeing." Though Aristotle in the *Poetics* places spectacle last among the six elements of tragedy—plot, character, thought, diction, music, spectacle—the emphasis remains on seeing. We go to see a play not to hear one.

Although many segments of American Protestantism have witnessed a movement for several decades toward more liturgical services, the unadorned worship in churches of the Reformed tradition continues in some places. In a recent visit to the Reformed Church of Hungary, I was struck by the brevity and simplicity of the Sunday morning services. Hymn singing provided almost the only opportunity for the people to participate. Furthermore, the high, prominent pulpits are a testament to preaching's importance. Here as elsewhere, the dominance of preaching emphasizes the use of reason in the service, in contradistinction of feeling and mystery.

The Church's Uneasiness

While drama has found a home in some Protestant churches, in many there is still some uneasiness about its use, the causes of which have their source in the writings of the early church Fathers and were strengthened during the Puritan attack on the stage.

In an ethos in which God's glory and majesty put into sharp relief the sinfulness and depravity of human nature, some saw drama as turning people's attention away form God, its rightful object, and toward the performer, thus encouraging idolatry.

When used in worship, drama is described by some as "enlivening" the service. For others, like its medieval and Puritan critics, drama makes the church a place of spectacle, where people are drawn by the "cheap tricks" and "false effects" of the theater. Far from enhancing worship, they say, drama

detracts form an atmosphere of worshipfulness and reverence.

Some fear that by imitating real life, drama introduces jarring crudities into a place where a reverential spirit should be cultivated. The language of the street and marketplace, gestures appropriate for profane transactions and attire suitable for the cocktail party are things that cause people discomfort when seen or heard in church. Some suggest that the pretense and human imagination that are drama's genius stand over against the majesty and glory of God, distort our understanding and confuse our perceptions about worship's true object.

Finally, in using drama in the church, we stand in danger of undermining the liturgy itself. "Some feel that it is not wise to bring drama into too close contact with worship, as the congregation may turn itself into an audience and confuse the distinction between the two." (Joyce Peel and Darius Swann, *Drama for the Church,* 2d ed. [Madras: The Christian Literature Society, 1970], 13). A good deal of the uneasiness about using drama in the church may be resolved by arriving at some clarity about drama's place and functions in those services of worship in which preaching is central.

Preaching and Drama

To those who think of a play only as a sermon in dialogue form, it should be pointed out that drama and preaching are fundamentally different, not only in form but in intent and function. Preaching is presentational; drama is representational. That, of course, is a general statement which for the moment ignores different styles of preaching and different styles of drama. The preacher proclaims the Word of God. She or he presents the claim of God on our individual and collective lives. The prophetic formula "Thus says the Lord" is the sermonic pattern, even though the language may vary. Using biblical stories, teaching, and exegesis, the preacher analyzes the human situation, delineates to the best of her or his ability what God requires of us, and exhorts us to do it. However embellished by dramatic incident, language, symbolism, or dramatic gesture, preaching's function is to declare clearly God's demand on us. Preaching is therefore direct, rationally oriented, instructional and motivational.

Shakespeare saw the function of dramatic art as holding up a mirror to nature. The figure of the mirror is an important one, for in the play we do not look at life directly but by way of a contrived imitation of an action, the essential parts of which the playwright has selected. Through the medium of human imagination, playwrights, actors, and audiences together construct a "reality" that we know is not an actual fact. Through their creation, our own existential situation is illuminated. The drama, as Picasso is credited with observing, is a small lie in the service of a big truth.

The play, then, cannot fulfill a sermon's function of declaring directly, clearly, and prophetically what our human situation is, how God has acted, and what response we are called to make. If the play attempts to do this, it runs the risk of becoming propagandistic. It simply imitates an action, the experience of which may illuminate the spectator's own experience and help to clarify his or her decision making. By allowing the spectators, in all their human vulnerability, to be exposed to a life situation with which they can empathize, response in freedom is made possible.

Drama, then, gives the spectators another place in which to stand to hear the truth. Preaching not infrequently puts the hearer on the defensive and elicits an adversarial response. Drama provides what Francis Ferguson calls "direct perception." It communicates through the intellect but also above, around, and below it, at the level of the subconscious as well as the conscious. "Because drama is written to be played, it both offers and requires a peculiarly immediate understanding" (Francis Ferguson, *The Idea of Theatre* [Princeton: Princeton University Press, 1968], 10). The immediate vision or understanding offered by the play may then be corrected and amplified by theologians, historians, and preachers. Indeed the sermon may complete the work the play has begun.

The Value of Drama's Ecclesial Use

To appreciate the potential value of drama in serving the church, we must distinguish among its several uses. There are plays that are suitable for use in the worship service itself. The nature of dramatic art does not make it inimical to worship. John P. Newport has reminded us that art refers to the aspect of that life that expresses itself in the creative, imaginative, and dramatic, and that the artist is one who awakens and heightens our faculties of perception ("The Arts in Worship," *Review and Expositor* 80:71–83). Through symbol, language, and theme, a play may move us to contemplation of God's good-

ness and majesty or to a sense of sin and repentance. Henri Ghoen's *Way of the Cross* is a profound meditation on the Passion, which has deeply moved congregations of very diverse traditions.

Some plays are unsuitable for the worshiping service but may be excellent for supplementing or complementing another preaching function: teaching or instruction. Drama is an excellent tool for teaching the Bible. As an incident or event is acted out, the participants gain an immediate and personal understanding of the situation and the play's interior action. This is especially true in creative dramatics where the participants make up their own play. The exploration of character, circumstances, and conflicts serve to bring to life even well-know biblical stories.

In India, I observed that Hindus for centuries have used drama as a primary means of religious realization and the transmission of the stories of heroes and heroines of faith. The Ras Lila, the dance of love, is a dance drama used to achieve a living experience of Lord Krishna. In October of each year, the Ram Lila (the play of Rama) is enacted in most of North India's towns and villages. The exploits of Rama, the ideal king-son-husband, are reenacted with great pageantry over a ten-to-thirty day period. Through these reenactments, devotion to Rama is deepened and the ideals of Hindu society are reiterated most memorably.

Of course, drama as a mode of instruction is not confined to biblical material; it is also an excellent means of exploring social and public questions as well as personal and domestic ones. The nature of drama does not admit of clean-cut answers to questions raised, nor is that result necessary or desirable, but the clarification and examination of issues is in itself of great value. Arthur Miller in *After the Fall* draws on the great symbolism of the Jewish and Christian traditions to illuminate both his hero's (Quentin's) ethnic experience (the Jewish Holocaust) and his personal dilemma focusing on two broken marriages. Standing in the tower's shadow (symbolic of the Nazi concentration camps) with the woman he's attracted to, but with whom he fears developing a relationship because of two failed marriages, Quentin's realization is twofold. On the social level, he acknowledges complicity in the world's cruelty: "My brothers built this place." Ironically, his recognition of this fact is gained by realizing his personal guilt in regard to the suicide of his second wife, Maggie. The play ends on a note of hope:

And the wish to kill is never killed, but with some gift of courage one may look into its face when it appears, and with a stroke of love as to an idiot in the house—forgive it; again and again . . . forever. (New York: Viking Press, 1964, 161)

Finally, drama can be an effective aid to evangelism, the speaking and showing forth of God's act of forgiveness and mercy toward the whole human race. Because the play makes no altar call and issues no decision cards, it engages those who watch in total freedom. But from that freedom may issue a willingness to hear God's direct claim on their lives. In this sense drama is a preparation for hearing the gospel.

Preaching is the stable, continuing element in most Protestant worship services, while drama waxes and wanes. The longstanding hostility between pulpit and stage should not prevent drama from fulfilling the functions it can perform in worship and church education. Preachers with vision should recognize that preaching and drama complement each other; and performers who, like Grotowski's "holy actor," empty themselves and sharpen their skills need to know that their playing may be done well and directed to God's glory.

Darius Swann[93]

338 • DRAMA IN THE SEEKERS' SERVICE

The recent development of the seekers' service has created many opportunities for drama in the church. The article describes the use of drama in the seeker services of the church who pioneered them, the Willow Creek Community Church of South Barrington, Illinois. In these services, which are not considered worship services per se, drama is used prior to the spoken message to depict a scene in everyday life that applies insights from the Christian faith to that situation. An example of a dramatic script used in a seeker service is presented in the next chapter of this volume.

In 1975, Willow Creek Community Church began in a rented movie theater in suburban Chicago. Founded with the expressed purpose of reaching the unchurched, today Willow Creek attracts upwards of 15,000 people to its weekend seekers' services.

Since the beginning, drama has been an integral part of Willow Creek's outreach. It differs from traditional church drama in that these sketches are short, six- to eight- minute, contemporary vignettes, rooted in real-life experience. Today many churches all over the country, both large and small, are using these sketches as a powerful part of their ministries.

The Message "Set Up"

These sketches are not intended to stand on their own. Rather, they are used to create interest in an issue by grabbing the attention of the audience and getting them to identify with the characters. Also, the sketches do not provide easy answers, but instead raise questions which the pastor then seeks to answer in the message. Much of the material in these sketches may seem "secular" in that there is no specific "Christian" content in the sketch itself. However, when the sketch is performed in connection with a biblically based message that addresses the same question or problem, it takes on spiritual significance. *Keeping Tabs,* for example, presents a character who is possessed by the idea of paying back people for kindness shown toward her. While the theme is comically explored, the point it makes is a serious one. Many have a difficult time accepting the mystery of grace—a gift given with "no strings attached." This "secular" sketch has a strong Christian application when presented along with a message on grace. (See the full script of this sketch in the next chapter.)

This separation of drama and message is a major difference between Willow Creek's approach to drama and that traditionally taken by many churches. While difficult for some people to accept, such a separation is supported by dramatic tradition throughout history. Dorothy Sayers, Christian playwright and novelist, summed it up well: "Playwrights are not evangelists." A dictum frequently repeated to aspiring playwrights is "if you have a message, send it to Western Union." At Willow Creek we try not to abuse drama as an art form by manipulating it to preach a message. Simply put, the sketches clarify the "bad news" so the pastor can bring the "good news."

The Audience "Set Up"

A sketch cannot "set up" a message if viewers do not, in some way, see themselves mirrored in the action. Drama works because people experience vicariously what characters act out on stage. We want to engage not only the minds, but also the emotions of our audience. And drama, which results in high identification, appeals to people's hearts as well as their heads.

At Willow Creek we use contemporary slice-of-life drama, rather than enacted biblical stories, because people more readily identify with characters who act and talk like they do and who confront the same daily issues. This approach helps us earn the right to be heard, because our seekers realize that the church is in touch with the real world, where real people live, work, and struggle. A character has power to communicate when it is rooted in what the audience can identify with.

We've discovered that the degree of audience identification directly parallels what we call the "reality factor." Drama earns credibility with an audience when it is honest and truthful in how it handles material. If drama comes off simplistic and naive, or presents trite, easy answers, it will not produce the desired result.

If drama for seekers is to be effective in the church, we must be passionately committed to being real, warts and all. We must avoid easy answers, because they ultimately don't help, even if they sound good. Seekers and believers alike want truth, not a sugar-coated, sanitized version of reality.

In his book *Open Windows,* in a chapter entitled "Pitfalls of Christian Writing," Philip Yancey laments:

> Sometimes when I read Christian books, especially in the fields of fiction and biography, I have a suspicion that characters have been strangely lobotomized. . . . Just as a lobotomy flattens out emotional peaks and valleys, Christian writers can tend to safely reduce life's tensions and strains to a more acceptable level. . . . A perverse fear of overstatement keeps us confined to that flatland realm of "safe" emotions and tensions—a fear that seems incredible in light of the biblical model.

The cause of Christ would be well served if the church would listen to Yancey. For it is truth-telling (which isn't very safe) that not only gives ministry integrity, but also opens up seekers to the possibility of transformation through the power of the gospel.

Getting Started

The sketch format is a fairly easy way for any church, regardless of size, to begin using drama. A little time, a few simple props, a couple of actors (in some cases just one), and a director are all the necessary elements.

Because sketches are short, the time demand for rehearsals is not excessive. Typically, we spend about four to five hours rehearsing each one. If you are working with relatively inexperienced people, however, it would probably be wise to plan more time. Our four hours is divided into two rehearsals. The actors pick up their scripts one week before the performance. Our first rehearsal is early in the week, during which time we discuss the characters and work out the basic movement (blocking). Because we have only two rehearsals, we ask the actors to memorize the script prior to this rehearsal, with the goal of being off the script by the end of the two-hour session.

For the second rehearsal—in our case, before it is performed for the first service—we rehearse one and a half hours, working on stage with the hand props and furniture we'll be using. During this time we polish the movement, work on character consistency, pacing, and the rise and fall of the action. If movement doesn't look natural because an actor is having a hard time making it look motivated, we change it. After we're off the stage, we run lines or work problem areas of blocking for an additional half to full hour. We also try to relax and enjoy each other's company before the service begins.

For props, we use only that which is absolutely necessary. In other words, we don't use furniture to establish setting, but only if it fulfills a necessary function in the sketch. If, for example, a phone is needed, we would use an end table to set it on. But if nothing needs to sit on the end table, why use one? Typically we do not use door or window units. If a window is called for, we mime it. However, rather than mime the opening and closing of an imaginary door, which gets cumbersome, the actors simply enter a room, a convention which an audience seems to accept.

A simple rule of thumb, then, for props and scenic pieces is to keep them simple, relying on the audience's imagination to fill in the details. Not only is this an easier route, but—unless you have a professional set designer—it is also the most effective. Furthermore, since props usually need to be set in place before a sketch and removed afterwards, the simpler you can keep it, the better.

While the technical elements necessary to produce a good sketch are fairly basic, assembling the right actors and someone to "lead the charge" might prove more challenging. Talent in drama, unlike the other arts, is somewhat difficult to assess quickly. If someone cannot sing a song or play an instrument, it is readily evident, but acting talent is more difficult to define. To further complicate the matter, drama seems to attract people who have an affinity for the arts but who lack specific talent or training. Someone reasons, "I can't sing, or play the piano, but I think I can act." Indeed, maybe this person has acting ability, but too often such people are drawn to drama because it appears relatively "easy," at least compared to the other arts. But doing drama well is more difficult than it appears. Unfortunately, many well-intentioned people, because they know little about the craft of drama, have not helped further the cause of drama in the church. God is not served when drama is done poorly.

Therefore, before getting serious about drama, even short sketches, the church must find a competent drama director. This person needs to have adequate people skills, the ability to assess acting talent, and an understanding of the basics of stage direction. If someone possesses great drama instincts but lacks formal training, it would be a wise investment for a church to enroll this person in some courses in acting and directing at a local college. A good course in directing can provide many of the basic principles necessary for staging drama effectively.

Having formally trained actors is an advantage, but most churches do not have this luxury—all the more reason to have someone with skill and training leading the team. Over time, talented lay people with good dramatic instincts can develop into strong performers, even if they have no previous drama experience, but their growth will be severely limited if their directors do not have sufficient training.

And finally, a word of encouragement. Once a person has understood some basic principles of theater—as simple as this sounds—that person learns to do drama by *doing* drama. Even the most inexperienced actors and directors can improve, as long as they are willing to learn from their mistakes.

Throughout our many years of doing drama at Willow Creek, we have made numerous mistakes. We still do. In the earlier years, for example, too many of our scripts were "preachy," and therefore stilted and manipulated. Today, periodically, we do a script that we think will work, but it ends up falling flat, due to a lack of conflict, identification,

humor, or any number of factors. Sometimes it is particularly frustrating because it's difficult to figure out exactly why a script appeared not to "go over." Such is the business of doing original drama. But as long as we try to learn from each experience, over time we improve the quality and increase our understanding of the craft of drama.

Steve Pederson[94]

339 • BEGINNING A DRAMA GROUP

Preparing drama for worship requires much time and skill. The following article identifies many of the issues that need to be addressed in beginning a drama ministry and describes helpful procedures for making this process efficient.

Religious drama is finding its way into the liturgy and pedagogy of religious institutions. Laypersons who wish to begin such a "drama ministry" need assistance in knowing how to form a religious drama interest and a performing group. They need to realize that drama has a historical connection to the church and can continue to be useful in presenting the Christian truth. Christ used narrative and stories to present his truth during His brief ministry here on earth. Humans seem to discover deeper aspects of their faith through stories and narratives, and today this form of storytelling can best be offered by means of dramatic production and presentation.

Religious leaders have had a "love/hate" relationship with drama throughout history. The early Hebrews composed group chants, praises, and prayers that were dramatically interactive in group and leader recitative. The basilicas of early Christianity were so immense that group liturgists projected the sound of doctrinal pronouncements so that those attending could hear and understand the tenets of the faith. From these beginnings the Mass evolved to incorporate segments of group reading, recitation, and drama. The early mystery plays portrayed aspects of the lives of Christ and the apostles in outdoor and cathedral settings.

For some well-meaning theologians and believers, the "drama" of the early church was suspected of participating inadvertently in evil, because believers portrayed other personae, potentially compelling the faithful to deception, false implications, or connections to the sinful secular culture. An early advocate of drama's distinct sacred potential was the tenth-century German nun Hroswitha, who came to the convent at Gandersheim in southern Germany from an educated life as a nobleman's daughter. Once converted to monastic Christianity, she disavowed all connections to her past love and appreciation for the Roman playwrights and decided to compose plays for a cloistered audience in Latin. Hroswitha was so concerned that her plays might be linked with secular stage productions that she specifically wrote stage directions that her plays be read rather than performed. Predating the modern readers' theater art form, Hroswitha's six plays regaled the local community with tales of saints tortured and abused for their faith. She called these dramas "comedies," because each saint went to spend eternity in heaven at the end of each reading.

Does drama have a place in the church today? Many realize that the answer is resoundingly affirmative. The topics presented in drama bring people to the edge of confrontation with social values and traditions. That tension is a given; good drama must have tension. But the good "play" with resolution, direction, or rhetorical premises seeks to provide answers to life's dilemmas. Drama in the church today should have five purposes: (1) worship; (2) education; (3) entertainment; (4) evangelism or conviction; and (5) mature growth and appreciation.

Drama can lead us in *worship* as we listen, hear, and meditate on the attributes of God: his work, his plan, his essence, and his majesty. Drama tells Bible stories to *educate* us and our children or to relate biblical injunctions for contemporary living. It can evoke feelings of happiness or sadness as our emotions *entertain* our passions and deepest thoughts. Drama can relay the message of *evangelism* in an unpredictable manner, leading to *conviction*. Finally, we become more balanced, more *mature* Christians as we absorb drama's efforts to instruct us on *growth* and change in the Christian life.

For the past twenty years, contemporary Christian music has revitalized the local congregation, introducing percussive instruments, contemporary rhythms, and even making inroads into secular culture with crossover artists like Amy Grant, Michael W. Smith, and Philip Bailey. But within the past five years, drama in the church, which had lagged behind in renewal, has begun to catch up with contemporary Christian music. Churches are recognizing the power of drama, incorporating scenes, skits, full productions, and pageants into regular services, as well as creating specialized formats for presentation. Reformed Jewish synagogues like Temple Beth Tikvah in Columbus, Ohio, have experimented with modern liturgical formats that involve the congregation in dramatic and choral recitation; they create a "theater of worship." Other ministries experiment with clowning or puppetry to tell stories to "media-raised" youth, enhancing traditional religious and spiritual training. Willow Creek Community Church in Illinois has been on the cutting edge of innovative approaches, coaxing the unchurched to attend through an emphasis on contemporary, locally produced drama. Proscenium full-staged productions to stark choral readings are part of the growing interest in bringing drama back to the church in our day.

Laypersons who have talent and experience in dramatic presentations have been neglected for too long in our churches. To utilize drama as a communicative system, a local training program may be needed. Consider the following pedagogical guidelines, suggestions, and resources for a local church to begin a "drama ministry."

Stimulating Interest in Drama

A good quality dramatic script and performance will stir interest in a congregation for more dramatic endeavors. As a stimulant, bring in an outside group to perform before starting dramatic training. A highly polished and prepared group will demonstrate to all, especially the cynics, the power and communicative impact of religious drama. Find a local church with a strong drama program and ask the members if they would perform at your church. Local Christian colleges (such as Biola University in California; Northwest Nazarene College in Idaho; or Gordon College in Massachusetts) have troupes that can be invited for local church gatherings. Parachurch dramatic organizations, such as Lamb's Players in San Diego or A. D. Players in Houston, can be contracted for various dramatic productions. A local civic theater may have a "secular" play with religious overtones, and the cast may enjoy an opportunity for interaction. A question/answer period following a presentation of *Amadeus, Luther,* or *J.B.* might stimulate religious thought and growth.

Other mechanisms to stimulate interest in drama might include:

1. A dialogue sermon in which two leaders speak in tandem, occasionally in choral-line delivery.
2. Readers' theater, a "Theater of the Mind," in which minimal staging and dramatized prose,

poetry, and drama selections call upon the audience to "imagine" actions and scenes.

3. A pre-sermon/homily monologue in which a biblical character or religious persona reacts to the principles of the day's message. This could be a costumed monologue or predictable dress presentation.

4. A choral reading of the Scripture passage by two or more readers, seated in various places among the congregation.

5. A combined choir and drama musical presentation. Various publishers listed at the end of this article offer many full-length plays with music for congregational use.

Any of these suggestions should stir interest in creating a local drama troupe. The congregational leader needs to be aware of drama seminars and source material available for production.

Look for local or area-wide drama specialists who will come to your church for a one- or two-day seminar on drama. Choose a seminar that offers information to the novice actor as well as stimulating the veteran drama enthusiast.

Source References for Dramatic Presentation

An annotated bibliography appears at the end of this chapter listing titles and publishers of religious drama. Though more Christian publishers are offering more dramatic script texts, entertaining, instructive, and powerfully compelling material is sometimes difficult to find. You may choose to write your own material, clip and adapt religious poems, essays, editorials, vignettes, and stories for use in creatively compiled skits or readers' theater productions. Try your hand at writing short or lengthy original material as well.

Locating the Drama Enthusiasts

Finding those members of the local religious center who are interested in dramatic performance can be frustrating. At first, a director will gravitate toward finding the performers for specific parts, but as an alternative, consider beginning with a survey card which indicates interest or background in all facets of drama. Most religious groups have an abundance of hidden talent just waiting to be asked or discovered.

Hand the cards out as a bulletin insert or at the door as worshipers come in for a service. If possible, augment the survey card with a public announcement of the need for performers, set designers, lighting, sound technicians, make-up artists, music, choral readers, costume designers, and publicity people.

In addition to basic information about name, age group, address, and experience, establish a planning session time, usually a week or two weeks from the distribution date. Appeal to all ages, and if the interest is high within an age grouping (e.g., high school) you may wish to cast performers from within the predominant age group. Drama has the ability to bridge the generation gap, so casting a multiaged group can bring the religious body together in a cross-generational activity.

At the planning session, find out how interested your attendees are. For those who want more information, indicate to them that you would like to start a drama ministry that would allow opportunities for the local church to put on shows similar to the kind performed by your guest troupes. Discuss with attendees that a drama ministry can augment the pulpit or liturgical presentations. Try to instill an enthusiastic anticipation for what a drama ministry could mean for the congregation and the participants.

Choosing a Performance Piece and Casting

When you have a good idea of the number and quality of those interested in drama, choose a dramatic program to present. If anticipated presentation is seasonal, select a holiday-themed program. You will need to write to the publishers for royalty information if you choose certain plays. If you compile a readers' theater program, copyright obligations may compel writing for performance permission. Some legal advisers believe that if nondramatic literature is presented to an educational audience or in a nonprofit setting, permission and/or royalties may be unnecessary. Some older literature is definitely in the public domain and does not require a royalty. You are clearly in violation of copyright laws if you charge admission for royalty-earning plays or equally designated nondramatic forms without writing for permission. A good rule of thumb is to check at the beginning of any published work to see if specific permission or royalty fees must be paid prior to performance.

You can meet separately with the technical crew as the preliminary plans progress. Inform the technical crew of their responsibilities and your needs and prepare them to run *their* "dress rehearsal" (cue-to-cue rehearsal) on one of the nights preceding the first performance.

At your planning session, you may wish to designate two times for performance auditions. During the auditions, hand out an "audition sheet." This sheet asks for basic information about name, address, telephones (work and home), age group, and an explanation of drama experience. The sheet should clearly indicate drama rehearsal times (e.g., Sunday afternoons, 3 P.M. until 6 P.M.; Saturdays, 10 A.M. until 12 noon; Thursday night dress rehearsal; Friday night dress rehearsal, etc.). Ask for a clear indication of days on which the performer cannot attend. Finally, leave a blank space for "director's comments" or helpful notes about each person who auditions.

At the auditions you will need to stress commitment to rehearsals and performances, but be a little more flexible than you might be with a school or "graded" class. Too much pressure will drive participants away, since they have no extrinsic reason to stay with the activity. You must build intrinsic commitment by emphasizing the ministry aspects and the opportunity to communicate in a novel and effective manner. The indication of rehearsal times on the audition sheet should preempt some, but not all, of the "no-show" problems. Try to instill in all the performers the necessity of being at rehearsals on time, because you will be committed to letting them out on time. Set the example as a director by always being on time and keeping to a clear schedule. You should cast performers who will commit themselves to the practice times and performances. Drop a cast member who fails to meet the rehearsal times regularly. Allowing this kind of behavior brings down the performance level and morale of the whole cast.

Auditioning can be accomplished by any number of methods. The following patterns may be useful:

1. Audition individually. You make script copies available ahead of time or have a "cold" session. Bring in each performer separately and feed them cue lines.
2. Audition by small group (2 to 5 people). Divide up the scripts and allow several combinations to read and reread short one-minute to three-minute sections of the script.
3. Call-back auditions. If you choose to narrow the field of performers for one last decision-making audition, set up an additional audition time by posting, phoning, mailing a "call back" list. Some directors feel more secure when they cast one or two alternates or understudies.

During an audition, the drama leader should choose performers with enthusiastic dedication to the rigors of the endeavor. As a director, listen for such variables as vocal tone and range; believability; appearance; abilities to portray personae (e.g., older or younger people; those with regional dialects or noticeable psychological characteristics); cooperative attitude; and the somewhat enigmatic but powerful concept of stage presence.

Sometimes after casting, and once you have begun rehearsals, you may wish to ask some performers to switch parts or line reading. Try not to make it seem like a promotion or demotion, but rather a fine-tuning of the best combination for presentation.

Adapting to the Performing Area

Religious centers are seldom built for "proscenium" or theatrical presentations. But the space available for performing—"found space"—can be adapted for presentation by altering the environment or using the space as is. The church sanctuary platform area may have a removable pulpit, but choir banister and loft seats are often permanently attached to the floor. You may choose to use the already existing steps to the pulpit area or add risers or leveling platforms over the stationary choir seats. If the congregational seats are movable, a theater-in-the-round format might be utilized. If a readers' theater format is chosen, you may use stools and boxes to stand or sit upon to represent staging areas.

Consider the focus for the performers. If a play is presented and the primary eye contact is on-stage, position the performers in such a way that most of the time they are readily visible from all parts of the congregation. If a readers' theater format is used, consider an off-stage focus (imaginary scene placement above the heads of the audience) or audience focus as the main means to keep performers in clear view.

The use of lapel mikes and mike cords can be a nightmare of entanglement. Ideally, try to perform without benefit of electronic amplification. If this is not possible, try to set up at least four omni-directional microphones at levels that will project most of the sound. Technology is constantly improving the means to amplify sound, but you still may be at the mercy of a microphone with a bad battery, external sound competition, or other mishap. Stress again and again the need to project all dialogue and recitations so all can hear and understand.

Rehearsal Practices and Training

The first series of rehearsals require that a director give direction and insights into the meaning and interpretation of the script. Read through the script around a table, pausing when necessary to ask questions concerning character analysis and motivation. Try to get your performers to discover the deeper layers of personality in their character parts by asking questions, or doing demonstration or role plays. Especially in preliminary rehearsals for readers' theater, work for energetic cue pick ups and matching pitch tones for multicharacter line readings.

Some directors have found that an initial ten to fifteen minute period of "theater games" provides good warm-up technique. Improvisations with characters from the presentation, calisthenics, and verbal scale recitations ("Ah, Ay, Eee, Oh, Ooh," etc.) can help prepare performers for a more in-tune presentation.

When the read-through rehearsals have led up to a point of familiarity with the script, blocking rehearsals should follow. If you are presenting a play or chamber theater, memorization of parts should accompany the blocking rehearsals. If you are presenting a readers' theater, stress that 60 to 70 percent of the time eye contact should be off the manuscript. If your performers are novices, you may wish to hand out a blocking pattern of the stage area. Divide a stage area into nine segments (e.g., upstage right, upstage center, upstage left, center stage right, center stage, center stage left, downstage right, downstage center, downstage left). Remind your performers that upstage is always away from the audience and downstage is toward the audience. The "power" stages are those central to the playing area and gain the most attention from audience observers. Have performers bring pencils so that they can mark blocking moves into their scripts or notebooks. As a director, you will need to schematically map out your blocking and staging moves ahead of time (e.g., diagrams in a notebook or amplified script copy) or ask the cast to move around for aesthetic decisions and composition variables of staging.

As blocking rehearsals continue, offer refining comments about cues, nuances of character movements, and entrances/exits. If necessary, offer to meet for individual coaching sessions. Usually, a cast will forget or lose some interpretive character business as they learn blocking, but with a gentle reminder the performance choices you desire in your actors will return, accompanied by the well-timed blocking moves.

For the first night's dress rehearsal, prepare your performers for a cue-to-cue technical rehearsal. Bring all of your sound technical crew together and walk your performers through each segment, pausing to insure that lighting, sound, and scene change crew members know their parts. For the next night's dress rehearsal, invite a small select audience to come, watch, and meet with the cast and crew afterwards for final corrections or reminders. When the performance night comes, meet early with the cast for prayer. Encourage them to do their best and to have fun.

Religious Drama Is Ministry

Continually stress that unlike any other performance, religious dramatic endeavors are meant to *minister* as well as entertain and provoke thought. Remember to be reasonable in your praise and kind in offering constructive criticism. Your cast will give you their best if they are encouraged and gently corrected rather than publicly disgraced or humiliated.

After the initial performances, consider other outlets for using religious drama. Speak to the pastor about augmenting the sermon/homily with a dramatic scene. Consider a summer dinner theater for your religious center. Use drama as a pedagogical tool (e.g., a production concerning pain and suffering and God's role, followed by a discussion). Encourage age-group drama troupes to form so that they can teach their peers. Take your production to another church and introduce drama and its possibilities to them. Religious dramatic presentations can minister in effective and dynamic ways, thereby increasing the number of ways to reach the needs of the various congregations.

Todd V. Lewis

340 • INVOLVING CHILDREN IN DRAMA FOR WORSHIP

Involving children in a drama ministry provides an appropriate way to use their unique gifts in the life of the congregation, encourages their spiritual growth, and makes an important contribution to common worship. These and other benefits of a children's drama ministry are described here.

Children's chancel dramas or musicals have become a popular means of bringing young people into active participation in the worship service. Often such musicals serve as the proclamation of the Word, sometimes even taking the place of the sermon; or they may serve as the anthem for a particular Sunday. Since children remember and reflect on the biblical texts and stories they have sung as anthems or performed in a chancel drama, these musicals are invaluable methods of Christian education.

A drama of any duration requires costumes, lights, blocking, and extra instruments, and may take many hours to prepare. The time is well spent when the focus is a chancel drama because its preparation offers multiple opportunities for children's spiritual growth in, for example, the following areas: (1) commitment and cooperation; (2) biblical and theological insight; (3) musical and dramatic skill; (4) awareness of church aesthetics; (5) mission awareness; and (6) a sense of ritual and "liturgy as theater."

Commitment and Cooperation

At the basis of any learning process is commitment. To have learned to give one's self and to take pride in that giving is a lesson that benefits all dimensions of a child's life. Children often exhibit a phenomenal capacity for love and commitment when they agree to participate fully in a project. When choir leaders and choristers share commitment, their rehearsals come alive.

In the presence of such vitality, a spirit of cooperation and teamwork is likely to follow. Openness and a desire to participate and learn develop a corporate sense among the children. Nothing is more satisfying to the group or its director than putting aside age and personality differences to work toward a common goal. Within such an atmosphere, a choir community can produce excellent music or drama while also participating deeply in the church's purpose and mission.

Biblical and Theological Insight

One criticism of chancel dramas is that the people in the pews often already know the biblical narrative being presented. Young and old have heard the stories of Adam and Eve, Jonah and the whale, Noah and the ark, the three wise men and other stories since their earliest years. Yet fresh insights into biblical stories are always being discovered by scholars, preachers, church educators, and musicians. Children can be part of an ongoing biblical exegesis as they explore and memorize the texts of anthems and act out Bible stories.

Stories are remembered in more detail and with greater understanding when they have been sung and dramatized. Children (and adults) begin to understand by role-playing how their character interacts with other characters, and how each player fits into the story line. For example, when I directed *Winter Star* by Malcolm Williamson, our choir worked at "getting into character" by talking about how each character or group of characters acts and reacts in the story.

During discussions and rehearsals, we also explored the story's theological symbolism. *Winter Star* is a retelling of the familiar tale of the three wise men. Among the insights that the children discovered for themselves were these: the star character is a symbol of God; Jesus is a gift of God's love for us; and the kings and shepherds are representative of humankind. The choir's retelling of the familiar story provided the children and others with fresh insights into Christian theology.

Musical and Dramatic Growth

To reap the immense rewards of participation in a chancel drama, the script must be chosen very carefully. Many musicals that have clever, easily-learned tunes and simple stories do not lend themselves to dramatic enactment. While they may be fun for the children and well received by the congregation, they have little educational and spiritual value. If a chancel musical is to be worthwhile and fulfilling to the children, the music and drama must be interesting, challenging and a joy to perform.

Interest can be heightened by the use of a variety of compositional techniques: canon, different meters (including ones like 5/8 and 7/8), different melodic notes, melodies that identify specific characters and "ensemble finale" endings in which all characters come together and sing their own thematic material. Williamson employs many of those techniques in *Winter Star,* and the result is a successful, creative dramatic expression. For example, he uses differences in modes and meter to create unique characterizations and atmospheric suggestions for each player and scene. The 7/8 march tempo of the kings gives the impression of the rocking movement of the camels on which they ride—though fortunately no live camels appear! The radiating star—a circle of five young girls with their backs to the center and arms clasped above them—revolves to the motif of consistent eighth notes, a sparkling star in sound and appearance.

Many of the choristers involved in *Winter Star* found that they were able to memorize much more music than ever before. Struggling with its various meters and modes, they learned unusual aspects of music that are often never encountered in the education of young church musicians. The musical success of the final project so increased their confidence that later they tackled difficult pieces and performed them with ease.

The children's growth as actors was facilitated by a talented local actress who volunteered as production director and choreographer. The children learned how to make the audience believe they were watching shepherdess, kings, angels, and a star; in other words, the actors learned how to become the person or things portrayed. After discussing each character, we took some time to allow each child to play at "getting into character." Several of the children had such fun that they signed up for drama classes in the local youth theater program.

Mission Awareness

Too often young people's singing groups offer their talents only once a month, usually at the "family service." It is important, however, that parishioners also become aware of the benefits of the children's choir as part of young people's Christian education. The young church people of today need a sense of belonging and affirmation for their contributions. A children's musical is an opportunity for such affirmation, especially if it is presented at all services.

The sharing provides an occasion for young churchgoers to participate actively in the parish's ministry to those within the church. An external ministry also occurs as the children bring their friends from outside the parish to participate in the chancel production. Once the newcomers are part of the drama, they often choose to stay with the choir for other events; the children's choir program gives young people a "hands on" experience of drawing others into the church.

Aesthetics in the Church

I believe that a chancel drama is one of the best ways to instigate reflection on church aesthetics. In such a project, children can be made consciously aware of all aspects of corporate worship. They concretely explore aesthetics in several ways: (1) by using the space within the church building in a variety of ways; (2) by using movement that is appropriate to a text; (3) by being made aware of a specific text as it relates to an entire church service; and (4) by learning to use different kinds of sounds and periods of silence.

In James Pottie's *More Profound Alleluia!* (Washington, D.C.: Pastoral Press, 1984), Erik Routley is quoted as saying that "art is a mode of human public conversation" (p. 64). Instead of a dictionary-like definiteness, the artist communicates subtle meaning and value. The art of music communicates with sounds and rhythms. The addition of a text couples useful information with beautiful sounds. Often if we recall those beautiful sounds, we can more easily understand and remember the words. Our subconscious is filled with biblical stories learned in this way.

Pottie likens the artistry we try to instill in our children's choirs to Jesus' communication with his disciples through parables.

> The artist, as Jesus does in his parables, invites us to go beyond the "letter," i.e. mere information, explicitness, usefulness, or instruction. Only the spirit gives life. Artistic forms participate in some way in the life-giving spirit. (Ibid., 64)

Art in all forms becomes part of the aesthetics of our worship. Worship involves the whole assembly: presiders, preachers, readers, musicians, architects, and of course all those who do not exercise a specific liturgical ministry. Music, as an integral part of the whole, must be carefully selected, prepared, and performed, not as a concert or entertainment, but as an offering.

This view of worship is an important concept that can easily be communicated by the director's attitude and actions. In my situation, I try to make time between rehearsals to discuss such matters. We often begin a time of vocal rest with a simple question about an attitude of worship; for example, "How does our anthem fit into this week's service?" or "What can the choir do to make the service more meaningful to the parish?"

———— The Sense of Ritual and Theater ————

Ritual involves an assembly of God's people who seek to communicate with one another and with God. The ritual is the communication; it weaves together signs, symbols, and events, such as the cross, the paraments, and the blessing of the vessels for Communion, into a structured order of service. Children and adults often perform rituals week after week without really entering into the communication process. One role of the children's choir is to teach the wonder and mystery that is liturgy, "the work of the people" and the church's most ancient forms of communication.

In _A More Profound Alleluia!_ Pottie devotes an entire chapter to the relationship between ritual and communication. He writes:

> Ritual, then, is corporate symbolic activity. In the context of a Christian worshiping community, it is the medium of communication revealing the God in Christ, who is the ground and reality to which the ensemble of signs and symbols refer. This ensemble serves also to communicate to the participants of the assembly gathered in faith the meaning and context of their coming together. On both levels, the ritual activity (i.e., the ensemble of liturgical signs) is the means of communication of the Christ-event to and among the assembled worshiping community. To know what aides and what hinders the flow of communication through the ritual action allows the ritual to do its proper task: the communication of life, meaning and value for the gathered. (p. 19)

A significant chancel drama-musical helps children to begin to understand this concept. Choir members and director need to examine the routine of ritual and discover how the choir's contribution can enhance and develop with the spoken word, the corporately sung word, moments of silence, gestures, and other ritual elements. With careful explanation, children can begin to see the entire scope of that communication while gaining a sense of belonging and participation in it. Under ideal circumstances, this reflection will take place even if the choir is dealing with less elaborate anthems.

The idea that worship is theater has been the subject of many theoretical writings. Erik Routley, for example, was a proponent of this concept. Theater and drama within a church setting include communication forms such as prayers, readings, music, and sermons. Each week the church presents a drama depicted in a way that connects with our own life settings. The service functions as a link between our spirits and God's. It is a delicate link; worship as theater encompasses, engulfs, and involves the entire person and the whole church community.

It is imperative that children know and believe that all the senses are involved in the church's dramatic action. Children are subconsciously aware of shape, color, movement, sound, and silence. Our job as church music educators is to help them develop an appreciation of themselves as members of a corporate worshiping body.

While anthems can be used to teach worship to our children, the larger chancel drama incorporates an even greater number of aesthetic, musical, and Christian ideals. Though much work is involved in any such production, the rewards are far greater. Through them we can enrich the lives of young church members with the ideals and love of Christ.

Jeannie Kienzle[95]

341 • Bibliography on Drama in Worship

Bennett, Gordon C. _Acting Out Faith_. St. Louis: CBP, 1986. Excellent resource for dramatic arts, comprehensively and practically considered with focus on technical aspects of church theater for worship and witness. History and variety of religious theater discussed. Special chapter on playwrighting, and twenty pages of resources. Perhaps the most complete, compact volume on the subject. Illustrations and diagrams.

Cassady, Marsh. _Acting: Step by Step_. San Jose, Calif.: Resource Publications, 1988. The beginner's Bible to acting, including chapters on: creative state, creative concentration, freeing the imagination, thinking and acting, the stage, body, voice, script, matter of technique, script and character analysis, and more. Tips on improvisation, rehearsal, and performance. Good for any presentation in the public forum. Illustrations and diagrams.

Cassady, Marsh. _Playwriting: Step by Step_. San Jose, Calif.: Resource Publications, 1984. Basic book that acquaints the reader with the elements and techniques of playwriting from concept to performance, along with helpful suggestions concerning planning, writing, and marketing the finished product. Illustrations and diagrams.

Deitering, Carolyn. *Actions, Gestures, and Body Attitudes*. Saratoga, Calif.: Resource Publications, 1980. An advocate for liturgical artistry, Deitering fully exposes and sensitively treats the church's rich tradition of ritual movement in a fresh way that both respects tradition and encourages creative innovation. The kinesthetic sense is applied to stillness, sitting, standing, sinking, skipping, song, story and more. Involves the use of the whole body, including its movement in relation to objects and architecture. Illustrations, exercises, and index.

Ehrensperger, Harold. *Religious Drama: Ends and Means*. New York: Abingdon, 1962. Author is concerned about the "amateurish" situation of religious drama. Volume is a primary text in drama and religious drama, with particular attention to chancel drama. Part three of the book includes standards for choosing a play, making a play come to life through directing and acting, organizing and rehearsing, and production imperatives. Appendices, lists of resources, and an extensive bibliography.

Litherland, Janet. *Getting Started in Drama Ministry*. Colorado Springs, Colo.: Meriwether: 1988. Concise, complete volume in three parts: (1) Possibilities—drama in education, worship, fun, fund-raising, dining and advertising; (2) Limitations—support system, facilities and scenery, and special effects; and (3) Challenge—directing, acting, leading, and learning. Excellent primer on the subject with illustrations, diagrams, and photos. Resource list and bibliography.

Miller, Paul M. *Create a Drama Ministry*. Kansas City, Mo.: Lillenas, 1984. A "getting started" handbook that provides a rationale for drama as ministry; explores the dramatic possibilities in the church; assists in organizing a ministry and production preparation (including budgeting); advises with respect to maximizing artistic talent; and considers in detail the technical side of staging, scenery, construction, lighting, sound, makeup, and costuming. Glossary, resource, and play lists.

Lewis, Todd V. *RT: A Readers' Theatre Ministry* [featuring "I Thought the Christian Life Was Supposed to Be a Piece of Cake"]. Kansas City, Mo.: Lillenas, 1988.

Lewis, Todd V. *RT Two: Two Scripts For Readers Theatre*. Kansas City, Mo.: Lillenas, 1990.

Robey, David H. *Two For Missions: Courageous Stories Come to Life Through Readers' Theatre*. Kansas City, Mo.: Lillenas, 1988.

Examples of Drama for Worship

This chapter presents several examples of dramatic scripts that can be used in worship. They represent different types of drama and are designed for use in a variety of services and parts of a worship service. Some of these depict a scriptural narrative; others portray a scene from modern life. Examples of dramatic renderings of scripture passages that might be used in place of the reading of a scripture lesson are not included here, but are printed in chapter 18.

342 • *Doubting Thomas: A Dramatic Script based on a Scriptural Narrative*

The following script is an adaptation of Thomas' confession of the risen Lord. It would be appropriate for use in conjunction with a service based on this theme, especially during the season of Easter.

Cast:
    Narrator
    John
    Thomas
Running Time:
    Approximately 6 minutes

This readers' theater piece is conceived for a variety of settings. It works equally well as a static piece (read at microphones with limited gestures) or as a staged reading. In a staged reading, scripts are still carried in a binder, but movement and gesture patterns are specifically determined. The following rendering of the script indicates only broad movement patterns. Obviously, you may stage it as you wish.

[Narrator *stands off to one side.* John *stands upstage right and motions to* Thomas, *standing downstage left.*]

John: Thomas!
Narrator: He cried hurrying down the crowded market street. Thomas motioned for silence and slunk down an alley.
John: Thomas!

Narrator: He cried again.
John: Thomas! Wait!

[John *crosses downstage to* Thomas.]

Narrator: Called John, the disciple loved by Jesus.

[Thomas *pulls him aside.*]

Thomas: Shh! Are you crazy? Be quiet! You'll get us killed. The Pharisees would like nothing better than to see us all go the way of the cross.
Narrator: Thomas, one of the twelve, was afraid.
John: Thomas! I saw! I saw our Lord!
Thomas: What?
John: Thomas, I have seen him! I saw the risen Christ!
Thomas: Don't mock me.
John: I'm not mocking you. It's the truth.
Narrator: John's words tumbled and spilled and rolled and sang out—for his delight was complete. He had seen his beloved Savior!
Thomas: Quiet! How can you be so reckless? People will think the rumors are true. They'll think we spirited away Jesus' body so that prophecy would be fulfilled.
John: It has been fulfilled, Thomas.
Thomas: That's crazy. They killed him three days ago.
John: No crazier than Lazarus, Thomas. He was raised after four days. Thomas, Jesus revealed himself . . . in the upper room. We have seen him.
Thomas: But I haven't. I wasn't there. He didn't reveal himself to me. Unless I see in his hands the print of the nails, put my finger in the marks of

the nails, and thrust my hand in his side, I will not believe.

[*As the* NARRATOR *begins to speak,* THOMAS *turns away from* JOHN *and crosses upstage—full back to audience.*]

NARRATOR: He could not believe. His sorrow and fear overwhelmed him. He refused to believe that the sightings of Jesus were anything more than manifestations of grief, and he ran. He kept himself apart from the brethren for seven days.

[JOHN *crosses upstage and faces full back as well— the two should be about five feet apart.*]

JOHN: Thomas! Let me in!

NARRATOR: John whispered through the door. Thomas cautiously opened it and admitted John.

[*At the word* "*door,*" JOHN *and* THOMAS *turn in toward each other and then out, facing the audience.*]

THOMAS: Did anyone see you come here?

JOHN: Be at peace, Thomas!

THOMAS: Peace! There's little peace to be found. Between the Pharisees and Romans on one side, and you and the others. . . . I haven't slept in a week.

JOHN: Thomas, we want you to share our joy.

THOMAS: I . . . I don't know what to think.

JOHN: I was there on Golgotha. I was at the tomb. The linen clothes and burial cloth were there— but not Jesus. Simon Peter was there; Mary was there; we all saw. The tomb was empty. He had risen!

THOMAS: That doesn't prove a thing.

JOHN: But then, Thomas, in that upper room, I saw his hands. Jesus showed us his pierced side. He came to us.

THOMAS: Sure. He came to you. But I am Thomas the lesser. It doesn't matter. Who am I anyway? Second son, second twin, second class. Didymus, the twin. "Hey, twin. Hey you!" Why did the Lord bother with me in the first place? Who am I? Nobody.

JOHN: Thomas, we're gathering together tonight to talk and pray. Please, come with me.

THOMAS: I'll come, but mind you, that doesn't mean I buy any of this. I meant what I said. When I see it, I'll believe it.

[*They both turn and cross upstage and face away from the audience. On* "*peace to you,*" *they both turn.* JOHN *kneels.* THOMAS *stares transfixed.*]

NARRATOR: So Thomas went and joined the others in the house. The door was closed and locked. Suddenly, "Peace to you!" said Jesus, the risen one. Jesus approached Thomas and gently placed Thomas's hand in his side and on the holes in his palms. "Do not be faithless and incredulous, but believe."

[THOMAS *kneels reverently.*]

THOMAS: My Lord and My God! I do believe.

[*End of scene*]

Debra L. Freeberg

343 • *THE UNFORGIVING SERVANT:* A DRAMATIC SKETCH BASED ON A PARABLE

The following sketch is based on Matthew 18:23-35. It could be used in a worship service in conjunction with the reading of this gospel lesson.

Participants:
JOSEPH CLARK
ANDREW COATMAN
THIRD SERVANT
FOURTH SERVANT
FIFTH SERVANT
KING

Use large books for the ledgers. Optional costumes are robes and crown for King, smocks or breeches for Servants.

[*Playing area is divided into two sections: imaginary courtyard occupies one-third,* KING'*s house the other two-thirds. An imaginary door connects the house and yard. Enter* CLARK, COATMAN, THIRD *and* FOURTH SERVANTS, *lolling about.*]

CLARK: I say, Coatman, I'll bet you two pounds you can't hit that wall *(gesturing to imaginary wall behind audience)* with a stone!

COATMAN: *(gazing directly out, looking at wall)* Fie! o'course I will!

THIRD SERVANT: I don't know, Andrew, it's quite a ways . . .

COATMAN: Here's my hand, it's a deal, Clark!

[*They shake on bet, then* COATMAN *seizes imaginary stone, gathers self together, hurls stone forward. All watch as it hurtles through air, then* CLARK *speaks as* COATMAN *makes rough, disappointed gesture.*]

CLARK: Ho! What did I tell you! Now, my two pounds, please! *(extending hand)*

COATMAN: Oh, Joseph, I haven't it wi' me just now! I'm sorry . . . I'll pay ye soon.

CLARK: See that you do, Andrew! See that you do, then!

FOURTH SERVANT: It's time we were gone, the master will be wanting us!

THIRD SERVANT: Aye! We're off then!

[*All exit R. Pause, then enter* KING *from L.*]

KING: Ho! Where are you now!

[*Enter* THIRD, FOURTH, FIFTH SERVANTS, *talking at same time, bowing.*]

THIRD SERVANT: Here, my Lord!

FOURTH SERVANT: Just coming, your Majesty!

FIFTH SERVANT: Yes, my Lord! Just here!

KING: Today is the day to sort my accounts. Where are the ledgers?

THIRD SERVANT: I'll just get them, Sire! [*Exit R;* KING *seats himself; other* SERVANTS *take positions U.* THIRD SERVANT *returns, carrying large book. Crosses to* KING, *opens book and reads aloud.*] Malcolm Albernathy—he works in the stables, Sire—two horses and fifty pounds. He has sent word he will pay by next week. Stephen Campbell, from the northern farms. One hundred and fifty bushels wheat. Payment will be made day after tomorrow. Frederick Winning, from the gardens. Two hundred and fifty pounds, uh, no, that came in yesterday. Joseph Clark, from the household, Sire, five thousand pounds. Uh, no word from him.

KING: Clark? Five thousand, is it? I think we must settle that account. How long has it been?

THIRD SERVANT: It's been . . . *(consulting book, then looking up wide-eyed)* it's been . . . ages, your Highness.

KING: I see. Well, go collect him.

[FOURTH SERVANT *exits R;* KING *and* THIRD SERVANT *carry on* sotto voce. *Loud knock,* FOURTH SERVANT *returns with* JOSEPH CLARK. CLARK *walks forward, falls before* KING *in low bow;* SERVANT *returns to former place.*]

KING: Joseph Clark.

CLARK: Yes, your Majesty.

KING: I am told you owe me five thousand pounds.

CLARK: Yes, my Lord. That I do, my Lord.

KING: Very well, Clark, pay me the debt.

CLARK: Oh my Lord, I can't.

KING: You can't, did you say?

CLARK: Aye. I have no money.

KING: But Clark, it's been years and years since you contracted this debt. And I pay you well. How do you not have any money?

CLARK: I, I have none, my Lord.

KING: The penalty for paupers, Clark is prison! Steward! (FOURTH SERVANT *steps forward*). Cast Clark and his entire family into prison. Go to their home, sell all they have, and bring the money to me as partial payment. The law is the law, Clark! You'll be released when you've paid your debt!

CLARK: Oh my Lord! *(throwing himself down, grasping* KING*'s feet, wailing)* Have mercy, I beg you! Have mercy! If you give me time, I swear I'll pay the whole debt! Have mercy!

KING: Well . . . all right! I'll be kind to you. I forgive your debt! Yes, I do, I forgive it! (CLARK *collapses in gratitude.*) Now, now, man! *(to* SERVANTS*)* Show him out.

[SERVANTS *take* CLARK *to "door" on R, put him out. They shut door halfway, then reopen it as the following ensues. Enter* ANDREW COATMAN R, *as* CLARK *is picking himself up off the ground.* CLARK *is brushing his clothes off and straightening them when he sees* COATMAN.]

CLARK: Coatman! Andrew Coatman! Come here, I say! *(Surprised,* COATMAN *crosses to* CLARK *who rushes forward to meet him, grabbing, shaking, almost choking him.)* You owe me money, Coatman! You owe me two pounds! Pay it!!!

COATMAN: *(struggling)* O, I beg you! Have mercy! If you give me time, I swear I'll pay it! Have mercy Clark!

CLARK: Mercy, fie! I'll have none! I want my money! You, your wife, your whole family will be imprisoned until you pay me! *(dragging him off R)* Constable! Arrest this man! *(They exit.)*

[*Aghast, the* SERVANTS *look at each other, then rush L to* KING. *In rapid succession:*]

THIRD SERVANT: Master! Master! Joseph Clark, whom you just forgave his debt! He's having Andrew Coatman from the stables, Sire—put in prison!

FOURTH SERVANT: For indebtedness, my Lord! Coatman owed him two pounds, and he couldn't pay!

KING: What? Coatman imprisoned? For owing Clark? Find Clark! Bring him immediately! (SERVANTS *exit R, return with* CLARK *who throws himself at* KING'*s feet, truly frightened this time.*)

KING: *(outraged)* Joseph Clark, you are *rotten!* You owed me five thousand pounds, and I forgave it because you asked me! But Andrew Coatman owed you two pounds, and you refused to forgive him! Oh, Clark! I was merciful to you for a great sum, you should have been merciful to him for such a small one! Now! *(to* SERVANTS) Cast him into prison, and let him stay there until he's paid all he owes me!!! (SERVANTS *drag* CLARK *off L.* KING *exits R, still fuming!*)

Patricia Beall[96]

344 ◆ *KEEPING TABS*: A DRAMA FOR USE IN A SEEKERS' SERVICE

The following sketch portrays a scene from everyday life involving a character who cannot accept a gift without wanting to pay it back. This sketch would appropriately be followed with a message on the mystery God's grace.

[*Setting:* DAN *is sitting on a sofa reading a newspaper.*]

NANCY: *(entering)* Oh, Dan.

DAN: Oh, what?

NANCY: Are you busy right now?

DAN: *(dropping paper)* Depends. Why?

NANCY: I thought today would be a good time to start planning your birthday party.

DAN: *(back to paper)* I'm busy.

NANCY: Dan.

DAN: Nancy, it's not for two months.

NANCY: I know. That's why we need to get started on it now.

DAN: Couldn't we just go out for a quiet dinner this year?

NANCY: Just the two of us?

DAN: Sorry, I must have lost my head for a moment.

NANCY: Oh, it's not that. It's just . . . Well, you know, we have to have a party.

DAN: Why?

NANCY: Because . . . well, take the Millers, for example.

DAN: For an example of what?

NANCY: Do you realize that we have been invited to their home six times in the last year?

DAN: So?

NANCY: So we've only had them here four times.

DAN: So?

NANCY: So we owe them.

DAN: Nancy, I really don't think they're keeping track.

NANCY: And then on top of that Linda calls me at least once a week.

DAN: What's wrong with that? I thought you liked her.

NANCY: I do, but I hardly ever call her.

DAN: Well, so?

NANCY: It makes me feel guilty. I don't like someone being so nice to me when I'm not as nice to them. And her calls just rub it in.

DAN: Nancy, don't you think you're being just a little neurotic?

NANCY: No. You know how people are. They keep tabs on things like invitations, gifts, and phone calls. And I'm telling you if we don't start catching up here, we're going to lose them.

DAN: Will you listen to yourself? You're talking as if we have to buy our friends.

NANCY: Not buy them, just stay even or get ahead. So, you see, that's why we have to have a party.

DAN: To pay back the Millers?

NANCY: Not just the Millers. The Whites, the Langstones, the Addisons.

DAN: And what do we "owe" the Addisons?

NANCY: Oh, honestly. Have you no cells in your brain? Don't you remember what they gave us for Christmas two years ago?

DAN: Silly me, but no, I don't.

NANCY: *(gets a computer printout form from an end table or on floor next to sofa)* All right, I'll show you.

DAN: What the heck is that?

NANCY: It's a computer printout showing what people have given us in the last few years.

DAN: *(looking at it)* You've got this alphabetized . . .

NANCY: And categorized. You see, in this column I have their name and a number which represents the number of times we've been invited to their house. I've also entered the gifts they gave us, along with the food they served. Now, over here in this column it lists the number of times we've had them here, our menu, and the gifts we gave them.

DAN: Nancy, this is ridiculous. I've never heard of anyone keeping an account like this.

NANCY: Well, maybe not like *this,* but people have it all in their heads, I guarantee you. Now look at this, Dan. Look at the number of blanks in our column compared to everyone else. See the Addisons here: three times . . . ribs, turkey, filet . . . napkin rings. Us: nothing. The Langstones: five times . . . roast pig, shish kebabs, steak, steak, steak . . . silver goblets! Us: burgers and a deck of cards. I am *so* embarrassed.

DAN: *(referring to her neurosis)* You should be.

NANCY: How are we going to pay all these people back?

DAN: We're not going to.

NANCY: What?

DAN: Honey, when someone has us over and gives us a gift, they do it because they want to.

NANCY: Oh, Dan, grow up! Nothing is given without expecting something in return. There are always strings attached. So, I've come up with an idea that I think should take care of our problems.

DAN: You set up an appointment to see a therapist?

NANCY: Dan, I'm serious.

DAN: So am I. *(doorbell rings)*

NANCY: I'll get it. *(she exits)*

DAN: *(picking up printout)* I don't believe this. What difference does it make? I mean, look at this . . . half this stuff we've sold at garage sales.

NANCY: *(entering)* Well, for heaven's sake, Dan, look at this. I got flowers. I wonder who they're from? Oh, here's the card. "To a terrific person." *(pause)* There's no name. There's no name?

DAN: Must be a secret admirer.

NANCY: Well, there has to be some mistake. I'll just call the florist.

DAN: Why?

NANCY: To see who sent them.

DAN: Why do you have to know?

NANCY: So I can return "the favor."

DAN: *(getting angry)* Nancy, will you get a hold of yourself? Someone sent you flowers simply be-

cause they like you, because they think you're a "terrific person." Why can't you just accept that?

NANCY: *(pause, we think he's getting through, then . . .)* I bet it was Lois. It would be just like her to do something like this.

DAN: Nancy, you're not listening to me.

NANCY: Well, I'll just call the florist.

DAN: Ok, I sent them.

NANCY: Oh, you did not!

DAN: I did so.

NANCY: Why?

DAN: Because I love you.

NANCY: Don't be ridiculous!

DAN: *(growing angrier)* Nancy, I'll show you the receipt. I've got it in my wallet.

NANCY: *(taken aback)* You sent them?

DAN: Yeah. Sorry to disappoint you.

NANCY: *(pause, cocky)* All right, let's hear it. What do you want?

DAN: Nothing.

NANCY: Nothing. You never send me flowers. You must be after something.

DAN: I'm not "after" anything . . . *(tenderly)* except maybe you.

NANCY: Oh, so that's it!

DAN: I give up. I try to do something special for my wife because I love her and she doesn't trust me.

NANCY: *(looking through printout)* Williams, Williams. Here we are. Dan Williams.

DAN: You've got me in there too?

NANCY: Well, of course.

DAN: Forget it, forget it. *(grabs flowers)* I'm throwing these things out.

NANCY: Dan, don't be ridiculous.

DAN: *(totally exasperated)* Ridiculous. I'm not ridiculous. I just don't want you to feel obligated to "return the favor," to "even the score." I give you something simply because I love you.

NANCY: And I love you too, hon. I was just surprised, that's all. Now, come on, how about if you put these beautiful flowers in some water for me . . . please?

DAN: But . . .

NANCY: Please?

DAN: *(very reluctant)* Oh, all right. *(pause)* But I'm only doing it . . .

BOTH: "Because I love you."

NANCY: I know. *(He leaves. She waits until he's gone, then goes back to printout.)* Dan Williams. *(writing)* Flowers. June 14, 1993. Occasion: *(pause, looking out, reflective)* Because he loves me.

[*Note: The way she says the last ''Because he loves me'' gives the impression that maybe she has understood Dan's point.*]

[*Fadeout*]

Sharon Sherbondy[97]

345 • *I Was There:* An Example of First-Person Portrayal of Scriptural Narrative

The following is a complete service for Christmas Eve that features three first-person accounts of Christ's birth. These monologues, along with a brief homily, are interspersed among Scripture readings and Christmas hymns.

Gathering for Worship: We prepare for worship in the Gathering Space. Welcome!
Choir: ''On Christmas Night''
Processional: ''Once in Royal David's City''
Scripture Reading: Isaiah 9:2; 42:5-9
''Yes, I Was There'': The Innkeeper's Wife

''Yes, I was there that night. We'd had a busy day at the inn. People arrived from all over for the registration, and we were full by mid-afternoon. In fact, we had to turn away five families. But somehow I didn't have the heart to turn away the young man and pregnant young woman, so I fixed them a place to sleep in the barn. I could tell her time for delivery was close, so I stayed with her. A woman needs another woman at a time like that.

''It was a night I'll long remember. The young mother told me some strange stories about her baby. At first I thought she was covering up her shady past, but later I started to realize that what she said might be true. After the baby was born, and we had swaddled him properly, there was a knock on the barn door. A bunch of shepherds came in with another bizarre story. They said that they had seen and heard angels who told them that this was a special child—a Savior not only of our people, but of all people!

''We can sure use a savior. Times are tough. The soldiers are always roaming through town, and our children—especially our girls—are never safe. We feel like captives all the time. And although most of us can scratch out a living, some of the really poor may not make it through this winter.

''There's also been a lot of fighting in the village lately, and our neighbor is carrying on with someone else's wife. So few people seem to walk in the way of the Lord anymore. These are dark and lonely times for our people.

''But I do remember an old prophecy we hear at the synagogue:

> The Spirit of the Lord God is upon me,
> because the Lord has anointed me
> to bring good tidings to the afflicted;
> he has sent me to bind up the
>   brokenhearted,
> to proclaim liberty to the captives;
> to comfort all who mourn,
> to give the oil of gladness instead of
>   mourning.

''Who knows? Maybe this baby will be involved in that wonderful freedom. At any rate, it sure was a night I'll never forget.''

Hymn: ''Come, Thou Long-Expected Jesus''
Solo: ''Come Children See Him''
Scripture Reading: Luke 2:8, 15-20
''Yes, I Was There'': A Shepherd Boy

''Yes, I was there.

''It was a night that began like most other nights I remember. My older brothers and I had taken care of the sheep many nights before. I was only eleven, but I had already learned a lot about sheep. I had once even chased away a lion. I was learning to become a good shepherd.

''But this ordinary night soon became very unusual. I saw it first. Way up in the sky, I saw the light coming. Before long it was so bright, we could hardly stand it, and we were scared out of our wits. Then that voice—I'll never forget it. 'Don't be afraid,' the voice said, and it told us about a Savior. And then came those hundreds of other voices—the most beautiful sound I'd ever heard, a song about glory and peace. I don't cry much, but I sure got a lump in my throat when I heard that.

''When they were gone, it was pitch dark and so quiet we could hear the sheep breathe. After a while I said, 'Let's go.' Some of the others weren't quite sure. 'We can't leave the sheep; they may all be gone when we get back.' But I told them I wanted to see that Savior. I was so excited, I was willing to take a chance—nothing like this had ever happened to me before. When I had convinced the others, we ran all the way into town and found the barn. And it was just as the angels had said! I'll never forget that night.

"On our way back to the field, we told everybody we met about what we had seen and heard, and you can imagine their reaction. Some said we must have had a little too much moonshine, and others thought we were just making the whole story up. I told them I could never make up anything like that!

"We were so happy on our way back to the field that we started singing psalms and some of the song that the angels sang. We're not the greatest singers, but it sounded OK. It sure was a night I'll never forget."

Hymn: "Infant Holy, Infant Lowly"
Choir: "The First Noel"
A Christmas Eve Litany:

LEADER: If our lives are dry and parched, Lord, send the living waters of your Spirit:
PEOPLE: To revive us, to enliven us, to bring forth new life. Immanuel, come quickly.
LEADER: If our times are empty and barren, Lord, grant us a rich harvest:
PEOPLE: Send us home with sheaves of blessing, fill us with your abundance, and teach us to share the harvest with others. Immanuel, come quickly.
LEADER: If our bodies are weary and heavy laden, Lord, fill us with laughter:
PEOPLE: Give us shouts of joy, envelop us with your gladness. Immanuel, come quickly.
LEADER: If our lives are small and trivial, Lord, make us see great things:
PEOPLE: Enlarge our vision, widen our borders. Immanuel, come quickly.

Scripture Reading: Luke 2:9-14
Hymn: "Angels We Have Heard on High"
"Yes, I Was There": An Angel

"Yes, I was there.

"I was one of the angels in that choir. Of course, I'm not as important as Gabriel. He was sent on a few solo trips to Zechariah and Mary, and I'm not sure I'll ever get to carry those kinds of messages. But I did get in on the singing message.

"At first I nearly started laughing when those shepherds saw us. I guess they had never seen an angel before. They were so scared they started running for the hills. But the angel of the Lord calmed them, and our song was so beautiful that they stayed and listened. We sang 'Glory to God' over and over. I could have sung it all night.

"Of course, our song told them only a little bit of the story. Gabriel told us the rest of it, but I'm not quite sure I understood it all. Our great God saw no other way to save the world, to bring wholeness back to the people—except by becoming one of the people. Somehow that baby we sang about is also God!

"I must admit, it was a bit of a shock when we heard that God was going to be born in a barn as a helpless baby. We were even more shocked to hear that this baby/God may have to die. But we were overjoyed to learn that our God is going to come back to us as our great King.

"I don't quite understand all of that, but when we were singing, I got the main point: God is going to straighten out the world. God's going to save his people from their crooked ways. God's going to bring peace. And, though it's hard to believe, this baby Jesus is going to be involved in it all. Even though I may not understand it, I'm going to keep singing about peace on earth, good will to all people, and glory to God."

Choir: "Rejoice, Earth and Heaven"
Offertory: "A Little Shepherd"
Scripture Reading: John 1:1-14
"Yes, We Are There": A Word to the Congregation

"You no doubt remember the old spiritual, 'Were You There when They Crucified My Lord?' Tonight we're asking the same question about Jesus' birth. The innkeeper's wife was there. The shepherd boy was, too. So was the angel. And their lives were all affected by the events of that wondrous night.

"And, of course, we were not there. We are here, Christmas Eve. But we can still ask if and how our lives are affected by that wondrous night.

"Like the innkeeper's wife, we're not always so sure that Jesus is for us. Is he for real? Does he make a difference? And we also know about the dark corners in our world. There are dark corners of fear and loneliness in the ghettos of our large cities, as well as in in quiet neighborhoods in small towns.

"In all of these places, it's important that we say to ourselves and to each other, 'This Christ child brings good tidings to the afflicted; he will bind up the brokenhearted. This Christ is for us too. We need and want to be near the Savior.'

"The shepherd was full of excitement after the angels sang their message. He could hardly wait to get to the stable, and he was willing to take some risks to get there. After his encounter with the Child, he went back to work whistling and singing, telling his story to all who would hear.

"We, too, must show some of that holy impatience. We, too, must look for Christ's kingdom with eager anticipation. We want Christ to rule in our hearts and lives and in this world—NOW. But are we willing to take risks for the gospel? Are we willing to give of ourselves, our time, and our money—for the church, for those in need, for missions?

"And after meeting Christ, do we tell our story of meeting him? On the way back to work, the shepherds said, 'Guess what we heard! Guess what we have seen! Would you believe . . . ?' After we meet Christ in worship, in prayer, in Bible study, in meditation, do we go and tell 'Guess what I have seen! Do you believe there's an honest-to-goodness Savior?' That's part of our story, and we should make people wonder at what we tell them. We also can identify with the angel. We are full of wonder, full of amazement. God loved so much! God cared so much that he gave his only Son—he gave himself. And that wonder and amazement makes us sing the angels' song two thousand years later."

Hymn: "Go, Tell It On the Mountain"
Recessional: "Silent Night"

Harry Boonstra[98]

346 ◆ *KING OF KINGS*: A FESTIVAL MUSIC DRAMA

The following is an example of a festival music drama on the theme of the lordship of Jesus Christ. It could well be used on the Feast of Christ the King, the final Sunday of the Christian Year, the Sunday immediately preceding Advent.

Cast of Characters:
    CHRIST THE KING
    JEDIDIAH, THE HIGH PRIEST
    DAUGHTERS OF JERUSALEM I, II, III
    GATEKEEPER
    MESSENGERS I, II
    ACOLYTE
    BANNER BEARER I, II
    CONGREGATION OF ISRAEL: the Congregation
    OTHERS: Trumpeter, Organist, Musicians

(This is a master script which is used by leading characters. The CONGREGATION *is given a smaller insert script that includes its lines, or the lines can be shown on an overhead projector.)*

──────────── **Part I** ────────────

[*On the chancel there is a raised platform on which a huge throne sits. Behind the throne is a large banner with a crown and a cross on it. Beside the throne are two large menorahs. Another large banner on the back wall has the star of David on it. On the front left side of the chancel there is a kneeler. Toward the end of the center aisle is a "gate"—the temple gate where the* GATEKEEPER *stands. Each of the* DAUGHTERS OF JERUSALEM *is in her starting position.* DAUGHTER I *is seated on a pew on the right aisle.* DAUGHTER II *is seated on a pew on the left aisle.* DAUGHTER III *is seated on a pew at the back of the center aisle. The* GATEKEEPER *and the* TRUMPETER *stand by the gate.*]

TRUMPETER: *(sounds a short alarm)*

GATEKEEPERS: Citizens of Jerusalem! We're in danger! Messengers from Megiddo report that our armies have been defeated. The kings of the North are now marching towards our holy city! We must pray! Our Deliverer must come!

DAUGHTER I: *(rises from her seat and walks down the center aisle towards the chancel. As she does she directs her prayer to God)* O God, do not be silent. Hear us! For centuries our city has been ravished. We have not known peace, O God, only war and strife. My husband, a great captain, and his company have all been killed in Megiddo! He is dead! Killed by the enemy's hand of hate! *(When she reaches the chancel, she goes to the kneeler and remains in silence; then she faces the* CONGREGATION *and says)* Pray with me, people of God, for our Deliverer, the Prince of Peace, to come quickly and bring in his reign of love and harmony.

DAUGHTER I AND CONGREGATION: *(She leads them in singing the following words to the tune of* ST. THOMAS*)*

> Bring in thy reign of peace
> And purity and love
> Then shall all hatred cease
> As in the realms above.

DAUGHTER II: (DAUGHTER I *is seated in a front pew.* DAUGHTER II *arises from her seat and walks down the left aisle towards the chancel and prays to God)* O God of Israel, will you reject us forever? How long will you be angry with us? My betrothed, along with thousands of our young men, has died in a battle lost. Do not prolong the suffering of your people. Come and save us. *(When she reaches the chancel, she kneels in silence at the kneeler. Then she faces the* CONGREGATION *and says)* Pray with me for the Lord of life to come and save us from death and destruction. We have grieved over our loved ones too often. Pray that the promised kingdom come now.

DAUGHTER II AND CONGREGATION: *(She leads the* CONGREGATION *in singing these words to the tune of* ST. THOMAS*)*

> Bring now the promised time.
> So death shall be no more.
> Let war, oppression, crime and hate
> Flee from thy kingly face.

DAUGHTER III: *(*DAUGHTER II *is seated on the front pew.* DAUGHTER III *arises from the pew in the back of the center aisle. She walks down the center aisle towards the chancel and prays to God.)* O Lord God of Hosts, when will you come and install your king on Mt. Zion? The rulers of this world have killed all our great leaders. My father, the chief commander, lies slain on the fields of Megiddo. Break them with your iron rod! Save us and establish your kingdom. *(When she reaches the chancel, she kneels in silence. Then she faces the* CONGREGATION *and says)* Pray with me, you who love the Lord and his holy hill. Pray the Lord of Lords to come and deliver us, that he establish the throne of David.

DAUGHTER III AND CONGREGATION: *(She leads them in singing the following words to the tune of* ST. THOMAS*)*

> Thy kingdom come, O God
> Thy rule, O Christ begin
> Break with Thine iron rods
> The tyrannies of sin.

JEDIDIAH: *(*DAUGHTER III *is seated in the front pew. After singing this hymn,* JEDIDIAH, *the High Priest, walks down the center aisle. He addresses the* CONGREGATION *and walks towards the kneeler.)* Blessed be God, ruler of heaven and earth!

CONGREGATION: And blessed be his Kingdom, now and forever.

JEDIDIAH: The cries of these daughters of Jerusalem echo the cries of our own broken hearts: cries for love to be known among all people; cries for life,

abundant and full; cries for a righteous ruler and justice. Let us pray that our deliverer, our Messiah, will arise in his great might, deliver us from our enemies, and bring love, life, and justice to our holy nation.

JEDIDIAH AND CONGREGATION: *(*JEDIDIAH *than kneels at the kneeler and facing the* CONGREGATION *leads them in singing these words)*

> We pray thee Lord, arise
> And come in thy great might.
> Revive our longing eyes
> Which languish for thy sight.

JEDIDIAH: Brothers and Sisters, we languish for our *(standing)* hearts are filled with fears and doubts. We fear we shall not be saved. We doubt that our deliverer shall come. Let us confess our sins of fear and doubt. *(*JEDIDIAH *returns to kneeler and kneels:* CONGREGATION *kneels)*

JEDIDIAH: *(The following responses are all sung to music)* Almighty God, we are afraid of the enemy. Have mercy.

CONGREGATION: Lord, have mercy.

JEDIDIAH: Almighty God, we doubt our deliverer shall come. Have mercy!

CONGREGATION: Lord, have mercy.

JEDIDIAH: Almighty God, our hearts are faint as we wait for thy coming. Have mercy!

CONGREGATION: Lord, have mercy. Lord, have mercy. Lord, have mercy.

JEDIDIAH: Let us strengthen our hope in his coming by *(standing)* the hearing of the word of the Lord. *(*JEDIDIAH *is seated while* DAUGHTER I *rises and walks to the front of the church)*

[DAUGHTER I *reads the first lesson while the* ORGANIST *may play softly "Comfort ye, Comfort ye" from Handel's* Messiah]

First Reading: Isaiah 40:1-5 and 9-11, followed by "This is the Word of the Lord."

CONGREGATION: Thanks be to God.

*(*DAUGHTER I *exits to the back of the church)*
*(*DAUGHTER II *stands and walks to the front of the church and recites the second Old Testament passage, while the* ORGANIST *softly plays "The People Who Walk in Darkness.")*

Second Reading: (from several sections of Isaiah) Nevertheless that time of darkness and despair shall not go on forever. The people who walk in darkness shall see a great light; And they that dwell in the land of the shadow of death, Upon them the light will shine. For Israel will again be great; filled with joy like that of a reaper when the harvest time comes. Come sing, then, O daughter of Zion. Shout, O Israel, be glad and rejoice with all thy heart. O daughter of Jerusalem, the Lord hath taken away thy judgments. He hath cast out thine enemy. The king of Israel, even the Lord, is in the midst of thee; Thou shalt not see evil any more. The Lord, thy God in the midst of thee, is mighty. He will save; he will rejoice over thee with joy. He will rest in his love; he will rejoice over thee with singing.

CONGREGATION: This is the word of the Lord. Thanks be to God.

(DAUGHTER II *exits*)

——————— **Part II** ———————

GATEKEEPER: *(excited)* A messenger . . . a messenger of the Lord is coming here!

MESSENGER I: *(walks down the center aisle with excitement)* Citizens of Jerusalem. Daughters of Jerusalem Rejoice! Rejoice! Our deliverer has come! He has defeated our enemy! He is now marching to Jerusalem. (MESSENGER I *then sings and circulates among the people*) Rejoice greatly, O daughters of Jerusalem, for your King has come and has defeated all your enemies. He has crushed them with an iron rod. He has dashed them in pieces like a potter's vessel. He has entered the gates of Jerusalem. And let all the inhabitants of the land rejoice before Him.

[MESSENGER I *exits, and* JEDIDIAH *arises and shouts.*]

JEDIDIAH: The Lord has heard our prayers. The king of glory comes! Riding in victory!

[JEDIDIAH *leads in singing the song* "The King of Glory Comes," *and the* CONGREGATION *responds by singing the chorus. Some words have been changed to suit this occasion. During the singing of this praise song, the* DAUGHTERS OF JERUSALEM *(if they are dancers) will dance together and then exit when the song is over.*]

JEDIDIAH: He has come to redeem his own chosen people; he is Emmanuel, the promised of ages.

CONGREGATION: The King of Glory comes, the nation rejoices; He rides in victory, all praise goes before Him.

JEDIDIAH: Blessed is he who comes now, son of the highest; he shall reign over us with love and with justice.

JEDIDIAH AND CONGREGATION: The King of Glory comes, the nation rejoices; he rides in victory, all praise goes before him.

JEDIDIAH: Sing then of David's son, Our saviour and gov'ner, in all of Israel was never another!

JEDIDIAH AND CONGREGATION: The King of Glory comes, the nation rejoices; he rides in victory, all praise goes before Him.

GATEKEEPER: Another messenger comes!

[MESSENGER II *walks through the gate and down the center aisle and sings this verse of "Prepare ye the Way" as he/she walks towards the chancel. Some word changes have been made.*]

MESSENGER II: I've seen the King coming o'er the mountain; I've seen him marching this way. I've seen the king marching to this temple, And he says, Prepare ye the way.

MESSENGER II AND CONGREGATION: Prepare ye the way. Prepare ye the way. Prepare ye the way of the Lord!

MESSENGER II: BEHOLD! The King of Kings is here! He stands at the temple gate!

(MESSENGER II *exits, and* JEDIDIAH *arises and begins to sing the following rendition of Psalm 24 which includes sung responses from* GATEKEEPER *and* CONGREGATION.)

JEDIDIAH: Open up the gates, Be lifted up, ye everlasting doors. For the king of glory shall come in.

GATEKEEPER: Who is this King of glory?

JEDIDIAH AND CONGREGATION: The Lord strong and mighty, The Lord mighty in battle.

JEDIDIAH: Open up the gates, Be lifted up, ye everlasting doors. For the King of glory shall come in.

GATEKEEPER: Who is this King of glory?

JEDIDIAH AND CONGREGATION: He is the King of glory! *(The* TRUMPETER *plays a short voluntary)*

GATEKEEPER: Arise, shine for thy king has come.

[JEDIDIAH *(lifts up his hands indicating that the* CONGREGATION *stand. This processional is led by an* ACOLYTE, *followed by two* BANNER BEARERS. *One banner reads "Lord of Lords," and the other "King of Kings." Behind them is* CHRIST THE KING. *They process toward the throne as the* CONGREGATION *sings the following hymn with word changes to the tune* NATIONAL HYMN; *used with "God of our Fa-*

thers.'' *When the processional party reaches the throne, the* ACOLYTE *places the candle between the menorahs and exits; the* BANNER BEARERS *place their banners on either side of the throne and exit to seats nearby.* CHRIST *sits on the throne.*]

JEDIDIAH AND CONGREGATION: All hail to Jesus, king of all the earth, Prince of all peace, O mighty counselor. Now here on earth to rule and reign in peace. O mighty King, to Thee be glorious praise.

JEDIDIAH AND CONGREGATION: King of all Kings, the Lord's anointed One, Lord of all Lords, the people praise thy name; now here on earth to rule and reign in peace. O mighty king, to thee be glorious praise. (CHRIST *now stands and recites this Gospel proclamation*)

CHRIST: I shall be called the Son of the highest, for the Lord God hath given unto me the throne of my father David. And I shall reign over the house of Jacob forever. And of my kingdom there shall be no end. (JEDIDIAH *and* CONGREGATION *sing this response*)

JEDIDIAH AND CONGREGATION: Alleluia, Alleluia, opening our hearts to Him, singing Alleluia, Alleluia, Jesus is our King.

VOICE OF GOD: *(on tape)* You are my Son, this is your coronation day. I will give you the nations for your inheritance. The ends of the earth will be your possession; in you I am well pleased.

JEDIDIAH AND CONGREGATION: Alleluia, Alleluia, opening our hearts to Him, singing Alleluia, Alleluia, Jesus is our King.

(Everyone is now seated. CHRIST THE KING *gives a ten-minute inaugural address or sermon. Then* JEDIDIAH *leads the congregation in the Apostles' Creed. During the recitation of the creed, the* DAUGHTERS OF JERUSALEM *take the same positions that they had in the beginning.)*

––––––––––– **Part III** –––––––––––

JEDIDIAH: O Daughters of Jerusalem, God has heard your prayers and our prayers. The holy city is saved; his Kingdom has come. Offer to him the gifts we have longed to give.

[DAUGHTER OF JERUSALEM I *walks down the right aisle towards the throne and speaks to* CHRIST. *She holds a red crown in her hands.*]

DAUGHTER I: O Mighty King, we, your people, have suffered greatly. Our enemies have hated us and

sought to destroy us. Many have died, as did my husband at their cruel hands; but you have come to redeem us from all strife and hatred. We offer you this crown of love. *(She lifts it high for all to see. As she places it on his head, she says . . .)* Blessed art thou, Lord of Love.

CONGREGATION: We bless and praise you forever.

[JEDIDIAH *leads the* CONGREGATION *in singing a verse of "Crown Him with Many Crowns" with the following words.* DAUGHTER OF JERUSALEM I *kneels before the throne.*]

JEDIDIAH AND CONGREGATION:

> Crown Him the Lord of love,
> All hatred now shall cease,
> From pole to pole all strife is gone
> All people live in peace.
> His glories now we sing, who rules with love
>   and peace,
> The King of kings to whom is giv'n
> the matchless name of Love.

(DAUGHTER OF JERUSALEM II *walks down the left aisle toward the throne and speaks to* CHRIST. *She holds a blue crown in her hands*)

DAUGHTER II: O mighty King, many of your people have died, as did my betrothed, by the sword of our enemies who have prevailed over us. But you have come; death and the grave shall be no more. In your kingdom, our young and old shall know life and life abundant. You have come to redeem us from all strife and hatred. We offer you this crown of life. (DAUGHTER OF JERUSALEM II *lifts it high for all to see. As she places it upon the red crown, she says . . .)* Blessed art thou, Lord of Life.

CONGREGATION: We bless and praise you forever.

(JEDIDIAH *leads the* CONGREGATION *in singing another verse of "Crown him with many crowns." The* DAUGHTER OF JERUSALEM *kneels before the throne.*)

JEDIDIAH AND CONGREGATION:

> Crown Him the Lord of life,
> Who triumphed o'er the grave,
> Who rose victorious in the strife
> For those He came to save.
> His glories now we sing,
> Who died and rose on high,
> Who died eternal life to bring.
> And lives that death may die.

(DAUGHTER OF JERUSALEM III *walks down the center aisle towards the throne and speaks to* CHRIST. *She holds a purple crown in her hands.*)

DAUGHTER III: O mighty King, we, your people, have been trampled upon by the kings of this earth for thousands of years. Our kings and generals, like my father, have been defeated, and our land ravished. But the times of the gentiles have been fulfilled. You have come to rule over Israel and all the earth with righteousness, justice, and mercy. We offer you this royal crown, O Lord of Lords. (DAUGHTER OF JERUSALEM III *lifts it high for all to see. As she places it upon the blue crown, she says*) Blessed art thou, Lord of Lords.

CONGREGATION: We bless and praise You forever.

(JEDIDIAH *leads the* CONGREGATION *in singing the last verse of "Crown him with many Crowns."* DAUGHTER OF JERUSALEM III *also kneels before the throne*)

JEDIDIAH AND CONGREGATION:

> Crown Him the Lord of lords,
> Enthroned in glorious praise,
> Crown Him the king to whom is given
> The matchless name of Love.
> His reign shall know no end
> As thrones before Him fall.
> Bring forth the royal diadem,
> For He is king of all.

JEDIDIAH: *(shouts)* ALLELUIA! THE LORD GOD OMNIPOTENT REIGNS!

CONGREGATION: *(shouts)* ALLELUIA! THE LORD GOD OMNIPOTENT REIGNS!

DAUGHTER I: *(stands and shouts)* LORD OF LORDS

CONGREGATION: *(shouts)* LORD OF LORDS

DAUGHTER: *(stands and shouts)* KING OF KINGS

CONGREGATION: *(shouts)* KING OF KINGS

DAUGHTER III: *(stands and shouts)* ALLELUIA! HE SHALL REIGN FOR EVER AND EVER!

CONGREGATION: *(shouts)* ALLELUIA! HE SHALL REIGN FOR EVER AND EVER!

JEDIDIAH: *(shouts)* KING OF KINGS AND LORD OF LORDS, ALLELUIA!

CONGREGATION: *(shouts)* KING OF KINGS AND LORD OF LORDS, ALLELUIA!

CHRIST THE KING: My beloved people, come to the feast I have prepared for you.

[*During the singing of a hymn such as "Hail to the Lord's Anointed,"* CHRIST *descends from the throne and the* ACOLYTE *and* BANNER BEARERS *come and take the candle, banners, etc. and exit.*]

This concludes the first part of the service. The second part of the service can be a celebration of the Eucharist, or it can be a banquet, after the wedding feast of Rev. 19:7-8, in the parish hall. Christ will sit at the head table and the banners will hang above him. During this banquet, the celebration continues with song and dance.

[This service can be copied and used in your church or organization for a *production* fee of $100.00. A list containing descriptions of other festival drama services for Christmas and Easter is also available free of charge. Please address all correspondence to Star Song Publishing Group, 2325 Crestmoor, Nashville, TN 37215.]

James Speck

347 • BIBLIOGRAPHY ON EXAMPLES OF DRAMA FOR WORSHIP

Barker, Kenneth S. *Dramatic Moments in the Life of Christ.* Atlanta: Knox, 1978. Seven plays for troupes of various sizes. Though offered as "chancel dramas," imaginative spinoffs from biblical texts and theological themes can be used in a variety of settings. Script only.

Brown, Margie. *The Stick Stories.* Saratoga, Calif.: Resource Publications, 1982. Unique volume which contains "a series of biblical animations where a stumbling clown and a simple stick lead us through characters and conversations of our Judeo-Christian heritage." Written as stories in poetic format in order to encourage performer's imagination.

Milgrim, Sally Anne. *Plays to Play With in Class.* San Jose, Calif.: Resource Publications, 1985. Eight creative short plays featuring drama and mime for adolescents on themes such as responsibility, conflicts, independence, job-hunting, romance, moral and contemporary issues, and family relations. Script and "Director's Notes" (scenery, setting, sound effects, costumes, props).

Moynahan, Michael. *How The Word Became Flesh.* Saratoga, Calif.: Resource Publications, 1981. Twelve imaginative short-story dramas occasioned by liturgical celebrations or feasts. May be used in many contexts, especially worship. Study questions with relation to biblical texts following each play. Explanatory notes and script with stage direction.

Mullaly, Larry. *The Golden Link*. San Jose, Calif.: Resource Publications, 1985. Nineteen parish playlets for education of varying age groups. Their brevity makes them useful in a wide variety of situations, and each play highlights a celebrative occasion in the church year. Catholic orientation.

Mulholland, James. *The Drama of Worship*. Kansas City, Mo.: Lillenas, 1989. A resource for traditional worship services which includes eighteen short dramas and one dramatic worship service. Authors suggest uses of plays as worship openings or closings, dramatic litanies, children's dramas or stand-alone Bible stories, and sermon starters. Two are choral dramas. Script, Scripture reference, brief director's notes.

Paticucci, Karen. *Three-Minute Dramas for Worship*. San Jose, Calif.: Resource Publications, 1989. Seventy-two sketches with topic, theme, Scripture references, and director's notes. Wide range of topics from anger to apologetics, Christmas to counseling, Jesus' deity to our own self-image. Special sections on writing and producing sketches with script ideas and Scripture index.

Robertson, Everett. *Extra Dimensions in Church Drama*. Nashville: Broadman, 1986. Unique collection of seventy-four plays, pantomimes, improvisations, speech-choir materials, reader's theater works, creative dramatics, and children's theater works for a full-dimensioned dramatic arts endeavor.

————. *Monologues for Church*. Nashville: Broadman, 1982. More than a hundred useful and unusual monologues divided into sections covering biblical characters and situations, special events (Christmas, etc.), general subjects, and humorous selections. Approximately twenty-five selections concern women in the Bible.

Smith, Judy Gattis. *Drama Through the Church Year*. Colorado Springs, Colo.: Meriwether, 1984. Season-appropriate plays and ideas for drama as it relates to the church calendar. Especially helpful for worship planners/coordinators. Ideas include—but are not limited to—family fun nights; parades, processionals, and pageantry; chancel and street drama, and movement and liturgical dance.

Sullivan, Francis P. *All Eyes and Blind*. Kansas City, Mo.: Sheed and Ward, 1990. Unique compendium of over sixty personal faith stories and contemporary parables related to the church year. Story lines are sophisticated and startling, demanding attention, imagination, and participation. An excellent and unusual resource.

Waddy, Lawrence. *Drama in Worship*. New York: Paulist: 1978. Collection of thirty plays for the church calendar year with a drama calendar reference guide. Play lengths: 5 to 10 minutes. For various-sized groups. Scriptural themes, some with texts. Helpful ideas on directing and executing drama in a liturgical context.

SEVENTEEN

The Dramatic Arts in Scripture Proclamation

The various literary genres found in Hebrew and Christian Scriptures suggest that God's written word was intended to be presented aloud. Each genre has its own dramatic quality. Poetry, parables, oratory, epistles, and even narrative have rhythmic, intonational, and affective qualities that set them in dramatic categories. Using the Bible exclusively as a reference book and forgetting that it is also a literature book has deprived many worshipers of the experience of hearing Scripture presented dramatically. This chapter presents a brief history of Scripture reading in worship, as well as suggestions for enhancing Scripture presentations in worship.

348 • A Brief History of Scripture Reading

The reading of Scripture has been a significant part of both Jewish and Christian worship, an appropriate liturgical priority for a religion that is based on God's revelation. This article traces the history of the reading of Scripture in worship throughout the history of the church.

So Moses wrote down this law and gave it to the priests, the sons of Levi, who carried the ark of the covenant of the Lord, and to all the elders of Israel. Then Moses commanded them: "At the end of every seven years . . . during the Feast of Tabernacles when all Israel comes to appear before the Lord your God at the place he will choose, you shall read this law before them in their hearing. Assemble the people—men, women and children, and the aliens living in your towns—so they can listen and learn to fear the Lord your God. . . ." (Deut. 31:9-12)

These verses formally introduce the institution of Scripture reading in the history of Judeo-Christian worship. No longer binding his communication to the ephemeral thunderings on Sinai, the spatially confined burning bush, or the fleeting prophetic pronouncement, God now commands the repetition of a text as his immanent and permanent voice incarnate. Thus, reading the Word of God becomes the very core of worship, affording each hearer an opportunity for personal encounter with the divine (J. Edward Lantz, *Reading the Bible Aloud* [New York: Macmillan, 1959], 43).

The homage reserved for presenting God's recorded Word is evident in the honored position the reading of Scripture has held in the liturgy, doctrine, and history of the Christian church. The verses quoted above from Deuteronomy introduce that portion of its suzerainty structure where the arrangements of the covenant between God and his people are scheduled for public review (R. K. Harrison, "Deuteronomy," in *New Bible Commentary Revised,* ed. D. Guthrie and J. A. Motyer [Grand Rapids: Eerdmans, 1970], 202; Meredith Kline, "Dynastic Covenant," *The Westminster Theological Journal* 23 [1960]: 13, 15). Thus, as early as the writings of the Pentateuch, oral reading of Scripture became a normative worship practice. Because these books laid the foundation for the Jewish concept of covenantal worship, this practice of public reading assumed seminal significance for later developments in Christian worship (Richard G. Moulton, *The Literary Study of the Bible* [Boston: D. C. Heath, 1906], 268).

As the Jewish worship traditions developed, standards emerged for the habitual reading of various Scriptures in the synagogue. The liturgy essentially consisted of two readings: the first came from the Law (i.e., the books of Moses) and the second from the prophets (see Luke 16:16; Acts 13:15) (Pius Parsch, *The Liturgy of the Mass,* 3d. ed., trans. H. E. Winstone [St. Louis: B. Herder, 1957], 72).

While Scripture reading was required in synagogue worship, preaching was optional (Luke 4:16-

20) (Arthur T. Pierson, *How to Read the Word of God Effectively* [Chicago: Moody Bible Institute, 1925], 3–4; Lantz, *Reading Aloud,* 3). Preaching naturally developed in ordinary worship services as an exposition or hortatory application of what was read, but sermons were based on the readings (Edwin C. Dargan, *A History of Preaching,* vol. 1 [New York: Hodder and Stoughton, 1905], 39). Further, as was demonstrated annually in the Passover observances of individual families, worship of the highest order could always be oriented around the Word and prayer without sermonic exposition (Joseph A. Jungman, *The Mass of the Roman Rite,* German rev. ed., trans. Francis Brunner [New York: Benzinger Bros., 1950], 8; *The Union Hagadah,* rev. ed., [New York: the Central Conference of American Rabbis, 1923]). The Christian church did not revoke this aspect of its Jewish worship heritage nor subordinate the importance of Scripture readings. Instead the readings were expanded.

New Testament worship services echoed the Jewish synagogue patterns for prayers, readings, and exposition; but apostolic writings were added to the canonical materials (cf. 1 Thess. 2:13; J. H. Srawley, *The Early History of the Liturgy,* The Cambridge Handbooks of Liturgical Study, 2d ed. [Cambridge, U.K.: Cambridge Univ. Press, 1958], 188; Dargan, *History of Preaching,* 39). As the Old Testament prophets arranged for the perpetuation of their message in the readings of the temple, the New Testament messengers created literature for repeated use in the church (Acts 15:23-31; 2 Cor. 3:1-3; 1 Thess. 5:27). In his Colossian letter Paul commands, "After this letter has been read to you, see that it is also read in the church of the Laodiceans and that you in turn read the letter from Laodicea" (Col. 4:16). The Scripture poem of Philippians 2:6-11 is apparently intended for liturgical use, and Paul specifically commands his protege Timothy, "Devote yourself to the public reading of Scripture, to preaching and to teaching" (1 Tim. 4:13).

Readings of the newer writings did not replace the Old Testament readings, but augmented them. That the apostolic writings were being read in the churches along with the ancient Scriptures is apparent from Peter's commentary on Paul (2 Pet. 3:16), and Paul's own commands for the continued use of the Psalms (Eph. 5:19; Col. 3:16). Further, the reading of the New Testament gospels and epistles, with their many Old Testament quotations and analogies,

would necessarily keep both testaments echoing in the church.

Sensing the continued respect of the apostolic writers for the older Scriptures, the church continued reading publicly from both testaments in the early centuries of the Christian era. By the end of the fourth century the dominant liturgical pattern included three readings: one from the Old Testament and two from the New—an epistle and a gospel. The last reading was always the gospel, and the people stood during this reading (James D. Robertson, *Minister's Worship Handbook* [Grand Rapids: Baker, 1974], 52).

As with most key features of Christian worship, the reading of Scripture has also occasionally been the focus of abuse and controversy. In Elizabethan England, debates boiled between Puritans and the established church over John Whitgift's rhetorical question, "Is not the word of God as effectual when it is read as when it is preached? Or is not reading preaching?" (Donald J. McGinn, *The Admonition Controversy* [New Brunswick, N.J.: Rutgers Univ. Press, 1949], 176. The great debate between Whitgift and Cartwright is conveniently abridged in this most helpful work that topically arranges the original arguments of Cartwright's *Admonition,* 1572, Whitgift's *Answere,* 1572, Cartwright's *Replie,* 1573, Whitgift's *Defense,* 1574, and Cartwright's *Second replie,* 1575, and *The rest of the second replie,* 1577). The divergent viewpoints were argued expertly and expansively by Whitgift when he was Bishop of Worcester, and also by the Puritan scholar Thomas Cartwright (Edwin Hall, *The Puritans and their Principles,* 2d ed. [New York: Baker and Scribner, 1846], 108; McGinn, *Admonition Controversy,* 145–147).

Whitgift's insistence on the sufficiency of readings, though argued on theological grounds, was a political necessity. In order to suppress Puritan teachings and provide services in parishes whose ministers had been removed (i.e., defrocked, imprisoned, or executed), a series of approved readings and homilies were prepared for reading in the churches (Hall, *Puritans,* 110–112). Approved clergymen made the rounds through the rebel churches presenting nothing but these readings (Ibid., 109).

Cartwright argued for the Puritans, "It may be that God doth work faith by reading only, especially where preaching cannot be, and so he doth sometimes without reading by a wonderful work of his Spirit; but the ordinary ways whereby God regenerateth his children is the Word of God which is preached."

Whitgift adroitly replied, "Did not St. Paul preach to the Romans when he writ to them? . . . Was not the reading of Deuteronomy to the people a preaching?" (McGinn, *Admonition Controversy,* 186–187)

The argument progressed with increasing vehemence. Cartwright eventually concluded that "reading [i.e., dictated homilies and Scriptures] is not feeding, but it is as evil as playing upon a stage, and worse too" (Ibid., 189–191). While the harsh words of Cartwright and the harsh measures of Whitgift's church may tempt the modern reader to take sides in the ancient debate, there are more fruitful conclusions to draw. The fact thrown into historical relief by the Elizabethan controversy is that Scripture reading is an inherent and indispensable feature of Christian worship.

Even when events were so exceptional as to cause the merits of reading Scripture to be weighed against preaching, no one argued for excising Scripture from worship. The Puritan preachers insisted that preaching be an exposition of Scripture (Irvonwy Morgan, *The Godly Preachers of the Elizabethan Church* [London: Epworth, 1965], 25). While they vigorously opposed "bare readings," they never argued for bare preaching (i.e., preaching apart from Scripture reading). Cartwright might argue, "The word of God is not so effectual read as preached" (McGinn, *Admonition Controversy,* 176). But he would conclude, "[M]en's works ought to be kept in and nothing else but the voice of God and holy Scriptures, in which only are contained all fullness and sufficiency to decide controversies, must sound in his church. . . ." (Ibid., 169) Thus, at the very time in the history of the church when events and passions would seem poised for the denigration of Scripture reading in certain worship traditions, all factions continued to treasure the practice.

Since the Reformation, divergent commitments to fixed forms of worship exemplified in conflicts between English Puritan and established church leaders have influenced Scripture reading practices in Protestantism. Traditions valuing nonprescribed forms of worship tend to deemphasize Scripture "reading," viewing "interpretation" of the Word in preaching as the focus of worship. Traditions maintaining a high regard for ritual often organize worship around Scripture "readings" in liturgical forms while giving less attention to formal exposition of those texts.

Recent movements in a number of denominations have sought to unite the strengths of the Word of God, which is promoted both by its reading and preaching. Musical and dramaturgical influences have also added new creativity and power to the way Scripture is "read" in both regular and special services. The force of these movements stems from the ancient ethic—confirmed throughout the church's liturgy, theology and history—that the public reading of Scripture is a touchstone of authentic worship.

Bryan Chappell

349 • AN APPROPRIATE STYLE FOR SCRIPTURE PROCLAMATION

Reading Scripture effectively can bring the text to life. This article argues that the best way to do that is through a typical conversational tone of voice. Scripture readers are encouraged to carefully study and rehearse each passage they are to read.

Many studies have been done on the parts of worship—where people fall asleep and where they wake up. Whatever else researchers conclude about the flow of liturgy, they all agree that people stop listening as soon as the Scripture is being read, and return to consciousness, perhaps, after it is over. The Scripture reading is presented as a somber pill we have to take, its meaning to be grasped later in the sermon.

I suggest that before we add various artistic tools to the communication of Scripture, we learn how to read the Scripture, word for word, in a way that is surprisingly fresh and alive. Because it is fresh and alive! We are not adding that to the reading. We are allowing it to be, giving room to what is already there.

There are three ways to read from a text. One way is to use a "reading voice." This is the one that you recognize when a congregation reads something in unison. There is a set cadence, regardless of the grammar or sentence structure, that sounds like everyone is riding a horse: "Ta-da-da-da-dah, ta-da da-da-dah," rising in pitch then falling with a thud at the end of the phrase.

The second voice is not so monotone; it is trying

to be more expressive. This is what I call a "memorized voice." Again there is a sing-song cadence to it, but the sentence goes up at the end: "Ta-da-da-da-dah, ta-da-da-da-dah." There is an affected theatrical quality to it, expressing the power of the total piece, but still not regarding the individual words. This is the voice which you hear when you listen to something that was obviously memorized, and the reader is making a valiant effort to be properly dramatic.

The third kind of voice is what I call the "talking voice." This is the voice I am encouraging for reading Scripture. The reader recognizes that there is a beauty in the written word, but a different kind of beauty in the spoken word. You use one kind of language to write a term paper and another kind of language to explain your research to a friend. Just as the Good News must be translated from Greek to English for our understanding, so it must be translated from written to oral language for us to feel its immediate presence.

The technique of the "talking voice" recognizes that the cadence of one's voice is influenced by many factors besides the grammatical structure of the text. For example, when talking we often ignore the punctuation that would be present if the text were written. We speed up and slur our words, in a hurry to get to the good part. We slow down to stall for time as we get our thoughts together. We add humor and drama to the little phrases instead of them being only subservient to the larger grandiose concept. We are relaxed, taking our time and enjoying the weave of the story. We use our faces and hands as paintbrushes picturing our total presence in the story. We add "um's" and "uh's" and "so's" and "like's" and "y'know's." We repeat ourselves. We drop words. We use contractions and make up our own contractions. We smile and scowl and glance sideways at imaginary characters.

Each word counts! That doesn't mean that each word is given equal weight or length. But as emphasis or throwaway, each word holds within it a little magic which can take us off the page and into the breathing present.

I am suggesting that each word or phrase be read in the same voice you would use to speak to a friend. This requires studying and practicing the text beforehand, until you develop the ability to "translate" extemporaneously. It needs to come off comfortably and relaxed, or appropriately full of true pain or poignancy—dramatic, but not theatrical.

To begin understanding the concept, read just one sentence out loud. It is helpful to do this with a class or partner at first, because others have more objective ears and can help you hear how you are saying something. Listen carefully to the inflection you use. Would you say it that way in real life?

Listen, for example, to the stern voice quality or, on the other hand, the breathy earnest quality, which is often used to say: "Jesus said, 'Love one another as I have loved you.'"

Now compare this to the voice used to say: "Hey you guys, Mom said to stop fighting and come on in the house."

Likely, in the Jesus sentence, you tend to use a lower voice and an even tone drifting downward. In the mom sentence, you use a higher voice and you bring your voice up on hey, Mom, stop, come, and house.

Another example.

"Jesus wept. Then said the Jews, 'Behold how he loved him!' And some of them said, 'Could not this man, who opened the eyes of the blind, have caused that even this man should not have died?'"

> "Jesus (pause) wept. (pause) Then *some* Jews said, (very quietly) Behold! (a little louder, awe and questioning in voice) *how* he *loved* him! (sarcasm in voice) Then some *others* said, (add sneer to voice and face) *couldn't* this man, . . . *this* man who *opened* the eyes of the *blind*, . . . (said quickly on one pitch) couldn't he have caused that even (raise pitch to a question and keep it up throughout the phrase) *this* man shouldn't have died?"

There is not, of course, one right way to do it. I recommend that, as you work on a text, you read it first in a reading voice, then again in a memorized or theatrical voice, to hear it again and get those styles out of your system. Then read it in a number of talking voice styles, experimenting until you find the rhythm that is both true to your own speaking, and also true to the text. The more somber styles may seem more true to our expectation of holy Scripture, but they wash over the congregation like a Cecil B. DeMille sound track. This talking style is truer to the text, because it is actually paying attention to what each word is saying.

Some people have told me that they are afraid that they will get in trouble if they don't read the Bible in the boring way; that the minister won't let them; that they're not allowed to "change" it; that the congregation isn't ready for this; that their own performance will get in the way of the reading; that people will laugh at them. These are concerns to be addressed with care. Understand that they are not actually questions of biblical exegesis, but questions of theology, pastoral relationship, and congregational community. If you feel like you're performing, or being foolish, it may mean that you are using the theatrical voice and trying too hard. The change in the talking voice comes more from your own internal relationship with the text.

Jesus did not speak in King James or Revised Standard English. Our present Scripture is translated from translations, even as the gospel writers pulled their material from different sources. It is not that we are changing the Scripture if we repeat a phrase, add a pause, or drop a long list of unpronounceable geographical names that nobody has ever heard of, or if we change "heretofore" to "so that." Jesus told the story, therefore we must tell the story.

I gave a class assignment to pick one of the healing stories, go home and memorize it; then (without the written page) tell the story to one person at least once a day. The partner would be unchanging so that a relationship with the story developed rather than the performance skills which would happen if it was told to different people. When the students came back to class, they agreed that at first they had wanted to "fix" the story—throw in little exegetical comments to make it more clear or to repair inconsistencies in the text. But as time went by, that need dropped away and they just let themselves enter in the story.

We sat informally in our carpeted classroom, and I asked them not to applaud after the stories—applause is such a loud, mood-breaking thing. But people need to respond, so I invited them to gently wave their hands, which is both applause and the word "hallelujah" in the deaf community. This effectively took away the performance mood and enabled a mood of prayer instead.

The students got up whenever they felt ready and told their stories without introduction or explanation. Three hours passed where we heard only Bible stories. We were falling on the floor laughing at times; we were in tears at other times. The humor and pathos was coming from the very words themselves, straight from the text. We agreed afterwards that the evening had been a very healing experience, just as they had discovered the weeklong homework assignment to be healing for themselves.

One student had thought, "I don't believe in healing stories," so he had picked the story of the healing of the storm (the disciples fear was healed in that story, too). Our usual expectation in that story is for Jesus to rise up from sleep, drift like a ballerina across the boat, and in a gentle voice summon the storm—"Peace! Be still!"—then waft back to his place in the boat and all is well.

In this student's interpretation, the speed and intensity of his voice rose with the anguish of the disciples until in anger they called for Jesus to wake up (doesn't he care?). Jesus got up, rubbed his eyes, looked with disgust on the disciples, clomped across the heaving boat, and in an impatient voice at the top of his lungs shouted, "Peace! Be still!" After looking at the disciples with a disappointed sigh and shake of his head, Jesus then clomped back across the wet floorboards to collapse in a sleepy heap again.

Without his adding a single word to the text, we saw this interaction take place before our eyes and understood why the closing sentences showed that the disciples were even more confused and afraid. Who is this guy? The traditional voice inflection of gentle Jesus, meek and mild, puts a sugarcoating veneer over the power of the text. The power of Jesus was displayed not in his magic act of the stilled wind, but in his very presence and confidence.

At the end of the class, this particular student said that he was now willing to consider the possibility of there being real healing stories! The class said, "Okay, this worked with the stories. But you couldn't use this technique with other parts of Scripture, like the epistles or Revelation." I said, "Think of images that you remember from the non-gospel New Testament books, and call them out to me." I made a long list on the blackboard (parts of the body of Christ, gifts of the Spirit, etc.). Then I said, "You can't choose any of these! We remember these because of the story quality of these images. Pick something different, like a discussion on circumcision, go home, and tell it to your partner every day, just like before." Many groans. The next week, as we gathered in the small carpeted class room we had made our home for six weeks, I told them I had a surprise. I led them all across campus into the large stone chapel. The air was cold; the pews were hard. I told them that they might or might not use the pulpit, but that they were to create the same intimacy and presence that we had found last week, taking into consideration the acoustic and spatial differences.

It worked. Fully half of the chosen pieces were from such obscure texts, but told with such fullness of presence that everyone afterwards whispered, "That was great! But, is *that* the Bible?" We had been touched, healed, brought to laughter or tears or "aha!" from the text itself, and not because we *knew* it was Scripture and, therefore, it should be good for us.

The class moved on to work with the Bible stories using the dramatic arts, which I was more accustomed to teaching. But the quality of the creations was heightened, compared to what I had received from other classes.

It is not a question of one or the other—should the Scripture be read word-for-word, or made contemporary through the dramatic arts? Rather, it is an issue of remaining true to the text in either style. The word is God's saving action within history, our community, and ourselves. It is that calling and claiming of salvation, that inner relationship shouted out, which makes the Scripture reading the keystone of worship. Writings and reader stand hand in hand, sharing the good news.

Margie Brown[99]

350 • GUIDELINES FOR READING SCRIPTURE EFFECTIVELY

The public reading of Scripture is a skill that can be developed with experience and practice. Becoming sensitive to the nature of the scriptural text and the way in which listeners hear public reading is also an important aspect of this skill development. This chapter prescribes a series of helpful approaches to Scripture reading and gives several examples for how a given passage may be brought to life through public reading.

Stress Verb Action

As a sample reading, take the second reading for the fourteenth Sunday in Ordinary Time, Cycle C.

Read through Galatians 6:14-18 slowly and prayerfully to gain a sense of the whole passage.

Go back to the first sentence. Your first impulse may be to give emphasis to the words, "our Lord Jesus Christ!" Your proclamation would go some-

thing like this: "May I never boast of anything but the cross of OUR LORD JESUS CHRIST!"

That is a mistake in emphasis. Jesus is important. But what is said and done must be the focus of attention.

To sense the movement in the reading, underline all the verbs: "May I never *boast* of anything but the cross of our Lord Jesus Christ! Through it, the world has been *crucified* to me and I to the world. It *means* nothing whether one is *circumcised* or not. All that *matters* is that one is *created* anew. Peace and mercy on all who *follow* this rule of life, and on the Israel of God. Henceforth, let no man *trouble* me, for I *bear* the brand marks of Jesus in my body. Brothers, may the favor of our Lord Jesus Christ *be* with your spirit. Amen."

Reread the entire passage aloud. As you do, push out the verbs which give a correct picture of what is going on. Sense the action and movement. Notice how the nouns, pronouns, and other words take their rightful secondary positions. Prepositions, which are the least important words (of, through, to, on, with, etc.), fall into correct place as you catch the flow and movement in the reading.

Once you sense the movement, you are ready to interpret the emotions in the passage.

Express Emotions

Sunday worship becomes shared belief when liturgical ministers openly express their feelings and emotions. But emotions scare some people who are still embarrassed by feelings displayed in a community setting.

The two writers of this handbook are convinced that Roman Catholics and other mainline Christian denominations are in no immediate danger of becoming overemotional in worship. If anything, we need to begin to express our honest feelings as a sign of our full relationships with God and with the community.

There is legitimate variety of interpretation among lectors. What impresses one lector may not impress another. Taking that difference into consideration, how can lectors capture and express the emotions contained in the Scriptures? How do we proclaim with the intense feeling of a Jewish prophet? How do we convey the tenderness, anger, and worry often expressed in Paul's letters?

In the previous section of this chapter, you learned how to emphasize verbs in order to convey the movement in Galatians 6:14-17. As you did, you may have also noticed Paul's emotions, and, at the same time, how your own emotions were stirred.

Listen to what your feelings are telling you. Are you touched in some way? If so, stop and circle the emotion-filled words and phrases. Your task as proclaimer is to unlock and express these emotions. Paul's letters are quite a challenge for proclaimers who wish to capture his tenderness and concern for early Christian communities. Proclaim Paul's letters as though it is as important for you to get the message across as it was for him to express it.

When you practice the reading aloud, try to express the various emotions you feel. That is the way the Lord works through us. The way you are touched by a reading is the way you can proclaim it—if you give yourself permission to do so! Through you, the risen Jesus will touch others in the assembly.

During your proclamation, pause long enough to make certain you can shift gears emotionally. The proclaimer who takes the time to unlock the emotions in proclamation will do much to encourage the assembly to look up from their participation booklets and begin listening to God's Word. Wouldn't that be a nice change?

Become Sensitive to Hebrew Poetry

Read through Isaiah 66:10-14, the first reading for the fourteenth Sunday in Ordinary Time, Cycle C.

What difference do you detect in the way emotions are expressed by Paul and by Isaiah? Jesus, Isaiah, and all Jewish prophets expressed their emotions in a unique style found throughout the Bible, especially in the Old Testament. The style is called Hebrew poetry.

The lines of Hebrew poetry are balanced. The same idea, mood, or emotion is repeated over and over again in concrete images.

Jewish poetry is probably different from the poetry familiar to you. The key to understanding this poetry is an appreciation of the parallel, balanced structure. Dom Celestin Charlier gives an excellent description:

> Parallelism is the natural mold for an idea which can only be evoked by repetition and suggestion. Its purpose is not only to enrich the primary statement by giving it precision, but also to create a gradual and insistent rhythm. The result can be compared to a succession of waves, ebbing and flowing over a

rock, or to a series of concentric circles rising in a spiral around an axis. (*The Christian Approach to the Bible* [New York: Paulist Press, 1967], 138)

Look again at the reading from Isaiah. How many different moods are expressed in parallel fashion? Basically, one emotion is expressed, that of jubilant rejoicing. In the five verses of the reading, that emotion is expressed several times. How many parallel expressions do you find? We find at least twelve.

If you proclaim the Isaiah reading as prose or narrative, you will completely lose its meaning. To proclaim biblical poetry effectively, first recognize and study the parallel lines. Sense the main feeling in the passage. Experience the emotion rhythmically, like ocean waves hitting a beach. In your proclamation, convey this same feeling in a deliberate, unhurried manner. Your timing is essential. Pause briefly between parallel images. As you proclaim the rhythmic lines, paint concrete images.

Another example of Hebrew poetry is the responsorial psalm for each Sunday. The main emotion is expressed in the refrain. The refrain for Psalm 66, the psalm for the Fourteenth Sunday, Cycle C, is "Let all the earth cry out to God with Joy!" This sentiment is repeated in all 15 or 16 parallel lines.

> Let all the earth cry out to God with joy
> Shout joyfully to God, all you on earth
> Sing praise to the glory of his name
> Say to God, 'How tremendous are your deeds!'

And so forth throughout the psalm.

This rhythmic, balanced style is found in the Psalms, the prophets, and the Old Testament wisdom literature, such as Proverbs, Sirach, and the Book of Wisdom. Soon you will easily recognize and enjoy proclaiming the poetic structure of Hebrew poetry.

Nervousness—Friend or Foe?

Getting rid of nervousness is uppermost in the minds of most lectors, especially those who are beginners in the ministry. Only two lectors out of more than 2,000 that we have worked with ever claimed they do not feel nervous. It is normal to experience the jitters before doing something in public, whether acting in a play, giving a talk, or proclaiming the Word. Professionals who earn their livings in the public eye tell us nervousness actually aids in their effectiveness.

In our proclamation workshops, we have heard many successful remedies for the proclaimer's Sunday morning case of the nerves. Here are some suggestions that have worked for others:

First of all, admit to being nervous. That admission will begin to take the edge off you nervousness. At least you are no longer in the denial stage.

It may also help you to know that your nervousness is largely undetected by the assembly. (By the way, it is sound advice not to make eye contact with your children when you are proclaiming.)

Thorough preparation is the best deterrent to run-away jitters. The better your preparation, the less nervous you become.

Arrive early. Coming to church just on time is unsettling for you and the other liturgical ministers.

Do you worry about difficult-to-pronounce proper names? During your preparation sessions, telephone someone who can help you with the correct pronunciation. You may prefer to check a Sunday Lectionary Pronunciation Guide. It is best not to wait until Sunday morning to settle on the pronunciation you will use.

Take some deep breaths before starting the proclamation—not through the microphone, of course!

Offer your proclamation as a gift of love to your assembled sisters and brothers. This prayer, said silently right before the moment of proclamation has helped control the nervousness of several lectors: "Father, I proclaim your Word because I love you and I love your people."

Another way to control the shakes is to hold the lectionary in your hands during proclamation. As you hold the book, nervous energy is released without the notice of the assembly. When the lectionary lies flat on the stand, or when your hands are tightly gripping the side railing, you have no chance to relieve your nervous feeling. Try holding the lectionary. It will relax you.

Nervousness often indicates a preoccupation with self. What will happen if you make a mistake? Chances are you will survive, and so will the assembly.

What should you do when you make a mistake? If your mistake has not changed the meaning of the passage, relax. Continue the proclamation. If your mistake does change the meaning, relax. Without words of apology, simply go back and repeat the phrase or sentence.

No assembly has a right to expect perfection in proclamation. If fact, a faith-filled proclaimer who occasionally makes mistakes is preferred over a perfect but lifeless lector.

Do you still feel nervous? That's normal. Properly channeled, your nervousness will help you become a better proclaimer.

Your Body Speaks

Dress appropriately for the occasion. Your Sunday best will do. Choir robes or clerical vestments seem out of place for this ministry. The Word you proclaim is a Word that has become flesh in our world. Lay garb makes a statement to that effect.

In many parishes, the lector carries the lectionary in procession. Hold the book high enough to be seen, but not so high that you feel awkward. Be dignified. Walk with a purpose. Don't rush. When carrying God's Word, there is no need to bow or genuflect.

Proclaim from the large dignified lectionary, not from a flimsy paperback.

When you are at the podium, act natural. Be yourself. Stand with your two feet firmly planted on the floor or platform. Your parish liturgy committee may wish to provide a small stool at the podium so that shorter lectors can be easily seen.

Your body also speaks through eye contact and gestures, which will be treated later in this chapter.

Effective Breathing

Though our lungs have been taking in air all our lives, many of us do not know how to breathe deeply and correctly. The following exercises will help you breathe effectively.

Stand up. Place your hands on your sides, above your hips, just at the base of your rib cage. Breathe through your nostrils. Inhale deeply. As you inhale, your diaphragm expands, and you feel your hands being pushed away from your sides.

Exhale slowly and let the air completely out of your lungs. As your diaphragm contracts, you feel your hands sink into your sides.

Repeat several times, with your hands on your sides. Inhale deeply. Exhale deeply.

When you first attempt this deep breathing exercise, there is a good chance you may feel dizzy. If this happens, sit down and relax. The dizziness will pass. Through correct breathing, you have merely taken in more oxygen than you are accustomed to.

Continue the exercise. Inhale. Your diaphragm expands and your hands are pushed away from your sides. Exhale. Your diaphragm contracts and your hands sink into your sides. Inhale. Exhale.

In deep breathing, there is no reason why the sound of your breathing should be much louder than your normal breathing. When you are breathing correctly, you can take in a great deal of air without a whooshing sound picked up by the mike system.

When you breathe, your shoulders should remain level. Movement of the shoulders actually constricts breathing. In deep breathing, there is great expansion of the diaphragm and some expansion of your chest.

Practice the breathing exercise until you have mastered it well enough to feel your diaphragm expand and contract without having your hands on your sides. Correct breathing will help you in volume and voice projection.

——— Volume and Voice Projection ———

Most new lectors have to learn to project their voices. Even the most excellent microphone system does not compensate for a lack of voice projection and poor volume.

Get familiar with the mike system in your church. Arrange to have a practice session with another lector. Turn off the microphone. Have one lector stand in the back of the church. That person asks the lector at the podium to repeat each line with greater voice projection until the lector can be easily heard by the person standing in the rear of church. That is probably the level of projection needed with a live microphone when the church is full for Sunday liturgy.

Every word is important. Attack the first word: "A READING FROM . . . ." When you project your voice adequately, volume takes care of itself.

Voice projection is not the same as shouting. Projection is a skill everyone can learn, even people who are soft spoken in normal conversation.

Be sure to ask someone for feedback after the liturgy. You will soon become aware of the progress you are making, and you will feel better about yourself as a proclaimer.

——— Clear Enunciation ———

Exaggeration is the key to good enunciation. Use your lips, your teeth, and the tip of your tongue. Guard against lazy lips and a lazy tongue. Your diction for ordinary conversation probably falls short of what is needed in your proclamation.

A tape recorder used during a practice session will reveal which sounds you tend to slur. Do you say "Peter and Paul," or "Peter 'n' Paul"? Do you habitually swallow final syllables? Try to distinguish between final "t" and final "d." Is the word "lend" or "lent?"

Every lector needs to improve his or her diction to some degree. One lector who had had speech therapy received the following exercise to achieve clearer diction: Say "B D F L M P T V" as quickly and distinctly as possible.

Another diction exercise is to say quickly: "Use the lips, the teeth, the tip of the tongue."

One lector recommended that as you drive to church make the "BBBRRR" sound that children use when they play with toy cars. That sound will get the blood flowing in your lips, thereby improving your diction.

Finally, we should mention that good diction is attainable only if you open your mouth sufficiently.

Try all these suggestions. Find out what works best for you.

——— Pace, Pauses and Eye Contact ———

Most lectors, regardless of experience in the ministry, are rapid public readers. Nervousness only compounds the speed problem. If your pace is too rapid, you will be unable to use pauses and eye contact effectively.

A tape recorder in a practice session will reveal your pace as rapid or slow. The best way to counteract rapid pace is to slow down deliberately, right from the first words of your proclamation: "A READING FROM . . . ." Pauses and successful eye contact go hand in hand. Plan them during your practice session. Use a pause and eye contact at the conclusion of a thought so that your listeners have time to grasp the thought. You are familiar with the thought. The assembly has one chance to catch it.

Eye contact is also appropriate when a strong emotion is delivered. A few well-planned eye contacts are usually sufficient.

Some lectors avoid eye contact because they fear losing their place on the page. To keep your place, have one hand always on the lectionary page. Don't run your finger back and forth across the page, but let your hand slide down the page as you go through the reading. Place your finger at the exact place where you will resume after making eye contact.

New lectors are generally at one of two extremes with regard to eye contact. Some try to use too much eye contact, which lessens its effectiveness. Others are wary of eye contact. All lectors can safely make deliberate eye contact in at least two places in each reading: Right after announcing the reading, "A Reading from the Prophet Isaiah," and just before concluding with, "This is the Word of the Lord!"

Beware of too much eye contact. Some lectors look up too frequently and without reason. What results is the bobber effect. Meaningless eye contact distracts the assembly and causes the flow of thought to be lost. Pause briefly, with your head bowed, after each reading. No explanation is necessary for the assembly to understand the gesture. Your bowed head gently invites the assembly to reflect on the Word just proclaimed.

Any Other Gestures?

Occasionally, we hear of someone who argues in favor of free and extensive gestures for the lector. Only three gestures are appropriate: carrying the lectionary in procession; holding the lectionary during proclamation; and an occasional well-planned eye contact.

Keep your eyes primarily on the lectionary page. You are proclaiming the Lord's Word from the lectionary, not your own thoughts or ideas.

A completely memorized proclamation should also be avoided. Attention becomes focused on the performer.

Sharing Faith Convictions

From childhood, many of us have been discouraged from expressing negative feelings: Don't be angry, fearful or jealous. And so we are generally uncomfortable with negative reactions in ourselves and in others. The result is that when we turn off expressions of negative feelings, we also become unable to share positive feelings freely. Therefore, many of us have to learn how to share our faith with others.

Make the decision to share your faith as you proclaim the Word. Gradually you will improve in your ability to do so. If you become discouraged, keep trying.

How can you tell when you are making progress? Ask yourself the following questions: Am I expressing genuine enthusiasm when I proclaim the Word? Is my faith conviction transparent? Do I proclaim the readings as an urgent invitation to Eucharist?

Jerry and Gail Du Charme[100]

351 ✦ WAYS OF PROCLAIMING SCRIPTURE DRAMATICALLY

Here are some helpful guidelines to enliven Scripture readings and thus communicate the Word of God more clearly. Six ways of rendering Scripture dramatically are presented, along with a variety of practical suggestions for preparing dramatic readings for use in worship services.

The Case for Drama in Worship

As an instructor, I taught that drama, from its earliest beginnings in Greece, had three functions: to exalt, to edify, and to entertain. The Greeks used drama to praise their gods, teach history and religion, and not bore everyone to death in the process. Isn't that exactly what we should be doing in worship?

As a student of educational methodology, I learned that drama was the most basic tool of communication. Edgar Dale promoted a theory which justifies the old adage, "Experience is the best teacher." Indeed, lessons are learned most readily and most vividly by experience.

According to Dale, the next best teacher is dramatization. If you can put people in a contrived situation so that they can experience the event, the process, or the feelings firsthand they can gain new insight, expand their perceptions, and gain new per-

Worship Bell. The bell has always been a symbol of the call to worship.

spectives. In addition, through empathy, they can relate to situations they see dramatized before them.

Of course, theater in general and actors in particular, have often enjoyed a distinct lack of trust by the church. The Catholic church banned both after Rome fell, but brought drama back to the liturgy when attendance waned. Priests donned costumes to perform the mass in an effort to win back the people with the *Quem Queritas*. Indeed, there are strong historical precedents for the use of drama as a tool of communication in worship.

So, if we use drama to communicate the Scriptures, won't they be more exciting, more relevant, and more meaningful? I think the answer to all those questions is a resounding ''Yes!''—if we keep in mind that drama is only a means of communicating. It is not an end in itself, i.e. the play is not the thing, nor is the performance. The purpose is the message.

The Dramatic Options

1. Use a Different Translation. Sometimes the answer to a boring presentation is simply to read the lesson from another translation. Just hearing the same thoughts expressed in slightly different words will provide some listeners with new perspectives. Familiar, especially literary passages such as those found in Handel's *Messiah* may be read best from the King James. *The Good News Bible (Today's English Version)* may provide more contemporary language; *The Jerusalem Bible* may be less stilted, but not too ''modern.''

I'd like to insert a word here about inviting the congregation to ''read along in their pew Bibles.'' Why do it? Really. It's not a reading test. ''Let those who have ears hear.'' By asking them to read along, you stifle their ability to hear new interpretations and perspectives. Allow them the freedom of visualization and imagination. Read it to them with the expression and care you would use to read a story to a child.

2. Rewrite the Lesson. Perhaps, after reading the various translations, you determine none of them are exactly what you want. Rewrite it—with the blessing of the pastor, of course. Make it relate to the sermon or another part of the worship service. Make it relevant, not just to contemporary life, but to the events and selections of that specific worship service.

This is especially helpful to the youth who are always asking what the events of 2,000 years ago

have to do with life today. Also, it's refreshing to those who have heard it so often they could recite it from memory and are inclined to ''tune you out.''

3. Adapt the Reading for Multiple Voices. Many of the biblical passages are stories which readily lend themselves to division for multiple readers. For example, Genesis 3:8 begins a conversation among God, Adam, and Eve. Why not employ different voices for each? Sometimes it may be helpful to add a narrator to provide the transitions: ''Then God said to Adam.'' Often, there is no need for any rewriting or additional material; just divide up the verses. For example:

> NARRATOR: That evening, Adam and Eve heard God walking in the garden, and they hid among the trees.
> GOD: Adam? Where are you?
> ADAM: I heard you in the garden; I was afraid and hid from you because I was naked.
> GOD: Who told you that you were naked? Did you eat the fruit that I told you not to eat?
> ADAM: The woman you put here with me gave me the fruit, and I ate it.
> GOD: Eve, why did you do this?
> EVE: The snake tricked me into eating it. (Gen. 3:8-13 [New English Bible])

4. Choral Reading or Readers' Theater. Numerous passages lend themselves to group reading, especially the more poetic and literary selections. Alternate voices and groups of voices using different parts of the sanctuary, if possible. The prophetic Isaiah passages also used by Handel were especially well-suited to this adaptation.

> READER 1: The people that walked in darkness have seen a great light; and they that dwell in the land of the shadow of death, upon them hath the light shined. For unto us a child is born, unto us a son is given: and the government shall be upon his shoulder, and he shall be called:
> READER 2: Wonderful Counselor!
> READER 3: Mighty God!
> READER 4: Everlasting Father!
> READER 5: Prince of Peace! (Isa. 9:2, 6 [KJV])

Choir members could read this passage from the rear gallery, calling out from various places.

Especially long passages, such as the Passion reading, are actually interesting and tolerable when presented as readers' theater. *Handbook of the Christian Year,* published by Abingdon Press, carries all three gospel passages in this effective format. We have placed speakers on stools and scripts on music stands for the reading.

5. **Rewrite the Passage as a Scene.** For Pentecost, I wanted to bring the event into contemporary terms and got the idea to present it as a press conference from *Short Dramas for the Church* by Dorcas Diaz Shaner. We created a woman as a witness to the event, and a press secretary introduced her. She told the story in a brief statement before answering direct questions from our press corps. We startled a number of congregation members at first, but they really liked it!

6. **Rewrite the Passage as a Dramatic Monologue.** Many readings can be recounted from the perspective of one character. Such first-person adaptations promote involvement by the congregation. The story of the Magi is easily adapted as such.

> Excuse me. Could you spare me a moment or two? I am sorry to impose on you like this, but I've just had the most wonderful experience . . . and if I don't tell someone I fear I might explode!
>
> Do you remember the promises of Isaiah, that a child would be born in Bethlehem who would become a leader to guide Israel? Yes, that's right—from Jesse's family. Well . . . he is here! I have seen him. Such a beautiful baby, and his mother, so young—still a child herself. What? How did I know where to find him? All right, let me go back to the beginning. . . . (Matt. 2:1-12)

It is generally more effective to memorize monologues, but a good speaker can carry it off with quick references to the script. If you don't feel confident to do the writing yourself, Mary E. Jensen's *Women of the Bible Tell Their Stories* and *Monologues for Church* by Everett Robertson offer great resources. Other valuable books include: *Acting Out Faith* by Gordon C. Bennett, a good basic text with practical guidelines for use of drama throughout the programs of the church; Shaner's *Short Dramas for the Church,* which provides a wealth of material for use in worship, church school, or other church programs; and *Introduction to Church Drama* by Everett Robertson.

Practical Hints and Helps

Casting can make or break any dramatic endeavor. In worship don't look for acting or actors—just people willing to share their voices with others. Practically speaking, you do need people who will speak clearly and can be heard since your object is to communicate.

Look first among friends in the choir. As singers, they have had some training in articulation, vocal production, and projection and will feel fairly comfortable in front of people.

Naturally, regular worship leaders are fair game, but it's important to encourage others to participate in this leadership. Individuals who use oral communication skills in their occupations or professions, such as teachers, coaches, lawyers, and salespersons, generally make good speakers.

We find it beneficial to use a variety of people, especially those with no acting background. Some ''actors'' will not be appropriate because they can't sublimate the performance to the message. God will provide all the inspiration needed for use in worship. Almost anyone with the willingness to participate can bring it off. We like the congregation to know that regular people, like themselves and their neighbors, can serve as leaders.

As far as rehearsals are concerned, use material that allows people to read rather than memorize, then allow them to get familiar with it. Make it easy for people to participate by not asking for much of their time.

Remember the three purposes of drama: to exalt, to edify and—to entertain. Make it fun as well as meaningful. Be flexible and adaptive; capitalize on spontaneity. Just set up the opportunity to communicate and put your faith in the Lord.

There are no new ideas, just new twists on old ideas. I'm sure there are others using drama to breathe new life into the Scriptures, and I hope this will encourage them to share their experience, thoughts, and resources.

Carole J. Carter[101]

352 • RESPONSIVE READING OF SCRIPTURE

This article calls for vibrant congregational responsive reading that can be achieved through congregational rehearsal and creative adaptation of biblical text. Several examples of the authors' work appear in the next chapter of this volume.

Think about it for a moment. Isn't a "responsive reading" supposed to be *responsive?* But, honestly, aren't most of the responses you hear from your congregations what you might call "less than exciting?" Are they not too often slow, in low voices, and tedious—like a large, cumbersome sound, a mumbling, perhaps—concentrating more on keeping up with the rest of the voices rather than *responding in the gladness and joy of worship?* In congregational singing you hear excitement, harmonies, soprano voices, deep bass parts resonating. In responsive readings too often everything is in dull, lifeless monotone.

Part of the problem simply centers in what we expect of a congregation in terms of spontaneity. Would God object if we rehearsed the congregation and introduced it to exciting reading that corresponds to the excitement of its experience with Christ?

Responsive readings are not new to most churches or worship leaders. For most of us, they have been a part of our Christian worship heritage for as long as we can remember. In that regard this form is not new.

We have drawn from four common dramatic forms in composing readings for the congregation: traditional responsive form, readers' theater, traditional drama, and choral reading. Those familiar with these forms will recognize some of the techniques for maintaining interest, attention, and involvement.

Both of us have experienced lifeless responsive readings in worship. We were sure something could be done to improve our involvement. With that in mind, we began writing. We decided that worship leaders may encourage their congregations all they wish, but they need the help of a well-written reading as well.

Traditionally, responsive readings have simply called for repeating verses of Scripture arranged alternately for reader and congregation. It has apparently mattered little how long these passages are. But in congregational reading, the longer the passage, the less enthusiastic the response becomes, unless there is some rehearsal with the group (which virtually never happens).

Responsive readings may expand beyond this traditional approach. The congregation may be cast in various roles (as in drama) where it responds as a character in the story (as in readers' theater). The congregation may play the fool, the Pharisee, the publican, God, the believer, the skeptic. Good reading is easy to achieve (as in choral reading), and the congregation gets to answer and suggest corporately (as in traditional responsive readings). At all times we have worked at keeping the responses short so that the monotony of untrained reading would be avoided, and a minimum of rehearsal or instruction would be needed.

Melvin Campbell and Edwin Zachrison[102]

353 • BIBLIOGRAPHY ON THE DRAMATIC ARTS IN SCRIPTURE PROCLAMATION

Arnold, Charlotte E. *Group Readings for the Church.* Grand Rapids: Baker, 1973. Eight plays that are read rather than memorized constitute this small volume of condensed biblical passages and stories from the lives of such significant individuals as Helen Keller and Thomas Cranmer. Helpful pointers on presentation of the readings and valuable direction to all public readers.

Bennett, Gordon C. *Readers' Theatre Comes to Church.* Atlanta: Knox, 1976. A collection of eleven informal dramas that may be read in the public context. Sample scripts are taken from the Bible, the works of O. Henry, Henrik Ibsen, and C. S. Lewis, and episodes of *Les Miserables.* Bennett's primary contribution may be found in the opening chapters, which acquaint the newcomer with methods for developing a readers' theater. Suggested materials list and bibliography.

Du Charme, Jerry and Gail. *Lector Becomes Proclaimer.* San Jose, Calif.: Resource Publications, 1985. The DuCharmes wish to recover the ministry of the lector as proclaimer of God's word. The eight-chapter volume is divided into five parts that emphasize the Lord's call to proclamation, provide an explanation of the Sunday Lectionary and its structure, suggest prayerful methods of preparing and interpreting readings for "faith-filled proclamation," and present practical tips, techniques, and resources to improve effectiveness. Ecumenical.

Sparough, Michael. *This Is the Word of the Lord.* Chicago: Liturgy Training Publications, 1988. This work is a comprehensive series of twelve fifteen-minute lessons on three audio cassettes with a manual that covers all aspects of lector training from a theology of the lector, to effective communications techniques, to understanding the intention behind the text. The manual's reading and resource list is excellent. Ecumenical.

Wallace, James C. *The Ministry of Lectors*. Collegeville, Minn: Liturgical Press, 1981. Good primer for lay readers in a short volume. Theology and theory of "the Word" is followed by three chapters of technical and practical suggestions. Booklet in "The Ministry Series." General audience.

Williamson, Audrey J. *The Living Word*. Kansas City, Mo.: Beacon Hill, 1987. A complete volume on oral interpretation that technically prepares the participant for reading. The book also alerts one to the hermeneutic element in public proclamation through "voices of the Bible," its interpreters, storytellers, teachers, poets, prophets, and its theological formulations. The appendix contains over forty pages of special occasion readings.

EIGHTEEN

Examples of Dramatic Arts in Scripture Proclamation

The following examples illustrate how Scripture passages can be proclaimed dramatically. A variety of types of readings are presented here as models to guide worship planners in individual congregations.

354 • AN EXAMPLE OF READERS' THEATER: *PSALM 65*

The following script calls for Psalm 365 to be read by four readers and the congregation.

READER 1: Praise awaits you, O God, in Zion: to you our vows will be fulfilled.

READER 2: O you who hear prayer, to you all people will come.

READER 3: When we were overwhelmed by sins, you atoned for our transgressions.

READER 4: Blessed is the one you choose and bring near to live in your courts!

ALL: We are filled with the good things of your house,

READER 1: of your holy temple.

READER 2: You answer us with awesome deeds of righteousness, O God our Savior,

READER 4: *(Hushed)* the hope

READERS 4 AND 3: the hope

READERS 4, 3, AND 1: the hope

ALL: the hope of all the ends of the earth and of the farthest seas.

READER 1: who formed the mountains by your power,

READER 3: having armed yourself with strength,

READER 2: who stilled the roaring of the seas,

READER 4: the roaring of their waves

READER 1: and the turmoil of the nations.

READER 3: Those living far away fear your wonders;

READER 4: Where morning dawns

READER 2: and evening fades

READER 1: you call forth songs—

ALL: you call forth songs of joy.

355 • *ON THE ROAD TO EMMAUS:* AN EXAMPLE OF READERS' THEATER

This script calls for three readers to render the gospel lesson from Luke 24:13-35 (NIV).

READER 1: Now that same day

READERS 1 AND 2: the two of them were going to a village called Emmaus, about seven miles from Jerusalem.

READER 1: They were talking with each other about everything that had happened.

READER 2: As they talked and discussed these things with each other,

READER 3: Jesus himself came up and walked along with them;

READER 1: but they were kept from recognizing him.

READER 3: He asked them, "What are you discussing together as you walk along?"

READERS 1 AND 2: They stood still, their faces downcast.

READER 1: One of them, named Cleopas, asked him, "Are you the only one living in Jerusalem who doesn't know the things that have happened there in these days?"

READER 3: "What things?" he asked.

READERS 1 AND 2: "About Jesus of Nazareth," they replied.

READER 2: He was a prophet, powerful in word and deed before God and all the people. Their chief priests and our rulers handed him over to be sentenced to death, and they crucified him; but we had hoped that he was the one who was going to redeem Israel.

READER 1: And what is more, it is the third day since all this took place. In addition, some of our women amazed us. They went to the tomb early this morning, but didn't find his body. They came and told us they had seen a vision of angels, who said he was alive. Then some of our companions went to the tomb and found it just as the women had said, but him they did not see.

READER 3: He said to them, "How foolish you are, and how slow of heart to believe all that the prophets have spoken! Did not the Christ have to suffer these things and then enter his glory?" And beginning with Moses and all the Prophets, he explained to them what was said in all the Scriptures concerning himself.

READERS 1 AND 2: As they approached the village to which they were going,

READER 3: Jesus acted as if he were going farther.

READERS 1 AND 2: But they urged him strongly, "Stay with us,

READER 2: for it is nearly evening;

READER 1: the day is almost over."

READER 3: So he went in to stay with them. When he was at the table with them, he took bread, gave thanks, broke it and began to give it to them.

READERS 1 AND 2: Then their eyes were opened and they recognized him, and he disappeared from their sight.

READERS 1 AND 2: They asked each other, "Were not our hearts burning within us while he talked with us on the road and opened the Scriptures to us?"

READER 1: They got up and returned at once to Jerusalem.

READER 2: There they found the eleven and those with them, assembled together and saying, "It is true! The Lord has risen and has appeared to Simon."

READERS 1 AND 2: Then the two told what had happened on the way, and how Jesus was recognized by them when he broke the bread.

Jeannette Scholer

356 • EXAMPLES OF RESPONSIVE READING OF SCRIPTURE

The following examples all involve the congregation in the proclamation of Scripture. Each script is based on a portion of Scripture with some adaptation in order to highlight the dramatic qualities of the text involved.

—————— **The Lost Sheep** ——————

Background. This reading is based on the parable of Jesus in Matthew 18:10-14. The parable illustrates the value of human beings, especially of little children. Throughout Jesus' ministry, he interacted with children and noted that many of their characteristics are shared in some way with those who are a part of the kingdom of heaven. The parable of the lost sheep has been consistently overlooked as a parable about the significance of children! So we will underscore this point in the following reading.

Script/Participants:
  READER 1
  READER 2
  READER 3
  READER 4
  CONGREGATION

Position all four readers facing the CONGREGATION. READERS 1 AND 2 _should stand together in front on one side the platform and_ READERS 3 AND 4 _should stand together on the other side. The_ READERS _are in a teaching role in this reading. Their lines should be consistently read with the emphasis given according to the punctuation. For example, ellipsis (. . .) indicates a pause. This reading can sound fragmented, but with rehearsal the readers will be able to make these sentences smooth and will discover the delightful effect of several voices acting in cooperation to communicate a single thought._

READER 1: This is a parable
READER 2: about the kingdom of heaven.
READER 3: The kingdom is . . .
READER 4: like sheep.
CONGREGATION: Sheep?
READER 3: And a shepherd
READER 2: And little children who are lost.

READER 4: The kingdom is . . .
READER 2: like wandering,
READER 1: losing and looking,
READER 3: finding and laughing,
READER 4: maybe rejoicing!
READER 3: Tell me,
READER 4: what do you think?

READER 2: A man was counting
READER 1: his flock of sheep—
READER 3: one
READER 1: two

READER 2: three
CONGREGATION: four,
READER 3: Seventy-two
READER 1: Eighty-nine
READER 2: Ninety-eight
CONGREGATION: Ninety-Nine, One Hundred
READER 3: No, . . . just ninety-nine!
READER 2: One of them,
READER 1: One of the hundred,
READER 4: wandered off, got lost—
READER 2: hopelessly lost—
READER 4: in the hills—
READER 2: in the world—
READER 3: which left just
CONGREGATION: ninety-nine.

READER 4: A man owns
READER 1: A flock of sheep
READER 3: one hundred
READER 1: to be exact.
READER 4: But now it's
CONGREGATION: ninety-nine.
READER 2: He looks
READER 3: for the one lost sheep.

READER 1: He leaves the
CONGREGATION: ninety-nine
READER 2: on the hills or in the world—
READER 4: . . . or wherever—
READER 1: looks and finds
READER 2: the wandering lost sheep.
READER 3: This is the truth
READER 4: about shepherds and sheep,
ALL READERS: and God and people.
READER 2: When the shepherd
READER 3: finds the sheep,
READER 2: he is so happy.

Our Majestic God

Background. Worship has everything to do with the object of our adoration. Christians see God as One who deserves worship. Whatever we do and say should bear in mind this truth, and attempt to build up one's faith in God as a reasonable and worthy object of worship. The biblical writers showed God's worthiness by enumerating his accomplishments and actions. Psalm 8 is a meditation on God majesty. It lists some of the reasons why we worship him. The contrasts between God and humankind underscore this majesty, and this reading is designed

to emphasize those contrasts. We will be reminded that God is God and that any rulership we have is because of that fact.

Script/Participants:
  READER 1
  READER 2
  READER 3
  CONGREGATION

READERS 1 AND 2 *should stand together in front on one side of the platform and* READER 3 *should stand alone on the other side. The* CONGREGATION *should say their lines with feeling. The lines "Who am I?" and "I am wretched." should be said with passionate feeling.*

READER 1: O Lord—
CONGREGATION: Our Lord
READER 2: how majestic is your name in all the earth!
READER 3: Majestic?
READER 1: Excellent!
READER 2: Powerful!
READER 3: Authoritarian?
CONGREGATION: Loving!

READER 2: O Lord—
CHORUS: Our Lord!
READER 1: Yahweh!
READER 2: Adonai!
READER 1: Savior!
READER 3: Creator?
READERS 1 AND 2: Creator of all the earth!

READER 1: You have set your glory—
READER 2: not only in the earth—
READER 1: not only in the heavens—
CONGREGATION: but in our hearts!
READER 2: Your glory
CONGREGATION: is our hope
ALL READERS: and salvation.

READER 1: From the lips of children and infants—
READER 2: though their words of weakness—
READER 1: through their words of innocence—
READER 3: you have ordained praise.
READER 1: Out of the mouths of children
READER 2: comes openness,
READER 3: comes tolerance,
CHORUS: comes praise!
READER 1: So a little child shall lead them.

READER 3: When I consider the heavens,
READER 2: the work of your hands—
READER 1: when I think about
CONGREGATION: things bigger than I—
READER 1: the moon and stars,
READER 2: the Milky Way,
READER 1: the unknown that you have set in place—

CONGREGATION: who am I,
READER 2: that God would think of me?
READER 3: Who am I,
READER 1: that God should care for me?
READER 2: Who am I,
READER 1: that I should be crowned with glory and honor?

CONGREGATION: I am wretched
READER 2: and naked
READER 3: and blind.
READER 1: Yet I am crowned with glory and honor.
READER 3: God has made us rulers
READER 2: over His created works.
READER 1: Under our feet are the flocks of the hills,
READER 2: herds of the pasture,
READER 3: beasts of the field,
READER 2: birds of the air,
READER 1: fish of the sea.
READER 3: O Lord—
CONGREGATION: *Our* Lord!
READER 3: O Lord are we that glory?
READER 2: The lost coins that were found?
READER 1: The pearls that were purchased?
READER 3: The treasure that was uncovered?
READER 1: That you have set us above the heavens?
READER 2: How majestic is your name in all the earth.
READER 3: All of us are—
CONGREGATION: because God is!

Promise for a New Year

Background. Some have seen the "Day of the Lord" as so much pessimistic talk or doomsday-ism. Others have taken heed, reformed, and then been disappointed. Their expectations were dashed when God did not carry out what their prophet or interpretation had suggested. In the Old Testament, the "Day of the Lord" was a notion that summed up all expectations of God's people about his deliverance. Christians, too, have always seen profound meaning for the salvific action of God in judgment. Judgment is after all a declaration that God's people have chosen the right side of the controversy between good and evil. In this reading we see judgment as a promise of deliverance.

Script/Participants:
    READER 1
    READER 2
    READER 3
    CONGREGATION 1
    CONGREGATION 2
    CONGREGATION 3
    CONGREGATION 4

The CONGREGATION *should be arbitrarily divided up by the worship leader. Obviously, it is crucial that people know clearly what part of the* CONGREGATION *they will be in if they are to fully participate.*

READER 1: Hear this—
READER 2: this is the word of the Lord!
READER 3: Listen to this—
ALL READERS: All you church people!

READER 1: Tell it to your children—
READER 2: let your children tell it to their children—
READER 3: and let their children tell it to the next generation.

READER 1: A nation has invaded my land—
READER 2: a nation powerful and without number—
READER 3: a nation with the teeth of a lion—
READER 1: a nation with the fangs of a lioness.
ALL READERS: Joy has withered away.

CONGREGATION 3: Mourn!
CONGREGATION 1: Wail!
CONGREGATION 2: Spend the night in sackcloth!
CONGREGATION 4: Declare a holy fast!
CONGREGATION 1: Summon all who live in the land!
ALL: Cry out to the Lord!

READER 1: The day of the Lord is near!
CONGREGATION 3: Blow the trumpet in Zion!
CONGREGATION 4: Sound the alarm!
READER 1: At the very sight of this army, nations are in anguish—
READER 2: every face turns pale!
READER 1: God's soldiers will rush upon the city.
CONGREGATION 3: Let all who live in the land tremble—
CONGREGATION 1: For the day of the Lord is coming.
ALL: It is close at hand.

READER 1: With a noise like that of chariots—
READER 2: God leaps over the mountaintops!
READER 1: Like a crackling fire consuming stubble—
READER 3: God's mighty army is drawn up for battle!

READER 1: At the very sight of this army, nations are in anguish—
READER 2: Every face turns pale!
READER 1: God's soldiers will rush upon the city.
READER 3: They will run along the wall.

CONGREGATION 2: They will climb into the houses—
CONGREGATION 4: Like thieves they will enter through the windows.
READER 1: The Lord thunders at the head of his army.
READER 2: His forces are beyond number,
READER 3: and mighty are those who obey his command.
READER 1: Return to me with all your heart—
READER 2: with fasting and weeping and mourning!
READER 3: Rend your hearts and not your garments.

CONGREGATION 1: Return to the Lord your God—
CONGREGATION 3: for he is gracious and compassionate—
CONGREGATION 1: slow to anger—
CONGREGATION 4: abounding in love.
CONGREGATION 1: He may turn
CONGREGATION 2: and have pity
CONGREGATION 3: and leave behind a blessing.

READER 1: Blow the trumpet in Zion!
READER 2: Declare a holy fast!
READER 3: Call a sacred assembly.
CONGREGATION 1: Gather the people!
CONGREGATION 2: Consecrate the assembly!
CONGREGATION 3: Bring together the elders!
CONGREGATION 4: Gather the children!

READER 1: Let the priests weep
READER 3: between the temple porch and the altar.
READER 2: Let them say,
READER 3: "Spare your people, O Lord."
READER 1: Then the Lord will be jealous for his land
READER 3: and take pity on his people.
READER 2: Then the Lord will satisfy you fully.

CONGREGATION 3: Be glad, O people of Zion!
CONGREGATION 2: Rejoice in the Lord your God!
READER 1: He has given you the autumn rains in righteousness.
READER 2: He sends you abundant showers.

CONGREGATION 4: We will eat
READER 3: until we are full
CONGREGATION 1: We will praise the name of the Lord your God.
READER 2: He has worked wonders for you.
READER 1: Never again will my people be shamed.

READER 3: Then you will know that I am in Israel,
READER 1: that I am the Lord your God,
READER 2: that there is no other.
ALL READERS: Never again will my people be shamed.
READER 1: And everyone who calls on the name of the Lord will be saved.
ALL: There will be deliverance.

The New Heart

Background. The Scriptures are Christ-centered from beginning to end. The message God sends his believers is wrapped up in the promise for divine deliverance. The Old Testament narrative presents God as a delivering God. The New Testament interprets these delivering acts as the divine activity centered in Jesus Christ. With this deliverance from enemies, powers, and places comes deliverance from the "old man of sin," or depravity and evil desires. A new heart is promised to those who wish to be delivered. This new heart does not simply empower believers to reach their goals, it *alters* these goals. In this reading we meditate on the new-heart theme of Ezekiel 11 and 36.

Script/Participants:
READER 1
READER 2
READER 3
CONGREGATION

The CONGREGATION *is responding as the people who have gone astray. They have been beaten by the enemy, and they are sitting in captivity. They have been humbled. The* READERS *are giving the message of God to the people.*

READER 1: Hear what the Sovereign Lord says.
READER 2: I will gather you from the nations.
READER 3: I will bring you back from the countries,
READER 2: where you have been scattered
READER 1: and return your land.
CONGREGATION: What will we do, Lord?

READER 1: You will return to the land.
READER 2: You will remove all your vile images
READER 3: and detestable idols.
CONGREGATION: But we love them, Lord.
READER 2: I know.
READER 1: I know.

READER 1: But in my faithfulness to you
READER 2: I will give you an undivided heart,
READER 3: I will put a new spirit in you,
READER 2: I will remove your heart of stone,
READER 1: and give you a heart of flesh.
CONGREGATION: What good will that do?

READER 1: Because of that you will follow my decrees
READER 2: and you will find it more natural to be careful
READER 3: to keep my laws.
READER 2: For you will be my people.
READER 1: And I will be your God.
CONGREGATION: What if we don't want that?
READER 1: For those whose hearts are devoted to their vile images
READER 2: and detestable idols,
READER 3: I will bring down on their heads what they have done.
CONGREGATION: Is that a threat?
READER 2: Yes—
READER 1: You could look at it that way.

READER 1: Or you could be wise and learn from it.
READER 2: It could be seen as information.
CONGREGATION: Explain yourself, Lord.
READER 3: You could see it as a promise—
READER 2: A promise—
READER 1: of deliverance!
CONGREGATION: Of deliverance?!

READER 1: When my people lived in their own land
READER 2: they defiled it
READER 3: by their conduct—their actions—
READER 2: So I poured out my wrath.
CONGREGATION: We know!
READER 1: Of course, you know.

READER 1: Which do you detest more—
READER 2: my wrath?
READER 3: or my actions?
READER 2: There is a connection, you know—
READER 1: between your hardship and your wickedness
CONGREGATION: We are learning, Lord.

READER 1: Because of your unfaithfulness to me
READER 2: you tested my faithfulness to you.
READER 3: And I let you know
READER 2: what it would be like
READER 1: to live without me.
CONGREGATION: We are thick between the ears, Lord.

READER 1: You lived without me
READER 2: and you got beat up
READER 3: by the world.
CONGREGATION: Yes!
READER 2: The world without me,
READER 1: is not a friendly place.

READER 1: Everybody knows you now!
READER 2: Yes—everybody knows you now!
READER 3: They all know that you are my people
READER 2: and because you were unfaithful
READER 1: you lost your land.
CONGREGATION: Everybody knows us now.

READER 1: But it was not the witness I wanted—
READER 2: I wanted them to know my faithfulness-
READER 3: Not *your faithfulness*—
CONGREGATION: So, what now, Lord?
READER 2: Will you try again—
READER 1: Now that you have learned?

READER 1: I will take you out of the world
READER 2: and gather you back to your own.
READER 3: I will sprinkle you clean,
READER 2: I will remove your heart of stone,
READER 1: I will give you a heart of flesh.
CONGREGATION: What will we do?
READER 1: You will remember your evil ways and wicked deeds—
READER 2: you will loathe those sins you commit—
READER 3: you will know my faithfulness—
READER 2: you will act out of your new heart—
READER 1: You will be my witnesses.
CONGREGATION: And everybody will know you through us!

New Things

Background. God clearly cares about our need to feel the freshness of life. Scripture has much to say about "new" things. We can look at *new* in two ways. We may see the idea of being "brand" new, that is, never before in existence. I go to the shoe store, I buy a pair of "new" shoes. These are different from the other shoes I own. They are "brand" new. Or we may understand *new* as "renewed," or made over. You go to the shoe repairman and he resoles your shoes. They are now new shoes, that is, they have been remade or made over. In Scripture the great promises are *new* in this latter sense of *renewed*. The new covenant is actually very old, given to our first parents. But being renewed with each generation and finally renewed in Jesus, it is "new." In this reading we review many of the new things that biblical writers mention. This reading is for any occasions when renewal is emphasized—the new year, resolutions, Easter, Christmas—or when sermons stress repentance, new birth, and other like ideas.

Script/Participants:

    READER 1
    READER 2
    CONGREGATION 1
    CONGREGATION 2
    CONGREGATION 3
    CONGREGATION 4

The READERS *should be positioned at separate microphones and face the audience. They can stand next to each other or at opposite sides of the platform. The* CONGREGATION *needs to be divided into four equal parts. You simply do this before reading as if you were leading a round.*

READER 1: Every teacher of the law—
READER 2: who has been instructed
READER 1: about the kingdom of heaven—
READER 2: is like the owner of a house,
READER 1: who brings out of his storeroom
READER 2: new treasures as well as old.
ALL CONGREGATION: New treasures?

READER 1: I am revitalizing everything,
READER 2: said the voice from the throne!
READER 1: Write this down,
READER 2: for these words are trustworthy and true.
ALL CONGREGATION: What is this? A new teaching?
READER 1: Yes! and with great authority!
READER 2: He even gives orders
READER 1: to evil spirits and they obey him.

READER 2: In his great mercy
READER 1: he has given us new birth
READER 2: into a living hope
READER 1: through the resurrection
READER 2: of Jesus Christ from the dead.
ALL CONGREGATION: New birth?

READER 1: He told them a parable:
READER 2: Do you pour new wine
READER 1: into old wineskins?
READER 2: If you do,
READER 1: the skins will burst,
READER 2: the wine will run out
READER 1: and the wineskins
READER 2: will be ruined.
READER 1: We don't sew patches of unshrunk cloth
READER 2: on an old garment.
READER 1: If we do, the new piece
READER 2: will pull away from the old,
READER 1: making the tear worse.
READER 2: New wine must be poured
READER 1: into new wineskins
READER 2: so we may become a new creation!
ALL CONGREGATION: May we know this new teaching?

READER 1: Christ is the mediator of a new covenant,
READER 2: that those who are called
READER 1: may receive
READER 2: the promised eternal inheritance,
READER 1: now that he has died as a ransom
READER 2: to set them free from their sins.
ALL CONGREGATION: A new covenant?
READER 1: In the same way,
READER 2: after the supper he took the cup, saying
READER 1: This cup is the new covenant in my blood
READER 2: poured out for you.
ALL CONGREGATION: New covenant!
READER 1: At the place where Jesus was crucified,
READER 2: there was a garden.
READER 1: And in the garden a new tomb,
READER 2: in which they laid him.
READER 1: We were therefore buried with him
READER 2: through baptism into death,
READER 1: so that just as Christ
READER 2: was raised from the dead
READER 1: through the glory of the Father,
READER 2: we too may live a new life.
ALL CONGREGATION: New life?

READER 1: He opened a new and living way
READER 2: through the curtain of his body.
CONGREGATION 1: A new way!
READER 1: Therefore,
READER 2: he is a new creation!
CONGREGATION 2: A new creation!
READER 1: The old has gone,
READER 2: the new has come!
CONGREGATION 3: The new!

READER 1: We are now created to be like God
READER 2: in righteousness and holiness.
READER 1: As believers
READER 2: you have put on the new self.
CONGREGATION 4: The new self!
READER 1: Which is being renewed in knowledge,
READER 2: in the image of its Creator.
ALL CONGREGATION: Renewed!

READER 1: A new command I give you:
READER 2: You may now love one another!
READER 1: As I have loved you,
READER 2: so you may love one another!
CONGREGATION 1: We don't need to hate anymore?
CONGREGATION 2: We don't need to criticize anymore?
CONGREGATION 3: We don't need to be judgmental anymore?
CONGREGATION 4: We don't need to act like babies anymore?
ALL CONGREGATION: We may now love—all the time??
READER 1: Neither circumcision
READER 2: nor uncircumcision
READER 1: means anything—
READER 2: Works of the law mean nothing—
READER 1: What counts is a new creation.
READER 2: His purpose was
READER 1: to create in himself
READER 2: one new person—
READER 1: To be made new
READER 2: in the attitude of your minds.
ALL CONGREGATION: A new attitude!

READER 1: In keeping with God's promise,
READER 2: we are looking forward
READER 1: to a new heaven and a new earth—
READER 2: the home of righteousness.
READER 1: Whoever has an ear,
READER 2: hear what the Spirit says!
READER 1: Whoever overcomes,
READER 2: I will give a new name.
ALL CONGREGATION: A new name!

READER 1: To those who overcome
READER 2: I will give the city of my God,
READER 1: the new Jerusalem,
READER 2: and I will write on them
READER 1: my new name.
CHORUS: His new name!

READER 1: Go, stand in the temple courts,
READER 2: and tell the people the full message

READER 1: of this new life.
CONGREGATION 4: All right!
CONGREGATION 3: Amen!
CONGREGATION 2: Yes!
CONGREGATION 1: OKAY!
ALL CONGREGATION: We will!

READER 1: And I saw
READER 2: a new heaven
READER 1: and a new earth,
READER 2: for the first heaven
READER 1: and the first earth
READER 2: had passed away.
CONGREGATION 1: Praise be
CONGREGATION 2: to the God
CONGREGATION 3: and Father
CONGREGATION 4: of our Lord
ALL CONGREGATION: Jesus Christ!

Melvin Campbell and Edwin Zackrison[103]

357 ◆ BIBLIOGRAPHY OF EXAMPLES OF THE DRAMATIC ARTS IN SCRIPTURE PROCLAMATION

Betten, Mary. _People of the Passion._ Kansas City, Mo.: Sheed and Ward, 1988. Nine monologues designed to "unsettle" the audience through the encounters of real and imaginary characters with Jesus during the Passion. Personalities include the servant girl in Caiaphas' court, the woodcutter of the tree that became the cross, Pilate's wife, and more. Eleven more monologues acquaint the reader with "Mary M.", the Magdalene's musings of Jesus as told to others.

Glavich, Mary K. _Acting Out the Miracles and Parables._ Mystic, Conn.: Twenty-Third Publications, 1988. Fifty-two five-minute dramatic presentations of parables and miracles with director's handbook for staging, props, costuming, and so on. Developed to augment religion programs or incorporate in liturgy. Simple scripts. Points for discussion follow dramas.

Langdon, Harry N. _Twenty-Six Biblical Playlets for Learning and Liturgy._ Liguori, Mo.: Liguori, 1988. The volume contains three divisions of playlet (1–3 minutes) material: (1) historical—categorized by event, parable and miracle; (2) contemporary; and (3) interpretive. Appendices match playlets to the lectionary schedule and provide a guide to special occasion use. Simplicity and symbolism are advocated. Script and director's notes.

Richardson, Don. *Eyewitnesses: Dramatic Voices From the Gospels*. Wheaton, Ill.: Harold Shaw, 1988. The author highlights the drama of thirteen life-transforming encounters with Jesus through intimate and intriguing monologues and dialogues that may be used in a variety of settings. All have been field tested, refined, and set in chronological order to progressively reveal the gospel message through confrontation with the characters portrayed.

NINETEEN

Dance, Movement, and Posture in Worship

Movement is the essence of life. From the moment of conception until the moment of death, human beings are in a constant state of movement. We breathe by moving; we grow by moving; we learn by moving; we love by moving. We move toward God on our journey of faith, slowly discovering the nature of that Spirit who moved over the face of the deep.

Dance emerges from the repetitive movements and patterns of life that become stylized and are given significance. Folk dances, improvised movement, fully choreographed works, or ballroom dances are organized patterns of meaning and purpose set in specific contexts. They explore the nature of relationships: their joy, pain, tension, love. Often dance fleetingly reveals something of the mysterious power of bodies, spirits, and souls meeting in a common rhythm or caught up in a common pattern. Through dance we explore strong feelings that elude the power of words to capture. For good reason, dance has been a significant metaphor for understanding the relationship between God and humankind.

Movement, dance, and posture are also fundamental elements of worship. They can be used to express the many moods of worship: joy, sorrow, reverence, submission. They can also be used to both accompany and respond to the proclamation of God's Word. This chapter outlines ways in which dance, posture, and movement can be intentionally employed in common worship and provides reasons for doing so.

358 • A BRIEF HISTORY OF DANCE IN WORSHIP

Christian dance has persisted throughout the history of the church, despite many official decrees against it. Christian churches that have incorporated dance and other stylized gestures in worship have benefited from a profound way of expressing their praise and enacting the gospel message. Dance as worship is one manifestation of the Spirit's ongoing activity in the church.

The New Testament church was not born into a vacuum, but into a Jewish culture filled with heritage and saturated with rich traditions. T. W. Manson has commented:

The first disciples were Jews by birth and upbringing, and it is *a priori* probable that they would bring into the new community some at least of the religious usages to which they had long been accustomed. (T. W. Manson, quoted in Ralph P. Martin, *Worship in the Early Church* [Grand Rapids: Eerdmans, 1974], 19)

Christianity entered into a tradition of already existing patterns of worship, including music and dance, as found recorded in both the Bible and ancient writings.

King David danced exuberantly in God's presence (2 Sam. 6), while Miriam the prophetess led the women to dance with tambourines in response to their mighty deliverance from the pursuing Egyptian army (Exod. 15). Women are seen dancing in Shiloh at a feast (Judg. 21:21-23) and before David as a response to his military victories (2 Sam. 29:5). Visual images show both the bride and the bridegroom dancing: he leaping in dance (Song 2:8) and she as two dancing companies or armies with banners (Song 6:13). The Psalter commands the dance (Ps. 149:3; Ps. 150:4).

Other writings provide accounts of dancing in Jewish history. The Mishna describes a major ceremony of Sukkot, the seventh and final feast of the Jewish sacred year celebrating God's rains and the increase of crops. The ritual is called *Nissuch Ha-*

Mayin, in Hebrew meaning the water drawing. "The water-drawing ceremony was a joyous occasion, replete with grand activity and high drama" (Mitch and Zhava Glaeser, *The Fall Feasts of Israel* [Chicago: Moody Press, 1987], 175). "Levitical priests, worshipers, liturgical flutists, trumpeters, and a crowd carrying *lulax* (branches) and *etrog* (fruit) celebrated together in a great display of symbolic activity and festival rejoicing" (Sukkah 5:1). It was probably the viewing of this ceremony to which Jesus makes reference in his great teaching on the outpouring of the Holy Spirit in John 7:37-39.

Another celebration, which occurred on the first night of the feast of Sukkot, was the illumination of the Temple. Enormous golden candlesticks were set up in the court of the women.

> The mood was festive. Pious men, members of the Sanhedrin, and heads of the different religious schools would dance well into the night holding burning torches and singing songs of praise to God. (M. and Z. Glaeser, *Fall Feasts of Israel,* 182)

The Glaesers go on to report: "Not only did they play instruments with fervor, but the Levitical choir stood chanting and singing as the leaders of Israel danced" (M. and Z. Glaeser, *Fall Feasts of Israel,* 183).

Dr. Sam Sasser writes:

> Recognized Norwegian scholar Sigmund Mowinckel, in what is believed to be one of the best books written on the Psalms in Israel's worship, and a standard text in most graduate schools and seminaries, notes in definition: "Together with song and music goes the dance, which is a common way of expressing the encounter with the body. The dance is a spontaneous human expression of the sense of rapture. . . . At a higher religious level it develops into an expression of the joy at the encounter with the Holy One, an act for the glory of God (2 Sam. 6:20ff). It behooves one to give such a visible and boisterous expression of the joy before Yahweh." (Sam Sasser, *The Priesthood of the Believer* [Plano, Tex.: Fountain Gate Publishers], 111)

The church from A.D. 30 to A.D. 70 was undergoing transition. There was a separation from Temple worship, and those elements in the old covenant which would not be continued in the new covenant. The epistles and the book of Acts outline the forms and ceremonies of Judaic worship that would be eliminated in the church. Blood sacrifice (Heb. 9), Levitical priesthood (Heb. 7:11-28), the practice of circumcision (Acts 15:5, 28-29), and the keeping of new moons and Sabbaths (Col. 2:16-23) were to be discontinued. However, there is no commentary about discontinuing the use of musical instruments, singing, and dancing. Nowhere are these condemned or forbidden. On the contrary, the following Scriptures seem to indicate the continuing practice of inherited worship patterns (Col. 3:16; Eph. 5:19-20; Acts 15:13-16; 1 Cor. 5:13, 14:26). It is noteworthy that historically the book of Psalms has been the basic hymnbook for the church and her worship patterns, as David Chilton describes:

> When the church sang the Psalms—not just little snatches of them, but comprehensively, through the whole Psalter—she was strong, healthy, aggressive, and could not be stopped. That's why the devil has sought to keep us from singing the Psalms, to rob us of our inheritance. If we are to recapture the eschatology of dominion, we must reform the church; and a crucial aspect of that reformation should be a return to the singing of Psalms. (David Chilton, *Paradise Restored* [Tyler, Tex.: Reconstruction Press, 1985], 8–9)

Although Jewish tradition is replete with accounts of dancing, Ecclesiastes 3:1 and 4 state, "To everything there is a season, and a time to every purpose under the heaven / A time to weep, and a time to laugh; a time to mourn, and a time to dance." The New Testament church was soon to experience seasons of mourning and weeping. Lamentations 5:15 says: "The joy of our heart is ceased; our dance is turned to mourning." Laughing and dancing would again find their season in the church as God brought times of restoration, healing, and revival. Jeremiah 31:4 promises, "Again I will build thee, and thou shalt be built, O virgin of Israel: thou shalt be adorned with thy tabrets, and shall go forth in the dances of them that make merry."

Separation from Jewish heritage was not the only point of adaptation for the new church. Until the time of Constantine, A.D. 323, the church experienced extreme persecution at the hands of the Roman government. Christians were captured, used as human torches, compelled to fight in gladiatorial combat, and fed to lions in elaborate spectacles called Roman games. The games reflected the immoral decadence, monstrous abuses, unwieldy influence, and imperial sadism into which Rome had fallen. Incorporated into these games was the Roman dance, an art form borrowed from other cultures, mainly Greek, and consigned to slaves.

Christians had seen their friends and fathers martyred in amphitheaters where their agony was merely a prelude to, or an incident in, the shows. That the church Fathers would honestly have denied any desire to employ consciously a trace of taint from Roman spectacle we have no reason to doubt. Church history is full of the courageous and violent denunciations that the early Fathers launched against the shows.

As early as A.D. 300 a council at Elvera decided that no person in any way connected with circus or pantomime could be baptized. In 398, at the Council of Carthage, a rule was established excommunicating anyone who attended the theater on holy days (Lincoln Kirstein, _Dance: A Short History of Classic Theatrical Dancing_ [Little Rock: Revival Press, 1982], 59–60).

Although church history of the first millennium finds the weight of evidence to be in opposition to dance, there are quotes from writings of the church fathers which indicate some trace of dancing remained in the Christian church.

"Of those in heaven and those on earth, a unison is made, one General Assembly, one single service of thanksgiving, one single transport of rejoicing, one joyous dance." _Chrysostom_ (A.D. 386)

"Everything is right when it springs from the fear of the Lord. Let's dance as David did. Let's not be ashamed to show adoration of God. Dance uplifts the body above the earth into the heavenlies. Dance bound up with faith is a testimony to the living grace of God. He who dances as David dances, dances in grace." _Ambrose_ (A.D. 390)

"To keep the sacred dances, discipline is most severe." _Augustine_ (A.D. 394)

"Could there be anything more blessed than to imitate on earth the dance of angels and saints? To join our voices in prayer and song to glorify the risen creator." _Bishop of Caesarea_ (A.D. 407)

"I see dance as a virtue in harmony with power from above." _Thodoret_ (A.D. 430)

"Dance as David danced." _Bishop of Milan_ (A.D. 600)

"Dance as David to true refreshment of The Ark which I consider to be the approach to God, the swift encircling steps in the manner of mystery." _St. Gregory of Nazianzus_ (A.D. 600) (all quoted from Debbie Roberts, _Rejoice: A Biblical Study of the Dance_ [Little Rock: Revival Press, 1982], 39–40)

In his book on dance, Lincoln Kirstein records a few examples of dancing in Christian churches:

The Abbot Meletius, an Englishman, upon the advice of the first Gregory, permitted dancing in his churches up to 604. . . . The Jesuit father Menestrier, whose history of dancing published in 1682 is full of valuable data about his own time as well as of curious earlier tales, tells of seeing in certain Parish churches the senior canon leading choirboys in a round dance during the singing of the psalm. The Parish Liturgy reads "Le chanoine ballera au premier psaume." ("The canon will dance to the first psalm.") (Kirstein, _Dance,_ 63)

Continuing in this vein, Kirstein records three more examples:

Scaliger said the first Roman bishops were called praesuls and they led a sacred "dance" around altars at festivals. Theodosius says that Christians of Antioch danced in church and in front of martyrs' tombs. Los Seises, the dancing youths of the Cathedral of Seville, whose annual performance on the feasts of Corpus Christi and the Immaculate Conception was connected with the ancient Mozarabic rite, are often described as ritual dancers, though their dance was really an independent votive act, peculiar to the towns of Seville and Toledo. (Ibid.)

The writings of Augustine in the fourth century issue a complaint against dancing.

It is preferable to till the soil and to dig ditches on the day of the Lord than to dance a choreic reigen. Oh, how times and manners change! What once was the business of lute players and shameless women only, namely to sing and to play, this is now considered an honor among Christian virgins and matrons who even engage masters in their art to teach them. (Walter Sorell, _The Dance through the Ages_ [New York: Grosset and Dunlap, 1967], 36)

On the one hand condemned and on the other hand embraced, dance seems to have never completely disappeared from church history. Especially in the Mediterranean countries and the Orient, people never gave up dancing. Here, the clergy applied less coercive measures to restrain dance. However, taking the gospel to the north, the clergy had an uphill struggle to uproot the rituals and pagan rites.

> With the Christian way of life taking root, the heathen quality was lost, but the people retained what they liked about the old way. How many things in which we still indulge nowadays have their roots in ancient pagan rituals, such as the idea of a June bridge, Halloween, or Yuletide! Or who would think today of the Maypole as a phallic symbol and of the dance around it as a fertility dance? (Ibid., 38)

Although dance was more often condemned by the millennium church than sanctioned, there were exceptions.

> As Alordyce Nicole writes, in his exhaustive work on the period, had this been actually enforced half of Christendom, including a section of the clergy, would have been out of communion with the church. . . . From East to West, in Constantinople, in Antioch, in Alexandria, in Rome, the mimic drama flourished, uniting together old pagans and new Christians in the one common enjoyment of pure secularism. (Kirstein, *Dance,* 60)

Because of the increase in heresy, the leaders desired more centralization of authority and a set pattern of doctrine. A series of traceable events, beyond the scope of this article, gave rise to priestly class and eventually the formation of the Roman Catholic church.

> From the scriptural position of the priesthood of all believers there grew up a distinct priestly class. . . . The early leaders warned against falling from this idea, but soon a priestly class was developed and the priests began to do things for common Christians that, they were told, they could not do for themselves. This was not only a retrogression to Jewish days, but was also a compromise with paganism. If the ministers were to be priests they had to interpret the items of worship in such a way as to give themselves special functions and to justify their position. . . . Along with these developments was a general increase of ceremonialism. Simple services became ritualistic. (F. W. Mattox, *The Eternal Kingdom* [Delight, Ark.: Gospel Light Publishing House, 1961], 151)

Combining the practice of asceticism and the sharp cleavage between clergy and laity, this period finds little expression of dance in the church; and what can be found is in the ceremony and service of the priests. Hence, the rise of the Mass. The Mass is based on Christ's passion. It is called Eucharist or Thanksgiving, since those celebrating give thanks for the bread and wine. The Mass continued to be arranged until it supported "an astonishing exuberance of minute detail, each tiny point related to a central truth of the religion" (Kirstein, *Dance,* 70).

The expression of one's beliefs and feelings through movement is the very foundation of dance. Though the worship form of dance was removed from the people and repressed in the priesthood, the basic element of dance found its expression in the Mass. It is the indirect contribution of the Mass with which we are occupied but even so, there were definite preordained movements and postures for the participants. However, we do not infer nor should we "easily assume that basilicas were sacred opera houses, or the Mass was a holy pantomime" (Ibid., 67). But dancing as a form of worship is not an isolated phenomenon or an ancient relic of our distant Hebraic ancestors. Therefore, we must understand the forms worship may take when it emerges as the dance.

Outside the walls of the church, people were still expressing religion in dance, although their belief was more a fear of death than faith in the living God that prompted Israel's dance.

> In no other epoch besides the late Middle Ages has the dance been more indicative of social phenomena. It reflected frightening aspects of the plague and the fear of death.
> At Christian festivals people would suddenly begin to sing and dance in churchyards, disturbing divine service.
> Hans Christian Anderson tells of little Karen who was cursed to dance without stopping and who could not find rest until the executioner cut off her feet. (Sorell, *Dance through the Ages,* 40, 42)

The church leaders tried to stamp out these obscene dances, which often began in the churchyard cemetery with people dancing around tombstones then moving through the town attracting more and more people as they went. This dance, also known as dance macabre, reached a climax as the bubonic plague swept Europe in the fourteenth century. These dances of violent nature occurred everywhere. In Germany, they were called St. Vitus' dance. In Italy it was called tarantella and these dances indicated the tenor of life, particularly during the period of the plague (Ibid., 40).

The clergy maintained that the millennium would be the day of reckoning, Judgment Day. When the year 1000 passed without any visible changes, some of the fear subsided.

> The Church remained powerful and the spirit of medievalism lingered on, even while man awakened to a new inner freedom. From the crudeness of his carnal lust and mortal fear of it, he escaped into chivalry; checking his growing freedom, he forced himself into the straitjacket of ideal codes. (Sorell, _Dance through the Ages,_ 39)

The fourteenth century introduced more change for the world and the church with the beginning of the Renaissance, the great revival of art and learning in Europe in the fourteenth, fifteenth, and sixteenth centuries. The world was revolting to set the soul and body free.

> Above all, Renaissance man had a visual mind, as his accomplishments in printing, sculpture and architecture prove. The eye became used to seeing in patterns. And it was geometric design which inspired the first attempts at ballet. (Ibid., 90)

The Renaissance, emphasizing the dignity of the human person, laid the foundation for an independence of thought which eventually broke the grip of Catholic theology. A revitalized interest in the study of the Scriptures caused people to be aware that the New testament church was vastly different from the church in existence in Western Europe.

> The religious and moral corruptions now could be effectively combated because of the intellectual freedom which had been encouraged by the Renaissance. Men began to see in the Scripture that the claims of the clergy were unfounded, and with a new intellectual basis for their criticism, ideas of opposition to the hierarchy spread rapidly. (F. W. Mattox, _Eternal Kingdom,_ 240)

The sixteenth century began the Reformation. Notable leaders sought to eliminate the unscriptural doctrines and practices of the Catholic church and, through reforms, return the church to New Testament patterns. One of first reformers was Martin Luther (1483–1546). Along with emphasizing justification by faith, Luther stressed the priesthood of all believers. This was a preeminent step to releasing

the people to express their worship unto God, which would eventually release all the Davidic expressions of praise, including dance.

John Calvin (1509–1564) was a leader of the Reformation in Switzerland who laid down principles which have influenced a large part of the Protestant world today.

> The church of Luther experienced and preached the ideal of renunciation of the world more strongly than the Reformed church, which desires to proclaim the glory of God in all areas of life. The Reformed Churches do not view this world as a vale of tears, but as the vineyard of the Lord, which is to be cultivated. They do not shun the world, but meet it, accepting the danger of becoming secularized in order to magnify God's name within it and by its means. Thus in the last analysis they subject nothing to a judgment of absolute condemnation. Everything must and can serve to the glorification of God, even art. We may recall the thought of the Neo-Calvinist Abraham Kuyper. Basically, the art of the dance should also be capable of being incorporated into the service of God. (Gerardus Van Der Leeuw, _Religion in Essence and Manifestation_ [Princeton, N.J.: Princeton University Press, 1986], 51–52)

Writings on the Renaissance and Reformation periods are scattered with accounts of a revitalized interest in dance in the church. Giovanni Boelaccio of the fourteenth century mentioned the _carole,_ a dance in a ring to singing voices, originally performed in May only, but whose popularity grew until the carole was sung and danced throughout the year.

> Variations of the carole arose everywhere. The minnesingers in Germany called it Springtang and put into it a great many hops and small leaps. . . . The people identified the carole—today known only as a Christmas song—with religious images as they appear in many "Last Judgment" paintings of the early Renaissance which show angels in heaven enjoying a carole. (Sorell, _Dance through the Ages,_ 41)

The varied artistic styles of the Renaissance reflect the concept of dancing in the heavens. The works of Leonardo da Vinci pictured the entire cosmic order as dancing. Dante, famous writer, poet, moral philosopher, and political thinker of his day saw the dance of the saints in heaven.

When those bright suns so gloriously singing
Had circled three items 'round about us
    turning,
Like stars which closely 'round the pole go
    swinging,
They seemed like women who are not yet
    willing
To dance, but to the melody stand clinging
While the new rhythm mind and ear is
    filling. (Van Der Leeuw, *Religion,* 30)

The works of Vondel reveal the same visual imagery:

. . . for the guests so merry
At the wedding, must not rest,
Since their dance is necessary.
Heaven holds no ghost nor quest
who with holy dance and singing
Does not spend eternity. . . . (Van Der Leeuw,
    Religion, 30)

Vondel also sees how the church dances with God:

As air through many organ pipes is guided
One spirit is to many tongues divided,
In equal time through field of equal sound,
Where Church and God together dance the
    sound.
The angel hosts from heaven's height
    descending
Dance deeply down, our sacrifice
    attending,
About Christ's body on His altar-stone. . . .
    (Van Der Leeuw, *Religion,* 30)

Apparently, the prevailing philosophy embraced dancing in heaven. "To die on earth as a martyr brings heavenly joy. . . . In Fra Angelico's *The Last Judgment,* the virgins and martyrs dance the heavenly dance" (Van Der Leeuw, *Religion,* 68). Luther, describing heaven's garden for his young song, portrays "a small beautiful meadow, which was arrayed for a dance. There hung lutes, pipes, trumpets, and beautiful silver cymbals" (Van Der Leeuw, *Religion,* 68). Although the church may have somewhat embraced the concept of dancing in heaven, the practice of dancing on earth was, for the most part, shunned if not declared anathema.

No longer under the heavy restraints of the church, Renaissance society was, therefore, dancing. Two opposite poles of dance developed in Europe between the twelfth and fourteenth centuries: the peasants, or the populace at large, stood for the earthiness and crude joy, while the nobility replaced the primary impulses with refinement and polish. "The court dance was subjected more and more to rules. Contributing to this development was, no doubt, the reliance of the nobility on professional entertainers" (Sorrel, *Dance through the Ages,* 45).

Further refinements and more popularity came to dance because of Catherine de Medici, a daughter of a great house in Italy who came to France to marry Henry II. "She brought with her a company of musicians and dancers from her native city of Florence to supervise her artistic presentations, and highly impressive they were" (John Martin, *The Book of Dance* [New York: Tudor Publishing Company, 1963], 26). In 1581, with the expertise of Balthasar de Beaujoyeux (an Italian by birth though bearing a French name), Catherine de Medici produced what is considered the first ballet, *Ballet Comigue de la Rein.*

The populace was also dancing. Folk dances such as the egg dance, the country Thread-the-Needle, and ring-shaped or choral dances grew in popularity. Labyrinth dances signifying resurrection themes were popular in many parts of the world, sometimes even being incorporated into Christian holidays. At Easter, in the province of Twente, in Oatmarsum, the children danced or processed through the entire town in a serpentine motion singing a very old Easter song:

Hallelujah! The happy melody
Is now sung loud and prettily.
Hallelujah! Hallelujah!

This dance is sluip-door-kruip-door in Dutch, Magdeburger in German, forandole in French, and the cramignon of Limburg. These also had two other names, taken from Biblical antiquity and the classics: Jericho and labyrinth.

From the Reformation period until the present, the church has experienced many spiritual awakenings or revivals, including the restoration of many New Testament truths. The energies of the clergy, theologians, and even whole denominations has been to embrace and preserve the truths that were being revealed. If the loss of truth or the embrace of heresy propelled the church into the dark ages (which is the prevailing philosophy of church historians), then the converse is also true. Embracing truth is responsible for returning the church to her calling, commission, and glory. Scripture compares truth to walls and salvation (Isa. 26:11; 60:18; Ps. 51:18). The rebuilding of truth is analogous to the rebuilding of the walls of Jerusalem after captivity, defeat, and judgment (Ezra 9:9; Neh. 2:17; Isa. 26:1). In Israel of old, such restoration was the promised season of release, rejoicing, and dance (Jer. 31:1-13; Neh. 7:1; 12:27-30). Likewise, as the church has experienced reforming and rebuilding, rejoicing and dancing have accompanied each season of restoration. (Below you will find quotes from various revival periods and special religious sects that validate this view.)

A unique group called the Shakers was founded in England in 1747. The term *Shaker* came from the rapid up-and-down movement of their hands, mostly in their wrists. Shaking the hands with the palms turned upward as if to receive a blessing meant they were expressing the open petition, "Come, life Eternal." Shaking of the hands with the palms turned downward to the floor was a symbolic motion that they were shaking out all that was carnal.

The Shakers believed that by keeping their inner and outer lives in perfect order they were reflecting the perfect order of God's kingdom. The practicing Shaker was held accountable to his religion when he stepped out of bed, when he dressed, when he ate, when he spoke, and when he worked. Worldly lusts were suppressed by rules: carnality was held at bay by a dress code that insured modesty, by a series of orders restricting the body's movements and appetites, and by architectural designs that segregated the sexes. Unity was enforced by the requirements of obedience—the submission of the individual to the authority of God's appointed leaders.

On Sundays the Shakers danced to the honor of God. Their worship—in vivid contrast to the restrained order of their weekday lives—was an exuberant spectacle that veered unpredictably through many hours of the day. Formal dances could at any time break off into spontaneous displays of whirling, weeping, and shaking. Scathing or uplifting sermons were delivered extemporaneously by the elders, or by individual worshipers who were suddenly seized by the power of God and compelled to speak. Throngs of spectators—"the world's people"—packed the little meetinghouses to be entertained, shocked, or inspired. No one who witnessed Shaker worship, whether horrified or enraptured, ever forgot it.

The first ordered dance of the Shakers, the "Square Order Shuffle" was introduced by Joseph Meacham about 1785. In 1820 a variation was introduced, men and women shuffled forward and backward in a series of parallel lines, weaving, in imaginative designs, a fabric of union and love.

A 19th Century American engraving called "Shakers Dancing" can be seen at the Dance Collection, Performing Arts Research Center, The New York Public Library at Lincoln Center. (Amy Stechler Burns and Ken Burns, "The Shakers," *American History Illustrated* [Summer 1988], 27)

During the early 1800s in the slave community, dance was an important part of their worship. A syncretism of African and conventional Western religious beliefs, the praise meeting in the quarters was unique in the United States. While whites might be carried away by religious frenzy at occasional "awakenings," slaves had an even more intense emotional involvement with their God every week. In contrast to most white churches, a meeting in the quarters was the scene of perpetual motion and constant singing. Robert Anderson recalled that in meetings on his plantation there was much singing. He noted, "While singing these songs, the singers and the entire congregation kept time to the music by the swaying of their bodies, or by the patting of the foot or hand. Practically all of their songs were accompanied by a motion of some kind." A black plantation preacher testified to the uniqueness of the religion in the quarters when he asserted: "The way in which we worshiped is almost indescribable. The singing was accompanied by a certain ecstasy of motion, clapping of hands, tossing of heads, which would continue without cessation about half an hour; one would lead off in a kind of recitative style, others joining in the chorus. The old house partook of the ecstasy; it rang with their jubilant shouts, and shook in all its joints (John W. Blassingame, *The Slave Community* [New York: Oxford, 1972]: 27). Two outstanding features of the slave community worship were the "ring shout" and the "juba." H. G. Spaulding gave an excellent description of the "shout" on the Sea Islands in 1863:

After the praise meeting is over, there usually follows the very singular and impressive performance of the "Shout" or religious dance of the negroes. Three or four, standing still, clapping their hands and beating time with their feet, commence singing in unison one of the peculiar shout melodies, while the others walk round in a ring, in single file, joining also in the song. Soon those in the ring leave off their sing-

ing, the others keeping it up the while with increased vigor, and strike into the shout step,
observing most accurate time with the music. This
step is something halfway between a shuffle and a
dance, as difficult for an uninitiated person to describe as to imitate. At the end of each stanza of the
song the dancers stop short with a slight stamp on
the last note, and then, putting the other foot forward, proceed through the next verse. . . . The shout
is a simple outburst and manifestation of religious
fervor—a "rejoicing in the Lord"—making a "joyful
noise unto the God of their salvation." (Blassingame,
Slave Community, 65–66)

Accompanying their singing was the practice of the
"patting juba."

When slaves had no musical instruments they
achieved a high degree of rhythmic complexity by
clapping their hands. Solomon Northup, an accomplished slave musician, observed that in juba the
clapping involved "striking the hands on the knees,
then stroking the hands together, then stroking the
right shoulder with one hand, the left with the
other—all the while keeping time with the feet, and
singing. . . ." Often the rhythmic patterns used in
juba were little short of amazing. After viewing a
performance in Georgia in 1841, a traveler from
Rhode Island observed that, while the slaves were
patting juba, it was "really astonishing to witness
the rapidity of their motions, their accurate time,
and the precision of their music and dance." (Ibid.)

The world was in a period of change. The Industrial
Revolution followed the Reformation changing the
character of life as people had known it. Likewise,
the reformers continued to bring change to the
church. The late 1800s produced a church concerned about holiness, some Christians even seeking a second work of grace called sanctification.
Holiness evangelist, pastor, and church leader Ambrose Blackman Crumper, a licensed Methodist
Episcopal preacher, was determined to establish the
holiness message in his native state of North Carolina. "Everywhere he went, people shouted, danced
before the Lord, and 'fell under the Spirit' when
they received the second blessing."

The Holiness movement spawned the great outpouring of the Holy Spirit at the turn of the century.
Pentecostalism was born on Azusa Street, prompted
in part by the Great Welsh Revival. Seekers of the
baptism of the Holy Spirit would receive the gift of
tongues. "Dancing in the spirit" was often a regular

happening at their meetings. Dancing in the spirit
is physical movement akin to dancing, presumably
done while under the influence and control of the
Holy Spirit. "Most older Pentecostal believers who
have participated in spiritual revivals over a period
of years have witnessed what is known as 'dancing
in the spirit'" (Stanley M. Burgess and Gary B.
McGee, eds., *Dictionary of Pentecostal and Charismatic Movements* [Grand Rapids: Zondervan,
1988], 236). According to the *Dictionary of Pentecostal and Charismatic Movements,* various
phrases applied to the dance movements observed
in the Pentecostal believers included: holy roller,
orgiastic worship, physical agitation, physically
demonstrated praises, orgasmic worship, noisy and
expressive worship, holy jumpers, and others.

Dancing is a phenomenon closely tied to the fresh
encounters with God found in the message of sanctification, baptism of the Holy Spirit, or healing revivals. One famous woman healing evangelist, Maria
Woodworth-Etter, whose meetings journal has
many accounts of people dancing, had this to say
on the subject:

David danced with all his might before the Lord.
The word is full of dancing. Where dancing in the
Bible is mentioned, it always signified victory for
the Lord's hosts. It was always done to glorify God.
The Lord placed the spirit of power and love of the
dance in the Church, and wherever the Scripture
speaks of dancing it implies that they danced in
inspiration, and were moved by the Spirit, and the
Lord was always pleased, and smiled His approval;
but the devil stole it away and made capital of it. In
these last days, when God is pouring out His Spirit
in great cloudbursts and tidal waves from the flood-
gates of Heaven, and the great river of life is flooding
our spirit and body, and baptizing us with fire and
resurrection life, and divine energy, the Lord is doing His acts, His strange acts, and dancing in the
Spirit and speaking in other tongues, and many
other operations and gifts. The Holy Ghost is con-
firming the last message of the coming King, with
great signs and wonders, and miracles. If you read
carefully what the Scripture says about dancing, you
will be surprised, and will see that singing, music
and dancing has a humble and holy place in the
Lord's Church. . . . All the great company was
blessed but Michael, and she was stricken with bar-
renness till the day of her death, so you see she
sinned in making light of the power of God in the
holy dance (just as some do today), and attributed it
to the flesh or the devil. They always lost out, and

many are in darkness till death. (Maria Woodworth-Etter, *A Diary of Signs and Wonders* [Tulsa: Harrison House, 1981], 524–525)

The Pentecostal revival was not limited to the United States, but spread quickly to the European continent, bringing with it the Holy Spirit's gifts, anointing, and also the dance. Between the two world wars, a revival of Christian drama won wide popularity, especially in Germany.

I shall never forget seeing one of these bands of German young people as they produced a thrilling version of the Totentanz (Dance of Death) before a Chinese student-group in Peking. Being chiefly a dance, with music but no words, it spoke an international language; and the intensity of the emotion among these oriental and largely non-Christian observers aroused by this European and thoroughly Christian play was surprising and extraordinary. (Richard H. Ritter, *The Arts of the Church* [Boston: The Pilgrim Press, 1947], 97–98)

From that time until the present day, dancing has been incorporated by many evangelistic groups. Currently, two outstanding examples are YWAM (Youth With A Mission), founded by Loren Cunningham, and Toymaker's Dream by Impact Productions. The year 1948 hosted another outpouring of the Holy Spirit known as the Latter Rain Movement. With a strong emphasis on the gifts of the Holy Spirit, laying on of hands, and prophecy, this visitation, like earlier revivals, hosted manifestations of spiritual dancing. Rev. Charlotte Baker, a modern day prophet and anointed teacher, comments on that outpouring in her book *On Eagle's Wings:* "Dancing is not new to the Christian who is familiar with worship in the realm of Pentecostal churches. Since the outpouring of the Holy Spirit at the turn of the century, dancing in the Spirit has been a part of Pentecostal praise and worship." However, a shift began to take place in the understanding of teachers such as Charlotte Baker. Although not doubting the validity of dancing while yielded to the Holy Spirit's influence, she and others also believed dancing as a voluntary act is a true act of worship. She goes on to comment:

It must be noted, however, "dancing in the Spirit," the term which has been so widely used throughout the years, is not found in God's Word. Careful study of the Word reveals that the appropriate expression

is dancing before the Lord. For example, David danced before the Lord with all his might at the time of the return of the Ark of the Covenant to Israel. "Dancing in the Spirit" suggests that the Holy Spirit takes hold of the Christian, causing him or her to enter into uncontrollable motions and contortions, all supposedly manifestations of the Spirit. "Dancing before the Lord" suggests the worshiper's strength, training, and expertise as fully under the control of the dancer, who expresses worship and joy in actions and steps which bring pleasure to the heart of God. While it is true that the believer is admonished to "leap for joy," it is also true that there are many Scriptures which indicate that intricate steps, marches, group dances, twirling, and twisting were part of the expression of the dance. There is a growing conviction among the people of God that He is most pleased when we offer to Him, as an act of worship, all of our ability whether it be in art, in the dance, or in any other creative expression with which the Lord has blessed us. Every activity of life is designed to become an act of worship. In the past five years we have seen many gifted dancers come to Jesus for salvation and add to the Body of Christ a wonderful ability to express, in an excellent manner, their worship unto Him in dance. Just as there are those who have been given the ability to sing and to edify the Body through excellence in song, so are there those who have been given the ability to pour out to God a similar ministry through the dance. Room should be made within the worship structure of the Church for the full expression of each individual; such expression should always remain within the confines of the Word and under the leadership of the ministries. (Charlotte E. Baker, *On Eagle's Wings* [Shippensburg, Pa.: Destiny Image Publishers, 1990], 101–102)

In the 1950s and 60s a few churches pioneered new territory in choreographed dancing, pageants, dance troupes, and trained artists. Among these were The King's Temple in Seattle, Washington, pastored by Rev. Charlotte Baker, a disciple of the late Reg. Layzell, and Living Waters Fellowship in Pasadena, California, pastored by Willard and Ione Glaeser.

By the early 1960s the charismatic renewal movement was building momentum, sweeping people from every denomination into the outpouring of the Holy Spirit. An outstanding feature of the charismatic meetings was the importance placed on singing Psalms and other Scriptures. "The rise of singing psalms and Scripture songs, as well as the rebirth of dance in worship, in the charismatic movement is directly attributed to Old Testament examples'' (Burgess and McGee, *Dictionary of Pentecostal and Charismatic Movements,* 689). Exuberance and freshness marked the worship services: "As in the early days of the Pentecostal revival, it is not unusual to find charismatic worshipers singing, shouting, clapping hands, leaping and even dancing before the Lord as they offer him sincere praise and thanksgiving'' (Burgess and McGee, *Dictionary of Pentecostal and Charismatic Movements,* 693).

In 1978 God raised up four men—Rev. Larry Dempsey, Rev. Barry Griffing, Rev. Steve Griffing, and Rev. David Fisher—to begin a teaching worship conference called the International Worship Symposium. This worship seminar, along with one of its offshoots, and the International Feast of Tabernacles Celebration in Jerusalem have done much to encourage local assemblies to begin creative worship in the area of dance.

Dancing in churches currently ranges from simple folk style steps in which whole congregations participate, to traveling professional artists such as Ballet Magnificat. Liturgical dance, the name having been just recently coined to identify the style of dance, is becoming more common.

> Practiced by liturgical artists, dance serves and functions as a conduit from the inner workings of the spirit to the outer expression of today's worship. . . . dances for the liturgy change with the seasons: fall, winter, spring, and summer match advent, Christmas/Epiphany, Lent/Easter, and Pentecost. Becoming immersed in the cyclical process, a dancer discovers that he or she has become a student of religion. Dances are designed from personal reflections on the spirituality of the liturgical season. Scripture and prayer, mingled with the urgings of the dancer's soul, and enriched by the experience of life, are shaped through the medium of dance. (Doug Adams and Diane Apostolos-Cappodona, eds., *Dance as Religious Studies* [New York: Crossroad, 1990], 153–154)

It appears that there is an inescapable link with restoration and rejoicing, with rebuilding and responding—"going forth in the dances of them that make merry'' (Jer. 31:4). Indeed "to everything there is a season." The season of weeping over our spiritual captivity has come to an end, for He has "turned our mourning into dancing."

Patti Amsden

359 • A Case for Dance in Worship

The church's uneasiness about including dance in worship stems, in part, from the dualism that equates the body with evil and the spirit with good. Worship demands physical and spiritual involvement that can transcend this dualism.

In the beginning there was dance. Before Israel, there was dance. Before Jesus' birth there was dance. Before the writing of the Scriptures there was dance. Before words there was dance. "Dance" has been described and performed in many different ways from one worshiping community to another throughout history. Here I will examine dance historically, practically, and theologically by addressing some common questions, concerns, and opinions about this most ancient form of worship.

Why Should Dance Be Part of Christian Worship?

Many people fear the idea of dance in worship because their visions of "dance" include the awkward stumbling of children's dance classes, memories of dance forced upon them by overzealous physical education teachers, or even the experience of watching poorly executed dance within the context of worship. The word *dance* is often accompanied by feelings of embarrassment and discomfort. Here I will propose helpful, natural, and appropriate

Harp and Lyre. The harp and lyre have always been a symbol of praise and worship.

ways in which dance can be utilized within worship.

I define dance in a more general way than perhaps many have in the past. Some may be surprised to hear that they are already dancing in worship! When arms are raised in prayer, when we make the sign of the cross to remember our baptisms, or when we kneel to express humility, we are participating in a form of liturgical dance. Any expressive movement of our bodies within worship can be considered, in a general sense, liturgical dance.

In the beginning God *moved* over the waters and *created*. If we accept the definition of dance as expressive movement, we need no further proof of the importance of dance. Expressive movement is an integral part of the human worship experience.

From Shiva, India's deity, who danced the world into being and through dance holds it in sacred order, to the Shakers, who dance to receive the gift of prophecy, dance appears in some form within most human expressions of spirituality.

To witness the natural human response of dancing, we need only look at our children. Even before a child has mastered speech, he or she will likely whirl and jump in dancing movements. In responding to the wonders of creation, which unfold daily in the life of a young child, it is probably not words but movement and music which come most easily and naturally as a response. In the perception of many children, all of nature seems to sing and dance.

Dance was one of the first forms of worship for humankind, and it was also one of the first forms of Christian worship, inherited from the Jews. Dance in worship is part of our Christian heritage. It was practiced earlier than our creeds, most of our hymnody, and even our naming of God as Triune. Yet, while historical precedent goes far toward justification of a practice, I will not use that argument for the continuance of dance. As with any religious practice, we should examine our reasons for maintaining or discarding it regardless of historical precedent. We must judge dance using the criteria we use to judge all practices we call "Christian": does it enrich our worship, carry spiritual meaning for us today, and reflect the good news of grace and forgiveness we have through Christ?

As a child I looked around at the stony faces of adults in church pews and wondered how they could sing. "We praise Thee, we bless Thee, we worship Thee, we glorify Thee, we give thanks to Thee for Thy great glory" with faces and bodies absolutely devoid of expression! When I could understand the message these words were intending to proclaim I was at first puzzled, then amused, and finally saddened and frustrated. The love and grace we proclaimed were incredible; the God we worshiped, awesome. How could these people have the restraint to keep from dancing, shouting, embracing, or at least smiling?! I could not understand or accept a response limited to reluctant vocal chords.

Why should we embrace dance as a valid, even necessary part of our worship? Because expressive bodily movement is fundamental to our humanity. When we hear the gospel of Jesus the Christ, how can we help but express our joy with all of our being? The question now becomes one of form.

How Can We Dance Appropriately in Worship?

Some think that no dance is appropriate in worship and consequently use a very narrow definition of dance. Others feel that only congregational movement is legitimate. Some insist that any spontaneous movement by anyone at any time during worship is acceptable and a gift of the Spirit, while others insist dance should be done only by those who are properly trained.

By defining dance as I do, it becomes an action done by nearly all worshiping people and includes a wide variety of things. Different forms of dance are appropriate in different settings. Here I will mention a number of specific forms dance can take, some of which are not acceptable in every congregation or in every worship setting:

1. **Common Worshiping Movements**. These movements include special postures of praise or reflection (e.g., kneeling, raised arms, folded hands, bowed heads, and embracing) in the name of Christ. Unlike simple walking, standing, or sitting, these movements are done not merely for the practical reason of moving from point A to point B so the service may continue, but they are done by the individual to express something specific and meaningful about his or her faith. Under this definition, one who presides at a worship service does a considerable amount of dancing.

2. **Communal Movement**. This includes movement shared by an entire congregation which helps to emphasize equality and community among the worshipers. The movements generally resemble simple

folk dances, if they are structured at all. The movements of charismatic congregations come under this heading, where the movements are extemporaneous and unrestrained. This form of "dance" is difficult to classify, as it may be done by many or only a few within a congregation; and whether it promotes unity or equality may be debated. Historically, communal movement has been accompanied by singing or chanting. The most common forms are circular and processional.

3. Fine Art Dance. This is performed by one or more dancers with technical training in dance and a sensitivity to liturgical practice. This involves the community in a less direct manner. These dancers help to set the mood for a community's worship, using their particular gifts to express the community's praise, repentance, gratitude, sorrow, or joy. It is more refined and ordered, using instrumental accompaniment more often than vocal accompaniment.

4. Mime and Clowning. While these expressions of the Christian message fall under our definition of dance as expressive movement, they should be seen as separate expressions of worship and faith. Confusion results when these things are lumped together with liturgical dance in the forms of communal or fine art dance. While all three are expressive movement, they are very different and should be studied separately.

5. Drama. This too deserves a classification all its own. While drama involves much expressive bodily movement, it is confusing to speak of it as dance.

In what form then, should dance be a part of worship? I consider any of these forms appropriate as long as it is done in the proper setting and with willing participants. The choreography must fit the occasion and contribute to a worship experience that enriches the faith of all involved. Where it is possible, communal movement is a wonderful vehicle for enriching the worship of a congregation. It beautifully illustrates our oneness as the body of Christ. More realistic, however, is the performance of fine art dance. In twentieth-century America, this form, in most instances, best expresses our cultural identity. Dance is no longer a part of our shared communal identity, woven into our culture as it once was through folklore, recreation, celebration of life events, and natural cycles. If the dance is properly done, the dancers do in fact dance for the whole congregation. The more experienced the dancers are with both dance and liturgy, the more naturally this bond is formed.

If Dance Was Once Part of Christian Worship, Why Did It Not Continue?

The debate over dance and what forms are appropriate within the context of Christian worship has gone on since the church's first days.

The Old Testament references to dancing make clear that dance was inseparable from Jewish worship. J. G. Davies tells us: "The religion of ancient Israel was without question a dancing one" (J. G. Davies, *Liturgical Dance: An Historical, Theological and Practical Handbook* [London: SCM Press, 1984], 96). Dance for Israel was a sacred expression of faith, one worthy of heaven itself. Daniels writes, "The idea of heavenly beings encircling the throne of God and singing his praise goes back to the Talmud, where dancing is described as being the principle function of the angels" (Marilyn Daniels, *The Dance in Christianity, A History of Religious Dance through the Ages* [Rams, N.J.: Paulist, 1981], 18).

As Christians considered the "new covenant" in Jesus the Christ, many forms of Jewish worship, including dance, were adopted as a natural part of early Christian worship.

> The string of dancing prophets continues with Jesus, as described in the Acts of John. The often violent opposition to dancing by the Church Fathers throughout the centuries has made us forget the significant role of the dance in the life of the early Christians. (Walter Sorrel, *The Dance through the Ages,* [New York: Grosset & Dunlap, 1967], 19)

The Acts of John (C.E. 120), an apocryphal writing, describes dancing at the Last Supper. The disciples gather around Jesus and perform a circle dance, with Jesus speaking the words, "Whoso danceth not, knoweth not the way of life. Now answer thou to my dancing" (Sorrel, *Dance through the Ages,* 20–21; Daniels, *Dance in Christianity,* 14).

Eusebius tells of the worship of the Therapeuts, which consisted of an all-night festival, including sacred dancing:

> They all stand up in a body and in the middle of the banqueting-place they first form two choroi, one of the men and the other of women, and a leader and conductor is chosen for each, the one whose reputa-

tion is greater for a knowledge of music; they then chant hymns composed in God's honor in many meters and melodies, sometimes singing together, sometimes one chorus beating the measure with the hands for the antiphonal chanting of the other, now dancing to the measure and now inspiring it, at times dancing in procession, and at times set-dances, and then circle-dances right and left. (Sorrel, _Dance through the Ages_, 20)

Throughout the ages many leaders of the church have loved and promoted dance as a form of worship, defending it against many false perceptions. In the second century Lucian of Samasta called dance "an act good for the soul, the interpretation of what is hidden in the soul" (Ronald Gagne, Thomas Kane, and Robert Ver Eecke, _Introducing Dance in Christian Worship_ [Washington, D.C.: The Pastoral Press, 1984], 39). In a late fourth-century sermon on the text of Luke 7:32, Ambrose, the Bishop of Milan, gives this defense of dance:

The dance should be conducted as did David when he danced before the ark of the Lord, for everything is right which springs from the fear of God. Let us not be ashamed of show of reverence which will enrich the cult and deepen the adoration of Christ. For this reason the dance must in no wise be regarded as a mark of reverence for vanity and luxury, but as something which uplifts every living body instead of allowing them to rest motionless upon the ground or the slow feet to become numb. . . . This dance is an ally of faith and an honoring of grace. The Lord bids us dance. (Daniels, _Dance in Christianity_, 18–19)

There are numerous references to dance as a beneficial and welcome part of liturgy in the early church, including those from Gregory of Nazianzus, Bishop of Constantinople, Basil the Great (334–407), Bishop of Caesarea, Jerome (340–407), Ambrose (who requested that persons about to be baptized approach the font dancing), Hippolytus, and Clement, among others. These people judged dance according to its place in Scripture and tradition and encouraged sacred dance as an acceptable, even necessary form of worship and praise.

The first limiting factor for dance was space, since Christians met (often secretly) in private homes. In days when Christians were persecuted and driven into hiding, dance was limited for practical purposes.

Official prohibitions against dancing began for a variety of reasons. When people were converted to Christianity from other religions, they sometimes wished to bring with them the dances of their former religions. This was troubling to the early church leaders and led to a fear of dance becoming a pagan intruder into Christianity. Not all of these dances borrowed from other religions lent themselves well to the purpose of expressing the Christian faith.

Some early church leaders also tried to prohibit dancing in order to set Christianity apart from Judaism. For this reason many Jewish practices were "spiritualized." Christian practices may also have fallen victim to spiritualization due to the Hellenistic dualism of flesh and spirit, body and soul which was a part of the culture into which Christianity came.

Under Constantine dance faced another obstacle. While Christianity was made the state religion and grand, ostentatious worship spaces were built, a wedge was driven between clergy and laity. Participation of the laity in worship, especially in the form of dancing and singing, was discouraged.

Dance nevertheless continued. Some of the most well known dances were the "Dance of Death" and the "Mozarabe." When plagues swept through Europe, touching the lives of all (especially the Black Death, 1347–1373), peasants believed that if they could catch the devil (who caused this terrible malady), they could drive him off. In the Dance of Death this was symbolically done.

The Mozarabe was a seventh-century dance where a wooden arc of the Testament was carried through the cathedral in procession with eight boys dressed as angels, dancing and singing. In 1439 it was forbidden by Don Jayme de Palafox, the Archbishop of Seville. The dance was so beloved that the people of Seville collected money and sent the young dancers to Rome to dance before Pope Eugenius IV, who responded, "I see nothing in this children's dance which is offensive to God. Let them continue to dance before the high altar" (Daniels, _Dance in Christianity_, 22–23).

The reaction of church officials to dancing appears to be a subjective thing throughout the church's history. In 539 the Council of Toledo condemned dancing in church processions in Spain and dancing in churches during vigils on saints' days. In 633 the Council of Toledo forbade the Festival of Fools with its singing and dancing. In 678 the Council of Toledo suggested that the Archbishop Isidore of Seville compose a ritual with much sacred choreography (Gagne, et al., *Introducing Dance in Christian Worship,* 82; Daniels, *Dance in Christianity,* 22). Many such examples can be found throughout the history of the church.

Where Do We Go from Here?

Dance began as an expression of the faith of common people as inherited from the Jews and was used to express faith through the centuries despite the warnings and prohibitions of the church hierarchy. The rationale for these prohibitions ranged from legitimate concerns about inappropriate practices making their way into Christian worship, to clericalism, to a confusion between sensuality and sensuousness.

Sensuality arises when the body is objectified and is thus stripped of its sacramental meaning. Sensuousness is a natural and good aspect of being human that needs to be recognized in our worship. We cannot worship as disembodied spirits. James Nelson writes:

Because the human body is vitally and spontaneously sexual, many Christians in their dualistic alienation have been offended by the radical implication of the incarnation. . . . The Victorian within still winces at the thought that the incarnation might be "a tale of the flesh." (James B. Nelson, *Embodiment: An Approach to Sexuality and Christian Theology* [Minneapolis: Augsburg, 1979], 74)

Why is dance not a more widely used expression of worship today? If we hesitate to use dance but not song because we feel one form of worship has more historical precedent, we must look more closely at our history. And if dance is omitted from worship solely out of our fear of causing someone to notice the beauty of the human body and of its movement, we need to confront our own fears and ask whether they are valid reasons for prohibiting someone's worship of God. Deiss writes

[Humans are] not only spirit, but also flesh. Our creator has given us bodies endowed with beauty and grace, and expects us to use them—not as a hindrance in our progress toward [God], not as "weapons of iniquity" in the cause of sin, but rather as "weapons of justice for God" (Rom. 6:13). It is, therefore, natural that the inner prayer of the soul express itself outwardly through the body. (Lucien Deiss and Gloria Gabriel Weyman, *Dancing for God* [Cincinnati: World Library of Sacred Music, 1965], 3)

Worshiping as whole people should not frighten us. We should, in fact, look for ways in which we can "offer our bodies as a living sacrifice, holy and pleasing to God" (Rom. 12:1). Our worship should incorporate all of our being: our voices, our minds, our eyes, our ears, our hands, and our feet. Worship cannot be restricted to one day per week and certainly should not be restricted to watching the show in the chancel. Jay Rochelle writes:

Dance in church still seems offensive to many not only because of the focus of the human body, but because of the active nature of that body as instrument of worship. Our sense of the passive, even quietistic, uses of the body as receptor may block us from seeing the body active in offering, thanksgiving, and praise. (Jay C. Rochelle, "The Contemplative Ground of Craft," *NICM Journal* [September 1977])

Our liturgy does not occur in a vacuum, it reflects the whole of our Christian life. If we will greet one another in the name of friendship, why do we hesitate to greet others in the name of Christ? If we will leap for joy when the Chicago Cubs hit a home run, why will we not leap for joy at the good news of Jesus the Christ? And if we feel the unquenchable impulse to dance, as Gene Kelly declared in "Singing in the Rain," shall we not dance also for our God?

Deena Borchers[104]

360 • INTEGRATING DANCE IN THE LITURGY

This article offers a rationale for incorporating dance in worship as well as guidance for understanding the purpose of various types of movement.

If dance is to become an acceptable feature within a church service, then it must be integrated with and not just added to the celebration of the liturgy. If it is a mere decoration that neither deepens nor focuses devotion at the point where it takes place, then it should be excluded, since the accusation of gimmickry would be justified. In other words, liturgical dance must be protected from becoming the intruder that ballet once was in opera—when the pace seemed to be dropping and interest possibly flagging, a dancer or a troupe was introduced to enliven the proceedings; this added nothing to the opera and was a prostitution of ballet itself. This is certainly not what is needed in church. Dancing will be integrated with the Eucharist only when and if it corresponds with the nature of worship itself.

When dance is an act of praise or witness, then it is not a filler that brings the course of the liturgy to a halt. An inadequate relationship between dance and worship has been fostered if members of a congregation are prompted to think: _Now the service proper has to be stopped for a few minutes in order to experience this particular art form. No doubt it will proceed shortly_ (_Environment and Art in Catholic Worship;_ G. Huck, ed., _The Liturgy Documents. A Parish Resource,_ Liturgy Training Program, Archdiocese of Chicago, Chicago, 1980). To avoid this, dance has to serve the ritual action; it has to be an enrichment of the whole cultic act. It has indeed to manifest grace, using that term in the sense defined by Martha Graham: "Grace in dancers is not just a decorative thing. Grace is your relationship to the world, your attitude to the people with whom and for whom you are dancing."

She, of course, was speaking as an individual dancer, but she was perfectly well aware that a solo in the course of a service when legitimate is or should not be a performance. In this respect Judith Rock's view is very opposite: "An effective religious dance is an effective dance which springs from someone else's relationship with God and the world, to illumine my own relationship with God and the world" (J. Rock, _Theology in the Shape of Dance_ [Austin, Tex.: Sharing Co., 1978]).

This means that when dancing in a church, he or she must be aware that they are being invited to contribute to an event in which God is encountered, not to execute a program seeking applause. Here is hallowed ground—not in the sense that some ecclesiastical formula has been uttered over it, but of a place where God can be met; if the dancing aids that meeting, its integration with worship has been achieved. The reference here is of course to dance which in itself is an act of devotion, but this statement has to be freed from ambiguity by defining precisely what kind of dance is in mind, since there are many varieties, not all of which could be identified in this way with worship.

The old distinction within dance, which has previously been given some attention when seeking to outline modern developments, is that between story telling and movement. The liturgical viability of the former is not difficult to discern.

1. Narrative dance can accompany biblical readings, both illustrating and supplementing them. When a scriptural passage recounts an event, such as the entry of Jesus into Jerusalem on the first Palm Sunday, this can be represented in dance. In this way one of dance's major uses by the world religions will be recovered for Christianity, namely, the function of reenacting the sacred history that is the foundation of the faith. When the lection itself consists of a story, e.g., the parable of the Pharisee and the publican, this story can obviously be mimed. Teaching, e.g., some verses from a prophetic book, frequently cast in concrete images, can be supplemented by dance.

2. Narrative dance can replace a sermon, not simply of the didactic but also of the kerygmatic type, i.e., through a dance, the proclamation of the gospel may take place. One should not only preach one's religion but dance it; one should not just pay verbal testimony to one's faith but incarnate it. Athenaeus, writing _c._ A.D. 200, could refer to a particular person as "a philosopher-dancer" on the grounds that "he explains the nature of the Pythagorean system, expounding in silent mimicry all its doctrines to us more clearly than they who profess to teach eloquence" (Athenaeus, _Deipnosophistae_). If philosophy can be danced, so can theology.

3. Narrative dance in a dramatic form can be used to accompany and be a commentary upon spoken prayers, as well as hymns and carols, and also psalms. Psalm 68, to give an illustration, is a reenactment of God's conquest of chaos and it included, and can still include today, dancing and singing (J. Eaton, "Dancing in the Old Testament," in Davies [II. G. 9], 4–15).

4. In narrative dance the meaning of the stories can be explored physically. We are apt to think that understanding is something we achieve through mental processes alone; in fact a group that has danced, say, the parable of the Talents may come to a deeper perception of responsibility than that which a verbal analysis alone can achieve. Or to dance the tension between Mary Magdalen and Jesus, the former attracted to and yet inadequate before the figure of Christ, is to become more sensitive to personal interaction. This exploration may also be related to the prophetic character of dance. Prophecy, to use a familiar cliché, is not so much foretelling as forthtelling. It calls things into question—actions, policies, behavior, preconceived ideas. It has an iconoclastic aspect, breaking down barriers to new understanding. It witnesses to reality

deep-down in things, brings awareness, witnesses to the possibility of the new. Prophecy summons us beyond the now and encourages hope in the future, i.e., it deals with the present in the light of what is to come. Dance too can assist us to find the ultimate in the immediate by transcending the present and opening it up to eschatological possibilities. Prophetic dance does not simply mirror the present nor depict solely the historical context of an original story; it points beyond that which is to what may be. It can awaken responsibility and lead to an appreciation of values rooted in actual living.

5. Narrative dance fosters identification. To identify through dance with the Samaritan woman in John 5 is to share her initial doubts about Jesus and so discern and feel some of the problems that his challenge presents—problems such as we ourselves have in the shape of our own individual doubts. Indeed we cannot appreciate our own faith without being conscious of and living with the questions that continually rise against it—faith and doubt are the sides of a single coin. To identify with Christ himself through dance is to take a step towards greater Christlikeness. Mimesis arouses the sentiments imitated (see Aristotle's *Politics*), and here may be found some of the ethical and educative value of liturgical dance of the narrative kind. The dancer has to use imagination and make an image of that which may be more beautiful and more sublime than he or she really is: this promotes identification with the image—in Christian terms—with the image of God.

We turn next to the other main category of dance—movement. This may be understood as that which either expresses something or is simply a kinetic flow that does not "mean" anything; the former is the general understanding of modern dance and the latter of what may be called postmodern dance. In either case movement can have a liturgical relationship. As expression, dance, e.g., after the act of Communion, would give bodily shape to gratitude—we respond in dance and dance our thanks in celebration of the goodness and bounty of God, experienced through partaking of the bread and wine. As movement, it may consist of the creation of abstract patterns: this too can be at home in the liturgy if the dancers are intending to weave patterns to the glory of God, i.e., offering in his honor the best of which they are capable. The dances of Fred Astaire and Ginger Rogers could have belonged to this category; they did not mean any-

thing; they did not express anything, but they can be liturgically related in terms of the exercise of their creative gifts before him who bestowed them. However, these particular dances may be included in another variety, namely, the spectacular: this introduces a different typology, not simply one of narrative and movement, but one which embraces, in addition to the spectacular, the recreational, with the expressive coming in again as a third variety.

The spectacular itself can also be subdivided into the mimetic and the abstract—and no more need be said about these two. The recreational on the other hand comprises dances from the minuet to rock and roll, from ballrooms to discotheques. On the face of it, it might appear that there is little to be learned from this category that might be applicable to liturgical dance, since its very title suggests a mere pastime, a relaxation of not very profound significance. However, the origins of folk dance are often to be found in ritual, e.g., in marriage ceremonies or in the celebration of the seasons. It is essentially communal and its purpose is not to entertain an audience, but to involve the participants in a group activity. In this sense, it can be very suitable for corporate worship, and especially for the Eucharist, one of whose essential thrusts is towards unity so that the members of the community may become progressively one in Christ—a round dance, for example, is an effective symbol of such togetherness. This is to affirm that this kind of dance can have practical results, which is how many religious dances in the past have been understood—a hunting dance was believed to lead to success in running down a quarry, and so on. Of course when dance is regarded as an art, there is a tendency, under the lingering influence of the slogan "art for art's sake," to deny that it can have any effect. Yet this primitive way of interpreting it cannot be ruled out; liturgical dance may be properly understood in terms of cause and effect, in this instance the circular dance is the cause and a greater sense of fellowship is the effect.

Of the expressive or expressional dance something has already been said, but it does demand further brief consideration. Expressive dance, as it has been understood by Balanchine, is nonmimetic and nonrepresentational. The movement itself is held to be self-explanatory so that the expressiveness is perceived to be intrinsic to it (J. Highwater, *Dance, Ritual of Experience* [New York: A & W Publishers, 1978]). Without repeating previous statements, it should perhaps be emphasized here how the expression of, for example, sorrow in a penitential dance is inseparable from the dance itself, which in its turn is indistinguishable from the dancer who is the instrument of his or her own art. The dance *is* the penance.

If this is difficult for those unfamiliar with dance to grasp, some help may be forthcoming from Barbara Mettler. She describes what it is to dance fire. It does not mean pretending to be fire; what is necessary is to sense in the muscles the quality of fire movement and then to move as fire itself moves (B. Mettler, *Materials of Dance as a Creative Art Activity* [Tucson, Ariz.: Mettler Studios, 1979]). Let us apply this to the expression of sorrow in a penitential dance. This does not mean pretending to be sad or mimicking how we think a mourning person may behave. On the contrary, it is to experience sorrow bodily and then to move accordingly. The dance then *is* the penitence. Similarly, in a dance of praise to express gratitude, the dance *is* the praise.

William of Malmesbury, the twelfth-century historian, showed his appreciation of this in his life of Aldhelm, when he described the saint's return from Rome *c.* 701. He was welcomed by monks with songs and incense, while "a part of the laity danced, stamping with the feet (*pedibus plaudunt choreas*); and a part expressed their inner joy with diverse bodily gestures" (William of Malmesbury, *de Gestis Pontificum Anglorum* [*Rolls Series,* ed. N.E.S.A. Hamilton, Longman; Trubner; Parker, Oxford; Macmillan, Cambridge, 1870], 373f.). The Latin verb *plaudere* in its intransitive form means to applaud, to give signs of approval, to praise, so the burden of the report is that Aldhelm was praised in the dance with the feet—this is a practical application of the psalmist's "Praise him with dance" (Ps. 150.4).

When dance is integrated with worship, then there is a gain in three respects. Diversity is increased, creativity is encouraged, and participation is intensified. A glance at Paul's account of worship at Corinth reveals a great variety within every service. A Shaker recipe for the liturgy provides a charming comment on this.

> Sing a little, dance a little, exhort a little, preach a little, pray a little and a good many littles will make a great deal. (D. W. Patterson, *The Shaker Spirituals* [Princeton, N.J.: Princeton University Press, 1979])

Paul was also concerned that every member of a congregation should play a part: "When you come together, each one has a hymn, a lesson, a revelation, a tongue, or an interpretation" (1 Cor. 14.26). The parts played were determined by the Holy Spirit who revealed his presence through his gifts: teaching, prophecy, and so on. When and if these gifts are suppressed or not given expression, inevitably there is a quenching of the Spirit (1 Thess. 5.19), leading to a decay of the *charismata.* What then of those whose gift it is to dance? Are they to be ruled out of a liturgical celebration? Is the divine source of their unique gift to be denied by neglect? Are talents to be unused and their exercise inhibited, thus incurring condemnation? (Matt. 25:14-30). If music and singing and sculpture and painting—all the arts—have a place in the Christian cultus or its setting, why not dance? "All words and art forms," say the North American Roman Catholic bishops, "can be used to praise God in the liturgical assembly" (*Environment and Art in Catholic Worship,* 215–243]). This is applicable to those individual artists who can and wish to worship God by dancing. To deny them the opportunity is to subject them to an almost intolerable restraint that those responsible for leading worship need to understand sympathetically. Ruth St. Denis tells of an occasion in a St. Louis restaurant when the orchestra began to play.

> The music went through me like a shock. I did not have the audacity to spring up then and begin to dance . . . I sat still and suffered, every fibre of me responding to the rhythm, every nerve stiffening in my effort to stay in my chair. (Ruth St. Denis, *An Unfinished Life* [New York: AMS Press, 1991; reprint of 1939 ed.)

This reaction could be identical at a church service where there is no freedom to exercise one's gift. Indeed this applies to all gifts and not only to that of dance. In the early days of Miss St. Denis's career such liberty was little known.

> Intuitively I tried to restate man's primitive use of the dance as an instrument of worship, and the result was a profound evolution in myself but no answer to the question, *What temples will receive these dances?* (Ruth St. Denis, *An Unfinished Life*)

At the level of individual devotion, as distinct from that of a body of corporate worshipers, there is also a problem. When visiting a famous cathedral, such as that at Canterbury, we are usually exhorted to kneel and pray. Suppose, however, we have the gift of dance: why should we not dance before the altar, quietly so that our form of devotion does not interfere with others of the more cerebral kind?

In stressing the importance of removing barriers to liturgical dance, it is necessary to recognize that there is a risk involved. Religious dance can be like saccharine, sweet but lacking any real substance. It can neglect, to its detriment, the dark side of human existence. It can become sentimental, superficial, and anything but a fitting rendering of glory to God. But once the expert, who does not readily give way to these temptations, is allowed into church, the result is likely to be disturbing. Creativity does not fashion a safe haven: it challenges. This can upset members of a congregation, many of whom will be conservative and, even if prepared to tolerate dance, will want it to be inoffensive. This could be to impose shackles on creativity and it has called forth this heartfelt complaint from another dancer, Judy Bennett.

> Everything is peaches and cream kind of dance. . . . Only trouble is, life's not always pretty, and I want to dance about life, and offer that dance to God, but it's hard to do that in the church: there's no market there for dances with guts. . . . I won't, as a dancer, compromise what I know to be worthy and true just to pacify church ladies with "body-hangups." (Carlynn Reed, *And We Have Danced. A History of the Sacred Dance Guild, 1968–1978* [Austin, Tex.: The Sharing Company, 1978])

Of course not every Christian has a gift to enable him or her to be a solo dancer of distinction and originality or a choreographer of stature. Nevertheless some worshipers may have powers unknown to themselves which can come into play if there is the possibility of bodying forth their aspirations (M. N. H'Doubler, *The Dance and Its Place in Education* [New York: Harcourt, Brace, 1925]). Moreover it was a Shaker conviction, and one that all Christians can share, that "dance is the greatest gift of God that ever was made for the purification of the soul" (Patterson, *The Shaker Spirituals*)—something then for all, even if most will fall short of perfection.

Because it is for all, dance can be integrated with worship to increase participation. It may further this in several ways. First, it reduces the threshold of shyness and so promotes corporateness. Second, it draws people out of isolation since the movements are visible, the emotions and rhythm are common

and the enjoyment of God becomes the shared activity of a fellowship. Third, dance enables each one to become part of a totality that is greater than him- or herself. Fourth, through dance each person can have an active role in the service—such was the case with the mystery religions contemporary with the birth of Christianity and in part accounted for their popularity since the adherents were able to feel themselves involved (G.-P. Wetter, 'La danse rituelle dans l'eglise ancienne' *Rev. d'hist.et de lit. relig.* 8 [1928]: 254–75). Fifth, the Eucharist is a celebration of love; this relatedness (for that is what love is) is possible because of our common bodiliness which itself may come into play through dance. Finally the Eucharist concerns not only bread and wine but people, and what they do should be a sign of that unity which it is one of the purposes of Communion to advance: an effective symbol of this is the dance, especially in its ring form. Such dancing corresponds to a change in the art that has accompanied the development of democratic ideals. In the past, prima ballerinas and subservient corps de ballet corresponded to kings and queens and their courtiers. Today it is the group, where there is a relationship of equals, that is to the fore. In a congregation where a hierarchic concept predominates, the dancing group will be less welcome than in one where fellowship is the ideal (Doris Humphrey, *The Art of Making Dances* [New York: Rinehart, 1959]). But the Eucharist is not only about oneness, it is about liberation, and with this the question of the interpretation of dance, which has already emerged at several points, must become the prime object of attention.

J. G. Davies[105]

361 • CATEGORIZING THE MOVEMENTS OF WORSHIP

Since movement is a normal part of life it has to be a part of worship forever. However, highlighting or emphasizing actions is the purpose of dance. These articles describe sources and means for utilizing movement more fully in worship.

Gestures denote the movements of a part of the body as distinct from the whole. Wagging the ears, shaking the fist, stamping the feet—these are gestures. One can gesture with the fingers (beckon), with the shoulders (shrug), or with the eyes (wink). Smiling too is, strictly speaking, a gesture, since only part of the body is mobile—the face. We clap with the hands, nudge with our elbows, frown with our foreheads, embrace with our arms, kiss with our lips, etc. Gestures are not always easy to interpret. We scarcely need a Hamlet to know that one may smile, and smile, and be a villain. The meaning of a gesture may be modified by a posture: I may shake my fist at someone, but if my whole bearing is one of good humour, with a smile on my face, I obviously intend to communicate a playful threat and not some warning of doom to come.

Posture, according to the OED, denotes the position and carriage of the limbs and of the body as a whole when it is in a state of immobility. Under posture then are to be grouped a long list of words that designate total body shape. A person is said to be standing, sitting, squatting, crouching, kneeling—these are all postures. To assert that someone has a threatening posture is to indicate that his jaws, shoulders, legs and feet are thrust forward aggressively and that his hands have been made into fists. A posture of exhaustion points to hanging heads, drooping shoulders, dangling arms and unsteady legs. While posture thus relates to a condition of stillness, this stillness, as Martha Graham has emphasized, can be dynamic and not static: it may be the body at its most potential efficiency (S. J. Cohen, ed., _Dance as a Theatre Art: Source Readings in Dance History from 1581 to the Present_ [Pennington, N.J.: Dance Books, 1977]). Posture can also involve, in the words of Carolyn Deitering, either complete tension or complete relaxation which "are the two poles of _no movement_ between which all movement takes place" (C. Deitering, "Creative Movement Expression," _Momentum_ [Journal of National Catholic Education Association], [1974]: 18–23), while movement itself can take any one of three forms: gesture, which has already been mentioned, together with posture adjustment, and locomotion.

Posture adjustment denotes the action whereby one changes one's body shape. I am standing (posture) and I then lie down on my back (posture adjustment) and so adopt a new posture of supineness. In this movement every part of the body has been involved. Posture adjustment also signals a change of attitude. A woman standing erect, with head held high and a haughty expression on her face, who then bows down and prostrates herself on the ground is adjusting her posture from one of independence and possibly defiance to one of servitude and humility. She has disposed herself bodily in a

particular posture. So a distinction has to be observed between a participle which may denote a posture (e.g., kneeling) and an active verb which describes posture adjustment (e.g., I kneel or am in the process of kneeling down). Posture then calls attention to a completed movement while posture adjustment specifies the actual motion.

Locomotion, as its etymology indicates, involves movement or motion from one place _(loco)_ to another. It denotes therefore not movement on the spot but through space. In the horizontal plane one runs or walks, while in the vertical it is possible to jump or hop.

Directions

The several adjustments of posture may each be placed on a scale that can be read either downwards or upwards. If we start in a standing posture, then bowing, sitting, kneeling, and lying on the ground are successive stages of descent to the earth, with falling as a precipitous way of achieving the same end. If we start from a supine posture, then the posture adjustments we can make are all concerned with ascending or rising movements. The meaning of the adjustments derives largely from the significance attached to the directions of up and down, but turning, since it involved changes of direction on a horizontal plane, has to be interpreted differently.

Directions have indeed always been important for human beings. Jews pray towards Jerusalem; Muslims face towards Mecca; Christians orient their churches to the east. Although we are perfectly aware that God does not dwell on the top of our atmosphere, height symbolizes that which is more important (a higher position) and indeed the upward direction is interpreted as Godward while downwards is the direction of the creature, of the grave, and even of hell itself.

The expressiveness of directions has been admirably set out by Joan Russell:

Reaching to the high point directly above gives the feeling of aspiration, a reaching beyond oneself into the endless space above. Movement in the opposite direction, deep, is helped by the pull of gravity and has a feeling of stability and security. Movement across the body brings about a closing-in movement, almost as though cutting oneself off from everyone else. Movement to the open side brings about an awareness of others with an almost welcoming attitude. Movement backwards gives a retreating expression, while movement forwards has an advancing, reaching expression. (Joan Russell, *Modern Dance in Education* [London: MacDonald & Evans, 1958])

The Sources of Christian Movement Vocabulary

With these distinctions in mind, it should now be possible to set out a movement vocabulary, but there is one other factor to be considered, and that is the determination of what source or sources should be drawn upon. To attempt to adapt the Hindu vocabulary, as a number of Christians in India are very properly doing (R. Englund, "Christian Dances in India," *Journal of World Association for Christian Communication* 27:2 [1979]; R. Englund, "Sing a New Song," *Now* [Methodist Church Overseas Div.] [1983]: 8f), would not be a sensible proceeding in Western societies where the culture and movement conventions are so different. Another point of departure has to be sought. In the first place, past Christian practice presents itself, already hallowed by tradition and use. This practice has the virtue of familiarity. To this can be added, in the second place, Shaker movement patterns that are sufficiently distinct from mainline Christianity to come under a separate heading. In the third place, it is reasonable to suppose that an extension of them by reference to the Bible would be generally acceptable. Such an extension is unlikely to prove difficult because the biblical anthropology knows nothing of the body-soul dualism and uses, therefore, psychological concepts to characterize bodily parts and movements. Hence over and above their strict physiological meaning, organs and limbs have a further significance attached to them. To give an illustration: the word in Hebrew translated as *throat*—that is its anatomical designation—can also mean breathing, life, and desire. Indeed the main Hebrew terms for worship are verbs of physical movement such as "to prostrate oneself" or "to raise the hand to heaven." Worship then can never be exclusively mental or spiritual; it has to be physically embodied. Precisely because of this perspective, the Bible is likely to provide a rich source for movements, and indeed there are only a few limits to be observed.

First, it has to be accepted that some parts of the body have no meaning ascribed to them either in themselves or in use. The legs, for example, apart from being bent in prayer (and even then it is customary to speak rather of the bending of the knees), are afforded no special significance. Then some organs are, as it were, neutral in that they only acquire meaning from the way they are used, e.g. lips can flatter, lie, or praise. Moreover, since the interpretation of gestures is in part a question of conventions subject to cultural change, not every biblical interpretation will commend itself at the present day—to give an example: winking the eye is an expression of contempt according to the Old Testament, whereas in modern Western society it is a come-hither signal.

There is a fourth source which should not be neglected, and that is ancient Middle Eastern iconography (O. Keel, *The Symbolism of the Biblical World: Ancient Near Eastern Iconography and the Book of Psalms* [New York: Seabury, 1979]). This serves to supplement the biblical material as well as to illustrate it. Postures and gestures can be studied on coins, seals, and painted mummy cases; they are represented in statues and bas-reliefs, while archaeological finds of all sorts have their own contribution to make.

Finally of course there are the meanings attributed to conventional gestures which often coincide with their functions (e.g., to clench the fist is to show aggression precisely because that is what a boxer does in order to fight). Natural positions too have their inherent meanings, e.g., kneeling is a near-fetal posture expressing dependence and need. Moreover, to kneel is often a painful thing to do, especially in Eastern churches where there are no foam-padded kneelers and no bench in front against which to support oneself. Penitence then becomes a bodily condition (A. Chirovsky, "Revelation and Liturgy: The Epiphanic Function of the Human Body in Byzantine Worship," *Diakonia* 13:2 [1978], 111–19).

J. G. Davies[106]

362 • THE POSTURE OF KNEELING FOR PRAYER

In addition to formal dance, the postures taken for the various acts of worship are an important aspect of movement in worship. Posture both reflects and shapes the attitudes that we bring to worship. One of the most important postures for many Christians in worship is that of kneeling for prayer. This article traces the history of the use of kneeling in worship and commends this practice to all Christians.

Anglicans traditionally kneel to pray, although worshipers in many parishes are now invited to "sit or kneel," which suggests a growing uncertainty about what is appropriate. Most Protestants sit; some stand; and many of the Nonconformist traditions object to kneeling on the grounds that it is unacceptably ritualistic or Romish or both. Should we, or should we not kneel to pray, and does it matter?

Here is what Screwtape writes to his young charge in C. S. Lewis's *Screwtape Letters:*

> One of their poets, Coleridge, has recorded that he did not pray "with moving lips and bended knees" but merely "composed his spirit to love" and indulged "a sense of supplication." That is exactly the sort of prayer we want. . . . Clever and lazy patients can be taken in by it for quite a long time. At the very least, they can be persuaded that the bodily position makes no difference to their prayers; for they constantly forget, what you must always remember, that they are animals and that whatever their bodies do affects their souls.

The argument here is that since we are bodily, "animal" creatures, our desires and aspirations necessarily find expression in bodily form. When we are joyful or fearful, sad or angry, we will most naturally seek to manifest this in some appropriate outward and physical fashion. For someone hungry or thirsty it is not enough merely to adopt an attitude of eating and drinking. So also the posture we adopt in prayer is an outward and visible expression of our real (and not just inward!) need for God.

For this reason, although it is of course fundamentally a matter of Christian freedom and discretion rather than of absolute right and wrong, we may be well advised to ask what Scripture and tradition have to say about the appropriate posture for prayer.

The Old Testament

The Old Testament views kneeling as a gesture of humility or of prostration before God or even Baal (1 Kings 19:18) or another figure of authority such as a prophet (2 Kings 1:13). The call to worship in Psalm 95 (the *Venite* of the traditional liturgy) includes the phrase: "O come, let us worship and bow down; let us kneel before the LORD our Maker" (v. 6).

Other, similar forms of prostration are found. Abraham's servant bows his head in worship after being invited to lodge with Rebekah's family (Gen.

24:26). Joshua and the elders fall on their faces before the ark after being routed at Ai (Josh. 7:6). Elijah on Mt. Carmel bows down to the ground and puts his face between his knees (1 Kings 18:42). Jehoshaphat (2 Chron. 20:18) and Ezra (Neh. 8:6) each lead the people in bowing their heads to the ground in worship. The exilic hope for redemption included the trust that one day "every knee shall bow" to God, in submission and worship (Isa. 45:23); in the New Testament, Paul takes up this hope and applies it to Jesus (Rom. 11:4; 14:11; Phil. 2:10).

Despite Psalm 95, kneeling specifically for prayer or worship is in fact relatively uncommon in the Old Testament. It does, however, occur in three important stories. Solomon prays his prayer of dedication for the new Temple kneeling and with his hands spread up to heaven (1 Kings 8:54; 2 Chron. 6:13). Ezra offers a prayer of repentance on his knees and with his hands spread out to God, because of Israel's intermarriage with pagans (Ezra 9:5). And three times a day Daniel kneels down in his upper room with his windows open toward Jerusalem, to pray and give thanks (Dan. 6:10). There are probably just two instances of "sitting before the Lord" in prayer. After the war against the Benjamites, the children of Israel went up to Bethel, wept, fasted, and sat before the Lord all day (Judges 20:26). David went into the sanctuary and "sat before the Lord" and prayed after Nathan had announced to him God's everlasting covenant with the house of David (2 Sam. 7:18; 1 Chron. 17:16). This shows that sitting in prayer is not entirely unthinkable for the Old Testament; but it may on the other hand be significant that the same expression ("to sit before" someone) is used elsewhere to denote the attitude of attentiveness which disciples have for their master (2 Kings 4:38; Ezek. 33:31; Zech. 3:8). Our two instances of sitting before the Lord both suggest situations of extended, attentive, listening prayer.

The normal prayer posture in Old Testament times was to stand: Hannah stands at the sanctuary to pray for a son (1 Sam. 1:26); the people of Israel stand to confess and repent of their sins, to read from the Law and to worship God (Neh. 9:1-3, 5); and numerous other texts speak of standing before God in worship (2 Chron. 20:13, 19; Ps. 24:3, 134:1, 135:2; cf. Lev. 9:5; Jer. 7:10). The Levites stand every morning and evening to thank and praise the Lord (1 Chron. 23:30), as indeed in a wider sense they stand ministering before the Lord (e.g., Deut. 10:8, 17:12, 18:5, 7; 1 Kings 8:11; 2 Chron. 5:14; 29:11,

35:5; Ezek. 44:15; Luke 1:11; Heb. 10:11). Similarly, Elijah appeals to the authority of the God of Israel "before whom I stand" (1 Kings 17:1, 18:15; cf. 2 Kings 3:14, 5:16). To "stand before" someone was to serve and recognize that person's authority (e.g. 1 Kings 1:2, 10:8; 2 Chron. 9:7; cf. Zech. 6:5; Luke 1:19, Rev. 20:12), although we also hear repeatedly that humans are not worthy or able to stand before God (1 Sam. 6:20; Ezra 9:15; Job 41:10, Ps. 76:7; 130:3).

Ancient Judaism

The later Jewish literature from the Second Temple period quite consistently suggests that Jews stood for prayer, facing Jerusalem. Solemn prayers for deliverance and penitential prayers, however, were offered while kneeling. In the Prayer of Manasseh, a little gem of intertestamental spirituality, the penitent king will "bend the knee of my heart," pleading for God's kindness and forgiveness (v. 11). Similarly, Simon the High Priest prays on his knees and with outstretched hands for help against the invading enemy, the Emperor Ptolemy (3 Macc. 2:1). There are various other examples of prostration or kneeling in prayers of confession or desperate need dating from around the time of Christ.

In the emerging liturgy of the synagogue, the main prayer (the Prayer of Eighteen Petitions) was in fact also known as the *Amidah,* literally, the "standing prayer." While the daily *Shema* ("Hear O Israel," Deut. 6:4) could be recited while traveling or lying down, the *Amidah* could only be said while standing.

Rabbinic literature, written after the destruction of the Temple, reflects widely on prayer. Prayer was seen as the true service of God, and greater than sacrifice. It must be engaged in from the heart, with earnest intention and concentration; our prayer is not accepted unless we pray with our heart in our hands. Prayer should never become a mindless routine or be done absent-mindedly.

Among the rabbis, standing for prayer is assumed to be the norm. Simon the Pious (fl. *c.* 200 B.C.) reputedly taught that in prayer God's very presence stands before us. Rabbi Eliezer (early second century A.D.) taught his disciples, "When you pray, know before whom you stand!" (*Babylonian Talmud,* Berakhot, 28b). Nevertheless, we are told about the famous Rabbi Akiba (second century A.D.), who while in public prayer was brief but in private given to much kneeling and prostration.

The New Testament

A similar pattern holds true in the Gospels. Standing in prayer is assumed throughout. Jesus teaches, "Whenever you stand praying, forgive if you have anything against anyone; so that your Father also who is in heaven may forgive you your trespasses" (Mark 11:25, Mt. 6:25). Even Pharisees and tax collectors stand for prayer in the synagogue (Luke 18:11, 13). The only reference to a kneeling prayer is in Luke's account of Jesus' solemn, agonizing struggle with his death in the Garden of Gethsemane (Luke 22:41; in Mark 14:35, Jesus prostrates himself on the ground).

In the Acts of the Apostles, however, there are several interesting examples of praying in the kneeling position. As he is being stoned, Stephen kneels down (perhaps involuntarily?) and asks God not to "hold this sin against" his persecutors (Acts 7:60). Peter kneels to pray in the upper room for Dorcas/Tabitha to be revived (9:40). After Paul's farewell speech to the Ephesians elders, they all get down on their knees to pray (20:36); similarly the disciples at Tyre kneel down on the beach to pray with Paul and his companions, having escorted them out of the city on their way to Jerusalem (21:5). One other relevant New Testament passage about kneeling is Paul's prayer that God will powerfully strengthen his readers "through his Spirit in the inner man, and that Christ may dwell in your hearts by faith"; for this prayer Paul says that he bows his knees before the Father (Eph. 3:14-17). The book of Revelation envisions the angels and the saints standing before God in the heavenly worship (7:9, 11; 8:2, cf. 20:12).

In summing up the biblical and intertestamenal evidence, it is probably fair to say that standing to pray was normal, although a kneeling position was assumed for particularly solemn, earnest, or penitential prayers. The function of kneeling seems to be to express humility and prostration before God.

Ancient Christianity

The early church witnessed a further refinement of this view. As the biblical precedent suggests, both standing and kneeling in prayer was practiced. There was at first no uniform custom; in fact several different prayer postures are attested: standing upright or with the head and back bent forward, kneeling, or fully prostrating oneself face down.

In formal settings, kneeling was primarily reserved for penitential occasions, although informally and in private devotion Christians might kneel more frequently. Writing around the year A.D. 96, Clement of Rome encouraged the church at Corinth to put aside strife and disloyalty and instead to "fall down before the Master, and beseech him with tears that he may have mercy upon us" (1 Clement 48:1). Early church tradition reports of the piety of James the Just (the brother of the Lord) that he "used to enter alone into the Temple and be found kneeling and praying for forgiveness for the people"; we are told that in the course of his constant penitential kneeling on behalf of the people his knees become calloused like those of a camel . . . ! (Hegesippus, *c*. A.D. 170, quoted by Eusebius, *Ecclesiastical History,* 2:23:6). The author of the Shepherd of Hermas (c. A.D. 140) repeatedly kneels to confess his sins during his visions (Vision 1:1:3; 2:1:2; 3:1:5; 4:1:7, v. 1). And Origen (*c*. 185–254) in fact considered kneeling to be a necessary expression of humility and submission for those wanting to confess their sins and to ask God's forgiveness (*On Prayer,* 31:3). For the ancient Christian, to kneel was to give outward expression to his or her unworthiness and humility before God.

Other instances of kneeling prayer occur in the context of earnest entreaties in the face of disaster. Tertullian (*c*. 160–225) and Eusebius (*c*. 260–340) refer to efficacious kneeling prayer at times of drought, and supplication on one's knees was also practiced at the time of death or other serious need.

As for corporate worship, the repeated references to church custom in some early writers seem to suggest that kneeling was very much the norm here, too. But although this may have been the case at certain times and places, it would be misleading to assume that kneeling was in fact universally practiced in worship. It is true that for a while the first part of the liturgy was said kneeling, followed by the rest of the service, for which the communicants stood. Catechumens and those not admitted to Communion for reasons of penance had to leave the service after the reading of the Scripture and the kneeling prayer; for this reason penitents were sometimes referred to as "kneelers" (*genuflectentes*).

In time, however, an ecumenical consensus emerged that explicitly restricted the occasions on which kneeling for public prayer was permitted. If kneeling is an appropriate bodily sign of penitence and humility, then times of triumph and joy would seem to call for a different posture. Tracing such a custom to the apostles, Irenaeus (*c*. 130–200) insisted that kneeling is appropriate during the six weekdays as an expression of sinfulness, but on the Lord's day *not* kneeling manifests our rising again by the grace of Christ and being delivered from our sins. Others who agree with Irenaeus but ban kneeling both on Sundays and from Easter to Pentecost include Tertullian, Hilary, Epiphanius, Basil, Jerome, Augustine, and numerous later church fathers and canons. In keeping with this consensus, Canon 20 of the Council of Nicaea (A.D. 325) determines that "since there are some who kneel on the Lord's Day and even during the days of Pentecost, in order that all things should everywhere be uniformly observed it has seemed right to the Holy Synod that prayers to God should be made standing."

Conclusion

Following biblical precedent, the ancient Christians knelt and stood for prayer. Kneeling was appropriate for confession and for solemn entreaties at times of need. Corporate public worship on Sundays and during the Easter season, however, was offered standing up. "In fact," says an acknowledged Anglican authority on the matter, "few customs are more frequently mentioned by early Christian writers than the practice of praying in the standing posture" (V. Staley, "Position and Posture of Minister and People," in George Harford and Morley Stevenson, eds., *The Prayer Book Dictionary* [London: Isaac Pitman and Sons, 1925], 596).

At the outset I quoted C. S. Lewis on the subject of kneeling. A rather similar perspective was offered by St. Augustine. God, he says, does not of course need our outward gestures of kneeling, raising our hands, or prostration in order for our hearts to be open to him. Nevertheless, the outward gesture is of great benefit because it helps motivate us to pray more fervently. And although the decision to pray is of course inward and spiritual, the outward and physical motion curiously reinforces our heart's commitment:

I do not understand why, although these motions of the body cannot be made without a prior act of the mind, nevertheless by performing the outward and visible motions the inward one which caused them is itself increased. Thus, the heart's affection which caused the outward motions, is itself increased because they are made.

We may of course pray seated if we must, but in any case the witness of Scripture and of the ancient church should encourage us to think about what we are expressing with our bodies.

Should we kneel to pray? Yes, by all means let us kneel to ask earnestly for God's forgiveness and to implore his help in conflict and adversity. And then let us stand, too, to praise and worship for our liberation.

Markus Bockmuehl[107]

363 ✦ FOLK DANCE IN WORSHIP

Folk dances express the ethos of a culture in much the same way that music and poetry do. Shared cultural sentiments and beliefs take shape in folk dance patterns that can be learned with little difficulty. These dance styles can be used in worship with many members of the congregation participating.

Before examining the role of folk dance in worship, one must investigate the subject of folk dance, defining it, discovering its origins, and identifying its purposes. Most simply defined, folk dance is the dance of the folk or the common people. Dancers and scholars disagree as to what can actually be labeled folk dance.

> Discussions dwell upon the confusion between such terms and concepts as "folk dance," "primitive dance," "ethnic dance," and "stage dance" and on the distinction between folk dance and modern recreational forms of ballroom dancing. (*Encyclopedia Britannica,* Book 7 [1976 ed.], s.v. "Folk Dance," 449)

Whereas some authorities do not differentiate between the terms ethnic dance and folk dance, the famous American dancer Ted Shawn does. Mr. Shawn believes:

> . . . ethnic dance subsumes folk dance as a subspecies. He considers pure, authentic and traditional racial, national, and folk dance to be "ethnic"; he calls the theatrical handling of them "ethnologic," and he refers to the free use of these sources of creative raw material as "ethnological." (Ibid.)

Folk dance, therefore, is the root out of which ethnic dancing grows and is the treasure which comprises the dance culture of a country. Walter Sorell agrees with this sentiment, reporting:

> . . . it may be difficult to draw an exact line between folk and ethnological dance, but the latter have developed a distinct traditional style, a technical terminology and a clearly defined school of instruction. No longer done as a communal experience, they have become art dances executed for the enjoyment and edification of spectators. The ethnological dance was a folk dance first before it became the art expression of a race. (Walter Sorell, *The Dance through the Ages* [New York: Grosset & Dunlap, 1967], 76)

Perhaps we could conclude that folk dance is the dance from which the art dance of a nation grows, both in technique and in spirit.

Whether dance is professional or folk, John Martin proposes that both are outgrowths of "basic dance."

> To understand it is simplicity itself. Nature has so constituted us that movement is the medium in which we live our lives, not only in our internal physiological mechanisms but in our outward conduct as well. . . . For example, when we are worried we do not skip about the room hugging ourselves, and when we are startled by a sudden noise we do not walk the floor. The movements themselves actually have in them the essential nature of the emotional experience, even though we have not rationally directed them and they do not specifically "mean" anything.
>
> It follows, then, that any emotional state tends to express itself in movements which may not be practically useful or in any way representational, but nevertheless reflect the specific character and quality of that emotional state. Working on this principle, consciously or unconsciously, dancers have evolved all kinds of emotional dances. . . . Thus, at the root of all these varied manifestations of dancing (and of countless other manifestations, as well) lies the common impulse to resort to movement to externalize states which we cannot externalize by rational means. This is basic dance. (John Martin, *Book of the Dance* [New York: Tudor Publishing, 1962], 7–8)

Although the basic dance may be a universal urge, it does not manifest itself in a universal form. Geography, climate, religion, and labor help to define a people's dance. The occasions which inspire it, the traditions which define it, and the very passage of time itself, affect the ways in which people translate their lives into dance.

Let's examine an important principle that transforms basic dance, the need to express oneself through movement, into folk dance, the specific dance common to a given group of people. God created humans to be receptively recreative. That is, to receive information from their environment and then to recreate or reform their environment in response to their perception of the data which they had received. This principle governs a human's activities in all areas of life. A mother may hear the cry of the child in need of food, utilize the raw material in the refrigerator or pantry, and recreate the groceries into a meal. An entrepreneur perceives the need in the market place, gathers materials existing in one form, and reforms or recreates a new product to meet the demand. An artist, inspired by a sunset, takes the materials of oils and canvas to recreate and fashion a painting. Humans create things to bear the image they possesses or the impressions that are impressed upon them. Richard Ritter defines this to be the process of the formation of art.

There are three great elements in every work of art: an object outside of the artist which is sensed or perceived; a relationship of some sort between that object and the artist; and an outward response to his perception on the part of the artist. . . . The third element—the response of the artist to his object, or to his perception of the object—produces the work of art itself. Art, then, is perception, relationship, and reaction. (Richard H. Ritter, *The Arts of the Church* [Boston: The Pilgrim Press, 1947], 3)

Culture is built as humans refashion the world around them. The word *culture* is derived from the Latin word *colo* and can be translated cultivate or inhabit. For example, people cultivate the soil, tilling and preparing the earth to recreate food for their need or to produce flora for beauty. This is called agriculture, the culture of the soil. Webster's dictionary defines culture as the improvement, refinement, or development of study, training, and so on. Humankind continuously cultivates and inhabits the world around it, taking the raw materials of the world and building civilization.

The Bible tells us that humans are God's image and workers.

And God said, Let us make man in our image, after our likeness: and let them have dominion over the fish of the sea, and over the fowl of the air, and over the cattle, and over all the earth, and over every creeping thing that creepeth upon the earth. (Gen. 1:26, KJV)

God is creative and has made humans, his image, to be creative. God's manner of construction is creating all things to bear His image. "The heavens declare the glory of God; and the firmament sheweth his handiwork" (Ps. 19:1, KJV). Romans 1:20 affirms this truth by stating, "For the invisible things of him from the creation of the world are clearly seen, being understood by the things that are made, even his eternal power and Godhead." James Jordan comments:

Everything in creation, and the creation as a whole, points to God. Everything is a sign or symbol of God. . . . Man is the only symbol that is also a symbol-maker. He is inevitably so. He cannot help being so. He generates good symbols or bad ones, but he is never symbol-free. Man's calling is to imitate God, on the creativity level. (James Jordan, *Through New Eyes* [Brentwood, Tenn.: Wolgemuth & Hyatt, 1988], 30–32)

This brings us to one closing comment along this line of thought. We have stated that humans perceive the environment and then build culture or art as a response to that perception. In other words, culture is developed based upon human beliefs. An affirmation of this can be found in the Latin word *colo,* the root word for our English word *culture,* which is also the root word for *cult,* or worship. The Bible affirms that the object which humans worship creates an imprint or image in them, which they in turn imprint upon their culture. Listen to Romans 1:21-25 from the perspective of this principle:

Because that, when they knew God, they glorified him not as God, neither were thankful; but became vain in their imaginations, and their foolish heart was darkened. Professing themselves to be wise, they became fools, and changed the glory of the incorruptible God into an image made like to corruptible man, and to birds, and four footed beasts, and creeping things. Wherefore God also gave them up to uncleanness through the lusts of their own hearts, to dishonor their own bodies between themselves: Who changed the truth of God into a lie, and worshiped and served the creature more than the Creator, who is blessed for ever. Amen.

As commented earlier, humans are receptively recreative. They are not originally creative. Only based upon that which they receive, do they create. If humans do not worship and serve God, thus stamping God's image on their recreative activities, then the image of that which he does worship and serve will be reflected in their creations, their culture, their art, and their dance.

With the understanding of this principle, we return to the subject of folk dance. In the early beginnings of the dance of a nation or people, the dances reflect their worship and their beliefs about common areas of life. In his book *The Dance Through the Ages,* Walter Sorell comments on the early dance of humans:

> With primitive man on the level of primeval tribes dance is synonymous with life in all its major aspects: with love, work, and ritual. But in his mind these three aspects are closely interrelated. For instance, the members of the Mexican Indian tribe Tarahumara knew only one word for dance and work. Almost everywhere dance and growth, i.e., fertility, were part of one and the same magic. And how inseparable the religious aspect from dancing is could not be better proved than through the natives along the Swan River in Africa who, when first introduced to the sacrament of communion, called it a dance. In the mind of primitive man the borderline between the concrete and the symbolic is blurred. This is why in putting on a mask he tries to implant in himself another being, or the spirit and magic of the god image. He sees the supernatural as a living force and needs to identify with it. Since early man had no other means with which to express himself and, above all, to communicate his "within-ness" than through movement, the concept of the dancing god has been in the foreground in many cultures.
>
> No dancer in primitive society is a performing artist in our sense of the word, although in time many tribes began to have their professional dancers, too. For all ceremonies and feasts they were as important as the priests are for our churches. They were held in great esteem and their tribes cared for them. They had nothing to do but to dance. (Walter Sorell, *Dance Through the Ages,* 14–15)

An outstanding example of a people's belief or cult influencing the forms and styles of their dance can be seen in the dances of the East. Sorell's insight is valuable.

> According to Hindu legend all this began in heaven: the world was created by Lord Shiva in a dancing mood, and with a divine dance Shiva annihilated his monster enemies. Ever since then, the gods have danced. And with the principle in mind that "what delights the gods, must delight man" dance was received from the gods as their great gift to man. Probably in the fifth century, the sage Bharata established artistic principles and a system of training— the rigid rules for the gesture language called the *natya shastra.* (Ibid., 52)

For centuries the *natya shastra* was the dancers' bible. These ancient forms stylize the dances of India and the East today.

Whereas Eastern dance is basically focused on contemplation and idolization of god, Western dances, from the Renaissance period, moved away from their religious roots. Because the church during the Middle Ages embraced the gnostic belief that everything connected with the flesh was evil, people did not use the body and the dance to express the beliefs of the church. They did, nonetheless, dance; and their dance focused upon "the causes of man's [sic] inner conflicts in their relation to the world, but mainly as they reflect his being" (Ibid., 50).

Western dances became dramatic, conquering space, much in contrast to Eastern dancing. It is impossible for us to say one style of folk dance is right and another wrong or even to evaluate better or worse. All styles arose out of the inner need to express the nation's beliefs or feelings in dance.

Because culture, art, and the dance of the folk reflect the beliefs of humans, these are subject to change as their beliefs change. For example, as human knowledge grew in the area of agriculture, people relied proportionately less upon harvest dance rituals. As their understanding of principles that ensured success increased, some aspects of the basic drive that created the folk dances faded into the background. In most areas of the world folk dances have undergone extensive changes as history has developed around them.

As the English scholar Douglas Kennedy pointed out, when primitive religion weakens, some of the mystery and the magic departs from the dances that express it. The dancer becomes less a medicine maker than a performing artist as ritual changes imperceptibly into art. In short, man's social adjustment to the environment, for purposes of survival, created both the original dance rituals and their subsequent functional or formal changes. (*Encyclopedia Britannica,* Book 7 [1976 ed.], 499)

No form of dance is permanent; only the basic principle of dance is enduring. Dancing falls into two major categories. John Martin describes these categories as

that which is done for the emotional release of the individual dancers, without regard to the possible interest of a spectator; and that, on the other hand, which is done for the enjoyment of the spectator either as an exhibition of skill, the telling of a story, the presentation of pleasurable designs, or the communication of emotional experience. The second category is largely an outgrowth of the first, but both play important parts in the picture as a whole. (Martin, *Book of the Dance,* 18)

As folk dance evolves to become an art or theater dance, the life spring from which the dance originated begins to dry up. Unless the choreographer or the dance participants research the roots and experiences which precipitated the dances, the steps begin to communicate the dancer's skills more than the folklore. Artistic dancing also departs from folk dancing because the pleasure or entertainment of the spectator demands theatrical and choreographic enhancements. Repetitious and simplistic folk steps must be augmented and aggrandized to avoid boring the audience as well as to challenge the dancer. Dress of the common folk lacks the embellishments and visual stimulation to evoke an emotional response from the viewer; therefore, color and sparkles are added to ameliorate the original.

It could be maintained that when folklore leaves its immediate environment or place of origin, it must of necessity lose its character. Through breathing the air of a world of make-believe, it is tempted by the artificial and spectacular. How to preserve its basic characteristics, its rudimentary powers, its emotional impact while shifting from the healthy joy of participation in a folk dance to the pleasurable edification of viewing it as a spectator may depend on the innate theatricality of the material. Also of importance is the skill of the choreographer in finding a happy balance between being inspired by a

source he uses without imitating it and keeping intact that source which inspires imagination. However useful the theater dance may be in serving and preserving the folk dance—theater always claims victims and crowns its victors—folk dance will remain a life-giving force. (Sorell, *Dance Through the Ages,* 87)

Losing the origin and inspiration of the folk dance is problematic for the common folk as well as for the professionals. Distanced by time and environment, dancers look backward at tradition instead of inward at creation. Steps that were once spontaneous and alive can become mechanical and stagnant because of superficial repetition. When this happens, the dance of the folk renews itself.

In every barren period, accordingly, rebels arise who break through the entrenched traditionalism and set up fresh currents to replace it. No form is permanent, definitive, ultimate; only the basic principle of dance is enduring, and out of it, like the cycle of nature itself, rises an endless succession of new springs out of old winters. (Martin, *Book of the Dance,* 16)

Note the insight of John Martin:

It is a cycle that must inevitably continue, for recreational dancing, done solely for the sake of providing the dancer with a release for his inner compulsions, no longer serves its purpose when that release is denied. No matter how pretty a dance may be to watch, unless it gives something to the dancer it is doomed. (Ibid., p. 24)

The *Encyclopedia Britannica* well summarizes this evolution of folk dance:

If a dance does not die of old age, of having totally outworn its function and of having a form or spirit out of tune with a new age, it will continue to gain new life from improvised variations on basic steps or ground plans or from conscious elaborations of its forms by professional directors of ethnic dance groups and programs. Such kinds of creativity, individual and group, contribute to that constant cycle of orderly change within traditional parameters which accounts for the rich variety of the dances of the people.

Although the origins of many traditional dances are lost in a nebulous past, the folk arts are represented in the social organizations of people throughout the world. Numerous troupes exist, from professionals like Ballet Folklorico de Mexico under the direction of Amalia Hernandez, to local groups who gather for good fellowship, healthful exercise, and, to some measure, ethnic unity. An outstanding example of revitalization of traditional dance structures by present day choreographers can be seen in modern Israeli dance. Today's folk dance movement in Israel began its unified growth in 1944, when, with the backing of the Inter-kibbutzim Music Committee, the first folk dance meeting was held at Kibbutz Dalia. Under the direction of Gurit Kadman, founder of the Folk Dance Movement, 200 dancers gathered at Kiryat Machon, also known as Dance Village. On the second night, 3,500 people gathered to watch the first Israeli folk dance performance. The dances were a potpourri of styles, many without any Israeli quality. That first event began a new creative process that was felt in every village, settlement, kibbutz, and city group. The various cultural patterns of the races, who were now the essence of Israel's population, were to meld into a pleasing and unique style.

Israeli folk dance has gained wide acceptance and popularity throughout the nation of Israel, in Jewish cultural centers across the world, and in dance clubs in many major cities. Folk dances are being choreographed by leaders such as Yankele Levy, Ruth Goodman Burger, Shlomo Bachar, Dani Dassa, Shmulik Gov-ari, Shlomo Maman, Rivkah Sturman, Gurit Kadman, and many others.

Israeli folk dances are being incorporated in many of the Christian churches, which are actively restoring the arts in their worship patterns. There are several predominant reasons why Israeli folk dance is receiving more popular acceptance than the folk dances of other countries. Some Christians seek to establish a natural link with Israel through such things as tours to the Holy Land, celebrating Hebraic holidays, and dancing Israeli folk dances. The proliferation of dances and the accessibility of training has made Israeli folk dance a ready source of material. Also, the styles of dances (i.e., the Yemenite with its soft undulating movement of the whole body) are easily adapted to praise dancing. However, there is no biblical reason to utilize Israeli folk dance over other ethnic dances, especially since popular Israeli dances are of recent origin and not authentically ancient Davidic-style dance.

Because folk dance is the dance of the people of a given region and because folk dance degenerates when removed from its place of origin, Christian churches which embrace Israeli folk dance or the style of any other nation will find difficulty in maintaining the deep roots or heart of the dance. Therefore, it is reasonable to assume that the learned steps and patterns of any style of folk dance will become a vehicle of expression of the heart of the new ethnic, the holy nation of the church (1 Peter 2:9). Whether the style of dance utilized in Christian worship is classic ballet, modern dance, Israeli folk, or a combination of many styles, the life spring must be the dancers' encounter with God.

There are many benefits to incorporating folk dance into the repertoire of a church dance program. Because folk dance is designed to be danced by the common people, the basic steps can often be executed without years of intense training. Hence, more people can become participants. The more people who can share in the corporate worship expressions, whether they be singing, recitation, giving, or dancing, the greater the unity and sense of community.

One example of a church that has effectively adopted the use of folk dance is Son-Life Church in Collinsville, Illinois. They have incorporated approximately 50 Israeli folk dances into the training program of their dance troupe and their Christian school. These dances serve several functions. Learning the combination of steps and perfecting the styles becomes an excellent training tool for developing the skills of both children and adults who desire to function in the dance ministry. The dances themselves are easily adaptable to many modern day praise choruses. Therefore, the dance team can dance to a large number of songs throughout the worship services by making small modifications and adjustments to the set menu of dances. This eliminates the enormous work load of choreographing and remembering a new dance for each new song assimilated into the treasury of an assembly's psalms, hymns, and spiritual songs.

Folk dancing can enhance the spirit of rejoicing during congregational worship. Simple dances or even single steps, such as the Israeli *hora* or *grapevine,* can be easily taught to all members of the congregation who wish to participate. Children and the senior citizens can praise God together in the dance. Especially in this form does the spirit of folk dance, the emotional release of the dancer in response to his or her environment, remain alive.

Because it is composed of every kindred, tongue,

people, and nation, the church is an ideal environment to incorporate folk dances from many nations. It is important to note that each particular style helps to define the application and extent of utility the folk dance affords the church. For example, the vigorous hip movements of the island dances or the gymnastic exploits of some Russian folk movements may be inappropriate for application into praise or worship. However, the lovely hand motions of Hawaiian dance or the vigorous foot stomping and kicks of the Russian style could be utilized to reflect the mood of a song, especially one arranged to represent a particular style or ethnic sound. The more education the dancers and the whole church assembly can receive concerning the use of any style folk dance, the greater will be the appreciation for and sense of common heritage with that ethnic group.

Caution arises when embracing dances whose origins are temple worship. Although, as we have seen, the primitive beginnings of most folk dances were of a religious function, the dances of the Eastern world have a more current cult tie than do the folk dances of the Western hemisphere. Prudence and discrimination are advisable.

Transported into Christian worship, folk dance is placed into a new environment. Executed by Christian participants, the various folk dance patterns and movements are now expressing new inspirations, not the beliefs of their ritual origins. The dances will, of necessity, lose their ethnic heritage or folklore and reflect a new ethnic group, the church. As the church worships and receives inspiration from the heavenly realm, she will recreate her art, including dance, to reflect God's glory. Whether the style is Israeli, Russian, German, or Latin-American, the folk are Christians and their lore is redemption. That must be the life spring of the church as she dances.

Patti Amsden

364 • INTRODUCING DANCE IN THE LOCAL CHURCH

This article gives practical guidance for introducing movement into congregational worship for the first time.

Congregations who have had no experience in dance are willing to enter into congregational movement and dance if they are introduced to it properly.

With a greater emphasis being placed today on the physical body and with our increased time for

Guitar. _The guitar has become a significant instrument for leading contemporary worship._

leisure, there is an open opportunity to portray through dance a positive Christian standard of bodily expression. But care and skill need to be used so that this new and sometimes controversial experience is a helpful and positive one. Our bodies are amazing creations; they should not, on the one hand, be flaunted as sexual objects, nor, on the other, be ignored, despised, or neglected. They should be celebrated and cared for as part of all that we are as we live out our life for God and others.

My vision is to see churches with congregations free enough to express their worship and fellowship in movement; where there is a warmth and joy in being able to join hands as a congregation or march together around the church; where new church buildings are designed with space for movement; where dance groups are encouraged in the same way as singing groups.

The Possibilities

Dance and movement have been accepted with enthusiasm by some congregations. Others see their introduction as new and suspect, often not realizing the long tradition they have in Jewish and Christian history. Their acceptance in the church has ebbed and flowed throughout history but has been gathering momentum in this century. For a while, predominantly in the eighteenth and nineteenth centuries, dance almost totally disappeared, surviving only in isolated pockets and in a few accepted movements in the Eucharist and other liturgies.

Dance in biblical times was primarily a communal expression of rejoicing and worship. In congregations today it may also help the ministry of the church in such areas as intercession and prophecy, healing, teaching, and evangelism. The expression may be simple movements to songs and prayers that people in the congregation can do during worship or in the privacy of their own homes. Or it may be a community dance. It could also be presentations done by a specialist group as part of the ongoing worship and teaching of the church or as an outreach to the wider community.

A Language Without Words

Movement is a language that can speak without words. It can either reinforce or detract from the words we speak. A slumped body, a clenched fist or a hand reached out to touch can say as much or more as any spoken words. The postures used in the Bible for prayer and worship—bowing, kneeling and standing with hands raised—are still widely used today and can express to God our love, reverence and humility. These movements are mentioned in many of our songs and hymns. It can be helpful to encourage people to use such expressions rather than merely singing "bow down before him" or "we lift up our hands" without any movement.

Movement can also help us to be still. We need a balance between action and rest, between doing and being, between giving and receiving. Jesus commended Mary for sitting and listening because Martha's service, though well-intentioned, was distracting her from listening to what Jesus had to say (Luke 10:38-42). But just quieting our bodies is not always enough—wandering thoughts and anxieties can still be running around in our minds, preventing us from hearing. Simple rhythmic movements or the use of prayer gestures and postures may help to slow our minds down and center our thoughts without sending us to sleep, and so bring us to the point of being able to listen and commune with God.

The word *worship,* used in its broadest sense, refers to our attitude of service. It is the honor and love we offer to the Lord in all that we do. It can also be used to refer to the expression of awe, reverent homage, and adoration in our times of public and private prayer.

As we worship, we begin to enter into a deeper awareness of God's presence, offering ourselves, our awe, devotion, and adoration to him in a more intimate and quiet way.

Movement was an integral part of worship in biblical times. Many different movements were encouraged in the expression of worship. For example, in the Psalms we read:

- Come, let us worship and bow down; let us kneel before the Lord our Maker (Ps. 95:6).
- Lift up your hands in the sanctuary and bless the Lord (Ps. 134:2).
- O clap your hands, all peoples; shout to God with the voice of joy (Ps. 47:1).
- The singers went on, the musicians after them, in the midst of the maidens beating tambourines (Ps. 68:25).
- Let them praise his name with dancing; let them sing praises to him with timbrel and lyre. For the Lord takes pleasure in his people (Ps. 149:3-4).

There has been a surge of interest in the dance and other arts over the last few years among Christians and much of it, I believe, has been inspired by God.

Dance and prayer movements can be meaningful and symbolic ways of expressing worship with everything that we are—our hearts, minds, souls and strength (Mark 12:30). We are encouraged in Scripture to use our strength and activity as well as our words and stillness, presenting our bodies as living sacrifices (Rom. 12:1).

Introducing Movement and Dance

When starting to introduce more movement to a congregation, it is a good idea to bring to people's attention the meaning of the movements they already do. Encourage them to move with more of an awareness of what they are doing to help make it a real part of their prayer and praise.

As you explain their need to move towards God with their whole being, also explain that there are times they need to be still and allow God to move towards them. Movement can help to bring us to an inner quietness and concentration. The movement artist, aware of the importance of both, can effectively lead the congregation in stillness as well as movement.

---------- **Before the Service** ----------

In planning to lead the congregation in movement, it is helpful to keep the following points in mind. To avoid introducing too many new things at once, use already well-known or easy hymns, choruses, or spoken words. If you feel you need to use a new song, introduce it two or three weeks before you plan to lead the movement participation.

- Choose movements that are meaningful to people's lives.
- Remember those who are older or physically handicapped and either make the movements ones they can manage or suggest adaptations.
- Try out the movements and the explanation on one or two other people or in a small group to check for meaningfulness and clarity.
- Make sure you consult whoever is leading the service to coordinate when and how the participation will take place.

---------- **In the Service** ----------

- Explain to the congregation that this is a way of offering to God their whole selves—body, mind and spirit—and give some passages from Scripture as support.
- It may also be appropriate to mention the history of movement in the church, explaining, for example, that many of the choruses in seventeenth-century carols and hymns were danced.
- Present the movements and explanation simply and prayerfully with enthusiasm and assurance. People need to feel confident about what you are asking them to do.
- Give the meaning of the movements, using Scripture where appropriate, so that people are motivated to worship through them and so the movements are not perceived as being in the same realm as actions in children's songs. For this reason, it is better to use the word *movement* rather than *action*. The explanation will also help people enter into the worship more fully rather than feel embarrassed.
- Each movement needs to be "performed" as you show it, so people can see and feel what it

means to you and begin to enter into the feeling and focus of the movement for themselves.
- Remember in demonstrating that you need to mirror the congregation. If they are to move right, you will need to move left.
- Invite and encourage people to participate, but don't force them to or make them feel awkward if they don't want to. Here is an example of an introduction the movement leader might give:

> I'd like to invite your to worship God in the next song with simple movement as well as with your hearts, minds, and voices. God created us body and spirit, and Jesus tells us to love God with all our heart, mind, soul, and strength. So let's offer our whole selves to him this morning. As the psalmist says in Psalm 149, "Let Israel be glad in his Maker . . . for the Lord takes pleasure in His people." This may be something new for you. Many people immediately find a new release and meaning in their worship as they express it in movement. Others feel self-conscious and awkward at first. But I encourage you to try it. Paul says in Romans 12:1, "I urge you therefore, brethren, by the mercies of God, to present your bodies a living and holy sacrifice, acceptable to God, which is your spiritual service of worship." Your sacrifice of worship this morning will be pleasing to God.

---------- **Understand Resistance** ----------

Not everyone will immediately warm to the thought of participating in movements, and it is important to understand the points of resistance that may consciously or unconsciously hinder people from joining in wholeheartedly.

This possible resistance increases the importance of adequate teaching along with the participation. You must encourage people that using movement in worship is very biblical, that it has a long history in the church, and that it can be a very positive experience for most if they give themselves the chance to try it and get used to it.

Mary Jones[108]

365 ✦ Dances for the Seasons of the Christian Year

The seasons and feasts of the church year offer numerous possibilities for congregational movement and choreographed dance. Significant dimensions of these celebrations are best experienced through such action.

The liturgical celebrations during the seasons provide variety, color, texture, emotion, and richness of theme to what would be a rather unexciting "ordinary time." Each season has its own particular symbols as well as those that are part of the ritual throughout the year, such as bread and wine, water, and oil. In Advent, the symbols are darkness and light; at Christmas, light and birth, evergreens, and angelic choirs; in Lent, ashes and palms; in Easter, water, light, oil, flowers, and signs of new life; at Pentecost, fire, wind, and dancing people. There is a dramatic sequence to the events of the year that call forth special ritual response in symbolic moments. These "moments" are most often built into the rituals of the year, such as the Easter vigil. The problem that often arises, however, is that somehow these symbols are blurred and do not speak clearly. Many persons who have used liturgically danced prayer have discovered that gestures, movements, and dances in some form can indeed make the symbols of the seasons "come alive" and "speak" to the assembly. Because these celebrations are so special, they demand a special attention to the symbols and the way in which these symbols are allowed to communicate. Dancers in the liturgy serve as "symbol-bearers"; the first and foremost symbol being the human body itself . . . a body that is called to be the place of divine and human interaction. A look at some of these seasonal celebrations can yield specific suggestions to make them expressive of the human desire to communicate with God and God's desire to speak an incarnational language.

Advent and Christmas

"The people who walked in darkness have seen a great light" (Isa. 8). The primary symbols of the Advent season are darkness and light. It is a season of expectation and hope that is expressed in the flickering lights of candles glowing in the darkness and the enduring hope captured in the symbol of the "Advent wreath," a circle of evergreens, claiming a promise soon to be fulfilled and a longing that will never die.

A traditional song of the Advent season is "O come, O Come Emmanuel." It has been the source of many Advent processionals. What I would suggest is a simple walking pattern with a pause or

lunge on the "Rejoice! Rejoice!" section of the song. What can make the processional beautiful and interesting, however, is the movement of the lights. This can be done holding the candles in both hands or one, moving them in a clockwise or counterclockwise direction. With the Advent wreath carried in the middle of the processioners, the effect of the lights dancing around the wreath is created. Once one verse is established in its movement, a simple choreographic device can be used in geometric patterns that change the visual perception (do not, however, confuse the dancers by adding extra "steps"). The basic pattern can be done around the altar in a circle or using diagonal lines through the celebration space. Even the most inexperienced choreographer can devise an interesting processional movement with a simple walking base, some upper arm/body movements, and the use of geometric patterns. This procession of lights for the Advent season can be an effective and solemn way to engage the assembly in the symbols of light and darkness. An advantage is that this does not demand trained dancers; it can be done by most members of the community who are willing to learn and practice.

Many of the readings during the Advent season speak of God's glory. Another effective use of the symbol of light would be to keep the electric lights extinguished even after the opening processional. As the liturgy of the Word continues, a few more candles are lit. The *Alleluia* proclamation could then become a dance of lights around the gospel book. This would bring to expression the Word as light in the lives of the faithful people: "your Word is a lantern." There is a beautiful *Alleluia* setting in Peloquin's "Lord of Life" that is solemn, reverential, and very suitable to the theme of the Word incarnate in the Advent season. Again, there could be a simple movement of the feet, a basic walking pattern, with more movement of lifting, lowering, turning, and passing the light as it shines on the gospel book.

All through the liturgy, during the preparation of gifts, the creed, and so on, more lights could be lit. The gradual impression of light building can be an effective means of having the assembly "come alive" to the light. By the conclusion of the liturgy the space would be ablaze with light. At this point, as a closing expression of faith, the song "City of God" from the St. Louis Jesuits' *Lord of Light* could be sung and danced. The lyrics speak of the light in the darkness, our tears turned into dancing, and other appropriate expressions of the Advent season. Depending upon the assembly, space, and time of preparation, this could be danced by those trained in the community or be simplified as a congregational dance given the requirements of space, time for preparation, and openness to this kind of communal prayer expression. If it is impossible with the assembly, it is possible to use a simple, but lively dance in a triple meter that many could do with willingness and preparation. This closing song and dance would express the primary symbol of a people who share their faith, their hope, their love, and their desire to "build the city of God."

—— Alternative Advent Suggestions ——

First Sunday—Year A. Begin the liturgy with the proclamation of the first reading, Isaiah 2:1-5. The image is walking together in the light of the Lord, streaming toward God's holy mountain. Immediately following the proclamation (ideally done in some other gathering place) the whole assembly or selected members and ministers would "go up with joy to the house of the Lord." Carrying the symbols of the season, the procession would in fact *do* what the first reading and psalm are speaking about: a joyful journey in faith and hope. A simple tripudium step; three forward one back could be the basis of this easy, rhythmic procession. Another new addition to the musical repertory is Peloquin's "Let us Go Rejoicing" from his *Songs of Israel II*.

Third Sunday—Years A and C. There are certain readings that are meant to be simply "listened" to and reflected on. There are others, however, that can vividly be "expressed" through mime, drama, or dance. There is something about certain readings that calls for an appropriate visualization as well as a clear proclamation. In the third Sunday of Advent, the theme of rejoicing is most explicit. In Isaiah 35:1-6 and Zephaniah 3:14-18, the readings use images of physical exultation, of life-giving expression. These readings could be "interpreted" by competent members of the community who have some training and background in mime or dance. The important caution, however, is that it not be a *literal* interpretation, using gestures or movements that say the same thing as the verbal text. The idea of this kind of interpretation is to capture the underlying emotions and conflicts and give them life through the movement. It is not to "picture" or "act out" what the words are saying. Its purpose is to enliven

the spirit, not to burden it with repetitive images. The difficulty is that this kind of interpretation demands much planning and work with the reader of the text. Because there is no musical support, the rhythm of the language and the dancer's body have to mesh into an expressive unity. This is a most difficult liturgical dance and yet it seems to be a frequent addition to liturgies. Anyone who feels "moved by the spirit" comes forward to "interpret" the reading or the psalm. Such movement can be a distraction to the community. Because this interpretation demands so much coordination, it demands sufficient preparation to enable the movement to speak its own language and not be imitative of the verbal language.

Isaiah 35, for example, describes very clear and precise images: the desert blooming, feeble hands, weak knees, eyes of the blind opened, ears of the deaf cleared. The literal way of presenting this reading would be an attempt to find nonverbal images that correspond to the verbal images. One would be at pains to find explicit images for blindness, deafness, or weak knees. It is better to leave this to the imagination of the listener. An alternative is for two dancers to reveal the underlying expectation, excitement, and miraculous joy that stems from the experience of God's transformation. The challenge is to bring alive the emotional content of the reading and bring that to expression for those who are hearing and feeling that excitement. Meeting the challenge with this kind of liturgical movement is rewarding if it is done well. It enables the living Word to come to life.

First Sunday—Year B. The first reading of this liturgy, Isaiah 63, has been set to music by the St. Louis Jesuits ("Redeemer Lord," *Lord of Light*). The driving rhythms, and the musical dissonance make this a very interesting piece of danceable liturgical music. (Often the unchanging rhythms of much liturgical music do not aid the dynamics of dance.) Through music and movement the Isaiah passage could be effectively communicated.

The climax of the Advent season is the celebration of the birth of Christ, the Incarnation. On this feast, it is especially appropriate to "incarnate" the church's liturgy through movement prayer. Christmas is a season of wonder. The liturgy of this season needs to capture this sense of wonder, especially as it is embodied in the lives of children.

The *Directory for Masses with Children* encourages, "the development of gestures, postures, and actions . . . in view of the nature of the liturgy as an activity of the entire man and in view of the psychology of children" (33). It goes on to say that

> the processional entrance of the children with the priest may help them to experience a sense of the communion that is thus constituted. The participation of at least some of the children in the procession with the book of the gospels makes clear the presence of Christ who announces his word to the people The procession of children with the chalice and gifts expresses clearly the value and meaning of the presentation of gifts. The communion procession, if properly arranged, helps greatly to develop the piety of children. (34)

The liturgy of Christmas should embrace these instructions and let the children give expression to their wonder in specific shape and form. There are numerous Christmas carols that can be used in procession. The story of Christmas can be told through different carols with the children dancing or miming. The origin of the carol is rooted in dance forms that were used in conjunction with the music. The Christmas liturgy would be an excellent opportunity to use the musical settings designed for children, such as Peloquin's "Unless You Become." This work affords many opportunities for movement acclamation, especially during the *Alleluia* and Eucharistic prayer.

The Advent/Christmas season is rich with symbols of hope, of longing, of wonder and promise. In the liturgies of this season, gesture, movement, and dance can incarnate what is hoped for and what has already been fulfilled in the coming of Christ.

——————— Lent ———————

The Lenten season has its own richness of symbolic expression beginning with the celebration of ashes and culminating with the powerful symbols of Holy Week. It is a season in the church's liturgy that allows the experience of the life, death, and resurrection of Jesus to be remembered in the lives of the assembled faithful. It is most important during this season that the assembly be engaged in embodied prayer so that it may experience its unique participation in the Easter event. The renewed place of the catechumenate during this season has been helpful in letting the assembly claim the process of conversion as its own. The following are some suggestions for the involvement of the whole assembly as well as specific examples of dance during the Lenten/Easter season. It is a time of penitence, journeying, growth in self-knowledge, a time to deepen one's knowledge of the person of Jesus, especially in his humanity, a time to celebrate the ultimate victory of life over death. It is a time to dance.

Ash Wednesday. This day that begins the Lenten season has the power of linking the past and looking forward to the future. The symbols are strong and clear. It is important that people see the burning of last year's palms so that there is a link with the past experience of Lenten conversion. (The cyclic nature of human ritual needs to be brought out more clearly.) Bread and wine should be seen and tasted as food for the journey. If possible, the signing with ashes should be done by members of the assembly to each other so that the symbol may be touched, felt, and seen. The liturgy can begin with proclamation of Joel's "call to repentance" from within the assembly. The presider enters in silent procession and prostrates himself before the assembly. The members of the assembly kneel to express their need for conversion and repentance. There is time for silent prayer. On rising, the presider invites the community to further reflection and all sing a selection such as "Grant to us, O Lord" by Lucien Deiss. Following the homily and silent reflection, the presider burns some palm, blesses the ashes, and invites members of the assembly to sign each other as a beginning symbol of solidarity with the Lord and with each other during this Lenten journey. At some point in the liturgy, a single member of the assembly could dance to "Be Not Afraid" as an expression of hope and trust during the Lenten season. People can be drawn more deeply into the truth and beauty of the words of this song and the shared human experience they articulate.

The Sundays of Lent. The Liturgy of the Word during the Lenten season offers many opportunities for creative proclamation. The long gospels of John during Cycle A can be communicated through drama, mime, or dance. A model of this kind of presentation is given in the work of the Fountain Square Fools. This group of professional actors, mimes, and dancers has integrated the gospel story with imagination, energy, and conviction. The group's portrayal of the parable of the Prodigal is exceptionally powerful.

The following are some suggestions for dance in the Sundays of Lent:

- **1st Sunday**: The theme in all cycles is the temptation of Jesus in the desert. The song, "Jesus the Lord," can be used as a response to the gospel reading. The slow, reflective antiphon repeated four times can lead the assembly into a simple gesture prayer. The music breathes the name Jesus and the gestures/movement should be an extension of the rhythmic pulse set up by the breathing in and out on the name "Jesus." (It is important for those who design the movements for the assembly to explore all the possibilities of raising and lowering the hand and arms, so that all gestures do not look and feel alike.)

- **2nd Sunday**: The theme in all cycles is the Transfiguration. Michael Joncas's "On Eagle's Wings" captures the spirit of this theme of transformation, light, and special protection. This particular piece of music with its intricate rhythms demands a certain expertise of the dancers who perform it. If the movement is to be faithful to the form and intent of the musical composition, it is important that the choreographer recognize the complexity of the music and not trivialize it with a too basic movement. The choreography for this piece in the repertoire of the Boston Liturgical Dance Ensemble, for example, includes arabesques on half-pointe, en penche, Soutenu turns, attitudes en promenade, and reverses. These movements are visible to the assembly but need trained dancers to execute them.

- **3rd Sunday**: In cycle A, the gospel is the woman at the well and the liturgy has a strong baptismal theme. John Foley's "Come to the Water" can be an effective response to the Liturgy of the Word and a bridge to the Liturgy of the Eucharist. In a liturgy at St. James Cathedral in Brooklyn, New York, the Boston Liturgical Dance Ensemble danced with members of the assembly who had been trained the day before. A white cloth twenty yards long was drawn through the building by twenty dancers. Working the cloth in an undulating motion, the dancers gave the impression of water flowing, enveloping the assembly with the symbol. Two dancers near the altar danced more complex movements. The cloth was drawn over them and then placed on the altar to become the altar cloth. The two dancers the presented the gifts to the presider and the liturgy continued.

The variety of themes during this season afford many more opportunities for nonverbal expressions. The theme of forgiveness and reconciliation can be embodied through gestures of healing, through enacting the gospel stories of reunion, through expressing the affective dimension of reconciliation in the psalms of the season (Ps. 23, 130, 137, 51, 34). The musical settings of these psalms vary in style and will effect the movement interpretation. Certain musical forms are more conducive to the necessary tension within dance composition. Many of the psalm settings of Peloquin, for example, have a musical tension that elicits an expressive movement response.

Holy Week

Holy Week is clearly the high point of the church's liturgical year. The celebration of the life, death, and resurrection of Jesus demands a liturgy rich in word and action, mood and symbol. The Holy Week liturgies need to involve the whole person in prayer. The reality of Passover is incarnated in bodies that move. This movement emerges naturally from the existing ritual and does not have to be superimposed upon it. The following are examples of places in the ritual that call for "embodiment."

Passion Sunday. _Procession with Palms:_ (a) the whole community gathers outside the building and enters in procession carrying the palms; (b) with the community already assembled, dancers carrying royal palms enter in rhythmic procession to "All Glory, Laud, and Honor." The procession uses a simple walking base, punctuated by lunges. The dancers open and close the palms, turn and reach with them. The royal palms have a majesty that conveys the solemnity of the occasion.

Proclamation of the Passion: There have been many different approaches to dramatic presentations of the Passion. One effective presentation that has been used employs a combination of dramatic reading and mime. A long purple cloth is used as the unifying symbol throughout. It functions as the cloth of the Last Supper and delineates the different places: the garden, the house of Annas, Pilate's palace. It becomes the cloth thrown over Jesus, the cross itself, and then the burial cloth. The narrative is read by trained lectors and the dance/mime is done by dancers and actors. This particular rendering of the Passion has engaged the assembly with the powerful emotion, even though they did not "do" anything.

The Assembly's Acclamations: The original Palm Sunday event had people in the streets of Jerusalem acclaiming Jesus as King. During the acclamations of the eucharistic prayer, the assembly should be invited to raise their arms with palms in hand, waving them with the words, "Hosanna in the highest, blessed is he who comes in the name of the Lord," and at other points of acclamation.

Holy Thursday. *Washing of Feet:* An important gesture embodying the gospel which precedes it. This is a case where form and content are inextricably bound. The command of Jesus to "love one another" is tied to a specific symbol of service. This sign should not be neglected for the sake of convenience or speed. It is also important that it be done in such a way that it is a visible sign to the whole assembly.

Preparation of Gifts: The symbols of bread and wine should be given an even greater emphasis on this night. A more elaborate procession may be called for. The symbols must be clearly visible and genuine; bread that is baked by someone in the community, wine held in a lovely carafe.

Transfer of the Eucharist: A simple but powerful movement that can engage people in reverence and prayer.

Stripping the Altar: This silent ritual has an extraordinary psychological effect on people. It can be a striking prelude to the experience of Good Friday.

Good Friday. *Prostration:* Prostration is an important gesture of penance, humility and dependence. The silent procession and the prostration is a stark beginning to the Good Friday liturgy.

Orations: "Let us kneel. Let us stand." The Good Friday liturgy tries to involve the assembly in postures that embody reverence and respect for the solemnity of the celebration. The community should take time to kneel in silent prayer so that the movement "kneel-stand" is expressive of an attitude of reverence and respect rather than an empty gesture of inconvenient effort.

Veneration of the Cross: A movement that involves the whole assembly in procession and praise. It affords the opportunity to express an attitude of loving reverence not only for Jesus' sacrifice but for

all of life which is embraced by the symbol of the cross.

Easter Vigil

On this night the church uses all of its basic symbols to allow a rich experience of new life and hope. The elements of fire, water, bread, and wine become the sacramental manifestation of the presence of God. The form and structure of the celebration, from the lighting of the new fire, the procession of light, the proclamation of the exalted, the stories of God's activity in the world, the baptismal event, to the new Passover meal that is shared, proclaim the single most important affirmation of the Christian faith. "He is risen. *Alleluia!*" All of the symbolic elements of this ritual are involved in this proclamation. That is why it is so important on this night to allow the symbols to speak. The following are some suggestions for an effective ritual:

Lighting of the Fire: If feasible, begin outside so that all can see the fire. The procession should only begin when all have their candles lit. The final acclamation should be intoned only when all have assembled in the celebration space. During the "Exsultet," candles should be kept burning. The lights (electric) should be left off until the *Gloria.*

Liturgy of the Word: In darkness, except for the light of the paschal candle and any light necessary for the lector, the readings are proclaimed. For the Genesis reading, six lectors are stationed throughout the church, each with an unlit candle. As the story of creation begins, a dancer comes to the paschal candle and draws the light from the candle. He or she then goes to the next reader bringing the light. At the end of the seven days there are seven lights symbolizing the creation. The positions of these readers around the perimeter of the space can create the impression of being surrounded by creation.

Gloria: Out of the darkness comes a dancing people! As the final response to the Ezekiel reading is being sung, all the candles are lit again. As the *Gloria* is intoned, the first image the assembly has is women and men dressed in white and gold, dancing to this song of praise.

Alleluia: The first *Alleluia* of the Easter season should be embodied in a joyful dance around the gospel book. This could be done as a procession with the book or as a special incensation with dancers moving around the book, carrying bowls of incense.

The entire liturgy of Easter cries out for the full participation of the assembly. In the baptismal and Communion rites that follow the proclamation of the Word, the people should be engaged by the symbols in the acclamation: "Christ has died, Christ is risen, Christ will come again! Alleluia!" It is the task of those working with movement and gesture in liturgy to continue to find suitable ways to make the Easter event come to life.

Pentecost

Pentecost gives another opportunity to ritualize the Easter event, but where the focus of Easter is the proclamation "Jesus is risen," the focus of Pentecost is "Where are God's people?" This is the celebration of a people filled with the Spirit of God. It is an appropriate time for dance as an expression of the joy, the ecstasy, and the liveliness of the Spirit. There are a number of musical settings appropriate for a festive opening procession. Peloquin's, "Lord, Send Out Your Spirit," The Monks of the Weston Priory's "Spirit Alive," and Peloquin's "Praise to the Lord" have all been used by the Boston Liturgical Dance Ensemble as opening processionals to enliven the celebration space on this special feast. In these pieces, red material is used to suggest the tongues of fire and capture the breath, vitality, and dynamic movement of the first Pentecost.

There are many other celebrations during the year that can call for a special use of dance. Two that have been exceptionally effective for me have been a baccalaureate and a wedding. In the baccalaureate liturgy at Boston College, which takes place every year in a sports complex, the dance brings a visual beauty and focus to the celebration that it would lack without it. In alternative spaces for liturgy that are used for very large groups (convention center, stadium) the "secular" can be transformed into the "sacred" through movement and color that provides beauty and graciousness. In the Boston College baccalaureate, the most successful use of dance has been with Peloquin's _Lyric Liturgy_ and his _Lord of Life_.

This particular wedding ritual had a special meaning since the bride and groom were both dancers and dance had become the way in which they expressed their faith. Their friends, other dancers, carried floral arches in procession that could be brought together to make a bridal arch, combined to form the symbol of the ring or simply make a beautiful visual pattern in the front of the space.

After the exchange of vows, the dancers returned with the floral arches, dancing to Laetitia Blain's _Song of Meeting,_ surrounding the newly married couple, finally creating a floral canopy over their heads. Since this was a special dance liturgy, in which the medium of dance was the primary mode of communication, there were many points in the liturgy that were danced. During the water rite the dancers passed flowers to all in the assembly. The responsorial psalm, Michael Joncas's "I Have Loved You," was danced as was his "Praise His Name" for the gospel acclamation. The bride and groom led the assembly in gesture prayer to a chanted "Our Father." The communion meditation, "Be Not Afraid," was danced as was the closing hymn "Ode to Joy" (with special wedding lyrics). The entire ritual was a beautifully effective realization of the power of dance to communicate as a symbol in liturgy. Although it may seem to one who has only heard the ritual described that there was "too much" dance, the experience of the people who were present was not that at all. Because of who the couple was, and given the integration of the dances into the flow of the ritual and the participation of the whole assembly in spirit and body, it was a ritual that communicated what it intended, namely, the love of two people as a sign of new life in the church.

A renewed sense of the place of dance in liturgy is a sign of life for many in the church. For others, it is a threatening manifestation of disintegration of standards and morals. Many will continue to fight vigorously against its inclusion as a valid means of religious expression in liturgical worship. If there is to be a meaningful dialogue between those who approve and those who disapprove, there must be an openness to learn from each other's perceptions and experiences, but in the last analysis people must be able to worship their God in ways that honestly express their faith. _Environment and Art in Catholic Worship_ says:

> Christians have not hesitated to use every human art in their celebration of the saving work of God in Jesus Christ, although in every historical period they have been influenced, at times inhibited, by cultural circumstances. In the resurrection of the Lord, all things are made new. Wholeness and healthiness are restored, because the reign of sin and death is conquered. Human limits are still real and we must be conscious of them. But we must also praise God and give God thanks with the human means we have

available. God does not need liturgy; people do, and people have only their own arts and styles of expression with which to celebrate.

Robert Ver Eecke[109]

366 ♦ FIVE TYPES OF DANCE IN WORSHIP

Below are five different types of supportive dance that can be used in worship. They are not to be seen as performance dances because they do not stand outside of the liturgy. Rather, they are "liturgical" because they express what is happening in worship.

——— 1. Processional Dance ———

The processional dance can be used at the gathering, as an accompaniment to the reading of the gospel, at the presentation of the gifts of bread and wine, and at the closing of the service. Thomas Kane summarizes these dances as follows:

	Function	Source Material
1. Entrance or gathering	gathers the community opens the celebration sets the theme accompanies the minister to the celebration space	sung or instrumental music
2. Gospel	accompanies movement to the ambo solemnizes the gospel proclamation	*Alleluia*/ acclamation
3. Gifts	accompanies the presentation of gifts of bread and wine by the assembly	sung or instrumental music
4. Closing	closes the celebration accompanies the minister from the celebration space	sung or instrumental music

——— 2. Proclamation Dance ———

The proclamation dance adorns the reading of the word of God. In some cases it may proclaim the actual Scripture reading itself (the story) or it may simply augment the reading of the word by preparing the hearts of the hearers. Thomas Kane summarizes the proclamation dance this way:

	Function	Source Material
1. Scriptural	to announce to inspire and instruct to reveal to witness to challenge	Hebrew and Christian Scriptures Creed
2. Spiritual/ historical	to inspire to witness to challenge	thematic spiritual/liturgical writing

——— 3. Prayer Dance ———

Although the entire service of worship is a kind of prayer, there are special prayers within a service of worship that can be expressed through dance.

Function	Source Material
to acclaim to invoke	Kyrie (Lord, Have Mercy) Sanctus (Holy, Holy, Holy) Eucharistic Acclamation Great Amen Doxology to Lord's Prayer Lord's Prayer Blessing

——— 4. Meditation Dance ———

A meditation dance is a reflective dance done as a response to a proclamation part of the service of worship. It is associated with a quiet time in the service of worship. The people are called upon to meditate on the presentation of truth found in the reading of Scripture, in a sermon, or in Communion.

	Function	Source Material
1. Psalm dance	to respond meditatively to the first reading	psalm

	to draw the community into a reflective spirit	
2. homiletic	to share with the community the implication and impact of the good news (prophetic) to witness to the truth of the good news (evangelical)	Scripture texts
3. after Communion	to reinforce the theme of the celebration to inspire to give thanks (communal)	sung or instrumental music

——— 5. Celebration Dance ———

A celebration dance is usually used at the prelude and postlude of a service. It either prepares the congregation for worship or brings the service to a close. Often celebration dances involve the entire worshiping community in some simple gestures or in movement such as a circle dance.

Function	Source Material
to prepare the assembly for festivity	sung or instrumental music
to conclude the celebration in a special way	

In summary the various kinds of dances can appear in a service or worship in the following places:

Relationship of Dance ——— Types to Elements of ——— Eucharistic Celebration

The Eucharistic Liturgy	Liturgical Dance Types
Prelude	(5) Celebration

INTRODUCTORY RITES:

Opening song/Music	(1)	Procession
Penitential Rite (Kyrie)	(3)	Prayer
Glory to God (Gloria)	(3)	Prayer

LITURGY OF THE WORD:

First Reading	(2)	Proclamation
Psalm Response	(4)	Meditation
Second Reading	(2)	Proclamation
Alleluia	(1)	Procession
Gospel	(2)	Proclamation
Homily	(4)	Meditation
The Creed (Credo)	(2)	Proclamation

LITURGY OF THE EUCHARIST:

Preparation of Bread and Wine	(1)	Procession
Holy, Holy (Sanctus)	(3)	Prayer
Acclamation	(3)	Prayer
Amen	(3)	Prayer
The Lord's Prayer	(3)	Prayer
Communion	(4)	Meditation

CLOSING RITE:

Blessing/Dismissal	(3)	Prayer
Closing Song/Music	(1)	Procession
Postlude	(5)	Celebration

Thomas Kane[110]

367 • BIBLIOGRAPHY ON DANCE IN WORSHIP

Adams, Doug. _Congregational Dancing in Christian Worship_. Richmond, Calif.: The Sharing Company, 1984. This book examines biblical material and demonstrates the need and benefit for dancing in four areas: community, repentance, rejoicing, and redemption. It practically answers the question: "What dance [movement] should be made during different parts of the worship service so as to increase the effect of the liturgy?" Good emphasis on responsibility and appropriateness in worship. Excellent annotated bibliography.

_____. _Dancing Christmas Carols_. San Jose, Calif.: Resource Publications, 1983. A resource for adding movement and gesture to Christmas carols. Subjects include a history of dancing to carols, folk dancing and carols, moving to carols in liturgy, updating Christmas carols to jazz, dancing carols with children, and a carol choreography workbook. Fully one-half of the book focuses on designs for dance choirs and companies which are complete in text, staging, music, and choreography.

Adams, Doug, and Diane Apostolos Cappadona, eds. *Dance as Religious Studies*. New York: Crossroad, 1990. A primary text in three parts which (1) explores the Judeo-Christian tradition in detail with (2) special attention to women who danced and (3) contains a large section on theory and praxis regarding liturgical dance. Contributing writers are expert in their special considerations. Excellent bibliography. Many illustrations. For the serious reader/participant.

Andrews, Edward D. *The Gift to Be Simple: Songs, Dances, and Rituals of the American Shakers*. New York: Dover Publications, 1962.

Backman, E. Louis. *Religious Dances in the Christian Church and in Popular Medicine*. London: Allen and Unwin, 1952. A chronicle of dance from Judaism to the modern era, dividing subject matter between sacred and popular church dances. Covers medieval period in 100 year increments and notes significant developments and groups. Very complete. Pictures and illustrations.

Daniels, Marilyn. *The Dance in Christianity*. New York: Paulist, 1981. A readable summary of pre-biblical, biblical, and ecclesiastical references to dance in worship to the twentieth century. Knowledge of history and the notion of a modern post-literate civilization are employed to encourage new expressions of Christian dance that will transcend "barely recognizable . . . symbolic movements of the clergy."

Davies, J. G. *Liturgical Dance*. London: SCM, 1984. Historical, theological, and practical handbook with plates and figures. Considers condemnation of and dancing in churches; sacramental, biblical, and liturgical dancing; developing movement in liturgy and Christian education; and role of the dance choir. Special section on physical disability.

Deitering, Carolyn. *The Liturgy as Dance*. New York: Crossroad, 1984. Volume exposes types of dance as reflected in liturgy and liturgical history. The liturgy is a dance and the movement artist's role is of transparent servant. The "language of movement" is variously considered regarding ritual and creative beauty, gift and burden, sacred act and priestly office, and more. Challenges clergy to develop a language of celebrational movement; congregants to sensitively embrace common gestures and movements; and dance artists to create edifying artistry for ministry.

_____. *Actions, Gestures, and Bodily Attitudes*. San Jose: Resource Publications, 1983.

De Sola, Carla. *The Spirit Moves: A Handbook of Dance and Prayer*. Richmond, Calif.: The Sharing Company, 1986.

Fisher, Constance. *Dancing the Old Testament*. Richmond, Calif.: The Sharing Company, 1980.

_____. *Dancing With Early Christians*. Richmond, Calif.: The Sharing Company, 1983.

Gagne, Ronald, Thomas Kane, and Robert Ver Eecke. *Introducing Dance in Christian Worship*. Washington D.C.: The Pastoral Press, 1984.

Hoeckmann, Olaf. *Dance in Hebrew Poetry*. Richmond, Calif.: The Sharing Company, 1977.

Kirk, Martha A. *Dancing With Creation: Mexican and Native American Dance in Christian Worship and Education*. San Jose, Calif.: Resource Publications, 1983. The volume advocates the use of Mexican and Native American dance in Christian worship. Its primary focus on a more holistic, bodily approach to spirituality through these forms. There are at least fourteen movements or dances described which may be used in worship. Insights to Native American and Mexican spirituality are offered as background in an invitation to a unique cross-cultural experience.

Knoll, Barbara. *A Time to Dance*. Shippensburg, Pa.: Destiny Publications, 1991. Advocates reinstitution of liturgical dance for corporate and personal worship. Theology of dance is interspersed with types of expression such as prophetic or celebratory dance. Some discussion regarding objections to "movement ministry" in liturgy. Practical value of the art form is the focus.

Manor, Giora. *The Gospel According to Dance: Choreography and the Bible from Ballet to Modern*. New York: St. Martin's Press, 1980.

Reed, Carlynn. *And We Have Danced: A History of the Sacred Dance Guild, 1958–1978*. Austin, Tex.: The Sharing Company, 1978.

Roberts, Debbie. *Rejoice: A Biblical Study of the Dance*. Shippensburg, Pa.: Destiny Publications, 1989. Popular volume traces the history of "social dance" and early-modern attempts at liturgical dance as distinguished from the contemporary "restoration" of spiritual dance in renewal contexts. Biblical and church history is employed to advocate use of the art form for "priestly ministry" and the church's edification.

Rock, Judith, and Norman Mealy. *Performer as Priest and Prophet: Restoring the Intuitive in Worship through Music and Dance*. San Francisco: Harper and Row, 1988. A two-voice (musician and dancer) consideration of the nonverbal communication of the Word of God. Philosophical and practical considerations are mixed with historical and theological insights to flesh out the priestly and prophetic role of dancers and musicians who bring us closer to the vision of God through artistic ministry.

Taussig, Hal. _Dancing the New Testament: A Guide to Texts for Movement_. Richmond, Calif.: The Sharing Company, 1977.

_____. _New Categories for Dancing the New Testament_. Richmond, Calif.: The Sharing Company, 1981.

_____. _The Lady of Dance: A Movement Approach to the Biblical Figure of Wisdom in Worship and Education_. Richmond, Calif.: The Sharing Company, 1981.

Taylor, Margaret F. _A Time to Dance_. Aurora: The Sharing Company, 1967, 1976. Concentration on the "art of symbolic movement in worship." Many practical suggestions for starting a "symbolic movement choir," using dance in festive services, and dramatizing religious ideas. Good resource for dance types and idea. Historical section.

_____. _Hymns in Action for Everyone: People 9 to 90 Dancing Together_. Richmond, Calif.: The Sharing Company, 1985.

Winton-Henry, Cynthia. _Leaps of Faith: Improvisational Dance in Worship and Education_. Richmond, Calif.: The Sharing Company, 1985.

TWENTY

Examples of Dance in Worship

The articles in this section outline for the congregation simple movements to well-known hymns or stories. Some suggestions for forming movements and elaborating set patterns are also given.

368 • A GIFT TO BE SIMPLE

If one thinks of religious dance in America, the Shakers always come to mind, for they were a religious sect for whom dance was an integral aspect of worship. Founded in England, they came to the East and Midwest in the late eighteenth century and created many songs and dances to express their delight in God.

"A Gift to Be Simple" is one of the best known examples of their dances and songs. This dance was taught to Carla DeSola by a person living in the vicinity of a Shaker village.

Opening formation: a circle, all facing center.

- *"It's the gift to be simple, it's the gift to be free"*: All take four steps toward the center, beginning with the right foot (r, l, r, l). Hands are held in front of the body about waist height, palms facing upward. Initiated by a gentle wrist movement, the hands pulse upward and downward. (This up and down movement with upturned hands was thought of as a gesture to receive grace.)
- *"It's the gift to come down where we ought to be"*: All take four steps back to place (r, l, r, l). The palms face downward as you walk backward, and shake in a small down and up direction. This movement, with turned down palms, was used to signify shaking out bad influences, or "all that is carnal." (There is a Shaker song with the words, "Come life, Shaker life, come life eternal, shake, shake out of me all that is carnal.")
- *"And when we find ourselves in the place just right, we will be in the valley of love and delight"*: Repeat the above pattern; four steps into the center and four steps back to place.
- *"When true simplicity is gained"*: Bring hands to prayer position (palms together, fingertips pointing upward). Step to the right with the right foot and bring the left foot to meet the right, bending both knees. Reverse to the left on the words, "simplicity is gained."
- *"To bow and to bend we shall not be ashamed"*: Repeat the above pattern (stepping and bending to the right and then to the left).
- *"To turn, turn will be our delight"*: Keeping hands in the same prayer position, turn in place by making a small circle to the right (step r, l, r, l). End facing the center.
- *"Till by turning, turning we come round right"*: Reverse. Make a small circle to the left (stepping l, r, l, r).

Carla De Sola[111]

369 • THE LORD'S PRAYER

It is possible for a dance to the Lord's Prayer to be simple enough for a whole assembly to learn. The text used here is one prepared in 1975 by the International Consultation on English Texts.

Opening position: Cross your arms in front of your body and take the hands of the person on each side of you. Still holding hands, bend over and remain in this position for a moment, with a sense of stillness and prayer.

- *Our Father in heaven, hallowed be your Name; your kingdom come, your will be done, on earth as in heaven:* Slowly raise your torso and at the same time lift your arms up in a smooth continuous way, holding your neighbors' hands until you naturally let them go as your arms lift high. (Avoid any pulling.) Uncross your arms (there will be a lovely moment of expansion when everyone does this at the same time) and hold them in an open, praising position, head and chest upraised.

- *Give us today our daily bread:* Lower your arms, bringing your hands together in a gesture of petition (palms face upward, arms stretched out in front of you about chest height).
- *Forgive us our sins:* Bow forward folding your arms to your chest with a sense of contrition.
- *As we forgive those who sin against us:* Come out of the bow and take the hands of the person on either side of you as a gesture of reconciliation. (Do not cross your arms this time.)
- *Save us from the time of trial:* Holding hands, all bow deeply.
- *And deliver us from evil:* Hold bow.
- *For the kingdom, the power, and the glory are yours, now and forever. Amen:* All raise arms and torsos, hands still joined. Rise to toes, and letting go of neighbors' hands, raise hands even higher in an exuberant Amen!

Carla De Sola[112]

370 ◆ PSALM 36

This is a psalm prayer in movement to be done in pairs by an even number of persons.

- *How precious is thy steadfast love, O God!* Take partners and spread out. One member of each pair begins by kneeling, or sitting back on his or her heels, body bent over; the other begins by standing, facing the partner. Hold this position while the first line is slowly sung or read. Then in response the person kneeling raises his or her back and lifts up his or her hands, palms upward, as the standing person (a "God figure" of love) bends forward and lowers the hands, palms downward, till they meet the upraised hands of the partner. This is done very slowly, so that the meeting of the hands becomes a meaningful moment.
- *The children of men and women take refuge in the shadow of thy wings.* While the line is sung or read, the lower person in each set rises to his or her knees and each couple then slowly embraces, folding arms around one another, each in his or her own way.
- *They feast on the abundance of thy house.* The "God figure" helps the kneeling person to rise, then grasps with the right hand the partner's left

hand and steps backward in a small circle as the partner walks forward. The "God figure" leads the other gently around, gestures with the free hand as if showing the "house"—the river of delights. Think of it as a thanksgiving in movement for God's bounty.

- *And thou givest them drink from the river of thy delights.* The "God figure" bends down as if scooping imaginary water and rising, passes it to the partner who with cupped hands and swaying body accepts it in a variety of ways (such as drinking deeply, bathing in a fountain, and so on). This passing and receiving can be done a number of times.
- *For with thee is the fountain of delight.* Both persons gradually stop the gesture and come to a standing position facing each other, a few feet apart. Both persons place their hands with palms facing inward, a few inches in front of their own face.
- *In thy light do we see light.* All slowly separate their hands as if parting a curtain and look at their partner face to face, receiving "light" from one another. This position is held for a few seconds.

Note: This is simply an outline for a movement meditation. Each couple must make it their own. If possible, go over the text beforehand and have someone lead some movement warm-ups.

Carla De Sola[113]

371 ◆ A MEXICAN DANCE

This colorful dance reflects on themes of aging and hospitality and broadens our appreciation of the spirituality of other cultures.

The Mexican people have always had a deep respect for old persons. This is not a dance laughing at the elderly, but a dance laughing with them as they express their joy in a long life. They know God's promise: "Even to your old age I am the same, even when your hair is gray I will bear you" (Isa. 46:4).

The dance of little old men could be used to inspire intergenerational discussions by raising key questions and ideas: What perspectives can age bring? How can these lead one to dance in the face of that which might have brought one to a paralyzing fear earlier in life? Age brings insight: the elderly Simeon and Anna had the ability to recognize a baby in the temple as the Christ while others did not (Luke 2:29-38). How can one keep doing the inner dance as the body begins to stiffen? What types of social dances have been done by different generations? How have these been parts of their lives offered to the Christ? In the end, we have no wealth, but only the dance of life to bring before God.

The dancers wear white shirts and pants, with colorful bandannas around their necks. Usually they have flat brimmed *sombreros* of straw with colorful ribbon and fringe on them, though sometimes dancers wear no hats, but thick white wigs made of straw. Wrinkled benevolent masks and canes upon which the dancers lean give the dance its particular charm and humorous flavor. The dancers hobble and do the whole dance bent over, leaning on their canes. They mime gestures of holding their aching backs, expressing weariness, and almost tripping, yet they continue to delight in the dancing. The leader of the dance taps his cane on the floor, and the others echo the taps. They stomp in different rhythmic patterns, jump as they would in a game of hopscotch, land with feet and knees apart, and shake as they try to steady themselves. In Mexican villages, this folk dance is often continued for hours: perhaps an allusion to the endurance that old age demands! Patterns of movements may be worked out by the dance group. The dance should evoke both empathy and delight. A *Zapateado* (a Mexican dance with rhythmic foot work) melody could be used.

While a congregation can share in these movements as spectators, the themes of hospitality and of aging can touch people even more deeply if they are invited to participate in the dance in some way. People could be invited to try some of the movements or to discuss how the themes touch their lives. These folk dances do not require professional skill.

Through dances we can come into contact with the spiritualities of people of diverse cultures which can enrich the imaginations and the prayer of our communities. Mexican and Native American dances reveal a sensitivity to the earth, to the life cycle, and to all of creation. These dances can provide incarnational ways to experience Christian seasons and sacraments profoundly.

Martha Ann Kirk[114]

372 • A Congregational Dance

This article describes four patterns of congregational dance that are relatively easy for people of all ages to learn.

A child is in each person, and each child is a person. There really is no basic generation gap. Too often in our churches we have segmented our member into children, youth, women's guilds, laymen's fellowships, and senior citizens. There is a very simple art of communication that spans these divisions. It is found in exploring the joy of dramatic dance or symbolic movement, in moving together with expressive gestures and simple patterns of group designs.

Everyone can participate in the patterns of standing (even if in pews), circling (the basic pattern used through all the centuries), walking together in processionals (with gestures during refrains), and cluster groups gathered to express dramatic moods (as in a sculpted composite). These four patterns will be illustrated here.

In order to involve a group of people of various ages and abilities, movements must be simple and somewhat repetitive. Also, the symbolism must be clear and genuine. Then everyone can join in the joy of moving together in meaningful designs.

1. While standing in rows of pews, informally in a room, or outdoors, we can relate to each other as we sing "Shalom," the greeting of peace. This Hebrew folk song ("Shalom, Shalom") should be learned by the groups before movement is added. (It is found in many of our songbooks.)

Congregational Singing. Singing has always been a vital expression of Christian worship.

Shalom, my friend, Shalom, my friend: Everyone joins hands with the ones on either side. Hands will remain joined.

Shalom: Look up and raise hands high (aware of the peace of God).

Shalom: Look down and lower hands (aware that God's peace is here among us).

May peace be with you. Look around at others and smile.

May peace be with you. Look at others in another direction.

Shalom: Look up and raise joined hands.

Shalom: Lower hands and smile at one another.

Now repeat this design. No one needs to worry about what to do next. The joined hands and repeated words make it easy for everyone. If the group is in rows or pews, have them turn toward the center aisle so those on the two sides are facing each other. Then repeat the same pattern, this time with hands reaching out to those in the adjacent pews. This time, during "May peace be with you," everyone looks across at those who are on the opposite side, and the smiles carry the dimension of caring about them.

2. If we are in a circle or in concentric circles, we can add more movement:

Shalom, my friend. Shalom, my friend: The same gesture patterns as used with a group standing in rows.

May peace be with you, May peace be with you: All circle to the right while looking around at each other.

Shalom, Shalom: All stand and use the upward and then downward gestures.

Another variation involves two concentric circles. Those in the inner circle turn to face those in the outer circle. Hands are joined, arms out to the sides with elbows bent as in a folk dance.

Shalom, Shalom: Stand still to raise and lower arms as in previous patterns.

May peace by with you, May peace be with you: Groups circle to their right while greeting each other with smiles.

Shalom: All stand and reach up. This time release hands for high stretch.

Shalom: Lower hands outstretched to touch the hands of those opposite, while looking at each other. Usually there are fewer in the inner circle, so the hands that touch may not be evenly matched.

This design can be repeated a number of times because each time there will be some new persons to greet with outstretched hands in the closing "Shalom." As you see, this folk song may be danced in many ways, and your group may create other patterns.

3. Processionals provide an active participation for all ages. "Rejoice, Ye Pure in Heart" has the lines, "Bright youth and snow-crowned age," and "From youth to age, by night and day, in gladness and in woe," with the refrain. "Rejoice, rejoice, rejoice, give thanks and sing." How natural to have persons of all ages process through the aisles with upward swings of their arms during these joyous refrains!

Hymnals can be a burden during these processionals, so one remedy is to have 5 x 7 cards with the words of the stanza. Curve the card over your wrist and hold it here with one or two elastic bands. In this way, those processing can sing the stanzas and still be free for movements during the refrains. Some churches project the hymns high on a wall or screen. In this way, everyone is free from holding hymnals.

"Praise the Lord, his glories show, Alleluia" has the repetition of an "Alleluia" at the close of each line. As young and old process through the aisles they can be like antiphonal choir members, responding with a strong upward swing of the arms held high, heads uplifted, joyously singing, "Alleluia." As the congregation sings the lines from their hymnals, those in procession continue walking with arms lowered by anticipating the next "Alleluia." The congregation will respond with increased vitality, for they will catch the mood of this processional hymn and won't be burying their heads in their hymnals.

Enjoy exploring processionals with your people. You will find many songs and hymns with refrains or repeated phrases that lend themselves to symbolic movement. They will enliven and deepen the moods of each season of the church year.

4. Cluster group designs evolve surprisingly with a sequence of "Amens." The refrain of the "Amen" spiritual folksong is a good musical background, but other fivefold "Amens" can be used if preferred.

An "Amen" should be portrayed with conviction, for it is a strong personal affirmation that people use as a response. The build-up of five "Amens" will evolve into a living sculpture of strong affirmations. Everyone gets into a group of five persons, perhaps in the aisles or before the chancel, in a room, or out on the grass. Within each group the people, standing in a circle, number off in sequence. As everyone sings, each person in turn takes and holds a strong position that has meaning to him or her. Number one takes a position while the first "Amen" is sung; number two takes another position as the second "Amen" is sung, and as they take their statuelike positions they stand close to each other. Numbers one, two, and three take any posture that instantly occurs to them; perhaps a contrite kneeling, or an upward thrust of seeking or exaltation, or reaching out in angular confusion. Numbers four and five now are responsible to use a gesture related to one or more of the first three persons. Four and five bring the others into a sculptural whole. At the end of this sequence, have all the groups remain frozen in their clusters while one or two groups are chosen for the others to observe.

When repeating this sequence, have each of the people in the groups renumber themselves so that each person has an opportunity to start as number one, but also the challenge to be a closing relating number.

Children, youths, and adults contribute a variety of gestures as they throw themselves totally into dramatic stances. Amazing living sculptures happen each time. Diversity and community are found in each cluster.

Margaret Taylor Doane[115]

373 • The Ten Lepers

The themes of healing and restoration are portrayed vividly in this creative dance interpretation of Luke 17:11-19.

When attempting to express the miracles, or any other story, using creative movement, you should first place yourself inside the situation you wish to interpret; feel the ground beneath your feet and see the scene as it was. Become a part of it, and when you move, interpret what you see. Let the expression flow out from within, rather than confining yourself to a set routine.

The story we have chosen as an example is the miracle of the ten lepers from Luke 17:11-19. The movement in this story is from confinement (leprosy) to freedom (health). We will detail first the reflection process and then a visual expression of the story. The first half of the reflection enables us to experience the freedom we already possess in our bodies. From there the second half of the reflection process draws us into the bodies of lepers who await the freedom Christ will bring.

Process of Reflection

What you will need:

A tambourine, a Bible, a cleared space large enough to move around freely

Find a space in the room . . . this is your own personal space. Slowly stretch your arms out all around you. Feel the space . . . reach up high . . . reach out to your sides . . . reach down low . . . stretch your whole body and explore every bit of the space that surrounds you, and then relax.

Walk freely around the room, naturally and at a regular pace. Keep on walking . . . swing your arms as you walk . . . keep well away from the others. Now with your whole body, walk as slowly as you can . . . get slower and slower all the time. . . . gradually feel your body becoming heavier and heavier . . . slow right down . . . and freeze.

Walk around the room again . . . just walk naturally again and at a regular pace. Now slowly begin to quicken your steps . . . faster . . . faster . . . and even faster still.

Now take large steps and begin to slow down to the regular pace again. Make your steps larger and larger . . . giant steps. Now take small steps . . . tiny steps. . . . even smaller than you are taking now.

Now take bouncy steps . . . bounce up and down, up and down as you walk along . . . bounce. . . . bounce. Now walk with smooth even steps . . . no bounce at all.

Can you walk in a curved path? Now walk a straight line . . . walk forward . . . backward . . . sideways.

Make up as many original walks as you can. See how many different ways you can walk.

Walk freely again around the room . . . keep your whole body straight and your head up high . . . walk with a spring in your step. Now walk backwards again looking over your shoulder, to see where you are going.

As you walk forward again, show how you might walk if you were angry. How would you walk if you were sad? How would you walk if you were bored? How would you walk if you were in pain?

Slowly walk back to your own space and relax.

In your own space, lie flat on your back . . . feel completely relaxed . . . let your whole body sink into the floor underneath you. Become aware of your own breathing, in and out, in and out. (At this point the story of the ten lepers should be read, Luke 17:11-19.)

Now take your time and sit up very slowly. What do you know about leprosy? What parts of the body does it strike? How were people warned that lepers were approaching? Where did this story take place? What was that countryside like? Try to make a mental picture of the countryside. Perhaps the road is hot and dusty. Maybe the sun is beating down upon your back. Feel its warmth on your face. Place yourself in the picture and stand up slowly.

Imagine that you are a leper . . . where has leprosy struck you? Is it in the arm? Or perhaps a leg . . . maybe it's your back. You may have it in more than one part of your body. Make your body into a twisted shape. Find your own level . . . you may still be standing, you may be crawling, or you may be dragging yourself along on the ground. Find your own level. Now make another twisted shape, keeping in mind where leprosy has struck you. How does it feel being a leper? Are you ashamed? How do you think you appear to others? Can you look at others face to face? How do you react when others look at you? Where does it hurt you most of all? Move very, very slowly . . . not hurrying at all. Some of you may want to move more slowly than others. How do you communicate with the other lepers? Say something to another leper using gestures only . . . what are you saying?

Putting these movements together and using a tambourine, the scene may look something like this:

A Visual Expression of the Ten Lepers

The reading may be read before or after the expression if you wish.

1. Four slow beats of the tambourine. Lepers enter slowly in their own twisted shapes. They look at their own bodies. (Remember to use different levels.)
2. Shake the tambourine. Lepers quickly recoil hiding their faces.
3. Four slow beats of the tambourine. Lepers try to communicate with each other.
4. Shake tambourine. Lepers recoil again.
5. Four slow beats of the tambourine. Lepers stretch their arms out in all directions: some upward, some out to the sides, some downward.
6. Shake tambourine. The lepers recoil again.
7. Shake tambourine. Jesus enters.
8. Shake tambourine. Lepers look curiously at each other and then at Jesus.
9. Shake tambourine. Various expressions of surprise and curiosity cover their faces. Here we add voices to accompany the movement. Each of the lines could be repeated several times for an echo effect (rather like the rhythm of a train).

> LINE 1: "Who's coming, who's coming? (Each of these lines should be repeated about four times.)
> LINE 2: "Who is it?"
> LINE 3: "Jesus."
> LINE 4: "Go away."
> LINE 5: "We're lepers."
> LINE 6: "Heal us." (This said only once and in a loud, sharp, crying voice.)

As these lines are spoken, the lepers huddle in a small group. Jesus walks around the group and takes up a position in the center behind the group. Each leper as he or she is touched by Jesus must show through his or her body and face the change which has taken place in his or her body. As each is touched he or she moves out away from the group and freezes in an attitude of joy, disbelief, or astonishment. The movement would finish here.

Another way creative movement could be used with this story would be to go through the reflection process and then choose some suitable music and ask the group to improvise the story of the lepers through movement.

In this case the group could experiment with shapes, from twisted distorted shapes to strong healthy whole shapes. (Suitable music for this could be _Oxygene 1_ by Jean Michel Jarre.)

You may discover, after your own reflection, a better way of interpreting this story visually. That is the beauty of creative movement, the freedom it allows us.

Cathy Lee and Chris Uhlmann[116]

374 • MOVEMENT PRAYER

Hand motion is vital to movement prayer. This article introduces some basic gestures that can be incorporated with congregational prayer.

"Every part of the body is an expressive instrument of the soul. The soul does not inhabit the body as a man inhabits a house. It lives and works in each member, each fibre, and reveals itself in the body's every line, contour and movement" (Romano Guardini, *Sacred Signs* [St. Louis: Pio Decimo Press, 1956], 15). Watch any person while he or she talks, and you will find feeling being expressed, not just in the words being spoken, but in the whole being of the person speaking in movement and gesture. Watch particularly the hands. Apart from the face, the hands may be most expressive. They may move animatedly when the person is excited, be clenched if he is worried, or lie quietly in his lap if he is speaking thoughtfully or pausing momentarily in his thought. The movement of a person's hands can also belie his words. The hands may indicate that the person is feeling the opposite of what he is saying.

Hands are instruments of truthful expression. They are also instruments for work, for doing violence, or for loving. Hands give, take, and receive. They surround and hold, and they release and send forth. Expressive and useful as they are in the ordinary business of life, it cannot "but be that in prayer, where the soul has so much to say, so much to learn from God, where she gives herself to him and receives him to herself, the hand(s) should take on expressive forms" (Guardini, *Sacred Signs*, 16). The church has traditionally encouraged and maintained some prayer movements of the hands. Let us look at them and see how they serve the soul in its conversation with God.

Close your hands, one over the other, interlocking your fingers, draw your closed hands in toward your body, allowing this movement to draw your head and upper body down over that space deep within you where God dwells . . . hold this position . . . pray . . . sense how this position affects your prayer . . . rather than being a prayer of exuberant praise, it is more likely that your prayer is quiet, private, personal, a meeting with the Lord who is hidden deep within and who is waiting patiently for you to come and be alone with him. On some occasions in your prayer life, come to this physical and spiritual place to meet the Lord.

Next, open your hands and place the fingers and the palms flat against one another . . . hold this position for a moment. . . . There is no power in your hands. They can neither inflict injury nor be put to active service. They are, as it were, bound invisibly in a position of defenseless obedience. Close your eyes and pray in this position. . . .

Now, open your hands wide, palms up . . . In this position, your hands are ready to receive or to give. They can absorb healing or offer praise. Close your eyes and pray. . . .

With one hand (the one you use most often), make a fist . . . bring your fist down across your breast and strike yourself several solid blows . . . When you strike your breast, make sure you give yourself an "honest blow" (Guardini, *Sacred Signs*, 30). This gesture must speak to your soul of its need for repentance and contrition. It must awaken your senses to the need to shatter the old self and put on the new. Pray this movement prayer several times, slowly and with concentration. Let it communicate its meaning to the soul and to the Lord.

Allow these movement prayers of the hands to assist you in your private and your public prayer. If you lead congregational prayer, teach your people to raise their hands in praise at the beginning of the preface; to hold their hands, palms together, in reverent attentiveness during the eucharistic prayer; to strike their breasts in earnest at the "Lamb of God" or during "Lord, I am not worthy. . . ."

Here is a penitential rite (Form C) which you might want to teach to your congregation.

Because we have been afraid to be ourselves.
Draw your hands back tightly and protectively against your body
Free us to be what you have created us to be.
Relax your hands and arms, open them out wide and free
Lord have mercy.
Because we have hurt others by what we have said or done.
Make fists of your hands and raise them forward as if to strike out
Help us to bring healing instead.
Cup your hands as if to hold a soothing ointment, and then turn your hands over to let that ointment run down over those you have hurt
Christ have mercy.
Because we have been greedy with our time and our possessions,
Claw your fingers in tightly toward each other with a feeling of grasping
Teach us to give and to share.
Open your hands and arms, spreading your fingers wide, in an expansive movement

Lord have mercy.
May Almighty God have mercy on us, forgive
us our sins and bring us to life everlasting.
Amen.

Carolyn Deitering[117]

375 • A DISMISSAL DANCE

A dismissal dance helps to emphasize and energize the closing words of a worship service. Included in this article are creative suggestions for sending worshipers into the world with a strong sense of God's presence.

During the final hymn, choir members moved down the aisles, and each stopped at the end of a different pew to sing the words directly to the people in that pew: "Go tell it on the mountain / Over the hills and everywhere / Go, tell it on the mountain / That Jesus Christ is born!" In another church, all the people were directed to face others around them while singing the benediction "God Be With You Till We Meet Again." And in a third church, the people processed out singing the final hymn: "Forth In Thy Name, O Lord, We Go." As we see in these three examples, dismissals and benedictions should give us a strong personal sense of God's presence and direction to send us forth.

By contrast, we know of churches where the people begin leaving before the dismissal is spoken. In some congregations, the dismissal is spoken so indirectly that many are not aware they are being addressed. To make dismissals more meaningful, embody the direction suggested in the words of the closing hymn. When the words speak of our interaction, direct the people to face each other. When the words speak of spreading the good news and God's activity beyond the church, direct the people to sing those words while they move out beyond the church building.

Some people cannot envision the presence of God outside the place of worship. One such example occurred when a worship service concluded with all the people processing out of the church singing "God of Grace and God of Glory" as the benediction. One person complained that the moving disturbed his sense of God's presence, for he could not imagine God moving with us outside the church. I responded that the benediction and/or dismissal should stress that God leads us outside the church to the rest of the world throughout the

week. Unfortunately, always saying and hearing benedictions and prayers in a static position has made it difficult for our people to sense God moving in the world; we need more moving dismissals to help our people sense God in world events as well as in our lives outside the church building.

Directions for simple movement to dozens of hymns are given in my book *Dancing Christmas Carols;* many of these are appropriate as moving dismissals not only in Advent, but also in the first months of the new year. As outlined in that book, certain theological guidelines emerge from biblical and historical studies to aid the worship leader in designing contemporary worship with dance. Most important, the processional march is the paradigmatic form of dance in both Jewish and Christian worship.

The theological significance of the march is best seen when contrasted with the circle dance. In both forms of dance the individual is incorporated into the community. In the circle dance, the community is oriented inwardly upon itself. God transcends the group, yet is envisioned at its center, focusing attention with the group. In the march, the community is oriented beyond itself. God again transcends the group, but is envisioned as leading the people out into the world beyond themselves. The circle dance leads the worshiper over and over the same ground, cultivating a cyclical view of events; the march leads the people out of cyclical or static world views into a forward movement more in keeping with a faith that makes history meaningful.

Although the circle dance is more congenial with some Eastern religions and the march with Western religions, both Judaism and Christianity may utilize circle dances at times. But the march is appropriately the most frequent dance in Christian worship.

A most effective closing to worship combines a meaningful gesture of benediction within the context of a processional march using the historic tripudium step in which one takes three steps forward and one step backwards, three steps forward and one step backwards, etc. (See "Triumph and Tripudium," pages 58–59, in Eileen Freeman's *The Holy Week Book* for a historic use of the tripudium step appropriate for Lent and Holy Thursday dismissals.) Through this dance step in a processional march, the people sense a heightening of community, repentance, rejoicing, and rededication.

An illustration of the use of this march was at Washington Cathedral when we used this pattern as a moving dismissal. The choir began by repeatedly singing "Alleluia," and the congregation joined in the singing. Then the choir began moving with the tripudium step around and around the Communion table as they continued singing. They did not move in single file nor in rows of two or three abreast with arms linked; instead they moved as a massed group with each person having a hand placed on a shoulder of one person ahead. After they have moved around the altar in that way a few times, they invited others from the congregation to join them as they continued to move in that pattern. After a few more times around the altar, they continued singing "Alleluia" and moved in a massed group (with many of the congregation joining in) through the cathedral hall and outside into the city.

Doug Adams[118]

TWENTY-ONE

Mime in Worship

Gestures heighten our interest in conversations, speeches, sermons, and the narratives of story-tellers. But more significantly, gestures reveal a great deal about our experiences, thoughts, and feelings regarding the words we speak. Gestures and movements clarify our relationship to what we say.

Mime takes the natural qualities of gesture a step further. By acting out narratives, mime reveals meanings or insights into relationships and feelings that can not be experienced through words alone. Whether acted in silence or with background music, mimes highlight important dimensions of their stories with exaggerated gestures and action sequences. By the end of the mime, the viewers' eyes and heart perceive what their ears have frequently ignored.

As a medium of narration and proclamation, mime is no stranger to the church and its worship. In spite of abuses, mimes have acted out the Christian gospel for generations. In recent years, mime has regained a place in worship as a medium of proclamation and evangelism. The following articles describe the history of mime in the Judeo-Christian tradition and outline its specific uses and abuses in the church.

376 • MIME IN THE BIBLE

Nonverbal actions can communicate many powerful feelings and truths. The prophets of Israel used the medium of mime to reveal profound messages of judgment and promise. Mime was also used in joyful celebration and praise on occasions of military and spiritual victory. Although scriptural evidence does not always clearly explain the nature of the mimetic gestures used, it does indicate the movements and gestures were an important aspect of both proclamation and praise.

Prophetic Mime

Throughout Scripture, God used dramatic expression to communicate his will and his Word. Mime is one such dramatic expression. Mime or pantomime is listed by Finis Jennings Dake as occurring 40 times throughout the Bible (Ezek. 3:26; 4:1-17; 5:1-17; 6:1-14; 7:23-27; 12:1-26; 20:45-49; 21:1-23; 24:1-27; 32:17-21; 37:1-25; Jer. 13:1-14, 18, 19; 25:15-36; 27:1–28:17; 43:6-13; 51:62-64; 1 Kings 11:30-40; 2 Kings 13:15-19; Isa. 20:1-6; Hos. 2–3; Acts 21:10-13; Rev. 18:21).

There are also explicit references to God's dramatic action. Consider, for example, this verse from Hosea:

I have also spoken [to you] by the prophets and I have multiplied visions [for you] and [have appealed to you] through parables acted out by the prophets. (Hosea 12:10, Amplified Bible)

The phrase *parables acted out* is a translation of the Hebrew word *damah,* which indicates a silent enactment of judgment. Other versions translate this passage as: *similitude,* a representation of another thing (KJV), *representation,* an active illustration (Septuagint), *parable,* by active comparison (Knox), and *perish,* judgment of God by the prophets (Moffatt). All of these translations refer to an active demonstration of the prophetic word by the prophets.

In addition, there are many other appearances of "Jewish mime." Jewish mime is not related to modern white-faced mime or the masked Greek and Roman mime. Here the word *mime* is used in the generic and widest sense of the word, referring to a form of silent gestural communication. The word *mime* or *mimetic* is also the best word to describe the willed and developed actions of the prophets. Their gestures were often highly stylized and placed in specific order to help support a concise thought.

Jewish mime is the use of stylized gestures to communicate a thought, story, truth, or prophecy.

Generally, mime was only performed by the prophets to communicate the word of the Lord, although there are some references to mimes done in praise and worship (Ps. 149:6-9 [by tradition enacted], Exod. 15:20 [Latin Vulgate *saltator* or pantomimed dance).

Prophetic mime was delivered in the following manners:

1. Actions without words (Ezek. 3:26, 4:1-3).
2. Actions with words preceding or following action (2 Kings 13:14-19).
3. Actions with words delivered at the same time (Acts 21:10-13).

Prophetic mime shows us that God not only speaks to us through words, but also through gestures. Hosea 12:10 reveals that he has more than one way for revealing his word, listing three different voices for the word: (1) the uttered word, (2) the revealed word, (3) the dramatic word. The messengers who used this prophetic voice of drama include Agabus, Ahijah, an angel in Revelation, Elisha, Ezekiel, Hosea, Isaiah, and Jeremiah.

There are many reasons why God might have used mime. Eighty percent of human communication is nonverbal. The message delivered with mime can be powerfully clear and very well communicated. Mime involves the observer's "eyegate." God used mime when the people would no longer listen to the spoken word alone, as in the cases of Jeremiah and Ezekiel when the children of Israel listened to the false prophets and had closed their ears to the truth. Now they would *see* the Word of the Lord that they had chosen not to hear. Mime challenged the people to reflect upon the meaning of the gestures used to open themselves to the truths being presented. A parable is a story that reveals truth to those who were ready to receive it at their own level. The same is true for mime, a parable acted out.

Mime is used to show God's judgment (1 Kings 11:30-40); to show God's provisional will (2 Kings 13:15-19); to illustrate judgments of shame (Isa. 20:1-6); to foretell and warn (see the prophecies of Ezekiel and Jeremiah); and to make clear the results of one's actions (Acts 21:10-11). Mime is used to clarify, illustrate, and demonstrate.

Ezekiel. Ezekiel stands out as the prominent Jewish mime of Scripture because of his unique call and the conditions during which he prophesied. In 597 B.C., Nebuchadnezzar attacked Jerusalem, plundered the city, and deported king Jehiachin and many others to Babylon. Ezekiel was deported at this time and took residence at Tel-abib beside the river Chebar along with the majority of the exiled ones. While in captivity, the thirty-year-old Ezekiel received his commission from Yahweh. He then ministered through mime, speech, acting, visions, symbols, allegories, and parables. Because the Jews would not listen to the Word of the Lord in spoken form, the Lord made Ezekiel mute: "I will make thy tongue cleave to the roof of thy mouth, that thou shalt be dumb, and shalt not be to them a reprover: for they are a rebellious house" (Ezek. 3:26, KJV).

The only time Ezekiel was able to speak during the early years of his ministry was when God spoke through him saying "thus saith the Lord" (3:27). The rest of the time he was silent and mimed his prophecies. His use of mime extended throughout his ministry. Over one-third of his prophecies are in mime and "parabole," that is, in figure, illustration, comparison, or parable. We note this in his first prophecies, seen in chapters 4–6.

An Example of Jewish Mime. In Ezekiel 4:1-3, Ezekiel is commanded by God to enact the capture and defeat of Jerusalem. He is to do so in silence. He first draws the city of Jerusalem on a brick and sets this brick in front of him. Then he shows the different stages of attack that the city will go through by attacking the brick. After showing the siege of the city, he then shows that there is a barrier between the city and God (seen by the use of the iron pan). It is possible this barrier was created by the rebellious sins of Israel. This barrier stopped God from helping them, and because of it they could not get through to God with pleas for help. This prophecy is fulfilled in 2 Kings 23:23–25:30 and 2 Chronicles 35:20–36:23.

Mime in Praise

Mime in praise is a natural extension of the joy or happiness expressed through gestures in everyday life. The victory dances of the Old Testament illustrate the connection between movement, joy, and everyday experience. The developed style of Jewish mime is evidently only truly found as a form of prophecy. However, there are possible occurrences of Jewish mime as praise which are worth analyzing. They are found in Psalm 149:6-9 and Exodus 15:20.

It is not certain that these were indeed "Jewish mime," and different interpretations are possible. Psalm 148:6-9 reads as follows:

Let the high praises of God be in their mouth, and a two-edged sword in their hand; to execute vengeance upon the heathen, and punishments upon the people; to bind their kings with chains, and their nobles with fetters of iron; to execute upon them the judgment written: this honor have all his saints. (KJV)

This passage deals with expressions of praise, including singing, dancing, rejoicing. The action continues into the spiritual warfare of the believer. The Hebrew word used for high praises is *romemoth,* which means to rise exultantly, to lift up praise in an active sense. The praises are from deep within and are expressed in an outwardly acted fashion. This is seen with the loud audible praise of God that issues from the worshipers in a grand outburst of spiritual song. Their praises commemorate and retell the high and mighty acts for which God is to be praised, including our salvation and his victory over sin and death.

Psalm 149 depicts the worshipers as they take the two-edged sword (the Word) (Eph. 6:17; Heb. 4:12) in their hands and mime the spiritual warfare of believers (Eph. 6; 1 Tim. 1:18; 2 Cor. 10:4-5). Israel once battled physical enemies with songs of praise for God in their mouths (2 Chron. 20:15-17, 21, 28; 1 Sam. 17:47). Now God's people can fight spiritual enemies in the same way.

C. H. Spurgeon said, "We will not copy the chosen people in making literal war, but we will fulfill the emblem by carrying on spiritual war. . . . we sing joyfully and war earnestly with evil of every kind. Our weapons are not carnal, but are mighty, and wound with both back and edge. The word of God is all edge; whichever way we turn it, it strikes deadly blows at falsehood and wickedness . . . the verse" (C. H. Spurgeon, *The Treasury of David* [Grand Rapids: Kregel, 1977]). Thus, Psalm 149:6-7 indicates a happy blending of the chorister and the crusader: "When Godly men give battle to the powers of evil each conflict is high praise unto the God of goodness. Even the tumult of our holy war is a part of the music of our lives" (Ibid.).

The hearts of such active worshipers are seen "in their performance [of high praises]: the Lord . . . [requires] the duty of high praise to be performed with a great measure of Scripture-light, with a high degree of effectual faith, and with a more ample proportion of practical holiness than any other of the most solemn exercises of his public worship" (selections from a sermon entitled "The Prisoner's Praise" (1650) by Samuel Fairclough, quoted by Spurgeon in *The Treasury of David*).

In fact, just as Israel executed judgment on the heathen and punishments (1 Sam. 17:45; 2 Sam. 8:1; 2 Sam 1:18; 2 Cor. 6:7; Neh. 4:17, 6:17-19; Heb. 4:12 [example of the heathens to be judged, and the saints who brought judgment]), we shall overthrow evil and judge the world (Rom. 6:13 [instruments: weapons]; 2 Cor. 10:4-5; 2 Cor. 10:4; Ps. 44:5; Luke 10:19; Rom. 8:37; 1 John 5:4; Rev. 2:26; 3:5, 12, 21; 21:7). As Israel humbled their great enemies by the power of God, so are the chief powers of evil restrained. Evil shall be bound by a great chain and cast into the bottomless pit to be trodden under the feet of all (2 Sam. 22:39-41). Jesus has and will always win this battle for us as we enact what he has already done. We celebrate this victory when we mime and express in movement the spiritual battle we have won: "this honor have all his saints" (Ps. 149:9).

With these thoughts a scenario unfolds. The following is an adaptation of Psalm 149:6-9, applying the principles found in Ephesians 6 for spiritual warfare. The worshipers take the two-edged sword, which is the Word of God, into their hands (power and means). They overcome evil by the power of the sword of the Spirit, and swing the mime sword in mime of war as they proclaim the Word of the Lord. The enemy is slain by the word of truth and the judgment of the blood overcomes the power of sin and death, bringing the effects of sin in life to an end. They mime the binding of kings and nobles, binding them with the actions of his praise and life, and with the spoken word they bind principalities and powers of darkness. Evil is placed under their feet as they are shod with the gospel of peace. We are all spiritual warriors fighting the good fight.

Psalm 149 was both a literal event (2 Chron. 20:15-17, 21, 28; 1 Sam. 17:47) and a commemorative mime of the battle won. The text gives us the guidelines for the story, though it leaves out the actual gestures. Battle dances and commemorative dances were common to the ancients. Greece and Rome had their Pyrrhic (military) mime/dance. The Egyptians acted out the battles of the gods and kings. In the Middle East it was common to greet the victor of a battle with mimic dances, which reflected the battles won. It is for this reason that the dance of Miriam in Exodus 15:20 is considered as a mime/dance commemorating God's victory over the Egyptian armies. The children of Israel might have been affected by the Egyptian traditions of dance in which the mime/dance leader, called the first-dancer or leading dancer like the Greek *archimimus,* leads the others in song, dance, and mimetic interpretation. Miriam could be considered the first-dancer (mime leader) as she leads out in this mimetic dance of victory. The victory dances of the Old Testament may well have been mimetic dances set to music.

The influence of the Egyptians on the Hebrews can be seen by the dance of Exodus 32 (dancing before the golden calf) and the prohibition against Egyptian art (idolatrous art) in the Ten Commandments. Scholars debate this hypothesis, arguing that the Hebrew children seem to have a mimetic tradition of their own without the influence of Egypt. The Hebrew word used in this verse (32:19) is *macholah,* suggesting a dance company or chorus (mime). The Greek Septuagint used the word for chorus, suggesting a "pantomimic dance done to song." The Latin Vulgate uses a form of *saltator* meaning "to dance" which is a synonym for "a pantomime." These words do not mean that the Israelites mimed in a Greek or Roman fashion; they simply identified a movement style which related a story or had mimetic qualities, in addition to expressing feelings of joy. (The expression of dance in Scripture is used as a synonym for joy [see Eccl. 3:4, Ps. 30:11]. The dance of Miriam portrayed the battle as well as expressed the joy of victory, and thus is as much a mime as it is a dance. The same is true for the dances listed in 1 Samuel 18:6, 21:11, 29:5.) In Scripture, dance is considered "the physical expression of the internal joy" and it generally does not express a story. In contrast, mime expresses thoughts and stories. Miriam's "dance" retold the story of God's victory in throwing the Egyptian army into the sea. Therefore it qualifies more as a mime than a dance. A mixing of popular translations of Exodus 15:20-21 recreates a mimetic picture of the event:

> Miriam the prophetess, the sister of Aaron, (KJV) went out with a tambourine in her hand, (Knox) and all the women went out after her with timbrels, (KJV) with flutes, (8PRL) with choruses [mime], (YLT) and with tambourines with which they danced. (BER) And she (Miriam) led them in the refrain, (NAB) "Sing ye to the Lord, (KJV) For He hath triumphed, He hath triumphed, (8PRL) hurling horse and chariot into the sea." (Moffatt)

Consider the following: Miriam leads the women out of the camp. The men sing with Moses and Joshua the story of God's victory. As the men sing, the women with Miriam repeat the words and mime the actions of the song with the accompaniment of the flute and timbrels, just as the pantomimes of Rome were to mime to the sound of the flute centuries later. Miriam's gestures recreate the horse and the rider as they are thrown into the sea by the right hand of God. The whole story told in Exodus 15 is full of mimographic imagery (gestural illustration). It shows God's arm in battle and the very elements doing his bidding as the enemy is overwhelmed by the forces of the deep, fire, and the earth itself. The poetic retelling of this story is a mime's delight.

Miriam may have been influenced by Egypt in this style of mimetic dance, or it could have been an existing Hebrew custom. However, even if it was not, it became a custom in celebrating victories (see 1 Sam. 16:6 and Judg. 21:21). These dances were in all probability mimed.

Mimetic Movement and Praise

There are different types of gestures: natural gestures—those which we are born doing (crying, laughing, smiling); learned gestures—those which are learned for comfort and by living (sitting, walking, crossing the arms or legs); cultural gestures—those which we do by the influence of education and society (hugging in greeting, waving hello, thumbs up for approval, shaking hands); mimetic gestures—those which copy life or represent an idea or foreign thought (playing an animal, pretending to fly, posing as mad, faking a smile). Scripture is full of mimetic gestures used in praise and worship.

Mimetic gestures include clapping the hands (Ezek. 25:13; Ps. 47:1) to represent triumph; lifting the hands (Ps. 23:2; 63:4; 119:48; 134:2; 141:2; 143:6) to show praise and surrender; bowing (Ps. 72:9; 95:6) to show the humbling of our human stature; lifting our head (Ps. 24:7) to give total attention to God; kneeling (Ps. 95:6—*barak:* to kneel expectantly and quietly before Him, to bless the Lord; Ps. 145:21; 34:1; 63:4; 72:15) to humble ourselves; laughing (Gen. 21:6; Ps. 126:2) with the joy of the Lord; washing each others' feet (Luke 7:44, 1 Tim. 5:10; John 13:4-14; Gen. 19:2) as a sign of servanthood; sharing Communion (Matt. 26:26; Mark 14:22; Acts 10:37; 13:24) in commemoration of the death and resurrection of our Lord; being baptized (Acts 2:38; Rom 6:3; Col. 2:12; 1 Pet. 3:21) as a sign of putting away the old nature and rising in new nature by the resurrection power of Jesus, taking off one's shoes (Exod. 3:5; 2 Sam. 15:30) on holy ground to show we are not worthy and have no ownership or rights before God, we become sensitive to his will; rending clothes (Josh. 7:6; 1 Sam. 4:12; Lam. 2:10; Rev. 18:19) as a sign of mourning; hitting one's chest (Luke 18:13) in sorrow; putting dust (Josh. 7:6; 1 Sam. 4:12; Lam. 2:10; Rev. 18:19) on one's head to represent the worthlessness of oneself; fasting (Matt. 6:16) to be seen as holy, etc. The list continues, pointing out the fact that mimetic gesture is a very strong part of Scripture.

Mimetic movement is used in the simplest expressions of life and in the celebration of the cornerstone of our faith, Communion. Therefore, mime and gesture can open people to a greater understanding of the word and our devotion to God in praise and worship.

Todd Farley

377 ✦ Mime in the Early Church

The following article outlines the role of mime in the church and society during the first centuries after Christ. In this period, as in others, mime was a significant medium of instruction and communication for believers and nonbelievers alike.

Mime was performed in the middle of the period of controversy and social change that riddled both the falling Roman Empire and the young church struggling to establish an identity. By the end of the fourth century, mime was on its way to virtual extinction, but not before it had been used in the church as a medium of evangelism and ministry. To understand the history of mime in the church, we must understand the place and history of secular mime in Rome before the birth of Christianity.

Mime in the Roman Empire

The popularity of mime and pantomime grew with the population explosion of the Roman

Singing in the Spirit

Empire. The Empire grew from 1,200,000 to 120,000,000 in the span of 300 years. It absorbed dozens of nations and became a vast polyglot society of heterogeneous peoples. The problem of communication was great. Mime and pantomime were the only forms of communication which transcended the language barriers. Mime communicated in the international, multilingual art of gesture, which everyone could understand.

The mime artists became the news tellers of the day. They were seen in the homes of the aristocrats and on the corners of the streets, and through pantomime they enacted the news and daily gossip. As their name suggests, mimes loved to mimic life (mime is associated with the Greek word *mimesis,* "to imitate life"). They portrayed all things good or bad, but they had a special love for satire and comedy. They would mock a leader's faults and the hypocrisies of life. "They based their work on life itself, and never looked beyond; they ridiculed the legends of the old gods just as later they ridiculed the Christian rites" (Allardyce Nicoll, *Masks, Mimes, and Miracles: Studies in the Popular Theatre* [New York: Cooper Square, 1963], 18, 121). They made the gods more human and reachable in a negative way by creating them with laughable faults, a practice accepted or at least tolerated by the Greeks and Romans. For the Christians, mocking Christ and his church was blasphemy and a reproach. They came to see mimes as enemies. To the mime artists, the Christians were just another subject of life to imitate.

When Christians began to be persecuted, the mimes picked up on the strange and unique beliefs and practices of the Christians and their faith in a crucified God. St. Gregory of Nazianzus said "nothing on the stage was more pleasing to auditors and spectators than the comic Christians" (ibid). Mocking the Christians and Christian rites became a popular theme among the mimes and the public. Theater historian Allardyce Nicoll writes that "nothing . . . seems to have amused them more than the Christian rite of Baptism. The dipping of a man in a tub as part of an ecclesiastical ceremonial tickled their secular minds, and according to the testimony of the Acts Sanctorum, the mime which ridiculed this rite was most popular of all" (ibid).

The church leaders did not always help their own case. As the early years went by, divisions and hypocrisy grew in the church. The mimes, being true to life, imitated and mocked this infighting. Nicoll says "the mimes had been . . . amused at Christianity, and when they saw the adherents of this new church quarreling with one another they shook their sides in undisguised merriment. Theological controversy was the mightiest jest of all, and ceremonies of a spiritual significance left them merely smiling" (ibid). So they mimed water baptism and the baptism of the Holy Spirit; they mimed healings, conversions, and controversies.

The Evolution of Greek and Roman Mime

The Egyptian mystery plays and imitative dances (2500 B.C.–550 B.C.) influenced the growth of the masked dance and dithyrambs of Dionysus (the god of wine and festival) in the Corinthian Isthmus, Megara. This base style of mime is called Dorian mime. Dorian mime (fifth century) birthed Greek mime and Roman phlyax mime (northern Italy). The Phlykes (improvisational mime) inspired the development of The Fabula Atellana or Atellan farce (in southern Italy), which is a much more literate style. At first the themes of the mimes were the stories and legends of their gods; however, the popularity of the art and humanistic philosophy caused the focus to fall from their gods to men. Mime became

the act of imitation, showing life in all of its secular glory. Entertainment replaced religion. Devotion was sold out to pleasure. Mime birthed all Western theater and dance as people learned to use the arts to worship humankind in the name of education and entertainment.

Types of Ancient Mime

There were many styles and types of mime and pantomime in existence by the first century of the church. *Greek mime (mimus)* used stock character masks and gestures to accent spoken words. *Histriones* was a general term for all actors. *Planipes* were barefoot mimes. Roman pantomime (*pantomimus:* all mime) was the art form supposedly created by a mime actor who lost his voice, Livius Andronicus (c. 240 B.C.). He is said to have had another actor speak/sing for him as he gestured the story. Pantomime also used music (especially the flute) and chanted lyric.

Phylades and Bathylus are said to have brought the art to its perfection under the patronage of Caesar Augustus. Rome also bred mimetic dances, pyrrhic dance/mime (war mime/dance), *funambuli* (tight tope walkers), mime dancers *(saltator),* archmimes *(archimimus)* who were the leaders of mimes, Roman mime (Roman *mimus*) a vulgar sort of burlesque mime. The writer of a mime play is called a mimograph *(mimographus),* the directions in the play are called the mimography, and the play itself is referred to as a mime (as in the player: *mimus*). *Atellanae fabula* was the Roman theater form of stock masked characters. Moral and educational pantomime was called *ethologues*. The *ludi* were "games" both athletic and theatrical, distinguished by the event: *Ludi Circenses* (circus games), *Ludi Scenici* (theater games).

Jewish mime (gestures and actions used to prophesy or worship) was not unique and seems to have been absorbed into the refined and popular arts. Greek and Roman mime did have a long and great heritage. We must remember, however, that before Thespis created the first drama in the sixth century B.C., before Epicharmus wrote Dorian mime (the parent form to Greek mime) in the fifth century B.C., or before Livius Andronicus did the first Roman pantomime in the third century B.C., we see the mimes of prophets hundreds of years earlier ministering the Word of the Lord. It should not surprise us when God redeems even the other arts for his glory.

Mime and Martyrs

In the midst of the persecution of Christians something wonderful happened. The mimes began to meet Jesus, and their jest became the "mime of life" in more than just their sayings. (The "mime of life" reflects the Greek concept that our life was but the game of the gods. Christians adapted this to portray that life on earth was but a reflection of heaven's afterlife, a small portion of time in comparison to eternity. Those who talk about the "mime of life" include the Emperor Augustus, Suetonius, St. Gregory of Nazianzus, Seneca, Leone Di Somi.) The mimes were converted by their mimed parodies. The most famous account of a mime being saved in recorded in *Acts Sanctorum* (Sacred Acts [of the martyrs]).

In the year A.D. 304, Diocletian came to Rome to celebrate his triumph over the nations and over the Christian impiety. In celebration of this victory he went to the theater to watch the famous mime Genesius mock the conquered Christian faith. The story Genesius told in mime was that of a mock baptism. However, in the process of being baptized in jest, Genesius had a revelation of Jesus Christ and was baptized in truth. When he exited the tepid water that was in the tub on stage, he proclaimed to his audience "I saw a hand which came from heaven, and shining angels above me. They read in a book all the sins I had committed since my infancy, and washed them in the water in which I had been baptized, and presented me with the book, which was whiter than snow" and "I am truly a Christian!" (Darras, *The History of the Church,* vol. 1, and Nicoll, *Masks,* 122). The mime arose a Christian, shattering the lie of Diocletian's victory over the Christians. The mime who Diocletian wanted to mock the Christians was mocking him. Diocletian had Genesius tortured and beheaded. Diocletian had lost face while Genesius won eternity.

Another legend comes from the reign of Diocletian; this one from Egypt (Nicoll, *Masks,* 17–18; and Lincoln Kirstein, *Dance: A Short History of Classic Theatrical Dancing* [Brooklyn: Dance Horizons, 1969], 61). The story tells of a weak-willed deacon who came into the town of Antinoe where the prefect Arianus had proclaimed that all visitors must make sacrifice to the gods of Antinoe or be slain. This law persecuted the Christians and the Jews who would not offer sacrifices to a false god (the polytheistic people of the Roman empire did not care how many gods they worshiped and offered the sacrifice without problem). This law separated the Christians and Jews from the polytheists, making the Christians and Jews look like fanatic and unreasonable extremists.

In this setting, the deacon knew both that he would not offer sacrifice and that this defiance would lead to his death. Instead of facing martyrdom, he asked the famous mime Philemon to take his place at the altar of sacrifice and make the offering for him. This jest was the type in which any mime would glory. The opportunity to fool the whole town was too much to pass up, and Philemon donned the holy man's robes. The plan worked up to the point of the sacrifice, when a miracle happened. Just as Philemon was about to commit the sacrifice, a voice from heaven spoke to him, and he had a revelation of Jesus. He spoke out the words "I am a Christian, and I will make no sacrifice." This statement was not a surprise to the people; it would have been expected from the deacon. What did surprise the people was that as Philemon spoke he pulled back his hood to reveal not the deacon, but the town mime. Great confusion ruled as the crowd tried to understand what had just taken place. Arianus was pressured to dismiss the whole incident as a bad joke. However, Philemon would not compromise by making the sacrifice and continued to proclaim his faith in Christ. No matter how the mob and Arianus tried to persuade him, whether by guilt, promised fame, proclaimed love, or wealth, Philemon remained constant and was finally put to death along with the deacon. His dying words were: "Good people of Antinoe, be not distressed at the blows I have received. I doubt not ye remember the time when I was a mime—how to my shame in the theater blows were rained on me by my fellow-actors. You laughed at those comic blows then, but the angels wept. Now, therefore, it is just that your tears should not weigh against the joy which the angels feel at my salvation" (excerpt from Nichol, *Masks*).

These are but two examples of the many mime martyrs—Philemon (A.D. 287), Masculas (A.D. 486), Ardalio (A.D. 298), Gelasiunus (A.D. 297), Genesius (A.D. 303), Porphyrius (A.D. 362), Porphyrias of Caesarea (A.D. 275)—who died for their faith in Jesus. Theodoret said that the mimes

came upon the stage and suddenly entered into the ranks of the martyrs, gaining the victory and seizing the crown; who by the attestation of their faith cast error into the breasts of the devils whose slaves they had formerly been. . . . A number of mimic actors, during the third and fourth centuries gained canonization (sainthood) at the hands of the catholic church because of their constancy." (Nicoll, *Masks*, 121, 122)

The Issue of Mime in the Church

Not all mimes who were saved become martyrs. Some survived to use their art to glorify God. This meant changing both the form of their art and their costumes (for one thing, they had to remove all phallic symbols from their costumes). The stories they told were of the crucifixion, the Lord's Supper, baptism, and healing. Their characters resembled the anti-Christian mime characters: a hero, a friend, a judge and attendants, a bishop and acolytes, soldiers, guards, neighbors, and Christians, or Bible characters or saints. One of the most famous mimes was the arch-mime (mime leader or master) Masculas, who mimed for the Lord and died for this faith during the invasion of the Vandals.

The church Fathers used mime in evangelism to compete with the worldly draw of the arts. Mimograph (mime writer) St. Gregory of Nazianzus (A.D. 329–390) was well versed in mime. He stood against its secular usage, but redeemed its form by writing after the style of the Syracusan Sophron. He redeemed mime's *canticum* (story song with music). He is credited with writing *The Passion of Christ*, which is a mime play after the Attic style with the hymns of the church substituting the original choruses (Katharine Lee Bates, *The English Religious Drama* [Port Washington, N.Y.: Kennikat, 1966]). *The Passion of Christ* borrows from Aeschylus (*Prometheus Bound*) and Euripides (*Bacchanals*). The story was narrated by the character of Mary, and her lament of Christ's death is directly taken from Euripides' play. (There is a contention, however, that this work was written in the tenth century rather than in the fourth century and was supported by the labors begun by Ignatius, a deacon of Constantinople and a supporter of the ministering arts.)

Another famous religious figure who used mime was Arius of Alexandria (A.D. 260–336). Arius was a presbyter who developed a heretical theology that created a great controversy in the church. He was a mimograph (mime writer) who styled the *Egyptian Sotades*. The Arians (those who followed after his beliefs) used liturgies that were called "stage books."

Nicoll states that "when we hear a prominent Arian described as 'the leader of the Arian stage ballet,' we realize that here we are in the midst of a religious movement which is attempting to counter the activities of the mimes by introducing some of their characteristic methods of appeal into the church services. Gesticulation, variety of vocal tone, and, later, music came to be used for this purpose" by all of the church.

Arius wrote the drama *Thalia*, whose mimography (instruction for gestures) included a pantomime of the crucifixion. This work supported his doctrinal positions, which were later rejected by the council of Nicea. When Constantine exiled Arius, Athanasius, the Bishop of Alexandria, destroyed all records of *Thalia* and Arian mime traditions. Arians tried to make their theology popular through the arts and were prepared to make the services more popular by using mimic gestures and inflections. Chrysostom hated the Arian use of mime, saying,

> they show themselves . . . no better than madmen, agitating and moving their bodies, uttering strange sounds, engaging in customs foreign to the things of the spirit. They introduce the habits of mimes and dancers into sacred places. Their minds are darkened by what they have heard and seen in the theaters. They confuse theatrical action with the ceremonials of the Church.

Chrysostom thought that all drama was "for those who execute the will of the devil." Prejudice like this caused great confusion in the church.

However, mime and mimetic dance seemed to have become a very active part of the church's life. Plays were being written by many different factions. The Gnostics (who believed in salvation by knowledge) wrote a gospel on Christ called the Acts of John. In it is mimetic dance said to have been done by Jesus after the Last Supper. In this *saltatio* (mimed dance), the disciples circled around Jesus, singing and gesturing by his directions.

> I will pipe. Dance, all of you—Amen. I will mourn, beat you all your breasts—Amen. . . . to the Universe belongs the dancer . . . He who does not know what happens. . . . I am a door to you [who] knock on me . . . I am a way to you [the] traveler. Now if you follow my dance, see yourself in Me who am speaking . . . You who dance, consider what I do, for yours is this passion of Man which I am to suffer. . . . After the Lord had so danced with us, my

beloved, he went out [to be crucified]. (excerpts from the Gnostic writings, Acts of John, vv. 94-97)

This *saltatio* (mime/dance) was apparently influenced by the mime styles that incorporated a hymn and mime of the mysteries of the universe. Mystery dances were common among Egyptians, Greeks, and Romans. It is logical that the people of the early church were acquainted with this form of presentation and incorporated it into their explanations of church mysteries, as the mimography of this passage suggests. The Acts of John were mentioned by St. Augustine and show that mime was accepted in the early church, enough so that Jesus is pictured miming—without the church considering this an outrage. (The Acts of John was considered uninspired and unworthy to be called Holy Scripture and was therefore not included in our New Testament. The writings had a different view of Christ and created a spiritual Christ who was not wholly man, but was rather wholly Spirit in the form of man. This book contained imperfect doctrine and was considered to be a more devotional work.)

The quote from the Acts of John is reminiscent of Jesus' rebuke to the unresponsive generation of his day (Matt. 11:17 and Luke 7:32). They would not mime or dance to his piping (that is, understand the truths that he and John the Baptist brought): "We have piped unto you, and ye have not danced; we have mourned unto you, and ye have not lamented."

Other modern translations of this passage present other possibilities for understanding it in terms of mimetic gesture:

We have played the flute to you, [Rotherham] we played at weddings, but you wouldn't dance. [Phillips] We sang a lament, [Rotherham] we sang a funeral song, [Beck] and you would not beat your breasts. [Moffatt]

Matthew Henry comments that this passage is parable to show the extremes to which God will go to get our attention. It speaks of the joyful dance, a wedding dance, as representing Jesus' good news of salvation and the dance of the bride of Christ (Rev. 19:7), while the dirge, a funeral dance, is associated with the call of John the Baptist for repentance, baptism, and the burial of the old nature. Both dances were rejected by the children of Israel. Instead they called Jesus a drunkard and John a possessed crazy man. If Jesus is willing to use analogy

in the form of mime, it is not surprising that his church would use mime and the arts to explain and illustrate other mysteries of God.

Other examples of mime in the early church include the second century efforts of a Jew named Ezekiel, who wrote a mime based on Exodus. Its characters included Moses, Sapphora, and God seen in the similitude of the burning bush. In the fourth century the priest Apollinarius (the Elder) of Laodicea, disciple of Athanasius and contemporary of Gregory of Nazianzus, wrote parts of the Old Testament in homeric hexameters; his son, Apollinarius, rewrote the New Testament in Platonic dialogues, which were enacted stories. All of these examples show a general popular use of mime in the church as part of its worship and ministry.

Mime was embraced by the church when it evangelized and ministered to those who could not understand their message due to differences in language or culture, when it illustrated a doctrine or truth, when it was used in prophecy, when it proclaimed a philosophy to be embraced, or when it helped in expressing worship. It was also embraced as a popular form of celebration, a form which later degenerated into mere entertainment and began the process that led to the fall of mime in the church.

The Fall of the Arts

The church stood against the worldly mime of the Romans and the Greeks, even as it embraced it as a form of ministry. By the fourth century, the secular art form of mime had bred many forms of drama that were ungodly and unholy. Much like our television and movies of today, they contained explicit sex and violence. In response to this, the church cast out mime. The following were important considerations in this development.

1. **Associations with Sin.** The theaters were well attended by members of the Christian church. These Christians attended love feasts *(agape)* and festivals, some of which were vulgar, lustful events that incorporated degenerate Roman *mimus* (burlesque mime) and other base forms of drama such as the *Floralia* (naked courtesans who were *histriones* [actresses]). The church rose up against these gatherings, promising to punish those who participated in them with exclusion from the Lord's Table or even excommunication. The festivals of the pagans were slowly replaced by Christian festivals. But until that

time they remained a threat to the church. The feasts that the church fought in particular well into the Middle Ages were the feasts of fools, the feast of the ass, the feast of the boy bishop, and the ancient Saturnalia.

2. False Doctrine. Athanasius destroyed the mimography of Arius because the Arians were using it to perpetuate condemned doctrines. The gnostic Acts of John was also cast aside with the erroneous doctrines of the gnostics. The church tried to purge itself of all doctrines which might cause division and eliminated those things related to the doctrines—the good with the bad.

3. Association with the Sorrows of the Christians. Many Christians were tortured during the violence of the *Ludi Circenses* (circus games) by gladiators or wild animals. Tacitus wrote that "the Christians . . . were dressed in the skins of wild beasts, and exposed to be torn to pieces by dogs in the public games . . . they were crucified, or condemned to be burnt; and at nightfall served in place of lamps to lighten the darkness, Nero's own gardens being used for the spectacle." Augustine wrote against its lure, speaking of how he lost his friend Alypius, who was drawn to the blood lust of the games of the gladiators. Christians had seen their friends martyred for the pleasure of the public shows while other people were lost to its lusts. St. Paul wrote in 1 Corinthians 4:9 that "God has exhibited us Apostles at the very end of the procession [Goodspeed] . . . like doomed gladiators in the arena! [Moffatt] . . . to be gazed at in a theater by the whole world, both men and angels" [Conybeare].

The church became a very serious and contemplative place; at points laughter was even considered unworthy conduct for the Christian or even to be evil. Many church leaders tried to fight this error, arguing that joy and laughter came from God and not from the devil, as Chrysostom would have had them believe. The mimes did not fit Chrysostom's somber frame of mind; they were a joyous lot who made fun of the very serious.

Some Christians tried to find release from their sorrows in the ungodly, lustful theater of the Roman mime and *Floralia*, drawn like bugs to a flame, devoured in the pleasures of a theater form that would destroy their souls. The confusion of the early church toward drama and mime was largely due to the fact that degenerate mime was mixed with the godly mime. The church threw out both.

4. Association with False Worship. Cyprian complained

> They put on the stage the wanton Venus, the adulterer Mara, and Jove, that old wretch, prince of the realm of love not less on account of his own vices that on account of his position. They show him majestic with his thunderbolts, or made white with the feathers of a swan or descending in a golden shower.

Augustine wrote, "In the theaters the spectators may behold some counterfeit god Jove, committing adultery and hurling his thunderbolts at one and the same time." Mimes commonly mocked the gods just as their earlier counterparts worshiped them in the goat song. However they still worshiped the false god by mentioning their existence and glorifying their sins.

5. Mockery of Church Disputes. The quarrels of Patriarch Chrysostom with the bishops Severianus and Antiochus, and of St. Gregory of Nazianzus with Maximus of Alexandria became the subject matter for the mimes. Gregory of Nazianzus exclaimed "My tragedy is become a comedy for my enemies. Through this we of the church are bandied to and fro and are brought upon their stages."

All these reasons caused church leaders such as St. Tertullian (in his *De Spectaculis*), St. Chrysostom, and St. Cyprian to write avidly against all theater. The evil associations found in the arts caused the early church fathers to raise a voice of protest against all *ludi* (mime, dance, juggling, athletics, etc.). The arts in general were condemned because of their associations, just as the violence and sex of drama today causes the church to condemn art.

Mime was frequently condemned throughout the early history of the church. The councils which in some way condemned actors, mimes, and feasts, included the Council of Arles (314); Laodicean Council (341–381); Council of Carthage (397); Canons of Hippolytus [3d century: lost], Constitutions of the Apostles by Clemens Romanus, the African Council of 408, the seventh Council of Carthage, the second Synod of Arras in 452, Council of Agde in 506, Concilium Trullanum of 692, the second Council of Cloveshow in Mercia 747, Synod of Nicea of 767, the Synodus Turonensis of 813, Synodus Cabilonensis of 813, the canons of the Concilium Aquigranense of 816, the Concilium Parisiense of 829, and the thirteenth canon of the Concilium Moguntinum of 847. These documents prove that mime was alive throughout the centuries despite the church's opposition.

Mime in Worship

Eventually, the church debated the proper use of the arts. Language became a problem in evangelism and later in ministry. Much of what was preached had to be supported in pictures, mimetic movements, and even mime. Mime was an integral part of the church and worship. Nicoll writes that "almost all the average man knew of his faith was through what he could see . . . ritual was visual . . . and dramatic." The Mass evolved out of the mimed dramas of the early church in order to illustrate the truths of the Lord's Table and other mysteries. Of necessity the church became more and more visual in its ministry because fewer people spoke Greek or, in later years, Latin. The church added statues, paintings, and ceremonies and relied on a liturgy of gestures as complex as the most difficult mime. Reluctantly, the church came to reconsider the mimetic arts it had once wholeheartedly condemned.

Todd Farley

378 • MIME IN THE MEDIEVAL CHURCH

The pattern that began in the early church continued in the Middle Ages: official pronouncements squelched mime even as some leaders found creative and helpful ways of incorporating it into their practice of the Christian faith.

A.D. 300–1000

Synods, canons, and councils struggled throughout the Middle Ages against the secular use of mime that survived from Graeco-Roman culture. The mime traditions had been carried forward by artists known as *mimes (mimus), jongleurs,* and *histriones,* which later evolved into the medieval artists known as *minstrels, jongleurs,* and *troubadours.* The councils of the church threatened to withhold Communion from mimes and, in the worst cases, excommunicated them. The immoral use of the arts was condemned by the church, yet the arts still flourished. Both priests as well as lay persons participated in hosting the mimes. The English priest Alcuin advised Bishop Higbald of Lindisfarne that "it is better to feed the poor from your table than the actors . . . it is better to please God than the actors;

it is better to have a care for the poor than for the mimes." The Archbishop of Lyons, Agobard, denounced ecclesiastics who "gave food and drink to actors, to the basest of mimes and to the most wretched of jesters" while leaving the poor to starve. All of this points to the fact that mime was not dead and was in fact a very active part of life in the medieval church . . . but at great expense. Buchnell states "the migratory professional entertainer was always in trouble with the church even though he may have influenced the style and manner of the sacred services."

Mime in the Mass. While the councils struggled against secular mime, liturgical mime was evolving in the church. The seed that had been planted by the early church mimes began to grow. By the tenth century the Mass had become largely mimetic due to the language barrier caused by the use of Latin. Its ceremonies used mime, movement, costume, color, and furniture. Each element had symbolic meaning that the people understood; in this way they participated in the Mass. Peter Buchnell, in his book *Entertainment and Ritual,* states

those who had participated for sometimes (in the Mass) grew to read the meaning beyond the symbol whilst the fully initiated discovered a personal divine truth . . . almost all the average man knew of his faith was through what he could see. Ritual was visual . . . and dramatic.

The drama of the Mass served the same purposes as the parables of Jesus insofar as they allowed everyone to understand the truth being presented at his or her own level.

The Mass replaced the Greek/Roman theater in many ways. It was not drama in the sense of impersonation, it was dramatic in presentation. The Mass was believed to be a recreation of the sacrifice of Christ, where Christ's blood and body was believed to be rebroken literally for the church (transubstantiation). Because of the idea that this was a literal event, many disqualify the Mass as drama, though it is dramatic. The priest's mime, movement, costume, color, furniture, bread, and wine became more than just objects and gestures; they took on the nature of what they had represented. For a Roman Catholic, the Mass was not considered a drama representing Christ's sacrifice, it was Christ sacrificed. In the tenth century this changed, and the Mass gave birth to theater.

The introduction of the Mass was called the *introit,* and it was during the Easter Introit that mime and drama were first introduced. The liturgy of the church also included *tropes* [from the Latin *tropus* meaning added melody]. Tropes are embellishments to the sung parts of the medieval liturgy. These embellishments included movement, dress, and mimetic gestures as part of their execution. The tropes that were part of the Easter Introit began to introduce mimed gestures of the Marys at the tomb, the visitation of the angels who proclaimed Jesus had risen, and the transformation of the Marys' sorrow into joy at hearing the good news. The playlet, called *Quem queritis,* was first performed at the monastery of Saint Gall (A.D. 970).

Rubrics (stage directions which include mimography) were added to the tropes in the tenth century. An example of these rubrics is seen in St. Ethelwold's code of rules for Easter celebration in his diocese. In the rubrics of *Planctus Marias et a liorum,* the Marys and angels were instructed on how to enact each section of the trope with the specific mimed gestures and postures indicated. Their pointing, beating their chest, falling at Jesus' feet, wringing hands, etc., were all indicated in mimography. The actors were clergy, holy sisters, choirboys. The play was chanted to music rather than spoken in a stage voice, and the gestures were simple. The theater was now the church, containing the plates (place for performance) or the open space containing an altar, and for the auditorium, the open space surrounding the altar accommodated the worshipers.

The rites and actions found in the liturgy were referred to as the *officium* (office). As certain *officium* became more dramatic they were referred to as the *representatio* (representation). As the *representatio* became more of a play then a rite, it was referred to as a *ludus* (twelfth century). *Ludus,* the old Roman word for a "play," now referred to a biblical narrative presented in a dramatic form. The *ludus* was introduced into the Easter introit and was met with great enthusiasm by the celebrants and congregation alike. Because drama increased the joy of worshiping God's triumph in the resurrection, it was retained as a worthy ceremony, and was also used for occasions such as Christmas and other Christian holidays. Drama was embraced by the church completely and began to develop artistically.

Irene Mawer states that mime was used in religion as it had been in the false worship of Dionysus.

When the Church at last turned to illumine by it her most sacred mysteries, mime made alive the loving sufferings of Our Lady as it had pictured those of Demeter, and with the same simplicity of purpose told the life of Christ as it had that of Dionysus. Whether the altar that was the center of the story and the 'stage' were in the church in Italy, France or England, or in an open place among the hills of Greece, it mattered little. In every age when the heart of the world grows young again, mime will tell that story which most it cares to hear, by giving it life and color and action.

Drama and Dance in the Western Empire

Mime, dance, and drama did appear sporadically throughout the history of the West. In the early church there were the Arians, gnostics, and the Sect of the Unbended-Knee (who used gesture to expel evil spirits), the battle-songs of the Teuton warriors who told the story of a blond-haired Christ, and the dances of the Roman churches. In 604 Abbot Meletius of England was advised by Gregory the First to allow dance in the church. The church in Paris had priests leading the choir boys in a round dance during the singing of the psalm. Historian Lincoln Kirstein states

Scaliger said the first Roman bishops were called *preasuls* and they led a sacred "dance" around altars at festivals. Theodosius says that Christians of Antioch "danced" in church and in front of martyrs' tombs.

In the seventh century processionals are recorded in which a reenactment of the death and burial of Christ were done in Jerusalem. In the tenth century a Benedictine nun named Hiroswitha of Gandershem, Saxony, wrote and acted plays on martyrdom and the glorification of chastity. She was styled "the Christian Sappho" and was influenced by the writings of Terence. These events seemed to happen outside of the development of the liturgical musical drama. Even if this is true, it reflects the fact the church was ready for the reemergence of drama. This was also encouraged by the view perpetuated by the allegorical interpretation of the bible and the Mass as promoted by a contemporary of Charlemagne, Amalarius, bishop of Metz. Allegorical interpretation opened the way for drama, dance, and mime.

Mime in the Eastern Empire

Mime in the Byzantine Empire lasted longer than in the Western Empire, probably due to the popularity of what Sathas calls "liturgical drama" promoted by the Arians. In the first century Nicholas of Damascus wrote tragedies and comedies. In the second century Ezekiel, a Hellenized Jew, wrote a play called *Exodus* dealing with the exodus of the Jews from Egypt, with the characters of Moses, Sepphora, Chus, Raguel, God, and a messenger. The play was quoted by Christians for centuries to come. In the fourth century we not only find the mimograph Arius, but also Metodius of Byzantium, who wrote *the Banquet of Chastity* and the dialogues *Freewill* and *The Resurrection*. In the eighth century Eustathius states that the religious play *Susanna* was probably written by John of Damascus. The *Death of Christ* was written in Greek by Stephanos the Sabbaite in 790, two centuries before the tropes of *Quem queritis*. The play *Christ's Suffering*, was probably encouraged by Ignatius, a deacon in Constantinople, and created by a group of writers in the eleventh century. The tradition of mime seems to have never died completely in the Byzantine church. Liudprand, Bishop of Cremona, stated that the Church of St. Sophia was turned into a theater where religious plays could be performed, like the prophet play called *Elijah*. However, Liudprand is from the tenth century and predated the prophet plays of the West. Sermons were also said to be mimed or acted out in the Byzantine church and Western drama might have been influenced by the Eastern church.

Mime in the Early Plays

From the tenth century onward, there was a rebirth of theater. *Passion plays* (about Christ), *mystery plays* (about Scripture), *miracle plays* (about miracles of the saints), *prophet plays* (about prophets), and *morality plays* (about moral truths) were all products of the church, from which modern theater was to evolve. Mime was an essential part of these church dramas, with actors miming the song or chant of the choir or soloist. When drama evolved into the Passion play proper, the actor spoke and the parts of the mime were replaced by mimetic movement, which accompanied the speaking.

Leone di Somi wrote "the actor's movements . . . are of so great importance that perhaps the power of words is not more than the power of gesture."

About mime he said that "this corporal eloquence . . . is of tremendous importance, called . . . the soul of rhetoric." He believed that the actor was "above all other things to render whatever is spoken thoroughly effective, with suitable alteration of tones and appropriate gestures." Bucknell states that "early Christian drama must have required . . . training of the voice and a strong technique in mime and gesture from its actors." This is supported by evidence in the rubrics for a play about Adam and Eve:

> Adam shall be trained to speak at the right moment so that he may come neither too soon nor too late. Not only he, but all, shall be well practiced in speaking calmly and making gestures appropriate to the things they say.

The rubrics of a mimed vignette in a play about Cain and Abel are as follows:

> Abel shall have a saucepan beneath his garment against which he (Cain) shall knock when he pretends to kill Abel. Abel shall lie stretched as if he were dead.

While mime was being employed in dramatic presentations, it was also used in its purely silent form. Leone di Somi wrote about silent comedies, a type of mime familiar in certain parts of Europe "wherein the story is so clearly and pleasantly presented by means of action alone that only those who have witnessed this kind of play would credit its force." Mime took on new forms and was used in the dumb show (silent play), in the stories of *mummers, jesters,* and later the *Commedia dell' Arte.*

In this period of creativity, mime became an extension of human worship of God and God's ministry to humankind. Priests were said to have mimed and gestured their text; laity and whole cities joined together to act out God's Word, using every art available. The church delivered the message of Christ in a visual medium that supported its spoken word.

The increased use of drama in the church revived an art form that then was also used for ungodly entertainment. Such dramas created sinful Herods and demons who were more popular than saints. It portrayed false gods to laugh at because God was too serious to be comic. Sin became more pleasurable than piety, and people turned to the popular fleshly desires. The church had to throw out the theater it had created. The spoken theater was to evolve into Jacobean drama and produce the plays of Shakespeare. Mime was to be lost to the *Commedia dell' Arte.* Dance was to be lost to the Ballet of the Courts. The church was to lose all but the most basic pulpit-supporting dramas and specials play for Christmas and Easter. Though the church had ruled the arts for hundreds of years, she allowed it to become sinful and lost it to the secular world in the early years of the 1500s.

Todd Farley

379 • Mime in the Contemporary Church

Mime and clowning have returned to the church in the twentieth century, providing an important means for presenting the good news in a form which is not verbal. The eye may comprehend what the ear fails to hear. This article describes various ways in which mime is being used in public ministry.

Beginning in the 1970s the church began to awaken to the worship and ministry potential of the arts. At first, these awakenings happened in isolated circles, but as the arts grew in popularity they began to cross over the barriers of denominations and sects. The motivation for accepting drama into the church was based on acceptance of the arts as

1. Christian entertainment
2. Evangelism
3. Worship
4. Ministry and Prophecy

Contemporary Mime Artists

French mime Marcel Marceau introduced America to the art of mime in 1955 with appearances on Broadway and major television programs, such as the Ed Sullivan Show, the Red Skelton show, and Johnny Carson; in 1992 he appeared with Arsenio Hall. Marceau is considered the father of theatrical mime in the twentieth century; he made the art form a popular expression. Many performers followed his lead and benefited from his popularity.

The style of mime that Marceau executed is French lyric mime or classical mime. Lyric mime is beautiful to watch; its highly stylized gestures focus on the emotions and clarity of story. Marceau's stories in the early years of his creativity were Chaplin-like, many times told by his character Bip. The charming stories and the beautiful style in which they were presented helped the church accept

mime as a moral art form. It came to view mime as a viable form of entertainment.

As a result of Marceau's popularity, Americans developed a form of street mime that was based on illusion and body isolation control. In the process street mime lost the depth of emotion evoked by Marceau. It focused on the technical execution of illusions such as walls, walks, and robots. Shields and Yarnel were an American couple who hosted a short-lived television program which showcased American mime. Their execution of robot motions made them famous and increased the popularity of illusionary mime. They were followed by many impersonators, but the American public grew tired of illusions and body isolations that carried no meaning. Mime began to lose popularity, but not before the church began to see possibilities for evangelism. Mime had been made acceptable by Marceau, and street mime was seen as a vehicle for Christian entertainment and street evangelism.

In the 1970s, Youth With A Mission (YWAM), now a worldwide ministry, created a mime-drama called *Toymaker and Son,* an allegory of Creation, the Fall, and redemption through Christ. The actors did not speak; instead, they performed gestures to a musical track with words. The gestures were copied easily, enabling YWAM to create many troupes which perform *Toymaker and Son* to this day. YWAM also created other dramas for ministry after the popular reception of this original production. In the 1980s, a group called Impact Productions recast this original work using more recent music.

MIMEistry International was created by Marceau-trained mime artists Todd and Marilyn Farley in 1989. Todd Farley has mimed in the church since 1978, toured worldwide using the art form, has written books and produced videos on mime, the arts, and biblical foundations for the arts. He is also an ordained minister, supporting art as ministry rather than entertainment. His ministry program is comprised of vignettes of 5–18 minutes and retells stories from Scripture, using the back-ground of contemporary Christian music. Like YWAM's *Toymaker,* Farley's mimography has been frequently copied by soloists and groups. Mime and actress Marilyn (Clark) married Todd Farley in 1989, and she coined the name MIMEistry (mime in ministry). With her encouragement Todd formalized the organization he had been creating since 1985 and MIMEistry was birthed. MIMEistry has been involved in street evangelism, prison work, missions, school educational programs, university courses, theater performances, fairs, conferences, and local ministry in churches and is represented in Europe, the Americas, and the Orient. MIMEistry has started groups around the world and has made use of hundreds of mimes forming the largest skilled mime network. Its purpose is to train others in the ministry of mime, balancing technical understanding and excellence with theological foundation.

Another mime artist of repute is J. Geoffrey Stevelson, an American who now resides in England. His style is English mime, which uses basic illusion and more natural gestures than French mime to tell stories. He performs in silence, using music and poetry. He has had a major effect on mime in England and has written two books on the subject. He has done a great deal of work with Tear Fund, a Christian charity, as well as ministering in countries where the organization works. He uses mime to crossover cultural barriers. Therefore many of his mimes are not overt "ministry" as much as moral and cultural expressions with Christian principles.

Randall Bane is an American who has encouraged the development of the movement arts. Bane trained in acting in New York, then later applied his knowledge to the creation of a clown character named Obie Good. In 1983 he began overseeing dancing at the Feast of Tabernacles in Israel. He has travelled the world using a mixture of movement arts (acting, clown, basic mime, gesture, and dance) and now encourages people to enter the ministry of movement.

Todd Farley

Mime in Worship. This ancient art form is enjoying new attention as a powerful and expressive means of worship.

380 • PLANNING AND LEADING MIME IN WORSHIP

Mimetic gestures have been increasingly used in worship in recent years, especially among charismatics. This article describes ways in which mime has been used in worship and gives suggestions for developing a mime ministry.

Mime is not new to worship, although it is not as common as dance. Mimetic movements have been done for years in songs like "Father Abraham," "This Little Light of Mine," and "His Banner over Me Is Love." In the 1980s mimes began to enjoy greater expression in the church's worship, expressing songs like "As the Deer Panteth for the Water," and "Glory to the Lamb." It has also been used to inter-

pret the song of the Lord. This shows an advancement of mime from children's church into the main sanctuary. The idea of using mime interpretation during worship has been introduced at conferences such as the International Worship Symposium.

When mime is used to interpret the song of the Lord, it usually occurs with visually oriented songs. The difficulty the mime faces is clearly hearing the words of the new song. It is better when the singer works with the mime as he/she interprets. The singer does this by watching the mime and giving him or her time to express each phrase and by repeating the phrase if necessary. The interpretation of the song of the Lord works especially well with antiphonal songs (songs that have repeating lines), and songs being translated into other languages.

This gives the mime time to compose an interpretation to perform during the translation. Since the meaning of movement does not change, the mime can add interest for all watching.

If a mime is to be used in a worship service, it should be used only with permission of the worship leader or pastor. Mime is done as an extension of the people and not as a personal expression, which would only distract from worship. The possibility to mime a song does not qualify it as a good time to mime. It must flow with the service overall and be understood as an expression of the people. If it does not express the praise of the people, it does not belong in the service as an expression of worship.

Mime in Preaching

Mimes' most encouraged role is in the function and expression of preaching ministry. Mime can be used to support the message of the pastor as "pulpit support" or in what has been called "illustrated sermons." A full mime presentation can be used to bring the full message of the Word into a living context. It is best presented in the time used for preaching. Mime can also be used in the support of or presentation of prophecy. In all of these ways mime can say what cannot be said in the spoken word, or what will not be heard as a spoken word. Its ministry potential lies in the fact that it reaches beyond the intellect and touches the heart, soul, and spirit of people where God can do His work.

Pulpit Support. The illustrated sermon has been used since leaders began to preach. Gestures give words emphasis and added strength to their meanings. Stories can be used to communicate the idea or applied thought behind the message being preached. Both seeing and hearing the word creates a stronger form of communication. For all these reasons mime is a good form of pulpit support.

When is pulpit support best used? When the subject matter is a story; when the subject matter is better approached by comedy than dissertation; when the subject needs to be applied and seen in everyday life to be fully understood; when the illustration adds emphasis; when the people will not hear the truth; when the people need to experience the truth—all of these are appropriate occasions for mime.

Where pulpit support is placed in the service depends upon its purpose. At the beginning of the sermon a mime can be used to introduce its subject.

In this case, the sermon can refer to the mime as a point of reference. A mime can also be used at the beginning of an event, to break the ice, or to warm up the public at the beginning. An unresolved mime may be used as the spring board for ministry, being presented before the sermon and allowing the preacher to resolve the issue in the sermon. In this way the mime becomes a cliffhanger, or the hook for the sermon.

Pulpit support may also be used in the middle of a sermon when it is necessary to illustrate a specific point. The mime does not need to have a conclusive thought; its focus is to emphasize the complete thought of the preacher. For example, if the sermon is on the process of conquering the Promised Land, the mimes might illustrate the isolated story of Jericho. The mime can also be used to complete the preacher's thought or statement. Pulpit support used at the end of a sermon usually creates a summary of what has been preached by capturing the main theme. This supports the message visually and leaves a lasting reinforcement of the sermon. A fitting example of this is the song and mime "Moses" by Ken Medema, which was originally created for this purpose. The song/mime not only summarized the sermon, but left the congregation with the need to respond to the call of God. Various types of ministry or altar calls are appropriate after this type of pulpit support.

Creating a Pulpit Support

The following worksheet may be helpful in preparing a pulpit support mime. Each of the questions that follow call attention to an important consideration in the development of a pulpit support.

1. What is the subject matter?
2. Who is the crowd?
   a. the church
   b. the youth
   c. the saved or unsaved
   d. secular venue
3. Determine the placement of the mime. Does the mime:
   a. introduce the sermon?
      1. as a reference point for the sermon
      2. as a spring board for the sermon
   b. illustrate a point in the middle of the sermon?
      1. the mime doesn't have to be complete of itself

2. the mime might complete the thought
3. the mime might illustrate the whole isolated thought
c. conclude the sermon?
    1. by summarizing the whole sermon or the theme
    2. by setting up the altar call or ministry time
4. Is it comic or tragic?
5. What are the specifications for the use of space, props, and technical backup (sound and lights, etc.)?
6. Should it be done as a mime, dance, drama, song, etc., or a mixture of arts?
7. Examine the text to be illustrated. A mime may be delivered in three manners:
    a. actions without words
    b. actions with words before or after
    c. actions with narrative at the same time
    (All of these ways can be presented with or without music.)
8. Is the preacher going to participate in the illustration?
9. How many people are to be in the piece and how much time do you have to prepare? (This might alter who is in the piece or the piece itself.)
10. Mimography (mime choreography). This step involves writing out the gestures of the mime.

The following are an example of answers to each of these questions.

1. **Subject**: giving God your ministry and letting him be in control of and empower it.
2. **For whom**: the church
3. **Placement**: at the end of the sermon, to prepare the people for an altar call given by the pastor.
4. **Comic or tragic**: should be comic with a serious end (comedy loosens people up and opens them up to become serious).
5. **Conditions**: support song, MOSES (PA needed). 10 x 10 stage area clear, red lights and general lighting
6. **Art form**: mime with music
7. **Delivered**: music and song tell the story enacted by the mime (actions with narration [the song]).

8. **Preacher participation**: The preacher will introduce and have the altar call after the piece.
9. **Number of players**: one; preparation time: one day
10. **Mimography**: Moses with mimed rod before the burning bush. (Moses looks toward down center stage and up to identify the burning bush before him.) Moses responds to the statement made by God. Moses throws down the rod and jumps when the rod becomes a snake. He does a comic mime run around the stage to escape. He stops and picks up the snake (after arguing with God), the snake changes into a rod. He manipulates the mime rod while God demonstrates his power through it. Then the mime becomes the narrator and mimes "what do you hold in your hands . . . throw it down!" (For the full mimography, consult the mime video _Quiet on the Set!_ by Todd and Marilyn Farley.)

Mime Prophecy

Mime prophecy uses advanced techniques of improvisation and the principles of pulpit support. The term _mime prophecy_ refers to a mime inspired for a specific ministry to a specific audience. A prophetic mime can be the spontaneous interpretation of a prophetic word, or a pre-mimographed piece that becomes a _rhema_ or word to the observer. Biblical prophets learned their mimes and then performed them (Ezek. 4–7), unless the mime was very basic (Acts 21:11), or verbally instructed and done by another person (2 Kings 13:14-19).

The difficulty of spontaneously interpreting a prophetic word in mime concerns the clarity of the words spoken and the predictability of the prophecy. The argument is that if the mime is to interpret the words of the speaker, then he or she needs to receive the prophecy visually and then mime it as the speaker utters what he has heard in his spirit.

If a mime enacts a prophecy, it is to be judged as prophecy, just like a spoken prophecy. It must be a clear and understandable expression, and it must be in agreement with the infallible Word of God. If it cannot be understood, it fails as a prophetic word. The purpose of mimed prophecies is to clarify and illustrate the word, not to confuse and obscure it.

Generally speaking, the mime receives images which in turn he or she translates into mime movements. Therefore, the mime will be limited to the vocabulary of movements which he or she knows.

Skilled mimes communicate more clearly because they have a richer mime vocabulary to do so. This skill, however, does not replace the anointing of the Spirit. Without anointing, a mime is only so much movement or at best a good story with no heart or spirit.

Before a mime ministers prophetically, he or she must have the mime approved by the leadership, thus demonstrating a submissive spirit. Since this style of spontaneous mime is less frequently used, it is better for it to be explained to and understood by the leadership and congregation before it is introduced as a ministry style, thus avoiding the danger of alienating people with something that is designed to minister to them. If people will not receive the spontaneously mimed prophecy, then both the prophecy and the mime have failed.

Prophetic mime has a power that goes beyond the traditional worship service, as the following two accounts indicate. The first describes a prophetic mime used in a political arena:

> During a visit to . . . New York, [Todd] Farley was called upon to deliver his "Sheep and Goats" message. The city's pastors and elected officials were divided over whether or not to support a Christian halfway house for the city's homeless. Farley's message not only brought unity among the pastors and favor for the project, but moved the secular city commissioners as well. . . . (from *Charisma,* March 1989)

The fact of the matter was that a church, pastoral council, and city was moved by a prophetic mime—not by the skill of the performer who had mimed the "Sheep and the Goats" for over three years, but by the power of God touching and ministering through the mime. The mime delivered a *rhema,* a word to the city.

A second example describes the use of prophetic mime in the context of worship. In 1991, during the Worship Symposium held at Living Waters Christian Fellowship in Pasadena, California, Rev. Charlotte Baker delivered a prophetic word which was spontaneously mimed by Todd Farley:

> She prophesied of being before the Throne of God: the mime showed being in awe of God. The prophecy spoke of the person asking God for various gifts to minister with such as song, music, and dance: the mime acted out receiving each of these gifts from God. The person spoke of ministering to the masses yet only some of them came to know God: the mime danced, sang, and played instruments before the crowd and was sad as only few responded to God. The person went back to the throne and asked God why it was that the people didn't come: the mime re-established being before the Throne and mimed the question with sorrow-ridden movements. God responded that the Gift was to be used to worship God, not entertain man: the mime danced, sang, and played instruments to worship God. Then as He played the people came, and came, and came. He mimed, she spoke "learn to sing and to play and to dance before your King. When you have learned this, then you will touch the World." (*Psalmist,* June/July 1991)

That is the ministry of mime.

Todd Farley

381 • An Example of Mime

The following instructions, called mimography, describe mimetic movements that may be used to portray Jesus' Parable of the Sower.

Copyrights on Mime Numbers

Mime numbers and a mime's face (make-up design) are copyrighted. This means they are the sole property of the mime. To use another mime's created piece without permission from the artist is against the law and is unethical. To perform another mime's work, it is necessary to contact the original creator of the piece and receive permission for performance.

Like sculpture and painting, the original works of mimography are always better than the copied work. Therefore, they are released by the artist for performance in local church ministry only. Any other use of this work for public performance is an infringement of copyright laws. Information for permission to perform another artist's number should be sought before the performance occurs.

The Sower, by Todd Farley

Mime Pulpit. *The Sower* is an example of a pulpit support mime (illustrated sermon) in which the preacher can play an active role as the narrator. This would be placed in the middle of the sermon. It can also be included in a regular mime concert or on the street.

Level of Difficulty. Beginner to intermediate.

Techniques Used. Variations of the "seed sower hand" and "march of the sower," stomping, and flight. The players should work on these techniques before trying to do the mime.

1. **The Seed.** The seed starts in a balled up position on the ground. The player sits on his or her feet, head forward to the floor; the arms are around the head on the floor.

The technique is described as an exercise where, through use of rhythms, the growth of a seed into a plant such as a flower transpires. Change the rhythm throughout the exercise to make the plant look like it is growing at an accelerated speed, like time-lapse photography (cf. Todd Farley, _Mastery of Mimodrame_).

The players _tocs_ (jerks) from the stomach to begin the process of growth into a plant. He or she should move each part of the body with a different rhythm, making vocal noises commensurate with the movement. The most important point to remember in executing the seed is variety of rhythm and movement: from slow to fast (with and without resistance), smooth (non-stop, _breath_) to sharp _(tocs, succade)_ and spasmodic.

2. **The Sower.** The hand position is a complex design using "lyric hand," "hand that takes" (or a variation of "claw hand"), "leaf hand" with "hand that gives." It then uses "marche Grecque" to transfer forward. (These techniques are illustrated on the video _Master of Mimodrame II_.)

Description of hand movement: The right hand starts at the side in "classical hand": a relaxed hand position in which the middle finger is slightly indented (as in ballet). The left arm is slightly opened to the side and to the front, similar to a ballet fourth position.

The right hand moves gracefully in a large arc right to left, continuing over the head to the open space between the left arm and the body. While the hand moves to this position, the palm is exposed to the audience in the "lyric hand" position (a flat hand position with the fingers together with the exception of the thumb and small finger).

When the right hand arrives to the space between the body and the left arm, it grabs imaginary seeds (a variation on claw hand) in a movement called "hand that takes." The palm is now toward the floor as the fingers close over the "seeds." Turn the right hand over and with a large horizontal arc, release the seed across the path, to the left and to the right. As the "seeds" are released, the right hand shakes ("leaf hand") in order to spread the seed.

After spreading the seed, the right hand returns to the right side of the body (ballet first) to begin the movement again. The left hand and arm remain in fourth position and do not move at all. The left arm is meant to create the illusion of the sack of seeds from which the right arm is getting seed to spread.

Add to these movements the "marche Grecque." The player breathes in and begins the movement of the right hand, while leaning back in preparation to take a step (backward balance). The player grabs the seed as he passes his central balance, then begins to step forward (and forward balance) onto the right foot while scattering seeds as he breathes out. When he steps on the left foot, he grabs the seed, and when stepping on the right, he scatters the seed. The steps are graceful and majestic. There is a slight _glissade_ (sliding) forward with each step; however, the balance is maintained over the forward foot even as it advances. This creates an appearance of each step floating onto the next.

3. **Flight.** "Flight" is the technique used for angels and birds. The arms begin in first position along the side of the body. The movement begins with the elbows bending upward lifting the arm. This movement is followed by the wrist and finally the hand. The whole movement is continued until the hands touch over head. After the arms are overhead, they come down by the elbow, twisting and bending down, beginning downward motion which is followed by the wrist and hand. The movement is finished when the arms reach the side of the body, at which time it starts over. The arm movements can be made smaller as the player learns to manipulate his/her elbows, then the movement can be contained within a chest-to-eye-level field of movement. "Oriental hand" or "wave hand" can be added to the end of this movement for extra effect.

While the arms are going upward the player goes into "demiplié" (bending the knees). When the arms are coming downward, the player is "tondue" (straightens up) and goes into "relevé" (onto his toes). This creates the illusion of flight.

4. **Stomping.** Stomping does not need to be refined. The focus is on the caricature of the destructive

bully. The "marche" should include a facial expression which is "frozen" like a mask and a one- and two-foot "stomp." The character has the freedom to grunt.

Cast:
    1 Sower
    3 Seeds
    1–3 Birds
    1–3 Stompers
    1 Sun
    2 Thorns
    1 Group of 30-fold Seed
    1 Group of 60-fold Seed
    1 Group of 100-fold Seed
      (30, 60, 100 can be repeats)
Minimum:
    4 Players

Scenario: [*The story is a retelling of the parable of the* Sower: *how he went out to plant his* Seed, *which is the Word of God, and how it was received or not received into people's hearts. It begins by showing the* Sower *sowing, continues by portraying the reason for the destruction of the first* Three Seeds, *and concludes by describing the success of the 30, 60, and 100-*fold Seed.]

──────── **Mimography:** *The Sower* ────────

Narrator: *(from off stage)* "Behold, a sower went out to sow the seeds of truth, and as he sowed, some seeds fell by the wayside where the wild birds swooped down and gobbled them up, and the truth was trodden down under the Evil One's foot."

Sower *(to upstage stage right) walks and sows* Seeds *taking three to six steps then stops. Give breath cue to* Seed.

First Seed *(center stage right) grows quickly and opens hands with fingers spread apart as if they were the petals of the plant's flower. The* Seed *is now presented as a plant. The player remains on his knees.*

Birds *(from upstage left) fly to* Seed *and surround the first* Seed, *one on either side of it and one behind it. Look at audience. Look at* Seed. *Look at audience and show hunger and wicked grins.* First Bird *slowly brings arms above head and back in a counterpoint then "picks" and eats the first petal (finger) on the plant. The* Second *and*

Third Birds *follow the example nodding encouragement to each other and cooing contentment. The eating becomes frenzied as the* Three Birds *attack the fingers in an eating rage. They fly off, licking their fingers happily, flying off with leaps and with arabesques.*

First Seed *As the* Birds *eat each petal (finger), bend the finger as if it has been removed and show fear of the* Birds. *Then show pain at their frenzied attack. Whimper at the audience as the* Birds *fly off. Show the audience stubby hands as a plea for sympathy.*

Stompers *stomp on stage and surround first* Seed *in a half circle, leaving opening revealing the* Seed. *Look at the* Seed. *Look at the audience, laugh wickedly at the audience, then at each other. Stop. The* Stompers *jump and grunt as they stomp around the* Seed, *complete one circle and stop.*

First Seed *reacts with jerking changes of positioning as the* Stompers *jump about. When they have finished, the* Seed *is all the way on the ground again, as in the beginning. The* Seed *tries to recover, shuddering and breathing in and looking to the audience as it struggles to rise.*

Stompers *see the* Seed *trying to recover and give one final great stomp.*

[First Seed *responds to the final stomp by being violently cast down in a slightly sprawled out position.* Stompers *laugh and stomp off.*]

Narrator: "Some of the seeds of truth fell upon rocky ground and some even on the rocks, where they had but scanty soil. They sprang up quickly in the shallow soil, shooting up and sprouting charismatically; like those who receive the Seed of Truth straightway with joy, but it takes no real root in them. They endure for a while but lack any staying power and are unable to hold out long against the affliction and persecution of the sun's heat. Therefore, the seed is scorched and because it has no roots it withers away, becoming dry and dead."

Sower *(to upstage stage center) walks and sows* Seeds *taking three to six steps then stops. Give breath cue to* Seed.

Second Seed *(center stage) grows quickly (staying on its knees) using gestures that resemble a charismatic Christian stereotype. Last pose is that of open hands up in a "hallelujah" and a big grin.*

Sun *(directly behind second seed) rises from behind the* Seed *facing the audience. As it rises it uses its* arms in large round sweeping movements which shoot above the head and then come back in a graceful arc to the sides. The hand and arm design is a variation on "lyric hand." The SUN beams down on the SEED with a malicious look. The SUN continues to move its arms in a round motion as the SEED.

SECOND SEED _begins to sweat, indicated by blinking, fanning itself, wiping its brow, and smelling its clothes: each gesture is separated for effect and accelerates in rhythm (increase speed and intensity). After each gesture the_ SEED _tries to look happy-go-lucky until it tries to relieve itself with another gesture during which it shows the audience its discomfort. The_ SEED _begins to wither whimpering and "oohing" as its hands melt closed, its arms retract, its body quivers and shrinks into itself until the_ SEED _is on the floor._

[_The_ SUN _interrupts its "beaming" to give a gesture of triumph toward the audience (thumbs-up, brushing its fingernails, or showing its muscles), then it sits still using the round movement of the arms until it is hidden behind the_ SEED _again._]

NARRATOR: "Another seed fell among the thorns of anxiety, thistles of worry, and the brambles of worldly care. As the seed grew, the thorns, thistles, and brambles shot up and offered the seed false glamor, wealth, and the lusts of life. While the seed was lost in its own cravings, the thorns completely choked its life out. Since it could not yield fruit it died with nothing to show for its life."

SOWER _(to upstage stage left) walks and sows_ SEEDS _taking three to six steps then stops. Give breath cue to_ SEED.

THIRD SEED _(center stage left) grows up with gestures of wealth, pride, and glamor (fixing its hair, polishing its fingernails, etc.). The last position is one of posing for a glamor photo, breathe out or hit the floor with foot to indicate to the_ THORNS _of finish. (As with the others the_ SEED _only grows up onto its knees.)_

THORNS _(two players: upstage and to either side of the_ SEED_) upon hearing the cue to go, shoot up with clawed hands in the air and evil faces grunting at the audience. Grunt toward_ SEED. _Grunt toward each other, snicker, and begin attack approach to the_ SEED.

[_The_ SEED _inhales dropping arms, looking forward in concern. Brief stop . . . on the stop_ THORNS _drop_

arms and assume an innocent facial expression. The SEED looks back sharply to see the THORNS and stops. The THORNS smile and wave at her. The SEED turns back slowly to the audience and shrugs her shoulders and refreezes with a toc into a glamor pose._]

[_The_ THORNS _then resume their evil aggressive attack, grabbing her around the throat and choking her to the ground. The_ SEED _shoots out its arms reaching for help, gasping like the lady victim of a Dudley Do-Right film._]

[_Once on the ground, the_ THORNS _grab a mime dagger and plunge it into the body of the_ SEED_; the_ SEED_'s body reacts, arching upward as the dagger is pulled out (this is comic rather than tragically done). The_ THORNS _then throw away the dagger, look toward the audience, laugh, and shoot back down to the floor._]

NARRATOR: "The last are those good seeds which are received in the soil of the open heart, where the word is accepted and taken in. Embraced by the good soil the seed of truth multiples in the lives of those who accept it, bringing forth fruit thirty times."

[_The_ SOWER _walks backward to upstage stage right._]

ALL OTHERS _While the narrative is being read all players roll into three groups. A_ LARGE GROUP _(thirty fold) of "_SEEDS_" center stage right, a_ MEDIUM GROUP _(sixty fold) of_ SEED _center stage, and a_ SMALL GROUP _(hundred fold) center stage left._

[_On the cue "thirty times," the_ SOWER _sows_ SEED, _then stops. The_ LARGE GROUP _(thirty fold) grows to sitting positions with arms up and faces shining._]

NARRATOR: "sixty times"

[_On the cue "sixty times," the_ SOWER _sows_ SEED, _then stops. The_ MEDIUM GROUP _grows up onto their knees with arms up and faces aglow._]

NARRATOR: "and a hundred times as much as was sown."

[_On "a hundred times," the_ SOWER _sows_ SEED, _then stops, and the last_ SMALL GROUP _grows to a standing position, arms up and faces aglow. All freeze._]

NARRATOR: "If any man has ears to hear, let him hear! Be careful how you listen, give your minds to that which you have heard by sight and sound: for from that which you have received you shall be able to give to others, and the more seeds of truth you measure and deal out to others, the more it shall be given and added unto you."

[*End mime with neutral walk off the stage by players. At this point the pastor would continue his sermon.*]

Todd Farley

382 • BIBLIOGRAPHY OF MIME IN WORSHIP

De Angelis. William. *Acting Out the Gospels.* Mystic, Conn.: Twenty-Third Publications, 1982. Nineteen clowning, miming, dramatic presentations for use in liturgy. Scripture texts and full notes on organization, set design, staging, and make-up. Material developed to coincide with events in the church year on Gospel themes, Bible personalities, seasons, and celebrations. Tested in an actual parish setting.

Farley, Todd. *The Silent Prophet.* Shippensburg, Pa.: Destiny, 1989. Farley draws on instances of the dramatic arts in Scripture to teach that God uses actions to speak louder than words and that human bodies and dramatic art forms are instrumental in delivering His message. Mime is his focus. The book is an apologetic for this and other dramatic art forms as prophetic ministry of the human body.

Farley, Todd and Marilyn. *The Mastery of Mimodrame,* 3 vol. Shippensburg, Pa: MIMEistry International, 1988. Books and videos on mime from professionals in the field. Volume one contains foundational material on movement, positions, and the first steps in classical mime. Volume two covers advanced hand designs, marches, double design, and transfer concepts of Marceau, Decroux, and Farley. Volume three includes an in-depth section on statuary mime and more transfer concepts.

_____.*Quiet on the Set!* (videocassette recording). Shippensburg, Pa: MIMEistry International. A collection of seven performance numbers of Christian mime that illustrates mime ministry in solo, duet, and troupe performances and combines it with dance, acrobatics and contemporary music.

Kalbere, Jan, and Jack Krall. *Finding the Clown in Yourself.* San Jose, Calif.: Resource Publications, 1987. The book is about discovery and description: (1) discovering the clown inside the Christian through consideration of the Scriptures and especially through the life of Jesus, and (2) describing how to become a clown through skills, techniques, and exercises. Exercises, tips, stories, and reflections.

Kelley, Gail. *Come Mime With Me.* San Jose, Calif.: Resource Publications, 1987. Creative, step-by-step approach to putting scriptural mime dramas together for children. Each of the ten dramas is complete with preparatory material, narrator's text, stage direction, performance notes, and reflective summary.

Kipnis, Claude. *The Mime Book.* San Francisco: Harper and Row, 1974. A graphically complete presentation of the art of mime as well as accompanying text. Subjects are divided into three parts: (1) body, (2) illusion, and (3) creating a world. Subheadings are clear and text/photos/illustrations are concise and accurate.

Liebenow, Mark. *Is There Fun After Paul? A Theology of Clowning.* San Jose, Calif.: Resource Publications, 1987. Thesis: Christians are fools for Christ's sake and are therefore clowns with accompanying characteristics of faith, joy, humility, hope, and celebration. Touching, healing, and nurturing are Christ-like functions of Christian ministry. Biblical, ecclesial, historical material on clowns and clowning. God's love of laughter and liturgical clowning are discussed. Vast bibliographic resource (65 pages) and a good resource list.

Martin, Ben. *Marcel Marceau: Master of Mime.* Ottawa: Optimum, 1978. Martin's attempt is a photo essay on Marceau which alerts the aspiring artist to positioning and style. Performance and private moments are included as well as technical information.

Robertson, Everett. *The Ministry of Clowning.* Nashville: Broadman, 1983. An invaluable resource in the how-to's of religious clowning. The ministry dimension is covered in the first two chapters and technical areas follow in the latter five. Topics range from "Choosing a Clown Character and Personality" to the nitty gritty of make-up, costumes, props and staging. Resources section and bibliography.

PART FIVE

The Art of Language in Worship

The Use of Language
in Worship

Language has always been at the center of discussions about worship. In highly liturgical churches, concerns about language are focused on a fixed text. In free churches, choice of language is primarily the domain of a pastor or worship leader, whose selection of words for prayers and introduction of the various parts of the service may be either extemporaneous or written beforehand. In almost every tradition, texts set to music are scrutinized.

Most often, when the language of worship is discussed, theological and cultural issues are central. Texts of prayers, sermons, and songs are analyzed for their faithfulness to Scripture and to the central tenets of the Christian faith. The same texts are scrutinized for how they respond to and are sensitive to all persons in the worshiping congregation.

But language also has aesthetic qualities. Metaphors and images make language more imaginative and meaningful. The rhythm and rhyme of language make it memorable and momentous.

This section will discuss the aesthetic qualities of language appropriate for worship in relationship to theological and pastoral concerns. Chapter 22 will address general concerns related to liturgical language, concentrating on the language of prayer. Chapter 23 focuses more specifically on the use of poetry—the most self-conscious of all the uses of language—in worship.

The language of prayer from one tradition to the next varies perhaps more than any other element of worship. Some liturgies feature carefully crafted prayers written by skilled poets and liturgists for use on a given occasion; others include prayers that have been refined through centuries of use; still others include only extemporaneous prayers conceived in direct response to what is happening in a given service. The following articles examine the implications of these various approaches to liturgical language. Each article at some point refers to the aesthetic qualities of language, including image, metaphor, diction, and rhythm. Each article combines these concerns with theological and cultural issues important to liturgical language. Taken together, these articles argue for giving more attention to the language of worship, including its aesthetic dimensions.

383 ◆ PHILOSOPHICAL AND THEOLOGICAL ISSUES REGARDING LANGUAGE IN WORSHIP

The nature of language is a topic of significant recent interest to liturgical scholars. The following article outlines some of the most difficult questions these scholars address. These questions can also be helpful to worship planners and leaders as they reflect on the language they use in worship.

Introduction

Language is one of the primary ways that a people's culture is indicated and transmitted. Liturgical language is that set of words, usually vernacular but not necessarily colloquial, with which the Christian assembly publicly prays. What are the many issues that concern us as we choose the language for our liturgy? In order to give our conversation specific focus, we shall consider the liturgical use of the tetragrammaton (YHWH as a name for God; cf. Exodus 3) as our primary case in point as we attempt to list the questions concerning liturgical language before the Christian churches today.

God's Unspeakability

We begin where all liturgical language begins: the Bible. In Exodus 3, in a written record of a long-past religious experience, we are told that God appeared to Moses in the mysterious form of a burning bush and revealed divinity as merciful. When Moses asks the divine name, the answer in our text is one typically Hebraic in its mystery: four sacred consonants are given, YHWH, perhaps meaning I AM WHO I AM, perhaps meaning something else. The story demonstrates a fundamental religious conviction of the Hebrew people: human language cannot articulate divinity. God cannot be completely grasped by the human being: only the revelation, here the tale of the burning bush, can be spoken. Thus, when the Hebrew people read this story in the liturgy, and when they inculturated this legend into contemporary use, since they believed that God's height and depth cannot finally be spoken, they refused to pronounce this divine name. This intuition concerning the unknowability of God lives on in the most profound theologians—Augustine and Aquinas, for example—as well as in Christian mystics, for whom the *via negativa* testifies to the inability of human language to speak fully of God.

Questions about God's Unspeakability. How much is the unspeakability of God a Christian concept, and to what extent ought this idea guide our decisions about liturgical language?

Biblical Roots

To circumvent pronouncing the divine name, the Hebrews substituted *Adonai,* a cultural title for the male authority figure, for the sacred name of God. This was not intended as an accurate translation, or, in the words of current translators, "a dynamic equivalent," but as substitution of an honorific title for God's proper name. Apparently the Jews felt free to adapt the scriptural tradition for purposes of liturgical use. Another example of this tendency occurred when the rabbis incorporated into their liturgy the passage describing God in Exodus 34. They were perplexed that the text stated that God would not forgive: since their experience was that God did forgive, their quotation of the Exodus passage reversed the negative. It is frustrating that the process of these decisions has been lost to us, who would probably find the controversies all too familiar!

Questions about Biblical Roots. In what ways is Christian liturgical language bound to biblical language? Can liturgical language alter or contradict biblical language? How do we come to agree on a new rendering of the original Hebrew and Greek?

How do we render the androcentric bias of the biblical languages?

Translation

The Hebrew text was translated into the Septuagint by the Hellenized Jews in yet another example of inculturation. Throughout the translation one can see Judaism influenced by the Greek theological idea that God can indeed be known and spoken by the philosophical mind. Plato believed that there was precise correspondence between the divine mind and the human mind. It was possible to attain, even to remember, divine truth. We see the Greek idea replacing the Hebraic, for example, as the Septuagint rendered *El Shaddai,* yet another mysterious name for God in the Hebrew Scriptures, as "God Almighty." A conceptual adjective has replaced the ancient and mysterious metaphoric image of divinity. In the Exodus 3 passage, the tetragrammaton drops out of the Septuagint completely, replaced first by the Greek words *Ego eimi,* and later by the Greek word for the male authority figure, *Kyrios.* This noun was used contemporarily both as the common title for a man and as the exalted title for the emperor.

Questions about Translation. Are there traditional translations of biblical language which because of contemporary culture we must now alter? How do we inculturate biblical ideas into our tongue without making the gospel captive to culture-bound categories?

Christology

As Christians redefined Hebrew religious language, Christianity became distinct from Judaism. "That Jesus is Lord" reuses both the image of Joshua and the title of Kyrios: in such redefinitions of central Hebrew terms, Christianity was articulated. The primary break from Judaism came in the Christian use of the Hellenistic Jewish title for God, Kyrios, as also the title for Jesus. That Easter baptisms are pascha, that there is in Jesus a new covenant, that we are anointed as priests, that we are the tribes of Israel renewed: these are only a few of the central Jewish words and images which acquire new meaning for Christians.

Questions about Christian Speech. How can Christianity continue to use Hebrew ideas and texts typologically, i.e., redefined with reference to Christ, without the anti-Semitic implication that Christians have replaced Jews in the heart of God? How can liturgical language remain christologically orthodox?

Analogy

As Christians continued the endless task of translation of the gospel, they came to rely on Thomas Aquinas's discussion of religious language for their intellectual foundation. Aquinas attempted to combine the Hebrew idea of the incomprehensibility of God with the Greek hope for Platonic correspondence in his brilliant concept of analogy. Aquinas hoped that analogy would allow Christians to speak truth about and to God. When language became too obviously metaphoric—God being a rock or a lion—Aquinas relegated it to a lesser position, for Greek inquiries into truth were biased against metaphor's "deficient resemblance." Concerning Exodus 3, Aquinas found "He Who Is" the best name for God, because it met perfectly his understanding of the philosophical nature of divinity: the name said best that God is God's essence.

Questions about Thomism. Is analogous language more true about God than metaphoric? Which liturgical language is analogous?

Metaphor

However, most of the twentieth-century world is no longer Thomist. The great chain of being is broken. Since a hierarchy of being is no longer assumed, analogical language cannot be trusted as more truthful than other language. Nominalism proposed that words were not God-given labels, and eighteenth-century philosophers suggested that language has its meaning only within a community of discourse. Contemporary theorists of language like Paul Ricoeur suggested that metaphor is the highest form of human expression; it is the addition and transfer of meaning, the creation of complex discourse, the building blocks of human thought. There is no clear distinction between literal and metaphoric language: words have meaning only within the sentence and within the community. Religious language is meaningful self-contradictory expression in which the community understands certain meanings by a series of noises it makes together.

Questions about Metaphor. How does the church inculturate its traditional belief in the truth of inspiration into a secular culture in which language has

no exterior proof? How does the metaphoric quality of liturgical language influence our composition of liturgical language? What is the relationship between metaphoric religious language and the doctrines of the faith? How do we teach metaphor to a computer age?

We have traveled from an oral Semitic legend about the sacred name of God to many current questions about what words Christians use in the liturgy. As far as I know, all contemporary Christian traditions use as the name for God and the title for Jesus a noun designating the male authority figure. There are obvious problems with this word: In American English the word _Lord_ is archaic; in many Romance and Germanic languages the word is the same title normally addressed to any male. Yet the christological significance of this word makes it extremely prominent in the liturgy. The layers of religious transmission are known only to a few, and the metaphoric quality of the word is seldom probed.

Of course, all these problems concern not only the sacred tetragrammaton. Scripture scholars remind us that the central image throughout the entire Bible is the royal metaphor. King, kingdom of heaven, city of God, majesty, to reign, to inherit, to anoint, the King of the Jews, the ascension, apocalypse, even Son of God: all this language is derived from the ancient near eastern religious idea of the divine origin of the monarch, and inevitably becomes altered in the history of translation, as well as being redefined in the light of Christ.

Liturgical language is the traditional and yet inculturated speech of the assembled community, the church's treasury of metaphors offered to honor God and to enrich the body of Christ. The past asks us in the present whether we are being biblical and orthodox, and the future begs us to alleviate human misery with the mercy of God. Our liturgical language must continue to address these great and many issues. It is clear that our tasks with service books and hymnals are never done.

Gail Ramshaw[119]

384 • THE NATURE OF LANGUAGE FOR WORSHIP

The language of worship is responsive both to the scriptural tradition in which Christians worship and to the cultural context in which the worship event takes place. The interplay between these forces is dynamic and formative, challenging the church to examine the language it uses in worship. This *article was written in the early 1980s in response to many of the changes in language in worship in the 1960s and 1970s. It discusses many issues pertaining to language for worship that remain important today.*

Someday church historians will sift the ashes of the 1960s and 70s and happen on the fact of liturgical renewal. During a twenty-year time span almost every branch of Christian community rewrote liturgy. Prayer books were published, draft services through to finished volumes. In addition, collections of prayers were put out (e.g., Huub Oosterhuis, *Your Word Is Near: Contemporary Christian Prayers* [Westminster, Md.: Newman Press, 1968]; Michael Quoist, *Prayers* [New York: Sheed and Ward, 1963]; Omer Tanghe, *Prayers from Life* [New York: P. J. Kennedy, 1968], and others) not to mention reams of experimental material. Not since the sixteenth century has there been such a dramatic recasting of forms for worship. Looking back, what can we say about the "new" language of worship?

—————————— I ——————————

Let us begin by bowing to the fact of inevitable change: *a new liturgical language was necessary.* Suddenly in mid-twentieth century the English language, along with the other world linguistic systems, changed. In 1934, the fat *Webster's Dictionary* contained about 450,000 words. By 1978, lexicographers guessed that perhaps 150,000 of the original 450,000 words were still in use. Meanwhile, particularly in the 1960s, more than 200,000 new words invaded the language (see David Buttrick, "Renewal of Worship—A Source of Unity?" *Ecumenism, The Spirit, and Worship,* ed. L. Swindler [Pittsburgh: Duquesne University Press, 1967], 215–236). Not since the collapse of the Greco-Roman world or the dissolution of the medieval synthesis has there been such awesome reconstruction of the language. For three hundred years school children have plowed through Shakespeare with some understanding, now they reach for a "pony": the world of words has radically altered.

Von Humboldt understood that people do not have a language, they live in a language. Language constitutes the world we live in and may also shape our identity in the world. So, when language suddenly alters, human consciousness is, in a sense, being reconstructed. All of which poses special problems for those who would scribble liturgy. Not only must prayers and forms of worship be translated into a new language, they must be reformed: the metaphors and images that speak faith to faith must be searched, weighed, and chosen anew. If, at present, theologians are mute, struggling to find referential language for "God-talk," those who write liturgy are equally confounded. Is it any wonder that liturgical texts penned in the 1960s and 1970s are necessarily transient, fabricated in between-the-ages language that will in time beg revision? Language of transcendence is usually the product of an interrelation between faith and cultural "models" (often cosmological). We live now in what must be described as the death of the Protestant Era (A Catholic Era having ebbed some four hundred years earlier!), and we do not yet know what shape Christian community will have in the future toward which God beckons us. So any liturgical language we attempt will require future revision. The worst mistake a committee constructing liturgy today could make would be to aim at "imperishable prose." When language changes we have to rewrite words for worship—we have no choice, but our liturgical language as all language is currently in transition. So our liturgical writing is at best makeshift: unstable words stammering in the face of Mystery.

—————————— II ——————————

Liturgical language relates to Scripture on the one hand and a community of faith on the other: it is a people's language responding to their constitutive revelation which is crystallized in Scripture. It was no accident then that liturgical renewal came hand in hand with the publication of new Bible translations. For centuries, Christian worshipers have sung Psalms, heard lections, and prayed remembering stories of God-with-us. Trace your way through twenty centuries of Christian liturgy and you will find in the forms of worship not only scriptural quotation but an astonishing wealth of scriptural allusion. So, quite obviously, contemporary texts for worship have been influenced in style and substance by new versions of Scripture—RSV, Jerusalem, NEB, NAB, Phillips, and the like. Those who complain that worship has lost loveliness or who long for elegant Elizabethan English usually bemoan recent translations of Scripture as well (although how anyone can translate crass *koine* Greek into soaring prose is a mystery!).

While liturgical language works off Scripture, it also relates to human language, to the speaking of a people. Therefore, historically, liturgical language has employed a minimal common vocabulary with theological precision. By speaking of a people's language and mentioning a minimal vocabulary, we are underlining the fact that liturgy uses *public* language. Liturgies created by individuals, charmed into poetic expression, have seldom worked well: liturgical language is for a people to *use,* not admire. While liturgy is in the language of people, it must express a confession of faith: thus the primary criterion for liturgical language is theology. While liturgy moves from Scripture and employs ordinary language of a people, historic confessions of faith govern liturgical expression. Like it or not, liturgies are theological documents, so that style, structure, image, and the like must be weighed theologically. Because communities of faith are in time and culture, ongoing theological controversies are bound to emerge in the production of liturgy and are usually resolved by means of political compromise (The committee that labored long over *The Worshipbook* argued over features of the Eucharistic Prayer for years!). All we are saying is that liturgical writing is a delicate theological pastime involving an interaction of Scripture and public language, not to mention technical matters such as rhyme, syntax, metaphor, and the like.

--------------------- III ---------------------

Of course, underlying all liturgical language are what might be termed "models," which in turn delineate fields from which metaphors may be drawn. For example, Daniel Stevick notes that the Anglican *Book of Common Prayer,* dating from the sixteenth century, draws heavily on the model of Sovereignty: God is King, his people are subjects; God is throned on high, his people bow in dependence (Daniel B. Stevick, *Language in Worship* [New York: Seabury Press, 1970], 41–52). Now, obviously, a quick tour of the book of the prophet Isaiah will convince anyone that the sovereignty model is biblical. But, just as obviously, the model was also cultural, for the prayer book was penned in a land unified by the majesty of a crowned head. (No wonder Anglophiles still trill Cranmer's cadences with glee!) There are many, many other biblical "models" and metaphors in Scripture which may be more useful, indeed meaningful, to our current cultural setting. The problem nowadays is that some biblical models, cosmological (e.g., a four-cornered earth with umbrella-like heavens above) and social (e.g., a

patriarchal society) may no longer speak for faith or to faith in our world. "Models" of transcendence are a peculiarly difficult problem for even though the seventies moved from *nihil* implicit in the fifties toward a sense of undefined Mystery, our sky (Henny Penny!) is still somewhat fallen. All we are noting is that liturgical metaphor will imply "models" and that such models will have to be carefully chosen.

Lately, we have heard a number of complaints to the effect that liturgical writings in the 1960s and 1970s failed to evoke a sense of transcendent wonder; as poetry they failed to convey any feel for "otherness"; a criticism which is no doubt true. Nevertheless, the complaint is worth analyzing more deeply. Obviously liturgical writers are stuck with a language at hand. Twentieth century English may well mirror our age: it is startlingly secular. A trip through Kucera and Francis's *Computational Analysis of Present Day American English* [Providence: Brown University Press, 1967] will confirm the suspicion that traditional sacral language has slipped out of use, and a study of metaphor may indicate what literary critics have idly noticed, namely that about the time of Proust, holy metaphor reversed and became a device to enhance the secular. Just as gender has largely dropped from language so that the world is no longer richly sexual, leaving us to contend with personal pronouns and plumbing alone, so a sense of the sacred is no longer alive in our language and we are left bereft—"then the angels went away."

Let us probe the matter more deeply still. Romantic hopes to the contrary, liturgical language is public language and therefore is less open to poetic systems than is supposed. Poetry is metaphor, but metaphor to function in public language must be in the public mind. A recent work by Lakoff and Johnson, *Metaphors We Live By,* confirms the notion that metaphors relate to "models" and that public metaphor is determined by models in public mind: no models, no public metaphor (Chicago: University of Chicago Press, 1980). For liturgy to regain a sense of transcendent wonder we may have to wait the re-forming of models in the cultural mind. What liturgy written between-the-ages can do is to go for what Paul Tillich termed "natural" symbols, namely basic metaphors associated with universal human experience—e.g., light, darkness, birth, death, height, depth, etc. while looking toward a rebirth of common faith and common "models" for faith. However, it is worth noting that great liturgies of the Western church have never been metaphorically elaborate or given to poetic flights; they have been remarkably matter-of-fact, terse, and governed by poetic restraint. No doubt, when framed, they were regarded as bland.

IV

A more difficult problem for liturgical writing has to do with form. Attempts at developing new forms have been less than successful, particularly in the deluge of experimental material that was hustled off presses in the late 1960s. Liturgical writing has always worked in forms or from forms, most notably the collect and the litany. Because forms are social products and are seldom the result of individual creativity, most successful attempts at liturgical revision are likewise seldom the result of individual creativity. Instead, such attempts have worked with inherited forms, modifying a given rather than fabricating something new. When in the 1930s poetry found new voice, it did so by recovering patterns that were already lying about in ordinary language. Liturgy can adopt much the same tactic: traditional forms may be modified by the vitalities in ordinary public language. What liturgy cannot do is to be formless.

The collect form, brilliantly studied in J. W. Sutter, Jr.'s famous essay, is probably indispensable because it is good theology and may be native to the movement of religious consciousness (*The Book of English Collects* [New York: Harper and Brothers, 1940], xv–liii). The *theo*-logic of the form is worth attention. While Sutter distinguishes three kinds of collects, we can examine what he labels "Type A," which is composed of: (1) an address, (2) descriptive clause(s), (3) petition(s) or thanksgiving(s), and (4) an ending. The address usually features an attribute of God (e.g., "Mighty God" or "God of Compassion") which is not only a confession of faith but may well be *raison d'etre* for praying. The descriptive clause which follows points to a basis for faith in revelation or in the community's system of belief. So, for example, Israel might pray, "Mighty God, you drew back waves of the sea and let your people go through the waters . . . ," remembering deliverance from Egypt through the Reed Sea. Usually the address and the descriptive clause relate: would Israel call God "mighty" if the marvels of deliverance were not remembered? The petition (or thanksgiving) in turn depends on the memory found in the descriptive clause. Remembering how YHWH liberated the people of Israel from Egypt, we dare presume a promise of liberation now, "Set us free from every bondage," and even guess God's purpose in liberation, "So we may ever praise you." The conclusion of a collect, in its simplest form, is "through Jesus Christ." The conclusion not only recalls the impulse for all Christian praying, namely confidence in God's love founded on revelation in Christ, but also affirms faith that our praying is mediated through the high priestly intercession of a Risen Lord. Though some collects keep form with greater care than others, every collect is a theological pattern with immense usefulness for public worship.

The collect has been with us for centuries, from the *Shmone 'Esreh* of Jewish worship to the present day and has survived surely because it is theologically precise and does match the natural movements of faith-consciousness. The problem for writers of contemporary liturgy is how to retain the form while avoiding infelicities such as "you who" at the beginning of the descriptive clause. *The Worshipbook* embraces collect form and contains numerous collects, some of which may work:

> Merciful God, who sent Jesus to eat and drink with sinners: lead us to your table and be present with us, weak and sinful people, that, fed by your love, we may live to praise you, remembering Jesus Christ our Savior. (*The Worshipbook,* [Philadelphia: Westminster Press, 1970], 15)

The collect form can, of course, be expanded or written loosely as a substructure within longer prayers, as in the following:

> Almighty God: by your power Jesus Christ was raised from death. Watch over dying men and women. Fill eyes with light to see beyond human sight a home within your love, where pain is gone and frail flesh turns to glory. Banish fear. Brush tears away. Let death be gentle as nightfall, promising a day when songs of joy shall make us glad to be together with Jesus Christ, who lives in triumph, the Lord of life eternal. (ibid., 185)

The astonishing thing about a collect form is that while it disciplines word with theological tough-mindedness, it also permits vitalities of ordinary language to function. Though the form is ancient it is open to contemporary usage. Here is a modified collect filled with colloquial expression:

Eternal God: your Son Jesus had no place to lay his head, and no home to call his own. We pray for men and women who follow seasons and go where the work is, who harvest crops or do part-time jobs. Follow them around with love, so they may believe in you and be pilgrim people, trusting Jesus Christ the Lord. (ibid. p. 190)

Notice, whether loosely built or tightly woven, the collect tends to produce disciplined terseness in prayer, poetic compression and intensity, as well as a framework that is theologically appropriate.

The other major liturgical form is litany, a responsive system which has pre-Christian roots and has been employed century after century in worship. "The Grey Book," a proposed revision of the English *Book of Common Prayer* printed in 1933, contains examples of the litany in its many stock forms, e.g., depreciations ("from . . ."); obsecrations ("by . . ."); suffrages ("that . . ."), etc. (This revision was published in America as *The Kingdom, the Power and the Glory* [New York: Oxford University Press, 1933. For a useful discussion of different litany systems, see W. Maxwell, *Concerning Worship* [New York: Oxford University Press, 1948].) Now, clearly, many of the stock systems contain archaic responses and sometimes cumbersome grammar, but nevertheless they may imitate natural modes of speaking before God.

Writers who employ litany form ought to become familiar with problems of internal sequence, as well as with a variety of possible constructions. If we adapt a form, or even break a form, we must first master the form itself in classical expressions. *The Worshipbook* contains a number of litanies, some of which are worth studying, such as the Litany for the Church, pp. 116–118 (by David Romig); the Litany of Thanksgiving, pp. 114–115, or perhaps the Litany for the Nation, pp. 127–129. These litanies work from classical patterns but modify form in various ways. Some of *The Worshipbook* litanies depart from traditional form experimentally, such as the less than successful Litany of the Names of the Church (pp. 121–123).

V

Before addressing matters of style, it may be well to rehearse an ancient controversy. The matter comes to a head in a little work by Luther entitled "A Short and Good Exposition of the 'Our Father' Backwards and Forwards" (*Luther's Works*, Weim-

arer Ausgabe, VI, 21–22). Luther remarks that the Lord's Prayer begins with a hallowing of God's Name before it turns to our needs. Should the pattern be reversed by putting our needs first, then by the time we turn to God we may desire him not for his own sake but as answer to our clamorous needs. What is the content of worship, our needs, our religious affections, or God's glory? The Reformed tradition has always opted for objective worship (e.g., Westminster Shorter Catechism, question #1— Q. "What is the chief end of Man?" A. "To glorify God and enjoy Him forever"). Of late, much liturgical writing seems to have plunged into subjective affect: "We are here, Lord, with our guilts and hang-ups, aware of our . . ." While we may well wish to investigate religious affections, reading them in mirrored reflections of God's presence to faith as some phenomenologially oriented theologians have recently done, the task is meditative and better suited to private devotion than to public acts of worship (see, for instance, R. R. Niebuhr, *Experiential Religion* [New York: Harper and Row, 1972], and Donald Evans, *Struggle and Fulfillment* [New York: Collins, 1979]). Our age seems to have been co-opted by the triumph of the therapeutic, so that worship may well be viewed by some as a psychoanalytic, on-the-couch speaking, but we may well be suspicious of liturgical language overloaded with "we" and "our" and "us." Before God's glory we may become aware of our human nature in a new way: the Lord's Prayer does move from God's will to human need, but the order of movement, as Luther observed, may be crucial. The object of our concern in worship is God remembered and anticipated, not a wallow of affections.

VI

What is liturgical language? Earlier we noticed that liturgy is influenced by Scripture but made out of ordinary public language. Now we must distinguish liturgical language with greater care. Though liturgy employs ordinary language, it does so in an extraordinary way, by speaking to God. Some churches of late have begun worship cheerfully with:

Leader: Good morning.
PEOPLE: GOOD MORNING!

They use ordinary language in an ordinary way, forgetting its extraordinary function. The usage is a come-down from:

Leader: The Lord be with you.
PEOPLE: AND WITH YOU.

So liturgy uses ordinary language in an extraordinary way and, in doing so, stretches language, elevates language, producing a certain oddness. Now the alteration of ordinary language in worship is not necessarily in the direction of poetic diction. Yes, any speaking of God moves toward metaphor, the stuff of poetry, because our only recourse in making God talk is either analogy or mystic silence (never a serious Reformed Church option). But analogy once ventured begs correction. To say, for example, "God loves us with a Mother's love," immediately prompts recognition of categorical differences, for surely God-love is of a different order than any pale human imitation. The tension between analogy and counter analogy has always filled liturgical texts. Insofar as liturgy must use metaphor (analogy), the stuff of poetry, it will be poetic; but in recognizing the danger of analogy it must break toward prose, or tumble into silence when speech fails. Likewise, because liturgy must confess our states of being before God, it will use metaphor ("objective correlatives"), but again move toward prose acknowledging that states of being before God may be unique. (The phrase "objective correlative" was coined by T. S. Eliot. Eliot argued that inner states of being could only be expressed by making metaphor. For discussion, see William Wimsatt, Jr., and Cleanth Brooks, *Literary Criticism: A Short History* [New York: Alfred A. Knopf, 1965], 667–669.) So, though liturgical language employs poetic devices it is ultimately too public and too practical to sustain poetic diction. Liturgical writers, slightly in love with the poetry of affect, tend to produce liturgies that sound something like second-rate T. S. Eliot: their language is seldom sayable by congregations (except with inward guffaws). (See for example material in *The Chicago Theological Seminary Register* LVII [May-July 1968]: 4–5.)

So liturgical language is woven out of ordinary public language used in an extraordinary way. Obviously liturgical texts must be said by a congregational "voice," and therefore will tend toward a manageable minimal vocabulary and a short phrasing to permit breathing. Difficult polysyllabic words (such as "polysyllabic") will of course be avoided, particularly words drawn from less-than-public spheres. Sociological terms and psychological jargon can be avoided, along with the lingo of management. Arthur Herzog's little book *The B. S. Factor* will provide countless examples of language to be avoided in the writing of liturgy, from "input" to "organization" to "share" (as a verb) to "dialogue" (as a verb) to "church-wise" or any other -*ize* or -*wise* word (Arthur Herzog, *The B. S. Factor* [Baltimore: Penguin Books, 1974]). In worship we dare stand before God, but not with cant! Child-talk is closer to the language of worship.

Liturgical languages uses *depiction:* it is filled with imagery: we must see before we can pray. If we are going to pray for the elderly sick then, we will avoid general terms such as "afflicted" as well as clichés like "beds of pain." We must imagine actual scenes. Recently we heard a young preacher pray for "people who are sick, who turn from side to side in pain, or stare at ceilings." His images, perhaps cumbersome, were at least better than usual clichés.

Now, the difficulty in choosing images is that pictures we select may not match with common experience, they may be occasional or idiosyncratic. Nevertheless liturgical writers can call to mind a range of images, assess them, and select those most likely to have a kind of "universal" validity. Dangers are many. One of the problems has to do with style, namely, adjectives. Adjectives in language designed for oral use are weak. While adding little, they increase words per line and therefore rhythmics. Too many "beats" per line will tend to obscure meaning or create a heaviness, a cloyed sound. So the problem for writers is to go for phenomenal precision for images, while at the same time avoiding the adjectival—no easy task. Another danger has to do with time and change. Images quite compelling, even "universal" in one moment, may no longer function as time passes. With social custom rapidly changing, we may have to acknowledge that all liturgical writing is transient, as transient as preaching. Though the *Book of Common Prayer* held up remarkably well for generations, perhaps such longevity is no longer possible. Opting for general, somewhat abstracted, language will not do, for instead of serving more people, it always serves fewer. Perhaps if cultural custom settles someday we may image with surety—fortunately such a day is not near (Are all eras of cultural stability idolatrous?). All we are saying is that good liturgy will image, will depict the concerns of prayer.

Liturgy uses *cadence.* In all fine liturgy there is rhythmic subtlety. Ideally, metrics in liturgy ought to be imitative, matching content, mood, or images employed. Because ordinary public language employs all kinds of rhythms in speaking, so will liturgy. Rhythms in liturgy are achieved by rhetorical and poetic devices; rhetorically, by double and triple phrasing; poetically, by internal vowel rhymes, occasional subtle end rhymes, by alliteration (sparingly), various tropes, etc. Virtually all of the collects in _The Worshipbook_ are marked by cadenced language: some work nicely while others do not. Look at a prayer chosen at random, not as excellent (actually, it is a rather poor prayer), but as typical:

> Almighty God: in the beginning you made men and women to join in shared affection. May those who marry be filled with joy. Let them be so sure of each other that no fear or disrespect may shake their vows. Though their eyes be bright with love, keep in sight a wider world where neighbors want and strangers beg, and where service is a joyful duty; through Jesus Christ the Lord. (p. 184, adapted)

In addition to variable length of sentence, the prayer picks up "j" sounds in the first two sentences with "join" and "joy," thus indicating, at least by sound, that joyful marriage is a fulfillment of God's planned "joining." "Fear," a short word, is balanced by a three syllable "disrespect." The internal rhyme of "bright" and "sight" speeds the last sentence in which staccato words "want" and "beg" follow on complex words "neighbors" and "strangers." The last phrase, though started out in parallel construction with a previous "where" clause, returns to pick up the earlier "j" sound with "joyful." The example chosen, a weak prayer, does at least indicate the sophisticated patterns employed by _The Worshipbook_ combining rhetorical phrasing and poetic devices. Now prayers can be overcadanced; they may overdo rhetorical phrasing—triads and doublets _ad nausaeum_—and may repeat poetic devices so that they become obvious, arty, and even "cute." Nevertheless, a kind of studied ease of speech (rhetorical patterns) and beauty (poetic diction) are found in Christian tradition.

Language of worship, we have argued, works off of ordinary public language. As such it turns from the archaic that is no longer useful and, at the same time, fears the colloquial that is either transient or decidedly subcultural. Because public prayer has become a _tradition_ through the centuries (collections have gathered "great" prayers of the ages), the tug of previous form is strong. Have we not all heard contemporary prayers (using "you") slip back into painful anachronisms such as "beseech" and even "vouchsafe," or more subtly into what may be termed the prayer subjunctive ("O Lord that we _might_ . . ."). On the other hand, who has not been jarred by _kitsch_ slanginess in "Give it to us good, Lord . . ." and other unfortunate phrases. _The Worshipbook_ has leapt into contemporary phrases more than other "official" prayer books. Most of these colloquial phrases may be found in the collection of prayers that concludes the book. Here you will find such contemporary expressions as "settle claims" (p. 179), "put down by" (p. 179), "hooked on" (p. 182), "grown up" (p. 184), "break up" (p. 186), "wide open to" (p. 187), "in touch with" (p. 187), "name-calling" (p. 187), "scorekeeping" (p. 187), "good times" (p. 188), "follow up" (p. 188), "go where the work is" (p. 190), "cover territories" (p. 190), "think things out" (p. 191), "lose track of ourselves" (p. 192), "no strings attached" (p. 194), "Weigh us down," "cash on hand," "travelling light" (all in one prayer on p. 199), "Go about your business" (p. 200), "fall in love with" (p. 200), as well as many others. _The Worshipbook_ chooses such phrasing not to be "trendy" but to take hold of conventions which have developed in ordinary language and use them in extraordinary work of prayer.

Of course the trick is to use ordinary expressions in a heightened, all but poetic diction, that brings out true meaning and, at the same time relates to levels of experience common and profound. Clearly _The Worshipbook_ is attempting to relate to deep levels of human experiences when it describes grieving,

> "We pray for those whose tears are not yet dry, who listen for familiar voices and look for still familiar faces. . . ." (p. 113. The repetition of "familiar," and the ambiguity of "still" is of course deliberate)

or in the odd participle ending of,

> "For growing up and growing old; for wisdom deepened by experience; for rest in leisure, and for time made precious by its passing. . . ." (p. 115)

Devices, systems, tropes—the words sound calculated, even manipulative. Nevertheless, liturgical writing is neither a calculated condition of other human minds nor a form of spiritual outpouring, the self-expression of a warmed heart: it is technical, hopefully useful language offered to neighbors for the praise of God.

——————————— **VII** ———————————

How does one write liturgy? A person who strives for immortality will end up sounding pretentious; one who tries to be "mod" will sound trite. Writing liturgy is a tough act, to say the least. You must be faithful to traditional faith in a language that is often less than serviceable. Our language is secular and, only now at the tag-end of a terrifying century, is coming alive again. For the liturgical writer, however, public language is all there is. The writer can scramble along the edges of language where transcendence finds expression, but it is not easy. Perhaps every liturgy is written before the time (better spelled THE TIME, perhaps). Note that in *The Worshipbook* the editor's only signature is found in a final prayer. It reads:

> Almighty God: you have no patience with solemn assemblies, or heaped up prayers to be heard. Forgive those who have written prayers for congregations. Remind them that their foolish words will pass away, but that your word will last and be fulfilled, in Jesus Christ our Lord. (p. 200)

David G. Buttrick[120]

385 • LITURGICAL LANGUAGE IN AFRICAN-AMERICAN WORSHIP AND PREACHING

Language used in black preaching has a musical ring and rhythm. The spirit and delivery of this language has much to do with the emotional vitality of worship in black churches, a fine example of how the aesthetic qualities of language shape the meaning and experience of worship.

——————— **The Pervasiveness of the Idiom** ———————

One who observes the black church from within the context of its life as a worshiping community is soon struck by the degree to which the preaching is musical. The spectrum of musical expression ranges from the sonorous delivery, which has a pleasant melodiousness, meter, and cadence, to the full-blown chant or song. To those who are a part of the tradition in which musical delivery is normative, such a form often emerges as the criterion for preaching. This valuation categorizes other styles of

delivery as mere speech, address, or lecture, but hardly as preaching. Consequently, the preacher uninitiated in the customs of this segment of the black church may be thanked for his or her "talk" as courteous intimation that "preaching" per se had not occurred. Although few credible preachers and even fewer homileticians would make musical delivery a measure for preaching, it remains a highly treasured aspect of the culture.

The manner in which black preaching speaks to the black experience in America with a divinely inspired word is doubtless its most distinctive feature. To a situation characterized by bleakness, despair, oppression, and frustration, a word of hope is declared, offering to a people the promise of a brighter day and strength to endure the times in which they find themselves. This preaching is not solely "otherworldly" nor simply "protest." Emerging from the depths of a religious consciousness in which God is trusted against all odds posed by history, black preaching is an affirmation concerning the will and power of God before it is a protest against or a gesture away from this world. It is celebration—that point to which the preacher leads the congregation in moments of thanksgiving and transport—wherein the skills of musical delivery are unsurpassed in attaining the exalted moment. Not only does such celebration enhance the understanding and retention of the gospel; it is, as Henry Mitchell asserts, essential to faithful communication of the gospel, without which there would be a "defacto denial of the good news" (*The Recovery of Preaching* [San Francisco: Harper and Row, 1977], 55).

This "celebration" is, of course, distinct from what Mitchell calls "cerebration." "Celebration" is more affective and emotional than "cerebration," which is reflective and intellectual. This is not to diminish the significance of the cognitive aspect, for celebration does not stand independent of responsible exegesis, careful penetration of the teachings of the church, and sensitive theological insight. The detail that is supplied by careful and tedious exegesis, analysis, and the application of theology and doctrine supplies the material used in celebration. Musicality expresses that which is beyond the literal word; it takes rational content and fires the imagination. Indeed, at the point of celebration all that has been generated in the cerebral process is offered up in the moment of exaltation.

The persistence and pervasiveness of this form of delivery from one generation of black preachers to the next is astounding when one considers the paucity of reflection on the idiom. Among those who appreciate and practice the art, it is almost as though it were a secret of the guild's oral culture. Whereas some academicians ignore or disdain the idiom, denoting it a vestige of "folk religion," black preachers who have come under their tutelage not only maintain the tradition but also practice the art with consummate skill. Restricted neither by denomination nor by educational status, it continues to span the gamut from the preaching of Father Andrew Bryan and Andrew Marshall at the beginning of the nineteenth century, to Martin Luther King, Jr. and Charles Adams in the twentieth century, from the "cornfield preacher" to the "Harvard Whooper," from the "No D" to the Ph.D., and "every D in between." It is no surprise, then, that contemporary black preaching resembles descriptions of preaching within the slave community (see Jon Michael Spencer, *Sacred Symphony: The Chanted Sermon of the Black Preacher* [Westport, Conn.: Greenwood Press, 1987], 1–16).

This skill of musical delivery is not possessed by all black preachers; neither is it a feature unique to black religion. On occasion it is found among white Pentecostals whose worship style is more closely aligned to that customarily found in the black church. Among these white preachers is television evangelist Jimmy Swaggart, who (perhaps because of his style of preaching) attracts a substantial black audience. However, the larger American culture greatly influenced by the Enlightenment and the rise of modern science, offered little support for a genre of preaching that even hinted of the mystical. In African-American culture, the idiom has been highly appreciated as a form of religious expression, and it is in this latter cultural context that insight can be gleaned into its religious meaning. Such a focus eliminates the necessity of having to account for an aberration in larger American culture by reducing the idiom to some modality that is an epiphenomenon of a truly religious expression. (An epiphenomenon is the representation of an event that is regarded as incapable of explanation in terms of itself. A religious experience is regarded as an epiphenomenon, for example, if it is considered explainable solely in terms of nonreligious categories such as psychology or economics.)

Any overlap between black and white cultures (between a Charles Adams and Jimmy Swaggart, for instance) invariably invites inquiry as to who is mim-

icking whom. Although perhaps valuable for determining the origin of the practice in North America, such questions do little for the description, interpretation, and preservation of the form. Therefore, the concern of this essay is not to validate musicality in preaching by recourse to homiletical canons. Rather, it is to explore the character of this musicality in the context of the culture which sustains it as a normal occurrence.

Musicality as Surplus in Preaching

The very definition of Christian preaching is an attempt to account for its transcendence over ordinary speech. Nearly all homileticians address this dimension wherein the preacher is "outside of self" and speaking in behalf of a divine power. Gardner C. Taylor, one of the most influential black preachers of this generation, correctly argues the awesomeness and presumptuousness of the task undertaken by one who supposes to speak for God:

Measured by almost any gauge, preaching is a presumptuous business. If the undertaking does not have some sanctions beyond human reckoning, then it is, indeed, rash and audacious for one person to dare to stand up before or among other people and declare that he or she brings from the Eternal God a message for those who listen which involves issues nothing less than those of life and death. (Gardner C. Taylor, *How Shall They Preach* [Elgin, Ill.: Progressive Baptist Publishing House, 1977], 24)

John R. W. Stott, the Director of the London Institute for Contemporary Christianity and one of the foremost evangelists and lecturers of the day, attends to the same dimension of this reality by noting that the preacher can speak only because God has spoken:

No attempt to understand Christianity can succeed which overlooks or denies the truth that the living God has taken the initiative to reveal himself savingly to fallen humanity; or that his self-revelation has been given by the most straight forward means of communication known to us, namely by a word and words; or that he calls upon those who have heard his Word to speak it to others. (John R. W. Stott, *Between Two Worlds: The Art of Preaching in the Twentieth Century* [Grand Rapids, Eerdmans, 1982], 15)

Stott illustrates the implication of this insight with a somewhat humorous anecdote from the career of George Whitefield, the eloquent and spellbinding preacher of the eighteenth century. During a preaching campaign in a New Jersey meeting-house, an old man fell asleep during Whitefield's discourse, provoking him to exhort:

> If I had come to speak to you in my own name, you might rest your elbows upon your knees and your heads on your hands, and go to sleep! . . . But I have come to you in the name of the Lord God of hosts, and (he clapped his hands and stamped his foot) I must and I will be heard. (Ibid, 32–33)

In spite of the keen and penetrating focus on "this world," preaching through the ages has been uttered as a word coming from another world. Because the order which it assumes as normative does not exist in history, human beings have found it difficult to utter in ordinary speech the extraordinary pronouncements which preaching requires. The ancient prophets often resorted to signs; the apostles of the early church accompanied their words with signs and wonders; the saints were known to retreat into prolonged silent contemplation, only later to emerge with pronouncement; still others have incorporated the enchanting and mystical powers of music in their delivery. Black preaching is an instance of this latter employment.

The very word *music* is derived from an ancient view of the world which considered the art forms essentially enchanted. Music was a means for evoking and expressing the rapture of the soul. To the present day it has been integral to the cultic life of nearly every culture and, by implication, inseparable from religion. Analysis and reflection by the ablest scholars of religion has revealed further that music, celebration, and ecstasy are crucial ingredients differentiating religion from philosophy. Anthropologist R. R. Marrett, who pondered and explored the threshold of religion, concluded, for instance, that "religion is more danced than thought out" (*Handbook on Religion* [London: Metheun and Co., 1914], xxi, 175).

Within the comparative framework of religion, black preaching (as human phenomenon) employs music in the delivery of meaning from another world. In a skillful and stalwart way, music is one of the instruments which bridges the chasm between the world of human beings and God who speaks to them through preaching. Establishing a direct link between the spirit within the preacher, the word being uttered, and the worshiping congregation, the surplus of musicality operates beneath the structures of rational discourse, producing a mystical and enchanting effect upon the audience waiting to hear what saith the Lord. There can be no denial of the potency within this form of preaching, which has been a source of untold healing and motivation for the strivings of the people.

Music in the African Tradition

One of the greatest errors that can be made in attempting to understand black culture is to assume that it is but a carbon copy of some monolithic American culture. Invariably when American culture is projected as such a mythical caricature, it is viewed as a reflection of European culture, thus obscuring the rich interpenetration of African and Amerindian civilizations and authenticity of truly American genre. Hence, there is no chance of coming to terms with the musical aspect of black preaching without a backward and sideward glance to Africa, for in African culture we can clearly observe the structures of meaning embedded within the religious consciousness of its people, which has allowed for the sustentation of music as a means of communicating the "surplus."

In traditional Africa, human life exists in synthesis with other forms of life and in relation to rhythmic patterns observable in the natural order. These patterns—the coming and going of daylight and darkness, the phases of the moon, the periodic varieties of rainfall, planting and harvest—indicate an essentially rhythmic structure to the forces that sustain life. Even biological life has a rhythmic fundament—the conception and bearing of children, the process of reaching puberty and adulthood, and the phase of aging and passing on to join the ancestors. The connection between the rhythm and life is the primal nexus from which the manifold expressions of culture flow. In its unity, rhythm/life surges forth in the multifarious forms through which the world is known: language, art, society, religion, government, and so forth. It is therefore only a short step to the realization that the very force of life that pulsates through individuals and communities is given objective tangible expression in rhythmic motion and music, and that musical rhythm is the aesthetic sanguification of the force of life sustaining the people.

In traditional Africa, one can find this principle of

structural unity from one tribal group to another. Among the Fon of Dahomey it is *Da,* represented by a serpent coiled under the world. Among the Dogan it is the *nommo pair,* which signifies a word full of power. Among the Bantu it is *ntu,* the root from which all categories of life are derived. This principle of motion graphically illustrates the pulsating force of life that connects all living things (including plants and animals) and establishes the tie between them and the cosmos. During moments of ecstatic dancing in the cultic shrine, the powers of the universe coalesced and surged through the living being in question. Rhythm, which undergirded trance possession and the resultant "preaching" gave extensity to the African soul and in turn to those Africans who were taken as slaves to North America. Every conceivable effort was made by the enslaved to preserve the primal connection between the noumenal world of deities, ancestors, and spirits and the objective world in which they found themselves. This consciousness, which Gayraud Wilmore calls "hierophantic nature of historical reality" (*Black Religion and Black Radicalism* [New York: Anchor/Doubleday, 1973], 4), preserved within Africans and their descendants an openness to spiritual power. However, the surplus of deep stirrings, intensity, and zeal within the African spirit, easily expressed in African languages by means of rhythm, tone, and pitch, found little correspondence with the vocabulary of the strange land. And drumming, a precise means of communicating with human beings and the deities, was strictly forbidden in the slave regime. But rhythm and musicality were sustained within the worship of the slave community, a portion of its residue being deposited in black preaching.

The presence of rhythm within the African and African-American worldview corresponds to the oppugnancy slaves felt toward the world. To them, rhythm was essentially numinous: it was the property of the deities, and it moved the community backward away from present reality into the time of the deities. The same atavistic influence operated upon the adherents of Afro-Christian faith: rhythm and music in preaching, operating beneath the structures of rational and discursive communication, moved the hearers away from the history that unleashed terror upon them (Cornel West, *Prophesy Deliverance: An Afro-American Revolutionary Christianity* [Philadelphia: Westminster Press, 1982], 19; Mircea Eliade, *The Myth of the Eternal Return* [New York: Harper and Row, 1959], 139). Only through perpetuating their quarrel with history while simultaneously sidestepping its terror could they forge a positive identity for themselves.

That the direction of black preaching has ever been "a gesture away from history" has understandably given rise to the charge that it is otherworldly. However, because there has never been a historical epoch in which blacks could behold their dreams fulfilled, the rhythm and music in Afro-Christian preaching, correlative to the content of the message, is an affirmation of the atavistic and the primal—the world that God has truly willed.

Preaching as Kratophany

Within the tradition of the black church, preaching is truly a manifestation of power, or (in a word used by Eliade) a *kratophany.* As in a "theophany," which is a manifestation of deity, some object is present which opens to the transcendent while simultaneously being rooted in the world of tangible, historical reality. With a theophany, the object may be a tree or a stone, as in African traditional religions, while with preaching the kratophany is spoken word and rendered gesture. Further, within the context of the culture that sustains black preaching, there is no modality more indicative of the presence of deity, power and intrusion from another order than that of the preached word entrenched in musicality.

As kratophany, more must accompany the preached word than the claim that it has power or a theory of preaching. Because the Word is like "fire shut up in the bones" (Heb. 4:12; Jer. 20:9, 23:29), something special is supposed to happen in preaching. Replete with drama and musicality, its performative power is expected to move people and to cause reaction. Nodding the head, shedding a tear, holy dancing, speaking in tongues, singing, humming aloud, and saying "amen" are responses to the power manifested in effective black preaching.

Words thusly preached are akin to ancient Hebrew tradition, wherein words were believed to have accomplished and performed the action contained in them, especially when spoken on behalf of God. Moreover, the spoken word could by no means be retracted. When, for instance, Balaam, the Mesopotamian diviner, was summoned by the king of Moab to curse the Israelites as they came up from Egypt, Balaam instead blessed Israel, declaring that he could not retract the spoken word under some circumstances (Num. 22:12-18, Jer. 23:29). Again, when Jacob surreptitiously received the blessing that should have gone to his brother Esau, their father Isaac insisted that once the word bestowing inheritance had been spoken reversal was impossible (Gen. 26:36-38). The prophets declared too that the word they spoke for the Lord would not return without doing what it was sent to do, and the that word was like "a hammer that breaks a rock into pieces" (Isa. 55:11). When caught up in the more intense musical phases of speaking the word, the trance-like state of the black preacher parallels that of the early Old Testament prophets, the nabiim, who claimed no responsibility for their speech under the conditions caused by the Spirit of the Lord upon them. They spoke what "thus saith the Lord" without fear of punishment or death (George T. Montague, *The Holy Spirit: Growth of a Biblical Tradition* [New York: Paulist Press, 1976], 17–33; see also Amos 1). The preacher who genuinely enters this state of spirituality is able to deliver discourse far exceeding that which had been prepared.

Down through the ages music has provided the added dimension of communication through which one spirit could reach another. This non-discursive level of communication is apparent in the way listeners experience musical performance. On the one hand, there is the objective dimension that can be set on the bar and governed by the scale, whereby a musician correctly executing the score will produce the expected sound. Technical correctness aside, there still remains the subjective element—the surplus. The exceptional artist is able to "touch the spirit" for the sake of the audience. Similarly, the music of black preaching can be understood as a sort of "singing in the spirit" (1 Cor. 14, 15), for there is surplus (glossa) expressed in music which accompanies a rational content (logos) expressed in words. The rational portion is contained in the formal structure of the sermon which reflects the homiletical soundness and the doctrinal tradition in which the preacher stands. For the glossal portion, the preacher becomes an instrument of musical afflatus: a flute through which divine air is blown, a harp upon which eternal strings vibrate. For the sake of the audience, the preacher becomes an oracle through which a divinely inspired message flows.

When preaching attains the level wherein rhythm and musicality are unrestrained—wherein the preacher "lets the Lord have his way"—it is customarily said that the preacher is "under the anointing"

and is "being used of God." In the vernacular of the culture, we say, "the preacher has come."

William C. Turner, Jr.[121]

386 • THE LANGUAGE OF PRAYER

The text of a prayer is only one element important in the act of public prayer. For the way in which a prayer is spoken, the attitudes that accompany it, and the nonverbal gestures which complement it often communicate as much of the meaning of the prayer as the text itself. This article looks at the whole act of public prayer, offering worship planners pastoral, liturgical, and aesthetic guidelines regarding prayer.

It is a sign of health and a cause for rejoicing that the shelves of bookstores carry so many resources for prayer in worship and books about prayer. In my reading, however, one crucial part of prayer in worship draws scant attention: namely, the ways that prayers are spoken and experienced in worship. This act of praying in worship is the focus of this article.

We have all had the experience of sitting in a congregation and having prayers spoiled by the way the leader speaks them: prayers of thanksgiving voiced in a desultory, dejected fashion; prayers of intercession undercut with a mean or arrogant edge, as though the congregation were being scolded for insufficient concern for the causes in the prayers. Several years ago, I was asked to speak briefly to a church study group. The assignment was to speak about love in the most thoroughly unloving fashion I could manage. I remember, incidentally, that I found it a disturbingly easy assignment and wished there were more demand for such speeches. That experience is called to mind when certain prayers are spoken in worship: the mood of the speaking violates the content of the words.

It is a bit surprising, then, that the voicing of prayer receives relatively little attention in the literature. Perhaps that inattention is because many of the people who write frequently about prayer have a nearly magical view of the power of words. There is, I suspect, an unvoiced assumption that the words for prayer, if written beautifully enough, will necessarily be prayer simply because they are so forcefully written. Such trust in the power of the right words can lead also to a kind of smugness about the worship being led and the prayers being offered. It occasionally seems as though we leaders of worship feel that as long as we have the right prayers to say, no criticism can touch us.

Some years ago, I heard a comparison of the worship of black churches with that of "high church" congregations. The worshipers in a black church, it was observed, knew that if Christ were to return and visit their worship, all their frail human attempts at praise would be burned away by the presence of God's holiness. In high church Protestantism, however, if the Lord were to return to worship, the leaders of worship would expect the Lord (a) to be impressed by the splendor of the style and the seriousness of the content, and (b) to take a seat quietly in the back and not disturb the flow of worship. This comparison might serve to point to a certain belligerent rightness, a false pride in some of our prayers which can make worship very difficult.

The concern that prayers in worship not be ruined by the way they are voiced is somewhat akin to a concern expressed by Professor Ralph Underwood ("The Presence of God in Pastoral Care Ministry," _Austin Presbyterian Seminary Bulletin_ 101:4 [October 1985]). Under the section of his article "Guidelines for Pastoral Prayers," Dr. Underwood calls for "prayer as authentic response . . . [as] opposed to the conventional prayer at the end of a visit, the pastor's ritual escape. . . ." He then offers three guidelines that would encourage this authenticity in prayers in pastoral settings. These guidelines are in the form of three questions:

1. "Is the prayer we have with people a response to God?"
2. "Is the prayer a response to the person or persons in whose presence we find ourselves?"
3. "Is the prayer a response to the God of Scripture?"

It is obvious that prayer in worship is different from prayer in pastoral care. Prayer in worship should not be as personal or unguarded as the prayer in moments of pastoral ministry. Prayer in worship has far more people praying with the leader and has some educational effect on these people; those who lead prayer in worship must strive to take account of them. In spite of these obvious differences in the kinds of prayers, there is still a great deal to be learned by using Dr. Underwood's guidelines to assess our prayers in worship, particularly those prayers spoken by the leader for the people.

Response to the People

It will be helpful to begin with Dr. Underwood's second question: "Is the prayer a response to the persons in whose presence we find ourselves?" Prayer in worship, like prayers in pastoral care, will be more nearly alive and authentic if the people invited to pray with the speaker recognize some of their experience reflected in the prayers. When the prayers voice thanks for what the congregation feels thankful and when they pray for what the congregation feels needful, those prayers are more likely to enrich and energize the worship of the people.

This reflection of the experience of the people will require both pastoral content with the people and some focused attention on that experience. Dr. James A. Jones, in a classroom lecture printed as an introduction to a volume of his prayers, told of following the example of F. B. Meyer (_Prayers for the People_ [Richmond: John Knox, 1967], 11). Mr. Meyer would go into the church and walk the aisles during the week. He knew where people sat, would sit in their pews and pray for them there. A discipline like that can make the prayers in worship an authentic response to the people.

The prayers in worship will be more nearly alive and authentic if the people find them reflecting not only their own experiences but also their own prayers. While we can never know fully the prayer life of a congregation, we can safely assume that people know their prayers are imperfect and inadequate. An awkward question needs then to be faced: can prayers in worship that are always carefully crafted and elegant be authentic prayers of the people? The question could be turned around: when our prayers in worship are always well turned and controlled, do we not teach the people that only perfect prayers are acceptable? Do the people not conclude that prayers less than elegant will (to use Dr. Underwood's phrase) "require suppression"? Raising a question about the effectiveness of well prepared prayers could be misused, of course, to justify the worst kind of sloppiness in worship prayers. Recognizing that danger does not, however, change the need for prayers that reflect, at least to a degree, the prayer life of the people in the congregation.

Dr. Underwood argues that prayers in pastoral care settings can be offered even out of our false consciousness or our confusion and still be an authentic response or, at least, can lead to that authenticity. The same argument can be made, given the proper guards against overuse, to apply to prayers in worship.

Mrs. Merel Burleson, a member of Trinity Presbyterian Church, Midland, Texas, an artist and art teacher, told me of her "blue bead theory" about certain types of Mexican art. Her theory developed out of two experiences. The first was a remark to her by her art teacher when she was a child. As she worked so very hard on a project to make things exactly right, he tried to ease the pressure on her by saying, "Only Christ was perfect." The second experience was in watching necklaces being strung with colored beads. The colors formed a repeated pattern: black, yellow, white, again and again. The pattern was perfect except for a solitary blue bead, a built-in flaw, spoiling the perfection. The two experiences set her looking for other "blue beads" in the works of artists, deliberate flaws which could serve as reminders that there is no pretense of perfection. She reports finding large numbers of works where patterns are set up and, in what is obviously not just an oversight, the pattern is broken. "Only Christ is perfect."

Perhaps if our prayers in worship had an occasional "blue bead" to remind us that prayers need not be perfect, our people would feel those prayers as an acknowledgment of and response to their condition. This presupposes that the pattern set up in worship is one of carefully prepared prayers. While it makes no sense to build in awkward prayers deliberately, it could be helpful to leave open a possibility of a prayer that stumbles. Perhaps one prayer—such as that for illumination or of dedication or one part of the intercessory prayers—could be left open to the moment. Or perhaps the prayers could, from time to time, acknowledge the inadequacy of all our prayers. The hope is that our people learn that prayers can be offered before they are perfected.

Response to God

Dr. Underwood's first and third guidelines ask us to examine whether our prayers are responses to God and, more specifically, to the God of Scripture. For purposes of brevity I will treat these two guidelines as one: our prayers need to be authentic responses to the God of Scripture.

The often-heard criticism of "read prayers" by people in the pew needs to be taken seriously. What that criticism longs for is not necessarily a spontaneous bravado in praying or spiritual exhibitionism; it

may be asking for some sense that the prayers are an authentic response to God. There are styles of speech and tones of voice which communicate nothing of life and involvement and which signal a mere going through the motions.

It is, I suppose, conceivable to deal with this problem by encouraging certain characteristics of voice and inflection that sound "sincere." That would run several dangers: trying to create a contrived authenticity and promoting prayer as a performance, among others. The only alternative I can see to that manipulation of prayers is to ask a very personal question of those of us who lead prayers: are our prayers in worship authentic responses to God? In this regard, Dr. Underwood's "Catch 22" can be paraphrased: there is no prayer in worship that has not begun before worship. If prayer in worship is our only prayer, it has little chance of being authentic. This demands that we pay some attention to the connection between our private life and our prayers in worship. It does not require that this private prayer be perfect or even exemplary; we all share the feeling, I suspect, that our prayer life is inadequate. It does, however, stand as a guideline and challenge: we need not expect that our prayers in worship will be (or will be felt to be) responses to God unless that response is well practiced in private.

There are various ways to conceive of this continuity between private and public prayers. Some of the variety can be hinted at by looking at three forms of prayers in worship which are spoken by the leader for the people: spontaneous prayer, prayer written by others, and self-prepared prayer.

Spontaneous Prayers

The dangers of spontaneous prayers are obvious: while they may feel spontaneous to the one praying, they most often sound like a reshuffling of stock prayer clichés; also they tend to overlook important elements in worship prayers because these are not thought of on "the spur of the moment." Some of those dangers are minimized, however, if spontaneous prayer is part of the private prayer life of the worship leader. In that discipline, a sensitivity that avoids overworked phrases can be developed, and the habits of including the basic elements of prayer can be well practiced. If spontaneous prayer in worship is not deeply rooted in long use of this style of prayer, however, it will scarcely seem an authentic response to God.

With spontaneous prayer in worship, the leader

also needs to arrange for some feedback from the people in the congregation on how these prayers are being heard. The one who voices an extemporaneous prayer may intend the words one way, but the people can hear them in ways altogether different. Example: persons who use phrases such as "I just want to thank you . . ." or "I just pray that . . ." may well intend the phrases as efforts at humility, avoiding pretense. These phrases can strike others, however, as calling undue attention to that humility or even as devaluing the reality of the prayer. Feedback as to how prayers are heard is helpful regardless of the form of the prayer; it is crucial when that prayer is spontaneous.

Prayers Written by Others

The dangers of using prayers written by others are easy to name: the temptation to read the words in a rote detachment, using these prayers as a substitute for one's own life of prayer. However, if the leader's own prayer life is rich in the use of these prayers by others, then these prayers will likely be alive in worship. A private prayer life that is guided by the prayers of others will discover particular prayers that are more readily made one's own and certain prayers that will be useful in giving voice to the hurts and hopes of the people. When these prayers have been prayed before, they can certainly be felt as authentic responses to God in worship. This is not to excuse, however, grabbing a book of prayers five minutes before the service and selecting a few we think we didn't use last week to get us through the prayers of the people.

Self-Prepared Prayers

The discipline of preparing one's own prayers for worship may have fewer necessary dangers than the other two forms. The most obvious danger is to give the preparation so little time that it consists of little more than a few notes to remind one of who is in the hospital. A second danger, perhaps not frequently encountered but nonetheless real, comes from spending plenty of time on the prayers but making them so self-consciously pretty that attention is called to the words rather than to the focus of prayer. The most frequent offenders are strings of alliterative words that do nothing but show off and analogies so graphic as to be grotesque.

Both of those dangers are avoided when prayer in worship grows out of prayer in private. One way to do that is to use a prayer diary in which are kept phrases, sentences, even full prayers that came out of a particular time of private prayer. Such a diary of prayer can serve as a resource from which to select those elements of prayers that fit in corporate worship.

In preparing one's own prayers for worship, the writing needs to be done for the spoken content. A part of the writing process involves speaking aloud the written prayers in order to judge, not only if they make sense, but also if they can be, when spoken, authentic responses to God and to the people. Spoken tests can be the occasion for inspired revision—and rejection.

The reflections in this article take aim at an event which can not be controlled, manipulated, or guaranteed. The intent and hope is that in our corporate worship the words spoken in prayer may so resonate with the lives of those praying, including the leader, that they claim God's reality in the present hour and give a faithful response.

William K. Hedrick[122]

387 • WRITING PRAYERS FOR WORSHIP

Writing prayers for worship calls for the creativity of a poet, the sensitivity of a pastor, the insight of a theologian, and the foundation of a living relationship with God. Weaving together these concerns, this article gives advice to the worshiper who is given the task of writing prayers for public worship. It suggests an approach that will be accessible for beginners and challenging for experienced worship leaders.

Prayer is the heartbeat of worship—our living, vital entrance into the presence of God.

It is also often the part of the worship service in which most people's minds go to sleep.

Is it possible to write prayers for worship that powerfully bring people into God's presence? Can written prayers help us to shake off the lethargy of our congregational prayers? Yes, it is possible—given some basic spiritual principles.

A Levitical Tradition

If you are writing prayers for worship, you are part of the tradition of Levites that goes back to the time of Moses. God set apart an entire tribe to be in charge of the Israelite worship, and many of our most beautiful prayers and songs come from Asaph and the sons of Korah. Written prayers, whether spoken or set to music, form the heart of the earliest Jewish and Christian worship.

Your calling, as a modern-day Asaph, is to find language and imagery that engages people's minds and hearts in honest, worshipful, heartfelt prayer to the living God. But why written prayers?

First of all, there is nothing wrong with spontaneous prayers. These can be as eloquent, moving, and effective as written prayers. But not everyone feels comfortable making up a prayer on the spur of the moment in front of a large group of people. Sometimes the pray-er forgets things that he or she had wanted to say—or says things later regretted.

Writing your prayers allows you to think out beforehand what the congregation needs to be saying to God in prayer at that point in the service. It enables you to word your prayers so that they apply to the entire congregation (especially important in prayers of confession and repentance or commitment).

Writing down the prayer beforehand also challenges you to use fresh language, to find images that will focus the congregation's hearts and imaginations on God. It will keep your prayers from being unnecessarily long and repetitious.

And written, responsive-type prayers allow the congregation to join you not only with their hearts and minds but with their voices as well.

Choosing Language Wisely

Choice of language is where the creative part of your worship gifts comes into play. Language, a gift from the Creator, can be a powerful force in touching people's spirits and bringing them to God.

It's too easy, when praying "off the cuff," to use prayer language that is overused and worn out. For example:

O most holy God, we come to Thee in the evening hour of this day to thank Thee for all that Thou hast done for us. We come before Thee now to ask that Thou wilt be with us, that Thou wilt bless us and guide us in all that we do. Hear us now, we pray, in the name of your Son, our Lord and Savior Jesus Christ. Amen.

There is nothing wrong with the thoughts expressed in this prayer. They are reverent and proper, and have probably been used, with some variation, in many church services down through the years.

But there's the rub. Like stones that have been rolled together for a long time, these words and phrases have tumbled through our consciousness so often that they have lost their sharpness. Even substituting "you" for the "Thees" and "Thous" does little to bring this prayer alive. There is no "edge" to the language. It has lost its ability to move us, to catch our imagination. Sadly, it will (and often has) put us to sleep.

Choose your language wisely. Use images for God that help people to picture the living Eternal One. There are many images we can use, of course; think of the one most appropriate to the service or mood or theme of that day's Scripture. (This is especially important, as the Scripture should shape and influence the whole of the worship service.)

If the focus is on God's tender care of us, for example, images like shepherd, father, mother, brother, and comforter come to mind. If it is on God's sovereign power, work with images such as wind and fire, the Creator who stretched out the heavens, or the "Lord who will march out like a mighty man, like a warrior."

Don't be afraid to use concrete, specific images for God: rock, water, fire, shepherd, friend, shield, mother hen, lamb, bread, and so on. God, knowing that we are unable to comprehend fully his nature, gives us these images in Scripture so we can at least understand him on the simplest of levels. And the wealth of scriptural images reminds us of the many facets of God's nature and his dealings with us. Focusing on one of these in prayer and using Scripture's own language to make it come alive is one of the most helpful things you can do in writing prayers.

Using visual imagery in language helps to touch people's imaginations and hearts, making them more aware of God's presence. But you have only a brief time—a few minutes at the most—to do this. So use only one picture or several related ones in each prayer. Make the picture as clear and sharp as it can be; avoid general, cliched language (without going overboard in poetic extremes).

Once you've chosen a scriptural word picture to use, work at making it a unifying theme of your prayer. For example:

Lord Jesus, you are our living Head. Teach us to be your body here on earth—your hands, your feet, your eyes and compassionate heart. Lord, send the impulses of your love into the sinews of this church. May your will and thoughts direct us. Let your hands, through our hands, supply food for our neighbors' hunger. Let them hear your voice as we visit and talk with them. Let the children come to us and sit in our laps, as they sat in yours. Without you as our Head, Lord, we are lifeless. We wait for your power, your word, your instruction. Fill us with your life and love, Jesus. Amen.

One other consideration in your choice of language is your congregation's preference for formal or informal liturgy. There are some beautiful prayers taken from the language of "high church" liturgy in the traditional responsive mode. Here is one example that can be used as a call to worship at Pentecost, taken from *Praise God: Common Prayer at Taize:*

L: Blessed be our God at all times, now and always and forever and ever.

P: Amen.

L: Glory to you, our God! Glory to you! Holy Spirit, Lord and Comforter, Spirit of truth everywhere present, filling all that exists, Treasury of good gifts and Source of life, come and dwell in us, cleanse us from all sin and in your love bring us to salvation:

P: God, holy; God, strong and holy; God, holy and immortal; have pity on us.

But if you prefer a more "low church" informality, you might use this Pentecost prayer instead:

L: Holy Spirit, you are the fire of holiness that surrounds the throne of God. You burn away our sin and blindness; you fill us with the beauty and purity of Jesus, our Lord.

P:: Come to us, Holy Spirit!

L: Burn in us this morning, Holy Spirit. We give you the places of our hearts that have been choked by the cares of this world. We give you our tiredness, our sin, our struggles with apathy. We wait your fiery cleansing.

P: Come to us, Holy Spirit!

L: May the Word of God this morning burn in our minds, our wills, our feelings. May we sense the light and heat of your presence in that Word. Speak to us, O burning power of God!

P: Come to us, Holy Spirit!

Praying the Scriptures

Much of Scripture is prayer: the Psalms, portions of the prophets, David's beautiful prayer in 1 Chronicles 29, the simple prayers of our Lord, the magnificent prayers of Paul's epistles. Use them as part of your written prayers; combine them, reword them, find the best places to break them into a back-and-forth echo between leader and congregation. For example, consider this adaptation of Psalm 84 as a responsive prayer to open worship:

P: This sanctuary is lovely to us, O God—O living, powerful Lord almighty! Deep within our spirits we long to be near you, to stay here in your courts and to worship you.

P: Our heart and our flesh cry out to you, O living God.

L: Even the sparrow is welcome here, to build her nest by your altars, O Lord of all the worlds!

P: It would be our greatest joy to live in your house and to praise you forever!

L: Those who find their strength in you will find this place full of living water, even if they pass through the valley of weeping.

P: To spend one day here in worship is better than a thousand elsewhere!

Pastoral Considerations

Appropriateness. If you are writing a prayer for your congregation, be sure that it applies to them. Do not make the congregation say something they are not ready or willing to say about themselves. Do not say, "We confess that we ignore our neighbors and fail to pray for them," for example, when it might be true of you but not true of 10 or 20 percent of the people participating in the prayer with you. A safer way is to say, "Forgive us *when* we ignore our neighbors . . ."

Brevity. Keep prayers as brief and as honest as possible. Take as your example the prayer of the publican: "Lord, be merciful to me, a sinner." Say what you need and want to say—no more than that. Avoid the length, flowery language, and self-congratulation of the Pharisee. As Jesus said, "When you pray, do not keep on babbling like pagans, for they think they will be heard because of their many words."

Honesty. Make honesty the hallmark of your prayers. People want and need honesty in religion— plainspoken honesty that gets past the nice words and speaks the truth with God's love. If your prayers lack an honest, direct grasp of the truth—by avoiding mention of divisions in your congregation, for example, or by smoothing over your lack of effectiveness in outreach or your struggle to make ends meet financially—then the congregation will get the message that prayer is just for "nice" things and not for the difficult, specific problems facing your church.

Audience. Do not use prayer as an opportunity to preach to anyone. You are not making points to remind your listeners of certain truths; your listener is God himself. Always be aware of this and say to God what you would if you were directly in his presence.

Here's a good thing to do as you are starting to write a prayer for worship: Before anything else, use your God-given imagination to place yourself in the court of heaven. See the God of Isaiah, who is high and lifted up, and whose train fills the temple. Smell the smoke and incense of the God of Revelation, and see the blinding white throne and the unbearable majesty that radiates from God's holiness. Hear the angels cry around the throne, "Holy, Holy, Holy is he who is and who was and who is to come!"

Hear also the gentle invitation to "approach the throne of grace with confidence, so that you may receive mercy and find grace to help you in your time of need." See with the eyes of your heart the figure of Jesus, our high priest and brother, standing and pleading before the throne for the needs of you and your congregation.

Then write your prayer, conscious that this is no ploy or trick of the imagination but rather the highest glimpse of reality that you will see. Do not write your prayers first of all with the people in mind; write them with the presence of God in your mind and heart. Then your prayers will speak; they will also lift people to the throne and presence of God. Your language will be reverent, humble, holy, full of praise, calling participants to join you in the Holy of Holies.

A Final Word

To write for worship is, in a sense, to be an Old Testament Levite. The Levites' calling required spiritual preparation: ritual cleansing, donning white linen garments, and so on. Before you begin to write for worship, make sure that you have put on the white linen of forgiveness and righteousness, having confessed your sins and asked God's Spirit to cleanse and fill you.

Does this sound pretentious or unnecessary? Not if you take God's holiness and his call to worship seriously. Even the most beautifully written prayer or litany is lifeless without the quiet presence of God's power. And that power can make the simplest prayer come alive for those who listen and participate.

Edith Bajema

388 ✦ A BIBLIOGRAPHY ON THE ART OF LANGUAGE IN WORSHIP

Bouley, Alan. *From Freedom to Formula*. Washington, D.C.: The Catholic University of America, 1981.

Fischer, Balthasar. *Signs, Words, and Gestures*. New York: Pueblo, 1981.

Hoffman, Lawrence. *The Art of Public Prayer: Not For Clergy Only*. Washington, D.C.: The Pastoral Press, 1988.

Jasper, David, and R. D. D. Jasper, eds. *Language and the Worship of the Church*. New York: St. Martin's Press, 1990.

Jungmann, Joseph. *The Place of Christ in Liturgical Prayer*, 2d rev. ed. Trans. A. Peeler. New York: Alba, 1965.

Ramshaw, Gail. *Searching for Language*. Washington, D.C.: The Pastoral Press, 1988.

Ramshaw-Schmidt, Gail. *Christ in Sacred Speech: The Meaning of Liturgical Language*. Philadelphia: Fortress, 1986.

Sparkman, G. Temp. *Writing Your Own Worship Materials*. Valley Forge, Pa.: Judson Press, 1980.

Stevik, Daniel. *Language in Worship: Reflection on a Crisis*. New York: Seabury, 1970.

Thistleton, A. C. *Language, Liturgy, and Meaning*. Grove Liturgical Study no.2. Bramcote, Notts., U.K.: Grove Books, 1975.

Van der Leeuw, Gerhardus. *Sacred and Profane Beauty: The Holy in Art*. New York: Holt, Rinehart, and Winston, Inc., 1963. See especially Part III: Beautiful Words.

Weil, Louis. *Gathered to Pray: Understanding Liturgical Prayer*. Cambridge, Mass.: Cowley Publications, 1986.

Zimmerman, Joyce Ann. *Liturgy as Language of Faith*. New York: University Press of America, 1988.

TWENTY-THREE

Poetry in Worship

More than any other type of literature, poetry pays attention to the aesthetic qualities of words. As a result, poems can compress worlds of meaning into a mere few words or lines. Poems convey ideas, images, and narratives in ways that can hardly be forgotten. Poems can paint vibrant word-pictures of even abstract images and mysteries. And poems can stimulate the imagination and convey emotion to an extent that can not be achieved by other forms of verbal language.

Given this potential for communication, poetry can be of great value in the practice of Christian worship. Poetry is most often used in the singing of hymns. Poems are also used in the contexts of sermons or homilies. This chapter discusses these common uses of poetry, but also goes further, suggesting ways in which poetry can be used throughout a worship service.

389 • HYMNS AS POETRY IN WORSHIP

The most common use of poetry in worship is the singing of poems as hymns. Despite their common use, however, hymn texts are rarely thought of in terms of their poetic qualities. Yet hymn writers are among the finest wordsmiths the church has known. Appreciating their art enriches the experience of all who sing.

Hymns are usually seen as low art and sub-zero theology. Theologians file them under "music." Literature departments file them nowhere. C. S. Lewis detested them. John Ruskin described hymns of his own day as "half-paralytic, half profane," consisting partly of the expression of what the singers never in their lives felt, or attempted to feel, and partly in the address of prayers to God, which nothing could more disagreeably astonish them than His attending to.

I want to suggest that at its best, the hymn is a complex minor art form, combining theology, poetry, and music. As such it merits attention from theologians and artists alike. But first I must admit the truth in the criticisms. Hymn-texts range from doggerel to poetry, just as hymn tunes range from cliché to classic. Yet we have moved on from the hymnody that repelled Ruskin and Lewis. Since 1960 there has been an explosion of new hymn writing in the English-speaking world, beginning in Britain and spreading to Canada and the United States. Its styles range from praise music through folk song to the classic stanza form, reborn in contemporary English. I work at the latter end of the spectrum, and do theology through the hymn-poems I write.

At their best, hymns are a complex art form. When read aloud, as a poem, a hymn text is time art. Each reading is similar, yet unrepeatable. When the poem is sung as a solo or choral item, it moves the listener as songs do. When sung by a congregation, it invites commitment. Though some congregations behave as if they didn't have bodies, singing together is an intensely corporeal, as well as corporate, activity. Diaphragm, lungs, larynx, tongue, lips, jawbone, nasal cavities, ribcage, shoulders, eyes, and ears come into play. When body attitude combines with deepest beliefs, singers are taken out of themselves into a heightened awareness of God, beauty, faith and each other. Finally, hymns deserve to be seen as visual art: like other poems, their appearance on the page enhances their attractiveness, or detracts from it.

As a writer of hymn texts, I am a theological poet serving church congregations. The title "poet" once seemed pretentious. I claim it now because I've repeatedly seen the power of hymn-poetry to move people at a deep level. I have also gathered evidence showing how strongly our language habits shape thinking and behavior, so that the way we sing about God and each other is cardinally important. The hymn is an art form through which a congregation expresses and commits itself to a theology.

Sunday by Sunday, most Christian traditions sing their faith and are shaped by what they sing. It is therefore a great mistake to classify hymns as "church music," as if they only mattered to singers, choir directors, and organists. They matter to preachers, theologians, and anyone concerned with the interplay between theology and the arts.

Good hymns are theological poetry, not theology in bad verse. The classic hymn poem is formally strict, with exact meter, stress-rhythms, and usually rhyme in each succeeding stanza. It needs imagery and phrasing clear enough to grasp at first sight (singers can't stop to look in the dictionary), yet memorable enough to give pleasure and meaning through repeated singing. It cannot give free rein to the poet's imagination because it is poetry in the service of its singers. The singers of hymns need poetry that will express their faith and enable them to be truthfully themselves as twentieth century worshipers in the presence of God. The greatest compliment a hymn poet earns is an unspoken YES from singers who grasp, delighting, and identify with the hymn-poem in the immediacy of singing it, yet rarely know or care who wrote the words or composed the tune.

As with any art form these restrictions both cramp creativity and enable it. The possibilities of the form are exemplified by Thomas Troeger's hymn, "These Things Did Thomas Count as Real." The briefest analysis of this poem would note its strong visual and tactile imagery (stanza 1); its economic use of paradox and antithesis (stanzas 2 and 3); its full, apt rhymes (including the brilliant "Braille/nail"); its careful attention to stress and sound sequence; and the achievement of all this in sixteen eight-syllable lines which evoke the story yet break it open afresh. Read aloud, it compels attention. Sung, we find ourselves critiquing Thomas while stepping into his psyche, so that Christ's "raw imprinted palms" reach out to us and question our post-Enlightenment assumptions about reality.

An example of my own work is a wedding hymn (No. 643 in the new United Methodist Church hymnal), written for a well-known folk tune for ease of immediate singing. Its four syllable lines compel simplicity, since it is hard to be polysyllabic in such a short line. I wanted to sing truthfully about some of the experiences of partners in a long-term relationship. The first stanza came quickly, appearing almost fully formed in consciousness;

When love is found / and hope comes home,
sing and be glad / that two are one.
when love explodes / and fills the sky,
praise God and share / our Maker's joy.

"When love explodes and fills the sky" is a simple but strong metaphor. It may derive from firework displays, but the allusion is indirect, enabling me to crystallize varied experiences in one phrase. People know what it means for them, when they look in the crystal.

I then had to decide where the hymn was going. What I had already suggested was that the first line of each stanza could set out the theme developed within it, which led to the following outline:

—When love is found . . .
—When love has flowered . . .
—When love is tried. . .
—When love is torn . . .
—Final wrap-up stanza of praise.

In the second stanza, I wanted to avoid a cozy image of the home as private castle, so I tried alternatives till I got the lines "that love may dare/to reach beyond home's warmth and light/to serve and strive for truth and right." The third stanza recognizes that personalities change over time, so that relationships have to be restructured or broken. The fourth stanza deals with betrayal. I can't remember how long I waited for "when love is torn" to appear as its first line, but there was some waiting time between deciding on the theme and getting that first line. Finding the rhyme fade/betrayed also took time, and involved listing some of the possible rhyme-words and trying out phrases. I was aware of quoting from 1 Corinthians 13 in the New English Bible in lines 3 and 4. At some point I opted for the relaxed rhyme scheme ABCB that came with the first stanza.

Love Song

1. When love is found and hope comes home,
   sing and be glad that two are one.
   When love explodes and fills the sky,
   praise God and share our Maker's joy.

2. When love has flowered in trust and care,
   build both each day that love may dare
   to reach beyond home's warmth and light,
   to serve and strive for truth and right.

3. When love is tried as loved-ones change,
   hold still to hope though all seems strange,
   till ease returns and love grows wise
   through listening ears and opened eyes.

4. When love is torn and trust betrayed,
   pray strength to love till torments fade,
   till lovers keep no score of wrong
   but hear through pain love's Easter song.

5. Praise God for love, praise God for life,
   in age or youth, in husband, wife.
   Lift up your hearts. Let love be fed
   through death and life in broken bread.

4. Old, aching God, grey with endless care,
   calmly piercing evil's new disguises,
   glad of good surprises, wiser than despair:
   Hail and Hosanna, old, aching God!

5. Young, growing God, eager, on the move,
   seeing all, and fretting at our blindness,
   crying out for justice, giving all you have:
   Hail and Hosanna, young, growing God!

6. Great, living God, never fully known,
   joyful darkness far beyond our seeing,
   closer yet than breathing, everlasting home:
   Hail and Hosanna, great, living God!

The writing process always has this partnership between rational and intuitive. Metaphors and phrases have to be set in order, rhymes collected and selected. Ideas must be clarified, then wait for the appearance of suitable phrases and metaphors. "Appearance" is itself a metaphor, suggesting the way in which phrases come to consciousness from the part of the mind which constructs them, and which is outside conscious control. Though much theology is still done as if we were talking heads inhabited by controlling rationality, the creative process shows otherwise. I am emboldened to question the patriarchal dualisms of our culture (mind over body, reason/logic over imagination/feeling, man over nature, the masculine over the feminine, and the root dominance of men over women) because they are not only dangerous and unjust, but untrue to creative experience. My search for more varied titles and word-pictures of God (as in the hymn "Bring Many Names") reflects that conviction.

Bring Many Names

1. Bring many names, beautiful and good,
   celebrate, in parable and story,
   holiness in glory, living, loving God.
   Hail and Hosanna! Bring many names!

2. Strong mother God, working night and day,
   planning all the wonders of creation,
   setting each equation, gen-i-us at play:
   Hail and Hosanna, strong mother God!

3. Warm father God, hugging every child,
   feeling all the strains of human living,
   caring and forgiving till we're reconciled:
   Hail and Hosanna, warm father God!

I said earlier that like other forms of poetry, hymns are visual art. Most Americans never see the poetry of hymns, because the only way they encounter them is with their poetic structure dismantled, the words cut into syllables and interlined (arranged between musical staves for ease of singing). Thankfully, the needs of an aging population are obliging hymnal producers to provide large-print editions, in which the poetry of hymns is once again seen on the page. Christian educators will find this makes poems easier to teach. Pastors and congregations will find hymns more readily available as poetry, fit for public reading (by solo voice or the congregation) and devotional use, and beautiful to look at: an art form in their own right, and a useful part of seminary courses labelled "Introduction to Theology."

Brian Wren[123]

390 ✦ USING POETRY IN WORSHIP

As a highly compact form of speech capable of stimulating the imagination, poetry can be effectively used in almost any of the various dimensions or acts of public worship. This article catalogues a variety of ways that poetry can be used in worship and gives guidelines to worship planners for selecting poems and readers.

When we come together to worship God, we are participating in an ancient ritual expressed through many traditions. The unifying factor is that we come as God's children to enter into a dialogue with him.

Though our worship may be experienced and expressed in various ways, a major dimension of worship is verbal. We hear God speak through his Word and through the words of his people. We respond in words and songs of praise and thanksgiving as well as confession and supplication. While many of the words come directly from Scripture, we often use words from other sources, including the words that spring from our own hearts and minds. The songs we sing, the prayers we pray, a call to confession, a litany of praise, an introduction to an offering, or a parting blessing—all of these may be human compositions of language used for divine worship. At its best, the language for such various elements of the worship service is thoughtful, artful, and edifying. Though this language need not be poetry, carefully selected poems can at times significantly serve the verbal dimensions of worship.

Poetry, by nature, is writing that articulates a concentrated experience or emotion or thought through image, sound, and rhythm. Like all arts—music, visual arts, dramatic arts—poetry is a creative gift from God that can be used to edify God's people and glorify the Creator. The Bible gives us many examples. The Book of the Psalms, the Bible's richest source of poetry, gives expression to a wide range of emotions, experiences, and thoughts (a point Luci Shaw makes in her "Poetry's Permanence: the Psalms"). Poetry is also found in Job, Ecclesiastes, Song of Songs, Isaiah and Jeremiah and other prophetic books, and occasionally in the New Testament, as in 2 Timothy and the glorious prose-poem of 1 Corinthians 13. These are God-inspired examples that give evidence of the wealth and uses of poetic language.

The hymns of the church offer another rich example of poetry used in worship. The case has been made in other places for the use of hymns (in addition to the singing of psalms) in the church. Many of our favorite hymns were originally written simply as poetry and set to music much later. We may think, therefore, of religious poetry as an unsung hymn, appropriate for adoration, celebration, thanksgiving, invitation, supplication, and confession.

But a good poem can also serve other purposes in worship. It can powerfully present a truth of human experience. It can make an old truth new again. It can so dramatically render an implication of God's truth that none can fail to listen. In all these ways and others, poetry can fulfill a sermonic function in worship.

There are many ways, then, to use poetry in worship. Poetry can be incorporated occasionally within any general service, or it can occasionally serve as the primary verbal medium of the service.

The Occasional Uses of Poetry in Worship

It's possible to find a poem whose rich imagery, poignant emotion, or profound thought expresses a particular idea so well that it could almost constitute the sermon. But it might be most appropriate to use such a poem as a complement to the sermon. The poem, such as the following, could serve as an introduction to the theme or as an opener for the sermon, or it could be used within the sermon as an illustration or clincher for a point made, or it could be used at the end to reinforce the main thrust of the sermon or to bring it into sharper focus.

I'm Tired

i'm tired, so tired
i can't . . .
oh Lord, i can't go on.
i'm going down
and i'll never rise again.
what use am i
if i am lying in the dust?
if i am fallen in the pit?

are you tired indeed?
then come to me
for i am meek and lowly.
and if you would have rest,
then come to me
in lowliness of heart,
and i will give you
my precious burden
my easy yoke
for it is never you who till alone
nor carry by yourself.
so come to me
and i will give you a parched
and thirsty land to till
and i will give you rest.
(Debbie Wallis)

There are many fine poems that were inspired by certain verses from Scripture or by certain biblical characters. If those verses or characters are key to the theme of the service, either the sermon or the reading of Scripture might be enhanced by an accompanying poem, such as "Prophecy" by Luci Shaw. Some poems also work very well paired with certain songs and hymns; for instance, George Herbert's poem "Let All the World in Every Corner

Sing" could be used to introduce the hymn "Praise to the Lord, the Almighty."

Special events such as baptisms and professions of faith offer unique opportunities for the use of poetry. For example, when a child named Blake was baptized, his aunt read "The Lamb" by poet William Blake as part of the baptismal ceremony. An appropriate poem read by a special person (as is true of a special musical selection) can add both significance and emotional impact to the occasion.

There are a number of good poems about the Eucharist or Lord's Supper service. Some might work well as an introduction to the service of communion; others might be appropriate as an offering of praise at the conclusion of the feast. Madeleine L'Engle's "After the Saturday Liturgy at Montfort" might be a fitting poem to use in this context, or "Covenant Celebration" by Nancy Todd.

In addition to being used to *accompany* or complement various elements of the service, poetry can also be used *in place of* a particular element. A good example of this is the offering of prayer. Prayer can be taken directly from Scripture, the words of a song (even the singing of a song can be a prayer), the words of St. Augustine or other Christian writers, the original words of the person praying—and from poetry. Examples from literary history abound, from Donne's "Batter My Heart" to e.e. cummings' "i thank you God." But poems can substitute for other elements of the service as well. A poem may serve as an invocation or call to confession or assurance of pardon, as Carlisle's poem illustrates:

Next of Kin

God remembers
our structure
and our texture
our congruity
with the grass
our continuity
with the dust.

More than a father
feels for his children
He senses our need.
Even when we
are too foolish
to fear or heed Him
He keeps His love
invariably available.
(Thomas John
Carlisle)

Expressions of praise and thanksgiving can come from the wealth of poetry which celebrates God's creation or His work in the human heart. Such poems might also be used as a response of gratitude or poetic offering (like a musical offering along with the offering of monetary gifts). "Pied Beauty" by Gerard Manley Hopkins is one that might work well; another possibility is "Individuation" by Nancy Thomas. There are even good benedictory poems that could be fitting at the conclusion of the service. Clearly, possibilities for the occasional use of poetry in worship are numerous.

Primary Uses of Poetry in Worship

Services can also be designed with poetry as a primary verbal expression. This can be done especially effectively within a particular liturgical season. Some of the most profound poetry deals with the suffering and sacrifice of Christ; carefully selected pieces can be combined with Scripture readings and music for a moving and meaningful service during Lent. Other poems are very appropriate for use in special services around Easter and Christmas.

There may be other occasions in which poetry can be a key ingredient of the service: the celebration of a church anniversary; a prayer day; a service with a biblical theme such as God's creation, sins of the flesh, the parable of the sower, or a Bible character. For example, the poems of Thomas John Carlisle in *You! Jonah!* could shape the design of a service about Jonah.

For any of these services, the planners must consider the congregation's interest and aptitude for poetry and allow that to guide both the number and type of poems used in a particular service. A worship service that consisted entirely of poetry would perhaps be neither judicious nor theologically sound. But if the poems are carefully selected and paired with readings from Scripture and appropriate songs (whether for choral or congregational singing) into a seamless worship experience, members of the congregation may discover in new ways the power of God's word and his gift of language.

Considerations for Selection of Poetry and Readers

Careful selection is critical to the successful use of poetry in worship. The primary consideration should be the thematic appropriateness of the poem. A pastor's favorite poem may not fit well into a particular service even though he or she may be tempted to make it fit. But a poem that does not enhance or enrich the thematic center of the service forfeits its function.

Many fine poems do not lend themselves to oral presentation. They are difficult to read aloud, difficult to listen to, and difficult to understand. Therefore, poetry for use in worship must be chosen for its readability, listenability, and comprehensibility.

This means that the language of worship poetry should be fairly contemporary and concrete. Imagery should have the power to engage the listeners' imagination readily. The rhythm should be close to that of natural speech. End rhyme, if it's there at all, should not be forced or artificial. Poems should not be so long as to become taxing to listen to. In sum, the best poems for oral interpretation in worship are those which evoke and enrich genuine experience within a spiritual context.

There may be only a few gifted poetry readers in any congregation. The people who actually read the poems aloud in a worship service should be carefully chosen and given ample opportunity for oral rehearsal, ideally with the help of a qualified coach. A reader should prepare thoroughly for the presentation of the poems and consider such aspects of delivery as these: poetry should be read at a pace that gives time for the images to take shape in the listener's imagination; the lines should be read according to the phrasing of ideas, not according to the length of the lines; the appropriate use of pauses and stresses for emphasis is crucial to conveying the ideas or emotions of the poem.

It is usually preferable not to print the text of the poems in the liturgy or bulletin because the poems will be better understood by hearing them read well than by reading them for oneself. When a service is planned which incorporates several poems, it might be helpful to provide copies of the poems after the service (making sure to follow any copyright rules) for those people who will appreciate being able to read the poems for further reflection.

Cynthia R. de Jong and Henry J. Baron

391 • A Bibliography of Resources for Poetry in Worship

*There are many good sources of poetry suitable for use in worship. Perhaps a particular congregation or broader church community has its own gifted poets in its midst and can benefit from their gifts (though not everyone who scrib-*bles lines on paper should be called a gifted poet—and that may become a sensitive issue). Many ecumenical publications, such as* Christianity Today, Eternity, Campus Life, *and* Perspectives *frequently print poems, as do many denominational publications. And of course there are numerous anthologies of poetry, even a few that are particularly Christian and designed for worship. A word of caution here: many of these anthologies include mostly older works and neglect the considerable riches of more recent poetry by Christian writers. The most useful volumes may be those small collections by individual poets (which unfortunately have a very short life in the bookstores). An annotated bibliography of some resources that we've come across and used frequently concludes this article.*

Alexander, Pat, comp. *Eerdmans Book of Christian Poetry.* Grand Rapids: Eerdmans, 1981. This book serves as an introduction to Christian poetry from the past 1300 years and contains mostly classic selections. Also included are a few recent short poems that should communicate readily to modern readers.

Armstrong, Karen. *Tongues of Fire: An Anthology of Religious and Poetic Experience.* New York: Penguin, 1985. This anthology of poetry from a wide variety of sources and cultures is arranged topically rather than chronologically. It also provides a helpful introduction and chapter notes which provoke deeper thought about religious poetry.

Avison, Margaret. *Sunblue.* Hantsport, Nova Scotia: Lancelot Press, 1978. Margaret Avison is a profoundly Christian poet and one of Canada's best. Though many of her poems are too elusive for public readings, this volume merits mention because a few selections are powerfully appropriate and effective for public worship, especially during the seasons of Advent and Lent. A more recent collection of her poems, skimmed from previous volumes, may also include good material for worship: *Selected Poems* (New York: Oxford University Press, 1991).

Bush, Roger. *Prayers for Pagans.* Pflaum Press, 1969. These "prayers" are really conversations with God in ordinary but often poignant and pointed language about many of the painful realities of the human condition, e.g., poverty, racism, old age, suicide, conformity.

Carlisle, Thomas John. *You! Jonah!* Grand Rapids: Eerdmans, 1968.

———. *Celebration!* Grand Rapids: Eerdmans, 1970.

———. *Mistaken Identity.* Grand Rapids: Eerdmans, 1973.

———. *Journey with Job.* Grand Rapids: Eerdmans, 1984.

———. *Eve and After.* Grand Rapids: Eerdmans, 1984.

———. *Beginning with Mary.* Grand Rapids: Eerdmans, 1986.

———. *Looking for Jesus.* Grand Rapids: Eerdmans, 1993. (This volume includes a very useful Scripture index for the poems.)

Most of the poems in these volumes are short and very usable for worship readings. They both edify and entertain, in the best sense of the word, and they cover a wide range of Bible topics, people, and events.

Davie, Donald, ed. *The New Oxford Book of Christian Verse.* New York: Oxford University Press, 1988. This anthology features religious poetry ranging from Anglo-Saxon times to the modern era, including some Christian hymns; some carefully selected poems can be appropriate for worship.

Davie, Donald. *To Scorch or Freeze: Poems about the Sacred.* Chicago: University of Chicago Press, 1988. Davie's poems encompass many themes, from songs of praise to righteous vengeance. Many of them could be used in a worship setting, though some of the imagery and allusions may be too complex for the average congregant.

Houtman, H. *Six Days: An Anthology of Canadian Christian Poetry.* Toronto: Wedge Publishing Foundation, 1971. The quality of poetry in this volume is uneven and the subject matter varies widely, but a few of the selections will be fitting for worship.

L'Engle, Madeleine. *The Weather of the Heart.* Wheaton, Ill.: Harold Shaw, 1978.

———. *A Cry Like a Bell.* Wheaton, Ill.: Harold Shaw, 1987.

In these volumes of poetry, Madeleine L'Engle's searchings and findings about herself and God are illumined as she writes about love and pain and adoration and joy. She sometimes speaks through the voices of biblical figures like Rachel, Isaac, Mary, and Andrew to give us fresh insight into God's grace.

Miller, Calvin. *The Singer.* Downers Grove, Ill.: InterVarsity, 1979. Calvin Miller's poetic retelling of the Gospels provides a rich resource for longer readings, many of which would function well as a coda to the sermon.

Meeter, Merle, compiler. *The Country of the Risen King.* Grand Rapids: Baker, 1978. An anthology of poetry by both modern and historic Christian poets that is often consulted first by many Christians for worship services. The book contains poems of a very personal nature, many reflecting on God's creation, and a number inspired by Scripture passages and worship experiences.

Post, Marie J. *I Had Never Visited an Artist Before.* Grand Rapids: Being Publications, 1973. This general collection includes several poems appropriate for readings at Christmas, Easter, and Ascension services.

Shaw, Luci. *Listen to the Green.* Wheaton, Ill.: Harold Shaw, 1971.

———. *The Secret Trees.* Wheaton, Ill.: Harold Shaw, 1976.

———. *The Sighting.* Wheaton, Ill.: Harold Shaw, 1981.

———. *Postcard from the Shore.* Wheaton, Ill.: Harold Shaw, 1985.

———. *The Risk of Birth: A Gift Book of Christ-Poems.* Wheaton, Ill.: Harold Shaw, 1974.

———. *Sightseers into Pilgrims.* Wheaton, Ill.: Tyndale House, 1973.

———. *Polishing the Petosky Stone: New & Selected Poems.* Wheaton, Ill.: Harold Shaw, 1990.

Shaw's poems are very readable, often capturing through telling images a biblical truth that revitalizes the Christian life. All the listed volumes include selections that are often used liturgically for Sunday worship. Some focus especially on the holy seasons. Others feature biblical characters and themes.

Shaw, Luci, ed. *A Widening Light: Poems of the Incarnation.* Wheaton, Ill.: Harold Shaw, 1984. This volume is a priceless treasure. The poems, by Luci Shaw and other contemporary poets, are arranged according to the life of Christ and our celebrations of those events throughout the year.

Shriver, Peggy L. *Pinches of Salt: Spiritual Seasonings.* Philadelphia: Westminster/John Knox, 1990. Many of these poems take on social issues or family-related themes while others are about the incarnation and grace; a number would fit into worship settings.

Steele, David. *God Must Have a Sense of Humor: He Made Aardvarks and Orangutans . . . And*

Me! St. Helena, Calif.: Illuminations Press, 1983. This book has humorous poems about various Biblical people and themes and is written in a childlike style. Its material may be most appropriate for children's messages or church school programs.

Wallis, Charles L., ed. *A Treasury of Poems for Worship and Devotion*. New York: Harper & Brothers, 1959. This older collection has a few good poems that are suitable for worship. Most, however, are of an archaic nature best avoided for public readings.

Walsh, Chad. *The Psalm of Christ: Forty Poems on the Twenty-Second Psalm*. Wheaton, Ill.: Harold Shaw, 1982. Many of these excellent poems could be used especially to augment sermons on Psalm 22. But several would also be very appropriate for the season of Lent.

Weems, Ann. *Kneeling in Bethlehem*. Philadelphia: Westminster, 1980.

———. *Kneeling in Jerusalem*. Philadelphia: Westminster/John Knox, 1992.

———. *Searching for Shalom: Resources for Creative Worship*. Philadelphia: Westminster/John Knox, 1991.

The poetry of Weems is fresh, full of faith, and often profound in its simplicity. The poems in the Bethlehem volume focus on Christ's birth; the Jerusalem volume takes us through Lent and Holy Week and into Easter. The third volume has many valuable poems that could fit the liturgical flow of a Sunday service; in addition it contains some dramatic scripts about certain women of the Bible and three sample worship services.

Cynthia R. de Jong and Henry J. Baron

Works Cited

1. Kathryn L. Nichols, "Music and Musician in Service to the Church," *Reformed Liturgy and Music* 20:2 (Spring 1986): 72–77.

2. Paul Westermeyer, *The Church Musician* (San Francisco: Harper and Row, 1988), 3–40.

3. Linda Clark, "Aesthetic Value in Church Music," *Liturgy* 6:3 (Winter 1987): 47–53.

4. Carl Schalk, *Music in Lutheran Worship* (St. Louis: Concordia Publishing House, 1983).

5. Calvin M. Johansson, "Singing in the Spirit," *The Hymn* 38:1 (January 1987): 25–29

6. J. Wendell Mopson, Jr., *The Ministry of Music in the Black Church* (Valley Forge, Pa.: Judson Press, 1984), 9–23.

7. *The Liturgy Documents: A Parish Resource* (Chicago: Liturgy Training Publications, 1991), 277–293.

8. *In Tune with Heaven: The Report of the Archbishops' Commission on Church Music* (London: Hodder and Stoughton/Church House Publishing, 1992).

9. Paul Westermeyer, "The Present State of Church Music: Historical and Theological Reflections," *Word and World* 12:3 (Summer 1992): 214–220.

10. Milburn Price, "The Impact of Popular Culture on Congregational Song," *The Hymn* 44:1 (January 1993): 11–17.

11. Anton E. Armstrong, "Music as a Force in Building Community: Challenges of a Multi-Cultural Church," *Chorister's Guild Letters* (April 1991): 249–250.

12. Andrew Wilson Dickson, *The Story of Christian Music: From Gregorian Chant to Black Gospel* (Batavia, Ill: Lion, 1992), 144–147.

13. Ibid., 150–155.

14. Ibid., 156–159.

15. Ibid., 160–165.

16. Ibid., 170–176, 177–180.

17. Ibid., 49–54.

18. Ibid., 182–190.

19. Ibid., 191–195, 196–199.

20. David T. Koyzis, "Straight from Scripture," *Reformed Worship* 11 (Spring 1989): 18–20.

21. For an earlier version of this article, see Roy Hopp, "Writing Hymn Tunes," *Reformed Worship* 4 (Summer 1987):16.

22. James Rawlings Sydnor, "How to Improve Congregational Singing," *Reformed Liturgy and Music* 21:3 (Summer 1987): 152–153.

23. Carl Reed, "Welcome Back to An Ancient Tradition: The Canon in Hymnody," *The Hymn* 40:4 (October 1989): 25–28.

24. Carol Doran and Thomas H. Troeger, "Choosing a Hymnal: An Act of Ministry on Behalf of the Whole Church," *Reformed Liturgy and Music* 24:2 (Spring 1990): 86–90.

25. Bert Polman, "Singing Scripture: A Healthy Revival," *Reformed Worship* 2 (Winter 1987): 39–40.

26. Michael G. Hayes, "The Theology of the Black Pentecostal Praise Song," *Journal of Black Sacred Music* 4:2 (Fall 1990): 30–34.

27. Carlos A. Lopez, "Hymn Singing in the Hispanic Tradition," *Reformed Liturgy and Music* 20:3 (Summer 1986): 156–157.

28. May Murakami, "Ethnic Hymnody in the Asian American Tradition," *Reformed Liturgy and Music* 20:3 (Summer 1986): 154–155.

29. John Ferguson, "Instrumental Color in Worship," *Reformed Liturgy and Music* 25:3 (Summer 1991): 115–118. Revised by the author.

30. John Ferguson, "Organ Design for Congregational Song," *GIA Quarterly* 4:3 (Spring 1993): 24–25, 42.

31. John Ferguson, "Electronic Keyboard and the Church Musician," *Chorister's Guild Letters* (September 1992): 33–35. Revised by the author.

32. Michael Silhavy, "Brass 101," *GIA Quarterly* 2:2 (Winter 1991): 16–17; "Woodwinds 101," *GIA Quarterly* 2:3 (Spring 1991), 18–19, 39; "Strings 101," *GIA Quarterly* 2:4 (Summer 1991): 18–19.

33. Bruce Stewart, "The Use of Musical Instruments in Worship," *The Outlook* (March 1991): 8.

34. David T. Koyzis, "Restoring Psalms to Worship," *Reformed Worship* 10 (Winter 1989): 30–31.

35. Sue Mitchell Wallace, "Easter Hymn Festival," *Reformed Worship* 10 (Winter 1989): 17–18.

36. George Shorney, "Copyright Rights and Wrongs," *Reformed Liturgy and Music* 18:3 (Summer 1984): 118–119.

37. Paul Westermeyer, "The Practical Life of the Church Musician," *Christian Century* 106 (September 13–30, 1989): 812–814.

38. A portion of this article was printed as John Ferguson, "The Organ as Catalyst for the Song of the Assembly," *GIA Quarterly* 1:1 (Fall 1989): 16–17. Another portion will be printed in a forthcoming issue of *American Organist.*

39. Emily Brink, "Choirs in Reformed Worship," *Reformed Worship* 2 (Winter 1987): 7–8.

40. Molly M. Macaulay, "Children's Choir as Participants (Not Performers) in Corporate Worship," *Reformed Liturgy and Music* 26:1 (Winter 1992): 16–19.

41. Rosemary A. Hudecheck, "Role, Gesture, and Mikes," *GIA Quarterly* 4:3 (Spring 1993): 18–19, 40.

42. Calvin G. Seerveld, "Relating Christianity to the Arts," *Christianity Today* 24 (November 7, 1980): 48–49.

43. Richard Ostling, "Africa's Artistic Resurrection," *Time* (March 27, 1989): 77.

44. Donald E. Saliers, "Liturgical Aesthetics," in *The New Dictionary of Sacramental Worship,* ed. Peter E. Fink, S.J. (Collegeville, Minn.: The Liturgical Press, 1990), 30–39.

45. Robert W. Hovda, "Symbol: The Language of Art and Liturgy," *Environment and Art Letter* 2:4 (June 1989): 2–3.

46. Gordon Lathrop, "How Symbols Speak," *Liturgy* 7:1 (Summer 1988): 9–13.

47. John Dillenberger, "The Visual and the Verbal: One Reality, Two Modalities," *Review and Expositor* 87 (1990): 563–568.

48. Rodney J. Sawatsky, "Mennonites and the Arts: An Immodest Proposal." *Conrad Grebel Review* 7 (1989): v–ix.

49 Barbara Miller, "Art as Proclamation and Prayer," *Reformed Liturgy and Music* 23:4 (Fall 1989): 183–185.

50. This article is made up of excerpts from Todd Farley, *The Silent Prophet* (Shippensburg, Pa.: Destiny Image, 1989).

51. Thomas H. Troeger, "Art in Worship: The Integrity of Form and Faith," *Reformed Liturgy and Music* 18:3 (Summer 1984): 122–125.

52. Grace M. Donaldson, "The Non-Verbal Languages of Prayer" *Liturgy* 4:4 (Spring 1985): 67–70.

53. "Environment and Art in Catholic Worship," in *The Liturgy Documents: A Parish Resource,* 319–338.

54. James F. White, "Liturgical Space Forms Faith," *Reformed Liturgy and Music* 22:2 (Spring 1988): 59–60.

55. Edward A. Sovik, "Church Architecture—A Public Language," *Cutting Edge* 7:4 (1978), copyright, Board of Church Extension, Disciples of Christ, reprinted in *Liturgy* 4:4 (Spring 1985): 83–89.

56. Thomas R. Slon, "What the Church Building Wants to Be," *Modern Liturgy* 19:4 (May 1992): 9–12.

57. Aidan Kavanuagh, *Elements of Rite: A Handbook of Liturgical Style* (New York: Pueblo Publishing Company, 1982): 14–22.

58. Ralph Keifer "From Devout Attendance to Active Participation," *Modern Liturgy* 3:5 (1976): 4–6, 14.

59. Harold Daniels, "Pulpit, Font, and Table," *Reformed Liturgy and Music* 16:2 (Spring 1982): 63–72.

60. John P. Newport, "Some Specific Shapes: The Baptist Journey," *Christianity Today* 25 (August 7, 1981): 21.

61. James A. Stahr, "Some Specific Shapes: Christian Brethren Simplicity," *Christianity Today* 25 (August 7, 1981): 21.

62. "Platform Arrangements," *Psalmist* (Feb/Mar 1989): 30–31.

63. Bill Beard, "Seating for Catholic Worship: A Primer," *Environment and Art Letter* 1:1 (1988): 2–3.

64. Walter R. Bouman, "Acoustics for the Church," *The Hymn* 41:3 (July 1990): 20–23.

65. Dennis Fleisher, "Acoustics for Congregational Singing," *The Hymn* 41:3 (July 1990), 7–10.

66. Karmen Van Dyke, "Does Your Worship Space Speak the Faith?" *Reformed Liturgy and Music* 22:2 (Spring 1988): 114.

67. T. Jerome Overbeck, "Building and Renovating a Church," *Modern Liturgy* 19:4 (May 1992): 14–16.

68. Mario Locsin, "Ambo and Book," *Modern Liturgy* 19:4 (May 1992): 20–21.

69. Richard Vosko, "The Community Table," *Modern Liturgy* 19:4 (May 1992): 17–19.

70. Kevin Seasoltz, O.S.B., "The Altar: Scriptural and Historical Perpectives," *Assembly* 15:4 (May 1989): 442–443.

71. Kavanaugh, *Elements of Rite,* 70–71.

72. Andrew Ciferni, "Christian Table Etiquette," *Assembly* 15:4 (May 1989): 444–445.

73. James Notebaart, "The Font and the Assembly," *Liturgy* 5:4 (Spring 1986): 59–65.

74. S. Anita Stauffer, "A Place for Burial, Birth, and Bath," *Liturgy* 5:4 (Spring 1986): 51–57.

75. S. Anita Stauffer, "Fonts for Function and Meaning: Three Worthy Examples," *Environment and Art* 10:2 (March 1988): 22–29.

76. Jeannette Angell-Torosian, "Windows on the Holy," *Liturgy* 8:3 (Spring 1990): 91–95.

77. Howard E. Galley, *The Ceremonies of the Eucharist: A Guide to Celebration* (Cambridge, Mass.: Cowley Publications, 1989), 15–17.

78. Andrew D. Ciferni, "The Significance of Liturgical Dress," *Liturgy* 5:4 (Spring 1986): 77–79.

79. Kevin R. Boyd, "Vestments," *Modern Liturgy* 9:7 (1982): 34–36.

80. Galley, *The Ceremonies of the Eucharist.*

81. Thomas Nicolls, "Improving Liturgical Banners," *Reformed Liturgy and Music* 18:3 (Summer 1984): 133–135.

82. Galley, *The Ceremonies of the Eucharist,* 8–11.

83. Galley, *The Ceremonies of the Eucharist,* 11–12.

84. Peter Mazar, "Using Flowers," *Environment and Art Letter* 2:1 (March 1989): 5.

85. Steven J. Melahn, "Stained Glass: A Primer," *Environment and Art Letter* 1:3 (May 1988): 2.

86. John Walker, "Use of Visual Arts in Worship," *Reformed Liturgy and Music* 18:3 (Summer 1984), 128–132.

87. Chris Stoffel Overvoorde, "Not Just for Looks," *Reformed Worship* 17 (September 1990): 18–20.

88. Nancy Chinn, *Evaluating Visual Art for Worship,* Schuyler Institute for Worship and the Arts, P.O. Box 790, San Carlos, CA 94070.

89. Mary Lou Weaver, "Artisans and Worship," *Liturgy* 5:4 (Spring 1986), 99–102.

90. Kenneth F. von Roenn, Jr., "Stained Glass in a Church Building Project," *Environment and Art Letter* 1:3 (May 1988): 3–4.

91. Catherine Kapikian, "Art and Theology: The Artist-in-Residence in the Church," Institute for Theology and the Arts, Australia.

92. Esther Wiens, "The Uses of Drama," *Direction: A Quarterly Publication of Mennonite Brethren Schools* 16 (Spring 1987): 63–67.

93. Darius Swann, "Drama and Preaching in Protestant Worship," *Liturgy* 8:3 (Spring 1990): 39–43.

94. Steve Pederson, "Introduction," from *Sunday Morning Live, Volume 3* (Grand Rapids: Zondervan, 1993), 11–16.

95. Jennie Keinzle, "The Children's Chancel Drama," *Liturgy* 9:1 (Fall 1990): 71–75.

96. Patricia Beall, "The Unforgiving Servant," Celebration Services (International) Ltd., 1977.

97. Sharon Sherbondy, "Keeping Tabs," from *Sunday Morning Live, Volume 3,* 39–46.

98. Harry Boonstra, "I Was There," *Reformed Worship* 21 (September 1991): 25–27.

99. Margie Brown, "Finding Your Voice," *Modern Liturgy* 15:5 (1988): 12–13.

100. Jerry and Gail Du Charme, *Lector Becomes Proclaimer* (San Jose, Calif.: Resource Publications, 1985), 49–67.

101. Carole J. Carter, "O God, How Can I Take the 'Ho-Hum' Out of the Scriptures?" *Reformed Liturgy and Music* 23:3 (Summer 1989):128–131.

102. *Destination: Responsive Readings That Live,* pp. iv–v.

103. *Destination: Responsive Readings That Live,* pp. 8–10, 16–19, 34–38, 50–54, 82–87.

104. Deena Borchers, "Dance in Christian Worship," *Currents in Theology and Missions* (June 17, 1990): 207–213.

105. Excerpted from J. G. Davies *Liturgical Dance* (London: SCM Press, 1984), 137–145.

106. Excerpted from Davies, *Liturgical Dance,* 137–145, 167–170.

107. Markus Bockmuehl, "Should We Kneel to Pray," *Crux* 26:3 (September 1990): 14–17.

108. Mary Jones "Dance into God's Presence," *Psalmist* (June/July 1989): 14–15.

109. Robert Ver Ecke, "Dances of the Seasons," in Ronald Gagne, Thomas Kone, Robert Ver-

Eecke, *Introducing Dance in Christian Worship* (Washington, D.C.: The Pastoral Press, 1984), 149–161.

110. Adapted from Thomas Kane, "Types of Liturgical Dance," in *Introducing Dance in Christian Worship,* 99–113.

111. Carla De Sola, *The Spirit Moves* (Washington, D.C.: The Liturgical Conference, 1977), 98–99.

112. Ibid., 30–31.

113. Ibid., 98–99.

114. Martha Ann Kirk, *Dancing With Creation* (San Jose, Calif.: Resource Publications, Inc., 1983).

115. For further information on this article, write Star Song Publishing, 2325 Crestmoor, Nashville, TN 37215.

116. For further information on this article, write Star Song Publishing, 2325 Crestmoor, Nashville, TN 37215.

117. For further information on this article, write Star Song Publishing, 2325 Crestmoor, Nashville, TN 37215.

118. For further information on this article, write Star Song Publishing, 2325 Crestmoor, Nashville, TN 37215.

119. Gail Ramshaw, "Language and Liturgy," *Studia Liturgica* 20:1 (1990): 65–69.

120. David G. Buttrick, "On Liturgical Language," *Reformed Liturgy and Music* 15:2 (Spring 1981): 74–82.

121. William C. Turner, Jr., "The Musicality of Black Preaching: A Phenomenology," *Journal of Black Sacred Music* 2:1 (Spring 1988): 21–29.

122. William K. Hedrick, "Prayer in Worship," *Austin Presbyterian Seminary Bulletin* 101:4 (October 1985): 45–50.

123. Brian Wren, "Poet in the Congregation," *The Arts in Religious and Theological Studies* 2:1 (Fall 1989): 10–12.

Index